Handbook of
Workplace
Diversity

Edited by
Alison M. Konrad, Pushkala Prasad
and Judith K. Pringle

SAGE Publications
London ● Thousand Oaks ● New Delhi

Introduction, conclusion and editorial arrangement © Alison M. Konrad, Pushkala Prasad and Judith K. Pringle, 2006

Chapter 1 © Carol T. Kulik and Hugh T.J. Bainbrdge, 2006

Chapter 2 © Ellen Ernst Kossek, Sharon A. Lobel and Jennifer Brown, 2006

Chapter 3 © Deborah Litvin, 2006

Chapter 4 © Yvonne Due Billing and Elisabeth Sundin, 2006

Chapter 5 © Anshuman Prasad, 2006

Chapter 6 © Deborah Jones and Ralph Stablein, 2006

Chapter 7 © Raza Mir, Ali Mir and Diana J. Wong, 2006

Chapter 8 © David A. Harrison and Hock-Peng Sin, 2006

Chapter 9 © Amy Thurlow, Albert J. Mills and Jean Helms Mills, 2006

Chapter 10 © Donna Chrobot-Mason, Alison M. Konrad and Frank Linnehan, 2006

Chapter 11 © Yvonne Benschop, 2006

Chapter 12 © Jeff Hearn and David L. Collinson, 2006

Chapter 13 © Karen L. Proudford and Stella Nkomo, 2006

Chapter 14 © Elissa L. Perry and Jennifer D. Parlamis, 2006

Chapter 15 © W. E. Douglas Creed, 2006

Chapter 16 © Eugene F. Stone-Romero, Diana L. Stone and Kimberly Lukaszewski, 2006

Chapter 17 © Maureen Scully and Stacy Blake-Beard, 2006

Chapter 18 © Myrtle P. Bell and Mary E. McLaughlin, 2006

Chapter 19 © Kiran Mirchandani and Alana Butler, 2006

Chapter 20 © Anne-Marie Greene and Gill Kirton, 2006

Chapter 21 © Amanda Sinclair, 2006

First published 2006

SAGE Publications Ltd
1 Oliver's Yard
55 City Road
London EC1Y 1SP

SAGE Publications Inc.
2455 Teller Road
Thousand Oaks, California 91320

SAGE Publications India Pvt Ltd
B-42, Panchsheel Enclave
Post Box 4109
New Delhi 110 017

British Library Cataloguing in Publication data
A catalogue record for this book is available from the British Library

ISBN 0 7619 4422 2

Library of Congress Control Number: 2005925395

Typeset by C&M Digital (P) Ltd., Chennai, India
Printed in Great Britain by The Cromwell Press Ltd, Trowbridge, Wiltshire
Printed on paper from sustainable resources

Contents

Notes on Contributors

Hugh T.J. Bainbridge is a Ph.D. candidate at the University of Melbourne, Australia. His research interests focus on how organizations can reduce the stigma and negative outcomes experienced by people with disabilities and their caregivers.

Myrtle Bell, Ph.D., is an associate professor of management at the University of Texas at Arlington. Her research focuses on diversity and social issues at work.

Yvonne Benschop is an associate professor of gender and culture at the Nijmegen School of Management, Radboud University Nijmegen, the Netherlands. Her research combines feminist organization studies and critical management studies.

Yvonne Due Billing works at the Department of Sociology, University of Copenhagen, Denmark. She has published widely within the field of gender and organizations. Her publications include *Understanding Gender and Organizations* (SAGE, 1997) and *Gender, Managers and Organizations* (de Gruyter, 1994), both co-authored with Mats Alvesson with whom she has also adopted Miha and Mathilda from Vietnam.

Stacy Blake-Beard, Ph.D., is an associate professor at the Simmons School of Management. She is a research faculty member with the Center for Gender in Organizations at Simmons. Her research has focused on gender and race issues in mentoring, the growing importance of women mentors, and the dynamics of formal mentoring programs in both corporate and educational settings. She consults with a number of organizations on diversity issues, including Chase Manhattan Bank, The Compact for Faculty Diversity, and PepsiCo. She sits on the advisory boards of Essence Magazine's Best Places for African American Women to Work, MentorNet, and the Harvard Project on Tenure.

Jennifer Brown is employed by the W.K. Kellogg Foundation as a Human Resource Specialist. She holds a BA in personnel administration and a Master's of Labor Relations and Human Resources from Michigan State University.

Alana Butler is a graduate of the Adult Education and Community Development program at the Ontario Institute for Studies in Education of the University of Toronto. Her recent thesis work focuses on anti-racist approaches to diversity training for the corporate sector.

Donna Chrobot-Mason, Ph.D., is an assistant professor in the Center for Organizational Leadership at the University of Cincinnati, and the Graduate Director for the Masters in Labor and Employment Relations Program.

David Collinson is Professor of Leadership and Organization at Lancaster University Management School. David's work develops a critical approach to key organizational issues such as management, resistance, identity, gender, masculinity, safety and humour. His current research focuses on critical approaches to leadership and followership. He is also founding co-editor of the refereed journal *Leadership*.

W.E. Douglas Creed whose work has appeared in the *Academy of Management Review*, *Organization Science*, *Research in Organizational Behavior*, *Journal of Management Inquiry*, and the *Journal of Management Studies*, currently researches change agents with marginalized identities, using the case of gay Protestant ministers.

Anne-marie Greene is a senior lecturer in industrial relations at Warwick Business School, University of Warwick. Her research interests include gender and workplace trade unionism and the use of new ICTs by trade unions. She is co-author of *The Dynamics of Managing Diversity: A Critical Approach* (Butterworth-Heinemann, 2005) and is researching diversity management in the UK funded by the European Social Fund.

David A. Harrison is a professor of management at the Pennsylvania State University. His research on work role adjustment, time and diversity, executive decision making, and organizational measurement has appeared widely.

Jeff Hearn is an academy fellow and professor at the Swedish School of Economics, Helsinki, Finland, and Research Professor in Sociology, University of Huddersfield, UK. His books include: *'Sex' at 'Work'* (Prentice Hall/Harvester Wheatsheaf, 1995), *Gender, Sexuality and Violence in Organizations*, co-authored with Wendy Parkin (SAGE, 2001), *Information Society and the Workplace*, co-edited with Tuula Heiskanen (Routledge, 2004), and *Handbook of Studies on Men and Masculinities*, co-edited with Michael S. Kimmel and Robert W. Connell (SAGE, 2005).

Deborah Jones is a senior lecturer at Victoria Management School in Wellington, New Zealand. With early degrees in English literature and sociolinguistics, she has drawn on her humanities education in her work in management studies. She has published on discourse analysis, feminist post-structuralism, diversity and equality, ethnicity and gender, and organizational communication. More recently she has been involved in research on older women's work, on pay equity, on national identity, and on creative industries, especially the New Zealand film industry.

Gill Kirton is a senior lecturer in the Centre for Business Management at Queen Mary, University of London. Her research interests include gender and race equality, diversity and employment relations, trade union education, and women's trade union careers. She is co-author of *The Dynamics of Managing Diversity: A Critical Approach* (Butterworth-Heinemann, 2005) and is researching diversity management in the UK funded by the European Social Fund.

Alison M. Konrad, Ph.D., is a professor of organizational behavior and holder of the Corus Entertainment Chair in Women in Management at the Richard Ivey School of Business, University of Western Ontario.

Ellen Ernst Kossek, Ph.D., is a professor at Michigan State University. She is a Fellow of APA and SIOP, and elected to the Academy of Management's Board of Governors.

Carol T. Kulik is a professor of human resource management at the University of Melbourne, Australia. Carol's research interests encompass cognitive processes, demographic diversity, and organizational justice.

Frank Linnehan, Ph.D., is an associate professor of organizational behavior and human resources in Drexel University's LeBow College of Business. His research interests include workforce diversity and school-to-work transitions.

Deborah R. Litvin, Ph.D., is an assistant professor of management at the Girard School of Business and International Commerce, Merrimack College.

Sharon Lobel is a professor of management at Seattle University's Albers School of Business and Economics. She is also a research fellow at the Center for Work and Family at Boston College.

Kimberly Lukaszewski received her Ph.D. from Albany State University of New York, and is now Assistant Professor of Management at the State University of New York at New Paltz. Her research interests include diversity in organizations, electronic human resources management (e-HR), and recruiting. She has published several book chapters on disability issues, e-HR, and online recruiting, and has presented a number of papers at meetings of the Academy of Management and the Society for Industrial and Organizational Psychology.

Mary E. McLaughlin is a faculty member in the Department of Management and Organization at Pennsylvania State University. She received her Ph.D. from the University of Illinois-Urbana in 1988.

Albert Mills is Director of the Sobey Ph.D. Program (St Mary's University). He is the author of *Sex, Strategy and the Stratosphere* (Palgrave, 2006) and co-author/co-editor of 11 other books.

Jean Helms Mills is an Associate Professor of Management at St Mary's University. She is the author of *Making Sense of Organizational Change* (Routledge, 2003) and is currently working on her sixth co-authored/co-edited book.

Ali Mir is an associate professor in the College of Business at William Paterson University. He is currently working on issues related to migration/immigration and the international division of labor. He is on the board of directors of the Brecht Forum in New York City.

Raza Mir is an associate professor in the College of Business at William Paterson University. His research mainly concerns the transfer of knowledge across national boundaries in multinational corporations, and issues relating to power and resistance in organizations.

Kiran Mirchandani is an associate professor at the Ontario Institute for Studies in Education of the University of Toronto. She has published on home-based work, telework, contingent work, entrepreneurship, transnational service work and self-employment. She teaches in the Adult Education and Community Development Program and offers courses on gendered and racialized processes in the workplace, critical perspectives on organizational development and learning, and technology, globalization and economic restructuring.

Stella M. Nkomo, Ph.D., is a professor of business leadership at the University of South Africa Graduate School of Business Leadership. A former scholar-in-residence at the Mary Ingraham Bunting Institute of Radcliffe College, her internationally recognized work on race and gender in organizations and managing diversity appears in numerous journals, edited volumes, and magazines. She is the past Chair of the Women in Management Division of the Academy of Management.

Jennifer Parlamis received her Ph.D. in social-organizational psychology at Teachers College, Columbia University in 2001. She completed a post-doctoral fellowship at Columbia University's School of Business in 2002 and is currently a lecturer of psychology and education and Director of the MA program in social-organizational psychology at Teachers College, Columbia University.

Anshuman Prasad, Ph.D., is Professor of Strategic Management and Organizational Analysis at the University of New Haven. His research interests include corporate legitimacy, workplace diversity, resistance and empowerment, and epistemology.

Pushkala Prasad is the Zankel Chair Professor of Management for Liberal Arts Students at Skidmore College. Her research interests are in workplace diversity, multiculturalism and organizational legitimacy. She has recently published Crafting Qualitative Research with M.E. Sharpe Inc.

Elissa L. Perry is an associate professor of psychology and education at Teachers College, Columbia University. She received an M.S. and Ph.D. in organizational behavior and theory from Carnegie Mellon University. Elissa has research interests in the role of demographic variables in human resource judgments, sexual harassment, and older workers.

Judith K. Pringle, Ph.D., is Professor/Organization Studies at Auckland University of Technology. Her teaching and research focuses on issues of workplace diversity, the constructed identities of women in organizations, gender issues and critical analyses of careers.

Karen L. Proudford, Ph.D., is an associate professor of management at the Graves School of Business and Management, Morgan State University. She is also a faculty affiliate with the Center for Gender in Organizations at the Simmons School of Management. Her research, writing and consulting interests include group and intergroup dynamics, leadership, diversity and conflict.

Maureen Scully, Ph.D., is an assistant professor at the University of Massachusetts Boston. She is a faculty affiliate with the Center for Gender in Organizations at the Simmons School of Management and a research advisor for the Aspen Institute Business and Society Program. Her research focuses on how inequality is legitimated in organizational settings and is sometimes contested by grassroots employees groups. She has studied a variety of organizational change initiatives including corporate ethics programs, employee affinity groups, work restructuring, and virtual work. She is currently working on a book, *Luck, Pluck, or Merit? How Americans Make Sense of Inequality*.

Hock-Peng Sin is a Ph.D. student in industrial/organizational psychology at the Pennsylvania State University. His research interests include causes and consequences of performance trajectories and interpersonal dynamics in the workplace.

Amanda Sinclair is Foundation Professor of management (diversity and change) at Melbourne Business School. Her two most recent books are *Doing Leadership Differently* and *New Faces of Leadership* (both published by Melbourne University Press, 1998 and 2002 respectively). Amanda teaches and conducts research in areas including leadership, change, ethics, gender and diversity. As a yoga teacher, she also has a keen interest in supporting people towards change and growth, at work and in life.

Ralph Stablein, Ph.D., is Professor of Management at Massey University in New Zealand. His research and teaching focus on inquiry in organization studies and critical management studies.

Dianna L. Stone received her Ph.D. from Purdue University and is Professor of Management and Psychology at the University of Central Florida. Her research focuses on diversity in organizations, electronic human resources management (e-HR), privacy, and reactions to selection techniques. The results of her research have been published in the *Journal of Applied Psychology*, *Personnel Psychology*, *Academy of Management Review*, *Organizational Behavior and Human Decision Processes*, and *Journal of Management*. She has also edited two books on e-HR, and is on the editorial boards of *Human Resources Management Review*, *Human Resources Management* and other journals. She is a Fellow of the American Psychological Society and the Society for Industrial and Organizational Psychology.

Eugene F. Stone-Romero (Ph.D., University of California-Irvine) is Professor of Psychology and Management at the University of Central Florida. He is a Fellow of the Society for Industrial and Organizational Psychology, the American Psychological Society, and the American Psychological Association. The results of his research have been published in such outlets as the *Journal of Applied Psychology*, *Organizational Behavior and Human Performance*, *Personnel Psychology*, *Journal of Vocational Behavior*, *Academy of Management Journal*, *Journal of Management*, *Educational and Psychological Measurement*, *Applied Psychology: An International Review*, *Journal of Applied Social Psychology*, *Journal of Educational Psychology*, *International Review of Industrial and Organizational Psychology*, and *Research in Personnel and Human Resources Management*.

Elisabeth Sundin is a professor at the Swedish National Institute of Working Life and at the Department of Business Administration, Linköpings University, Sweden. She has been doing research on gender and organizations for many years and was leading the organizational part of a public investigation on women and economic power in Sweden in the late 1990s.

Amy Thurlow is a Ph.D. student at the Sobey School of Business, St Mary's University, Halifax.

Diana J. Wong is an assistant professor of strategy and organization development at Eastern Michigan University. Her research interests include cross-cultural boundary spanning, photography as a research methodology, and strategic alliances.

Examining the Contours of Workplace Diversity

Concepts, Contexts and Challenges

PUSHKALA PRASAD, JUDITH K. PRINGLE
AND ALISON M. KONRAD

Few social phenomena have attracted as much attention in the late twentieth and early twenty-first centuries as that of diversity and multiculturalism. Debates and policies regarding both diversity and multiculturalism are to be found in many different social sectors including education, health, government, the media and the workplace. While the United States is often regarded as a pioneer in the diversity movement, its preoccupation with diversity is now echoed across the world in countries ranging from Australia and France to Israel and Jamaica. What was once a concern mainly for so-called 'new' immigrant nations such as Canada, Brazil, the United States and New Zealand has increasingly become an issue for 'older' countries in Europe, Asia and the Middle East as well. Recent large-scale population movements across the globe (Appadurai, 1990) in the form of refugees, guestworkers and immigrants have changed the erstwhile homogeneous face of many countries, and have triggered a range of cultural tensions and visible exclusionary practices within them. Not surprisingly perhaps, an interest in diversity can now be found across the world.

This handbook focuses exclusively on workplace diversity and all its attendant problems, tensions and achievements. Before entering into a detailed discussion of our project, we feel that the term 'diversity' is in need of some unpacking. The dictionary definition of diversity is of little practical value because, in the material world of workplaces, the term holds multiple overlapping and conflicting meanings (Hays-Thomas, 2004; Prasad & Mills, 1997). One reason is that so many stakeholder groups – managers, consultants, activists, unions and academics – all claim ownership over the term and offer their own interpretations of it. To complicate matters further, diversity has an ambiguous and intangible connection to North American legal practices, social movements and public policy initiatives such as Title VII of the Civil Rights Act, various pieces of anti-discrimination legislation, affirmative action (in the United States and Australia) and employment equity (in Canada and the UK). At the same time, it is important to remind ourselves that diversity, unlike discrimination, is *not* a legal term and has no legal force behind it (Prasad, 2001; Yakura, 1996). Rather, managing diversity has primarily emerged as a voluntary corporate initiative directed at the systematic recruitment and retainment of employees belonging to diverse social identity groups.

At its core, the concept of diversity is all about matters of *difference* and *inclusion*. However, there remains no easy agreement on either the nature of differences that should be considered or the kind of inclusionary measures that should be practiced. At one extreme, a section of the consultant discourse on diversity favors including all conceivable elements of difference including leadership styles, physical characteristics, cognitive patterns and personality traits in addition to demographic differences in age, gender, race, ethnicity and religion (Thomas, 1996). The problem with this approach is that it treats all differences as meriting equal attention, and fails to recognize that some differences (e.g. race or sexual orientation) are likely to present more severe disadvantage in the workplace than others (such as hair color or communication styles).

Others, such as Hays-Thomas (2004) and Linnehan and Konrad (1999), propose that a more meaningful understanding of diversity would focus on groups that have *systematically* faced discrimination and oppression at work. These *historically disadvantaged groups* would typically include non-whites, women, religious and ethnic minorities, individuals with physical disabilities, older employees, gays, lesbians and bisexuals, and transgendered people. In many industrialized and economically advanced countries, many of these groups also receive some measure of protection from discrimination under local laws. This protection is one reason why workplace diversity tends to be often equated with anti-discriminatory regulation and equal employment policies. Our position in this handbook is that workplace diversity is a more relevant concept if it focuses on those differences that have been systematically discriminated against, irrespective of whether or not they receive legal protection. Thus, from our perspective, gender and race differences (which are often covered by the laws of various countries) are still important as are differences in sexual orientation and body weight (which receive less protection under the law).

Our reasons for making this choice are twofold. First, differences in power and status resulting from ascriptive characteristics are inconsistent with the logic of merit-based rewards in organizations. As such, the contradiction between the meritocratic ideology espoused by many work organizations and actual differences in treatment and reward experienced on the basis of demographic group memberships creates a set of substantive problems in need of investigation and action. Second, the literature on individual differences in organizations has a long history, and variation in personality, cognition and behavioral style has always been present in work organizations. Managerial interest in the topic of diversity was not precipitated, however, until members of historically excluded demographic groups began to make inroads into desirable occupational, professional and managerial positions previously reserved for the dominant majority (Konrad, 2003). Attending to the genesis of the field is important for ensuring that our scholarship does not ignore fundamentally important features of the diversity phenomenon. Studies that assume away status and power differences between groups threaten to result in a misleading set of findings that could direct organizational efforts away from the problems and opportunities with the greatest impact on outcomes. Importantly, the disadvantages experienced by historically excluded groups have greater impact on the lives of organizational members, and directing our research toward giving voice to the experiences of those who have historically been disenfranchised may be helpful for making important material improvements to the lives of many.

It is important to note here that certain kinds of difference are likely to have greater salience in some places and at certain moments than in different times and in different places. In some Scandinavian countries, for instance, progressive laws accommodating women in the workplace have made gender differences less of a concern than in others such as Malaysia, where rampant gender discrimination is practiced, or the United States, where working women are at a tremendous disadvantage because of the meager maternity benefits provided by the state. Yet, within Scandinavia itself, differences in race and religion clearly play a tremendous part in sustaining employment discrimination. Again, employers in some Western European countries are noticeably open toward gays and lesbians, while simultaneously being adverse to hiring Asian and North African immigrants. By contrast, sections of the United States are aggressively hostile to individuals with alternative sexual orientations while being open to hiring credentialed foreigners from different parts of the world. Additionally, some dimensions of diversity intersect with conventional categories of difference and protected social identity groups in new and problematic ways. In both Canada and the United States for instance, linguistic differences are often responsible for prejudicial attitudes and discriminatory actions against Francophones and Hispanics irrespective of gender and race, and sometimes compounding issues of gender and race. In sum, therefore, diversity is a geographically and culturally contingent phenomenon, and needs to be understood as such.

In addition to raising questions about what constitutes difference, the diversity discourse also raises questions about the meaning of inclusion. At a simplistic level, workplace diversity is all about ensuring that diverse social identity groups are fairly represented in private and public organizations in any country. However, the cultural dimension of diversity also implies that diversity is much more than a matter of representation. Diversity is also about *respecting* and *valuing* differences, whether they are gender-, race- or ethnic-based differences in lifestyles, appearance, linguistic proficiency, communication and decision-making styles, etc.

These questions about cultural inclusion often get played out in contemporary debates on cultural assimilation versus cultural pluralism. Cultural assimilation has a long history of liberal support in the West, and broadly favors homogenization followed by inclusion under the rubric of integration (Glazer, 1997; Suarez-Orozco, 2002). Within assimilationist thinking, once cultural differences (language, rituals, communication styles, etc.) are voluntarily surrendered in favor of the dominant cultural practices, integration will automatically take place and group differences will cease to matter. Assimilation thus demands a considerable amount of cultural sacrifice in return for inclusion and acceptance in the broader society and organization. We would argue that from a diversity perspective, assimilation is actually relatively monocultural, and therefore fundamentally antagonistic to an acceptance of, let alone valuing, cultural differences.

In the last 20–30 years, the notion of cultural pluralism has gained popular support, and offers an alternate approach to dealing with difference. Rooted in the philosophy of multiculturalism (Spivak, 1987; Taylor, 1994), pluralism requires that the dominant culture (of either states or organizations) accepts rather than absorbs cultural differences through co-existence rather than integration. In other words, cultural pluralism is far more sympathetic to the notion of diversity and is aimed at developing policies and mechanisms of adjustment to difference. Needless to say, both cultural assimilation and cultural pluralism engender different kinds of conflicts and tensions. Assimilation leads to the suppression of cultural difference and results in resentment among minority groups and unrealistic expectations of cultural integration among majority groups. Cultural pluralism, on the other hand, leads to struggles over cultural spaces in organizations and societies. Many of the chapters in this volume will either directly or indirectly touch upon some of the issues raised here. Additionally, as workplace diversity gains increasing visibility and legitimacy in organizational and academic worlds, it is also confronted with a whole host of new challenges, opportunities and dilemmas. The remainder of this chapter addresses some of them in greater detail.

THE DIVERSITY LEXICON

As noted earlier, language in the field of workplace diversity is contentious and contested. The proliferation of terms and the implied and often ignored political implications present a literal and literary quagmire for scholars and practitioners alike. It is important to use language that situates diversity issues within specific historical contexts in order to avoid implications that particular identity groups are lacking or deficient in some way. One responsibility of diversity scholars is to be aware of their usage of terms in order to provide syntactical leadership in their discussions within and beyond academe.

We prefer terms commonly used in anthropology and sociology, such as 'systematically excluded' or 'historically disadvantaged', because they explicitly recognize the structural component of the diversity plus an asymmetric distribution of power. Language rooted in disciplines such as psychology or economics commonly situates the fundamental mechanisms driving diversity dynamics within individuals which make structural forces, historical contexts, and the influence of power elites less visible. Confusion around terminology is most apparent within gender studies with differences drawn between sex, sex role category and gender (West & Zimmerman, 1991: 14). Scholars in the tradition of critical race studies eschew the term 'diversity' because they see it diluting the interest of particular identity groups. A parallel argument occurs in gender studies, namely that diversity serves to further mute the concerns of women (Sinclair, 2000). As Nkomo and Cox noted in an earlier review, 'The concept of identity appears to be at the core of understanding diversity in organizations' (1996: 339). Furthermore, social identity, or that component of identity based on membership in social groups (Tajfel & Turner, 1986), theorizes that our identity does not have meaning independent of the larger societal context.

Some terminology has legal roots, which is useful because legal issues arise very clearly within historical and national contexts. At the same time problems arise because such language is peculiar to a specific legal system and consequently meanings differ internationally. A central example is the terminology of equal employment opportunity (EEO) and affirmative action (AA). The same language is used across countries but the meanings and workforce implications vary due to the specific legal framework of the nation. For example, the AA legislation in Australia (Hede, 2000) broadly incorporates both the EEO legislation and the President's executive order on AA of the United States (Konrad & Linnehan, 1999); while, in New Zealand, initiatives labeled as EEOs mirror the Australian situation (Sayers and Tremaine, 1994) but the legislation applies only to governmental organizations.

Selecting terminology incurs the risk of choosing the linguistic roots and historical assumptions that are infused in the word. The choice of term therefore becomes a declaration, a marker of one's ontology and polemic. Consequently the origin of the term is of key importance signifying the direction of the question: through whose eyes? We argue that all terminology is problematic given the infusion of power and privilege, disadvantage and deprivation, embedded in social identity group relations. Clearly, the labeling of significant identity groups is not straightforward.

Most research and discussion has focused on 'visible' characteristics such as sex and race (Foldy, 2002), although more recent developments (Kirton & Greene, 2005) have been to extend the research domain to 'invisible' diversity. Disabilities (Chapter 16) and ethnicity may be both visible or invisible (Chapter 13). An added layer of complexity to invisible diversity in the workplace is the individual's decision-making process of becoming visible or 'coming out' (Chapter 15). Without disclosure (verbal or non-verbal) the person may 'pass' as a member of, for example, the heterosexual dominant group, an option not afforded members of visible diversity groups.

The preferred labels of identity groups also may change over generations as the specific socio-political context shifts. For example, in the United States, older people may use and refer to themselves as 'blacks' while more common usage by younger people is 'African Americans'. Conversely, in the UK people of African origin color prefer to refer to themselves as 'black' (Chapter 21), while South Asians are less comfortable with this terminology which they see as being too invariant. Within groups, members may disagree over terms such as Hispanic or Latina. In Canada the indigenous people are referred to as 'First Nations peoples' and in the United States, 'Native Americans'. With the increasing strength of the political voice of indigenous peoples on a global scale there have been moves to adopt the preferred name by the group members such as 'Inuit' in Canada rather than a colonizer's term such as Eskimo. Within Australia (and to some extent the United States) there has been a noticeable shift from the encompassing label Aboriginal Australian to the specific tribal name, for example Koorie. A clear example of the historical context embedded in the language comes from New Zealand (NZ). The labeling of the indigenous people as Maori was implicitly a colonizing act, assimilating previously distinct tribes under a common term. In a somewhat reciprocal manner, the word developed by Maori for the colonizers (of largely British origin) is 'Pakeha' (King, 2003). Today the term Pakeha is embraced by some European New Zealanders while it is vehemently resisted by others, with rebuttals such as 'we are all New Zealanders' (Mikaere, 2004). For those individuals who consciously adopt the label Pakeha there is a recognition that they are descendants of the colonizers. Thus the term 'Pakeha' makes explicit the political and cultural history of colonization.

Some protagonists would identify this debate and degree of specificity as superficial 'political correctness', an overused and impotent rebuke aimed to belittle and undermine the concerns of groups who historically have had lesser power. For example, within the United States there is common recourse to the right to 'free speech' contained in the First Amendment to the Constitution. Free speech has parallels with the right to a free lunch in a business world. 'Free' carries obligations and responsibilities where there is interaction with others. Invoking this aspect of the Constitution to insult others is immoral, if not illegal. There are examples of nations where there is strong pressure not to use politically charged identity labels; for example, within post-war democratic Germany the use of the label 'Nazi' is in effect deemed unconstitutional and effectively banned.

There is much debate amongst scholars and consultant/practitioners over the lexicon of workplace diversity. Managing diversity was a human resource management intervention adopted initially in the United States and Canada (Agocs & Burr, 1996). 'Managing diversity' is the most common label for diversity-related work (Foldy, 2002) within businesses, although not necessarily government organizations. However, within this umbrella term there is a plethora of expressions: 'managing', 'affirming' 'valuing' and even 'tolerating diversity'.

Imbued in all these concepts are variable political assumptions of the 'rightness' of hierarchy and disbursement of power within and amongst identity groups. We briefly outline the discussion around each of the terms and highlight the diversity (*sic!*) within the language which is an intrinsic part of the following chapters. Some authors are explicit about their usage while others are not.

The dilution of the powered implications within social identity become apparent in the much cited definition by Thomas (1991: 12):

> Diversity includes everyone: it is not something that is defined by race or gender. It extends to age, personal and corporate background, education, function and personality. It includes life style, sexual preference, geographic origin, tenure with the organisation ... and management and non-management.

Such a definition of 'diversity' views every individual as different and equally valued. Consequently differential power between identity groups is ignored and any historical asymmetric positions of power and privilege continue to be enshrined.

Some writers have developed a hierarchy of appropriateness for the terms: for example, Thomas (1990, cited in Agocs & Burr, 1996) claimed that managing diversity is a more advanced concept than valuing diversity, which, in turn, is a higher form of organizational response than affirmative action. These responses are part of the progressive distancing and backlash against AA and EEO initiatives and illustrate the desire to shift discussion to a managerialist discourse focusing on measurable objectives, thereby seeking to obliterate power from the conversation. Prasad (2001) has also argued that the discourse of workplace diversity has adroitly pushed questions of recurring employment discrimination to the background, while simultaneously showcasing individual corporate efforts to fill a few positions with women and minorities. Managing diversity has been differentiated from EEO and AA by other writers (Cassell, 2001; Hays-Thomas, 2004) but suffice to say in contrast to the group focus of EEO, managing diversity requires individual assessment and treatment presumably in a way that does not incite discrimination or favoritism.

Managing diversity carries with it the legacy of managing: the traditional classic notions of control, leadership, organizing and power. This diversity framework is situated within the hierarchical corporate control systems where organizational authority lies with senior management. Workplace diversity then becomes the object of control and organizing, and senior managers are the legitimate instigators of organization change. They are in the ambiguous position of predicting and pre-empting the needs of multiple identity groups 'lower' in the organization. Managing diversity then becomes the task of 'double-guessing' the needs and desires of the marginal groups (Jones, Pringle & Shepherd, 2000) by managers who have greater power. Yet as Alvesson and Willmott (1996) argue, 'emancipation is not a gift to bestow' (p. 33) and acts of assimilation and integration can 'estrange the individual from the tradition which has formed his or her very subjectivity' (p. 174).

An alternate twist on managing diversity comes from the more functionalist approach of writers situated in a managerial frame. From this view managing diversity is extolled over 'valuing diversity' for its agentic virtues. A variety of nuanced conceptualizations have emerged: parallel with Thomas and Ely's (1996) 'access-and-legitimacy' are Kamp and Hagedorn-Rasmussen's (2004) cultural capital argument, and Billing and Sundin's (Chapter 4 in this volume) 'special contribution'.

A more recent usage is *diversity management*, which simply 'emphasizes the value of difference among people in organizations' (Kamp & Hagedorn-Rasmussen, 2004: 535) and avoids some of the hierarchical problems of managing diversity but does not avoid the focus on individuals and the eliminating of power differentials. Critics of the implicit hierarchical power of the term managing diversity view it as the power-holders' continued commitment to continued 'control ... under the guise of liberal affirmation' (Casey, 2002: 143).

Affirming or valuing diversity implies the need for 'mutual respect, collaborative work styles and employee empowerment' (Betters-Reed & Moore, 1992: 47) and is intended to be more ethically and morally driven (Kirby & Harter, 2003). It implies a broad organizational change effort (Mighty, 1991: 67) aimed at egalitarian outcomes with greater equity for minorities and women, as well as organization benefits (Agocs & Burr, 1996). *Tolerating diversity* implies that attempts to value differences between members of different social identity groups have failed or have become too difficult, moving the organizations into one of grudging tolerance.

Following Konrad (2003) we advocate a definition of diversity that emphasizes intergroup interaction and is inclusive of power differences, rather than focusing on individual differences. This means explicitly acknowledging the role played by past discrimination and oppression in producing socially marginalized groups today. Our vision of diversity is therefore not color blind, a theme we take up below.

THE PROBLEM WITH COLOR BLINDNESS

A recurrent argument raised against multiculturalism and diversity by both Liberals and Conservatives is directed against the supposed tearing of the social fabric that takes place when gender, racial, ethnic, generational, religious and other forms of diversity are recognized and celebrated. The main thread of this critique focuses on the neglect of our shared humanity, arguing that individuals in most modern democracies are equal under the law and have access to a uniform set of rights and privileges. Given both our common humanity and equal status under the law, any emphasis on gender, race, creed, nationality, ethnicity, etc., is believed to be needlessly divisive at a broader cultural level, and ultimately detrimental to the accomplishment of an integrated society (D'Souza, 1995; Lynch, 1997). Such a position is often described as being *color blind*[1] – that is, one that neither notices nor focuses on any kind of biological or socially constructed differences. In essence, color blindness holds onto sameness while ignoring difference (Bacchi, 1990).

Color blindness is invariably presented as a positive attitude – one that is impatient with a range of physical and cultural differences – and is consequently unlikely to result in any kind of protracted discrimination. In other words, a persistent refusal to acknowledge differences is believed to result in a permanently non-discriminatory orientation. While the idea of color blindness is certainly laudable at one level, we should also take note of some of its more problematic features.

First of all, color blindness overlooks the powerful cultural and economic legacy that centuries of exploitation and discrimination leave for historically disadvantaged groups. Entire epochs of slavery, patriarchy and colonialism have resulted in some social identity groups lacking the skills, confidence and institutional support to enter into and advance within work organizations. At the same time, they have also left us with a collection of adverse stereotypes toward women, African Americans, gays, etc., that prevent their full inclusion into the workplace. Given this legacy of discrimination, it is somewhat naive to imagine that an attitude of color blindness on its own can overcome systematic social and organizational discrimination. In sum, 'blinding' oneself to race, gender, sexual preference and other socially significant differences cannot, by itself, erase the consequences of many lifetimes of oppression and/or discrimination.

At a philosophical level, the promotion of color blindness has always posed a troublesome paradox for both Liberals and Conservatives. As Goldberg (1993) argues, while liberal philosophy in particular has espoused color blindness and equality for all human beings irrespective of race, sex, ethnicity, etc., it has also been tarnished by statements from leading liberal scholars including Hume, J. S. Mill, Freud, Kohlberg and others who have clearly made pejorative value judgments about the intellect or moral development of women, Blacks, Asians and individuals following non-Christian religions. In other words, liberalism's abstract rhetoric about equality and color blindness is rarely matched by concrete internal discussions regarding women, different nationalities and races.

At the level of everyday organizational practice as well, similar disjunctures are present. While many progressive laws and organizational policies designed to ensure equality and fair treatment at work exist in several multicultural countries such as Australia, New Zealand, Canada, the UK and the United States these laws are often disregarded or even violated in actual organizational situations. Thus, the mere presence of policies and laws does not always end discrimination at work. Hiring committees continue to rely on questionable stereotypes, promotion decisions that subtly discriminate against women and ethnic minorities are routinely made, and many historically disadvantaged groups continue to be ignored, dismissed or disparaged in a multitude of workplaces (Mighty, 1997; Prasad & Mills, 1997). Given these ongoing realities, maintaining a position of color blindness is arguably somewhat pointless and naive.

Additionally, proponents of color blindness posit that not only is difference unimportant, but it can also be problematic on occasion. This overlooks the fact that biological and cultural differences are both a fact of life and a source of pride and identity to many individuals. Biological differences are most obvious in the case of men versus women. Yet, a gender-blind orientation would argue that men and women should be treated identically in the workplace, and would regard maternity benefits as a form of preferential treatment toward women. What they are missing is that the material facts of pregnancy, childbirth and motherhood cannot be equated with fatherhood, and do indeed require a special kind of accommodation from employers.

Other differences have different connotational significance. Belonging to certain ethnic groups might mean that individuals express specific interactional and communicative styles that could be at odds with mainstream organizational cultures (Prasad, 1997). Both men and women from Far Eastern cultures tend to be socialized to be more self-effacing and reserved. Perhaps, as a result, Chinese–Canadian and Chinese–American men are systematically passed over for managerial promotions on the grounds that they lack initiative and leadership potential (Prasad, 2003). In this case, one brand of ethnic socialization turns out to be a cultural handicap even for talented managers at work. In this and other similar situations, the discourse of color blindness is not helpful in either identifying or dealing with more covert forms of discrimination.

Further, adopting a color-blind attitude fosters a certain amount of denial about the continuation of racism, homophobia and other discriminatory tendencies at work. By assuming that social identities are basically irrelevant, many individuals are also able to ignore the less obvious forms of institutional sexism and racism that pervades organizations in different countries, and on occasion, to even blame women, gays and certain ethnic minorities for their supposed inability to get ahead in the workplace. Worse, as Thomas, Mack and Montigliani (2004) assert, the color-blind approach can provide a shelter for aversive racists and sexists – who make damaging remarks about certain identity groups without necessarily intending to be discriminatory or prejudicial.

In sum, the arguments against a color-blind approach of sameness are indeed compelling, and persuade us in this handbook to eschew such an orientation, focusing instead directly on the unique problems and issues that are relevant to different social identity groups based on gender, race, sexuality, age, class, and so on. This enables us to identify the specific historical circumstances that undergird each group's subsequent encounter with organizations, and examine the institutional barriers they are likely to face at work.

THE SALIENCE OF CONTEXT IN WORKPLACE DIVERSITY

The macro context – history and socio-political influences – directly molds which diversity issues become salient. Crucial aspects of the context for understanding workplace diversity include the history and relative oppressive actions toward different groups, the legislation around access to education, work and health, human rights, the societal placing of diversity groups and the shifts in the salience of issues at different times, caused by the activism internationally and the local level. Understanding diversity issues across countries (and even subcultures) requires the analysis of the social meanings and relative power positions of diversity groups. Within this handbook we have chosen not to present an overview framed by nation (Haq, 2004) as the complexity that results from the interactions of historical factors and specifics of the legal environment within a single volume results in a necessarily descriptive outcome. Nevertheless, relevant illustrations from specific countries are noted throughout this introduction to explicate meaning.

Judgments about 'which diversity group' is more important depends upon the history of the social identity group coupled with the socio-political climate present. It is linked to shifts in relevant legislation (Hunter, 2003) as much as the political activism of the particular group (Prasad, 2001). The salience of issues for each group may ascend and 'fall' within specific epochs, for example the ascendance of women's issues during the 1970s, the subsequent fragmentation and 'fall' in the 1990s. This shift in the women's movement has occurred globally, partly due to the strong and valid critique from women in non-dominant ethnic groups (Calás & Smircich, 1996; hooks, 1984). For example, initially in the United States, African American women were most vocally critics of white women, whereas in NZ it was indigenous Maori women. Moreover, a number of Third World women's movements have been sharply critical of a particular genre of liberal Western feminism which makes unreflective assumptions about female oppression in the non-West. In the chapter on postcolonialism, Prasad examines one such issue in detail.

The choice of which diversity issues become salient is also the result of a dynamic interplay in the shifting power positions of societal groups. Increases in the expression and power of conservative groups will inevitably elicit a stronger reaction from liberal and oppressed groups. For example, in the United States the debate on same-sex marriage increased as a diversity issue in conjunction with the increasing power of the conservative political parties and a stronger voice from conservative Christians. The discussion of this issue, in conjunction with local activism, gave salience to sexuality issues internationally (e.g. in Canada and NZ). The societal debate then flowed into the workplace where sexual orientation increased as a salient workplace diversity issue. Thus workplaces and organizations, which constitute them both produce and reproduce societal power relations. As Alvesson and Billing (1997: 108) noted in their discussion of organizations, 'Gender is not simply imported into the workplace; gender itself is constructed in part through work.'

There is a general tendency to avoid contentious issues, especially by politicians crafting the legislation and corporate elites who are responsible for bringing them into the workplace. Hence the societal context may variously mask and highlight workplace diversity issues. This tendency for avoidance can be seen most sharply in times of more conservative political environments. For example, in Australia, the discourse of diversity is primarily about gender, not about the difficult issue of race. The large immigrant populations of the late twentieth century have been substantively assimilated and integrated, no longer the 'new Australians'. Issues between the white majority and the small indigenous population are too contentious to be the focus of substantive diversity scholarship[2] or practice. Significantly, Aboriginal Affairs has been recently folded into the Department of Immigration and Multicultural Affairs (Chapter 21). In NZ, diversity is not currently focused on gender partly because gender is synonymous with women, and women are dominant in the political public landscape, are featured as entrepreneurial success stories and, to a large extent, are no longer popularly viewed as a disadvantaged group in spite of statistical evidence to the contrary (EEOTrust, 2004). The diversity discourse in NZ/Aotearoa is more firmly located in a bicultural discourse centered on ethnicity and race led by Maori struggles for self-determination. Most advances in this struggle have been made through the establishment and sanctioning of separate development in areas of education, health and economic development.

Acts of exclusion are performed by many, if not all, groups. Some groups have deliberately sought space to initially find support and solidarity, 'consciousness-raise' and then take action. As Greene and Kirton (Chapter 20) argue, this strategy of separate development applied to/by women in trade unions has been a successful facilitator of positive change. These spaces of comparative sanctuary provide one of the few times and places where historically disadvantaged groups are able to be freed from 'doing the work of integration' (Higginbotham, 2001) – explaining, translating and maintaining the bridge with the majority.

In the UK (Kirton & Greene, 2005), most of the 'older' European Union (EU) countries, Australia and NZ, unions are key 'social partners' in employment negotiations and the evolution of the workplace environment. In contrast the United States, the originating site of the diversity discourse, is unusual in the context of Western countries where the voices of unions are not prominent. Thus discussions on workplace diversity within the EU is most likely to be embedded within an industrial relations discourse (European Foundation, 2005 www.eiro.eurofound.ie). The most detailed analysis has been on the basis of gender (e.g. participation statistics, gender pay gap, parental leave provisions) while people with disabilities, older people, black and minority ethnic groups are targets of anti-discrimination legislation (European Commission, 2005).

The establishment (and expansion) of the EU has increased the ease of Europeans to move easily across boundaries, yet this increased workforce mobility is simultaneously countered by attitudes of ethnocentrism and a strengthening of nation states. The anticipated benefit of belonging to a strong economic and political bloc like the EU provides crucial incentives for aspirant nations to enact legislative and policy changes to move toward greater equality and fairness of historically disadvantaged groups, often in the face of a historically patriarchal societal structure. However, in actual practice, 'so-called' progressive Northern European countries such as Denmark, the Netherlands and Sweden have turned into sites of marginalization and discrimination toward non-white immigrants. The important influence of the local environment therefore directs and contains the problematization of workplace diversity.

An understanding of diversity issues as context-specific guided us to include several chapters that go beyond the US perspective to cover topics such as unionization, globalization and postcolonial views. Furthermore, while not ignoring traditional quantitative work, we attempted to place at least equal emphasis on qualitative and critical conceptual perspectives, which emphasize the importance of placing knowledge and scholarship within the appropriate historical and societal context.

MINIMAL INTERGROUP OR MACRO-HISTORICAL PARADIGM?

Another problem with divorcing workplace diversity issues from the social and historical context surrounding them is that an understanding of power/dominance relations between groups is often lost. A number of conceptual frameworks that have been highly influential in the diversity literature lose sight of status and power differences between identity groups. For example, social identity theory (Tajfel & Turner, 1986) has provided an important conceptual base for the field of workplace diversity scholarship, but it has the potential to divert diversity from the examination of power and inequality due to the predominance of the 'minimal intergroup paradigm' in its research tradition. Social identity theory focuses upon the portion of people's self-concept arising from membership in socially significant groups, known as identity groups. Tajfel and Turner's (1986) original conceptualization of social identity theory suggested that identity group categories have many possible origins, including power differentials between demographic or cultural collectivities. Their early experiments showed, however, that power differentials are not needed for people to categorize themselves into ingroups and out-groups or 'us' and 'them'. All that was needed was the categorization itself. For example, in some of the early experiments, participants were randomly assigned to innocuous categories, such as the 'blue' or 'green' groups, and then asked to conduct various activities. The researchers found that the mere act of categorization resulted in participants engaging in in-group bias and outgroup discrimination. This result provided the foundation for the minimal intergroup paradigm, upon which a substantial literature documenting the effects of mere categorization is based.

Considerable work has replicated and honed the early research, demonstrating that mere categorization results in bias favoring the in-group, including enhanced evaluations, more internal attributions for positive behaviors, more external attributions for negative behaviors, and positive discrimination in the distribution of rewards (Brewer & Brown, 1998; Deaux, Reid, Mizrahi & Cotting, 1999; Gagnon & Bourhis, 1996). Scholars have concluded from this substantial body of literature that in-group bias and out-group discrimination are a fundamental dynamic present in all human groups that organizations should be aware of and try to mitigate. One method of mitigating the in-group bias effect is to develop a larger shared goal that serves to focus people's attention on their common/shared identity (Dovidio et al., 2000).

There are at least two problems with the minimal intergroup paradigm for the field of workplace diversity. First, this paradigm implies that all identity groups at all times engage in an in-group bias. This implication has been explicitly examined and critiqued by experimental social psychologists, and meta-analytic findings have demonstrated that members of higher-status groups are more likely to exhibit in-group bias than members of lower-status groups (Mullen, Brown & Smith, 1992). Ironically, low-status groups often favor the higher-status out-group (Hunter et al., 1997; Sachdev & Bourhis, 1987; 1991).

A second problem with the minimal intergroup paradigm is that the impact of in-group bias is the same regardless of the social and historical position of the particular identity group. Given that identity groups are unequally situated such that some have considerably more power and resources at their disposal, in-group bias practiced by highly privileged groups is likely to be considerably more costly to historically disadvantaged groups than the reverse. This issue is also applicable to other concepts in the social psychological tradition, such as the similarity–attraction paradigm (Byrne, 1971) and the processes of prejudice and stereotyping (Macrae & Bodenhausen, 2000). Historically privileged groups who exclude, stereotype and manifest prejudice against historically disadvantaged groups have a considerably more detrimental material effect on the outcomes of the out-group than vice versa.

Sociologists and critical scholars are more likely to emphasize the importance of situating diversity issues within the social and structural context surrounding them. In this perspective, intergroup biases arise from sources outside the individual, such as historical patterns of resource distribution between groups, although they are expressed through individual cognition and behavior such as differential expectations and differential opportunities to demonstrate competence. Power and privilege are identified as a major source of intergroup biases, and the negative view of the out-group arises because that group is located in a resource-poor structural position within the society. As a result of their location in a disadvantaged social space, members of certain demographic groups come to be viewed by members of the advantaged group as dangerous, untrustworthy, lazy, and/or intellectually or in other ways inferior.

For example, status characteristics theory in sociology argues that the reason certain demographic groups come to be viewed as inferior performers is because members of that group are systematically denied access to the resources necessary for effectiveness, such as education, developmental experiences or advantageous social networks. When members of historically privileged groups work with members of historically disadvantaged groups, the former are likely to perform more effectively, due to these differences in access to resources. Hence, expectations that historically disadvantaged groups will perform poorly are reinforced by experience, and status differences between groups become strengthened, not reduced, with greater contact between groups (Ridgeway, 1991; Webster & Hysom, 1998).

The macro-historical paradigm suggests that the remedy of emphasizing a larger shared goal may be insufficient for overcoming all of the issues arising from intergroup inequalities in society. Hence, bringing different groups together into an organizational culture and then emphasizing that 'we are all on the same organizational team' may not mitigate the effects of unequal access to power and resources.

Additionally, an understanding of context creates the possibility of asymmetries in the experiences of historically advantaged and disadvantaged identity groups. Specifically, a particular belief or behavior may have a qualitatively different meaning if it comes from a person in power than if the person is in a position of historical disadvantage. The material implications of beliefs and behavior of powerful and powerless people are asymmetrical as well.

One example of such asymmetries is expressed in Higginbotham's (2001) concept of African American women doing the 'work of integration'. The work of integration arises when a historically excluded group becomes included in an organizational setting and is constituted of daily interpersonal struggles to be heard, valued and accepted by the historically dominant majority. Additionally, these individuals must interact with members of the dominant group in a way that will put them at ease in order to overcome the social discomfort of difference. In contrast, members of the dominant majority are listened to, valued and accepted in the organization. Given that members of the minority find that the work of integration falls on their shoulders, it is not surprising that such individuals find solace in interactions with similar others. Hence, self-segregation among minority groups likely fulfills a fundamentally different function (i.e. stress reduction, restoration, validation in the face of adversity) than it does among historically advantaged groups.

GENRES OF WORKPLACE DIVERSITY RESEARCH

In order to depict the variety of workplace diversity scholarship, we have identified four dimensions along which we categorize several conceptual perspectives. The dimensions are intended to be continuous, but for convenience, we represent them as dichotomies in the Tables. Hence, perspectives sharing the same box in our Figures represent both less and more extreme examples of each genre. Our placement of any given perspective can certainly be debated, but we have attempted to consider the breadth of the field in making these distinctions. Hence, a perspective that might appear to be relatively low on any particular dimension from the perspective of scholars working within a particular genre may appear to be relatively high on that dimension when the full range of genres in workplace diversity research is considered. It is from this broader view that we have categorized the perspectives which follow.

The Four Dimensions

The four dimensions we have chosen to depict the conceptual space for workplace diversity draw from and build upon the work of Burrell and Morgan (1979). We are able to expand the number of dimensions for the field of workplace diversity because we are developing a categorization scheme for a more narrowly defined field, which allows us to elaborate dimensions with greater specificity. The four dimensions we have identified consider whether the perspective:

1   takes a positivist or non-positivist epistemological stance,
2   has a relatively low or high awareness of power relations between identity groups,
3   locates the driving causal forces of diversity dynamics at the individual, interpersonal or macro-structural level of analysis, and
4   identifies identities as fluid or fixed.

The positivist/non-positivist dimension is consistent with Burrell and Morgan's work. Positivist genres assume that the researcher *can and should* take an objective stance external to the diversity phenomenon of interest. In positivist genres, *methodological rigor requires* that researcher involvement, either psychological (value-laden conclusions) or material (demand effects), be *ruled out* as a possible explanation for the results of the study. Non-positivist genres assume that the researcher *cannot* be objective and external toward diversity phenomena. Additionally, in non-positivist genres, the involvement of the researchers' personal values to guide the conclusions and even the researchers' personal intervention in the diversity phenomenon of interest is not thought to vitiate scholarly rigor.

The second dimension considers whether a conceptual perspective contains a high or low awareness of power relations between identity groups. By categorizing perspectives along this dimension, we emphasize that many perspectives consider the relative power held by different identity groups to be a key causal factor driving diversity phenomena. We recognize that researchers can and have added the dimension of power relations to some of the positivist perspectives we have labeled as being low in power awareness (see e.g. Stevens & Fiske, 2000). Such work has been valuable for identifying useful moderators and/or qualitative distinctions in the dynamics affecting high- and low-power identity groups. But in cases where the central causal constructs of interest do not include power relations, we consider the conceptual perspective to be low in power awareness.

The third dimension specifies the level of analysis at which the conceptual perspective locates the causal forces driving diversity phenomena. These causal forces have been conceptualized as residing within individuals (micro), interpersonal or group processes (meso), or macro-level social structures. The structural level of analysis potentially includes the organizational level, but in most cases the focus is on the societal level of analysis. The issue of level of analysis is less relevant to non-positivist diversity perspectives because most of them (e.g. feminism, critical race theory, postcolonialism, etc.) tend to constantly move between different levels when considering material situations. Feminism, for instance, always emphasizes local meanings around diversity while simultaneously being cognizant of macro-structural forms of injustice. Similarly, postcolonialism and critical race theory examine how macro-institutional patterns are imprinted in the micro everyday world. Most non-positivist genres therefore tend to emphasize the importance of regularly transcending different levels.

The fourth dimension that we include focuses on the construction of identity. 'Fixed' identity refers primarily to the psychological traditions reminiscent of traits. This does not imply a necessarily essentialist position in the origin of such identity characteristics, for some scholars argue that the identity is modified in adulthood as the result of learning and experience, albeit slowly. The discussion of 'fluid' identity lies firmly within the social constructionist and post-structural discourses. The degree of fluidity can vary from malleability across situations

TABLE 1.1   *Non-positivist genres in workplace diversity*

Nature of identity	Power awareness	
	Low	High
Fixed	Symbolic interactionism	Feminist perspectives (e.g. psycho-analytic, radical, socialist) Critical race theory Postcolonial theory Institutional theory (e.g. the European tradition)
Fluid	Dramaturgy	Post-structuralism Postcolonial theory

TABLE 1.2   *Positivist genres in workplace diversity*

Level of analysis	Power awareness	
	Low	High
Individual	Trait theory perspectives Stereotyping Prejudice	Homophobia/heterosexism
Interpersonal	Network theory Similarity–attraction Social identity theory	Subtle, everyday racism Subtle sexism
Macro-structural	Market forces Cultural differences Sociobiology	Institutional theory (e.g. institutional economics) Status characteristics theory Structuralism

(reminiscent of role changes) to the annihilation of the core concept of identity that is replaced by not only rapidly changing identity constructions but also the simultaneous holding of contradictory and ambiguous 'selves'. The concept of identity as fluid or fixed is less relevant to positivist diversity perspectives because these perspectives treat identity as relatively fixed. In the positivist view, each individual may hold multiple social identities, and the salience of any given identity is seen as determined by both the individual and the situation. The identities are seen as firmly rooted in the self-concept, however, unlike the social constructionist and post-structuralist perspectives, which view identities as being created and recreated through the process of interaction.

Tables 1.1 and 1.2 give a variety of academic theoretical traditions that may be fruitful when used to interrogate questions within research on workplace diversity.

The depicted perspectives do not include all conceptualizations informing the extant literature, and we invite readers to situate additional perspectives along this same set of dimensions. We find this categorization useful for identifying which conceptual perspectives best fit a particular research question, matching epistemology and methodology, and suggest that scholars utilize it for selecting that combination of perspectives which will best suit their research aims.

CONCLUSION

One of the benefits of bringing the different genres of workplace diversity research together into a single volume is that scholars are provided with the full array of approaches available to bring to bear on any particular research question. If scholars find that research approaches within familiar genres are overly limiting for achieving particular research aims, awareness of other possibilities may provide alternative avenues of exploration. In other words, we can take our research further when we hit a wall.

In sum, we can strengthen our research. As such, we can live with what we preach to organizations and decision-makers. As a result, we will know more. This understanding will allow us to develop a common language and body of knowledge so that we can better support one another.

Another benefit is raising awareness of the potential limitations of one's preferred genre or genres and to identify useful possibilities for triangulation. Qualitative, non-positivist work might uncover new constructs which might be usefully assessed quantitatively to allow for comparisons across situations as well as generalization through a positivist frame. Positivist work might identify statistical associations that could be elaborated and contextualized with a non-positivist approach.

We also demonstrate openness to a variety of voices and ways of knowing by including a variety of scholarly genres within the same text.

An appreciation for the variety of forms of work in our field will better inform our research, teaching and practice by ensuring that scholars in our field are more effectively educated in the full range of the language of workplace diversity scholarship.

Another benefit of bringing the different genres of work together is to reverse the process of fragmentation occurring in the workplace diversity field. Knowledge of the work that has occurred and is going on around the world will help to prevent needless reinvention of existing constructs. Such knowledge will also minimize the proliferation of multiple labels for the same concepts, or at least allow us to identify the relationships among families of similar concepts.

Being fully educated and aware of each other's work, we will be more able to support each other, perhaps with the result that the field will develop more richly and rapidly. Being able to understand what makes for good scholarship in a variety of genres of workplace diversity research will allow us to review each other's work more expertly in order to identify and support the finest pieces so that they will be more widely read. This process will enhance the visibility and impact of our work.

NOTES

1 We are using the term 'color blind' here also as a synonym for other kinds of social 'blindness' including blindness toward gender, age, ethnicity, religion, etc.

2 The authors acknowledge the emerging work from the research of doctoral candidates (e.g. Appo, 2004; Foley, 2004).

REFERENCES

Agocs, C., & Burr, C. (1996). Employment equity, affirmative action and managing diversity: Assessing the differences. *International Journal of Manpower, 17*(4/5), 30–45.

Alvesson, M., & Billing, Y. (1997). *Understanding gender and organizations.* Newbury Park, CA: Sage.

Alvesson, M., & Willmott, H. (1996). *Making sense of management: A critical introduction.* London: Sage.

Appadurai, A. (1990). Disjuncture and difference in the global economy. *Public culture, 2,* 15–24.

Appo, D. (2004). Facing the brick wall: Hassles, buffers and organisational policies affecting the employment of the physically, mentally and socially (indigenous) disabled. Paper presented at Australian and New Zealand Academy of Management conference, Dunedin, December.

Bacchi, C. L. (1990). *Same difference: Feminism and sexual difference.* Sydney: Allen and Unwin.

Betters-Reed, B. L., & Moore, L. L. (1992). Managing diversity: Focusing on women and the whitewash dilemma. In U. Sekaran and F. T. L. Leong (Eds), *Womenpower: Managing times of demographic turbulence.* Newbury Park, CA: Sage.

Brewer, M. B., & Brown, R. J. (1998). Intergroup relations. In D. T. Gilbert, S. T. Fiske & G. Lindzey (Eds), *Handbook of social psychology* (Volume II, pp. 554–94). New York: McGraw-Hill.

Burrell, G., & Morgan, G. (1979). *Sociological paradigms an organizational analysis.* London: Heinemann.

Byrne, D. E. (1971). *The attraction paradigm.* New York: Academic Press.

Calás, M., & Smircich, L. (1996). From 'the woman's' point of view: Feminist approaches to Organisation Studies. In S. Clegg, C. Hardy & W. Nord (Eds), *Handbook of organization studies* (pp. 218–57). London: Sage.

Casey, C. (2002). *Critical analysis of organizations: Theory, practice and revitalization.* London: Sage.

Cassell, C. (2001). The business case and the management of diversity. In M. Davidson & R. Burke (Eds), *Women in management: Current research issues, Volume II.* London: Sage.

Deaux, K., Reid, A., Mizrahi, K. & Cotting, D. (1999). Connecting the person to the social: The functions of social identification. In T. R. Tyler, R. M. Kramer, & O. P. John (Eds), *The psychology of the social self* (pp. 91–114). Mahwah, NJ: Lawrence Erlbaum.

D'Souza, D. (1995). *The end of racism.* New York: Simon & Schuster.

Dovidio, J. F., Gaertner, S. L., Niemann, Y. F., & Snider, K. (2001). Racial, ethnic, and cultural differences in responding to distinctiveness and discrimination on campus: Stigma and common group identity. *Journal of Social Issues, 57,* 167–88.

EEOTrust (2004). *Diversity survey report 2004.* Auckland: Equal Employment Opportunities Trust.

European Commission Directorate for Employment and Social Affairs (2005). *Managing diversity.* Available at www.socialeurope.com/mandiv/en/summary.html (accessed 23 May 2005).

European Foundation for the Improvement of Living and Working Conditions (2005). *European industrial relations observatory online.* Available at www.eiro.eurofound.ei (accessed 24 January 2005).

Foldy, E. (2002). 'Managing' diversity: Identity and power in organizations. In Iiris Aaltio & Albert Mills (Eds), *Gender, Identity and the Culture of Organizations.* London: Routledge.

Foley, D. (2004). Where do indigenous Australian entrepreneurs fit into mainstream society? Paper presented at Australian and New Zealand Academy of Management conference, Dunedin, December.

Gagnon, A., & Bourhis, R. Y. (1996). Discrimination in the minimal group paradigm: Social identity or self-interest? *Personality and Social Psychology Bulletin*, *22*, 1289–1301.

Glazer, N. (1997). *We are all multiculturalists now*. Cambridge, MA: Harvard University Press.

Goldberg, D. T. (1993). *Racist culture: Philosophy and the politics of meaning*. Oxford: Blackwell.

Haq, R. (2004). International perspectives on workplace diversity. In M. Stockdale & F. J. Crosby (Eds), *The psychology and management of workplace diversity* (pp. 31–51). Malden, MA: Blackwell.

Hays-Thomas, R. (2004). Why now? The contemporary focus on managing diversity. In M. Stockdale & F. J. Crosby (Eds), *The psychology and management of workplace diversity* (pp. 3–30). Malden, MA: Blackwell.

Hede, A. (2000). Affirmative action in Australia: Employment equity at the crossroads. In M. Davidson and R. Burke (Eds), *Women in management: Current research issues* (Volume II, pp. 279–93). London: Sage.

Higginbotham, E. (2001). Working for the city: Workplace dilemmas for professional U.S. Black women. Paper presented at the Conference on Rethinking Gender, Work, and Organizations held at Keele University, Keele, Staffordshire, June 2001.

hooks, b. (1984). *Feminist theory from margin to center*. Boston, MA: South End Press.

Hunter, J. A., Platow, M. J., Bell, L. M., Kypri, K., & Lewis, C. A. (1997). Intergroup bias and self-evaluation: Domain-specific self-esteem, threats to identity and dimensional importance. *British Journal of Social Psychology*, *36*, 405–26.

Hunter, L. (2003). Research developments in employment relations and diversity: A British perspective. *Asia Pacific Journal of Human Resources*, *41*(1), 88–100.

Jones, D., Pringle, J. K., & Shepherd, D. (2000). Managing diversity meets Aotearoa/ New Zealand. *Personnel Review*, *29*(3), 364–80.

Kamp, A., & Hagedorn-Rasmussen, P. (2004). Diversity management in a Danish context: Towards a multicultural or segregated working life? *Economic and industrial democracy*, *25*(4), 535–54.

King, M. (2003). *Penguin history of New Zealand*. Auckland: Penguin Books.

Kirby, E. L., & Harter, L. M. (2003). Speaking the language of the bottom line: The metaphor of 'Managing Diversity'. *Journal of Business Communication*, *40*(1), 28–49.

Kirton, G., & Greene, A.-M. (2005). *The dynamics of managing diversity: A critical approach*. Oxford: Elsevier Butterworth-Heinemann.

Konrad, A. M., & Linnehan, F. (1999). Affirmative action: History, effects and attitudes. In G. N. Powell (Ed.), *Handbook of gender in the workplace* (pp. 429–52). Thousand Oaks, CA: Sage.

Konrad, A. (2003). Defining the domain of workplace diversity scholarship. *Group and Organization Management*, *28*(1), 4–17.

Linnehan, F., & Konrad, A. M. (1999). Diluting diversity: Implications for intergroup inequality in organizations. *Journal of management inquiry*, *8*, 399–414.

Lynch, F. R. (1997). *The diversity machine: The drive to change the white male workplace*. New York: Free Press.

Macrae, C. N., & Bodenhausen, G. V. (2000). Social cognition: Thinking categorically about others. *Annual Review of Psychology*, *51*, 93–120.

Mighty, E. J. (1991). Valuing workforce diversity: A model of organizational change. *Canadian Journal of Administrative Sciences*, *8*(2), 64–71.

Mighty, E. J. (1997). Triple jeopardy: Immigrant women of color in the labor force. In P. Prasad, A. Mills, M. Elmes & A. Prasad (Eds), *Managing the organizational melting pot: Dilemmas of workplace diversity* (pp. 312–39). Thousand Oaks, CA: Sage.

Mikaere, A. (2004). Are we all New Zealanders now? A Maori response to the Pakeha quest for indigeneity. Bruce Jesson Memorial Lecture, University of Auckland, 15 November.

Mullen, B., Brown, R., & Smith, C. (1992). Ingroup bias as a function of salience, relevance, and status: An integration. *European Journal of Social Psychology*, *22*, 103–22.

Nkomo, S. M., & Cox, T., Jr (1996). Diverse identities in organizations. In. S. R. Clegg, C. Hardy, & W. R. Nord (Eds), *Handbook of organization studies* (pp. 338–56). Thousand Oaks, CA: Sage.

Prasad, P. (1997). The protestant ethic and myths of the frontier: Cultural imprints, organizational structuring and workplace diversity. In P. Prasad, A. Mills, M. Elmes & A. Prasad (Eds), *Managing the organizational melting pot: Dilemmas of workplace diversity* (pp. 129–47). Thousand Oaks, CA: Sage.

Prasad, A. (2001). Understanding workplace empowerment as inclusion: A historical investigation of the discourse of difference in the United States. *Journal of Applied Behavioral Science*, *37*, 33–50.

Prasad, P. (2003). The rainbow ceiling: Invisible barriers to career advancement. Paper presented at the annual meetings of the Academy of Management, Seattle, August.

Prasad, P., & Mills, A. J. (1997). From showcase to shadow: Understanding the dilemmas of managing workplace diversity. In P. Prasad, A. J. Mills, M. B. Elmes & A. Prasad (Eds), *Managing the organizational melting pot: Dilemmas of workplace diversity* (pp. 3–30). Thousand Oaks, CA: Sage.

Ridgeway, C. L. (1991). The social construction of status value: Gender and other nominal characteristics. *Social Forces*, *70*, 367–86.

Sachdev, I., & Bourhis, R. Y. (1987). Status differentials and intergroup behavior. *European Journal of Social Psychology*, *17*, 277–93.

Sachdev, I., & Bourhis, R. Y. (1991). Power and status differentials in minority and majority group relations. *European Journal of Social Psychology*, *21*, 1–24.

Sayers, J., & Tremaine, M. (1994). *The vision and the reality: EEO in the New Zealand workplace.* Palmerston North: Dunmore Press.

Sinclair, A. (2000). Women within diversity: Risks and possibilities. *Women in Management Review*, *15*, 237–45.

Spivak, G. (1987). *In other worlds: Essays in cultural politics.* New York: Methuen.

Stevens, L. E., & Fiske, S. T. (2000). Motivated impressions of a powerholder: Accuracy under task dependency and misperception under evaluation dependency. *Personality and Social Psychology Bulletin*, *26*, 907–22.

Suarez-Orozco, M. M. (2002). Everything you ever wanted to know about cultural assimilation but were afraid to ask. In R. A. Shweder, M. Minow & H. Markus (Eds), *Engaging cultural differences: The multicultural challenge in liberal democracies* (pp. 19–42). New York: The Russell Sage Foundation.

Tajfel, H., & Turner, J. C. (1986). The social identity theory of intergroup behavior. In E. J. Lawler (Ed.), *Advances in group processes: A research annual* (Vol. 2, pp. 77–122). Greenwich, CT: JAI Press.

Taylor, C. (1994). The politics of recognition. In A. Gutmann (Ed.), *Multiculturalism: Examining the politics of recognition* (pp. 25–73). Princeton, NJ: Princeton University Press.

Thomas, D. A., & Ely, R. J. (1996). Making differences matter: A new paradigm for managing diversity. *Harvard Business Review*, *74*(5), 79–90.

Thomas, K. M., Mack, D. A., & Montigliani, A. (2004). The arguments against diversity: Are they valid? In M. Stockdale & F. J. Crosby (Eds), *The psychology and management of workplace diversity* (pp. 31–51). Malden, MA: Blackwell.

Thomas, R. (1996). *Building a house for diversity*. Boston: Harvard Business School Press.

Thomas, R. R. (1991). *Beyond race and gender: Unleashing the power of your total work force by managing diversity*. New York: American Management Association.

Webster, M., Jr, & Hysom, S. J. (1998). Creating status characteristics. *American Sociological Review, 63*, 351–78.

West, C., & Zimmerman, D. H. (1991). Doing gender. In J. Lorber & S. A. Farrell (Eds), *The social construction of gender* (pp. 13–37). Thousand Oaks, CA: Sage.

Yakura, E. (1996). Law and managing diversity. In E. E. Kossek & S. A. Lobel (Eds), *Managing diversity: Human resources strategies for transforming the workplace* (pp. 25–50). Cambridge, MA: Blackwell.

Part I

THEORETICAL PERSPECTIVES ON WORKPLACE DIVERSITY

1

Psychological Perspectives
on Workplace Diversity

CAROL T. KULIK AND HUGH T. J. BAINBRIDGE

The title of this chapter links two problematic terms: 'psychological perspectives' and 'workplace diversity'. These terms act as succinct, compact labels for two large, sprawling and essentially unruly literatures. On the one hand ('psychological perspectives') we have the psychological literature that focuses on the cognitive processes that underlie perceptions and judgments about people. On the other hand ('workplace diversity') we have the organizational literature that focuses on the range of applicant and employee attributes that contributes to organizational diversity. Our chapter is positioned at the intersection of these two literatures, and it has three distinct goals.

First, we introduce the reader to the fundamentals of social cognition. 'Social cognition' is a broad umbrella term encompassing a range of theoretical models that describe how a perceiver forms impressions of other people. We link the social cognition literature to two other related, but distinct, theoretical perspectives: social identity theory and status characteristics theory. We demonstrate, as much as possible, the extent to which these theories make parallel and divergent predictions.

Second, we review the recent (1995 onwards) workplace diversity literature that is based on these theoretical perspectives. In an effort to make this review manageable, we made some difficult choices. Most importantly, our review emphasizes what previous researchers have called the 'surface' diversity dimensions – 'overt, biological characteristics that are typically reflected in physical features' (Harrison, Price & Bell, 1998: 97). That is, we focus on characteristics such as race, sex, age and disability status.

Finally, we step back and consider the linkages forged between the psychological perspectives and workplace diversity. We reflect on the advantages and disadvantages of the recent diversity research incorporating psychological theories, and we suggest some avenues for future research.

SOCIAL COGNITION: THE FUNDAMENTALS

Imagine a typical person, navigating his or her way through life. This person (we'll call him or her the 'perceiver') has amassed a great deal of information and this information is stored in the perceiver's memory. The perceiver's memory is like a huge warehouse of sorting bins, each bin filled to bursting with information. Now the perceiver meets another individual (we'll call this person the 'target'). Some of the information stored in that warehouse is relevant to this encounter, and some is not. Our perceiver faces a serious retrieval problem – how can the perceiver find the right information in the warehouse to form an impression of the target? And once that impression is formed, where in the warehouse should the perceiver store the new information?

One common feature of social cognition theories is an assumption that people use cognitive categories (those metaphorical 'bins' in our example) to make sense of the world around them. In a well-designed physical warehouse, each bin would be carefully labeled, and bins containing similar contents would be grouped together in the same area of the warehouse. In the same way, the cognitive bins in the perceiver's mental warehouse are associated with cognitive structures that help the perceiver identify the right bins at the right time (Fiske & Linville, 1980). Within the psychological literature, these cognitive structures go by a variety of names: schemas (e.g. Kalin & Hodgins, 1984), prototypes (e.g. Fiske & Taylor, 1991) and stereotypes (e.g. Glick, Zion & Nelson, 1988).

A 'schema' is a general cognitive structure that represents knowledge about a concept or a type of stimulus, including its attributes and the relationships among those attributes (Bartlett, 1932; Fiske & Taylor, 1991). For example, our hypothetical perceiver might have schemas for birds, haircut appointments and librarians, with each schema summarizing what the perceiver knows about the given concept. A 'prototype' is a more specialized cognitive structure and represents the most typical category member (a typical example of what the perceiver might find if he or she goes rummaging in a particular bin) (Fiske & Taylor, 1991). The perceiver might have a fairly elaborate schema for birds that relates beak size to wingspan to habitat, but the perceiver's bird prototype (the most typical bird that the perceiver has ever encountered) might be a robin. Robins do all of the typical bird things – they sing, they fly, they eat worms. The term 'stereotype' is generally reserved for schemas about people. A stereotype organizes the information the perceiver has about different groups (e.g. librarians, women, Australians) and creates generalized expectations about new members of those groups the perceiver encounters (Fiske & Taylor, 1991; Wyer & Srull, 1989).

These definitions describe the nuances among the different kinds of cognitive structures, but many researchers use the terms interchangeably (Fiske & Taylor, 1991: 117). This is especially true in the organizational literature, where researchers are more likely to be studying the consequences of accessing one bin or another, rather than studying the specific cognitive structures involved in the access process. To avoid confusion, we consistently use the term 'stereotypes' in this chapter to describe the cognitive structures associated with the categories perceivers use to form impressions of other people.

Why Do Perceivers Develop Demographic Stereotypes?

Stereotypes develop as a function of repeated encounters with the same 'type' of person – as the perceiver encounters new targets of the same type, information about the new target is stored in the same bin as the previous examples. These encounters may be real or virtual (based on reading, television or hearsay). A perceiver can acquire a stereotype of Turks as cruel without ever having met one in the flesh (Holyoak & Gordon, 1984). Cues about a person's race, gender, age and (sometimes) their disability status are easily available as perceivers encounter new targets, and therefore these physical dimensions become a very convenient way to categorize information in memory. Research suggests, for example, that organizational perceivers (managers and other organizational agents) have stereotypes associated with sex (Deaux, 1995; Eagly, Makhijani & Klonsky, 1992), race (Devine, 1989), age (Finkelstein, Burke & Raju, 1995; Rosen & Jerdee, 1976), disability status (Bowman, 1987; Fichten & Amsel, 1986) and other social categories.

Once the perceiver has developed stereotypes associated with different demographic categories, he or she can use them to categorize new targets. In fact, some research suggests that categorization based on demographic dimensions is extremely automatic (e.g. Blair & Banaji, 1996; Devine, 1989; Perdue & Gurtman, 1990). Researchers working within the social cognition area frequently describe perceivers as 'cognitive misers' who try to avoid conducting an exhaustive analysis of all the information available to them. Perceivers are often willing to sacrifice accuracy in favor of processing efficiency (Fiske & Taylor, 1991; Heilman & Martell, 1986). Stereotypes help the perceiver to 'fill in' details of a target that have not been directly observed ('this woman must like to shop, because most women do'). However, stereotypes can also be remarkably inaccurate (Fiske & Taylor, 1991; Wyer & Srull, 1981). The perceiver's previous experiences and expectations may not apply to this newly encountered target, but the perceiver's subsequent decisions about the target are still going to be influenced by the stereotype.

Social identity theory

From a social cognition perspective, the stereotypes that a perceiver develops are largely based on the world 'out there'. Perceivers develop new categories (and associated stereotypes) on an 'as needed' basis. If the perceiver encounters a new type of target, the perceiver compares features of the target to the stereotypes already available in his or her mental warehouse. If no fit is found, a new category (with an associated stereotype) can be created. In contrast, social identity theory (Hogg & Abrams, 1988; Tajfel & Turner, 1979; 1986) places a greater emphasis on the perceiver's personal characteristics in determining which categories are likely to be salient, and which stereotypes are most likely to be developed.

According to social identity theory, people develop a personal identity based in part on the categories to which they themselves belong (Hogg, Terry & White, 1995). In effect, people stereotype themselves by attributing to themselves the attitudes, behaviors and other attributes they associate with membership in a particular group. This process of seeing oneself as a member of a group is described as self-categorization (Turner, Hogg, Oakes, Reicher & Wetherell, 1987). Social identity theory suggests that if the perceiver encounters a new type of target, the perceiver compares features of the target to the self. Development of a new category (with a new stereotype) will most likely occur when the features of the target significantly differ from those possessed by the perceiver.

Social identity theory also suggests that people regularly make social comparisons between the characteristics they (and other members of their group) possess and those possessed by other groups (Ashforth & Humphrey, 1993). Due to their visibility and salience, demographic attributes (e.g. race, gender, age) are often a basis for these comparisons. The perceiver is likely to see these characteristics as central to his or her own identity and therefore these characteristics are used to categorize others.

To this point, social identity theory and social cognition converge nicely. However, social identity theory adds an element of evaluation that is not necessarily associated with social cognition theories. In social cognition, categories may differentiate among targets without those categories necessarily developing an evaluative tone. Theoretically, at least, a person could observe differences between men and women and develop categories for these two types of observations without describing one category as better than the other. In contrast, social identity theory starts with an assumption that the perceiver's own category membership is positively valued. Membership in an identity group has an emotional significance for the perceiver (Tajfel, 1972) and therefore the perceiver is highly motivated to see his or her own category in a positive light – necessitating the devaluation of other categories to which the perceiver does not belong. This leads to a general in-group bias, in which comparisons between in-group and out-group members generally favor members of the in-group (Tajfel, Billig, Bundy & Flament, 1971). This in-group bias is a direct means of enhancing the rater's self-esteem; favoring the in-group while derogating the out-group makes raters feel better about themselves (Finkelstein et al., 1995). In-group bias is especially likely to be observed when society values one group more than another and group boundaries are not permeable (i.e. members cannot voluntarily move from one group to another) (Bettencourt, Dorr, Charlton & Hume, 2001).

Status characteristics theory

Status characteristics theory (Berger, 1977; Foschi, 1989; Wagner & Berger, 1993) also suggests that categories differ in their evaluations. However, while social identity theory argues that the evaluation is driven by the perceiver's own group membership, status characteristics theory views category evaluations as derived from societal consensus on the value of different groups. Therefore, members of both more valued and less valued groups are likely to agree on the evaluative implications of group membership (in contrast to the in-group bias predicted by social identity theory).

A status characteristic is any characteristic around which expectations and beliefs about actors come to be organized (Wagner & Berger, 1997). There are two distinct forms of status characteristics – diffuse status characteristics and specific status characteristics. Diffuse status characteristics describe attributes that are relatively permanent such as demographic factors (e.g. race or gender). These characteristics acquire status value as people within a society come to agree that membership in one demographic group is somehow 'better' than membership in another (Ridgeway, 1991; Ridgeway & Erickson, 2000). These characteristics then in turn become associated with cultural beliefs that members of the more valued group are also more competent. For example, research suggests that it is perceived as more worthy or valuable to be male than female (e.g. Broverman, Vogel, Broverman, Clarkson & Rosenkrantz, 1972; Eagly & Wood, 1982) and men are widely judged to be more generally competent than women (Eagly, 1987; Wood & Karten, 1986). Specific status characteristics describe characteristics of people relevant to their abilities on specific tasks and activities. In other words, diffuse status characteristics attribute status to an individual as a function of group membership, while specific status characteristics attribute status to an individual as a function of his or her personal skills.

Each status characteristic serves as a central focus around which specific inferences about the anticipated performance of an individual are clustered. For example, the demographic descriptor 'male' may act as a status characteristic around which inferences of personality such as 'strong, assertive and aggressive' are attached. While status characteristics theorists generally do not use the term 'stereotypes', the underlying process is similar to the schema concept so central to social cognition models. Basically, perceivers elaborate stereotypes around status characteristics.

However, status characteristics theory goes a step further in identifying the evaluative implications of different stereotypes. Individual characteristics are described as having value states that are hierarchically organized relative to each other (Pugh & Wahrman, 1983). Perceptions of individuals depend on the perceiver's aggregate assessment of the full set of status characteristics.

A person who is associated with several highly evaluated demographic groups is expected to perform better on tasks relative to those who are 'status poor' on similar dimensions. Furthermore, low expectations for members of a particular group are thought to influence how others treat them such that they are given less air time to speak, are more likely to be interrupted, and are given fewer chances to take on challenging tasks (Ridgeway, 2001). As a result of unequal treatment, members of high-status groups are likely to perform better than members of low-status groups, and these results reinforce the extant status characteristics in the minds of perceivers.

Can Perceivers Control the Impact of Stereotypes?

The preceding discussion suggests that stereotypes are tools used by perceivers to form impressions of people, and depending on the stereotype content (or, in status characteristics theory terms, the status of the characteristic around which impressions are formed) they can impact how the perceiver evaluates a new target person. But is stereotyping inevitable? While social identity theory has little to say on this point, the other two psychological perspectives (social cognition and status characteristics theory) suggest that people may, under some circumstances, be able to control the impact of demographic stereotypes and limit their impact in impression formation.

Dual process models

Within the social cognition literature, several authors have suggested that information processes fall along a continuum (Brewer, 1988; Fiske, 1982; Fiske & Neuberg, 1990). At one end of this continuum, perceivers engage in heuristic-based processing – processing that is quick and easy but potentially inaccurate. When perceivers are forming impressions of people, heuristic processing is likely to make heavy use of any stereotypes that are accessible in memory. However, at the other end of this continuum, perceivers suppress stereotypes and instead engage in careful, controlled processing of any individuating information available about the target. Several factors increase the likelihood that perceivers will engage in controlled processing. First, perceivers must have access to sufficient information about the target person. Perceivers are more likely to use heuristic processing (including stereotypes) when they are given limited information, such as a category label or a brief description (Fiske, Neuberg, Beattie & Milberg, 1987). Second, perceivers must be motivated to form an accurate impression of the target (Fiske & Neuberg, 1990; Kulik & Perry, 1994; Petty & Cacioppo, 1979). Finally, even motivated perceivers must have enough time and cognitive resources before they can effectively engage in controlled processing (Fiske & Pavelchak, 1986; Kulik & Perry, 1994; Martell, 1991).

Motivated perceivers with sufficient cognitive resources may be successful in controlling the stereotyping process – at least in the short run. Research participants who are instructed not to stereotype a target form impressions that are far more individuated (Macrae, Bodenhausen, Milne & Jetten, 1994) than participants who are given no explicit instructions. Ironically, though, stereotype suppression may make the stereotype even more likely to influence the perceiver's thoughts and behavior at a later point in time (Macrae, Bodenhausen & Milne, 1998). The perceiver's efforts to suppress the stereotype seem to strengthen the association between the category and the associated stereotype (Wegner, 1994). For example, in Macrae et al.'s (1994) research, all of the participants were later asked to form an impression of a second target. The participants who had previously engaged in stereotype suppression formed significantly *more* stereotypic impressions of the second target than non-suppressors.

While they use different terminology, status characteristics theorists also point to dual processes in impression formation. Diffuse status cues and specific status cues are both important when perceivers evaluate a target. In the absence of specific information, expectations are directed by diffuse status characteristics such as gender and racial characteristics (Dovidio, Heltman, Brown, Ellyson & Keating, 1988) – in other words, impressions based directly on diffuse status characteristics are likely to be stereotyped. However, if task-specific status cues are available, they can displace the diffuse status cues in the impression formation process (Berger, Fisek, Norman & Wagner, 1985; Dovidio et al., 1988). Task-specific status cues become the dominant driver of impressions if the perceiver has access to explicit information about the target's competence (Berger et al., 1985; Hembroff & Myers, 1984). In social cognition terms, perceivers who have access to information about how the target performed on specific tasks are increasingly likely to use this individualized information and engage in controlled processing to form an impression of the target (Fiske & Neuberg, 1990; Fiske et al., 1987).

LINKING PSYCHOLOGICAL PROCESSES AND WORKPLACE DIVERSITY

Researchers interested in workplace diversity have frequently drawn upon psychological theories to understand the impact that stereotypes have on the experiences and outcomes of different groups of people in organizations. Given the focus of the psychological perspective on the role of the perceiver, most of the research in this area has examined situations in which an organizational agent (e.g. a manager or a laboratory participant assuming a managerial role) forms an impression of a target person (a job applicant or a subordinate). This impression then acts as the basis for organizational decisions (e.g. hiring or promotion decisions) made about the target.

The application of psychological theories to human resource decisions involves the integration of two distinct groups of variables. One set of variables focuses on the perceiver, and includes the cognitive structures discussed in the previous section (e.g. stereotypes) and characteristics of the perceiver (e.g. the perceiver's motivation to make accurate judgments). The second set of variables includes contextual components that influence whether, and how, the perceiver's stereotypes will influence decisions. The fact that diversity researchers are interested in organizational settings is significant because context has two distinct impacts on these processes. First, aspects of the organizational context may make it more or less likely that stereotypes will be used in decision making. The psychological literature has demonstrated that holding individuals accountable for decisions (Cvetkovich, 1978) and providing more time and more information to decision-makers (Macrae & Bodenhausen, 2001) can encourage the use of more effortful (i.e. less stereotypic) cognitive processing. Variations across organizations in the extent to which decisions are monitored, the amount of resources (in time and information) available to the decision-maker, and the consequences of making inaccurate decisions, can all impact the decision-maker's motivation and/or ability to use or suppress stereotyping in the judgment process (Perry, Davis-Blake & Kulik, 1994).

Second, the organizational context also determines whether a particular stereotype, once activated, will have positive or negative consequences for the target. Several authors have described organizational hiring and promotion decisions as resulting from a matching process in which the organizational decision-maker compares his or her impressions of the applicant (which are influenced by any stereotypes in operation) and the job requirements (e.g. Cleveland & Hollman, 1991; Heilman, 1983; Perry, 1997; Stone & Colella, 1996). If there is a good match between these two sources of information, decision-makers form positive expectations about the individual's ability to perform successfully in the job. If there is a poor match, decision-makers develop negative expectations for the individual's job performance.

Empirical support for this matching model, in which the perceiver 'matches' applicant impressions to job requirements, is evidenced by a target demographic × job interaction. The model has received considerable support with respect to sex stereotypes, such that female applicants experience the greatest disadvantage when they are considered for male-typed jobs (i.e. jobs that are usually filled by men or are associated with male characteristics) (Cohen & Bunker, 1975; Futoran & Wyer, 1986). Further, Davison and Burke (2000) conducted an extensive meta-analysis on performance ratings and demonstrated that women received higher ratings than did men on feminine jobs, while men received higher ratings than did women on masculine jobs. Recently, organizational theorists have extended the matching model to explain why older job applicants experience discrimination when they apply for young-typed jobs (Perry, 1997) and why applicants with disabilities are seen as more suited for some jobs than others (Stone & Colella, 1996).

We conducted a review of the recent (1995 and later) literature to see how researchers interested in workplace diversity have been using psychological concepts and models in their research. It was not our intention to provide an exhaustive review of this literature – in fact, our review is decidedly selective. We limited our review to the literature focusing on the cognitive processes of organizational agents (managers or laboratory participants assuming managerial roles) and the practical consequences (e.g. hiring decisions, promotion decisions) of those processes for the target. We excluded research focusing on the perceptions of coworkers or on the psychological outcomes (e.g. stress) of the target.

Our literature search identified two distinct categories of organizational research based on the psychological perspective. We have labeled one category 'correlational organizational research'. These studies were predominantly field based, and focused on measured variables rather than manipulated ones. We have labeled the other category 'experimental organizational research'. These studies were predominantly (but not exclusively) lab based, and directly manipulated variables in order to examine a decision-maker's cognitive processes. Both forms of research have distinct advantages and disadvantages, as our discussion will explain.

The Psychological Perspective in Correlational Organizational Research

Studies in this category focused on two key issues. Some studies attempted to identify the content of stereotypes associated with different demographic groups (e.g. women and men). Others used a psychological perspective to predict, and document, differences in organizational outcomes experienced by members of different groups. We discuss each type in turn.

Stereotype content

Historically, the attributes associated with the 'female' stereotype have been largely non-overlapping with those associated with 'manager' and 'leader' positions (Powell, Butterfield & Parent, 2002). This perceived inconsistency between sex stereotypes and job type is so widely held that Schein (2001) describes it as the 'think manager, think male' phenomenon. Since women are perceived as not possessing the leadership qualities critical for managerial success, they are unlikely to be selected or promoted into management positions (Heilman, 1983). Even when women are described as managers (suggesting that they have at least some leadership characteristics or competencies), women are characterized as less agentic than men (Heilman, Block & Martell, 1995). This tendency to 'think manager, think male' has been documented not just in the United States (Powell et al., 2002), but in Germany and the UK (Schein & Mueller, 1992) and in China and Japan (Schein, Mueller, Lituchy & Liu, 1996). However, while people in

European and Asian contexts continue to view managerial positions as male typed (Schein, 2001), recent work has suggested that stereotypes in the United States and New Zealand may be moving away from a consistent 'think manager, think male' position (e.g. Sauers, Kennedy & O'Sullivan, 2002; Schein, 2001). Stereotypes associated with 'manager' or 'leader' positions in these countries have shifted over the past 15–20 years to include more 'feminine' traits (Sauers et al., 2002), and raters have been found to differentiate managerial stereotypes on the basis of gender (Atwater, Brett, Waldman, DiMare & Hayden, 2004; Martell & DeSmet, 2001). For male raters, several leadership attributes (delegating, inspiring, intellectual stimulation, problem solving) are more associated with men than with women; for female raters, several attributes (inspiring, mentoring, problem solving, rewarding and supporting) are more associated with women than with men (Martell & DeSmet, 2001).

A number of studies have focused on the content of age stereotypes. In the United States and in the UK, previous research has found older workers to be characterized as less flexible, less interested in training, and less motivated than younger workers (e.g. Hassell & Perrewe, 1995; Lyon & Pollard, 1997). In Australia, Steinberg, Donald, Najman and Skerman (1996) found that older workers were perceived as being more dependable, making better decisions, and doing a better job than younger workers, but as less creative and harder to train. These negative views regarding the training of older workers are also reflected in the work of Gray and McGregor (2003). In New Zealand, older workers are stereotyped as having low motivation towards learning new job skills, as unable to learn, and as unable to adapt to new technologies. Therefore, investment in training older workers is perceived to provide a poor return for employers (Gray & McGregor, 2003).

Chiu, Chan, Snape and Redman (2001) contrasted stereotypes associated with older workers in the UK and in Hong Kong – anticipating that the Hong Kong sample would associate more positive characteristics with older workers, consistent with the high deference toward old age accorded by Chinese culture. Compared to the UK sample, Hong Kong respondents did have a more positive view of older workers in terms of their ability to cope with change. But at the same time, Hong Kong respondents saw older workers as less effective than British respondents.

Research has also focused on the content of race-based stereotypes. Smith and Ho (2002) found that Americans held stereotypes describing Asians as competent but overly competitive and untrustworthy. In a study of British employees, Rana, Kagan, Lewis and Rout (1998) found that British Asians were viewed as a homogeneous group, whose members were tied down by family commitments and incompetent at work.

Outcome differences

Most of the 1995-onward research drew upon psychological perspectives to understand the outcomes experienced by different groups in organizations.

Some of this research used stereotypes (and associated discriminatory judgment processes) to predict main effect differences. That is, researchers predicted that differential outcomes (e.g. jobs, promotions, salaries) would be experienced by different groups. For example, Landau (1995) suggested that gender and racial stereotypes could explain why her research found that females were rated lower than males, and blacks and Asians were rated lower than whites, in terms of their promotion potential. However, Powell and Butterfield (1997) found no direct effects of applicant race on promotions in a US government department. Lyness and Thompson (1997) compared the career experiences of male and female managers and suggested that sex stereotypes should have a detrimental effect on women, resulting in lower-position authority, less compensation, and fewer developmental opportunities than men in comparable positions. They found mixed support for their hypotheses: while women did have lower-position authority (operationalized by the number of subordinates supervised) than the men, there were only limited differences between women and men in salary and developmental opportunities. In a meta-analysis of studies examining performance appraisals in field contexts, Bowen, Swim and Jacobs (2000) found little evidence of bias against women. Finally, Perry, Hendricks and Broadbent (2000) predicted that stereotypes about people with disabilities would result in college alumni with disabilities experiencing discrimination in the workplace. They found that individuals with disabilities, especially individuals whose disability required the use of a wheelchair, did report more difficulty in gaining employment than individuals without disabilities. However, contrary to predictions, Perry et al. (2000) found no evidence that individuals with disabilities experienced discrimination once they were on the job (e.g. in terms of salary).

Not all of the psychological theories predict main effect differences in the outcomes experienced by different groups. Social identity theory, for example, predicts same-race (and same-sex) biases such that white applicants will be preferred by white decision-makers – but not by non-white decision-makers. Several studies examined this prediction in the context of promotion decisions. Prewett-Livingston, Feild, Veres and Lewis (1996) found a same-race effect only when review panels were race balanced (contained an equal proportion of white and black decision-makers), and Powell and Butterfield (2002) found that white males were not favored in promotion decisions either by solo white male decision-makers or by homogeneous review panels composed of white males.

Summary

The correlational studies highlight both the advantages and disadvantages of studying psychological perspectives in natural settings. One of the key advantages is the ability to identify the stereotypes associated with actual organizational decision-makers, and the outcomes resulting from stereotyping experienced by actual job applicants and employees. However, while field settings provide realism of context, there is an inevitable tradeoff in terms of the researcher's ability to rigorously measure the phenomenon of interest (McGrath, 1982). Within field settings, group differences in outcomes (such as those observed by Perry et al. in hiring decisions and by Lyness & Thompson in position authority) may reflect bias resulting from stereotyping – or they may reflect actual differences in group members' qualifications or performance (Roberson & Block, 2001). When differences in outcomes are *not* observed, the lack of bias may be attributable to rater motivation (consistent with dual process models) or to contextual variations. For example, Lyness and Thompson (1997) note that the women in their research had already passed through the glass ceiling, suggesting that they exhibited unusually high levels of competence. When targets exhibit unambiguous performance information, decision-makers are less likely to rely on stereotypes as a basis for their decisions (Heilman, Martell & Simon, 1988).

However, field research provides the opportunity to study naturally occurring contextual variations that would be difficult to manipulate in laboratory settings. For example, Perry et al. (2000) were able to isolate differences between the experience of people with disabilities at the organizational entry and post-entry stages. The lack of discrimination reported by people with disabilities post-entry is consistent with psychological theories suggesting that stereotyping should be most likely when decision-makers have limited information about targets (as they do at the organizational entry stage, when decisions must be based on brief resumes and short-duration interviews). Powell and Butterfield (2002) point out that their findings' lack of support for predictions from psychological theories may have been a function of the pro-EEO culture of the department in which their research was conducted. Contextual factors such as a dominant EEO program may override or constrain opportunities for perceivers to act on their stereotypes, and the generally weak evidence for discriminatory outcomes reported in recent studies may simply reflect a growing use of formal hiring and promotion procedures in organizations that limit decision-maker discretion (Perry et al., 1994).

Contextual variations may also explain some of the differences in effects across studies. For example, Landau (1995) found strong race and gender effects in private organizations, while Prewett-Livingston et al. (1996) and Powell and Butterfield (2002) examined similar issues in government settings and found weaker effects. Diversity issues tend to be more closely monitored in public organizations than in private enterprise (e.g. Edelman, 1990; 1992; Pfeffer & Davis-Blake, 1992). Therefore, managers in government departments may be particularly sensitive to the implications of their decisions and be motivated to reduce the influence that demographics might otherwise have on decision outcomes.

The Psychological Perspective in Experimental Organizational Research

During the period covered by our literature search, several meta-analyses were published that found considerable support for predictions of the psychological perspective as tested in experimental contexts (age – Finkelstein et al., 1995;

sex – Davison & Burke, 2000). These reviews found that, consistent with the dual process model, bias against older (Finkelstein et al., 1995) or female (Davison & Burke, 2000) targets was more likely when raters had access to limited job-relevant information. Furthermore, consistent with in-group bias predictions based on social identity theory, Finkelstein et al. (1995) also found that bias against older workers was more evidenced by younger raters.

The experimental research published in 1995 and later focused on these key issues: empirical verification of the matching model, rater individual differences, subtle discrimination and contextual influences on discrimination. We examine each of these in turn.

Empirical verification of the matching model

Perry and her colleagues examined predictions of the matching model in relation to age in two studies using a simulated hiring context (Perry & Bourhis, 1998; Perry, Kulik & Bourhis, 1996). In both studies, older applicants were evaluated less favorably than younger applicants, especially for jobs that were strongly young typed. Heilman, Wallen, Fuchs and Tamkins (2004) demonstrated that the matching model has implications for evaluations even when jobholders are clearly succeeding in their demographically mismatched jobs. When raters received unambiguous information about a woman's success in a male-typed job, they evaluated the woman as competent and effective, but also as less likable and more interpersonally hostile. Colella and her colleagues (Colella, DeNisi & Varma, 1998; Colella & Varma, 1999) examined predictions of the matching model in relation to disability and found mixed results. In one study (Colella et al., 1998), disability had neither a main nor an interaction effect on performance ratings or predictions about future performance. The other study (Colella & Varma, 1999) also failed to find either a main effect or an interaction effect on performance ratings. However, the disability × job interaction was significant with respect to expectations of future performance. Expectations were lower when the individual's disability was a poor fit to job demands (e.g. when people with physical disabilities that limited movement were placed in physically demanding manufacturing roles). Finally, the matching model was examined by Hosoda, Stone and Stone-Romero (2003), who examined the interactive effects of race, gender and job type on job suitability ratings and selection decisions. These researchers found that the stereotypes associated with being black and female did not damage a black woman's job suitability ratings if the woman was highly educated and provided a good match to a job's cognitive ability demands. In fact, highly educated black women were rated as more suitable for jobs requiring high levels of cognitive ability than comparably educated white men, white women or black men.

Rater individual differences

Several studies examined the impact of individual differences of the rater in influencing stereotype use. For example, in the Perry et al. (1996) research mentioned earlier, researchers found that raters' age bias acted as a moderator. As the rater's bias increased, older job applicants were evaluated much less favorably than young applicants for young-typed jobs. Drawing on social identity theory, Finkelstein and Burke (1998) predicted an in-group bias where older raters would favor older workers, while younger raters would prefer younger workers. Using an in-basket exercise, Finkelstein and Burke (1998) examined hiring recommendations made by managers in four companies. The older target applicant was rated as less interpersonally skilled, less economically beneficial and less likely to warrant an interview than the younger applicant. However, they found no evidence that the rater's age moderated this effect.

Lewis and Sherman (2003) found that, when white and black raters were forced to choose between a marginally qualified black applicant and a marginally qualified white one, both groups of raters favored the white applicant. Lewis and Sherman (2003) suggest that this parallel outcome results from different psychological processes. For white raters, the decision reflects a same-race bias predicted by social identity theory. However, if the rater is already a member of a stigmatized group (e.g. if the rater is black) the rater may be unwilling to risk the self-esteem blow that would result from a bad hiring decision. This may make black raters less willing to make risky decisions involving marginally qualified black job applicants.

Subtle discrimination

Three studies suggest that researchers may miss some of the influence of stereotypes if they rely only on overt measures such as hiring judgments. Harvie, Marshall-McCaskey and Johnston (1998) found no evidence of gender bias on either the likelihood of a job offer or starting salary in a simulated hiring context. However, in a second study, they asked participants to adopt the perspective of the job applicant, and rate their expectations of a job offer and starting salary. Female applicants were more confident of getting the offer and anticipated a higher starting salary when they were being considered for a female-typed job. Male applicants, in contrast, had equally high expectations regardless of the type of job. Harvie et al. (1998) explain their divergent findings by suggesting that in study 1, applicants were aware of the potential for stereotyping and actively suppressed gender stereotypes in their decision making.

Frazer and Wiersma (2001) asked decision-makers to make hiring decisions immediately after interviewing applicants. Interviewers hired equally qualified black and white applicants in equal proportion – but one week later, interviewers recalled the answers to interview questions given by black applicants as having been significantly less intelligent than those of whites. Frazer and Wiersma (2001) suggest that interviewers were able to inhibit racial stereotypes during and immediately after the interview. But the cognitive effort involved in suppressing the race category permanently linked racial stereotypes to impressions of the applicant. When interviewers retrieved information about the applicant a week later, information associated with the inhibited category was retrieved as well, resulting in biased memory about the job applicants.

Hebl, Foster, Mannix and Dovidio (2002) sent confederates to apply for jobs at local stores wearing baseball caps printed either with the label 'Texan and Proud' or 'Gay and Proud'. The manipulation had no impact on any measures of overt discrimination (e.g. both groups were equally likely to be given job applications). However, employers were more verbally negative, spent less time and used fewer words when interacting with applicants wearing the 'Gay and Proud' hat.

Contextual influences

Finally, several studies focused on how contextual factors or organizational interventions might exaggerate or discourage the use of stereotyping. Two studies suggested that cognitive busyness (the extent to which decision-makers are distracted by competing work demands) make stereotyping more likely. In the Perry et al. (1996) study cited earlier, cognitive busyness operated as a moderator. Among high-bias raters, differentiation between old and young job applicants was greater in busy than in non-busy conditions. Martell (1996) asked participants to read a vignette describing a subordinate's behavior while they worked on another task and had a time limit. Participants evaluated the subordinate either immediately or five days later. More effective work behaviors were attributed to male subordinates than to female subordinates, but only among participants in the delayed condition. These two studies emphasize that if decision-makers lack the time or the opportunity to carefully process information, biased judgments may result.

Bauer and Baltes (2002) wondered whether asking raters to engage in a 'structured free recall' would reduce the effects of sex stereotyping on performance judgments. In structured free recall interventions, 'raters are instructed to recall behaviors that they have observed and to rely on those observations to complete the rating' (Bauer & Baltes, 2002: 468). Raters who have retrieved specific performance events should be better able to base their performance judgments on performance-related behaviors rather than relying on general sex stereotypes. Their results were consistent with their prediction: among raters who did not engage in the recall task, female ratees were evaluated less accurately by raters with strong traditional stereotypes of women. However, this effect was not found among the raters who engaged in the recall task.

Kulik, Perry and Bourhis (2000) investigated the effect of directly instructing decision-makers to suppress age stereotypes during the hiring process and manipulated both cognitive busyness and suppression instructions in a hiring simulation. Busy raters who had been told to try and suppress age-related thoughts evaluated an older job applicant less favorably than raters in other conditions. In other words, raters who had sufficient cognitive resources were able to suppress stereotypes effectively. But for busy raters, trying to suppress the stereotype ironically made it more accessible in memory and more influential in the judgment process (Wegner, 1994).

Summary

The experimental studies also highlight some distinct advantages and disadvantages. Most of the studies described in this section asked decision-makers to evaluate 'paper people' (or in some cases, 'videotape people'), and inevitably, these simulated job applicants and subordinates are less complex than those encountered in organizational contexts (Murphy, Herr, Lockhart & Maguire, 1986). At the same time, however, the explicit manipulation of target characteristics allows much stronger inferences about the cause-and-effect relationships between stereotypes and resulting judgments.

In addition, the experimental studies permit the collection of information about decision-maker characteristics (e.g. the rater's own demographics or personal biases), decision-maker behavior (e.g. recall) and interaction characteristics (e.g. duration and affective tone) that are generally not available in non-experimental contexts. These measures are critical, because they help to explain why we sometimes fail to observe discriminatory outcomes in the field, even when predictions are based on psychological theories that have received robust support in the laboratory. The experimental findings that subtle discrimination may be observed in the absence of overt discriminatory behavior is consistent with recent theorizing that social biases are evolving from 'old-fashioned' forms, in which negative attitudes are expressed openly and correspond directly with discriminatory behavior, to 'modern' forms, in which expressed attitudes become less negative over time and behavioral patterns become more complex and subtle (McConahay, 1986; Swim, Aikin, Hall & Hunter, 1995).

REFLECTIONS AND SUGGESTIONS FOR THE FUTURE

Our review in the previous section suggests that psychological theories are clearly enriching our understanding of workplace diversity. Psychological theories are a rich source of hypotheses about how decision-makers use the demographic characteristics of applicants and employees to make hiring, promotion and other decisions. However, at the same time, the diversity literature is having a strong influence in the opposite direction. There are several distinct ways in which researchers interested in workplace diversity are contributing to the psychological literature. We review these contributions in the following section, concurrently discussing issues that are restricting the value-added impact of ongoing workplace diversity research.

Diversity dimension expansion

In contrast to a heavy emphasis on race and sex in the basic psychological literature, organizational researchers have led the way in studying the impact of a target's age (e.g. Perry & Bourhis, 1998; Perry et al., 1996), disability status (e.g. Colella et al., 1998; Colella & Varma, 1999) and even sexual orientation (Hebl et al., 2002) on the judgment process. Perhaps it is not surprising that organizational researchers are at the forefront in applying psychological perspectives to an ever-broadening range of demographic dimensions. Organizational diversity researchers are well positioned to monitor current trends regarding the availability of diverse job applicants (e.g. demographic changes that contribute to an aging workforce), and to monitor their success in the employment process. Organizational researchers also are sensitive to the impact legislation has on organizational policies and procedures, and our interest in discrimination against people with disabilities has certainly been influenced by the passage of the Americans with Disabilities Act in the United States and parallel legislation in Canada, the UK and Australia.

Organizational researchers' interest in a large array of demographic dimensions has demonstrated the robustness of the concepts and predictions associated with the psychological perspective. Organizational researchers have demonstrated, for example, that parallel matching processes underlie sex and age discrimination (see Perry, 1997, for a review). Organizational researchers have also demonstrated that the factors that increase the potential for stereotyping (time pressure, busyness, limited information) do so across a range of demographic dimensions (Davison & Burke, 2000; Finkelstein et al., 1995; Kulik et al., 2000; Martell, 1996).

Unfortunately, despite the wide range of demographic dimensions being studied, there has been little attempt to investigate the joint effects of multiple demographic dimensions within the same investigation (see for exceptions, Hosoda et al., 2003; Powell & Butterfield, 2002). As a result, the field is developing parallel streams of investigation organized by demographic dimension. These parallel streams cause two problems. First, they do not reflect the complexity of actual organizational decision making, in which targets present themselves in terms of multiple salient demographic dimensions (e.g. race as well as sex). Second, they prevent research in one stream from capitalizing on theoretical developments from another stream, since researchers largely review and cite only the research on the particular demographic dimension they are studying. Until we begin to examine the simultaneous impact of multiple demographic dimensions, we will be unable to explain why psychological processes seem to have parallel effects across some demographic dimensions but not others. For example, we noted earlier that Perry (1997) has suggested that the matching model operates for both race and sex, but Colella and her colleagues (Colella et al., 1998; Colella & Varma, 1999) have found mixed results for the matching model with respect to disability. These differences may result from competing demographic cues displayed by the target (e.g. the target's race and/or sex) that impact the meaning of the focal dimension (disability status) and the impression formed by the perceiver.

Future work might wish to make greater use of the sociology-based multiple jeopardy/multiple advantage literature examining the effects of multiple diversity characteristics (Landrine, Knonoff, Alcaraz, Scott & Wilkins, 1995; Lorber, 1998).

In some circumstances, the effects of individual status characteristics appear to be cumulative such that the more devalued status characteristics displayed by a target, the more devalued the target's overall status. In other circumstances, devalued status characteristics appear to be operate multiplicatively, and the effects of displaying multiple devalued status characteristics are greater than the predicted additive effect (Landrine et al., 1995; Reid & Comas-Diaz, 1990). By focusing on multiple diversity dimensions, academic research would better reflect the realities of a diverse workplace and we would be better able to understand how organizational decision-makers respond to diverse job applicants and employees.

Tests of psychological theory across contexts

Organizational researchers are studying psychological processes in a variety of contexts: lab and field, private and public, manufacturing and services (e.g. Landau, 1995; Linehan & Walsh, 2000; Perry et al., 1996; Powell & Butterfield, 2002; Simons, Pelled & Smith, 1999). But context itself is rarely the direct focus of the investigation, despite the influence context may have on diversity related outcomes (e.g. Edelman, 1990; 1992). Moreover, we are not making sufficient use of naturally occurring organizational variations in our investigations of contextual influences on psychological processes. Laboratory experiments have demonstrated that factors such as competing demands, amount of information, training instructions and time pressure influence the extent to which decision-makers stereotype (Kulik et al., 2000; Martell, 1996; Perry et al., 1996). These factors are also likely to vary across organizations, or across departments within organizations. Measuring contextual variables in organizational settings would help to explain why we see stereotyping effects in some field studies and not others. Organizational diversity researchers should capitalize on their access to the range of contextual situations available in the organizations they study.

Organizational diversity researchers should also be on the lookout for contextual variables in the field that have received limited attention in the psychological literature. For example, organizational researchers are respected for identifying job characteristics as a moderating factor in the stereotyping process, and research examining the impact of job characteristics has helped to refine the psychological models (Perry, 1994; Perry & Finkelstein, 1999). No doubt there are other organizational variables (e.g. formal organizational policies, organizational climate) that, if studied systematically, could further inform our understanding of stereotyping in organizations.

Workplace diversity researchers also need to be wary of indiscriminately generalizing the US workplace diversity research to other contexts (Jones, Pringle & Shepherd, 2000). A substantial amount of diversity research is produced or heavily influenced by North American academics. However, key diversity issues in the United States (e.g. African American workplace advancement) may have only peripheral relevance in other countries. In addition, stereotypes associated with a demographic group may have different content across cultural contexts. For example, US respondents frequently report negative stereotypes about older workers (Finkelstein et al., 1995). But the content of older worker stereotypes held by US respondents may be broadly inaccurate in non-US settings (e.g. Taiwan, Hong Kong) where older employees are more respected for their accumulated experience (Chiu et al., 2001; Pelled & Xin, 2000). When describing their results, organizational diversity researchers should distinguish whether the stereotype content, stereotyping outcomes or stereotyping process are likely to be generalizable across contexts. At the same time, researchers need to exercise judgment in assessing whether the diversity issues, conceptual frameworks and research methodologies presented in the academic literature are applicable to their local environments.

A developing correlational–experimental schism

Our review demonstrates that psychological perspectives are being actively studied using both correlational and experimental methodologies. However, we are concerned that a deep schism is developing between these two groups of researchers. While both research strategies have distinct advantages and disadvantages (McGrath, 1982), more cross-fertilization would be beneficial. A few studies (e.g. Finkelstein & Burke, 1998; Hebl et al., 2002) in our review examined the effect of manipulated stimuli on the behavior of real-life decision-makers – this is a trend we would like to encourage. Investigations that test the same predictions in both a laboratory and a real-world setting would also be beneficial.

This schism between the correlational and experimental paradigms may be directly limiting our theoretical advancement. In general, the correlational studies are using psychological theories as a very broad theoretical framework or employing the general notion of stereotype to predict differences in group outcomes. In contrast, the experimental studies tend to be based on particular psychological theories and test more specific predictions. Neither approach is taking advantage of the fact that the psychological theories do, in some cases, make divergent predictions about whether we should expect main or interactive effects of target demographics. More tests of competing predictions from alternative theories in both lab and field contexts would enhance our understanding of how target demographics influence the treatment of diverse individuals in an employment context. In addition, the perceiver's own personal characteristics may have implications for which psychological theory is most descriptive of the perceiver's psychological processes. For example, in the Lewis and Sherman (2003) study reviewed earlier, the researchers suggested that raters from a stigmatized group may be particularly sensitive to social identity concerns when making hiring decisions.

The design of diversity interventions

Diversity researchers are ideally placed at the interface between psychological theory and organizational reality to drive the development of theory-extending workplace interventions. Indeed, workplace diversity researchers have already made important contributions to the applied psychological literature by developing interventions based on psychological theory. Much of this research has focused on training interventions aimed at altering stereotype content, or on interventions that disrupt or constrain perceivers' stereotyping activities.

For example, researchers have investigated how the content of stereotypes held by perceivers may be altered through contact with, or the presentation of information about, the target of these stereotypes (Liebkind & McAlister, 1999; van Oudenhouven, Groenewond & Hewstone, 1996). In this research, perceivers are provided with counter-stereotypical information with the aim of changing harmful stereotypes to more realistic appraisals. Researchers have demonstrated that a variety of interventions such as formal training programs, informal interactions, seminars or the provision of reading material are effective mechanisms of altering stereotype content (e.g. Brown, Vivian & Hewstone, 1999; Roberson, Kulik & Pepper, 2001).

Organizational diversity researchers have also considered how training decision-makers in cognitive processing techniques may reduce or remove bias. For example, the recent research examining free recall strategies (Bauer & Baltes, 2002) and suppression instructions (Kulik et al., 2000) can be directly transferred to organizational contexts. Asking decision-makers to engage in a structured free recall task before making performance judgments appears to be a simple, low-cost strategy for reducing the impact of sex stereotyping (Bauer & Baltes, 2002). Suppression instructions are frequently part of organizational diversity training programs (Geber, 1990). The Kulik et al. (2000) research suggests that these instructions are an effective strategy for reducing stereotype effects, but only if decision-makers are given sufficient time and cognitive resources during the judgment process.

Unfortunately, research findings often fail to transition from the academic literature into the workplace (Johns, 1993), and there is reason to be concerned that academic research on diversity is not meeting the needs of managers grappling with diversity issues. The basic psychological theories, at this point, are powerful and robust descriptions of perceiver cognition. However, the literature contains few tests of theory-based workplace interventions. In general, researchers have spent little time reflecting on how psychological perspectives such as social identity theory might help to identify or to design workplace interventions (see for exception, Terry, 2003). As a result, we may be neglecting avenues through which we could contribute to the development of the psychological perspectives discussed in this chapter.

Research focused on organizational interventions and subsequent perceiver behavior (rather than perceiver cognition) represents a domain in which workplace diversity researchers have unique expertise. Researchers should creatively consider how our knowledge of psychological processes can inform the development of theory-led workplace interventions. For example, variations in the content and delivery of diversity training may have important effects on training outcomes, but only a handful of studies have used psychological theory to develop and test predictions about the effects of diversity training (e.g. Roberson et al., 2001; Roberson, Kulik & Pepper, 2003). Research that assesses the appropriateness of a variety of interventions (e.g. types of training methods, training group composition, training content) across contexts is sorely lacking and would greatly inform both the academic and practitioner literatures on diversity. Organizational diversity researchers should also consider making greater use of the broader literature on training in the design of their research. A number of important contributions to the training literature have appeared in the 1995–2004 period (e.g. Arthur, Bennett, Edens & Bell, 2003; Colquitt, LePine & Noe, 2000; Salas & Cannon-Bowers, 2001; Salas, Cannon-Bowers, Rhodenizer & Bowers, 1999). This literature should be an important guidance to ongoing research into the design of diversity-related interventions.

CONCLUSIONS

In this chapter, we have drawn attention to the mutually enriching dialogue occurring between theorists presenting psychological perspectives on diversity and researchers studying workplace diversity. We have highlighted the positive aspects of this dialogue and identified ways in which each of these literatures is contributing to the other.

However, we have also identified several ways in which this dialogue has been constrained. We hope that researchers will begin to address the limitations we have discussed in this chapter. We specifically call for research that studies the simultaneous impact of multiple demographic dimensions, research examining the effects of contextual variations in and across organizations, research bridging correlational and experimental paradigms, and research focusing on the design of diversity-related organizational interventions.

As workplace diversity researchers, we are positioned at the interface between psychological theory and the organizational context. This privileged position presents significant research complexities but also makes available remarkable opportunities. Continuing the dialogue between psychological theorists and workplace diversity researchers, and extending their collaborative efforts to the design of interventions that help organizations to successfully manage diversity and reap its benefits, is a worthy challenge.

NOTE

The authors thank Alison Konrad, Karen Lyness, Elissa Perry, Judith Pringle and Loriann Roberson for their helpful comments on earlier versions of this chapter.

REFERENCES

Arthur, W., Bennett, W., Edens, P. S., & Bell, S. T. (2003). Effectiveness of training in organizations: A meta-analysis of design and evaluation features. *Journal of Applied Psychology*, *88*, 234–45.

Ashforth, B. E., & Humphrey, R. H. (1993). Emotional labor in service roles: The influence of identity. *Academy of Management Review*, *18*, 88–115.

Atwater, L. E., Brett, J. F., Waldman, D., DiMare, L., & Hayden, M. V. (2004). Men's and women's perceptions of the gender typing of management subroles. *Sex Roles*, *50*, 191–9.

Bartlett, F. A. (1932). *A study in experimental and social psychology*. New York: Cambridge University Press.

Bauer, C. C., & Baltes, B. B. (2002). Reducing the effects of gender stereotypes on performance evaluations. *Sex Roles*, *47*, 465–76.

Berger, A. S., Fisek, M. H., Norman, R. Z., & Wagner, D. G. (1985). The formation of reward expectations in status situations. In J. Berger & M. Zelditch, Jr (Eds), *Status, rewards, and influence: How expectations organize behavior* (pp. 215–16). Newbury Park, CA: Sage.

Berger, J. (1977). *Status characteristics and social interaction: An expectation-states approach*. New York: Elsevier.

Bettencourt, B. A., Dorr, N., Charlton, K., & Hume, D. L. (2001). Status differences and in-group bias: A meta-analytic examination of the effects of status stability, status legitimacy, and group permeability. *Psychological Bulletin*, *127*, 520–42.

Blair, I. V., & Banaji, M. R. (1996). Automatic and controlled processes in stereotype priming. *Journal of Personality and Social Psychology*, *70*, 1142–63.

Bowen, C. C., Swim, J. K., & Jacobs, R. R. (2000). Evaluating gender biases on actual job performance of real people: A meta-analysis. *Journal of Applied Social Psychology*, *30*, 2194–215.

Bowman, J. T. (1987). Attitudes toward disabled persons: Social distance and work competence. *Journal of Rehabilitation*, *53*, 41–4.

Brewer, M. B. (1988). A dual process model of impression formation. In T. K. Srull & R. S. Wyer, Jr (Eds), *Advances in social cognition*. Hillsdale, NJ: Erlbaum.

Broverman, I. K., Vogel, S. R., Broverman, D. M., Clarkson, F. E., & Rosenkrantz, P. S. (1972). Sex-role stereotypes: Current appraisal. *Journal of Social Issues*, *28*, 59–78.

Brown, R., Vivian, J., & Hewstone, M. (1999). Changing attitudes through intergroup contact: The effects of group membership salience. *European Journal of Social Psychology*, *29*, 741–64.

Chiu, W. C. K., Chan, A. W., Snape, E., & Redman, T. (2001). Age stereotypes and discriminatory attitudes towards older workers: An East-West comparison. *Human Relations*, *54*, 629–61.

Cleveland, J. N., & Hollman, G. (1991). Context and discrimination in personnel decisions: Direct and mediated approaches. In J. R. Meindl, R. L. Cardy & S. Puffer (Eds), *Advances in information processing in organizations* (Vol. 4, pp. 223–38). Greenwich, CT: JAI Press.

Cohen, S. L., & Bunker, K. A. (1975). Subtle effects of sex role stereotypes on recruiters' hiring decisions. *Journal of Applied Psychology*, *60*, 566–72.

Colella, A., DeNisi, A. S., & Varma, A. (1998). The impact of ratee's disability on performance judgments and choice as partner: The role of disability-job fit stereotypes and interdependence of rewards. *Journal of Applied Psychology*, *83*, 102–11.

Colella, A., & Varma, A. (1999). Disability job fit stereotypes and the evaluation of persons with disabilities at work. *Journal of Occupational Rehabilitation*, *9*(2), 79–95.

Colquitt, J. A., LePine, J. A., & Noe, R. A. (2000). Toward an integrative theory of training motivation: A meta-analytic path analysis of 20 years of research. *Journal of Applied Psychology*, *85*, 678–707.

Cvetkovich, G. (1978). Cognitive accommodation, language, and social responsibility. *Social Psychology, 41*, 149–55.

Davison, H. K., & Burke, M. J. (2000). Sex discrimination in simulated employment contexts: A meta-analytic investigation. *Journal of Vocational Behavior, 56*, 225–48.

Deaux, K. (1995). How basic can you be? The evolution of research on gender stereotypes. *Journal of Social Issues, 51*, 11–20.

Devine, P. G. (1989). Stereotypes and prejudice: Their automatic and controlled components. *Journal of Personality and Social Psychology, 56*, 5–18.

Dovidio, J. F., Heltman, K., Brown, C. E., Ellyson, S. L., & Keating, C. F. (1988). Power displays between women and men in discussions of gender-linked tasks: A multichannel study. *Journal of Personality and Social Psychology, 55*, 580–7.

Eagly, A. H. (1987). *Sex differences in social behavior: A social-role interpretation*. Hillsdale, NJ: Erlbaum.

Eagly, A. H., Makhijani, M. G., & Klonsky, B. G. (1992). Gender and the evaluation of leaders: A meta-analysis. *Psychological Bulletin, 111*, 3–22.

Eagly, A. H., & Wood, W. (1982). Inferred sex-differences in status as a determinant of gender stereotypes about social influence. *Journal of Personality and Social Psychology, 43*, 915–28.

Edelman, L. B. (1990). Legal environments and organizational governance: The expansion of due-process in the American workplace. *American Journal of Sociology, 95*, 1401–40.

Edelman, L. B. (1992). Legal ambiguity and symbolic structures: Organizational mediation of civil-rights law. *American Journal of Sociology, 97*, 1531–76.

Fichten, C. S., & Amsel, R. (1986). Trait attributions about college students with a physical disability: Circumplex analyses and methodological issues. *Journal of Applied Social Psychology, 16*, 410–27.

Finkelstein, L. M., & Burke, M. J. (1998). Age stereotyping at work: The role of rater and contextual factors on evaluations of job applicants. *Journal of General Psychology, 125*, 317–45.

Finkelstein, L. M., Burke, M. J., & Raju, N. S. (1995). Age discrimination in simulated employment contexts: An integrative analysis. *Journal of Applied Psychology, 80*, 652–63.

Fiske, A. P., & Pavelchak, M. A. (1986). Category-based versus piecemeal-based affective responses: Developments in schema-trigged affect. In R. M. Sorrentino & E. T. Higgins (Eds), *Handbook of motivation and cognition: Foundations of social behavior* (pp. 167–203). New York: Guilford.

Fiske, S. T. (1982). Schema-triggered affect: Applications to social perception. In M. S. Clark & S. T. Fiske (Eds), *Affect and cognition: The 17th Annual Carnegie Symposium on Cognition*. Hillsdale, NJ: Erlbaum.

Fiske, S. T., & Linville, P. W. (1980). What does the schema concept buy us? *Personality and Social Psychology Bulletin, 6*, 543–57.

Fiske, S. T., & Neuberg, S. L. (1990). A continuum of impression-formation, from category-based to individuating processes: Influences of information and motivation on attention and interpretation. *Advances in Experimental Social Psychology, 23*, 1–74.

Fiske, S. T., Neuberg, S. L., Beattie, A. E., & Milberg, S. J. (1987). Category based and attribute based reactions to others: Some informational conditions of stereotyping and individuating processes. *Journal of Experimental Social Psychology, 23*, 399–427.

Fiske, S. T., & Taylor, S. E. (1991). *Social cognition* (2nd edn). New York: McGraw-Hill.

Foschi, M. (1989). Status characteristics, standards, and attributions. In J. Berger, M. Zelditch Jr & B. Anderson (Eds), *Sociological theories in progress: New formulations* (pp. 58–72). Newbury Park, CA: Sage.

Frazer, R. A., & Wiersma, U. J. (2001). Prejudice versus discrimination in the employment interview: We may hire equally, but our memories harbor prejudice. *Human Relations, 54*, 173–91.

Futoran, G. C., & Wyer, R. S., Jr (1986). The effects of traits and gender stereotypes on occupational suitability judgments and the recall of judgment relevant information. *Journal of Experimental Social Psychology, 22,* 475–503.

Geber, B. (1990). Managing diversity. *Training, 27,* 23–30.

Glick, P., Zion, C., & Nelson, C. (1988). What mediates sex-discrimination in hiring decisions? *Journal of Personality and Social Psychology, 55,* 178–86.

Gray, L., & McGregor, J. (2003). Human resource development and older workers: Stereotypes in New Zealand. *Asia Pacific Journal of Human Resources, 41,* 338–53.

Harrison, D. A., Price, K. H., & Bell, M. P. (1998). Beyond relational demography: Time and the effects of surface- and deep-level diversity on work group cohesion. *Academy of Management Journal, 41,* 96–107.

Harvie, K., Marshall-McCaskey, J., & Johnston, L. (1998). Gender-based biases in occupational hiring decisions. *Journal of Applied Social Psychology, 28,* 1698–711.

Hassell, B. L., & Perrewe, P. L. (1995). An examination of beliefs about older workers: Do stereotypes still exist? *Journal of Organizational Behavior, 16,* 457–68.

Hebl, M. R., Foster, J. B., Mannix, L. M., & Dovidio, J. F. (2002). Formal and interpersonal discrimination: A field study of bias toward homosexual applicants. *Personality and Social Psychology Bulletin, 28,* 815–25.

Heilman, M. E. (1983). Sex bias in work settings: The lack of fit model. *Research in Organizational Behavior, 16,* 457–68.

Heilman, M. E., Block, C. J., & Martell, R. F. (1995). Sex stereotypes: Do they influence perceptions of managers? *Journal of Social Behavior and Personality, 10,* 237–52.

Heilman, M. E., & Martell, R. F. (1986). Exposure to successful women: Antidote to sex discrimination in applicant screening decisions. *Organizational Behavior and Human Decision Processes, 37,* 376–90.

Heilman, M. E., Martell, R. F., & Simon, M. C. (1988). The vagaries of sex bias: Conditions regulating the undervaluation, equivaluation, and overvaluation of female job applicants. *Organizational Behavior and Human Decision Processes, 41,* 98–110.

Heilman, M. E., Wallen, A. S., Fuchs, D., & Tamkins, M. M. (2004). Penalties for success: Reactions to women who succeed at male gender-typed tasks. *Journal of Applied Psychology, 89,* 416–27.

Hembroff, L. A., & Myers, D. E. (1984). Status characteristics: Degrees of task relevance and decision-processes. *Social Psychology Quarterly, 47,* 337–46.

Hogg, M. A., & Abrams, D. (1988). *Social identifications: A social psychology of intergroup relations and group processes.* London: Routledge.

Hogg, M. A., Terry, D. J., & White, K. M. (1995). A tale of two theories: A critical comparison of identity theory with social identity theory. *Social Psychology Quarterly, 58,* 255–69.

Holyoak, K. J., & Gordon, P. C. (1984). Information processing and social cognition. In R. S. Wyer & T. K. Srull (Eds), *Handbook of social cognition* (Vol. 1, pp. 39–70). Hillsdale, NJ: Erlbaum.

Hosoda, M., Stone, D. L., & Stone-Romero, E. F. (2003). The interactive effects of race, gender, and job type on job suitability ratings and selection decisions. *Journal of Applied Social Psychology, 33,* 145–78.

Johns, G. (1993). Constraints on the adoption of psychology-based personnel practices: Lessons from organizational innovation. *Personnel Psychology, 46,* 569–92.

Jones, D., Pringle, J., & Shepherd, D. (2000). 'Managing diversity' meets Aoteatoa/ New Zealand. *Personnel Review, 29,* 364–80.

Kalin, R., & Hodgins, D. C. (1984). Sex bias in judgements of occupational suitability. *Canadian Journal of Behavioural Science–Revue Canadienne Des Sciences Du Comportement, 16,* 311–25.

Kulik, C. T., & Perry, E. L. (1994). Heuristic processing in organizational judgments. In L. Heath, R. S. Tindale, J. Edwards, E. J. Posavac, F. B. Bryant, E. Henderson-King,

Y. Suarez-Balcazar & J. Myers (Eds), *Applications of heuristics and biases to social issues* (Vol. 3, pp. 185–204). New York: Plenum.

Kulik, C. T., Perry, E. L., & Bourhis, A. C. (2000). Ironic evaluation processes: Effects of thought suppression on evaluations of older job applicants. *Journal of Organizational Behavior*, *21*, 689–711.

Landau, J. (1995). The relationship of race and gender to managers ratings of promotion potential. *Journal of Organizational Behavior*, *16*, 391–400.

Landrine, H., Knonoff, E. A., Alcaraz, R., Scott, J., & Wilkins, P. (1995). Multiple variables in discrimination. In B. Lott & D. Maluso (Eds), *The social psychology of interpersonal discrimination* (pp. 183–224). New York: Guilford Press.

Lewis, A. C., & Sherman, S. J. (2003). Hiring you makes me look bad: Social-identity based reversals of the ingroup favoritism effect. *Organizational Behavior and Human Decision Processes*, *90*, 262–76.

Liebkind, K., & McAlister, A. L. (1999). Extended contact through peer modelling to promote tolerance in Finland. *European Journal of Social Psychology*, *29*, 765–80.

Linehan, M., & Walsh, J. S. (2000). Work-family conflict and the senior female international manager. *British Journal of Management*, *11*, 49–58.

Lorber, J. (1998). *Gender inequality: Feminist theories and politics*. Los Angeles: Roxbury.

Lyness, K. S., & Thompson, D. E. (1997). Above the glass ceiling? A comparison of matched samples of female and male executives. *Journal of Applied Psychology*, *82*, 359–75.

Lyon, P., & Pollard, D. (1997). Perceptions of the older employee: Is anything really changing? *Personnel Review*, *26*, 245–6.

Macrae, C. N., & Bodenhausen, G. V. (2001). Social cognition: Categorical person perception. *British Journal of Psychology*, *92*, 239–55.

Macrae, C. N., Bodenhausen, G. V., & Milne, A. B. (1998). Saying no to unwanted thoughts: Self-focus and the regulation of mental life. *Journal of Personality and Social Psychology*, *74*, 578–89.

Macrae, C. N., Bodenhausen, G. V., Milne, A. B., & Jetten, J. (1994). Out of mind but back in sight: Stereotypes on the rebound. *Journal of Personality and Social Psychology*, *67*, 808–17.

Martell, R. F. (1991). Sex bias at work: The effects of attentional and memory demands on performance ratings of men and women. *Journal of Applied Social Psychology*, *21*, 1939–60.

Martell, R. F. (1996). What mediates gender bias in work behavior ratings? *Sex Roles*, *35*, 153–69.

Martell, R. F., & DeSmet, A. L. (2001). A diagnostic-ratio approach to measuring beliefs about the leadership abilities of male and female managers. *Journal of Applied Psychology*, *86*, 1223–31.

McConahay, J. B. (1986). Modern racism, ambivalence, and the Modern Racism Scale. In J. F. Dovidio & S. L. Gaertner (Eds), *Prejudice, discrimination, and racism* (pp. 91–125). San Diego, CA: Academic Press.

McGrath, J. E. (1982). Dilemmatics: The study of research choices and dilemmas. In J. E. McGrath, J. Martin & R. A. Kulka (Eds), *Judgment calls in research*. Beverly Hills, CA: Sage.

Murphy, K. R., Herr, B. M., Lockhart, M. C., & Maguire, E. (1986). Evaluating the performance of paper people. *Journal of Applied Psychology*, *71*, 654–61.

Pelled, L. H., & Xin, K. R. (2000). Relational demography and relationship quality in two cultures. *Organization Studies*, *21*, 1077–94.

Perdue, C. W., & Gurtman, M. B. (1990). Evidence for the automaticity of ageism. *Journal of Experimental Social Psychology*, *26*, 199–216.

Perry, E. (1994). A prototype matching approach to understanding the role of applicant gender and age in the evaluation of job applicants. *Journal of Applied Social Psychology*, *24*, 1433–73.

Perry, E. (1997). A cognitive approach to understanding discrimination: A closer look at applicant gender and age. *Research in Personnel and Human Resources Management, 15*, 175–240.

Perry, E., Davis-Blake, A., & Kulik, C. T. (1994). Explaining gender-based selection decisions: A synthesis of contextual and cognitive approaches. *Academy of Management Review, 19*, 786–820.

Perry, E. L., & Bourhis, A. C. (1998). A closer look at the role of applicant age in selection decisions. *Journal of Applied Social Psychology, 28*, 1670–97.

Perry, E. L., & Finkelstein, L. M. (1999). Toward a broader view of age discrimination in employment-related decisions: A joint consideration of organizational factors and cognitive processes. *Human Resource Management Review, 9*, 21–49.

Perry, E. L., Hendricks, W., & Broadbent, E. (2000). An exploration of access and treatment discrimination and job satisfaction among college graduates with and without physical disabilities. *Human Relations, 53*, 923–955.

Perry, E. L., Kulik, C. T., & Bourhis, A. C. (1996). Moderating effects of personal and contextual factors in age discrimination. *Journal of Applied Psychology, 81*, 628–47.

Petty, R. E., & Cacioppo, J. T. (1979). Issue involvement can increase or decrease persuasion by enhancing message-relevant cognitive responses. *Journal of Personality and Social Psychology, 37*, 1915–26.

Pfeffer, J., & Davis-Blake, A. (1992). Salary dispersion, location in the salary distribution, and turnover among college administrators. *Industrial & Labor Relations Review, 45*, 753–63.

Powell, G. N., & Butterfield, D. A. (1997). Effect of race on promotions to top management in a federal department. *Academy of Management Journal, 40*, 112–28.

Powell, G. N., & Butterfield, D. A. (2002). Exploring the influence of decision makers' race and gender on actual promotions to top management. *Personnel Psychology, 55*, 397–428.

Powell, G. N., Butterfield, D. A., & Parent, J. D. (2002). Gender and managerial stereotypes: Have the times changed? *Journal of Management, 28*, 177–93.

Prewett-Livingston, A. J., Feild, H. S., Veres, J. G., & Lewis, P. M. (1996). Effects of race on interview ratings in a situational panel interview. *Journal of Applied Psychology, 81*, 178–86.

Pugh, M. D., & Wahrman, R. (1983). Neutralizing sexism in mixed-sex groups: Do women have to be better than men? *American Journal of Sociology, 88*, 746–62.

Rana, B. K., Kagan, C., Lewis, S., & Rout, U. (1998). British south Asian women managers and professionals: Experiences or work and family. *Women in Management Review, 13*, 221–32.

Reid, P. T., & Comas-Diaz, L. (1990). Gender and ethnicity: Perspectives on dual status. *Sex Roles, 22*, 397–408.

Ridgeway, C. L. (1991). The social construction of status value: Gender and other nominal characteristics. *Social Forces, 70*, 367–86.

Ridgeway, C. L. (2001). Gender, status, and leadership. *Journal of Social Issues, 57*, 637–55.

Ridgeway, C. L., & Erickson, K. G. (2000). Creating and spreading status beliefs. *American Journal of Sociology, 106*, 579–615.

Roberson, L., & Block, C. J. (2001). Racioethnicity and job performance: A review and critique of theoretical perspectives on the causes of group differences. *Research in Organizational Behavior, 23*, 247–325.

Roberson, L., Kulik, C. T., & Pepper, M. B. (2001). Designing effective diversity training: Influence of group composition and trainees experience. *Journal of Organizational Behavior, 22*, 871–85.

Roberson, L., Kulik, C. T., & Pepper, M. B. (2003). Using needs assessment to resolve controversies in diversity training design. *Group & Organization Management, 28*, 148–74.

Rosen, B., & Jerdee, T. H. (1976). Influence of age stereotypes on managerial decisions. *Journal of Applied Psychology*, *61*, 428–32.

Salas, E., & Cannon-Bowers, J. A. (2001). The science of training: A decade of progress. *Annual Review of Psychology*, *52*, 471–99.

Salas, E., Cannon-Bowers, J. A., Rhodenizer, L., & Bowers, C. A. (1999). Training in organizations: Myths, misconceptions, and mistaken assumptions. *Research in Personnel and Human Resources Management*, *17*, 123–61.

Sauers, D. A., Kennedy, J. C., & O'Sullivan, D. (2002). Managerial sex role stereotyping: A New Zealand perspective. *Women in Management Review*, *17*, 342–47.

Schein, V. E. (2001). A global look at psychological barriers to women's progress in management. *Journal of Social Issues*, *57*, 675–88.

Schein, V. E., & Mueller, R. (1992). Sex role stereotyping and requisite management characteristics: A cross cultural look. *Journal of Organizational Behavior*, *13*, 439–47.

Schein, V. E., Mueller, R., Lituchy, T., & Liu, J. (1996). Think manager – think male: A global phenomenon? *Journal of Organizational Behavior*, *17*, 33–41.

Simons, T., Pelled, L. H., & Smith, K. A. (1999). Making use of difference: Diversity, debate, and decision comprehensiveness in top management teams. *Academy of Management Journal*, *42*, 662–73.

Smith, E. R., & Ho, C. (2002). Prejudice as intergroup emotion: Integrating relative deprivation and social comparison explanations of prejudice. In I. Walker & H. Smith (Eds), *Relative deprivation: Specification, development, and integration* (pp. 332–48). Cambridge: Cambridge University Press.

Steinberg, M., Donald, K., Najman, J., & Skerman, H. (1996). Attitudes of employees and employers towards older workers in a climate of antidiscrimination. *Australian Journal on Ageing*, *15*, 569–91.

Stone, D. L., & Colella, A. (1996). A model of factors affecting the treatment of disabled individuals in organizations. *Academy of Management Review*, *21*, 352–401.

Swim, J. K., Aikin, K. J., Hall, W. S., & Hunter, B. A. (1995). Sexism and racism: Old fashioned and modern prejudices. *Journal of Personality and Social Psychology*, *68*, 199–214.

Tajfel, H. (1972). Some developments in European social psychology. *European Journal of Social Psychology*, *2*, 307–22.

Tajfel, H., Billig, M. G., Bundy, R. P., & Flament, C. (1971). Social categorization and intergroup behavior. *European Journal of Social Psychology*, *1*, 149–77.

Tajfel, H., & Turner, J. C. (1979). An integrative theory of intergroup conflict. In W. G. Austin & S. Worchel (Eds), *The social psychology of intergroup relations* (pp. 33–47). Monterey, CA: Brooks/Cole.

Tajfel, H., & Turner, J. C. (1986). The social identity theory of intergroup behavior. In E. J. Lawler (Ed.), *Advances in group processes: A research annual* (Vol. 2, pp. 77–122). Greenwich, CT: JAI Press.

Terry, D. J. (2003). Social identity and diversity in organizations. *Asia Pacific Journal of Human Resources*, *41*, 25–35.

Turner, J. C., Hogg, M. A., Oakes, P. J., Reicher, S. D., & Wetherell, M. S. (1987). *Rediscovering the social group: A self-categorization theory*. Oxford: Blackwell.

van Oudenhouven, J. P., Groenewond, J. T., & Hewstone, M. (1996). Co-operation, ethnic salience and generalization or interethnic attitudes. *European Journal of Social Psychology*, *29*, 741–64.

Wagner, D. G., & Berger, A. S. (1993). Status characteristics theory: The growth of a program. In J. Berger & M. Zelditch Jr (Eds), *Theoretical research programs: Studies in the growth of theory* (pp. 23–63). Stanford, CA: Stanford University Press.

Wagner, D. G., & Berger, J. (1997). Gender and interpersonal task behaviors: Status expectation accounts. *Sociological Perspectives*, *40*, 1–32.

Wegner, D. M. (1994). Ironic processes of mental control. *Psychological Review*, *101*, 34–52.

Wood, W., & Karten, S. J. (1986). Sex differences in interaction style as a product of perceived sex differences in competence. *Journal of Personality and Social Psychology*, *50*, 341–7.

Wyer, R. S., Jr, & Srull, T. K. (1981). Category accessibility: Some theoretical and empirical issues concerning the processing of social stimulus information. In E. T. Higgins, C. P. Herman & M. P. Zanna (Eds), *Social cognition: The Ontario symposium* (Vol. 1, pp. 161–97). Hillsdale, NJ: Erlbaum.

Wyer, R. S., Jr, & Srull, T. K. (1989). *Memory and cognition in its social context*. Hillsdale, NJ: Erlbaum.

2

Human Resource Strategies to Manage Workforce Diversity

Examining 'The Business Case'

ELLEN ERNST KOSSEK, SHARON A. LOBEL
AND JENNIFER BROWN

In this chapter, we discuss the human resource management (HRM) perspective on workforce diversity. This viewpoint highlights the development and implementation of organizational initiatives that (1) increase the numerical representation of historically excluded groups; (2) empower a diverse workforce once it is in place to participate fully in organizational decision making; and (3) ensure the inclusion of a diverse workforce in every aspect of organizational life (Kossek & Lobel, 1996). The business case for HR diversity strategies links recruitment, selection, development and retention of a diverse workforce to business goals, labor market shifts, globalization and competitive advantage (Yakura, 1996).

Data from the US Department of Labor (2004) illustrates the continuing need for diversity strategies. Whites hold a larger than proportionate share of management occupations (88.4%) relative to other races and ethnicities (e.g. 5.7% for blacks, 5.9% Hispanics). If proportions mirrored the population, we would expect whites to comprise 75% of management, with blacks and Hispanics doubling current rates. In 2002, women represented 47.5% of the managerial and professional occupation, but mainly occupied 'female-dominated', relatively lower-paid occupations (e.g. school teachers) within these professions, while men were nine times as likely to be engineers and scientists. Turning globally, the Gender

Promotion Programme of the International Labor Organization (www.ilo.org) concludes that while globalization has created unprecedented economic opportunities, it has also deepened social inequalities. Only 54% of working-age women are in the workforce worldwide compared to 80% of men. Further, women continue to dominate the 'invisible care economy', which relates to caregiving and domestic work. The ILO report notes that although more and more women are obtaining paid work, most new employment in developed countries has been in part-time jobs, while in developing countries women have gone mainly into the informal sector and home-based work. Globally, women earn 20–30% less than men and hold only 1% of chief executive positions.

Table 2.1 gives an overview of diversity management strategies, which involve setting objectives (first column), translating objectives into programs and policies (second column) and finally establishing measurement outcomes (third column). For example, the organization might establish attracting a wider pool of talent as an objective. Then managers develop methods of achieving the objective, such as ensuring that women and minorities are on the interview shortlist for potential hires. Measurement outcomes might reflect the ratio of acceptance of job offers, and turnover exit interview data.

In this chapter, we review three principal research streams on the effectiveness of HRM diversity strategies (see Figure 2.1). The first stream investigates how particular HR practices influence workforce diversity. As Table 2.1 shows, diversity strategies can target individual, group and/or organizational outcomes. The second stream examines how the presence of diversity in the workforce affects outcomes, and the third stream directly links HR practices to outcomes.

We conclude with future research suggestions and a critique of the business case.

HR PRACTICES AND WORKFORCE DIVERSITY

HR diversity practices have broadened beyond affirmative action (AA) and equal employment opportunity (EEO) staffing efforts. Additional best practices include establishing a visible Diversity Advisory Committee, conducting mandatory training, and targeting communications to different affinity group members (Jackson, 2002).

The first research stream examines the effects of adopting specific HR practices on measures of workforce diversity. For example, Goodman, Fields and Blum (2003) surveyed HR managers in several hundred employers in Georgia. They found a positive relationship between emphasizing employee development and promotion and the representation of women.

Typically, researchers are interested not only in overall numbers, but in representation at different levels. In a cross-sectional study of over 100 organizations, Konrad and Linnehan (1995) found that identity-conscious HRM structures – those that explicitly address demographic group representation in HR decision making

TABLE 2.1 *Objectives and indicators of effective diversity*

Objectives of HR strategies	HRM initiatives in organizations	Indicators of achievement of objectives
Enhanced organizational effectiveness:		
Meet a moral imperative; do the 'right thing'	• Recruiting efforts that highlight the organization's commitment to, and efforts to support, diversity in the workplace and external community • Developmental assignments that expose employees to multiple cultures • Implement formal and informal mentoring programs • Incorporate diversity issue items into employee attitude surveys • Encourage network and support group areas and potential skill-building/advancement opportunities	• Assessment of corporate citizenship • Positive feedback from multiple stakeholders (shareholders, employees, labor organizations, communities) • Outside recognition, reputation • Structural integration (across levels, functions, titles, privileges) • Inclusive work environment; all voices encouraged and heard
Reduce labor costs	• Maintain database of workforce demographics to identify potential areas in need of intervention • Reward managers who effectively manage diversity	• Absenteeism • Turnover • Productivity
Reduce legal costs associated with lawsuits and grievances	• Monitor recruiting, hiring, promotion and compensation systems for compliance and equity • Implement 'open door' policies and other processes to facilitate employee communication of grievances • Articulate 'zero tolerance' of harassment and discrimination and diligently observe this commitment • Expanded job posting	• Number of EEO complaints and grievances; associated costs • Distribution of economic and social benefits, e.g. rates of advancement, access to training and development opportunities
Enhance the organization's reputation	• Market the organization's commitment to diversity through various channels, such as the organization's website, targeted trade and other group-affiliated periodicals, local newspapers and sponsorship of community events	• Public knowledge and assessment • Awards
Have policies and programs that are responsive to the changing demographic profile of employees	• Flexible benefits that address a broad range of employee work and family needs • Employee feedback incorporated into management performance evaluation • Linking organizational awards, such as promotions and compensation, to the achievement of diversity goals	• Number of relevant programs and policies (e.g. training) • Program utilization rates • Employee satisfaction with programs and policies (measurement not limited to beneficiaries) • Management accountability

(Continued)

TABLE 2.1 (Continued)

Objectives of HR strategies	HRM initiatives in organizations	Indicators of achievement of objectives
Attract a wider pool of talent	• Expand recruiting efforts to specifically targeted audiences through periodicals, job fairs, selected colleges and professional affiliation groups • Offer recruitment incentives; tap into the network groups of current employees	• Demographic characteristics of candidates • Demographic characteristics of hires
Retain a wider pool of talent	• Implement formal and informal mentoring programs • Incorporate diversity issue items into employee attitude surveys • Encourage network and support groups	• Demographic characteristics for voluntary and involuntary turnover populations • Retention rate of high-potential employees • Retention rate by function, level
Effect cultural change consistent with program and policy changes	• Implement formal and informal mentoring programs • Identify high-potential employees • Incorporate diversity issue items into employee attitude surveys • Encourage network and support groups	• Cultural audit • Integration of diversity with other programs, e.g. orientation • Top management support • Number and level of managers involved in diversity initiatives • Frequency of communication about importance of diversity in organization
Offer better service and marketing for a diverse customer base	• Incorporate customer feedback into performance appraisal • Provide recognition and/or rewards for employees who contribute to customer service initiatives	• Customer satisfaction with quality of products and services • Market share for target population or region
Enhance ability to innovate because of utilization of diverse perspectives	• Provide training and resources for diverse teams • Provide team-based recognition and/or rewards for contributions to successful design and marketing efforts	• Quality and profitability of new products and services • Diverse composition of decision-makers
Reinforce business strategies	• Recruit and retain a committed workforce by ensuring a work environment that values and includes all employees	• Profitability • Increased market share • Progress toward globalization • Quality • Customer service and marketing

(Continued)

TABLE 2.1 (Continued)

Objectives of HR strategies	HRM initiatives in organizations	Indicators of achievement of objectives
Enhanced individual and work group effectiveness:		
Improved job satisfaction and performance of individuals	• Conduct regular employee attitude surveys • Implement effective means to solicit and respond to employee concerns • Provide appropriate training to all employees	• Individual job satisfaction and performance • Existence of support networks; frequency of meetings; impact • Promotion rates of trainees
Increased awareness and understanding of issues	• Provide awareness training for all staff • Provide cross-cultural skill-building opportunities and resources • Maintain reference library and promote its use	• Changes in perception, e.g. stereotypes
Improved quality of team problem solving	• Provide resources and time to facilitate team socialization • Communicate team's accomplishments throughout the organization • Provide formal team feedback	• Team commitment and performance
Improved abilities to work with and manage people of diverse backgrounds	• Provide conflict-management training • Provide managerial training • Include hiring and climate measures in performance appraisal criteria for managers	• Satisfaction with coworkers • Managerial skill development (e.g. flexibility, interpersonal and communication skills) • Individual accountability for climate, hiring records

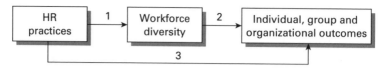

FIGURE 2.1   *HRM diversity research streams*

(e.g. setting diversity hiring goals) – are linked to the greater representation of women and minorities in management. Reskin and McBrier (2000) used data from the National Organization Survey (Kalleberg, Knoke, Marsden & Spaeth, 1994) and found that organizations with formalized HR practices (e.g. written documents for hiring and firing) had higher percentages of women in management. They theorized that status positions or opportunities in large organizations are less likely to be distributed based on ascribed characteristics (i.e. sex stereotypes of productive managers) when formalized personnel practices exist (cf. Elvira & Graham, 2002).

Leck and Saunders (1992) studied compliance with Canada's Employment Equity Act, the legislation to increase workplace representation of women, disabled persons and minorities. They found that employers who had more formalized programs hired more women. They measured formalization through an Employment Equity Program (EEP) effectiveness scale. Regression analyses showed the strongest effects between EEP compliance and the representation of managerial women.

French (2001) developed a typology of effective equal employment implementation for the entire population ($n = 1976$) of large Australian private sector organizations. She identified four equity profiles: traditional (non-compliance), anti-discrimination, AA and EEO. Only the AA approach to equity management resulted in increases in women in management across all tiers.

A major unpublished Ford Foundation study of non-profit boards shows a cascading effect from hiring practices (Burbridge, Diaz, Odendahl & Shaw, 2002). By hiring more than one female or minority board or staff member, a cascade effect followed as these hires make subsequent recruitment easier through their access to networks and talent pools. This expansion shaped institutional cultures and made retention easier.

In some research, HR diversity practices have not been associated with increases in diversity. In their study of Society for Human Resource Management (SHRM) members, Rynes and Rosen (1995) found little support for the notion that the adoption of diversity training correlates with top management diversity or increases in workforce diversity. Konrad and Linnehan (1995) found no relationship between formalized HRM structures and percentage of minorities at higher ranks of management. Moreover, Blum, Fields and Goodman (1994) found that companies that have more women and blacks sometimes can be worse places to work (e.g. lower salaries, more turnover), highlighting the issue that demographic diversity is not a proxy for diversity initiatives.

Furthermore, although academics and practitioners hope that diversity initiatives will have positive outcomes, there are occasionally undesirable impacts – those that

perpetuate disparate treatment of women and minorities. Cox and Blake (1991)
argued that organizations that valued diversity would have greater marketing
capability by mirroring increasingly diverse markets. By matching customers and
service providers on racial characteristics, Brief (1998) shows how Shoney's
restaurants enacted the business case argument to the detriment of black employees.
Throughout the chain, 75% of black employees held jobs in three low-paying, non-
customer-contact positions. Senior leadership espoused the business justification that
the restaurant's white customers preferred to be served by white employees.

Collins' work (1997) also exemplifies unintended consequences. She interviewed 76 of the most successful black executives in Chicago. She examined
their job descriptions and coded them as racialized if the position had some link
to African American issues, or mainstream if the job involved roles without racial
implications. She documents how these executives are often relegated to what she
calls 'racialized roles' in organizations, such as marketing to blacks or the job
of equal employment officer. Those with racialized roles had lower advancement
and mobility rates and less skill development than those with mixed or mainstream job histories.

Indeed, many leading corporations have been effective in hiring women and
minorities to mirror their increasingly diverse markets and win over new customers
(Perlman, 1992); but they have been less successful in retaining and promoting
those hired (Blum, Fields & Goodman, 1994; Goodman et al., 2003). Observing
this trend, Thomas (1990: 108) encouraged employers to move 'From affirmative
action to affirming diversity', arguing that 'women and minorities no longer need a
boarding pass, they need an upgrade'. For this reason, Cox (2001) advises companies to measure the identity profile or demographics of defined work groups. Using
this data, an intervention may be designed to increase the representation of minorities and women in top management, in line functions that have direct profit and loss
responsibility, or in functions where they have been historically under-represented
such as engineering. Thomas and Gabarro (1999) recommend that firms address
specific racial barriers to advancement at each career stage.

Overall, studies in this research stream have generally shown a positive association between formalized HR practices and workforce diversity. Increasing
workforce diversity is only one piece of the puzzle, however. Important questions
about effectiveness can be answered by examining links between diversity and
performance outcomes as discussed below.

ASSOCIATION OF WORKFORCE DIVERSITY WITH INDIVIDUAL, GROUP AND ORGANIZATIONAL OUTCOMES

The second research stream measures associations between the presence of diversity and performance outcomes measured at individual, group or organizational
levels. At the individual level, researchers have measured relationships between

demographic diversity and attitudes and performance ratings. At the group level, researchers have measured effects of group diversity on variables such as cooperative behavior and social cohesion. At the organizational level, outcome variables include turnover rates, productivity per employee and profitability.

Workforce Diversity and Individual Outcomes

Today, there are many individuals who view overt prejudice against women and minorities as socially and organizationally unacceptable. They believe that organizational decision-makers hold the same beliefs and therefore view discrimination as an outdated issue. Because 'modern racists' believe that discrimination is a thing of the past, they may believe that women and minorities are using unfair tactics to demand workplace advantages, which they do not deserve on the basis of merit (Brief & Barsky, 2000). Regarding workplace relations, modern racism does not result in hate toward minorities and women, but rather discomfort, fear and avoidance by majority members (Brief, 1998), which lessens majority members' commitment to the diverse group and organization.

Some studies show that individuals have more favorable attitudes toward diversity initiatives when their work groups are more demographically diverse. Kossek and Zonia (1993) found that regardless of one's individual demography, faculty in work groups with greater gender diversity had more favorable attitudes toward organizational efforts to increase diversity, relative to individuals in other units with less diversity.

Kanter (1977) emphasized how a minimum number of employees, who represent a minority in a group, create a critical mass that can protect the minority members from negative stereotypes. Ely (1995) reported that an increase in the proportion of women in upper management is associated with a reduction in stereotyping. Kossek, Markel and McHugh (2003) note the importance of identifying tipping points, defined by Kanter (1977) as having a sufficient critical mass of minorities in groups, for effectiveness in diversity change strategies. Webber and Donahue (2001) suspect the relationship between amount of group diversity and performance may be curvilinear: too little or too much diversity may be detrimental to group functioning.

Tsui and Gutek (1999) summarized consistent findings that show higher demographic similarity between supervisors and subordinates on age, race or gender correlates with HR outcomes such as higher ratings on performance, organizational citizenship, and lower role ambiguity and conflict. Leck, Onge and LaLancette (1995) found that Canadian organizations with higher representation of managerial women also have the most rapidly decreasing wage gap; however, the wage gap was widening for visible minority, Aboriginal and disabled women.

Overall, increasing workforce diversity seems to be associated with more favorable attitudes toward diversity and better performance ratings and wages. The effects of diversity on individuals are often intertwined with effects on groups.

Workforce Diversity and Group Outcomes

Results from studies examining effects of diverse group composition on group attitudes and performance are mixed. McLeod, Lobel and Cox (1996) found that more diverse groups had better-quality solutions on a brainstorming task, relative to homogeneous groups, and displayed more cooperative behavior (Cox, Lobel & McLeod, 1991). Yet major reviews of the diversity literature (Milliken & Martins, 1996; Tsui & Gutek, 1999; Williams & O'Reilly, 1998) conclude that the greater the demographic diversity in groups, the lower the social cohesion. Members who are different from others are more likely to exhibit turnover, as Elvira and Cohen's (2001) examination of the personnel records of employees at a Fortune 500 company suggests. Women were more likely to turn over when fewer women were employed at their job level. Finally, Webber and Donahue's (2001) meta-analysis found no relationship between diversity or type of team on work group cohesion and performance.

Researchers recognize the importance of measuring the tenure of members on the team; as individuals get to know each other better, the negative effects of diversity often subside (Watson, Kumar & Michaelsen, 1993). Besides demographic diversity, other variables such as congruence in values (Harrison, Price & Bell, 1998) are relevant.

Benschop (2001) observes that most of the research showing positive relationships between diversity and group performance is limited to laboratory studies or experiments with MBA students (Cox et al., 1991; Watson et al., 1993) and generally has not been replicated in organizations.

We need more complex studies within organizations to understand these issues.

Workforce Diversity and Organizational Outcomes

A workforce that is diverse may increase customer demand for related products and services (Richard, Kochan & McMillan-Capehart, 2002). Resource-based strategic theory predicts that firms with greater cultural diversity will be better able to mirror increasingly diverse product markets and have more complex inimitable social resources (Richard, 2000).

Drawing on federal records, Cordeiro and Stites-Doe (1997) showed that the 1992 percentage of the representation of women managers in the largest US firms was positively related to firm performance (return on equity, return on assets). The effect persisted even after controlling for growth in resources.

Catalyst (2004) conducted a study of linkages between the gender diversity of top management and business performance in Fortune 500 companies. After controlling for size and industry, the study showed that firms with higher top management gender diversity had 35% higher return on equity and 34% higher total return to shareholders than other firms.

A large multi-employer field study on the effects of racial and gender differences on group and organizational performance indicates the importance of time lag and cross-level effects within firms. The research was conducted at four major

US firms that were leaders in supporting workforce diversity (Kochan et al., 2003). Comparing the performance, group process and financial results for comparable teams or business units by industry (information processing, financial services or retail), the authors concluded that there were few direct effects of workforce diversity on organizational performance.

Research increasingly suggests that the relationship between the presence of diversity and organizational performance may not necessarily be a simple direct positive or negative relationship. Instead, the relationship may depend on the type of strategy followed (e.g. innovation, growth). Richard's (2000) survey of over 500 banks found that those with more racial diversity and a growth strategy experienced higher return on equity and net income per employee, relative to organizations with a diverse workforce and a no-growth or downsizing strategy. Richard and colleagues resurveyed a subset of this sample several years later, and found a moderation effect: workforce racial diversity only significantly improved performance when the firm followed an innovation strategy (Richard et al., 2003).

Frink et al. (2003) suggest an inverted U-shaped relationship between gender composition and performance that may vary by industry. Relying on several national datasets, they found that increases in the representation of women are related to perceptual measures of productivity per employee and profitability only up to the point when an equal proportion of jobs are held by men and women – no higher. Richard et al. (2002) bemoan the fact that cross-sectional studies comprise most of the literature on organizational outcomes. In other words, the second research stream we have reviewed does not address the question of *causality* (i.e. whether diversity caused these outcomes or whether HR practices were at all relevant) – issues tackled by the third research stream.

HR PRACTICES AND INDIVIDUAL, GROUP AND ORGANIZATIONAL OUTCOMES

The third research stream investigates how HR practices lead to individual, group or organizational performance outcomes. Cox and Blake (1991) argued that heterogeneous organizations that valued diversity would have higher-quality group decision making, greater creativity and innovation, more organizational flexibility due to the possession of divergent thinking, greater ability to attract and retain the best talent, and greater marketing capability. These objectives can be realized via organizational change strategies and interventions. Interventions such as altered selection processes (individual focus), conflict management (group focus) and top management commitment (organizational focus) might all contribute to the effect that diversity has on firm effectiveness. Interventions target not only formal bottom-line outcomes, such as turnover and productivity, but also intermediate and informal process-oriented outcomes, such as the cultural experiences and quality of member interactions, teamwork and cooperation, and individual commitment and identification with organizational goals.

HRM Strategies to Change Individuals

Workplace diversity generally impacts organizational-level outcomes indirectly through effects that begin at the individual level (Rynes & Rosen, 1995). Diversity training is the most prevalent individual-level intervention (SHRM *Diversity Surveys*, 1998, 2000, 2002). Ford and Fisher's (1996) review states that training programs aim to change employees' attitudes (affective and cognitive) and behaviors to 'value diversity' and reduce subtle forms of discrimination and exclusion that hinder effective working relationships. They note three main types of training objectives. Programs fostering assimilation provide education about the norms and goals of the dominant culture and might target minorities. Programs focused on accommodation emphasize adjustment of the majority to the changing workforce. Programs emphasizing multiculturalism (where members of two or more cultures are allowed to retain key aspects of their cultures) involve a bilateral process jointly focused on the majority and minorities.

Training topics typically include stereotyping, prejudice, communication styles, and attitudes toward AA (Nkomo & Kossek, 2000). However, there is very little research analyzing the differential effectiveness of various training designs, such as whether they are mandatory or voluntary or emphasize moral or business arguments.

Lobel's (1999) review described the positive impact of diversity initiatives such as training on attitudes. Using a survey of SHRM members, Rynes and Rosen (1995) published one of the few refereed studies on the effectiveness of diversity training. While 75% of respondents state trainees leave diversity training with positive diversity attitudes, only 9% believed trainees enter with favorable attitudes. Similarly, 68% believed that employees are skeptical prior to training, whereas only 7% reported skepticism after training. Importantly, these were HR managers' estimates rather than actual measures of attitude change. Training success was also correlated with managerial mandatory attendance and rewards for increasing diversity, long-term evaluation of training results and defining diversity broadly. Despite these positive perceptions, this same study found that only one-third of organizations viewed diversity management training efforts as having lasting change.

Others have been unable to document the advantages of diversity training (MacDonald, 1993). One reason training may have limited impact is that most training programs reinforce norms, values and perspectives of the dominant organizational culture; the focus is on helping members of the non-dominant group to adapt to the majority (Tung, 1993). Another reason is that the training, itself, may not incorporate what we know about transfer of training. The training context may be different enough from the ongoing work context so as to make it difficult for trainees to exhibit behaviors similar to those learned in training (Ford & Fisher, 1996). A third reason may relate to insufficient skill levels of diversity trainers.

Roberson, Kulik and Pepper's (2003) review recommends that companies systematically conduct a training needs assessment. Additionally, training objectives – whether to raise awareness or develop multicultural skills or both – need to be clarified. Social psychological research on stereotyping and linkages to prejudice reduction might also be more tightly incorporated into training design. Devine (1989) conducted several lab studies and found that change processes to support prejudice reduction were most likely to occur when a person was able to make active associations between both their personal belief structure and their stereotype structure. Regardless of whether a person tended to be a high or low prejudiced person, her research suggests that cognitive change is most likely to occur in training situations when social desirability demands are low.

Mentoring is another strategy targeting change at the individual level. Here a successful senior mentor is matched with a more junior woman or minority, with the objective of enabling under-represented demographic groups to move through 'glass ceilings' – the traditional, invisible barriers to advancement (Ragins, 2002; Thomas & Gabarro, 1999). Formal mentoring programs create a structure for pairing individuals; informal mentoring programs evolve from interactions individuals establish in the course of working together. Using a national sample drawn from professional associations, Ragins, Cotton and Miller (2000) conducted a mail survey on mentoring. The study showed that satisfaction with a mentoring relationship was a stronger influence on career attitudes such as commitment, job satisfaction, intention to turnover, and perception of organizational justice than program design or the mentor type (formal or informal). *Post hoc* analyses showed that although both men and women received similar mentoring information and had similar levels of satisfaction, women in formal programs had lower career commitment, suggesting that the selection of effective mentors though informal processes may be especially critical. Formal HR diversity strategies may be less effective for members of traditional out-groups, unless supported informally. Ragins (2002) urged firms to recognize that while formal programs help protégés deal with their jobs, informal programs help them deal with their lives.

Incorporating principles from research on intergroup contact, attitude change, persuasion and stereotype reduction may increase effectiveness. Developing 'affective ties' with out-group members, which increases information and empathy regarding the out-group and fosters social connections, reduces prejudice (Pettigrew, 1998). Rather than designing diversity initiatives to only focus on task issues such as imparting information, it may be useful to include opportunities to enhance social interaction.

Petty and Cacioppo (1990) argue that when persuasion depends on emotional appeals and values such as equality, it is less likely to produce lasting change. Rational appeals to the recipient's current goals and outcomes are more effective over the long term. Rather than using rhetoric emphasizing that diversity is the 'morally right thing to do', communication strategies might focus more on how these initiatives will help individuals personally be more effective on the job or help their company be more competitive. Individuals are more favorable toward affirmative action if it is framed as equal opportunity and not reverse discrimination (Bosveld, Koomen & Vogelaar, 1997).

Wood (2000) notes that behavioral influence strategies are more effective in changing attitudes when they involve participation in public acts that are designed to alter the social definition of an object. These influence strategies can be more effective in shifting relevant privately held attitudes by focusing on changing the meaning and definition of an object instead of focusing on only changing attitudes toward an object. For instance, using 'affinity group celebrations' as an example of an object, having Hispanic–American employees design activities for an Asian–American affinity month (Jackson, 2002), rather than simply exposing them to announcements about the importance of affinity activities or cultural facts, illustrates one method that could be used to change definitions. In this way, attitudes toward affinity group celebrations may become a source of pride for those outside the affinity group, and yield not only a better cross-cultural understanding of others, but also a new outlook and personal definition of how diversity is honored within an organization and the social meaning of and personal rewards from such celebrations. For individuals from outside the affinity group, the celebrations are now less likely to be defined as an 'activity that doesn't pertain to me'.

Richard and Kirby (1999) found that explaining the business case for implementing a particular diversity program, such as diversity training, has a positive effect on attitudes towards the program. We need more studies on employee perceptions of workplace diversity programs, and additional constructs such as respondents' legal knowledge of AA programs (Little, Murry & Wimbush, 1998).

In sum, HRM practices, such as diversity training and mentoring, have the potential to change attitude and career outcomes. We have learned how to make these efforts more successful, for example by incorporating social psychological principles into training design and by recognizing the unique advantages of informal mentoring.

HRM Strategies to Change Groups

Given evidence showing that work group diversity can lead to short-term, increased conflict among members (Pelled, Eisenhardt & Xin, 1999), focused training with an external facilitator may help the group to achieve higher levels of productivity in a shorter time. Training can target methods for raising, discussing and resolving difficult interpersonal, business and/or team-related process issues.

Some HR interventions at the group level involve identity-based networking groups, which are formal or informal associations of employees with common group identities. Friedman (1996) notes these separate affinity groups provide opportunities to connect socially and professionally to one another and enable members to make contacts that expand the range, strength and configuration of their social networks and reduce their isolation. Friedman and Holtom (2002) analyzed cross-sectional survey data from over 1000 minority employees in 20 networking groups for Asian, African American or Hispanic employees. Turnover intentions of managerial-level minority employees in networking groups were significantly lower than the intentions of minorities not in groups. They argued that more firms should establish networking groups, as these groups may have outcomes that extend beyond group members. For example, a case study at Digital Corporation found that the presence of valuing diversity discussion groups does seem to improve a company's reputation (Walker & Hanson, 1992).

However, formal sanctioning of identity-based groups may have unintended negative consequences when they are perceived to be exclusionary or threatening, particularly by white males. This perceived threat can lead to negative reactions, or 'backlash when minorities are seen as attempting to develop power by individual or collective means' (Chemers, Oskamp & Constanzo, 1995). Flynn (1999) notes few companies offer formal mentoring and networking groups for white men, which may be perceived as unfair and 'reverse discrimination' by white males, who do not see themselves as contributing to a problem (Flynn, 1999).

Caproni's management skills text (2001) notes that cultural barriers become exacerbated in virtual teams, unless team-building activities such as face-to-face workshops, followed up with regular email, rotation of team meetings and cross-cultural communication training are conducted. The British Council, with over 6000 employees in 109 countries, created technology-based teams with these methods (www.britishcouncil.org). Interventions in global teams can include discussion of how diversity influences team processes.

Many questions about impacts of group-level interventions remain. For example, does providing formal team feedback on diversity climate improve team building or make it easier to integrate diverse points of view? We also need research to identify how programs targeted at the individual or organizational level impact groups. Based on an organizational simulation of 248 MBA students, Chatman, Polzer and Neale (1998) found that groups in organizations that promote a collectivist culture, where people look out for one another rather than just for themselves, are more likely to reap the benefits of diversity. These observations crystallize the importance of showing how interventions directed at one level affect processes that occur at other levels.

HRM Strategies to Change Organizations

A successful diversity strategy must address organizational culture change to create a work environment that nurtures teamwork, participation and cohesiveness – characteristics of a 'collective' (versus individualistic) organizational culture (Dwyer, Richard & Chadwick, 2001). Cox (2001) suggests starting with a visioning exercise for change that specifically identifies what success in a multicultural organization might look like. A diversity council with credible people from a cross-section of functions should be charged with creating a business diversity strategy and serving as a resource. Diversity should be strategically integrated with the business objectives (Richard, 2000).

Top management should model leadership behaviors such as conducting the feedback sessions of the results of an organizational diversity climate survey. If diversity change efforts consist mainly of programs which lack the involvement of top managers and fail to address overall work processes, their long-term effectiveness in transforming the organizational culture is likely to be limited (Nkomo & Kossek, 2000). Thomas and Gabarro's (1999) study of US minority executives also echoed this theme: when a critical mass of senior executives were involved in supporting diversity efforts such as mentoring, or recruitment of minorities for top jobs, organizational diversity and upward mobility efforts were easier and more effective.

Establishing a formal measurement system is important early in the process to serve as a baseline for the current climate for diversity (Cox, 2001). Large amounts of data need to be collected to assess the dominant organizational culture and the perceptions of various employee groups. Cox stresses the importance of measuring the right indicators and identifies key organizational-level measures. These include the workforce identity profile to highlight demographic differences of defined work groups, cultural values and norms, power distribution between identity groups, whether employee acculturation fosters assimilation or pluralism, openness of informal social and communication networks, and HR policies and practices related to recruiting, promotion, pay, development, work schedules and the physical work environment. These measures yield information about the cultural barriers that may hinder the full and effective participation of all individuals and identity groups.

The outcome of diversity efforts should be systemic and structural organizational transformation (Litvin, 2002). Long-term culture change requires a significant commitment of resources and leadership (Cox, 2001). Organizations and researchers need to conduct regular employee attitude surveys about diversity and measure performance of managers. Organizational-level effects of this magnitude take time to materialize, with risks of setbacks and variable commitment over time. Few studies have been published using cultural audit survey data (an exception being Kossek & Zonia, 1993); most firms keep the data internal for fear of negative publicity or other adverse outcomes. Existing research provides some support for a contingency perspective on the effectiveness of diversity interventions targeting organizational outcomes (e.g. innovation). That is, the extent to which racial diversity will positively influence firm performance is contingent upon the firm's strategy and environment demands, and what it expects of its employees (Richard, 2000). The business case for diversity suggests that a diverse workforce and a supportive culture can bring about increased creativity. A diverse workforce, then, becomes a source of competitive advantage for firms that strive to achieve a high level of innovation.

Richard and Johnson (1999) conducted one of the few studies that investigates organizational advantages of formal diversity practices. They found that the adoption of formal diversity practices reduced turnover. While there was not a main effect of these practices on return on earnings, a strategic contingency relationship was supported: diversity practices correlated with improved productivity and market performance for firms following innovation strategies.

Turning to effective AA, Wright, Ferris, Hiller and Kroll (1995) note that while AA and managing diversity are not the same, discriminatory practices and guilty verdicts are examples of ineffective diversity management. Well-run AA programs indicate effectiveness in attracting a diverse workforce. Wright and colleagues used an event study methodology where one examines a significant change in stock price in the days immediately surrounding the event of interest. Focusing on 34 firms which received a Department of Labor award for their AA programs and another 35 firms which had major EEO settlements noted in the press, they showed that having an award-winning AA program was associated with better financial performance and having discrimination lawsuits related to worse performance. Arthur (2003) found a similar positive linkage for share price reaction to favorable press on work–family policies.

Stage models of organizational change and development may be helpful for organizing future research. Benschop (2001) supports further study of organizations that fall along the spectrum of minimal diversity strategies to all-inclusive HRM diversity strategies. Ely and Thomas (2001) documented three different perspectives governing how organizations respond to diversity. The *equality and fairness* perspective equates diversity with increasing the number of women and minorities on the payroll. The *legitimacy* perspective emphasizes that it is critical to mirror key customer demographics. Under the *integration and learning* approach, majority members assume they can learn from the minority members and the culture can be changed to reflect two-way adaptation and learning.

Comer and Soliman (1996: 478) attribute the lack of evaluation of diversity efforts to an unwillingness of many organizations to respond to what the research might demonstrate: for example, that efforts are ineffective or counter-productive, or that 'a radical upending of basic assumptions, patterns, and structures' is necessary. To augment research in this arena we will need to discover whether resource issues, a lack of interest, or fear of the results are key reasons for difficulties in measuring organizational outcomes. Perhaps companies believe that doing something is better than doing nothing at all. We need to know what kinds of incentives would be attractive to overcome the resistance. How can we put the measurement issue on the radar screen of those who have the authority to direct organizational resources toward research?

Future research should attempt to identify other factors that intervene in the effects of diversity practices on firm performance (Richard & Johnson, 2001). Models with intervening variables such as business strategy, HRM strategy and organizational environment should be tested to ascertain the effect of diversity on organizational performance.

Future research on organizational-level impacts might examine questions such as the following: Does including 'valuing diversity' in the mission statement elicit organizational unity and commitment? If so, does this facilitate a more favorable multicultural environment that yields stronger business results? Do organizations that value diversity because of the moral imperative do better on measures of organizational effectiveness, relative to those that value diversity because of the 'business case'?

CONCLUSION

Today, there is a wide spectrum of organizational response to managing diversity. There are some organizations responding to legal mandates; others are focused on discrete programs and policies; still others are implementing broad HR diversity strategies to foster change in culture and work processes.

In 2002, SHRM conducted a survey jointly with *Fortune* magazine to examine how the Post 9/11 economic challenges faced by many firms had affected diversity efforts. Although there were slight shifts, the 2002 survey showed that corporate spending on diversity initiatives remained constant, with even slight increases in funding for diversity training related to race and ethnicity (www.shrm. org/diversity/TalkingtoDiversityExperts.pdf).

In general, while most US multinationals have established diversity programs, a private research report indicates they are only beginning to establish parallel efforts in their overseas affiliates and subsidiaries. Most efforts are currently cosmetic and off-the-shelf US approaches that will likely be ineffective in the European Union (Eagan & Bendick, 2001). Around the world, valuing diversity faces competition from many other pressing HR issues (Wheeler, 1995).

Future work might be improved by more careful identification of relationships between specific HRM strategies, the target level of intervention (e.g. individual, group, organizational, or external stakeholder) and whether outcomes are related to process or productivity (Kossek et al., 2003). More research is needed on the interactions of the variables that contribute to positive outcomes of diversity, including time-continuum studies (Richard et al., 2002). For example, positive business outcomes from increasing diversity may depend on whether the firm emphasizes an innovation strategy or highly values retaining top talent.

In a survey of US firms examining the adoption of work/life policies and links to financial performance, Perry-Smith and Blum (2000) found that some policies may be more effective in impact if they are clustered or implemented with other HR policies than if they are adopted piecemeal. Building on their work, we suggest that diversity researchers examine the impact of policies not only separately but also in clusters with other HR practices and strategies. For example, diversity practices might be part of a high-commitment employer strategy as Osterman (1995) found for work/life policies. We need research not only on clusters of practices, but also on different forms of diversity (e.g. nationality, gender, ethnicity) and how these intersect with other important organizational characteristics such as leadership, top management composition, culture, representation across functions and industry key success factors.

BROADEN BEYOND THE BUSINESS CASE

Although organizations might express a desire for greater racial harmony, none, at least in the private sector, claims it as an important end in and of itself

(Brief & Barsky, 2000). Most organizations still require a business justification or a government influence, such as the European Union Directives, in order for these goals to be consistently articulated. Still, there are some important caveats to the business case for diversity strategy. Kossek (2005) argues that the business case emphasizes the shareholder over all other organizational stakeholders (families, employees, society). Business organizations are likely to be held increasingly accountable to multiple societal goals, such as promoting social change (Aaronson & Reeves, 2002; Anft, 2002). Lobel (1996) has advocated this approach for evaluating impacts of work/life initiatives. Corporations will not be healthy unless the society is healthy, and a healthy society in the twenty-first century will be one in which career opportunities are truly available to all races, ethnic groups (Gummer, 2000) and, indeed, all people.

REFERENCES

Aaronson, S. A., & Reeves, J. (2002). *Corporate responsibility in the global village: The role of public policy.* Washington, DC: National Policy Association.

Anft, M. (2002). Toward corporate change: Businesses seek nonprofit help in quest to become better citizens. *The Chronicle of Philanthropy*, September, 10, 12.

Arthur, M. (2003). Share price reactions to work-family initiatives: an institutional perspective. *Academy of Management Journal, 46*, 497–505.

Benschop, Y. (2001). Pride, prejudice, and performance: Relations between HRM, diversity and performance. *International Journal of Human Resource Management, 12*, 1166–81.

Blum, T. C., Fields, D. L., & Goodman, J. S. (1994). Organization-level determinants of women in management. *Academy of Management Journal, 37*, 241–66.

Bosveld, W., Koomen, W., & Vogelaar, R. (1997). Construing a social issue: Effects on attitudes and the false consensus effect. *British Journal of Social Psychology, 36*, 263–72.

Brief, A. (1998). *Attitudes in and around organizations.* Thousand Oaks, CA: Sage.

Brief, A., & Barsky, A. (2000). Establishing a climate for diversity: The inhibition of prejudiced reactions in the workplace. *Research in Personnel and Human Resource Management, 19*, 91–129.

British Council: www.britishcouncil.org (retrieved 13 July 2004).

Burbridge, L., Diaz, W., Odendahl, T., & Shaw, A. (2002). *The meaning and impact of board and staff diversity in the philanthropic field.* San Francisco: Joint Affinity Groups: http://www.nng.org/html/ourprograms/research/diversity_table.htm (Retrieved 20 November 2003).

Caproni, P. (2001). *The practical coach.* Upper Saddle River, NJ: Prentice Hall.

Catalyst (2004). The bottom line: Connecting corporate performance and diversity. New York: Catalyst: http://www.catalystwomen.org/2004fin_perf.htm (Retrieved 3 March 2004).

Chatman, J., Polzer, J., & Neale, M. (1998). Being different yet feeling similar: The influence of demographic composition and organizational culture on work processes and outcomes. *Administrative Science Quarterly, 43*, 749–80.

Chemers, M. M., Oskamp, S., & Constanzo, M. (1995). *Diversity in organizations: New perspectives for a changing workplace.* Thousand Oaks, CA: Sage.

Collins, S. M. (1997). Black mobility in White corporations: Up the corporate ladder but out on a limb. *Social Problems, 44*, 55–67.

Comer, D., & Soliman, C. (1996). Organizational efforts to manage diversity: Do they really work? *Journal of Managerial Issues, 7*, 470–83.

Cordeiro, J., & Stites-Doe, S. (1997). The impact of women managers on firm performance: Evidence from large U.S. firms. *International Review of Women and Leadership*, *3*(1), 1–20.

Cox, T. (2001). *Creating the multicultural organization: A strategy for capturing the power of diversity*. San Francisco: Jossey Bass.

Cox, T., & Blake, S. (1991). Managing cultural diversity: Implications for organizational competitiveness. *Academy of Management Executive*, *5*(3), 45–56.

Cox, T., Lobel, S., & McLeod, P. (1991). Effects of ethnic group cultural differences on cooperative and competitive behavior on a group task. *Academy of Management Journal*, *34*(4), 827–47.

Devine, P. (1989). Stereotypes and prejudice: Their automatic and controlled components. *Journal of Personality and Social Psychology*, *56*, 5–18.

Dwyer, S., Richard, O., & Chadwick, K. (2001). Gender diversity in management and firm performance: The influence of growth orientation and organizational culture. *Journal of Business Research*, *55*, 1–11.

Eagan, M., & Bendick, M. (2001). Workforce diversity initiatives of U.S. Multinationals in Europe. Research Report. Washington, DC: Bendick and Egan Economic Consultants.

Elvira, M., & Cohen, L. (2001). Location matters: A cross-level analysis of the effects of organizational sex composition on turnover. *Academy of Management Journal*, *44*, 591–605.

Elvira, M. M., & Graham, M. E. (2002). Not just a formality: Pay system formalization and sex-related earnings effects. *Organization Science*, *13*, 601–17.

Ely, R. J. (1995). The power in demography: Women's social constructions of gender identity at work. *Academy of Management Journal*, *38*, 589–634.

Ely, R. J., & Thomas, D. A. (2001). Cultural diversity at work: The effects of diversity perspectives on work group processes and outcomes. *Administrative Science Quarterly*, *46*, 229–73.

Flynn, G. (1999). White males see diversity's other side. *Workforce*, *78*, 52.

Ford, J., & Fisher, S. (1996). The role of training in a changing workplace and workforce: New perspectives and approaches. In E. Kossek & S. Lobel (Eds), *Managing diversity: Human resource strategies for transforming the workplace* (pp. 164–93). Oxford: Blackwell.

French, E. (2001). Approaches to equity management and their relationship to women in management. *British Journal of Management*, *13*, 267–85.

Friedman, R. (1996). Defining the scope and logic of minority and female network groups: Can separation enhance integration? *Research in personnel and human resources management*. Greenwich, CT: JAI Press (Vol. 14: 307–49).

Friedman, R., & Holtom, B. (2002). The effects of network groups on minority employee retention. *Human Resource Management*, *41*, 405–21.

Frink, D., Robinson, R., Reithel, B., Arthur, M., Ammeter, A., Ferris, G., Kaplan, D., & Morísete, H. (2003). Gender demography and organizational performance: A two-study investigation with convergence. *Group & Organization Management*, *28*, 127–47.

Goodman, J., Fields, D., & Blum, T. (2003). Cracks in the glass ceiling: In what kind of organizations do women make it to the top? *Group & Organization Management*, *28*, 475–501.

Gummer, B. (2000). Notes from the management literature: Workplace diversity and the global economy. *Administration in Social Work*, *22*, 75–93.

Harrison, D., Price, K., & Bell, M. (1998). Beyond Relational Demography: Time and the effects of surface and deep level diversity on work group cohesion. *Academy of Management Journal*, *41*, 96–107.

International Labor Organisation. The Gender Promotion Programme. Geneva, Switzerland: www.ilo.org (retrieved 5 February 2004).

Jackson, A. (2002). Competitive practices in diversity: http://www.shrm.org/diversity/hottopics/compprac.asp (Retrieved 5 February 2004).

Joplin, J., & Daus, C. (1997). Challenges of leading a diverse workforce. *Academy of Management Executive, 11,* 32–47.

Kalleberg, A., Knoke, D., Marsden, P., & Spaeth, J. (1994). The National Organizations Study: An introduction and overview. *American Behavioral Scientist, 37,* 860–71.

Kanter, R. (1977). *Men and women of the corporation.* New York: Basic Books.

Kochan, T., Bezrukova, K., Ely, R., Jackson, S. E., Joshi, A., Jehn, K. E., Leonard, D., Levine, D., & Thomas, D. (2003). The effects of diversity on business performance: Report of a feasibility study of the diversity research network. *Human Resource Management, 42,* 3–21.

Konrad, A., & Linnehan, F. (1995). Formalized human resource management structures: Coordinating equal opportunity or concealing organizational practices. *Academy of Management Journal, 38,* 787–820.

Kossek, E. (2005). Workplace policies and practices to support work and families: Gaps in implementation and linkages to individual and organizational effectiveness. In S. Bianchi, L. Casper, K. Christensen & R. Berkowitz King (Eds), *Work, family, health and well-being.* (pp. 97–116) Mahwah, NJ: Lawrence Erlbaum Associates.

Kossek, E., & Lobel, S. (1996). *Managing diversity: Human resource strategies for transforming the workplace.* Cambridge, MA: Blackwell.

Kossek, E., Markel, K., & McHugh, P. (2003). Increasing diversity as an HRM change strategy. *Journal of Organizational Change Management, 16,* 328–52.

Kossek, E., & Zonia, S. (1993). Assessing diversity climate: A field study of reactions to employer efforts to promote diversity. *Journal of Organizational Behavior, 14,* 61–81.

Leck, J., & Saunders, D. (1992). Hiring women: The effect of Canada's employment equity act. *Canadian Public Policy, 18,* 203–21.

Leck, J., St Onge, S., & LaLancette, I. (1995). Wage gap changes among organizations subject to the employment equity act. *Canadian Public Policy, 21,* 387–401.

Little, B., Murry, W., & Wimbush, J. C. (1998). Perceptions of workplace affirmative action plans: A psychological perspective. *Group & Organization Management, 23,* 27–47.

Litvin, D. (2002). Cracking the business case for diversity. Paper presented at the Meeting of the Academy of Management, Denver, CO.

Lobel, S. A. (1996). *Work/life and diversity: Perspectives of workplace responses* (Work-Family Policy Paper Series). Boston, MA: Boston College, Center on Work & Family.

Lobel, S. A. (1999). Impacts of diversity and work-life initiatives in organizations. In G. Powell (Ed.), *Handbook of gender and work* (pp. 453–74). Thousand Oaks, CA: Sage.

MacDonald, H. (1993). The diversity industry. *The New Republic, 2,* 22–5.

McLeod, P., Lobel, S., & Cox, T. (1996). Ethnic diversity and creativity in small groups. *Small Group Research, 27*(2), 248–64.

Milliken, F., & Martins, L. (1996). Searching for common threads: Understanding the multiple effects of diversity in organizational groups. *Academy of Management Review, 21,* 402–33.

Nkomo, S., & Kossek, E. (2000). Managing diversity: Human resource issues. In E. Kossek & R. Block (Eds), *Managing human resources in the 21st century: From core concepts to strategic choice, Module 9.* Cincinnati, OH: Southwestern.

Osterman, P. (1995). Work/family programs and the employment relationship. *Administrative Science Quarterly, 40,* 681–700.

Pelled, L., Eisenhardt, K., & Xin, K. (1999). Exploring the black box: An analysis of work group diversity, conflict, and performance. *Administrative Science Quarterly, 44,* 1–28.

Perlman, L. (1992). Turning Diversity into Opportunity. Conference Board Report #994: 75th Anniversary Symposia Series. *In diversity is strength: Capitalizing on the new work force,* pp. 15–16, New York: Conference Board.

Perry-Smith, J. E., & Blum, T. C. (2000). Work-family human resource bundles and perceived organizational performance. *Academy of Management Journal, 43,* 1107–17.

Pettigrew, T. F. (1998). Intergroup contact theory. *Annual Review of Psychology*, *49*, 65–85.

Petty, R. E., & Cacioppo, J. T. (1990). Involvement and persuasion: Tradition versus integration. *Psychological Bulletin*, *107*, 367–74.

Ragins, B. (2002). Understanding diversified mentoring relationships: Definitions, strategies, and challenges. In D. Clutterbuck & B. Ragins (Eds), *Mentoring and diversity: An international perspective* (pp. 23–31). Oxford: Butterworth–Heinnman.

Ragins, B., Cotton, J., & Miller, J. (2000). Marginal mentoring: The effects of type of mentor, quality or relationship and program design on work and career attitudes. *Academy of Management Journal*, *43*, 1177–94.

Reskin, B., & McBrier, D. (2000). Why not ascription? Organizations' employment of male and female managers. *American Sociological Review*, *65*, 210–33.

Richard, O. (2000). Racial diversity, business strategy, and firm performance: A resource-based view. *Academy of Management Journal*, *48*, 164–77.

Richard, O., & Johnson, N. (1999). Making the connection between formal human resource diversity practices and organizational effectiveness: Behind management fashion. *Performance Improvement Quarterly*, *12*, 77–96.

Richard, O., & Johnson, N. (2001). Understanding the impact of human resource diversity practices on firm performance. *Journal of Managerial Issues*, *XIII*(2), 177–95.

Richard, O., & Kirby, S. (1999). Organizational justice and the justification of work force diversity programs. *Journal of Business and Psychology*, *14*, 109–18.

Richard, O., Kochan, T., & McMillan-Capehart, A. (2002). The impact of visible diversity on organizational effectiveness: Disclosing the contents in Pandora's black box. *Journal of Business and Management*, *8*, 1–26.

Richard, O., McMillan, A., Chadwick, K., & Dwyer, S. (2003). Employing an innovation strategy in racially diverse workforces: Effects on firm performance. *Group & Organization Management*, *28*, 107–26.

Roberson, L., Kulik, C., & Pepper, M. (2003). Using needs assessment to resolve controversies in diversity training design. *Group & Organization Management*, *28*, 148–74.

Rynes, S., & Rosen, B. (1995). A field survey of factors affecting the adoption and perceived success of diversity training. *Personnel Psychology*, *48*, 247–70.

SHRM (1998, 2000, 2002). *Diversity Surveys*. Alexandria, VA: Society for Human Resource Management.

Society for Human Resource Management. Talking to diversity experts: www.shrm.org/divrsity/TalkingtoDiversityExperts.pdf (Retrieved 5 February 2004).

Thomas, D., & Gabarro, J. (1999). *Breaking through: the making of minority executives in corporate America.* Boston, MA: Harvard Business School Press.

Thomas, R. (1990). From affirmative action to affirming diversity. *Harvard Business Review*, *March/April*, 108.

Tsui, A., & Gutek, B. (1999). *Demographic differences in organizations.* Lanham, MD: Lexington Books.

Tung, R. (1993). Managing cross-national and intra-national diversity. *Human Resource Management*, *32*, 461–77.

US Department of Labor (2003). Highlights of women's earnings in 2002. Bureau of Labor Statistics. September: www.bls.gov (Retrieved 18 May 2004).

Walker, B. A., & Hanson, W. C. (1992). Valuing differences at Digital Equipment Corporation. In S. E. Jackson (Ed.), *Diversity in the workplace: Human resource initiatives* (pp. 119–37). New York: Guilford.

Watson, W., Kumar, K., & Michaelsen, L. (1993). Cultural diversity's impact on international process and performance: Comparing homogeneous and diverse task groups. *Academy of Management Journal*, *36*, 590–602.

Webber, S. S., & Donahue, L. M. (2001). Impact of highly and less job-related diversity on work group cohesion and performance: A meta-analysis. *Journal of Management*, *27*, 141–62.

Wheeler, M. (1995). *Diversity: Business rationale and strategies a research report.* New York: The Conference Board.

Williams, K. Y., & O'Reilly, C. A., III (1998). Demography and diversity in organizations: A review of 40 years of research. In B. M. Staw and L. L. Cummings (Eds), *Research in organizational behavior* (Vol. 20: 77–140). Greenwich, CT: JAI Press.

Wood, W. (2000). Attitude change: Persuasion and social influence. *Annual Review of Psychology, 51,* 539–70.

Wright, P., Ferris, S., Hiller, J., & Kroll, M. (1995). Competitiveness through management of diversity: Effects on stock price valuation. *Academy of Management Journal, 38,* 272–87.

Yakura, E. (1996). EEO law and managing diversity. In E. Kossek and S. Lobel (Eds), *Managing diversity: Human resource strategies for transforming the workplace* (pp. 25–50). Oxford: Blackwell.

3

Diversity

Making Space for a Better Case

DEBORAH R. LITVIN

In this chapter I analyze the business case for diversity to reveal the particular (social) constructions of diversity, human motivation and organizations upon which it stands, and from which it is produced. By making explicit these socially constructed, normalized meanings, I aim to interrupt their taken-for-grantedness. This clears a space for the consideration of alternative understandings of organizations, diversity and human motivation, and the proposition of rationales for diversity work not authorized within the mainstream management discourse.

Originating in the United States in the early 1990s, the business case for diversity is a management-focused, economic argument to promote corporate investment in workforce diversification. The business case links investments in organizational diversity initiatives to improvements in productivity and profitability. To 'make the business case' is to construct a detailed account of the ways in which employing (and effectively managing) a diverse workforce will improve a particular organization's 'bottom line'. One makes the business case to demonstrate to members of the organization that they should engage in diversity work for pragmatic, financial, *business* reasons.

Best diversity practice stipulates that the first step in launching any organizational diversity initiative is to develop and communicate the organization's business case for diversity (e.g. Launching an Initiative, n.d.; Robinson & Dechant, 1997; Wheeler, 1997). Citing actual examples and statistics, a well-crafted business case 'quantif[ies] the impact of diversity' on the organization (Simmons

Associates, 2002: 2) to show the specific ways in which diversity will enhance competitiveness and improve the bottom line. Investments in diversity efforts, just as in any other project, must be justified and legitimized by documentation of their anticipated ROI:

> Just as the head of Research and Development must present a compelling, fact-based business case to top management to gain the necessary commitment and resources from the organization to pursue a product initiative, so too must the head of Human Resources develop a case for diversity integration based on the competitive edge gained by optimizing the people resources of a firm. (Robinson & Dechant, 1997: 21)

An effective, '*wow!* business case' should specify for each department how its members' diversity efforts will enhance the organizational bottom line (Simmons Associates, 2002). Such a 'wow! business case' should then be widely disseminated throughout the organization in order to catalyze all members' participation in the proposed diversity initiative.

While of US origin, talk of 'diversity' and the business case for managing it has spread, gaining increasing acceptance, as well as triggering increasing study, as a 'globalizing vocabulary of difference' (Jones, Pringle & Shepherd, 2000: 364). This global expansion is most evident in the UK (e.g. Dick & Cassell, 2002; Kandola, 2004; McDougall, 1996) and other Anglophone countries, such as New Zealand (e.g. Jones, 2004; Jones, Pringle & Shepherd, 2000) and Australia (e.g. Cope & Kalantzis, 1996; Strachan, Burgess & Sullivan, 2004). Its reach, however, has become truly global, including Canada (e.g. Schmidt, 2004), the Netherlands (Gillert & Chuzischvili, 2004; Zanoni & Janssens, 2004), South Africa (Horwitz et al., 1996; Nyambegera, 2002) and Scandinavia (Kamp & Hagedorn-Rasmussen, 2004; Leijon, Lillhannus & Widell, 2003; Trux, 2002).

The Australian Department of Immigration and Multicultural and Indigenous Affairs has been notably prolific in its dissemination of the business case for diversity. A series of its media releases bear headlines such as 'Australian Business Profits from Diversity Management' (MPS 099/2000, 2000), and 'Boost for Development of Diversity Management Business Tools' (MPS 114/2000, 2000). Available on its 'Diversity Australia' website (www.australia.gov.au) are 'The Business Case for Productive Diversity and its Relationship to Corporate Sustainability' (Positive Outcomes, 2002) and several exemplary business cases. One, 'Australia's Halal Food Industry', features page headers such as 'Diversity is an Asset', 'The Importance of Diversity' and 'Benefits from Diversity in the Workplace'.

In the United States, prestigious, mainstream, not-for-profit organizations play a similar role. The Conference Board, whose membership includes executives from nearly 2000 companies in 60 countries (http://www.conference-board.org/memberservices/) and the Society for Human Resource Management (SHRM), with 190,000 members in 100 countries (*Who We Are*, n.d.), disseminate business case for diversity-focused models. They offer conferences, workshops, publications and websites to help those charged with creating diversity initiatives craft a properly compelling business case. For example, at its annual diversity workshops in October 2004, the Society for Human Resource Management offered four sessions, all of which offered help in forging the business case-required links between workforce diversity and the organizational bottom line:

- The Diversity Scorecard: How to Drive Measurable Performance and Results!
- The Bottom Line: Connecting Corporate Performance and Gender Diversity
- Successfully Integrating EEO/AA/Diversity into a Business Strategy
- Measuring Diversity Results for Improved Performance.

The description of 'The Diversity Scorecard' makes explicit the kinds of business-related documentation that will be required to obtain buy-in from managers:

> Many diversity professionals … have asked, 'How will we be able to demonstrate that diversity contributes to the organization's bottom line? How do we show senior executives and others that diversity is a strategic business partner that is aligned and linked to the strategic goals and objectives of the organization? How can we measure the impact of diversity on organizational performance and improved work environment? How does the strategic diversity process help our organization excel in the domestic and global marketplace and provide favorable returns to stockholders and stakeholders?' (Society for Human Resource Management, 2004)

Such workshops do not provide fora for discussion of possible alternatives, because there is no question about which arguments might prove effective. Among 'diversity professionals and others interested in diversity' it is already taken for granted that they must collect quantitative documentation of how diversity will enhance performance for their business. The workshop is necessary only to help them achieve compliance with the already-defined task.

Belief in the importance of 'making the business case' grew out of the acceptance of two underlying, testable, propositions:

1 Investing in diversity should be done for *business* reasons, as increased levels of (effectively managed) workforce diversity result in measurable increases in bottom-line, business performance. This is often called the (financial) value-in-diversity hypothesis.
2 Employees of the business will change their behaviors regarding diversity *because* doing so will enhance the business's profitability. Demonstrating how and why diversity efforts will generate those financial returns to organizations will cause employees to 'buy into' diversity efforts and change their behaviors.

Over the decade of the ideological dominance of the first proposition, the search for its validation has inspired both laboratory and field studies, culminating with a large-scale study conducted by the Diversity Research Network (Kochan et al., 2003). Researchers have sought empirical support for the proposition that increasing (well-managed) workforce diversity results in measurable increases in profitability.[1] Frustratingly, such empirical evidence of diversity management's promised bottom-line benefits has proven elusive.

Despite their efforts, researchers have failed to generate solid, unequivocal support for the proposition that engaging in diversity initiatives is a good investment for business, one that will pay back more than its costs (Kochan et al., 2003; Nkomo & Cox, 1996; Tsui & Gutek, 1999; Wentling & Palma-Rivas, 1997). This lack of empirical confirmation of the likely financial returns on their diversity investments has led to disappointment and some dismay on the part of corporate America (Hansen, 2003). Meanwhile, despite employers' investments in diversity work, claims of discrimination – and settlement costs – have increased:

> Employers spend billions on diversity programs, but there's little evidence of improved business performance, financial results, or accountability. Meanwhile, discrimination cases are on the rise. (Hansen, 2003)

Given these factors, one can reasonably conclude, at least for the present, that 'diversity's business case doesn't add up' (Hansen, 2003).

Researchers, no doubt, will continue their quest for evidence of financial returns to businesses from their diversity investments. In the meantime, however, executives of those businesses will have a hard time 'making the business case'. For example, how will their answers to 'hard questions' such as those below justify their expenditures on diversity work?

- What have we done in diversity that has strengthened the bottom line?
- Can we compare bottom-line benefits to the cost of the program?
- How do I prove the success of programs that are driving bottom-line benefits and protect those initiatives?
- Why do efforts that don't drive benefits still exist?
- Am I thinking like a line executive? (Diversity's Wake-up Call, 2001)

STATEMENT OF POSITION AND INTENTION

I approach this investigation of the business case for diversity from a pro-diversity position. I strongly support efforts by organizations to create inclusive, equitable workplaces in which human beings thrive, grow and willingly contribute their efforts to the accomplishment of goals they find meaningful and worthwhile. Thus, I undertake this work to support and encourage such diversity work by for-profit and not-for-profit organizations.

Second, my intention is not to disparage the many dedicated researchers and practitioners of diversity work, who find themselves continually reconstructing the business case for diversity. On the contrary, it is to free us all to speak about and engage in diversity work with members of our organizations and professions in ways unacceptable under currently prevailing norms, and to do so without the distraction and threat of the requirement to generate 'measurable metrics' to justify those efforts (Litvin, 2000). My primary purpose is to open a space for the development of non-business-case ways of talking about, thinking about and doing diversity work. The stance and methods of critical discourse analysis are useful to accomplish this purpose.

CRITICAL DISCOURSE ANALYSIS: A BRIEF INTRODUCTION

Critical discourse analysis (CDA) focuses upon the relationship between language and power. CDA examines how 'concepts, objects, and subject positions are constituted through language and how power relations are exercised in discursive activity' (Zanoni & Janssens, 2004: 55–6; for additional information on CDA see Phillips & Hardy, 2002; Van Dijk, 2001). Practitioners of CDA have political aims. They investigate 'how discourse constructs and maintains the relations of power in society' (McKenna, 2004: 15). Their project is to catalyze social change by piercing the discursively constructed armor of normality and inevitability that secures the economic and political status quo. To this end, the work of CDA is to 'make interpretive links between ... everyday texts and larger institutional and social configurations, often making inferences about the relationship of discourse change and material change' (Luke, 2004: 150). Belief in the material, social consequences of CDA grows from its ontological assertion that the 'phenomenally objective world of reality' is created through discourse and that this discursively constructed, 'objective world ... provides the practices, systems, knowledge, and rationality' of its members (McKenna, 2004: 15).

Discourse accomplishes its reality construction through the constitution of social identity. Who and what people can be or become, including their sense of self and relationships with others, are channeled by the discourses available to them. The ways in which one thinks and acts in the world, in turn, follow from the identities made available through discourses:

> As a person learns to speak these discourses, they more properly speak to him or her in that available discourses position the person in the world in a particular way prior to the individual having any sense of choice. As discourses structure the world they at the same time structure the person's subjectivity, providing him/her with a particular social identity and way of being in the world. (Alvesson & Deetz, 1996: 205)

Total quality management, religious, political and economic fundamentalisms, and reform or reengineering proposals put forward at every level of social organization are all ways of thinking and talking – discourses – that provide people's social identity and delineate simultaneously the ways they can and cannot be and act (Fairclough, Graham, Lemke & Wodak, 2004: 2). The business case for diversity is another such discourse.

CDA practitioners vary in the nomenclature and definitions they use for various forms and levels of discourse and in the analytical models they adopt. For the purpose of this analysis, I adopt the model and definitions introduced by Alvesson and Karreman (2000). I treat the business case for diversity as a Grand Discourse, which they define as 'an assembly of [local] discourses, ordered and presented as an integrated frame' (Alvesson & Karreman, 2000: 1133). Informed by their model of the 'ladder of discourse', my procedure is to study local discourses [small 'd'] about workplace diversity, as published in scholarly and practitioner-oriented books and journal articles, as well as Internet sites,[2] in order to delineate the Grand Discourse of workplace diversity, the business case for diversity. The Grand Discourse constitutes the 'normal', taken-for-granted, social 'reality' of diversity in the US workplace (Alvesson & Karreman, 2000; Fairclough et al., 2004).

Examining the brightly showcased (Prasad & Mills, 1997), familiar features of this Grand Discourse, I destabilize its taken-for-grantedness. Destabilized, its power to render 'common sense' and 'inevitable' its prescribed ways of thinking, talking and acting about diversity is interrupted. This interruption creates possibilities for the construction and practice of alternative discourses about people, diversity and organizations. The practice of different ways of speaking, thinking and acting will, in turn, constitute alternative organizational realities. Accordingly, as a practitioner of CDA, I present myself as a 'politically engaged participant in social change' and intend my work 'to make a difference in social transformation, [by] providing alternative understandings of what may be possible in organizational life' (Calás & Smircich, 2002: 26).

The remainder of this chapter presents my critical analysis of the Grand Discourse, the business case for diversity. First, I demonstrate that the normalized, institutionalized truths from which it is assembled are not necessarily so. Next, I theorize why, despite its shaky foundations, the business case not only has maintained, but has reinforced, its power to channel thinking, talking and acting about diversity. Finally, I sketch the outlines of one possible alternative discourse of diversity and argue that it will prove more effective than the business case to trigger individuals' engagement in the hard work of creating a truly inclusive, diverse workplace.

MAKING UP DIVERSITY MANAGEMENT

To interrupt the taken-for-grantedness of 'what everybody knows about diversity', it is necessary to examine the primary components of that 'knowledge'. There are two fundamental definitions upon which early diversity consultant–authors crafted the business case. They then used their creation to promote their new lines of diversity consultancy products to executives, HR and training managers, diversity training participants, and even casual readers of practitioner-oriented business publications (e.g. Copeland, 1988a–d; Copeland Griggs Productions, 1990; Thomas, 1990; 1991).

The first definition was that United States workforce diversity of the late twentieth and early twenty-first centuries was a new, unprecedented, dramatic and potentially threatening phenomenon, which, nonetheless, also presented new business opportunities. The second definition normalized through their writings and practices was that managing diversity was a 'business imperative', a pragmatic, business-oriented philosophy and set of practices. This made it fundamentally different from equal employment opportunity programs and affirmative action plans. A closer look at each of these definitions will reveal more clearly the construction of diversity and its management that the discourse of the business case has normalized.

'Workplace diversity' loomed as an object of interest and concern in the management literature in the late 1980s, when *Workforce 2000: Work and Workers for the 21st Century* (Johnston & Packer, 1987) was said to predict unprecedented, dramatic demographic changes sufficient to change the 'homogeneous' workforce of US businesses into a 'diverse' workforce. These alarming predictions took pride of place in diversity publications for over 10 years. According to the Social Science Citation Index (SSCI), references to 'Johnston & Packer, 1987' began in 1987, peaked in 1993–4 (when the number of *WF2000* citations amounted to 39% of the total number of diversity publications listed in the *Business Periodical Index*) and continued at least into 2004 (Litvin, 2000: 51). The influential *Workforce America! Managing Employee Diversity as a Vital Resource* (Loden & Rosener, 1991) provides an excellent example of such references:

> As we approach the next millennium, organizations throughout America are facing an extraordinary new challenge—unlike any they have confronted in the past. Analysts believe this current challenge will have a powerful impact on our future as a productive society. Yet few US institutions seem adequately prepared today to deal effectively with this momentous change—the increasing cultural diversity of the American workforce. (p. xvi)

Through their choice of vocabulary (e.g. extraordinary, powerful, momentous), the authors emphasize the threat to US businesses posed by their new workforce diversity.

Early diversity advocates cited another characteristic of the new workforce diversity that would challenge and threaten businesses: 'Unmeltable ethnics'. Ethnics of the past gave up their distinctive ethnic characteristics, throwing themselves willingly into the homogenizing American 'melting pot', but the new, diverse US workforce would be composed of ethnics (and other 'diverse others') who would cling (stubbornly?) to their ethnic characteristics, refusing to be 'melted' into US society. Metaphors used to describe the new diversity, thus, such as 'salad bowl', 'mosaic' and 'tapestry', focus on the composition of a whole from distinguishable units. Rather than melting into one another, the units, such as green, purple and red vegetables, tiles or threads, maintain their individual identities even when combined into a final product.

It would be difficult to overstate the influence of the demographic predictions attributed to *Workforce 2000* in the construction of the business case for diversity. Thus, it is ironic to note that a number of the alarming predictions attributed to it (including the apocryphal 'vanishing white male') were the results of the researchers' errors or readers' misinterpretations of graphs and tables in the *WF2000* Executive Summary.[3]

The second fundamental definition from which early diversity consultant–authors built was that managing diversity was a 'business imperative'. Indeed, organizations should manage diversity not only to meet the threats and challenges posed by their (newly threatening) diverse workforce, but also to capitalize upon it

e & Stone, 1995; Fernandez & Barr, 1993; Herriot & Pemberton, 1995).
siness-focused rationale stood as the defining difference between managing
ity and the EEO and AA programs of the previous 20 years. As the proposi-
that companies should engage in diversity work for business reasons is of
tral concern in this analysis, it is important to review the means by which it
came crystallized into 'common sense' as the business case for diversity.

The business rationale for diversity work was disseminated mainly through the
work of consultants and practitioners, notably R. Roosevelt Thomas, Jr (1990;
1991; 1992) and the team of Lennie Copeland and Lewis Griggs (Copeland,
1988a–d; Copeland Griggs Productions, 1990). As detailed by Lynch (1997a; b),
'diversity management' was created when United States consultants, who had
been making their livelihood by offering EEO/AA services to corporate clients,
detected a shift in the prevailing societal 'winds'.[4] The 1980s backlash against AA
and rejection of the very notion of 'protected groups' created a whirlwind which
threatened the consultants' professional lives. To rescue their livelihoods, they
invented a new way of talking, and thus, thinking and acting, about their professional services, namely 'managing diversity'. This allowed them to disassociate
themselves from what had become the increasingly divisive and unfashionable,
civil-rights-oriented discourse of EEO/AA and to market products more appealing
to their corporate customers.

Adoption of managing diversity was to be based on business reasons, such as
improved competitiveness, better customer service and enhanced profitability.[5] Early
diversity articles, published in 1989, strongly emphasize its differentiation from
affirmative action and EEO:

> It's a business imperative as opposed to the legal, moralistic and altruistic prior format-
> ting. (Solomon, 1989: 44)

> The workforce-diversity issue has no relationship to the old affirmative-action and EEO
> programs. Affirmative action and EEO were equity issues … Now, the issue is not social
> justice; it's employer demand … New language is coming out of the presidents' and
> CEOs' offices … EEO language is out … Valuing diversity isn't concerned about fair-
> ness, filling quotas, or forcing things because they are moral, ethical or legal … Valuing
> diversity says that we have a diverse workforce, and diversity can be an advantage if it
> is managed well. (Jones, Jerich & Copeland, 1989)

Fifteen years later, the Society for Human Resource Management (SHRM)
enshrines this discursive differentiation – this avoidance of the language of social
justice, morals or ethics – in its online resources. Its 'Workplace Diversity Toolkit'
site rescues those who might otherwise be accused of starting diversity initiatives
'just because they are the "right thing to do"' by stipulating the correct business-
oriented arguments:

> [C]ritics of diversity initiatives charge that such initiatives operate as an outgrowth of a
> 'politically correct' environment. They contend that organizations have diversity initia-
> tives just because they are the 'right thing to do.' It has become increasingly apparent,
> however, that appropriate management of a diverse workforce is critical for organiza-
> tions that seek to improve and maintain their competitive advantage …

The following are a few key factors that make diversity initiatives important to businesses for reasons beyond social or moral responsibility. They should be included in any argument you make on behalf of the business case for diversity at your organization:

- Diversity initiatives can improve the quality of your organization's workforce and can be the catalyst for a better return on your investment in human capital …
- Capitalize on new markets; customer bases are becoming even more diverse than the workforce …
- Recognized diversity initiatives and diversity results will attract the best and the brightest employees to a company …
- Increased Creativity … One byproduct of capitalizing on differences is creativity.
- Flexibility ensures survival … Making adaptations required by diversity keeps an organization flexible and well-developed. (What is the business case for diversity, n.d.)

As I have shown, the core definitions of the post-EEO, diversity discourse construct a reality in which businesses should manage diversity, because doing so will transform the threat of workforce diversity into an engine of economic, competitive benefits to the organization. Businesses should invest in creating a more effective diverse workforce not because it is the legal, ethical or moral 'right' thing to do, but because it is the savvy, bottom-line-focused, pragmatic, self-interested 'right' thing to do. Through its wide dissemination and frequent repetition in business practitioner publications, company training materials and services marketed by diversity consultants, this way of thinking, talking and acting became sedimented as 'common sense', and what everybody already knows. An article in *Tax Executive* provides evidence of this sedimentation into 'facts' that are unquestioned and unquestionable, as they are already 'established':

> The purpose of this article is not to establish the Business Case for Diversity in the workplace. The need to value, to leverage, and to manage diversity has long been established … It is well established that, over time, heterogeneous groups outperform homogeneous groups … A diverse organization … is more flexible and adaptable and, therefore, better able to … survive. (Wheeler, 1997)

Evidence of the taken-for-grantedness of these facts is readily available in the resources made available to practitioners, not only by independent consultants, but also by established authorities, such as the Conference Board and the SHRM. Simmons Associates, Inc., a consulting firm, insists that a '*wow* business case' is what is needed to get employees to change their behavior:

> You're telling them to change … Not only that, but it's change in an area that will be especially difficult, being that it involves a subject I'm really not comfortable discussing. Nah. I'll keep my head down until it passes … To motivate behavior change, you need a *WOW!* business case. (Simmons Associates, Inc., 2002)

The SHRM offers online resources, workshops, conferences and publications to help managers create proper renderings of the business case for diversity. On its 'Launching an Initiative' page, 'Explain the Business Case' is the first of six essential communication points:

> Employees will naturally wonder why your organization is spending money, time, and energy on diversity. The first order of business is to explain its relevance to the objectives of the organization. How does effective diversity management impact the bottom line, productivity, and achievement of organizational goals? ... A few statistics or a specific case may make a point here. Do you need to serve an increasingly diverse customer base? Are you at a disadvantage in competing for top talent? Is turnover eating up profits and burning out remaining staff? Managing diversity is not an altruistic, feel good frill. (Launching an Initiative, n.d.)

Managers are urged to create a 'savvy' business case (Yarrow, 1996), one tailored with the appropriate details to convince even the reluctant to commit themselves to managing diversity:

> When confronted with a need to convince a reluctant management group about the need to manage diversity, you should start by referring to the business case and to an understanding of the value and benefits of a diverse work force. (Wheeler, 1997)

Such reliance upon the business case to promote diversity work leads logically to the requirement that its promised diversity return on investment, 'DROI' (Hubbard, 1999), be empirically documented. As noted earlier, attempts to provide such 'hard' empirical documentation have achieved very limited success. In their review of 89 diversity studies, Williams and O'Reilly (1998) report only two substantial findings of workforce diversity effects: 'Variations in group composition can have important effects on group functioning' and 'at the micro level, increased diversity typically has negative effects on the ability of the group to meet its members' needs and to function effectively over time (pp. 115, 116). Neither of these findings strongly supports the positive DROI contention of the business case.

More recently, the Diversity Research Network (DRN), a group of researchers from several universities, reported on its five-year, four-company field study, an ambitious effort to test the propositions of the business case for diversity. Members of the Business Opportunities for Leadership Diversity initiative (BOLD), citing the need for such evidence to support diversity work within their own organizations, had commissioned the researchers to conduct 'definitive, [large-scale, field] research to assess the diversity-performance link'. The Alfred P. Sloan and SHRM Foundations provided additional funding (Kochan et al., 2003: 3, 19). Their five-year quest failed to supply the still-elusive Holy Grail of definitive, empirical support for a positive diversity–performance link:

> There were few direct effects of diversity on performance—either positive or negative ... [Our findings] suggest the need to move beyond the business-case argument for advancing the practice of diversity in industry ... and ... modify this argument to reflect the complexities we discovered in our research. (Kochan et al., 2003: 17, 4)

Despite their (Herculean) efforts, neither these nor other researchers have produced solid, unequivocal support for the business case for diversity's bottom-line-focused promise of DROI.

Perhaps it is time to take the DRN's advice and 'move beyond the business-case argument' to develop an alternative case for 'advancing the practice of diversity in industry'. Kochan and his colleagues take a step in this direction by proposing a 'reframed' business case:

> Diversity is a reality in labor markets and customer markets today. To be successful in working with and gaining value from this diversity requires a sustained, systemic approach and long-term commitment. Success is facilitated by a perspective that considers diversity to be an opportunity for everyone in an organization to learn from each other how better to accomplish their work and an occasion that requires a supportive and cooperative organizational culture as well as group leadership and process skills that can facilitate effective group functioning. Organizations that invest their resources in taking advantage of the opportunities that diversity offers should outperform those that fail to make such investments. (Kochan et al., 2003: 17, 18)

Note, however, that this is indeed a *reframing* of the business case for diversity and not a move beyond it. It backpedals from the 'normal' business case promise of DROI to offer only an (unquantified) probability of DROI after 'long-term commitment' at some unspecified time in the future. Such a reframing offers no assistance to diversity professionals working within the reality of the Grand Discourse. They know that they are expected to demonstrate their efforts' contribution to the bottom line, or face being 'written off' as a bad investment. Edward E. Hubbard, consultant and author of 'Diversity Return on Investment' (1999), clearly articulates these individuals' difficult situation:

> Diversity professionals and managers know they must begin to show how diversity is linked to the bottom line in hard numbers or they will have difficulty maintaining funding, gaining support, and assessing progress. Although interest in measuring the effects of diversity has been growing, the topic still challenges even the most sophisticated and progressive diversity departments. (Hubbard, 1999)

'Reframing' – modifying – the business case for diversity does not achieve a new discourse of diversity. The reframed language remains within the Grand Discourse, as it does nothing to undermine its foundation of underlying propositions. One must interrupt and shatter this taken-for-grantedness to make possible thinking, talking and acting outside of its crystallized ideological structure.

This has been the intent of this chapter, but it has not yet reached the source of the business case's strength and endurance. This is because the business case for diversity does not stand alone. It is supported by other, similar discourses, all of which spring from and reconstitute an even broader, more deeply rooted, seemingly all-encompassing Mega-Discourse (Alvesson & Karreman, 2000). To destabilize the business case for diversity, it is necessary to search out, attack and demolish the foundations of this Mega-Discourse.

THE BUSINESS CASE: A MEGA-DISCOURSE

The business case for diversity derives its position and strength from a normalized Mega-Discourse that enshrines the achievement of organizational economic goals as the ultimate guiding principle and explanatory device for people in organizations. More than 30 years ago, Georgiou noted its prevalence throughout United States management theory, calling it the 'Goal Paradigm' (1973). More recently, Chiapello and Fairclough referred to such discourse as the 'spirit of capitalism, [which] justifies people's commitment to capitalism, and ... renders this commitment attractive' (2002: 186–7). Its hold upon the way people think, talk and act solves a significant problem of the capitalistic system:

> Capitalistic accumulation requires commitment from many people, although few have any real chances of making a substantial profit ... This is an especially thorny problem in modern economies that require a high level of commitment from their employees, in particular from managers. (Chiapello & Fairclough, 2002: 186–7)

'Business case' vocabulary has developed as the contemporary discursive core of such thinking, so the business case for diversity now enjoys the discursive support of its younger siblings, the business case for work–family policies (e.g. Arthur & Cook, 2004), the business case for spirituality in the workplace (e.g. Giacalone & Jurkiewicz, 2003) and the business case for ethical, socially responsible behavior (e.g. Jackson, 2004). All are ardent worshippers within the Temple of Organizational Goals. Within this venerable, solidly constructed and capacious sanctuary, meanings, identities, beliefs, purposes and actions are constituted by and through a broad, universalizing, seemingly all-encompassing Mega-Discourse (Alvesson & Karreman, 2000). This Mega-Discourse anoints 'organizational goals', and, particularly, maximal financial return to owners, as taken-for-granted, terminal values, the ultimate ends toward which individuals strive and the most fundamental explanation for an individual's behavior.

In the reality constructed by and through this Mega-Discourse, the specification and communication of positive impact on the bottom line is the first and best means of securing the commitment of individuals to change their own behavior in support of organizational efforts to

1 Improve employees' opportunities to meet their commitments to both work and family.
2 Establish a workplace culture supportive of members' spiritual and emotional needs.
3 Encourage and maintain standards of ethical, socially responsible behavior.
4 Create an inclusive workplace characterized by equal opportunity, respect and acceptance of individual and group differences, and mutual growth and learning.

Pursuing the specific effects of the Mega-Discourse upon each of these areas is beyond the scope of this chapter, but its effects upon human diversity are instructive. Analyzing the discourse of 25 Flemish HR managers, Zanoni and Janssens found that these managers are 'not interested in the demographic difference *per se*, but rather in how that difference can or cannot be *used* to attain organizational goals ... diversity is conceived in a very selective and instrumental way with reference to the productive process in the specific organizational context'

(2004: 25). In other words, these HR managers valued the diversity of their workforces not as human beings, but as contributors to the bottom line.

Subject to the dicta of the Mega-Discourse, the colorful chaos of human diversity disappears into a synchronized, mutually indistinguishable chorus, whose members' only purpose is to function as instrumental, interchangeable cogs in the profit-making mechanism. Furthermore, this machine, the organization, is viewed as the supreme determinant of its parts, stripping them of idiosyncrasy or uniqueness. In the reality of the business case Mega-Discourse, the organization appears in Technicolor, while its constituents fade from view:

> [The organization is] so superior that it is effectively divorced from the influence of the parts … The whole is regarded not as the product of interaction between the parts, but as determining them. The organization is endowed with a personality while the individuals constituting it are depersonalized, role players in the service of the organization's goals. (Georgiou, 1973: 299)

The roles to be played by members of business organizations, as constructed by the Mega-Discourse of the business case, require individuals to strip their performances of idiosyncrasies, preferences and other 'differences', the better to fit into the overall pattern determined by the pursuit of bottom-line 'organizational goals'.

BEYOND THE MEGA-DISCOURSE

It is past time to liberate thinking, talking and acting about diversity (along with ethics, social responsibility, spirituality, work–family issues and other such prisoners) from this Mega-Discourse. As demonstrated in earlier sections of this chapter, diversity has eluded efforts to document its achievement of its financial, Mega-Discourse-specified goal, DROI. To continue to promote and pursue meaningful diversity work within the dictates of the Mega-Discourse (even by 'reframing' its business case) is to beg irrelevance and redundancy as 'investments gone wrong'.

What, then, might be a way of thinking, talking and acting about diversity that would prove effective at triggering personal and organizational change? What sort of discourse can champions of diversity, inclusion and opportunity create and disseminate, so that, in time, a more effective Discourse of Diversity will have been constructed?

Such a Discourse of Diversity must be rooted in a fundamentally different way of conceptualizing the origins and purpose of organizations. That is, it must grow out of the formation of an alternative Mega-Discourse. To do this, one must engage in a process of redefinition of basic vocabulary. Here are some possibilities:

1   The purpose of organizations – including business organizations – is 'to enhance human well-being' (Csikszentmihalyi, 2003: 21) and so the existence of an organization (no matter how profitable) makes sense only if it enriches the lives of its members.

2 Organization is 'the medium through which individuals pursue ... a diversity of personal goals' (Georgiou, 1973: 300).

3 'Human beings organise [*sic*] themselves into groups to get things done, but they also do it to overcome external threat, order their relationships with their fellows, overcome uncertainty in the environment and achieve continuity' (Stuart-Kotze, 2005).

4 Organizations can be seen as 'institutions that enable society to pursue goals that could not be achieved by individuals acting alone' (Ivancevich, Konopaske & Matteson, 2005: 637). As such, their proper purpose is to 'contribute to the sum of human happiness, to the development of an enjoyable life that provides meaning, and to a society that is just and evolving' (Csikszentmihalyi, 2003: 5).

Such a conceptualization of organizational purpose is not a utopian dream. The Good Work in Business Project studied 39 'visionary' business leaders. Many of these leaders claimed purpose beyond the growth of return on shareholder equity. They did not define themselves as 'profit-making machines' who existed only 'to satisfy escalating expectation for immediate gain' (Csikszentmihalyi, 2003: 10).

One of these 'Good Work' leaders, Robert Shapiro, former CEO of Monsanto, sketches a vision of purpose for business organizations – an alternative Mega-Discourse – that could give birth to an alternative case for diversity:

> Under the right circumstances, people could integrate ... within themselves and learn about themselves, could grow, develop, could connect within the context of a for-profit business organization. (Csikszentmihalyi, 2003: 202)

The *raison d'être* of a business organization and its leaders, according to Shapiro's vision, is to create the right circumstances for its people (identified or identifying with all social identity groups) *to learn, develop, grow, and connect* with one another. This vision is matched perfectly by the DRN's recommendations for effective diversity work:

> Organizations must ... implement management and human resource policies and practices that inculcate cultures of mutual learning and cooperation ... [They should] attempt to make diversity a resource for learning, change, and renewal. (Kochan et al., 2003: 19)

Similarly, researchers from the Simmons Center for Gender in Organization cite commitment to a process of learning from and about others as a key condition for successfully 'working across differences'. To be able to connect with others, one must commit to learning about their 'concrete histories, identities, emotions, needs, and aspirations'. This entails an ongoing pursuit of self-awareness, and willingness not only to ask risky and uncomfortable questions, but also to develop 'a critical understanding of how power and cultural legacies can make working across differences difficult' (Holvino and Sheridan, 2003).

Thomas and Ely's 'Integration and learning' perspective toward diversity is also related to the developing discourse. From this perspective, diversity work hinges on committing time and effort to process: to exploring one another's points of view and working out agreements on how to proceed with the task at hand. For the individual, successful diversity work means 'learning how to not be afraid of the differences, learning about conflict, and learning to be willing to go toward it and trying to talk about hard things ... to take risks ... to be willing to be wrong ... to be [seen as] politically incorrect ... to think about things differently' (Thomas & Ely, 2001). For the organization, successful diversity work translates to change in the organizational power structure. One evaluates diversity progress by 'the degree to which newly represented groups have the power to change the organization and traditionally represented groups are willing to change' (Thomas & Ely, 2001).

APOTHEOSIS

> Diversity transcends concerns of benefits and costs ... [Diversity is entwined] with organizing and being; diversity is thereby politicized. It is about ending domination and subordination. Diversity evolves with the end of hierarchy. It is about affirming the potentiality of life. It demands a risking of life, a commitment to transforming our consciousness of the world ... It is through diversity that life is affirmed and human beings help with the completion of the world. (Rodriguez, 2003: 115, 116)

This alternative Diversity Discourse is as political as the business case. It works to engender *change* in organizational power structures, just as the business case for diversity reconstructs and reinforces the political status quo. Each of these ways of thinking, talking and acting toward diversity grows out of its distinct Mega-Discourse. According to the business case, human beings are the means and the achievement of organizational goals the ends, the terminal value. According to the proposed alternative, organizations are the instruments, and serving the needs of their members and of society at large the ends. The growth, development, survival and happiness of human beings take their appropriate place as ends or terminal values.

One can build a better case for diversity from this foundation, one to catalyze individual commitment to thinking, talking and acting in ways that create inclusive, equitable workplaces – workplaces where people value each other's contributions to the achievement of their separate *and* common goals. But, to do so, one must break free from the Mega-Discourse of the business case and speak in a voice that risks – even *invites* – accusations of communist–utopian–Luddite hysteria. Having found this voice, I use it to offer an early draft of such a case, inspired by Rodriguez's vision, quoted above:

> Diversity is a reality in today's world. We are all interconnected, so we must learn how to live and work with one another. If we do not, eventually we will destroy one another. We should do what we can to create inclusive, equitable workplaces, in which we can develop and practice our ability to cooperate, learn, adapt, accept, and to persist in finding common ground. Workforce diversity can be understood as an opportunity for everyone in

an organization to learn from each other in order to enrich their lives, achieve their goals, and develop the skills necessary for human survival. A sustained, systemic approach and long-term commitment by the organization as a whole, as well as by individuals, will be necessary to support this process. Organizations that take this approach should find themselves composed of balanced, effective, emotionally-intelligent individuals with highly-developed interpersonal and intercultural skills.

To increase opportunities for all individuals to develop themselves through interaction with and learning from a pool of colleagues varied in perspective, background, strengths, disabilities, skills and assumptions may very well not always result in measurable, short-term financial contributions to the corporate bottom line. Investment in such efforts will, however, yield extraordinary returns over the long term. These returns on investment will come in the form of additions to the world's total stock of human capacities and the prospects for the survival of the human race. Insisting upon bottom-line enhancement as *the* reason for making these investments in human capital is, to borrow from Jim Collins (quoted in Frost et al., 2004: 262), 'like asking for a financial justification for breathing'. I invite other scholars and practitioners to join in the task of creating and disseminating new ways to think, talk and act about workplace diversity, ways that affirm life and further the completion of the world.

NOTES

1 For reviews of research on diversity and its management, see Nkomo and Cox (1996), Williams and O'Reilly (1997) and Litvin (2000).

2 For a detailed description of sources and methods of sampling and analysis see Litvin (2000).

3 Only 10 years later, with the publication of *Workforce 2020* (Judy, D'Amico & Geipel, 1997) did the Hudson Institute set right its *Workforce 2000* errors.

Interestingly, the results of a Google search on 'terminal values' argue that the term itself has been co-opted into this Mega-Discourse. Of the first 50 'hits,' only three led to sources defining or using 'terminal values' in ethical terms, as 'preferences concerning "ends" to be achieved. When an individual can no longer answer the question of "why" with "because", a terminal value has been reached' (Scholl, 2003). The other 47 hits led to sources defining 'terminal value(s)' as the total financial return on investment:

> The Terminal Value of a business plan or investment project = Annual Profits × Years + Economic Value of Earnings Beyond the Forecast Period. (http://vs31.cedant.com/dictionary/terminal-valuation.php)

> The dollar value of an asset at a specific future time. For example, a $1,000 certificate of deposit that earns an annual return of 9% has a terminal value of $1,539 in five years. (http://dictionary.reference.com/search?q=terminal%20value)

4 Kelly and Dobbin (1998) provide a similar account.

5 It is interesting to note that this 'good business' positioning was, in fact, not new to managing diversity. As Kelly and Dobbin point out, affirmative action had already been described as 'an essential management tool which reinforces accountability and maximizes the utilization of the talents of [the firm's] entire work force' (Feild, 1984: 49). They also cite a brief

filed by the National Association of Manufacturers in 1986, which described affirmative action as a 'business policy which has allowed industry to benefit from new ideas, opinions and perspectives generated by greater workforce diversity' (*Harvard Law Review*, 1989: 669 cited in Kelly & Dobbin, 1998). They suggest that these descriptions 'prefigured the diversity management discourse of the late 1980s and early 1990s' (Kelly & Dobbin, 1998: 969).

REFERENCES

Alvesson, M., & Deetz, S. (1996). Critical theory and postmodernism approaches to organizational studies. In S. R. Clegg, C. Hardy & W. R. Nord (Eds), *Handbook of organization studies* (pp. 191–217). Thousand Oaks, CA, Sage.

Alvesson, M. & Karreman, D. (2000). Varieties of discourse: On the study of organizations through discourse analysis. *Human Relations*, *53*(9), 1125–49.

Arthur, M. M., & Cook, A. (2004). Taking stock of work-family initiatives: How announcements of 'family-friendly' human resource decisions affect shareholder value. *Industrial and Labor Relations Review*, *57*(4), 599–614.

Australia's Halal Food Industry (n.d.). Case study produced by AUS-MEAT Limited (www.ausmeat.com.au) under contract with the Australian Government's Department of Immigration and Multicultural and Indigenous Affairs. Retrieved from www.diversity australia.gov.au/_inc/doc_pdf/halal.pdf.

Calás, M. B. & Smircich, L. (2002, August). The glass ceiling and the politics of knowledge: A cultural studies perspective on the possibilities of roads not taken. Paper presented at the annual meeting of the Academy of Management, Denver, CO.

Carnevale, A. P., & Stone, S. C. (1995). *The American mosaic: An in-depth report on the future of diversity at work*. NY: McGraw-Hill, Inc.

Chiapello, E. & Fairclough, N. (2002). Understanding the new management ideology: A transdisciplinary contribution from critical discourse analysis and new sociology of capitalism. *Discourse and Society*, *13*(2), 185–208.

Cope, B. & Kalantzis, M. (1996). An Australian watershed: Let's not squander our natural advantage. *The Australian*, 7 November. Also available at http://edoz.com.au/cwcc/docs/watershed/squander.html. Accessed 1 June 2005.

Copeland, L. (1988a). Learning to manage a multicultural workforce. *Training*, *25*(5), 48–56.

Copeland, L. (1988b). Ten steps to making the most of cultural differences at the workplace. *Personnel, June*, 58–60.

Copeland, L. (1988c). Valuing diversity, Part 2: Pioneers and champions of change. *Personnel*, *65*, 44–9.

Copeland, L. (1988d). Valuing workplace diversity: Ten reasons employers recognize the benefits of a mixed work force. *Personnel Administrator*, *33*(11), 38–9.

Copeland Griggs Productions (1990). Valuing diversity, Part I: Managing differences, Part II: Diversity at work, Part III: Communicating across cultures.

Csikszentmihalyi, M. (2003). *Good business: Leadership, flow, and the making of meaning*. New York: Viking.

Dick, P. & Cassell, C. (2002). Barriers to managing diversity in a UK constabulary: The role of discourse. *Journal of Management Studies*, *39*(7), 953–76.

Diversity's Wake-up Call (2001). Diversity.com, 11-1-01: http://www.simmonsassoc.com/html/diversitywakeup.html (Retrieved 28 July 2004).

Fairclough, N., Graham, P., Lemke, J., & Wodak, R. (2004). Introduction. *Critical Discourse Studies*, *1*(1), 1–7.

Feild, J. (1984). Affirmative action: A fresh look at the record twenty-two years after the beginning. Washington, DC: Center for National Policy Review.

Fernandez, J. P., & Barr, M. (1993). *The diversity advantage*. NYC: Lexington Books.

Frost, P. J., Nord, W. R., & Krefting, L. A. (2004). *Managerial and organizational reality*. Upper Saddle River, NJ: Prentice Hall.

Georgiou, P. (1973). The goal paradigm and notes towards a counter paradigm. *Administrative Science Quarterly*, *18*, 291–310.

Giacalone, R. A., & Jurkiewicz, C. L. (2003). *Handbook of workplace spirituality and organizational performance*. Armonk, NY: M.E. Sharpe.

Gillert, A., & Chuzischvili, G. (2004). Dealing with diversity: A matter of beliefs. *Industrial and Commercial Training*, *36*(4), 166–70.

Hansen, F. (2003). Diversity's business case doesn't add up: http://www.workforce.com/section/11/feature/23/42/49/index_printer.html (Retrieved 22 November 2004).

Herriot, P., & Pemberton, C. (1995). *Competitive advantage through diversity: Organizational learning from difference*. London: Sage.

Holvino, E. & Sheridan, B. (2003). Working across differences: Diversity practices for organizational change, CGO Insights Briefing Note #17. Center for Gender in Organizations: Simmons School of Management.

Horwitz, F. M., Bowmaker-Falconer, A. & Searll, P. (1996). Human resource development and managing diversity in South Africa. *International Journal of Manpower*, *17*(4/5), 134–51.

Hubbard, E. (1999). Diversity return on investment. http://store.diversityinc.com/cgi-bin/commerce.exe?preadd=action&key=HUBB02 (Retrieved 20 November 2004).

Ivancevich, J. M., Konopaske, R., & Matteson, M. T. (2005). *Organizational behavior and management* (7th edn). New York: McGraw-Hill/Irwin.

Jackson, K. T. (2004). *Building reputational capital: Strategies for integrity and fair play that improve the bottom line*. New York: Oxford University Press.

Johnston, W. B., & Packer, A. H. (1987). *Workforce 2000: Work and workers for the 21st century*. Indianapolis, IN: Hudson Institute.

Jones, D. (2004). Screwing diversity out of the workers? Reading diversity. *Journal of Organizational Change Management*, *17*(3), 281–91.

Jones, D., Pringle, J., & Shepherd, D. (2000). 'Managing diversity' meets Aotearoa/New Zealand. *Personnel Review*, *29*(3), 364–80.

Jones, R. T., Jerich, B., Copeland, L., & Boyles, M. (1989). How do you manage a diverse workforce? *Training*, *43*(2), 13–21.

Judy, R. W., D'Amico, C., & Geipel, G. L., (1997). *Workforce 2020: Work and workers in the 21st century*. Indianapolis, IN: Hudson Institute.

Kamp, A. & Hagedorn-Rasmussen, P. (2004). Diversity management in a Danish context: Towards a multicultural or segregated working life? *Economic and Industrial Democracy*, *25*(4), 525–54.

Kandola, B. (2004). Skills development: The missing link in increasing diversity in leadership. *Industrial and Commercial Training*, *36*(4), 143–7.

Kelly, E., & Dobbin, F. (1998). How affirmative action became diversity management. *American Behavioral Scientist*, *41*(7), 960–84.

Kochan, T., Bezrukova, K., Ely, R., Jackson, S., Joshi, A., Jehn, K., Leonard, J., Levine, D., & Thomas, D. (2003). The effects of diversity on business performance: Report of the Diversity Research Network. *Human Resource Management*, *42*(1), 3–21.

Launching an Initiative (n.d.). http://www.shrm.org/diversity/launch1.asp (Retrieved 13 March 2004).

Leijon, S., Lillhannus, R. & Widell, G. (Eds) (2003). *Reflecting diversity: Viewpoints from Scandinavia*. Göteborg: BAS.

Litvin, D. R. (2000). Defamiliarizing diversity. Unpublished Ph.D. Dissertation. Amherst: University of Massachusetts.

Loden, M., & Rosener, J. (1991). *Workforce America! Managing employee diversity as a vital resource*. Homewood, IL: Business One Irwin.

Luke, A. (2004). Notes on the future of critical discourse studies. *Critical Discourse Studies*, *1*(1), 149–52.

Lynch, F. R. (1997a). *The diversity machine*. NY: Free Press.

Lynch, F. R. (1997b). The diversity machine. *Society, 34*(5), 32–45.

McDougall, M. (1996). Equal opportunities versus managing diversity: Another challenge for public sector management? *International Journal of Public Sector Management, 9*(5/6), 62–72.

McKenna, B. (2004). Critical discourse studies: Where to from here? *Critical Discourse Studies, 1*(1), 9–39.

Nkomo, S. M., & Cox, T. J. (1996). Diverse identities in organizations. In S. R. Clegg, C. Hardy, & W. R. Nord (Eds), *Handbook of organization studies* (pp. 338–56). London: Sage.

Nyambegera, S. (2002). Ethnicity and human resource management practice in sub-Saharan Africa: The relevance of the managing diversity discourse. *International Journal of Human Resource Management, 13*(7), 1077– 91.

Phillips, N. & Hardy, C. (2002). *Discourse analysis: Investigating processes of social construction*. London: Sage.

Positive Outcomes (2002). The Business Case for Productive Diversity and its Relationship to Corporate Sustainability. Paper prepared by Positive Outcomes for the Department of Immigration and Multicultural and Indigenous Affairs, 28 March. Also available at http://www.diversityaustralia.gov.au/_inc/doc_pdf/business_case0402.pdf (Retrieved 25 May 2005).

Prasad, P., & Mills, A. J. (1997). From showcase to shadow: Understanding the dilemmas of managing workplace diversity. In P. Prasad, A. J. Mills, M. Elmes & A. Prasad (Eds), *Managing the organizational melting pot: Dilemmas of workplace diversity* (pp. 3–30). Thousand Oaks, CA: Sage.

Prasad, P., Mills, A. J., Elmes, M., & Prasad, A. (Eds) (1997). *Managing the organizational melting pot: Dilemmas of workplace*. Thousand Oaks, CA: Sage.

Robinson, G., & Dechant, K. (1997). Building a business case for diversity. *Academy of Management Executive, 11*(3).

Rodriguez, A. (2003). *Diversity as liberation (II): Introducing a new understanding of diversity*, Cresskill, NJ: Hampton Press.

Schmidt, P. (2004). An approach to diversity training in Canada. *Industrial and Commercial Training, 36*(4), 148–52.

Scholl, R. W. (2003). Encyclopedia of Organizational Behavior (online): http://www.cba.uri.edu/scholl/Notes/Encyclopedia.html#VAL.

Simmons Associates, Inc. (2002). Ten red flags in a diversity initiative: Flag #2: The 'blah' business case, *Profiles in diversity journal*. September/October: www.simmonsassoc.com (Retrieved 5 December 2003).

Society for Human Resource Management (2004) Workplace Diversity Conference and Exposition on New Challenges, New Opportunities. 25–27 October. Chicago, IL. Also available at http://www.shrm.org/conferences/diversity/2004/sessions.asp. Accessed 1 June 2005.

Solomon, C. M. (1989). The corporate response to work force diversity. *Personnel Journal*, August: 43–53.

Steyaert, C. & Janssens, M. (2002). Qualifying otherness. In S. Leijon, R. Lillhannus & G. Widell (Eds), *Reflecting diversity: Viewpoints from Scandinavia* (pp. 41–56). Göteborg: BAS.

Strachan, G., Burgess, J. & Sullivan A. (2004). Affirmative action or managing diversity: What is the future of equal opportunity policies in organisations? *Women in Management Review, 19*(4), 196–204.

Stuart-Kotze, R. (2005). Understanding organisations: http://www.theworkingmanager.com/articles/detail.asp?ArticleNo=126 (Retrieved 22 April 2005).

Thomas, D. A., & Ely, R. (2001). Cultural diversity at work: The effects of diversity perspectives on work group processes and outcomes. *Administrative Science Quarterly, 46*(2), http://web5.infotrac.galegroup.com/itw/infomark/411/459/58843926w5/purl=rc1_GBFM_0_A79829822&dyn=13!xrn_1_0_A79829822?sw_aep=ntn (Retrieved 13 March 2004).

Thomas, R. R., Jr (1990). From affirmative action to affirming diversity. *Harvard Business Review, March–April*, 107–17.

Thomas, R. R., Jr (1991). *Beyond race and gender: Unleashing the power of your total work force by managing diversity*. New York: AMACOM.

Thomas, R. R., Jr (1992). Managing diversity: A conceptual framework. In S. E. Jackson, S. E. & Associates (Ed.), *Diversity in the Workplace: Human Resources Initiatives* (pp. 306–17). New York: Guilford Press.

Trux, M.-L. (2002). Diversity under the northern star. In A. Forsander and M.-L. Trux (Eds), *Immigration and economy in the globalization process: The case of Finland.* Sitra Reports Series 20 (pp. 175–225). Helsinki, Finland: Sitra Publications.

Tsui, A. S. and Gutek, B. A. (1999). *Demographic differences in organizations: Current research and future directions*. Lanham, Maryland: Lexington Press.

Van Dijk, T. (2001). Critical discourse analysis. In D. Schiffrin, D. Tannen & H. Hamilton (Eds), *The Handbook of Discourse Analysis* (pp. 352–71). Oxford: Blackwell.

Wentling, R. M., & Palma-Rivas, N. (1997). *Diversity in the workforce: A literature review*. Report #1, MDS-934. Berkeley, CA: National Center for Research in Vocational Education, University of California at Berkeley.

What is the business case for diversity? (n.d.). http://www.shrm.org/diversity/businesscase.asp (Retrieved 13 March 2004).

Wheeler, R. D. (1997). Managing workforce diversity. *Tax Executive, 49*(6), 493–95.

Who We Are (n.d.). About SHRM: http://www.shrm.org/about/ (Retrieved 10 November 2004).

Williams, K. Y., & O'Reilly, C. A., III (1998). Demography and diversity in organizations: A review of 40 years of research. *Research in Organizational Behavior, 20*, 77–140.

Yarrow, J. (1996). The evolving case for diversity. *Cultural Diversity at Work, 8*(4), 8–9.

Zanoni, P. & Janssens, M. (2004). Deconstructing difference: The rhetorics of HR managers' diversity discourses. *Organization Studies, 25*(1), 55–74.

4

From Managing Equality to Managing Diversity

A Critical Scandinavian Perspective on Gender and Workplace Diversity

YVONNE DUE BILLING
AND ELISABETH SUNDIN

Gender is a relevant and important aspect of organizational diversity and consequently also of diversity in society. For obvious reasons gender is the most extensive diversity dimension from both time and space perspectives. It has, therefore, historically probably occupied a privileged position which, however, can be challenged by other dimensions in some contexts.

The concept of diversity emerged in the European debate in the 1990s. As with many other organizational concepts and theories, it was imported from the United States. The debate sounded like something we had heard before in gender-related discussions. Also, the way the problems were presented and the solutions seemed very familiar. Although gender was often implicit in the concept of diversity, like other individual characteristics such as handicap and sexual preference, it was, however, race, or rather ethnicity,[1] which was the most important dimension.[2] The other aspects were more or less loosely attached. Likewise, ethnicity was not often mentioned when gender was in focus. However, in gender research an ethnic dimension can be included and in ethnicity a gender dimension. Which of these is the most important seems to have been an ongoing discussion which reminds us of discussions which belonged to earlier decades – only these debates were about whether a class perspective or a gender perspective should be prioritized.

Although both concepts, gender and ethnicity in theory and practice, often have global similarities, there are always local interpretations, and we try to take notice of this in this chapter where we discuss gender in a diversity perspective and what that implies. What are the differences and similarities between a gender and other, especially ethnic, diversity perspectives? How does gender power operate in different ethnic groups? This last question is an issue which is important in itself, and we should be aware of the differences between the situation of families and that of communities. However, here we will deal only with the workplace perspective, which is a restriction, but nonetheless an important starting point as workplaces, that is organizations, *are* the labour market.

In the next section pioneer research on how to organize is presented. In some ways it seems very out of date and in others it is of great relevance even nowadays. What these different perspectives have in common is that they neglected gender (and/or diversity) dimensions which eventually triggered the sex and gender research that is introduced in the following section. Both areas, organizing and sex/gender, have great political relevance. Politics and research are connected. This is true also for the ethnicity/diversity area. We have written a special section on this theme before going into the 'diversity on the workplace' part of the chapter. Different themes are handled under that heading: gender versus diversity, arguments for diversity in the workplace, including gender, and how to manage diversity in the workplace. The last topic appear at the top of management literature lists and is an example of the political nature of diversity. We end the chapter with a discussion of the state of the art and what could be expected in the future, especially in relation to the gender dimensions of diversity.

This chapter adopts a Scandinavian perspective which will surface in different ways in various parts of the chapter. Under the present headings the Scandinavian touch will hardly be noticed as the strongest research influencing theory and practice within this region is international. Later on, the distinctive Scandinavian character is more pronounced. It will be explained why – as it seems to be a contradiction to the internationalization and globalization so often emphasized. In the last section we return to a more global perspective – although we are convinced that organizational practice is always local.

THE EARLY WORK/LIFE AND ORGANIZATION RESEARCH

In comparison with gender perspectives on studies of work and workplaces, the research on work/life and organization theory has a much longer history. This will be commented on as it is a necessary background for both theory and practice in the diversity field.

Among the classics within organization and workplace research we include the well-known Hawthorne studies (from the 1930s). The Hawthorne studies are important because their results eventually implied a paradigm shift from a Tayloristic way of 'seeing' the organization (scientific management) to much more emphasis on the human being in the organization (human relations school). The Hawthorne effect refers to the way people responded positively to being 'seen' as humans in the organization. These studies can be mentioned as examples of how the question of gender is treated in the early studies: in fact, it was not treated at all, as noticed by Acker and Van Houten (1972). Their re-examination showed that: (1) the treatment of men and women was different; and (2) women and men were recruited differently. These two factors together may have resulted in different outcomes. Acker and Van Houten accused the Hawthorne studies of being biased because the researchers did not notice the presence of gender dimensions – that is there was no awareness that there were work groups consisting only of men and others only of women, and that this might have led to some different reflections and results. The conclusion reached by Acker and Van Houten is that we may find that organizational processes are related to sex-based power differentials. Later, in the 1950s, Landsberger (1958) noticed that many of the female subjects in the study were also immigrants, a fact that was ignored in the first study. Even Landsberger, however, just mentions this and does not discuss it further. However, these immigrant identity locations clearly had implications for the women's relationship to work and the organization.

Top-down and Bottom-up Perspectives

After the Second World War the research and theory at the organizational level developed in different directions. To put it simply, many sociologists, who were more or less inspired by Marx, described and analysed workplaces from a bottom-up perspective while many management researchers and organization theorists were describing and analysing workplaces from a top-down perspective. The gap between these two approaches has widened and although empirical work is sometimes done in the same organization, the perspective and theories used could be very different. In both approaches, however, a gender perspective was missing, even though the theories and narratives were clearly gendered. It was the hard-working white (working-class) man, whom we were told about in various studies, which were mainly about industries (e.g. Hearn, 1992). The car industry was especially popular as an object of study (see e.g. Freyssenet, 1998). Braverman (1974) was one of the early influential writers and so were Burawoy (1982), Crozier (1964) and many others from different language areas. These classical theorists also tended to marginalize or ignore ethnicity along with gender.

RESEARCH ON SEX, GENDER AND ORGANIZATIONS

Along with the development of workplace research, research on women developed, partly because women in great numbers (in the Western world) became students at universities and some of them eventually researchers. Some of these women were aware that the history of workplaces (and organization theory) was actually *his* story. Eventually research developed which, to begin with, was mainly concerned with adding women where they were missed out – for example, in history, in literature and in art – and after some delay they were also studied and recognized in descriptions of the labour market and organizations (Alvesson & Billing, 1997). The research developed and passed the add-on-women stage towards a position where a woman's standpoint was emphasized. The latest post-feminist position has also been very influential and we return to this in the final section.

Within the gender research that focuses on the labour market and organizations a division of the kind mentioned earlier developed. The labour market perspective dominated, however, and many important questions were raised. What are the connections between women in the labour market and their roles in the family? Is capitalism or patriarchy to blame for women's situation or are they strengthening or opposing each other?[3] The feminist inclusion of domestic work changed the theoretical premises and challenged the basic conceptual definitions within neoclassical economics (Aaltio & Kovalainen, 2003, Ferber & Nelson, 2003). Even though economists often treat organizations as a black box, some realized that an understanding of gender segregation and gender biases in the labour market had to be looked for inside organizations. In particular, the question of wages was studied by many economists (Gonäs & Lehto, 1997; Maier, 1997).

Studies with a clear bottom-up perspective were conducted in most European countries, often published in national languages (see Rubery, 1997). Among the wide spread and important studies is 'Brothers' by Cockburn (1983), published in the early 1980s. Description and analyses of how new technology was implemented in the English printing industry were done from both a class and a gender perspective. Interesting studies in the Cockburn tradition have been conducted and presented in other parts of Europe too, such as Scandinavia. As examples we will mention the studies of women entering male-dominated organizations in Scandinavia by Kvande and Rasmussen (1994, Norway), Sundin (1995, Sweden), Pettersson (1996, Sweden) and Rantalaiho and Heiskanen (1997, Finland). These studies can also be classified as organization research, where the focus is mainly on barriers encountered by women. The top-down perspective, studies on women and management, is represented by some pioneers as well (e.g. Hennig & Jardim, 1977; Kanter, 1977). Before these classics, there was some sporadic early research on women in management (e.g. Gordon & Strober, 1975; Loring & Wells, 1972).

The origins of 'gender in organizations', 'gendered organizations' and now finally postmodern thinking on gender and organizations can be traced to both bottom-up and top-down perspectives. The culture perspective which was developed in the 1980s included paying attention to how the values of different groups influenced the way they acted within the organization. Finally, in the 1990s many researchers realized that organizations are not gender neutral but characterized by practices and processes which can be related to power differences, different values, etc. Gender was considered a significant dimension in research on organizations and the field expanded to become an important part in the organizational and gender areas (Martin & Collinsson, 2002). One of the early contributions to a critique of organizational practices was Ferguson's book (1984) *The Feminist Case Against Bureaucracy*, which made some connections between patriarchy and organizational structures. Later, Martin (1990; 1992) (among others) also made important contributions to the feminist critique about the taken-for-granted nature of gendered organizational practices. In line with other postmodern fields, what was earlier taken for granted on sex, gender and organizations has now begun to be questioned. From a post-structural perspective, gender is a cultural performance and work is seen as a place for the construction of gender. The construction of identity is emphasized as being an important element in the gendering of organizations.

We prefer to use the concept of gender in feminist studies, thus acknowledging that gender studies include studies on masculinity, an expanding area, which also focuses on men 'being men' (mainly being 'white men'), and on men's integration into women's workplaces. A field of special relevance in this organizational context is men and management. The title *Men as Managers – Managers as Men* (Collinson & Hearn, 1996) is illustrative of this new field, which seems to be far from the early studies on women in management not only in its empirical focus but with regard to the theoretical frames as well. Empirical findings and theoretical contributions made from feminist perspectives are otherwise surprisingly often neglected. Part of the field has been criticized by researchers – active in gender and feminist studies – for being too fashionable. There are also concerns over a switch in the political interest from gender and equality to men and masculinity (Aaltio & Kovalainen, 2003).

It is likely then that new themes will emerge and eventually become integrated, and in time further expand our understanding of work organizations and the people who act within them: 'The field of gendered organizations needs to expand beyond gender to embrace all forms of inequality which lack legitimacy in organizations that claim to use merit and performance as their evaluative standards' (Martin & Collinson, 2002: 257). One of these new themes is the concept of diversity, an even newer dimension than gender and one which is still under-researched in Europe. For example, 'ethnicity' is a heading with rather limited space in some of the articles in the state-of-the-art volume from the EU Commission published in 1997. Martin and Collinson (2002) state further that they expect the race/ethnicity trend to accelerate.

RESEARCH AND POLITICS

This chapter is written from a Scandinavian perspective. In Scandinavia there has been, and is, a strong connection between feminist research and politics, mainly around the question of equality between women and men often triggered by the shortage of labour as mentioned below (Aaltio & Kovalainen, 2003; Gonäs & Lehto, 1997). This 'political tradition' seems to be followed also for research in ethnicity and race. A political tradition implies that politicians support, and ask for, research on different topics.

Typically, the political concept has been used in a narrow way to imply decisions and actions taken by politicians. But 'politics' can also have a wider meaning referring to researchers' ambitions to give advice and support to groups of actors such as governmental decision-makers. In this meaning of the concept, research on organizations has from the very beginning been of a political nature. The normative ambitions are often stated by the researchers themselves. One of Taylor's famous books (1911) has the expression 'scientific management' in its title, underlining that the author's ambition was to help managers do their job in a good scientific way.

Shortage of Labour and Welfare Regimes

As mentioned above, research and analyses on women and the labour market have proceeded along different lines. Researchers' intellectual positions and focus are often influenced by the context in which research is done. Women's relations to the labour market vary between countries with regard to participation and working conditions, including working hours and salaries. The early research on gender and the labour market was connected to politics from different perspectives. Although working-class women have always worked, in many countries there have been marriage bars, meaning that women had to stop working when they married (Frangeur, 1998; Kessler-Harris, 1982; and many others). However, because of the labour shortage in many countries, (married) women eventually were regarded as a potential resource. Especially with regard to the labour market, the research was somewhat supported by the fact that there was a shortage of labour which led to an increased interest in expanding the workforce, among both politicians and managers.

Women and the labour market cannot be isolated from other parts of life, like the family and the welfare system (Esping-Anderssen, 1996; Sainsbury, 1996). These systems are of great importance for individuals' lives. One key element in the Nordic model has been the normalization of women's participation in gainful employment and a weak male breadwinner role, in contrast to Western and Southern European welfare models (Aaltio & Kovalainen, 2003). In Denmark and Sweden there was a labour shortage in the 1960's and there was a need to look for other 'unused' resources, married women being one big group[4] which joined the workplace in large numbers in the 1960s and 1970s. This became possible because of the expansion of daycare centres for children. In other Western countries there were (are) not the same 'generous' offers for mothers, and the breadwinner ideology differs from state to state. It is important to note that welfare regimes were established differently and the accompanying discourse on families meant (means) a great deal for women's, not only mothers', work possibilities and the conditions under which they were, and are, on the labour market (Haas, Hwang & Russel, 2000).

The political background for the great interest in research on women and the labour market resembles the present interest in diversity. Earlier immigrant workers were invited (often as an alternative to women) when there was a shortage of labour. The present situation in many European countries, including Scandinavian ones, has been of the opposite kind with great problems for immigrants (including refugees) to find a job. In the near future, however, there seems to be a need for more labour power, and immigrants can again be looked upon as a potential resource.[5] What has until now been looked upon as personal and individual problems for immigrants (of not getting work) has eventually transcended the 'personal' and become important societal issues which must be taken seriously and dealt with accordingly (see also Wright Mills, 1959).

Politics, Research Methods and Conclusions

As the empirical objects of social sciences are parts of these systems and regimes we can find significant differences also in the problems studied and the theories and interpretations used. In their article 'Over the pond and across the water', Martin and Collinson (2002) emphasise and exemplify the differences between US and European research on organizations. The differences concern both theories and methods and, of course, make comparisons and analyses tricky. Critical perspectives are hard to establish as 'North American "normal science" is globally dominant in management and organizational research, thereby blocking critical work on both sides of the pond' (p. 250).

Explanations and theories with the ambition of global relevance have to be looked upon with some suspicion. This standpoint has been taken by many Scandinavian researchers for more than two decades. The Americanization of the social sciences has been criticized as being not sufficiently appropriate to the local Scandinavian context. Local cultures have to be acknowledged as they are important in both theory and practice. This also goes for a lot of research with an American origin: 'even organization research stemming from North America might be less universalistic and more bound to a local way of working, organizing, and thinking than its proponents would have their readers believe' (Czarniawska & Sevón, 2003: 9). It must be mentioned that this privileged position of US research sometimes is maintained by Europeans themselves and that there is a vast critique of the positivistic mainstream research also in the US research community. There is also a strong tradition of research in the United States dealing with issues of race, gender and ethnicity at work in fields such as the sociology of work and corporate anthropology which European management researchers systematically overlook. It might be interesting to speculate as to why Europeans prefer to direct their critiques towards mainstream US research while ignoring the rich outpouring of non-positivist research that has been routinely produced in the United States over the last few decades.

The warning for over-generalization has to be sounded for the diversity field as well. As Wrench (2002) states in his overview of literature on diversity management, the differences in the US and European contexts are important. These differences concern plain facts like the size of the minority population and different ways of solving problems like the American readiness to resort to the courts.[5] Even inside Europe the differences can be great. In some countries there has been great resistance to both the diversity concept and its practice. As an example we will borrow Wrench's (2002: 88, 89) presentation of a French position: 'For some people in France the very word "diversity" has unacceptable overtones … Bourdieu and Wasquant, for example, criticise the "cultural imperialism" inherent in the assumptions that American academic ideas can be imposed on non-American environments.'[6]

Under the political heading we will also note that the literature on gender and organizations and on diversity and organizations tends to be overwhelmingly positive. There seems to be a 'political correctness' also among researchers and/or perhaps research in line with the historical tradition among researchers on organizations to help and give advice to managers and other organizational actors. This tendency is more obvious in the mainstream management diversity literature than in gender literature, which Wrench (2002) explains by diversity being a positive concept signalling efficiency and profits while equality and affirmative actions associate with fairness and costs.

THE WORKPLACE AND DIVERSITY

Sex, Gender and Diversity

In line with what was mentioned above, there are also specific European, and possibly also Scandinavian, traditions and practices for dealing with diversity. Like other characteristics such as disability and sexual preference, age, ethnicity and race (which are often described and classified as individual characteristics although they (also) are attached to social identity groups), gender was, and is, often implicit in the concept of diversity. However, it seemed to be race or rather ethnicity which was the most important dimension from the introduction of the concept in Scandinavia (de los Reyes, 2001). Our way of restricting ourselves to gender and ethnicity/race and neglecting other dimensions and characteristics, under the diversity heading, therefore reflects the broader Scandinavian discourse of diversity.

There are different perspectives on diversity and different definitions. From Thomas and Ely (1996) we learn that 'Diversity should be understood as the varied perspectives and approaches to work that members of different identity groups bring' (p. 80) and Osman (1999) states that 'Cultural diversity is a term generally used to signify the presence of different groups of people with different races, systems of belief (religion), languages, etc. in a geographical arena.' Consequently a variety of cultural diversity models has been devised. These models attempt to come up with a delineation of pluralism according to the following main descriptors: race, religion, gender, and language (p. 10).

We believe that in considering diversity at work, it is important to avoid what is known as the Wollstonecraft dilemma – which is either to be like the majority (often 'men') (white) and give up one's own values/perspectives, or stick to these and perhaps stay marginalized. This indicates the problem of acknowledging differences, in all the dimensions mentioned, and the right to equal opportunity, and parallels the multicultural discourse: that is, how to balance the right to be equal and the right to be different, and equal on whose conditions? Garcia (1995) presents another useful definition: 'The term multicultural diversity competence refers to the ability to demonstrate respect and understanding, to communicate effectively and to work collaboratively with people from different cultural backgrounds.' Even when individuals make efforts to integrate and give up their identities, they can still face exclusion. This is equally true for both women and minorities.

Differences and Similarities Between Gender and Diversity

What are the differences and similarities between a gender and a diversity perspective? Answers to these questions seem to be very complex as was illustrated above. In some studies, like Fine's from 1995, gender is treated as one dimension among others in cultural descriptions and analyses of organizations; that is, of the labour market. In others, like Wise and Tschirhart (2000: 33), it is emphasized that 'one dimension of workplace diversity can not be assumed to apply to other dimensions ... effects of sex diversity on performance ratings are not generalizable to racial diversity'. We will reflect on this statement below but start with an obvious similarity between all diversity dimensions – diverse means not being male, heterosexual, disabled and/or white. Gender is just 'one part of a complicated web of socially constructed elements of identity' and so are race and class. 'Each part may be manifested in its own peculiar and distinct way', Nkomo writes (1992: 507), and continues, 'the common factor is domination based on notions of inferiority and superiority'. The explicit or implicit norm (for these feelings) is the white male. Non-white and non-male represents diversity. But there are also some interesting differences between the diversity phenomena concerning gender and ethnicity that are worth mentioning:

- Early mainstream research did not provide a fair or just picture of the labour market. Women were often excluded although they were part of the labour market. The same cannot be said about ethnic groups. Although they are also partly there but hidden on the black market, their share of jobs seems constantly to be much lower than that of the natives. In this part of the world their share seems somehow to be dependent upon (1) how much they resemble the existing workforce[7] and (2) the need for more persons in the labour market. In the last mentioned perspective the similarities to the entrance of women on the labour market at a large scale are striking.

- Generally, women and men seem to be in different jobs, at different levels, etc. It is not easy to find a man and a woman who carry out the same work at the same time. And if they do, the tasks may have different labels. This seems to be a global, or at least an all-European, phenomenon (Rubery, 1997). We could add that the same might be said about ethnic groups. Segregation is then not just about women but also about ethnicity.

- With regard to gender segregation, it is interesting that the present segregation is always described as the most 'natural', whereas with regard to ethnic 'others' the employers' explanation for leaving them out/not hiring them is most often a matter of the 'others' not having the right qualifications and/or not being able to speak the language etc. In short, they lack skills, especially social skills. This theme repeatedly surfaces in the newspaper discourse in Scandinavia and among researchers (e.g. Osman, 1999). In the same way that labelling women as especially good at care-taking traps them into some specific work areas, there seems to be a corresponding danger that ethnic 'others' might be acknowledged as primarily good at cleaning, caring, serving and servicing (taxi-driving), whereas they are believed not quite to have what it takes to become a manager (or other jobs at higher levels). These lines of argument are illustrated further below under the alternative values and special contribution perspective.

- Women's position in the family is often an important and integrated part of the 'natural' argument referred to above, reminding us that the gender system works in all organizations, including the family. That means that members of different gender categories are living, eating and sleeping together. Some radical feminists would even argue that this is a case of sleeping with the enemy. At work, however, the other 'power' system often includes a separating spatial dimension. Let us give some examples. In the 'empirical world' women and men share daily lives, and are living under the same roof, while working-class people often live far away from upper-class people, do not send their children to the same schools, do not meet during their times off, etc. Different ethnic groups often marry inside their groups and have ethnic networks also in other dimensions. Ethnic separation along diversity lines is sometimes described as a problem, for example when it comes to housing and living.

- The relations between men and women on the labour market and in organizations are also characterized by a hierarchical dimension where what men do and is thought of as masculine is often valued higher and has higher prestige than what women do. How gender and ethnicity are related to each other from a hierarchical perspective is, however, not clear. There are several discussions about intersectionality, the topic of the intersection between race and gender that has interested both debaters and researchers (Acker, 2000; Andersen & Collins, 2000; hooks, 1989).

Models Supporting the Case for Organizational Diversity

The focus in this chapter is on organizations, gender and other diversity dimensions, mainly ethnicity. There is no single way of looking at organizational diversity. Billing and Alvesson (1989) developed a 'model' of how to understand the major reasons and rationales for the theoretical and practical interest in investigating and facilitating women's opportunities for attaining managerial positions. We adapt this model and expand it for our purpose to show the variety of differing views and underlying assumptions that are also present within the area of diversity. It should be noted that these positions should be seen as lines of argumentations, 'ideal types', and therefore not necessarily 'truths' about the different world views, and they may overlap. The four positions dealt with are the equal opportunities perspective, the meritocratic perspective, the special contribution perspective and finally the alternative values perspective. We will address each one of these.

The equal opportunities perspective

This perspective centres around the justice argument. It is based on a moral imperative that there should be equal opportunity with regard to work irrespective of one's biological or cultural background. There is no focus on profit maximization through diversity. It is mainly a 'political' approach, by which we mean that it is initiated by political parties and governments in power. It is perhaps most common within the diversity literature. The goal is anti-discrimination, which is in keeping with the ideals of the democratic nation state. The goal here would be to identify and remove all barriers to fair employment practices. Of course, at the same time, it is also important to get organizations to realize that they do in fact discriminate.

Many employers would argue that there is no discrimination, and that the reason there are few employees from different ethnic backgrounds (or old age etc.) is due to the applicants' lack of qualifications. This power to define 'the other' is essential to organizational control, as is the power to decide what is the standard (the qualifications) which we should be equal to. Likewise, there are fixed ideas about how the worker should look. Conflicts and problems often arise because the majority (in this case represented by the employers) have some 'natural' ideas about how things should be. In this instance, the question of lack of qualifications could be seen as clearly rooted in institutionalized discrimination in Scandinavia (compare the discussions of Osman referring especially to language). Even when minorities have attained greater access to organizations, this stereotyping can prevail, as when employers believe that women's working capacities are limited because of domestic and care-taking responsibilities, regardless of whether the women have children or not. One could imagine the same group-stereotyping about other minorities, but this would be based on myths of cultural differences instead of gender-based myths.

Within this perspective, the structures of the organization are believed to be of utmost importance to the advancement of minorities. Kanter (1977) has described the impact of the structural determinants of behaviour in organizations. She mentions the structure of opportunity, the structure of power and finally the proportional distribution of people of different categories. She argues that it is decisive for one's career progress to be centrally placed in the opportunity structure, to be on a career track and not to be in a dead-end job. For Kanter structure is believed to be more vital than the actor for the chances of getting ahead. With regard to numbers, she claims that when the minority is close to 15% there will be resistance against hiring more individuals from the same minority group. It is not until the minority comes close to one-third (critical mass) that it will be able to influence the workplace. When there are only a few members of a social identity group in an organization, they are likely to be regarded and treated as tokens. Tokenism is a response to these people being unique in the organization, who will, according to this 'theory', have to deal with stereotypes and other caricatures. People with different ethnic backgrounds in organizations are often, just like women, in lower positions, which according to Kanter's theory means that they are low in organizational power, and also in opportunity. There may be cultural circumstances which generate stereotypes that lead to prejudice and discrimination. The division of labour and the lack of network contacts (low in power structure) make it difficult for the different others to advance in the organization.

When individuals from diverse ethnic backgrounds are perceived as different, without adequate qualifications there is slim chance for equal opportunity actually to work. The equal opportunities perspective has clear political conclusions: the structural and cultural conditions lead to a bias in favour of white males, and it is thus necessary to have more regulations that ensure genuine equal opportunity. In some countries there are already regulations and requirements that minorities should be hired in organizations (see Lobel, 1997). Action may be needed for campaigns to affect attitudes or even a quota system. Others would claim that if discrimination were stopped, things would change; we just need a fairer approach. The difference between these two versions is marginal and more a matter of emphasis. The first version also views the removal of biases as significant, but complements this with measures aiming to 'empower', train or support women/ethnic others, while the other exclusively emphasizes external constraints and goes beyond the level of the subject in accomplishing change.

In modern societies (especially in Scandinavia) there is a strong conviction that everybody should be treated fairly, irrespective of race, ethnicity, gender, and such. It is simply unfair and immoral to prefer (white) men just because of their colour and sex; while this is often the case there is ample reason for examining the barriers to equal opportunities, including access to leadership positions. While subscribing to this normative position in theory, in actual practice the equal employment position finds little public support in Scandinavia (especially with respect to ethnic minorities) since most of the population is convinced of the intrinsic fairness of the overall social system.

The meritocratic perspective

The problem of conservatism, prejudice and stereotyping resulting in obstacles to competent persons being recruited or achieving higher-level positions can also be looked at from a meritocratic perspective. This perspective is interested in trying to get rid of obstacles that prevent maximum utilization of the resource potential in society. The argument is that a larger reservoir with bright and motivated people will make society/organizations function better (e.g. Adler, 1986/87). The primary goal is not equal opportunity but the organizations' possibility of using diversity in relation to how it markets itself and its service.

Here the argument is that the organization should mirror its surroundings in order to get access to different markets. An important assumption of this perspective is the organization's need for legitimacy in the media and the wider society, requiring that customers should be able to recognize themselves. To recruit more broadly is good for image reasons. Diverse resources can then be used to get more of the market share (see discussion in Thomas & Ely, 1996). Unlike the equal employment perspective which centres around justice, the meritocratic perspective is driven by a profits and efficiency motive. While this perspective encourages pluralism, it remains monocultural in its orientation rather than multicultural, with the white monoculture dominating the values of the organization. This argument (which is the prevalent one at the moment) argues that we should disregard gender, class, background, race, religion and other characteristics irrelevant to career patterns in modern society. Recruiting more diverse groups could be seen as a smart business practice fact because of the changing composition of people in post-industrial societies where the majority soon will be older people, and where there are more and more immigrants. On competitive grounds, labour shortages causes organizations to look in new directions for resources.

From this perspective it is not so much justice and fairness which are the focus since meritocrats are more concerned with the maximum efficiency of social systems. Ethics do not matter here. It is the full utilization of human resources, irrespective of gender, ethnicity, age, etc., which are important and not so much discrimination as such. Therefore, this perspective seeks to counteract irrational and old-fashioned cultural patterns. With its belief in market competition as the primary incentive, the question becomes one of attracting the best personnel irrespective of differences in race, age, gender, etc. This perspective therefore does not rely on legislation to take care of patterns of discrimination, but assumes instead that organizations have much to gain by recruiting competent individuals irrespective if race, age, gender, etc.

Both these perspectives seem to emphasize the commonality of people arguing that cultural differences are minor. Even when there are minor cultural differences, it is possible to see them as assets. This shows a total unawareness for example of how culture and underlying assumptions, about women, and about minorities, may effectively be a barrier for even recruiting minorities. Acker (1992) mentions the gendered substructure as a potential blockage for women entrants, and Wilson (1998) shows how a collusion between underlying assumptions and espoused values will have an effect with regard to whether minorities (like women) are 'seen' as career potential. This is certainly the case in Scandinavia where many ethnic minorities are not perceived as being 'qualified', even when they are highly educated and have considerable managerial experience but their credentials are from Eastern European and non-western countries.

The next two perspectives are much more interested in differences, the first in slight differences, while the second one makes a strong case for differences.

The special contribution perspective

This position holds that different 'others' (women, people from different ethnicities, older employees, the disabled, etc.) might be able to contribute to organizations with their different values, experiences, ways of thinking, etc. (Grant, 1988; Helgesen, 1990). There has been (and still is) a belief that women, because of different socialization, experiences, etc., have complementary qualifications and thus the potential of making important contributions to the workplace, and there have been many suggestions about women's abilities and skills (Gilligan, 1982) and what they could add. Billing and Alvesson (1989) suggest that there might be an exploitative dimension to this since women could very easily become the necessary oil to make the organization function better. In other words, they could be exploited and used as a potential tool for carrying out rationalizations more smoothly. This argument could be extended to other groups, like immigrants, ethnic minorities, older people, etc. Changes in society in the composition of people and demographic changes are forcing us to think differently about these potential resources for the labour market. These changes may also lead to necessary vital changes in the workplace.

A lot of different 'others' at the workplace could mean that formerly accepted norms might be questioned. These significant differences and the call for special contributions also make it impossible to recruit persons on the basis of some 'neutral' standards. We cannot use a single scale for recruitment. Instead it is perhaps reasonable to accept that people have different skills and therefore are suited for different jobs. The strategy is then not that we all compete on the same terms, but rather that we acknowledge our differences and see these as the vehicles for getting the job/position. Then the variety of perspectives can be seen as 'a knowledge asset that organizations are increasingly trying to optimize' (Thomas & Ely, 1996: 80).

We anticipate that when people are hired and 'used' specifically in relation to the unique difference they have, then there will easily be a culturalization of differences, where workers are identified with their cultural differences and therefore easily put in certain positions. The hierarchical and horizontal division of labour may then be reproduced. While categorizations might be reproduced, however, looking at resources contained in the differences will mean that the negative content might be reformulated as something positive, which then again could mean that even more persons with ethnically different backgrounds might be hired.

Also this perspective, like the others, has political implications. Problems are not over when persons with different ethnic backgrounds have been recruited. As we know from the feminist literature, there can be confrontations at the workplace, which must be dealt with before we can talk about successful integration. Similarly, Prasad and Mills (1997) assert that many organizations do not deal with these problems and managing diversity might easily become a showcase where there is only a focus on the positive side and where cultural differences are not acknowledged (Prasad, 1997). Further, Prasad (1997) observes that the fundamental structuring of many organizational practices is imprinted by cultural myths favouring Euro-male cultural traits and characteristics. This makes it very difficult for organizations even to recognize the so-called contributions of women and minorities. A number of Scandinavian organizations also suffer from this problem. While they are more frequently able to appreciate some of the special contributions of Scandinavian women, they are relatively unable to do the same with many ethnic minorities, especially those from the Middle East and Islamic countries (Prasad, 2005).

The alternative values perspective

The point made here is that there is a substantial difference between women and men. The key assumption is that in general women and men do not share the same interests, priorities and basic attitudes to life. This approach has some similarities with the special contribution view discussed above, but the alternative values position stresses the differences between typical 'male' and 'female' values more strongly, and also emphasizes conflicts between the two. This approach is basically critical of male-dominated institutions.

According to this position, traditionally women have been socialized to live by the values of the private sphere, to be nurturing, to serve others, to be emotional, etc., while men have been socialized to live by the values of the public sphere, to deny vulnerability, to compete, to take risks, wanting to control nature, etc. It could be claimed that the cultural norms and values characterizing the socialization of women and men belong to two different and more or less polarized worlds. An important stream here is psycho-analytic feminism. Other authors ground a distinct feminine orientation less in early socialization and psychology than in shared female experiences associated with the historical position as subordinated or an orientation developed as a consequence of the experiences of mothering (Cockburn, 1991). While special contribution advocates typically view female early socialization as crucial for the gender difference, alternative values advocates more clearly invoke social conditions, including political positioning. It is the marginal position of women which brings about a specific set of orientations.

These differences are believed to be much greater than in the former position and believed to influence how individuals look at competition (see Gilligan, 1982) and how they develop rationalities. This can certainly be extended to the advancement of minority social groups in work organizations. They will bring with them some very different characteristics and value orientations to the organizations (Thomas & Ely, 1996), a discussion which is also in Prasad (1997).

With regard to women, they are believed always to be marginalized in a capitalist society which is based on masculine values. If different ethnic groups are constructed (stereotypically) as being culturally different and this alternative culture is also seen as in opposition to the dominant masculinity, they will 'suffer' the same exclusion problems as women. This way of constructing diverse staff as being dependent on and behaving according to some other cultural norms (see e.g. Hofstede, 1990) will demand that more fundamental changes are needed if more than a minority of people are to fit into the organization positions and if all the different priorities/values and interests are to be taken seriously. Later we briefly go into a discussion of whose values to respect and the difficulties even in coming to an answer to this question.

Summary

The difference between the four positions is that within the equality strand, anti-discrimination and justice are the central pillars. This position urges that we fight against discrimination to increase the number of people with a different ethnic background and to achieve a balance between women and men. All are expected to adjust to the values and norms of the organization. Assimilation is the expected result.

The meritocratic perspective is a way of responding to the market, arguing that the organization's legitimacy is enhanced when it mirrors the diverse social composition that is found in its environment. Cultural differences are valued because they can be advantageous for competitive reasons, for the sake of efficient utilization of human resources, but there is a tendency to encourage segregation between the different member groups as they will be associated with their cultural backgrounds. Here again assimilation is the goal, but it takes place as a result of voluntary corporate action rather than governmental intervention or legislation.

The special contribution perspective suggests that organizations should value and use the resources of its diverse staff to develop itself. There is no demand that diverse employees should fit to the organization. Instead, innovation and new ways of thinking are valued. This way of thinking is usually framed as essentialist and is sometimes also referred to as celebrating diversity. To celebrate special alternative values would mean more 'female' ways of managing or, and better, organizing, that are mainly in the interest of women and preferably alternative organizations.

People with different ethnic backgrounds, and women (with different values), may then develop their own small (work) cultures and perhaps not be integrated in society. This last option seems to be most prevalent among immigrants at the moment in Scandinavia. But whereas (white) women may have the choice to enter the existing organizations and choose to create their own alternative organizations, minorities may not have this choice of entrance and may remain in separate subcultures as a reaction to this.

The four positions presented here indicate the variety of ways in which the topic of diversity may be considered. Equal opportunity expresses a liberal justice-based view, while special contribution and alternative values are weak and strong applications respectively of the feminist standpoint. Meritocrats may not be feminists at all, but if they are, the liberal–justice view is closest. The questioning and playing out of all approaches without advocating any 'best one' would be in line with postmodernist thinking.

The equal opportunity approach would rely on struggles within and outside organizations, legislation and, in the United States at least, bringing cases into court. Meritocrats would argue that effectiveness considerations and competition would provide sufficient incentives for change. Improved human resource management would be the major vehicle. Special contribution advocates would also rely on competition-induced pressure for effectiveness as well as the demands of particular female (but also male) subordinates. For alternative values advocates, the suggested route would be to develop alternative institutions, rather than try social engineering in the existing capitalist organizations.

There are problems with all perspectives. One general critique is that mainly the positive features of diversity management are emphasized, largely ignoring power relations and complex group dynamics. For example, while organizational assimilation may well be a desirable goal, none of the perspectives seriously address the question of culturalization of differences. A culturalization of differences takes place when the employed with different backgrounds are kept in specific job positions because they are supposed to have a specific group identity. It becomes a problem if competences are culturalized, meaning that the values and norms of the majority are implicitly the basis for the assessment of competences. This bias has been shown in gender research. At the same time one cannot deny that there might be a lack of competences (in some ethnic groups) which seem relevant in many cases, for example a lack of knowledge of the language, inadequate training, etc., which should be taken care of before we can expect any integration. However, one should also note that many employers in Scandinavia use the alleged lack of qualifications of immigrants as an excuse to not even consider them for employment (Prasad, 2005).

MANAGING DIVERSITY IN THE WORKPLACE

When we talk about diversity we talk about differences between social groups, but when we talk about managing diversity what does this actually mean? Who and what benefit from it? Some researchers and debaters state that 'management' indicates an owner/manager perspective where power dimensions are hidden behind the diversity concept. Prasad and Mills (1997) ask the relevant question about whether managing diversity is a way to hide that there are in fact discrimination patterns, as diversity management focuses on individuals and pays no attention to discrimination on the basis of ethnic background. Like all other concepts, diversity is not a neutral concept and the importance of this concept will probably last as long as it means something to be different. The concept of diversity is now an established (although a contested) paradigm and it will probably be an important issue as long as organizations do not pursue cultural heterogeneity and/or direct other diversity issues. Or, to use a well-known phrase, as long as it is possible to talk about 'them' and 'us' there will be a need to discuss diversity. Cox (1991) thinks that the multicultural organization is best in relation to integration and the possibility of benefiting from diversity in the organization (see also Fine, 1995). There is also research which shows that heterogeneous teams are more creative and innovative than homogeneous ones. This often presented 'fact' is challenged by others emphasizing that diversity, on both race and gender, has negative effects on group processes and performance (Wrench, 2002). The questionable support for diversity should not, from our point of view, be referred to as an argument against diversity. There could be, and probably are, very positive consequences above the organizational level of diversity including the ones mentioned by the meritocratic perspective.

As stated above, an ethnic dimension can be included in gender research, and in race a gender dimension. Which is the most important seems to have been an ongoing discussion, which reminds us of discussions that belonged to earlier decades, but then about whether a class perspective or a gender perspective should be prioritized. The discussion now sometimes seems to be very antagonistic. In a Swedish book on gender, class and ethnicity in the post-colonial society (de los Reyes et al., 2002), the authors firmly state that although knowledge from studies on gender and women can be of value for analyses on ethnicity, ethnicity and gender are different principles in the power systems. Traditional feminist researchers (Swedish)[8] are severely criticized for neglecting race and ethnicity and through taking part in the construction of immigrant women as a category of 'not-women'. Many Swedish scholars are obviously somewhat disturbed by de los Reyes et al.'s tone, which they describe as too antagonistic. At some level, this is not surprising, because Sweden is only now confronting the turbulent contests over civic space that multicultural countries like Canada and the United States have been facing for a long time. Scandinavians, however, are for the first time having to confront accusations about ignoring the realities of race and ethnicity, and learning to negotiate interactions with people from different ethnicities who have very different intellectual and cultural styles as well.

An Example – Gender Harder than Ethnicity

In the Scandinavian countries the diversity perspective has been thought of by many as imposed from above. For example, Berggren (2002) claims that the Swedish Defence Ministry was told by politicians in the 1980s to work hard for equal opportunity. This meant allowing women to have access to the army and being seen as potential officers. The presence of the female sex in the army increased the awareness of discrimination and also highlighted the small numbers of women in the army. That women might voluntarily not have wanted to join the army was not discussed at all. The chosen strategy was built upon an idea that women and men are different, the last two alternatives mentioned above. This was called the 'creative difference' – an essentialist perspective. When the concept of diversity entered the vocabulary in the army, it offered an opportunity to keep the taken-for-granted assumptions about women and men but to avoid the equal opportunity discussion. The diversity concept was acknowledged along with other diversity characteristics (some of them in fact automatically exclude certain individuals from the army – the disabled, people with extreme political convictions – and only Swedish citizens have to do national service in the army). Diversity turned out to be an excuse for taking the gender perspective out of the organizational agendas.

The above organizational reaction indicates that gender sometimes seems to be a stronger threat to organizational culture than ethnicity and race. This conclusion is probably not universal but at least relevant for some Scandinavian organizations where a gender 'order' is the prime order (see e.g. Abrahamsson, 2003; Sundin, 2002). This is sometimes hard to explain as the Scandinavian countries as a rule are near the top of equality lists. But 'Nordic countries are not a paradise of equality between women and men; gender regimes and gender contracts within worklife exist as they do in other countries' (Aaltio & Kovalainen, 2003: 197). Our conclusion is that ethnic diversity can be accepted as long as it is in line with established 'gender orders'. It should also be noted that in most private and public organizations in Scandinavia, women have made considerable inroads, while minorities remain highly under-represented.

GENDER AND ETHNICITY IN THE FUTURE WORKPLACE – THEORY AND PRACTICE

Practice, research and theory are connected. Both the present and the signs for the future are diverse. In our part of the world, Scandinavia, it is likely that demographic changes (as in many Western countries) will 'force' societies to look out for new labour power. In many Western countries, in a few decades there will be more retired people than people who work. The lack of people ready to be recruited supports the 'competitive strategy' emphasized both by researchers and diversity activists. It can be thought of as a solution to the lack of resources that will add competences, and promote legitimacy. This could be another narrative than thinking of ethnic immigrants as a burden (Thisted, 2003). Employers might be interested in recruiting persons with different ethnic backgrounds, because of the competitive advantage and because it increases the ability to compete.

As we know from the organizational literature, even without gender and ethnicity dimensions/perspectives there can be many confrontations at the workplace which must be dealt with. When the workplace has become more heterogeneous, how do we deal with these differences in the workforce? Problems are not over when people with different ethnic backgrounds have been hired. This will be more obvious when we confuse the picture by bringing in gender as an important diversity dimension. We can learn from postfeminist and postcolonial critiques that, first, not all women have the same experiences, and there are many standpoints and voices. There are also entire histories of neocolonial subjugation that have left a legacy of mutual hostility and suspicion between many ethnic minority groups and the dominant Scandinavian groups. Postfeminism and postcolonialism have also provided useful correctives to what is seen as a distorted Western view. This said, we should also recognize that diversity concerns more than gender and ethnicity. There is a growing recognition that age can intersect with gender and or ethnicity in interesting ways (Aaltio & Kovalainen, 2003). We should be sensitive to differences and not believe that it is possible to be culturally neutral. On the other hand, we should also be aware that too much focus on diversity could pose a problem of even articulating a 'we': inequalities might be seen as 'natural' and we therefore lose the possibility of seeing them.

Diversity management might be a tool with which prejudice and discrimination can be dealt so that ethnic minorities can be integrated in the labour market. Its point of departure is that the individual has resources and differences which are regarded as a force rather than a problem. In this sense it provides a positive narrative about people with different ethnic backgrounds. How can it then be used as a tool for integrating these people in organizations? What are the potentials and which problems can we expect? Taking all this into consideration is perhaps problematic, which the four presented alternatives showed. Promoting equal opportunity, acknowledging cultural differences and at the same time actively attempting to challenge the organization's way of doing things – if the workers with a different ethnic background are able to contribute in their culturally different ways – are not easy. The point of departure is an idea about cultural identity which forms how people experience, see and know the world. According to Ely and Thomas (2001), the best way to get integration is to use the diverse members' resources. It is of course a condition that the persons hired wish to keep whatever distinctions they have due to their cultural background. This on the other hand might pose a problem for individual free will and freedom to act, and then the power inequalities will still remain. While some people want to adapt, others may have a more fragmented or diverse identity[9]. Focusing on the differences and cultural competences which persons with a different ethnic background have can then keep them in a subjugated position. The ideal could be an organization where a multiplicity of complex constructed identities can flourish. Diversity in organizations should be cared for in order to create a 'healthy' work climate where people's potential is acknowledged and supported.

Globalization has had some contradictory effects in relation to these issues: on the one hand it has eroded some national identities. On the other hand, it has strengthened some local identities and also provided space for hybrid identities. Acknowledging that there are other standpoints is a starting point for changing organizations so there is more mutual respect and integration. By integration we mean that persons with diverse backgrounds get a stronger connection. In other words, they need the same possibilities that the hired already have. But how should the minority and majority adapt to each other's norms and values? Does integration mean changing the organizational culture and power structures? And what sort of competences should be looked for – are the 'local national' cultural norms seen as most important, and why? All this can only be answered through an empirical investigation.

Pluralistic integration demands that potential conflicts and power structures are dealt with (Cox, 1991). A few points are worth considering here that are pertinent to the Scandinavian situation. There is currently a strong feeling in Scandinavia that some (ethnic) men do not respect the women who work at the workplace and that these individuals are from ethnic groups which are still patriarchal and stick to a belief-system which denigrates women. There is also a strong feeling that such groups need to change their attitudes towards women. However, the Scandinavian discourse systematically ignores the fact that men from the same so-called patriarchal ethnic groups work alongside women in a number of multicultural countries including Canada and the United States. Second, this discourse systematically displaces patriarchal tendencies on a non-Western 'other' while conveniently ignoring mounting evidence of violence against women among European men themselves (Naravane, 2004). What this discourse inevitably produces is an invariant picture of non-Western immigrants (e.g. men as tyrannical, women as passive, etc.) that is not very helpful in the creation of a pluralistic society (Mohanty, 1987). It is hoped that with the forces of globalization, intellectuals in Scandinavia will also become more conversant with the kinds of discussions around postcolonialism and otherness that have been taking place in large sections of the world for a number of decades. Only with the changing of this discourse can there be genuine hope for a more pluralistic society in Northern Europe.

NOTES

We wish to thank Pushi Prasad for her patience and very helpful comments on earlier drafts of this paper.

1 Ethnicity is understood as a concept denoting 'collectivity and belongingness' while race is a way of constructing differences (Anthias & Yuval-Davis, 1992). Race has been looked upon more as an ideological construct, 'on the basis of an immutable biological or

physiognomic difference which may or may not be seen to be expressed mainly in culture and lifestyle but is always grounded on the separation of human populations by some notion of stock or collective heredity of traits' (Anthias & Yuval-Davis, 1992) and there has been a heated discussion on whether this term should be rejected or if it could perhaps be useful as the effects of this construct are important to note.

2 Parekh (2003) differentiates between different forms of diversity: subcultural, perspectival and communal. His concern and discussion is mainly about the last mentioned, which he believes is 'both easier and more difficult to accommodate depending on its depth and demands'. Communal diversity refers to 'several self-conscious and more or less well-organized communities entertaining and living by their own systems of beliefs and practices'.

3 There is a vast international literature on these topics. Among the many important contributions we will mention Hartmann (1979) and Walby (1986), and from Scandinavia, Ellingsaeter (1996). See also the bibliography in Rubery (1997).

4 In Denmark another large group comprised Turkish men who were 'invited' to work in the country in the beginning of the 1970s. The same could be said about people from Finland coming to Sweden after the Second World War (Häggström, 1990).

5 We are not thinking about well-educated and highly-credentialed people (who are said not to have quite the same problems of getting jobs) but rather those immigrants/refugees with hardly any education and many of whom do not speak the language. A big problem for countries with welfare systems which are paid for mainly by the tax payer is that it is difficult to attract 'Green Card' people and even to keep those who have come to the country. High taxes and a cold climate are claimed to be two main reasons for highly educated people leaving or not wanting a job in the country (Denmark) (*Berlingske Tidende*, 9 December 2004). However, this explanation seems to be reductionistic as, for example, Canada has the same characteristics but another immigrant policy influencing the number of immigrants. The well-educated also have problems in Scandinavia as they continue to face more difficulties on the labour market than the 'natives'. The somewhat smaller minority populations in Europe compared to the United States are sometimes seen as a result of protectionist European policies – an issue which in itself is a 'diversity' problem – but this is a much bigger discussion which we cannot go into here.

6 This critique in its turn has, however, been criticized for being a smokescreen for the continuing European neglect of internal diversity. See for example Grossberg (1996).

7 In Denmark in 1996 the unemployment rate among Danes was 7%, EU citizens 13%, Turks 41%, Africans 37%, Americans 16%, Pakistanis 40%, the rest (e.g. Arabs, Palestinians) 38%. In Sweden the unemployment rates among persons born outside Europe was three times as high as among immigrants born in the Scandinavian countries in the same year (Statistics Sweden, AKU table 52).

8 Just 20–25 years ago Sweden and the other Scandinavian countries were rather homogeneous societies.

9 Others have made the point that cultural identity is a matter of becoming as well as of being. The concept of diaspora consciousness shows that cultural identity is much more fluid and complex than politicians and employers seem to realize. Based on her study of Brazilians living in Australia, Duarte (2004) concludes that diasporic beings live 'in the betweens', 'in a condition of transnational liminality'.

REFERENCES

Aaltio, I., & Kovalainen, A. (2003). Using gender in exploring organizations, management, and change. In B. Czarniawska, & G. Sevon (Eds), *The Northern Light – Organizational theory in Scandinavia*. Malmö: Liber AB.

Abrahamsson, L. (2003). When it was important it turned male. In E. Gunnarsson (Ed.), *Where have all the structures gone? Doing gender in organizations* (Examples from Finland, Norway and Sweden). Stockholm: Center for Women's Studies.

Acker, J. (1992). Gendering organizational theory. In A. Mills & P. Tancred (Eds), *Gendering organizational analysis*. London: Sage.

Acker, J. (2000). Revisiting class: Thinking from gender, class, and organizations. *Social Politics*, 7, 215–43.

Acker, J., & van Houten, D. R. (1972). Differential recruitment and control: The sex structuring of organizations. In A. J. Mills & P. Tancred (Eds), *Gendering organizational analysis*. London: Sage.

Adler, N. J. (1986/87). Women in management worldwide. *International Studies of Management and Organization*, 16(3–4).

AKU (2004). *Table 52*. Stockholm: Statistics Sweden.

Alvesson, M., & Billing, Y. D. (1997). *Understanding gender and organizations*. London: Sage.

Andersen, M. L., & Collins, P. (Eds) (2000). *Race, class and gender: an anthology*. Belmont, CA: Wadsworth.

Anthias, F., & Yuval-Davis, N. (1992). Connecting race and gender. In F. Anthias & N. Yuval-Davis (Eds), *Racialized boundaries: race, nation, gender, colour and class and the anti-racist struggle*. London: Routledge.

Berggren, A. (2002). *Undercover operations in no-women's land. The Swedish armed forces through a gender lens*. Lund: Department of Psychology. University of Lund.

Billing, Y. D., & Alvesson, M. (1989). Four ways of looking at women and leadership. *Scandinavian Journal of Management*, 5, 2.

Braverman, H. (1974). *Labour and monopoly capital*. New York: Monthly Review Press.

Burawoy, M. (1982). *Manufacturing consent*. Chicago: University of Chicago Press.

Cockburn, C. (1983). *Brothers: Male dominances and technological change*. London: Pluto.

Cockburn, C. (1991). *The way of women*. New York: ILIR Press.

Collinson, D., & Hearn, J. (Eds) (1996). *Men as managers – Managers as men*. London: Sage.

Cox, T. (1991). The multicultural organization. *Academy of Management Executive*, 5(2), 34–47.

Crozier, M. (1964). *The bureaucratic phenomenon*. Chicago: University of Chicago Press.

Czarniawska, B., & Sevón, G. (2003). Introduction: Did the Vikings know how to organize? In B. Czarniawska & G. Sevón (Eds), *The Northern Light – Organizational theory in Scandinavia*. Malmö: Liber AB.

de los Reyes, P. (2001). *Mångfald och differentiering. Diskurs, olikhet och normbildning inom svensk forskning och samhällsdebatt* (Diversity and differentiation. Discourse, difference and the construction of norms in Swedish research and public debate). Stockholm: Arbteslivsinstitutet.

de los Reyes, P. et al. (2002). *Maktens (o)lika förklädnader: kön, klass & etnicitet I det postkoloniala Sverige: en festskrift till Wuokko Knocke* (Gender, class and ethnicity in the post-colonial society). Stockholm: Atlas.

Duarte, F. (2004). Living in 'the Betweens': Diaspora consciousness formation and identity among Brazilians in Australia. Unpublished paper.

Ellingsaeter, A.-L. (1996). *Gender, work and social change. Beyond dualistic thinking*. Report/ institutt for samfunnsforskning, 96: 14. Oslo: Institute for Social Research.

Ely, R. J. & Thomas, D. A. (2001). Cultural diversity at work: The effects of diversity perspectives on work group processes and outcomes. *Administrative Science Quarterly*, 46(2), 229–73.

Esping-Anderson, G. (1996). *Welfare states in transition. National adaptions in global economics*. London: Sage.

Ferber, M. A., & Nelson, J. A. (Eds) (2003). *Feminist economics today: Beyond economic man*. Chicago: University of Chicago Press.

Ferguson, K. E. (1984). *The feminist case against bureaucracy*. Philadelphia. Temple University Press.

Ferguson, K. E. (1994). On bringing more theory, more choices and more politics to the study of organizations. *Organization, 1*, 81–99.

Fine, M. G. (1995). *Building successful multicultural organizations. Challenges and opportunities*. London: Quorum Books.

Frangeur, R. (1998). *Yrkeskvinna eller makens tjänarinna? Striden om yrkesrätten för gifta kvinnor i mellankrigstidens Sverige* (Career women or servant to her husband). Lund: Arkiv.

Freyssenet, M. (1998). *One best way? Trajectories and industrial models of the world's automobile producers*. Oxford: Oxford University Press.

Garcia, M. H. (1995). An anthropological approach to multicultural diversity training. *Journal of Applied Behavioral Science, 31*(4), 490–504.

Gilligan, C. (1982). *In a different voice*. Cambridge, MA: Harvard University Press.

Gonäs, L., & Lehto, A. (1997). Segregation of the labour market. In J. Rubery & Plantenga, J. (Eds), *State of the Art Review on Women and the Labour Market: A Report for the Equal Opportunities Unit, DG-V*, European Commission: University of Utrecht, the Netherlands.

Gordon, F., & Strober, M. H. (Eds) (1975). *Bringing women into management*. New York: McGraw-Hill.

Grant, J. (1988). Women as managers: What can they offer to organizations? *Organizational Dynamics, 1*, 56–63.

Grossberg, L. (1996). Identity and cultural studies – is that all there is? In S. Hall & P. du Gay (Eds), *Questions of cultural identity*. London: Sage.

Haas, L., Hwang, P. & Russell, G. (2000). *Organizational change & gender equity*. London: Sage.

Häggström, N. (1990). *När finländarna kom: migrationen Finland-Sverige efter andra världskriget* (When they came from Finland: The migration from Finland to Sweden after the Second World War). Gävle: Statens institut för byggnadsforskning.

Hartmann, H. (1979). The unhappy marriage of Marxism and feminism: Towards a more progressive union, *Capital and Class, 8*, 1–33.

Hearn, J. (1992). *Men in the public eye. The construction and deconstruction of public men and public patriarchies*. London: Routledge.

Helgesen, S. (1990). *The female advantage: Women's ways of leadership*. New York: Doubleday Currency.

Hennig, M., & Jardim, A. (1977). *The managerial woman*. New York: Anchor Press.

Hofstede, G. (1990). The cultural relativity of organizational practices and theories. In D. Wilson & R. Rosenfeld (Eds), *Managing Organizations*. Maidenhead: McGraw Hill.

hooks, b. (1989). *Talking back: Thinking feminist, thinking black*. Boston: South End Press.

Kanter, R. M. (1977). *Men and women of the corporation*. New York: Basic Books.

Kessler-Harris, A. (1982). *Out to work: A history of wage-earning women in the US*. New York: Oxford University Press.

Kvande, E., & Rasmussen, B. (1994). Men in male-dominated organizations and their encounter with women intruders. *Scandinavian Journal of Management, 10*(2), 163–73.

Landsberger, H. A. (1958). *Hawthorne revisited*. Ithaca, New York: Cornell University Press.

Lobel, S. A. (1997). Impacts of diversity and work-life initiatives in organizations. In G. N. Powell (Ed.), *Handbook of gender and work*. London: Sage.

Loring, R., & Wells, T. (1972). *Breakthrough: Women into management*. New York: Van Nostrand Reinhold.

Maier, F. (1997). Gender pay gap. In J. Rubery & J. Plantenga (Eds), *State of the Art Review on Women and the Labour Market: A Report for the Equal Opportunities Unit, DG-V*, European Commission: University of Utrecht, the Netherlands.

Martin, J. (1990). Deconstructing organizational taboos: The suppression of gender conflict in organizations. *Organizational Science, 1*, 339–59.

Martin, J. (1992). *Cultures in organizations: Three perspectives.* Oxford: Oxford University Press.

Martin, P. Y., & Collinson, D. (2002). 'Over the Pond and Across the Water': Developing the field of 'Gendered Organizations'. *Gender, Work & Organization, 9*(3).

Mohanty, C. T. (1987). *Under western eyes: Feminist scholarship and colonial* discourses. In C.T. Mohanty, L. Torres & A. Russo (Eds), *Third world women and the politics of feminism.* Indianapolis: Indiana University Press.

Naravane, V. (2004). Within four walls. *Frontline*, 21 March, 13–26.

Nkomo, S. M. (1992). The emperor has no clothes. Re-writing race in organizations. *Academy of Management Review, 17*, 487–513.

Osman, A. (1999). *The 'Strangers' Among us: The Social Construction of Identity in Adult Education* (Linköping Studies in Education and Psychology No. 61). Linköping University.

Parekh, B. (2003). *Rethinking multiculturalism: Cultural diversity and political theory.* Basingstoke: Macmillan.

Pettersson, L. (1996). *Ny organization, ny teknik – nya genusrelationer? En studie av genuskontrakt på två industriarbetsplatser.* (New organization, new technology – new gender relations? A study of gender contracts in two industrial worksites). Linkoping, Sweden: Tema Teknik och social förändring, Linköpinps universitet.

Prasad, P. (1997). The Protestant ethic and myths of the frontier: Cultural imprints, organizational structuring and workplace diversity. In P. Prasad, A. Mills, M. Elmes & A. Prasad (Eds), *Managing the organizational melting pot: Dilemmas of workplace diversity* (pp. 129–47). Thousand Oaks, CA: Sage.

Prasad, P. (2005). Unveiling Europe's civilized face: Confrontations with diversity in the Scandinavian workplace. Paper to be presented at the Annual Meetings of the Academy of Management, Hawaii, August.

Prasad, P., & Mills, A. J. (1997). From showcase to shadow. In P. Prasad, A. Mills, M. Elmes & A. Prasad (Eds), *Managing the organizational melting pot: Dilemmas of workplace diversity* (pp. 3–27). Thousand Oaks, CA: Sage.

Rantalaiho, L., & Heiskanen, T. (1997). *Gendered practices in working life.* London and New York: Macmillan and St. Martin's Press.

Rubery, J. (1997). Overview and comparative studies. In J. Rubery & J. Plantenga (Eds), *State of the Art Review on Women and the Labour Market: A Report for the Equal Opportunities Unit, DG-V*, European Commission: University of Utrecht, the Netherlands.

Sainsbury, D. (1996). *Gender, equality, and welfare states.* Cambridge: Cambridge University Press.

Sundin, E. (1995). The construction of gender and technology. *European Journal of Women's Studies, 2*, 335–53.

Sundin, E. (2002). *Rationalitet som norm och hykleri som praktik: reflektioner kring betydelsen av organisationers genusordning* (Rationality as a norm and hypocrisy in practice: Reflections on the importance of organizational gender orders). *Kvinnovetenskaplig Tidskrift, 1*, 21–36.

Taylor, F. (1911). *The principles of scientific management.* New York: Harper & Brother.

Thisted, L. N. (2003). *Mangfoldighedens dilemmaer – hvad livshistorier fortæller om identitet, arbejde og integration* (pp. 15–47) (The dilemmas of diversity: What life stories tell us about identity, work and integration). København: Handelsskolen i Kbhvn.

Thomas, D. A. and Ely, R. J. (1996). Making differences matter: A new paradigm for managing diversity. *Harvard Business Review*, September/October, 79–90.

Walby, S. (1986). *Patriarchy at work: Patriarchal and capitalist relations in employment.* Cambridge: Polity.

Wilson, E. (1998). Gendered career paths, *Personnel Review, 27*(5), 396–411.

Wise, L. R., & Tschirthart, M. (2000). Examining empirical evidence on diversity effects: How useful is diversity research for public sector managers? *Public Administration Review, 50*(5).

Wrench, J. (2002). Diversity management, discrimination and ethnic minorities in Europe: Clarifications, critiques and research agendas. Mångfaldens praktik IV. *Occasional papers and reprints on ethnic studies,* 19. Centre for Ethnic and Urban Studies, National Institute of Working Life, Norrköping, Sweden.

Wright Mills, C. (1959). *The sociological imagination.* New York: Oxford University Press.

5

The Jewel in the Crown

Postcolonial Theory and Workplace Diversity

ANSHUMAN PRASAD

... it is from those who have suffered the sentence of history—subjugation, domination, diaspora, displacement—that we learn our most enduring lessons for living and thinking. (Homi K. Bhabha, *The Location of Culture*)

An identity is questioned only when it is menaced, or when the mighty begin to fall, or when the wretched begin to rise, or when the stranger enters the gates. (James Baldwin, *The Devil Finds Work*, quoted in George Lipsitz, *The Possessive Investment in Whiteness*)

... the [postcolonial] effort to present Europe as an Other involves ... a political impatience with the matter of Europe. (Gayatri Chakravorty Spivak, *A Critique of Postcolonial Reason*)

So it is said that when you know yourself and others, victory is not in danger; when you know sky and earth, victory is inexhaustible. (Sun Tzu, *The Art of War*)

For close to a hundred years after a country (an empire in the making) comes out with a ringing declaration on the equality of all of humanity ('We hold these truths to be self-evident, that all men are created equal, that they are endowed by their Creator with certain unalienable Rights') slavery involving the buying and selling of human beings as *things* continues to flourish in the country, and it takes another century for this country merely to enact legislation outlawing discrimination against sections of its own citizenry.[1] Some 150 years after a renowned nineteenth-century political thinker and *liberal* cultural icon of another empire writes celebrated essays laudatory of liberty and representative government (Mill, 1912), the chairman of the Commission for Racial Equality in that country, the UK, calls upon its non-white citizens to 'shed multiculturalism' and 'embrace Britishness' (Suroor, 2004).[2] More than two centuries after a country – later to become yet another of the great empires of the West – launches a revolution in the name of 'Liberty, Equality and Fraternity', it is convulsed by hysteria over headscarves worn by its Muslim female citizens (Terray, 2004).

Do these ambivalent and paradoxical histories of modern Western colonialism and its aftermath hold important lessons for management and organizational scholars investigating the dynamics of workplace diversity in the West? The answer, this chapter submits, is 'Yes'. Accordingly, the chapter will employ the intellectual resources of postcolonial theory with a view to furthering our understanding of the complexities of workplace diversity and multiculturalism. The usefulness of postcolonial theory for workplace diversity research will be briefly explained in the next section of the chapter.

As pointed out in various chapters of this handbook, recent years have witnessed a mushrooming of scholarly research on workplace diversity and multiculturalism (cf. Konrad, 2003; Nkomo & Cox, 1996). Despite such an explosion of research output, scholars in the field frequently express dissatisfaction with the current state of workplace diversity research, and emphasize the need for mobilizing new and critical perspectives for studying the phenomenon (e.g. Dick & Cassell, 2002; Linnehan & Konrad, 1999; Prasad, Mills, Elmes & Prasad, 1997). In keeping with such scholarly calls, this chapter seeks to utilize insights from postcolonial theory for understanding issues of workplace diversity and multiculturalism.

In what follows, this chapter proposes to: (1) briefly introduce postcolonial theory, (2) theorize, from a postcolonial perspective, 'Europe'/'the West' as the name of a complex problem, and (3) discuss the significance of those postcolonial theoretic insights for workplace diversity and multiculturalism. Before proceeding with this agenda, however, it needs to be emphasized that this chapter is primarily concerned with issues of workplace diversity *in the West*. Hence, the chapter's analysis and/or conclusions should not be viewed as being readily transferable/applicable – in a somewhat simple and straightforward manner – to considerations of workplace diversity in countries outside the West, even though the theoretical issues raised here may sometimes be helpful in channeling critiques of workplace diversity issues in those countries along new and productive lines.

POSTCOLONIAL THEORY: AN INTRODUCTION

Postcolonial theory (also called postcolonialism) is a somewhat recent approach for critical research, having become established in the wider academe only during the course of the 1980s (Ashcroft, Griffiths & Tiffin, 1995; Gandhi, 1998;

Goldberg & Quayson, 2002; Lewis & Mills, 2003a; Loomba, 1998; Mongia, 1996; Prasad, 2003a; Williams & Chrisman, 1994; Young, 2001). Notwithstanding its relative newness, however, postcolonialism has had a significant impact on a wide range of scholarly disciplines. This section of the chapter will offer a brief overview of the conceptual topography of postcolonial theory, and touch upon its usefulness for workplace diversity research.

During the course of a long and continuing history stretching over more than 500 years, modern Western colonialism and neo-colonialism have touched almost all corners of the globe. Not surprisingly, therefore, Western (neo-)colonialism and, equally important, non-Western anti-colonialism have deeply influenced the nature of our world, shaping in the process important aspects of the contours – economic, cultural, political, aesthetic, psychological, ideological, epistemologi- cal, philosophical, and the rest – of the world we inhabit today. Postcolonial theory may be understood as an attempt – from an intellectual perspective that insists upon, among other things, a persistent interrogation of Eurocentrism – to take stock of the consequences of the fateful colonial encounter between the West and the non-West and, in so doing, 'to investigate the complex and deeply fraught dynamics of modern Western colonialism and anti-colonial resistance, and the ongoing significance of the colonial encounter for people's lives both in the West and the non-West' (Prasad, 2003b: 5).

If the academic field of postcolonial theory and criticism can be said to have an inaugural moment, that moment, most certainly, was the publication of *Orientalism* (1978), Edward Said's highly influential study of colonial discourse.[3] A discourse, we may note here, is not simply 'writing and/or speech, narrowly understood' (Prasad, 2003b: 8). Rather, the analytic category of discourse func- tions to draw attention to the fact that knowledge (both scholarly as well as non- scholarly) and power *intersect*, and that institutions and practices serve as relays for the circulation of those diverse kinds of knowledges (e.g. political, economic, medical, penal, religious, sexual, etc.) that constitute and inform a specific culture at a given moment in history (see e.g. Mills, 1997; Weedon, 1997; Young, 2001).

Said's (1978) analysis of colonial discourse focuses upon what he calls Orientalism, the Western discourse with respect to the Middle East and Islam. Identifying the Orient as 'a European invention' – rather than a *fact* of geography – and 'one of … [Europe's] deepest and most recurring images of the Other' (p. 1), Said (1978) argues that the discourse of Orientalism is founded on the fictive assumptions that, ontologically and epistemologically, 'the Orient' and 'the Occident' are binary opposites that do not share in the same humanness, and that the essence of the Orient – and of being an Oriental – consists of such elements as 'despotism, splendor, cruelty, and sensuality' (p. 4), 'lack of logic, untruthful- ness, intrigue, cunning, lethargy, suspicion, irrationality, depravity, childishness' (pp. 38–40), 'eccentricity, backwardness, indifference, feminine penetrability, and supine malleability' (p. 206). Using these and similar other tropes, the discourse of Orientalism constructed an elaborate architecture of hierarchical dichotomies (see Table 5.1 for a list of some of these binaries) by means of which the Occident, that is the West, was conceptually maneuvered into a position of ontological superiority

TABLE 5.1   *The Hierarchical System of Colonialist Binaries*

West	Non-West
Active	Passive
Center	Margin/periphery
Civilized	Primitive/savage
Colonizer	Colonized
Developed	Backward/undeveloped/underdeveloped/developing
Fullness/plenitude/completeness	Lack/inadequacy/incompleteness
Historical (people with history)	Ahistorical (people without history)
The liberated	The savable
Masculine	Feminine/effeminate
Modern	Archaic
Nation	Tribe
Occidental	Oriental
Scientific	Superstitious
Secular	Non-secular
Subject	Object
Superior	Inferior
The vanguard	The led
White	Black/brown/yellow

Source: Prasad, 1997b: 291

over the Orient (or, by extension, over the entire non-West). Such an attribution of ontological superiority to the West – and of ontological inferiority to the non-West – implied that 'every [Western] writer on the Orient … saw the Orient [and the non-West] as a locale requiring Western attention, reconstruction, even redemption' (Said, 1978: 206) and, moreover, that Western colonialism came to be seen by many as a Western *moral obligation* 'designed to civilize, improve, and *help* those peoples who were 'lagging behind' in the March of History and Civilization' (Prasad, 2003b: 12; italics in the original).

Whereas Said (1978) focuses upon discursive aspects of colonialism and its ideology, the work of Nandy (e.g. 1983; 1987; 1995) primarily examines the psychology of colonialism. Nandy's emergence as a major theorist of colonialism was heralded by the publication of his important book, *The Intimate Enemy: Loss and Recovery of Self under Colonialism* (1983). Drawing, in part, on Mahatma Gandhi's cultural, ethical and political philosophy (Gandhi, 1927; 1928; 1938; see also Parekh, 1995), Nandy (1983) argues, among other things, that colonialism is psychologically destructive not only for the colonized, but even for the colonizers themselves. Hence, resistance to colonialism and its ideology becomes a project designed to save and liberate *both* the colonizers as well as the colonized. Nandy's writings, accordingly, are also concerned with developing an appropriate cultural strategy for resisting (neo-)colonialism.

In addition to Said and Nandy, Homi Bhabha and Gayatri Chakravorty Spivak represent two other renowned postcolonial theorists. Bhabha's (1994) contributions to postcolonial theory include celebrated elaborations of such important concepts as colonial ambivalence (which implies that colonial power is *necessarily* unstable, never hegemonic), and colonial mimicry and hybridity, which serve to undermine the colonizer's authority. Similarly, Spivak (1987; 1993; 1999) has greatly contributed to postcolonialism by scrutinizing the limits of First World liberal feminism, raising valuable questions of historiography, examining the usefulness of essentialism, and interrogating complex themes in philosophy, literature, history and culture. Other postcolonialist scholars have examined such important issues as the language and rhetoric of imperialism (Spurr, 1993), feminism (Lewis & Mills, 2003a; Mohanty, Russo & Torres, 1991), science (Prakash, 1999), nationalism (Chatterjee, 1986), history and historiography (Chakrabarty, 2000; Guha, 1997), cultural aspects of globalization (Appadurai, 1996), and so on.

Postcolonialism is useful to workplace diversity researchers because the colonial encounter significantly shaped Western perceptions of 'otherness' (e.g. other races, ethnicities, cultures, religions, etc.), perceptions that largely *continue to survive.* The continuation of colonialist perceptions can be seen, for instance, in somewhat widely held contemporary Western views of people of color (Cohen, 1998; Lipsitz, 1998), common Western stereotypes of social arrangements in Third World countries, the resurgence of anti-Muslim and anti-immigrant sentiments in several countries in Western Europe during recent years (Dawson, 2004; Jackson, 2002; Polakow-Suransky, 2002), and so on. Postcolonial theory is valuable also because colonialism profoundly influenced Western notions of sexuality and gender dynamics (Nandy, 1983; Stoler, 1997). In addition, postcolonial theory's analyses of social and cultural marginality are of great value to investigators of workplace diversity and multiculturalism, because the project of workplace diversity is linked to ameliorating the condition of those on the margins of the organization.

'EUROPE'/'THE WEST' AS THE NAME OF A PROBLEM

- Elizabeth I, Queen of England (1558–1603), seeks to deport 89 black African slaves because they 'threaten to overpopulate the land with their … *rampant sexuality*' (Dawson, 2004: 93; italics added).
- 'By the 1820s horrible things were happening in Tasmania. Sometimes the black people were hunted just for fun … Sometimes they were raped in passing, or abducted … We hear of children kidnapped as pets … woman chained up … men castrated … [White settlers] used to catch aborigines in man-traps, and use them for target practice' (Morris, 1973: 455–6).
- AD1876: 'I regret the death of the last Tasmanian aborigine, but I know that it is the result of a *fiat* that the black shall everywhere give place to the white' (Report in *The Hobart Mercury* on the death of Truganini, the last of the Tasmanian aborigines; quoted in Morris, 1973: 465; italics in the original).
- AD1876: Government of Canada Report: 'Our Indian legislation rests on the principle that aborigines are to be kept in a condition of tutelage and treated as wards or children of the state' (quoted in Neu, 2003: 201).
- AD1937: 'I do not admit … that a great wrong has been done to the Red Indians of America, or the black people of Australia. I do not admit that a wrong has been done to these people by the fact that a stronger race, a higher

grade race, a more worldly-wise race ... has come in and taken their place' (Winston Churchill, quoted in Ali, 2002: 92).

- AD1975: Australian Prime Minister Gough Whitlam during a conversation on Australian immigration policy: '[I am] not having hundreds of fucking Vietnamese ... coming into the country...' (quoted in Bowden, 2003: 48).

- The genitalia of Saartjie Baartman – the so-called 'Hottentot Venus' who died in 1815 – are on permanent display at the *Musée de l'Homme* in Paris (Gilman, 1985; Root, 1996).

- '[In Switzerland] more than one in five women is affected by physical or sexual violence in her lifetime ... In Spain, some 100 women are killed each year by abusive spouses or boyfriends and there are over 30,000 complaints of physical violence. In France, six women die each month at the hands of men who profess to love them ... In Britain ... one in every four women experiences domestic violence ... Strangely, the European press, which has devoted reams of paper—and rightly so—to [stories of female abuse] ... in Eastern Europe, Asia, Africa and Latin America, appears reluctant to speak out on the question of violence against women in its own backyard' (Naravane, 2004).[4]

- AD2001: Per Kaalund, Member of Denmark's Social Democratic Party: 'Denmark must not develop into a multicultural society' (quoted in Polakow-Suransky, 2002: 23).

- AD2001: Mogens Camre, Danish People's Party's representative to the European Parliament: 'All Western countries have been infiltrated by Muslims' (quoted in Polakow-Suransky, 2002: 22).

- AD2003: 'I knew my God was bigger than his [the Somali Muslim warlord's]. I knew my God was a real God and his was an idol' (US Lt. Gen. William Boykin, quoted in Prashad, 2004).

- 'Take up the White Man's burden – Send forth the best ye breed' (Rudyard Kipling, 1899).

Before fleshing out the notion of 'Europe'/'the West' as the name of a problem, it is worthwhile pointing out that, following a general postcolonial theoretic practice, this chapter uses the terms 'Europe' and 'the West' somewhat interchangeably. In the interest of avoiding some unnecessary confusion, it is important that we keep this terminological practice in mind. Wherever the chapter might deviate from this terminological practice, the different meanings of the two expressions will be fairly obvious. It is important to note also that, once again in keeping with a common practice in postcolonial theory, 'Europe' functions in this chapter as a *hyperreal* term, that is 'as a figure of the imaginary' (Chakrabarty, 1992: 1) with 'somewhat indeterminate geographical referents'. In other words, as employed in this chapter, the term 'Europe' should not be seen as 'neatly corresponding to ... a particular "race," ... or a particular geographical region' (Prasad, 1997a: 93). In addition, it might be helpful to keep in mind that, in Chakrabarty's (1992) usage, the word 'hyperreal' – borrowed from Baudrillard (1983) – holds a different meaning than the one employed by Baudrillard himself. Furthermore, while this chapter's use of sweepingly monolithic and homogeneous terms like 'Europe' or 'the West' might appear objectionable to some, postcolonialism insists on the continued *usefulness* of such terms because of their enduring material and symbolic significance, and because, frequently, the West has indeed 'spoken with one voice' (Radhakrishnan, 1996: 178, n.3; see also Chakrabarty, 1992; Prasad, 2003b: 34, n.5, etc.).

Notwithstanding the preceding caveats, however, to preface an analysis of 'Europe'/'the West' with a brief catalogue of some disturbing, violent[5] or xenophobic episodes from the West's past and present history might appear 'unfair' to some. To those readers, we would like to offer an assurance somewhat along the following lines. Our interest here is neither in narrowly exposing what some may see as the Grand Errors and Illusions of European/Western culture, nor in arguing that violence and xenophobia of the kind catalogued above offer a totalizing understanding of some *essentialized* European culture. Nor is the chapter interested in making the case, as Root (1996) seems to have done with great force and felicity, that 'the *critical mass* of histories, languages, and aesthetic and intellectual traditions that make up Western culture is *sick and predatory*' (pp. 201–2; italics added). And, needless to add, neither is the chapter seeking to argue that the West is the sole repository or source of all evils in the world.[6] In sum, it is *not* our objective here to adopt a prosecutorial stance and add up accusations.

The goal of the present exercise is altogether different. In brief, the preceding catalogue of the West's violence/xenophobia is intended to remind ourselves not only that the colonial/neo-colonial experience forms an integral part of Europe's history, but also that the violence and xenophobia that deeply inform varied aspects of Western colonialism – and of Western modernity (Bauman, 1989),[7] a historical phenomenon that grew and took shape in tandem with the European colonization of the globe – are not mere *aberrations* in an otherwise untarnished history, but are *constitutive* of the modern Western colonial project (Césaire, 1972; Davies, Nandy & Sardar, 1993; Dawson, 2004), and may be seen as having played a significant role in discursively producing[8] something approaching a grammar of action for the West's encounters with its Others. Our exercise, therefore, is symptomatic not merely of a pressing intellectual need to deny Europe the luxury of what Radhakrishnan (1996) calls 'a state of countermnemonic innocence' (p. 156) – which allows the West to 'freely and unilaterally (choose) what to remember and what not to remember from the pages of history' (p. 156) – but, more importantly, also of a scholarly recognition that (1) developing a sophisticated understanding of Western colonialism (and its continuation as neo-colonialism) is crucial to the task of generating new and productive insights about Europe's deeply fraught encounters – past as well as present – with its Others (racial, cultural, religious, epistemological, and so forth), and (2) that such insights have an indispensable role to play in adding important layers to our understanding of the enormously complex dynamics of diversity and multiculturalism in contemporary Western organizations.

The Idea of Europe

Recent postcolonial theoretic scholarship (e.g. Gandhi, 1998; Loomba, 1998; Young, 2001) has emphasized that the project of modern Western colonialism and neo-colonialism may be seen as manifesting a complex admixture of 'commercial ... financial [and geopolitical] interests, (religious) ideology and belief, military force and political cunning, and ... unimaginable violence and cruelty' (Prasad, 2003b: 4). Deeply enmeshed in it all – and lending, to the (neo-)colonial project, great ideological force, fervor, stability and grounding – lies something that may possibly be called the 'Idea of Europe' (Prasad, 1997a; see also Conrad, 1988: 10).

In a nutshell, the Idea of Europe refers to a broad set of notions that seek to lend 'Europe' coherence as a superior cultural entity. The Idea of Europe crucially anchors the project of modern Western (neo-)colonialism, and may be seen as gesturing toward a highly complex 'constellation of ideas, beliefs, values, images, desires, [variegated and shifting] discursive ensembles, and so forth' (Prasad, 1997a: 93). Considerations of space prevent us from undertaking a comprehensive analysis of the same within the confines of the present chapter.[9] Briefly stated, however, one of the key elements of the Idea of Europe would appear to be the claim that modern Europe represents the teleological endpoint of world history (cf. Prasad, 1997a; Shohat & Stam, 1994). Embedded in this claim is a progressivist view of *stages* of world history, according to which Europe is seen, for a variety of reasons, as the primary motor of history, and as being the first – the leader – to enter the modern era (or stage) of world history. From such an audaciously vanguardist view of Europe, the world is conceptually rearranged in a hierarchy of civilizations, with Europe occupying the very top of this hierarchy, and the remaining civilizations of the world – categorized as backward (or undeveloped/underdeveloped/developing) – are seen as still being in the *childhood* of humanity and, hence, as being comprehensively inferior to the *mature/adult* modern Europe in terms of cultural, intellectual, epistemological, religious, moral, ethical, political, economic, aesthetic, and other attributes.

Following from the preceding notions, modern colonialism has frequently come to be viewed as an instrument of Europe's *civilizing mission* – the 'White Man's Burden', in Kipling's memorable words – which imposes upon Europe a *moral obligation* to conquer and, thereby, civilize the non-West. In terms of the ideology of colonialism, therefore, the moral obligation of the civilizing mission demands that Europe drag the immature non-West – willingly or unwillingly – into modern history. It needs to be emphasized here that, according to the ideology of colonialism: (1) since the non-West is an immature child, it is often unable to recognize that such modernization is in the non-West's own supreme interest, and (2) because it is a child, the non-West is also incapable of implementing the universally desirable project of modernization on its own, that is *without* Western help and supervision. Therefore, it becomes a duty of the West (which is always already free, civilized, rational, modern, developed and liberated) not to 'grudge to [the non-West] ... an equal measure of freedom and civilization' (Lord Thomas Babington Macaulay, nineteenth-century British parliamentarian, colonial administrator and man of letters, quoted in Gandhi, 1998: 33), to use all necessary means (including force, coercion, conquest and violence, as needed) to *educate* the non-West about the virtues of modernization, and 'do the great work to which

... [the West has] been called: cultivate, enlighten and ennoble the human race' (Christopher Wieland, quoted in Gandhi, 1998: 33) and, in so doing, fulfill the promise held out to the entire world by Western humanism. As discussed by post-colonial critics of the modern paradigm of economic development, the organizational consequences of the civilizing mission can be seen in a range of global institutions (e.g. the World Bank, IMF, WTO, etc.), and the ruthless economic policies often imposed by them on many countries in the 'developing' world in the name of helping those countries modernize themselves (Alvares, 1992; Escobar, 1994).

From the preceding ideological perspective, however, Western (neo-)colonialism comes to be viewed as a selfless and disinterested project designed to confer on the non-West what the latter deserves as a *right*, and the West itself assumes the form of an instrument of providence. In such a narrative, the awesome violence of (neo-)colonialism is sometimes lamented, but such violence is generally seen in the nature of being an inevitable and unfortunate part of the overall project to *liberate* the world.[10] It is precisely an ideological narrative of this kind which may be seen as partly sustaining such a situation of terrible irony and paradox as, for instance, the general of a Western imperial army of occupation in Iraq claiming the mantle of a *liberator* even as the same army also drops large quantities of aerial bombs on the country it is occupying.[11] We continue to witness this kind of ideology in situations like the construction of the Exxon-Mobil Chad – Cameroon oil pipeline, where the destruction of the Aboriginal way of life is justified on the grounds of modernizing and liberating these two countries.

As suggested earlier, one of the necessary conceptual maneuvers – required in the attempt to produce certainty about the assumption of Western moral superiority – involved the construction of a seemingly fixed and impermeable boundary between the West and the non-West, a boundary frequently seen as being almost a product of nature. Related to this, colonialist ideology was further elaborated by such means, among others, as the construction of scientific theories of race and racial difference/hierarchy, cultural and legal prohibitions against 'miscegenation', valorization of hyper-masculinity as the source of imperial power and the attendant denigration of women/femininity (Nandy, 1983), repeated scientific and cultural representations of 'non-Europeans, especially women ... as libidinally excessive and sexually uncontrolled' (Loomba, 1998: 154–5), development of notions of 'deviant' sexualities and the idea of organic links between foreign lands and sexual deviance/excess (Gilman, 1985; Loomba, 1998; Young, 1995), and scientific consolidation of 'equivalencies ... between women, blacks, the lower classes, animals, madness and homosexuality' (Loomba, 1998: 160).

It is important to recognize here that these and related ideas, images, classifications and hierarchies came to be materially grounded, over centuries, in large networks of continually evolving institutions and cultural practices (e.g. law courts and legal systems, medical and health care practices, university departments, learned societies, educational curricula, museums, music and art, theater, colonial administration and tourism, journalism, organization of various sports on playgrounds in schools and universities, etc.). Simultaneously, these ideas and images took on the form of something akin to a *common sense* for the West and, hence, held enormous significance for the *identities* of Western individuals. A point that needs to be emphasized here, therefore, is that postcolonial theory is concerned with understanding such pejorative ideas and images not merely as the prejudice of the ignorant, but at the level of how prestigious and important institutions were (and often continue to be) routinely engaged in (re)producing them.

The significance of those ideas and images for individual identity, however, implied that the West became deeply invested in *defending* colonialism not only because of the economic and political benefits that colonialism brought, but also because of colonialism's important role at the level of the psyche. Here one needs to recognize also that, notwithstanding the formal demise of Western colonialism, and despite formal and informal efforts (in some Western countries) to promote diversity and multiculturalism, several of the ideas and images mentioned above continue to survive, often in new and troubling ways,[12] and continue to play important roles in the identities of individuals in the West (cf. Cohen, 1998; Gunew, 2004; Prasad, 1997b; Prasad & Prasad, 2002a). Hence, what postcolonial theory would suggest is that continued systematic discrimination (for instance, systematic discrimination directed against African Americans and other minorities in the United States, or against non-white immigrants in the countries of Western Europe) may offer not only material, political and economic pay-offs for dominant white groups in those countries, but also a psychological pay-off by way of safeguarding the concerned white individuals' sense of who they are (cf. Huntington, 2004; Lipsitz, 1998).

Postcolonial scholarship has noted that resistance to modern colonialism and its ideology is as old as European colonialism itself. Hence, it will be a mistake to believe that the Idea of Europe was ever fully and resplendently hegemonic (cf. Gramsci, 1971), or that it was not vigorously interrogated by those who opposed colonialism. Indeed, the history of colonialism and neo-colonialism teems with serious controversies and debates, many of which continue to the present day. Among such continuing debates, mention may be made, for instance, of the long-standing controversy around Christopher Columbus and its recent manifestation in the controversy over the 'celebration' of the Columbus Quincentennial in 1992 (cf. Shohat & Stam, 1994: 61ff.), the debate over the wearing of veil by many Muslim women in a number of societies around the world (cf. Lewis & Mills, 2003a), the comparatively recent debate over the so-called 'Western Canon' (cf. Bloom, 1994; Hirsch, 1987) and, perhaps the most vexing of them all, the controversy surrounding female 'circumcision' (Lionnet, 2003; Shweder, 2002). All these debates raise challenging questions for the Idea of Europe, create serious doubts about its attempts to 'naturalize' (and thereby legitimate) asymmetries of power across cultures and peoples and, in so doing, repeatedly bring it to crisis. Hence, revisiting these and similar other debates may be instructive for management scholars interested in understanding the complex challenges that invest issues of workplace diversity and multiculturalism. For reasons of space, however, it will not be possible here to look at more than one of the debates mentioned above. In what follows, we will briefly explore the controversy over African female 'circumcision', a cultural practice that is seen by many in the West as belonging to 'the list of *absolute evils*, along with ... the Holocaust, rape, lynching, and slavery' (Shweder, 2002: 219; italics added), and as a 'limit case' for the current discourse of diversity and multiculturalism (Lewis & Mills, 2003b: 12).

'Absolute Evil' in the 'Dark Continent'

We propose to use the term female genital alteration (FGA) to refer to that fairly widespread cultural practice (followed among African women in Africa, Europe and the United States) which, in the West, is often labeled as 'female genital *mutilation*' (Lionnet, 2003; Shweder, 2002). This terminological choice is mostly based on a scholarly concern that the word 'mutilation' seems to pre-judge the issue without due consideration. It is important to note, moreover, that the discussion that follows is primarily intended to examine the ideological scene of the controversy surrounding FGA, rather than to endorse or oppose FGA as a cultural practice. In part, we have chosen to focus upon the FGA controversy because it brings into sharp focus, at a somewhat paradigmatic level, important aspects of the West's engagement with 'otherness'. Any decision to support or oppose FGA, however, involves larger issues of morality and ethical responsibility (Miller, 1987; Nandy, 1995; Prasad & Prasad, 2003) that go beyond facile debates sometimes revolving around the notion of 'cultural relativism', and are too complex to be adequately addressed here.

In actual practice, FGA – generally understood as a 'coming-of-age and gender-identity ceremony' (Shweder, 2002: 223) – seems to exhibit considerable *heterogeneity*. Depending upon the ethnic and/or cultural context, different groups may hold the ceremony either at birth itself, or at any other time during teenage years (or sometimes even later). Similarly, the actual alteration of female genitalia may involve anything from a cut in the clitoral prepuce, to surgical removal of visible parts of the clitoris and external labia, to stitching of the opening of the vagina with a view to 'enhancing fertility, tightening the vaginal opening, and protecting the womb' (Shweder, 2002: 224). FGA is widely practiced in a number of countries, including Egypt, Ethiopia, Gambia, Mali, Sierra Leone, Somalia and Sudan, with prevalence rates ranging from 80% to 98%. In certain other countries (e.g. Ghana, Ivory Coast and Kenya), FGA is practiced only in specific regions (or by specific ethnic groups), but not all across the country. The practice does not seem to be prevalent in southern sections of Africa. Those African cultures that practice FGA consider this ceremony essential for the 'psychological, social, spiritual, and physical well-being' of women (Shweder, 2002: 218). FGA is seen in these cultures as making women 'more beautiful, more feminine, more civilized, and more honorable' (Shweder, 2002: 224). African cultures practicing FGA also commonly engage in male circumcision and, in these cultures, it would be virtually impossible for an uncircumcised male (or a woman who has not undergone FGA) to get married or find a sexual partner.

In the West, the African cultural practice of FGA has long been viewed as a dark, brutal, barbaric and primitive practice that maims, mutilates, disfigures and often kills women, and deprives them of their capacity for sexual response, enjoyment and fulfillment. The West has viewed FGA also as a particularly cruel example of how 'traditional' cultures may frequently exercise patriarchal domination by inflicting pain and controlling women's sexuality. As early as the 1920s, FGA was opposed by Western Christian missionaries, who seem to have seen the practice as truly representing the *essence* of Africa, the '*Dark Continent*'. Paralleling the efforts of the missionaries, several Western governments also sought to abolish what they regarded as a barbarous custom.

Interestingly, such Western opposition to FGA may be seen as being somewhat consistent with (and/or having conceptual overlaps with) instances of late nineteenth-century and earlier opposition to Jewish male circumcision (Gilman, 1999, cited in Shweder, 2002: 240). However, while opposition to various forms of male circumcision seems almost to have vanished from the cultural landscape of the contemporary West,[13] recent years appear to have witnessed a renewed strengthening of the Western campaign against African FGA. For instance, laws targeting FGA were passed in France in 1981 and in the United States in 1996, and courts in France have already handed down prison sentences under the new French law (Lionnet, 2003; Shweder, 2002).

Governments in the West tend to regard FGA as physical and sexual abuse of the women concerned, and as a violation of the human rights of these women. Western governments have expressed a desire to save and liberate these women by working toward eradicating what they view as a tyrannical and barbaric cultural practice. Toward these ends, the US government, for example, has established a policy of opposing international loans to those African governments that do not have official programs to abolish FGA. The Western campaign to eradicate FGA has also been supported by well-known organizations like WHO, UNICEF and Amnesty International. Although a number of factors (including geopolitical considerations) may be said to account for the renewed Western campaign against FGA, we are particularly interested in exploring the ideological scene of this campaign.

Before proceeding further, however, it may be interesting to note that recent critical research has shown the claims of the anti-FGA crusade to have been highly exaggerated. Based on this new stream of research, Shweder (2002) has pointed out that 'the widely publicized medical complications of African ... [FGA] are the exception, not the rule' (p. 219), that FGA does not deprive women of the capacity for sexual response/enjoyment, and women who undergo FGA 'continue to be orgasmic' (p. 221), and that 'alarmist claims' about FGA resulting in deaths of 'untold numbers of women and girls' appear untrue (p. 228). There are indeed instances in which FGA may result in medical complications. However, Shweder offers the argument that, just as a more reasonable reaction to unsafe abortions is to make abortions safe (rather than to abolish or criminalize abortions), in the case of unsafe FGA also an appropriate response can be to make FGA safe and reduce medical complications (2002: 229). That, however, is not what the Western campaign against FGA desires; the stated goal of this campaign is to completely eradicate FGA from the world.

Postcolonial critics (e.g. Loomba, 1998; Spivak, 1999) have noted that Western colonialism often justified itself by declaring that one aspect of colonialism's 'civilizing mission' involved the important project of saving/liberating/ rescuing non-Western *women* from the patriarchal oppression and domination of 'native' societies and cultures. Gayatri Spivak has sought to capture the complexity of this colonialist dynamic by way of formulating a sentence of the form: 'White men are saving dark women from dark men', or sometimes as 'White men *and* white women are saving dark women from dark men' (see. e.g. Spivak, 1999: 284 ff.). Embedded in such a dynamic, one may discern a number of ideological claims, including: (1) 'we' in the West are civilized, 'they' in the non-West are not; (2) 'we' are liberated, 'they' are not; (3) 'we' are active subjects of global history, 'they' are passive victims of 'traditional'/'tribal' cultures and/or of 'false consciousness', (4) women – being the weaker sex as a result of nature's design – need to be protected; (5) 'we' are a civilized society, and since 'we' are superior (morally, economically, militarily, etc.) it becomes our duty to protect and rescue 'their' helpless and powerless women who are *incapable* of defending themselves;[14] (6) 'we' are a civilized society not because we protect only 'our' own women, but because 'we' protect women all over the globe, and so forth. In this regard, Spivak, for instance, has noted that for the ideology of colonialism (or neo-colonialism), 'the protection of women (today the "third-world-woman") becomes a signifier for the establishment of a *good* society (now a good planet)' (1999: 288; italics in the original).

These and similar other ideological claims embedded in colonial discourse serve not only to reaffirm a starkly dichotomous view of 'us' ('good'/'developed') and 'them' ('evil'/'backward'), but they also ongoingly (re)produce and reinforce an all-important sense of Western civility, privilege and superiority, which can only be constructed in opposition to a non-West that must take its dutiful place as 'an area of darkness' (Naipaul, 1964). Hence, these ideological claims play a very important part in the formation of Western identities. It would appear, moreover, that such a sense of Western privilege and superiority is crucially linked – both as a cause as well as an effect – to what one may call a cultural grammar that seems to heavily lean toward producing quick judgments (with almost absolute certainty) on complex issues (such as FGA) relating to 'other' cultures.

The idea of the West's superiority – operating discursively with several other elements, including the kind of proclivity toward certainty mentioned above, a relatively unquestioned acceptance of the naturalness and stability of socially constructed categories/binaries (see Table 5.1), and a narcissism that seeks to convert the 'heathens' and remake them in the West's own image – seemingly prepares the ideological ground for a crusading world view, a world view that can survive only in and through prolonged and ongoing access to sites of 'rescue'/'redemption', and 'helpless' victims. Such sites of rescue and 'helping' (Gronemeyer, 1992) appear essential for safeguarding/defending the crusading world view, and the superior Western identity associated (as both cause and effect) with this world view, as also the power that such an identity confers on the West (and on Western individuals). It is not really surprising, therefore, to find that the *New York Times* seizes upon

FGA as 'a dream for Americans, *worthy* of their country …. the dream … that the US could bring about the end of a system of *torture* that has *crippled* 100 million people now living upon this earth … [in] *suffering, deprivation and disease*' (Rosenthal, 1995, quoted in Shweder, 2002: 220; italics added). FGA would appear to be a dream because, among other things, it is unlikely to be completely eradicated anytime soon and, therefore, it can keep alive the crusading world view (and the civilizing mission) for a long time.

Such a crusading stance, however, can be developed and maintained only by ignoring troubling questions about the givenness and/or universal validity and desirability of one's own cultural paradigm. Shweder (2002) suggests, for instance, that the anti-FGA crusade in the West can function only by learning not to question the validity and/or desirability of such Western cultural beliefs and practices as male circumcision, cosmetic surgery including the American Medical Association-approved 'clitoridectomies for young women who don't like the way their genitals look or feel' (p. 231), the valorization of the clitoris as 'the biological essence of femininity' (p. 233), and so on. Such a crusade, moreover, also requires that a highly complex and heterogeneous cultural practice like 'African' FGA be homogenized in representation and, thus, be simplistically reduced to a monolithic caricature of itself.

The complex dynamic adumbrated above, however, would also seem to imply that if, for whatever reason, the certainty associated with a 'cause' (or Western project of 'redemption') comes to be doubted or questioned, new causes – other sites for 'rescuing the helpless', 'saving the heathen' or 'improving the state of the downtrodden' – must necessarily be found (i.e. *discursively produced*, using all necessary means including military and economic power), because any prolonged interruption of the said dynamic would lead to a renegotiation of Western identity (with its embedded idea of superiority) and, hence, to that realignment or rearrangement of existing *relations of power* which invariably accompanies (re)negotiations of identity (cf. Bhabha, 1994; Prakash, 1999). In sum, what would seem to be suggested by the dynamic outlined above is a pressing need for the West to ensure relatively uninterrupted access to new and/or old 'causes', 'victims', and so on, otherwise the West's very identity may come under severe pressure and strain. The next section of the chapter briefly explores how the foregoing insights of postcolonial theory might be helpful in producing a deeper appreciation of the complexities of workplace diversity and multiculturalism.

POSTCOLONIAL THEORY AND WORKPLACE DIVERSITY

The preceding postcolonial theoretic analysis seeks to adumbrate an intricately articulated configuration (of power, identity, and material and symbolic interests and outcomes), the preservation of which may seem to crucially hinge upon preserving the *system of hierarchical binaries* discussed earlier. Arguably, therefore, it would be in the interest of those dominant sections of society that benefit from such a configuration (i.e. mostly the white privileged groups) to work toward preserving the said system of binaries. As suggested earlier, one way of preserving this system of binaries is to ensure *continued* access to groups of people (e.g. cultures, subcultures, etc.) that may be seen as being in *need* of help. For researchers of workplace diversity, however, this implies that the various organizational initiatives for promoting diversity and multiculturalism may sometimes need to be viewed in a somewhat new light.

It needs to be made clear, at this stage, that the following critique of workplace diversity initiatives does not imply that those initiatives have no value, or that we should eliminate such initiatives altogether. Over the past several years, these initiatives have indeed resulted in some gains for minority groups. Rather than fully rejecting workplace diversity programs, therefore, our critique is intended to alert management scholars and practitioners to the existence of multiple layers of complexity in which such programs are usually embedded, and to offer some ideas that might be useful in future discussions concerned with designing more effective diversity programs.

Conventionally, workplace diversity initiatives often tend to be viewed as organizational reform projects that would *empower* marginalized groups, and bring them to a position of equality with the white privileged groups. Taken to its logical conclusion, this view seems to suggest that, in due course, a series of successful diversity initiatives would result in organizational landscapes devoid of marginalized groups in *need* of further help and empowerment. In other words, this view seemingly argues that diversity initiatives are designed to put the marginalized groups on the same footing as the white privileged groups. However, what needs to be emphasized here is that, if such an outcome were to be actually achieved, the white privileged groups would lose further access to groups needing help, with somewhat obvious consequences for the all-important system of binaries. Hence, it would appear to be in the interest of the white privileged groups that diversity initiatives designed to help the marginalized groups be also *designed*, wittingly or unwittingly, to fail (and/or to discursively produce 'new' marginal groups in continuing *need* of help) and, in so doing, leave the hierarchical force of the said system of binaries relatively intact. Moreover, white privileged groups might also develop a conscious or unconscious investment in creating accounts that seek to explain failed diversity initiatives in terms of – at least to some degree – genetic, or cultural, or other supposed shortcomings of marginalized groups, in part because such accounts would work to further reinforce the system of binaries.[15] As a corollary to this, we might also expect that, in general, diversity initiatives would be unlikely to include elements that could seriously disturb the stability of the binaries in question. All this suggests at least two things for diversity researchers. First, when examining *failed* diversity initiatives, researchers may need to investigate such failures not merely in terms of mistakes related to the implementation of those initiatives, but also in terms of how the very design of such initiatives might include elements that *ensure* the failure of specific initiatives. Second, any examination of the potential *value* of specific diversity initiatives may also need to include an assessment of the degree to which such initiatives destabilize the binaries under consideration.

Postcolonial theory has frequently drawn attention to the ambivalence of colonial discourse (Bhabha, 1994). For instance, although colonial discourse considered the non-West to be weak and inferior, the same discourse also portrayed the non-West as a powerful threat that could destroy the entire Western world. Similarly, while colonialism found its moral fervor in the mission to civilize the (non-Western) savages, colonial discourse also saw savagery as an immutable biological condition that could never be changed. Or, in the contemporary context of the increasing 'Latinization' of the United States (briefly discussed later in this chapter), the Latin people are seen by (neo-)colonial discourse as being weak, lazy and shiftless but, *at the same time*, also as capable of swamping the Anglo culture of America and sapping its cultural strength (cf. P. Prasad, 2003). Colonial (or neo-colonial) discourse, in other words, is marked by a deep sense of schizophrenia. Past management research has noted that the complexity of workplace diversity issues is traceable, in part, to the continuing imprint of such colonialist schizophrenia (Prasad, 1997b; Prasad & Prasad, 2002a). Future research needs to examine the theory and practice of workplace diversity from scholarly perspectives that may adequately critique such colonialist imprints.

The ambivalence of colonial discourse also implied that the much needed system of binaries faced *constant* pressures and strains, and could never achieve a position of complete, final and hegemonic consolidation. Hence, preserving the binaries required ongoing discursive 'repair and maintenance' work. Bhabha seems to see the incessant repetitions of colonialist stereotypes – for example, the 'duplicity of the Asiatic or the bestial sexual license of the African' (1994: 66) – in the light of such unending need for discursive repair and maintenance. In the context of workplace diversity, the implicit and/or explicit use of cultural or other stereotypes (e.g. Asians as 'techies' incapable of corporate leadership) may need to be viewed in a similar vein.

The ambivalence of (neo-)colonial discourse may be seen as getting further aggravated as a result of certain ongoing, large-scale global developments, including significant population movements, declining birth rates in several Western countries, and the persistent shift *away* from the West of the world's political and economic center of gravity (Huntington, 1996; Wilson & Purushothaman, 2003). As a result, the system of binaries seems to be coming under increased pressure and strain and, hence, there may be a greater need for activities aimed at safeguarding the binaries. Given that workplace diversity initiatives may also serve as instruments for maintaining the binaries, there exists a possibility, under certain conditions, that these dynamics could lead to such paradoxical results as an increase in the number of diversity initiatives (or a greater pressure toward such an increase) and/or a greater investment on the part of white privileged groups in ensuring, consciously or unconsciously, the failure of those initiatives.

In addition to the foregoing, attention needs to be drawn also toward certain other developments that may introduce further complexities in the dynamics of workplace diversity. In brief, we would like to note four such developments:

namely, (1) increasing 'white backlash,' (2) the 'Latinization' of American society, (3) possible tensions at the intersection of race and gender, and (4) the struggle over 'soft power' (and not only over 'hard power') between dominant and marginalized groups (Prasad, 2004). These developments incorporate extremely intricate and complicated dynamics stretching across a range of elements, including race, ethnicity, gender, culture, power and identity. These developments are also likely to significantly alter the terrain on which issues of workplace diversity, multiculturalism, marginality and inclusion are currently negotiated between white privileged groups and others.

Past management research has stressed the importance of effectively dealing with the white backlash against organizational efforts aimed at promoting diversity within a North American context (Prasad & Mills, 1997). Since then, however, through a series of organized political, legal and intellectual efforts, the white backlash has assumed a much greater degree of institutional consolidation in the United States (Cokorinos, 2003). Moreover, the white backlash has become a significant social and political force in several Western European countries (Meyerson, 2002). This intensifying white backlash of transatlantic proportions may create fresh obstacles for those interested in promoting workplace diversity and multiculturalism.

On the other hand, the increasing 'Latinization' of the United States – in many ways a direct product of the expansion and consolidation of the American Empire (Gonzalez, 2000) – is expected to lead to a radical transformation of US society and culture. Hispanics, who formed only 5% of the US population in 1970, now constitute more than 13% of the country, and are expected to represent fully one-third of the US population by the end of this century (Ramos, 2004: xvii). In this process, while the United States moves further away from such celebrated ideas of the past as cultural assimilation and the nation as a monolingual community, new and difficult questions about the meaning and significance of workplace diversity, multiculturalism and the idea of 'inclusion' will be raised.

We may also expect new tensions to arise at the intersection of race and gender. Postcolonial theory has often critiqued white middle-class liberal feminism for, among other things, its complicity with reproducing the axiomatics of colonialism (Spivak, 1999), evacuating race from the category of gender, and claiming to represent – indeed to *lead*[16] – a global sorority's common and universal campaign against patriarchy (cf. Lewis & Mills, 2003a). Postcolonialism, in sum, is skeptical of white liberal feminism's claim that its interests are *fully* in common with those of all women, irrespective of race, ethnicity, and so on. Similarly, white liberal feminism's claims of representing a common interest come under some strain when confronted with, for instance, US statistics showing that Hispanic and African American women's earnings are, respectively, only 71% and 87% of white women's, or that official unemployment rates for African American women (9.2%) and Hispanic women (7.8%) are far worse than the 4.4% unemployment among white women (Kramer, 2005: 135). Somewhat similar differences with respect to earnings and unemployment can be found to prevail between white and non-white women in several Western European countries as well. These and other differences in the experiences and life chances of white and non-white women may add new tensions to workplace diversity dynamics.

Finally, we come to the matter of the so-called 'soft power.'[17] Consider, for instance, the following observations reported from two different work sites. An English-speaking white professional woman in the United States rebukes two Latina colleagues for, what she calls, 'unprofessional and exclusionary' behavior because – *after* the conclusion of a professional meeting, attended by several people, and conducted in the English language – the two Latinas use Spanish to make small talk between themselves. In Europe, during a professional dinner gathering of an international group of academics, a white male professor of Scandinavian ancestry uses several colonialist binaries (Table 5.1) to build a case in favor of the notion of 'hierarchy of cultures' and, upon being challenged by a non-white male professor regarding the questionable nature of such binaries, accuses the latter of not being familiar with the etiquette of polite dinner conversation, and brings the entire discussion to a dead stop.

One would be justified, of course, in viewing these incidents as instances of uncultured behavior on the part of the offending white individuals. However, it is useful to view these incidents also as attempts to mobilize and draw upon 'soft power'. Simplifying somewhat, soft power may provisionally be conceptualized as the symbolic power that flows from a relatively taken-for-granted and largely unquestioned understanding of what constitutes legitimate, appropriate or allowable behavior for different sets of people in specific cultural contexts (e.g. professional meeting in the United States, professional dinner-table talk in certain parts of Europe, etc.). From this perspective, soft power would often be mobilized in situations – including situations involving micro dynamics at the personal or group levels – where the system of colonialist binaries may be facing pressure and stress, with a view to defending not only the binaries alone, but also the individual identities that might have been formed through relying upon such binaries. Soft power has close links with 'hard power' (e.g. the power to control resource allocation in organizations) and identity. Hence, in view of the ongoing large-scale changes (including demographic ones) mentioned above, we may expect 'soft power' to become an increasingly contested matter. A result would be new complications on the workplace diversity front.

As this chapter has continually emphasized, issues of workplace diversity are closely tied with considerations of power. Postcolonial theory reminds us that power and power relations in contemporary organizations in the West have an intimate link with a hierarchical system of binaries discursively produced in the course of Western (neo-)colonial domination. In a somewhat fundamental sense, therefore, promoting genuine workplace diversity involves efforts aimed at destabilizing and subverting those binaries. However, since the power and identity of the white privileged groups (and, in important ways, the identity of white groups *in general*) are deeply implicated in this system of binaries, workplace diversity efforts frequently face strong opposition from such groups.

In the context of the project of creating a genuinely diverse and multicultural workplace, the above seems to suggest at least two things. First, since there does not appear to be sufficient reason to assume that the dominant groups are likely to willingly relinquish their structural positions of privilege, it may be somewhat naive to rely only on the goodwill of such groups for achieving a truly diverse workplace. And second, in some ways related to this, although attempts to *educate* the white (dominant) groups about the need to promote workplace diversity are undoubtedly important, postcolonial theoretic analyses of power and pedagogical efforts (e.g. Colla, 2003) sometimes also caution us against placing too much faith in the efficacy of education alone (including, for instance, corporate training and development programs) for making significant progress on the workplace diversity front. It may be useful, on the other hand, to view the terrain of workplace diversity as a discursive site of *resistance*, where the marginalized oppose the dominant and contest asymmetries of power. This would imply, however, that scholars and practitioners interested in promoting workplace diversity need to become deeply familiar with the intricacies and nuances of workplace resistance (see e.g. Prasad & Prasad, 1998; 2003).

In conclusion, promoting genuine workplace diversity and multiculturalism is also about 'inclusion'. Inclusion, however, does not mean the kind of tolerance for the 'other' that Hage (1994) has rightly critiqued (see also, Cavanaugh, 1997; Mirchandani & Butler, this volume). Moreover, while adequate representation of minority groups at all hierarchical levels in organizations is *essential*, numerical representation alone is not the be all and end all of inclusion (cf. Prasad, 2001; 2004). For inclusion also implies persistent material and ideological efforts – within organizations and in the society at large – designed to interrogate, resist and subvert that discourse of 'otherness' that has long sought to consolidate an ontological hierarchy between 'Europe and its Others' (Barker et al., 1985). Viewed thus, achieving genuine workplace diversity and multiculturalism in the West becomes an indispensable vector of the overall postcolonial project of '(relegating) the hyperreal Europe to an obscure corner of the universal ... imagination' (Prasad, 1997a: 106); that is, of the critical project for 'Provincializing Europe' (Chakrabarty, 2000).

NOTES

1 Despite the passage of the Civil Rights Act (1964) in the United States, however, white males continue to occupy about 95% of top executive ranks in US organizations (Carr-Ruffino, 2002: 4), and the median income of African American families, in 2002, was only 58% of that of US white families (*Harper's Magazine*, April 2004: 13).

2 Note, however, that although John Stuart Mill championed liberty and representative government for the *white races*, for the dark races of the world he firmly advocated 'vigorous despotism' (1912: 408).

3 *Orientalism* (1978) belongs to a long tradition of anti-colonial criticism, which was carried on by freedom fighters and scholars over centuries. Hence, it will be a mistake to think of *Orientalism* as inaugurating anti-colonial criticism per se; rather it is the scholarly field known as postcolonial theory (or postcolonialism) that *Orientalism* may be seen as inaugurating.

4 Naravane (2004) relies, in part, on a March 2004 Amnesty International report dealing with violence against women. Excerpts quoted from Naravane (2004) appear over different sections of his article.

5 Such violence, as our catalogue might suggest, comes in many forms, including military, economic, cultural, epistemological, aesthetic, and so on. Nevertheless, it will be a mistake to underestimate the role of sheer physical violence carried out on an enormous scale (e.g. large-scale killings not only in colonial military campaigns but also in the course of actions undertaken to preserve 'law and order' in the colonies, torture and brutality, systematic genocide, etc.) in modern Western colonial domination.

6 Postcolonial theory points out that any intellectual approach that views the West as the source of *all* evils is unremittingly Eurocentric (see e.g. Shohat & Stam, 1994: 3).

7. Bauman (1989) has argued that the European Holocaust that exterminated some 20 million people (including 6 million Jews) needs to be seen as a product of the processes under-girding Western modernity. In other words, the Holocaust took place not, as some say, despite the civilizing forces (so-called) of modernity, but rather, it was Western modernity that provided a '*necessary* condition' for the Holocaust (Bauman, 1989: 13; italics in the original). 'Without … [Modernity]' observes Bauman (1989: 13), 'the Holocaust would be unthinkable'. See Césaire (1972) and Nandy (1983), among others, for discussions of links between the violence of the European Holocaust (and the world wars), and the violence of modern Western colonialism.

8 Somewhat paralleling Spivak (1999: 3, n.5), this chapter uses the expression 'discursive production' to 'mean something that is among the conditions as well as the effect of a general system of the formation and transformation of statements', it being clearly understood here that the term 'statement' is not to be simplistically reduced to language alone. In this connection, see, for instance, Young's (2001: 401–3) discussion of the notion of 'statement'.

9 The Idea of Europe, of course, did not appear out of nowhere on the European scene under consideration. Scholars like Hulme (1986: 84 ff.), Root (1996: 154 ff.), etc., have drawn attention to the elaboration and consolidation of a European ideological identity during a period broadly stretching from the eleventh to the fifteenth century. This ideological consolidation took place in concert with such important and long-drawn historical processes as the Crusades (e.g. Ali, 2002; Reston, 2001), intensification of anti-Semitism and large-scale Jewish pogroms all across Europe, the organized witch-hunts that are estimated to have killed anywhere from half a million to 1.2 million women branded as witches (Barstow, 1994; Karlsen, 1987; Klaits, 1987), the workings of the Holy Inquisition, etc., all of which greatly contributed toward the development of elaborate and complex ideas and beliefs about Europe's Others ('internal' as well as 'external'). Those ideas about 'Europe and its Others' (Barker et al., 1985) were further worked over and fine tuned, discursively, during the course of European colonial expansion. See, in this connection, Carroll (2001) for the long history of the consolidation of anti-Semitism in Europe, with 'history's first large-scale pogrom' having taken place as early as 414 AD (p. 213).

10 Witness, for instance, Marx's (1972: 582) unfortunate comments, in the context of the terrible atrocities of British colonial rule in India, that 'whatever may have been the crimes of England she was the unconscious tool of history'.

11 The imperial general in question is Sir Stanley Maude, Commander of British Occupation Forces in Baghdad, in the early parts of the twentieth century (*Harper's Magazine*, May 2003: 31). Iraq under British occupation was the first colonized country to be bombed by the Royal Air Force (Young, 2001: 293). Does history repeat itself, whether – somewhat modifying Karl Marx (1963: 15) – as tragedy or farce?

12 Thus, while examples of fairly straightforward continuation of colonialist racial ideology like *The Bell Curve* (Herrenstein & Murray, 1994) are not hard to find, it has been pointed out that, in many parts of Western Europe, increasingly it is the idea of cultural difference (and culture) that serves as a proxy for the discriminatory notion of race (Dawson, 2004: 84).

13 For instance, about 65% of male babies are circumcised in the United States (Shweder, 2002: 237).

14 By way of highlighting the colonialist trope of the 'helpless native woman', Loomba quotes an 1898 editorial comment (by a British feminist) which, after referring to Indian women as 'helpless, voiceless, [and] hopeless', ends by concluding that 'these pitiful Indian women ... have not even the small power of resistance which the Western woman may have' (1998: 171).

15 A book like *The Bell Curve* (Herrenstein & Murray, 1994) may be seen as belonging to this genre of explanations.

16 Spivak (1999), for instance, has chastised 'so-called US feminists' for their 'ferocious leadership complex' (p. 384, n. 97).

17 Our view of soft power may have some overlaps with, as well as differences from, the one developed by international relations scholars (e.g. Nye, 2004).

REFERENCES

Ali, T. (2002). *The clash of fundamentalisms.* London: Verso.

Alvares, C. (1992). *Science, development and violence.* Delhi: Oxford University Press.

Appadurai, A. (1996). *Modernity at large.* Minneapolis: University of Minnesota Press.

Ashcroft, B., Griffiths, G., & Tiffin, H. (Eds) (1995). *The post-colonial studies reader.* London: Routledge.

Barker, F., Hulme, P., Iversen, M., & Loxley, D. (Eds) (1985) *Europe and its others* (2 vols). Colchester: University of Essex.

Barstow, A. L. (1994). *Witchcraze: A new history of the European witch hunts.* London: Pandora.

Baudrillard, J. (1983). *Simulations.* New York: Semiotext(e).

Bauman, Z. (1989). *Modernity and the Holocaust.* Ithaca, NY: Cornell University Press.

Bhabha, H. K. (1994). *The location of culture.* London: Routledge.

Bloom, H. (1994). *The Western canon.* New York: Harcourt Brace.

Bowden, C. (2003). Outback nightmares and refugee dreams. *Mother Jones*, March–April, 47–53.

Carr-Ruffino, N. (2002). *Managing diversity* (4th edn). Boston: Pearson Custom Publishing.

Carroll, J. (2001). *Constantine's sword: The church and the Jews: A history.* Boston: Houghton Mifflin.

Cavanaugh, J. M. (1997). (In)corporating the other? Managing the politics of workplace difference. In P. Prasad, A. Mills, M. Elmes & A. Prasad (Eds), *Managing the organizational melting pot* (pp. 31–53). Thousand Oaks, CA: Sage.

Césaire, A. (1972). *Discourse on colonialism.* New York: Monthly Review Press (originally published in 1955).

Chakrabarty, D. (1992). Postcoloniality and the artifice of history: Who speaks for 'Indian' pasts? *Representations, 37* (Winter), 1–26.

Chakrabarty, D. (2000). *Provincializing Europe.* Princeton, NJ: Princeton University Press.

Chatterjee, P. (1986). *Nationalist thought and the colonial world.* London: Zed Books.

Cohen, M. N. (1998). *Culture of intolerance.* New Haven, CT: Yale University Press.

Cokorinos, L. (2003). *The assault on diversity.* Lanham, MD: Rowman & Littlefield.

Colla, E. (2003). Power, knowledge, and investment. *Postcolonial Studies, 6*(1), 113–21.

Conrad, J. (1988). *Heart of darkness.* New York: W. W. Norton (originally published in 1899).

Davies, M. W., Nandy, A., & Sardar, Z. (1993). *Barbaric others.* London: Pluto Press.

Dawson, A. (2004). 'To remember too much is indeed a form of madness': Caryl Phillips's *The Nature of Blood* and the modalities of European racism. *Postcolonial Studies*, *7*(1), 83–101.

Dick, P., & Cassell, C. (2002). Barriers to managing diversity in a UK constabulary. *Journal of Management Studies*, *39*(7), 953–76.

Escobar, A. (1994). *Encountering development.* Princeton, NJ: Princeton University Press.

Gandhi, L. (1998). *Postcolonial theory.* New York: Columbia University Press.

Gandhi, M. K. (1927). *An autobiography: Or the story of my experiments with Truth.* Ahmedabad: Navajivan Publishing House.

Gandhi, M. K. (1928). *Satyagraha in South Africa.* Ahmedabad: Navajivan Publishing House.

Gandhi, M. K. (1938). *Hind swaraj: Or Indian home rule.* Ahmedabad: Navajivan Publishing House.

Gilman, S. L. (1985). Black bodies, white bodies: Toward an iconography of female sexuality in late 19th century art, medicine and literature. In H. L. Gates, Jr (Ed.), *'Race', writing and difference* (pp. 223–61). Chicago: University of Chicago Press.

Gilman, S. L. (1999). 'Barbaric' rituals? In S. M. Okin (Ed.), *Is multiculturalism bad for women?* Princeton, NJ: Princeton University Press.

Goldberg, D. T., & Quayson, A. (Eds) (2002). *Relocating postcolonialism.* Oxford: Blackwell.

Gonzalez, J. (2000). *Harvest of empire: A history of Latinos in America.* New York: Viking.

Gramsci, A. (1971). *Selections from the Prison Notebooks.* London: Lawrence and Wishart.

Gronemeyer, M. (1992). Helping. In W. Sachs (Ed.), *The development dictionary: A guide to knowledge as power* (pp. 53–69). London: Zed Books.

Guha, R. (Ed.) (1997). *A subaltern studies reader.* Minneapolis: University of Minnesota Press.

Gunew, S. (2004). *Haunted nations: The colonial dimensions of multiculturalism.* London: Routledge.

Hage, G. (1994). Locating multiculturalism's other: A critique of practical tolerance. *New Formations*, *24*, 19–34.

Herrenstein, R., & Murray, C. (1994). *The bell curve: Intelligence and class structure in American life.* New York: Free Press.

Hirsch, E. D. (1987). *Cultural literacy.* Boston: Houghton Mifflin.

Hulme, P. (1986). *Colonial encounters.* London: Routledge.

Huntington, S. P. (1996). *The clash of civilizations and the remaking of world order.* New York: Simon & Schuster.

Huntington, S. P. (2004). *Who are we? The challenges to America's national identity.* New York: Simon & Schuster.

Jackson, P. (2002). Geographies of diversity and difference. *Geography*, *87*(4), 316–23.

Karlsen, C. (1987). *The devil in the shape of a woman: Witchcraft in colonial New England.* New York: W. W. Norton.

Klaits, J. (1987). *Servants of Satan: The age of the witch hunts.* Birmingham: Midland Books.

Konrad, A. (2003). Defining the domain of workplace diversity research. *Group & Organization Management*, *28*(1), 4–17.

Kramer, L. (2005). *The sociology of gender* (2nd edn). Los Angeles: Roxbury.

Lewis, R., & Mills, S. (Eds) (2003a) *Feminist postcolonial theory.* New York: Routledge.

Lewis, R., & Mills, S. (2003b) Introduction. In R. Lewis & S. Mills (Eds), *Feminist postcolonial theory* (pp. 1–21). New York: Routledge.

Linnehan, F., & Konrad, A. (1999). Diluting diversity. *Journal of Management Inquiry*, *8*(4), 399–414.

Lionnet, F. (2003). Feminisms and universalisms: 'Universal rights' and the legal debate around the practice of female excision in France. In R. Lewis & S. Mills (Eds), *Feminist postcolonial theory* (pp. 368–80). New York: Routledge.

Lipsitz, G. (1998). *The possessive investment in whiteness.* Philadelphia: Temple University Press.

Loomba, A. (1998). *Colonialism/postcolonialism.* London: Routledge.

Marx, K. (1963). *The 18th Brumaire of Louis Bonaparte.* New York: International Publishers (originally published in 1852).

Marx, K. (1972). On imperialism in India. In R. C. Tucker (Ed.), *The Marx-Engels reader* (pp. 577–88). New York: W. W. Norton (originally published in 1853).

Meyerson, H. (2002). The Democrats and the Euro-left. *The American Prospect,* 3 June, 2–3.

Mill, J. S. (1912). *On liberty, representative government, the subjugation of women: Three essays by John Stuart Mill* (M. G. Fawcett, Ed.), London: Oxford University Press.

Miller, J. H. (1987). *The ethics of reading.* New York: Columbia University Press.

Mills, S. (1997). *Discourse.* London: Routledge.

Mohanty, C. T., Russo, A., & Torres, L. (Eds) (1991). *Third World women and the politics of feminism.* Bloomington: Indiana University Press.

Mongia, P. (Ed.) (1996). *Contemporary postcolonial theory.* London: Arnold.

Morris. J. (1973). *Heaven's command.* London: Penguin Books.

Naipaul, V. S. (1964). *An area of darkness.* London: André Deutsch.

Nandy, A. (1983). *The intimate enemy: Loss and recovery of self under colonialism.* Delhi: Oxford University Press.

Nandy, A. (1987). *Traditions, tyranny and utopias.* Delhi: Oxford University Press.

Nandy, A. (1995). *The savage Freud and other essays on possible and retrievable selves.* Princeton, NJ: Princeton University Press.

Naravane, V. (2004). Within four walls. *Frontline, 21*(6), 13–26: http//www.flonnet.com/fl2106/stories/20040326002109100.htm.

Neu, D. (2003). Accounting for the banal: Financial techniques as softwares of colonialism. In A. Prasad (Ed.), *Postcolonial theory and organizational analysis* (pp. 193–212). New York: Palgrave Macmillan/St Martin's Press.

Nkomo, S., & Cox, T. (1996). Diverse identities in organizations. In S. Clegg, C. Hardy & W. Nord (Eds), *Handbook of organization studies* (pp. 338–56). Thousand Oaks, CA: Sage.

Nye, J. S., Jr (2004). *Soft power: The means of success in world politics.* New York: PublicAffairs.

Parekh, B. (1995). *Gandhi's political philosophy* (1st Indian edn). Delhi: Ajanta Publications.

Polakow-Suransky, S. (2002). Fortress Denmark? *The American Prospect,* 3 June, 21–4.

Prakash, G. (1999). *Another reason.* Princeton, NJ: Princeton University Press.

Prasad, A. (1997a). Provincializing Europe: Towards a postcolonial reconstruction. *Studies in Cultures, Organizations and Societies, 3,* 91–117.

Prasad, A. (1997b). The colonizing consciousness and representations of the other. In P. Prasad, A. Mills, M. Elmes & A. Prasad (Eds), *Managing the organizational melting pot* (pp. 285–311). Thousand Oaks, CA: Sage.

Prasad, A. (2001). Understanding workplace empowerment as inclusion: An historical investigation of the discourse of difference in the United States. *Journal of Applied Behavioral Science, 37*(1), 51–69.

Prasad, A. (Ed.) (2003a). *Postcolonial theory and organizational analysis: A critical engagement.* New York: Palgrave Macmillan/St Martin's Press.

Prasad, A. (2003b). The gaze of the other: Postcolonial theory and organizational analysis. In A. Prasad (Ed.), *Postcolonial theory and organizational analysis* (pp. 3–43). New York: Palgrave Macmillan/St Martin's Press.

Prasad, A. (2004). The many benefits of diversity. (A conversation with S. Cornell). *Connecticut Business Journal,* April, 8–9.

Prasad, A., & Prasad, P. (1998). Everyday struggles at the workplace: The nature and implications of routine resistance in contemporary organizations. *Research in the Sociology of Organizations, 15,* 225–57.

Prasad, A., & Prasad, P. (2002a). Otherness at large: Identity and difference in the new globalized organizational landscape. In I. Aaltio & A. Mills (Eds), *Gender, Identity and the Culture of Organizations* (pp. 57–71). London: Routledge.

Prasad, A., & Prasad, P. (2003). The empire of organizations and the organization of empires. In A. Prasad (Ed.), *Postcolonial theory and organizational analysis* (pp. 95–119). New York: Palgrave Macmillan/St Martin's Press.

Prasad, P. (2003). The return of the native: Organizational discourses and the legacy of the ethnographic imagination. In A. Prasad (Ed.), *Postcolonial theory and organizational analysis* (pp. 149–70). New York: Palgrave Macmillan/St Martin's Press.

Prasad, P., & Mills, A. (1997). From showcase to shadow. In P. Prasad, A. Mills, M. Elmes & A. Prasad (Eds), *Managing the organizational melting pot* (pp. 3–27). Thousand Oaks, CA: Sage.

Prasad, P., Mills, A., Elmes, M., & Prasad, A. (Eds) (1997). *Managing the organizational melting pot: Dilemmas of workplace diversity*. Thousand Oaks, CA: Sage.

Prashad, V. (2004). In God we trust: Evangelism and American politics. *Frontline, 21*(6), 13–26: http//www.flonnet.com/fl2106/stories/20040326000506400.htm.

Radhakrishnan, R. (1996). *Diasporic mediations*. Minneapolis: University of Minnesota Press.

Ramos, J. (2004). *The Latino wave*. New York: HarperCollins.

Reston, J. (2001). *Warriors of God*. London: Faber and Faber.

Root, D. (1996). *Cannibal culture*. Boulder, CO: Westview Press.

Rosenthal, A. M. (1995). The possible dream. *New York Times*, 13 June, A25.

Said, E. (1978). *Orientalism*. New York: Vintage Books.

Shohat, E., & Stam, R. (1994). *Unthinking Eurocentrism*. London: Routledge.

Shweder, R. A. (2002). 'What about female genital mutilation?' and why understanding culture matters in the first place. In R. A. Shweder, M. Minow & H. R. Markus (Eds), *Engaging cultural differences* (pp. 216–51). New York: Russell Sage Foundation.

Spivak, G. C. (1987). *In other worlds*. New York: Methuen.

Spivak, G. C. (1993). *Outside in the teaching machine*. New York: Routledge.

Spivak, G. C. (1999). *A critique of postcolonial reason: Toward a history of the vanishing present*. Cambridge, MA: Harvard University Press.

Spurr, D. (1993). *The rhetoric of empire*. Durham, NC: Duke University Press.

Stoler, A.L. (1997). Making empire respectable: The politics of race and sexual morality in twentieth century colonial cultures. In A. McClintock, A. Mufti & E. Shohat (Eds), *Dangerous Liaisons: Gender, Nation and Postcolonial Perspectives* (pp. 344–73). Minneapolis: University of Minnesota Press.

Sun Tzu (1988). *The art of war* (T. Cleary, Trans.). Boston: Shambhala Publications (originally written during sixth century BC).

Suroor, H. (2004). Shed multiculturalism. *The Hindu*, April 4: http//www.thehindu.com/2004/04/04/stories/2004040401831401.htm.

Terray, E. (2004). Headscarf hysteria. *New Left Review, 26*(March–April), 118–27.

Weedon, C. (1997). *Feminist practice and poststructuralist theory* (2nd edn). Oxford: Blackwell.

Williams, P., & Chrisman, L. (Eds) (1994). *Colonial discourse and postcolonial theory*. New York: Columbia University Press.

Wilson, D., & Purushothaman, R. (2003). *Dreaming with BRICs: The path to 2050*. Goldman Sachs Global Economics Paper No. 99: http://www.gs.com/insight/research/reports/99.pdf.

Young, R. (1995). *Colonial desire*. London: Routledge.

Young, R. (2001). *Postcolonialism: An historical introduction*. Oxford: Blackwell.

6

Diversity as Resistance and Recuperation

Critical Theory, Post-Structuralist Perspectives and Workplace Diversity

DEBORAH JONES AND RALPH STABLEIN

'DIVERSITY' FROM THE MARGINS TO THE CENTRE

Those of us who want to intervene in organizations, in order to produce new power relations within them, inevitably risk various types of complicity with the already-dominant organizational powers. We must choose between the possibilities of being co-opted and the possibilities of being marginalized: we face 'the ethico-political choice we have to make every day … to determine which is the main danger' (Foucault, 1984: 343b). In this chapter, we draw on the resources of critical and post-structuralist thought as tools to help frame such choices, asking: how do these approaches help us understand the theory and practice of workplace diversity?

The rhetoric of 'workplace diversity' can act like a Trojan horse, providing a vehicle to resist and transform relations of organizational power, while speaking of human resource management (HRM) and demographic change. The language of 'workplace diversity' declares the existence of centres and of margins of organizational power, and of central and marginal identities. It can be, and to some extent has been, utilized to redistribute incomes and career opportunities, and to redefine identities and roles positively. In turn, 'diversity' can be resisted, and power can be recuperated – taken back, often in another form – by the powerful, through strategies such as co-option, marginalization and tokenism. 'The spectre of recuperation', as Sneja Gunew has described it, always haunts 'the relations between centres and margins' (Gunew, 1994: 87).

This chapter will critically address the language of 'diversity' in organizational theory and practice, exploring the ways that it can work as a form of resistance as it moves between the centres and margins, and can invoke a range of political possibilities for engaging with difference in organizations and in organizational theory. This range of possibilities runs from HRM practices of 'managing diversity' to radical postcolonial, anti-racist and feminist challenges to both organizational practice and theory. The lists of 'differences' addressed – gender, ethnicity, sexuality, class – are in themselves the results of political choices.

We begin by locating our critique within global diversity debates and go on to introduce 'critical' and 'post-structuralist' approaches as we will use them. The core of our discussion is the analysis of two exemplar texts which we take as talking points to develop our critique. The chapter ends with some propositions on further directions for critical/post-structuralist 'diversity' projects. Readers are encouraged to approach this chapter as an introduction to some 'propositions', as Michel Foucault described them, 'game openings', where those who might be interested are 'invited to join in', rather than 'dogmatic assertions' (Foucault, 1991: 74).

As authors, we 'live at the edge of the universe, like everybody else', as New Zealand poet Bill Manhire has put it (Manhire, 1991). 'Out' here in Aotearoa/ New Zealand[1] we have particular reason to be aware of the relationships between the margins and the centre. We live in a small postcolonial nation with a unique history, and in this context the language of 'managing diversity' is clearly marked by its origins in the demographics, history and cultures of the United States (Jones, Pringle & Shepherd, 2000). However, the inherent limitations of these origins are rarely acknowledged in the 'managing diversity' literature. In a comment on 'the language of diversity', American diversity scholar Taylor Cox has expressed frustration that the term repeatedly gets 'distorted' in 'international forums' where 'it is branded as an "American" issue' (Cox, 1994: 52). Cox argues that this 'distortion' means that non-Americans undervalue the importance of difference, and that they ignore the 'opportunities for transference of knowledge' from US accounts to their own national contexts. The model of 'knowledge transfer' here has the familiar implications of passing on the latest advances in knowledge and practice developed in the United States to less advanced nations. Cox argues further that 'conceptual clarity' is essential to advancing the study of 'diversity', and that the current 'confusion and ambiguity in terminology' undermines the value of the work (Cox, 1994: 51). Conversely, it can be argued that 'confusion and ambiguity' are an inevitable aspect of cross-cultural conversation. Some aspects of difference are incommensurable, and there can be no grand meta-language of diversity that transcends or comprehends all differences. This post-structuralist understanding of 'diversity' frustrates the desire of managers to divide the 'workforce' into governably diversified bodies according to a single universal 'best practice' code. It also disrupts those critical perspectives which want to reduce 'managing diversity' to a single truth of either resistance or oppression.

In this chapter the term 'difference' is used to refer to patterns of identity within networks of power – such as gender, ethnicity, sexuality. The term 'diversity' is reserved for a particular language of difference, one which treats difference in particular ways, especially within the framework of 'workplace diversity'. Living in Aotearoa/New Zealand, it is clear that the issues of difference that we struggle over in this country are unique – the issue of indigeneity is especially critical here – as they are everywhere. The particular political and legal histories of the United States, the United Kingdom, Australia and Canada, for instance, have given rise to varying models of affirmative action, Equal Employment Opportunities (EEOs) and 'managing diversity'. Their sizes and patterns do not fit all. More than that, the global export of dominant models continues the project of colonization within and between national boundaries. In a review chapter such as this, the focus is on shared understandings, but genuine recognition of difference must always welcome the 'unique case' that challenges them (Trinh Minh-ha, 1994: 15).

CRITICAL THEORY AND POST-STRUCTURALISM

'Critical theory' and 'post-structuralism' are not necessarily, or even usually, separate bodies of ideas. In this chapter we do not assume previous knowledge of these ideas. We separate them out to frame the beginning of our analysis, and then, in the process of discussing the exemplar articles, we will draw out and interweave these threads to argue *why* these relationships matter and *how* they work when we are doing specific kinds of reading or writing about workplace diversity. The 'diversity literature' reviewed in this chapter is not restricted to work in which the language of 'diversity' is explicitly used – although this is central – but also takes in issues of difference, identity and power as they occur more widely in the form of writings on gender, ethnicity, 'race', and so on. Following the authors' own trajectories, the chapter privileges feminist analysis, and a broad view of critical management studies (CMS), over the many other possible approaches to the triad of critical theory, post-structuralism, difference. We acknowledge that we are able here only to open few doors on what is a very complex series of debates, also raised elsewhere in this volume, and we encourage readers to follow the threads of our citations in developing their own trajectories.

'Critical theory' can be generally taken to refer to work in the tradition of Karl Marx ([1867–1895] 1992), which has at its heart a critique of capitalism and its power relations, and particularly of class relations within exploitative labour relationships. The objective of critical theory is to challenge contemporary capitalist ideology, which obscures its own processes of domination through distorting and mystifying knowledge. In resisting the dominance ('hegemony') of capitalist interests, critical theory offers instead emancipatory knowledge to enable 'the examination and exposition of situations of dominance and repression' (Ogbor, 2001: 591). In organizational terms, 'emancipation' means:

> Societies and workplaces that are free from domination, where all members have an equal opportunity to contribute to the production of systems which meet human needs and lead to the progressive development of all. (Alvesson and Deetz, 1999: 192)

Amongst critical scholars there has been a break with earlier scientistic versions of Marxism and a turn to the Frankfurt critical theory tradition, especially Habermas (1972), in search of a firm epistemological foundation for critique and for advocacy for disadvantaged organizational participants (Alvesson, 1987; Calás & Smircich, 1995; Stablein & Nord, 1985). Others have turned to post-structuralist writers, primarily Foucault, for an alternative epistemological position that explicitly rejects the need for, or even the possibility of, firm foundations, leading to a sometimes uneasy mix of structuralist, critical theory and post-structuralist critical research (e.g. Alvesson and Deetz, 1996).

The battles that laid down the groundwork for relationships between critical theory and post-structuralism have been fought in the galaxies of other disciplines far away and now relatively long ago (e.g. Best & Kellner, 1991; Poster, 1989). Nevertheless we intend to show how the questions they raise linger, especially in the domain of political and organizational action. They have slowly seeped into organizational and management studies (OMS), often via interpretations of the work of a small number of canonical writers drawing on French and German philosophical traditions: Derrida, Foucault, Habermas and the Frankfurt group (Calás & Smircich, 1995; 1997; Fournier & Grey, 2000; Linstead, 2003; Willmott, 2003).

Critical Management Studies

The recent formation of Critical Management Studies (CMS) groups and literatures includes streams with critical theory agendas outlined above, but also a much less explicitly marxian sense of the 'critical'. Broadly critical approaches to research on management have become institutionalized in the United States (the CMS workshops at the US Academy of Management began in 1998) and the United Kingdom (the CMS conferences began in 1999). The domain statement of the Critical Management Studies Interest Group (CMIG) of the Academy of Management summarizes its stance, which incorporates the critique of capitalism with some attention to difference and to praxis:

> Our premise is that structural features of contemporary society, such as the profit imperative, patriarchy, racial inequality, and ecological irresponsibility often turn organizations into instruments of domination and exploitation. Driven by a shared desire to change this situation, we aim in our research, teaching, and practice to develop critical interpretations of management and society and to generate radical alternatives. (CMIG, 2004)

The critical approach is always against exploitation, inequality and injustice. A critical approach to the study of workplace diversity would acknowledge a complex web of economic, social and political forces that constitute the positions of the dominant and marginally diverse employees, managers, interested academics, and associated workplace and research practices. In this context 'justice' no longer needs to be read as a universally agreed value with fixed meaning. A constituency for justice exists and can be mobilized in different ways, under different banners. For example, sometimes justice means equality of opportunity, sometimes justice means equality of outcome, sometimes justice means equality of treatment. The role of a critical approach is to trace the myriad effects of such realities, truths and powers (for recent overviews see Calás & Smircich, 2002; Fournier & Grey, 2000). At its best, a critical approach is engaged – it can connect knowledge and action to intervene on behalf of justice. But Fournier and Grey have argued that 'CMS has barely begun to consider engagements with the managed, with trade unionists, with women's groups and so on who might arguably be [an] obvious constituency' for this kind of intervention (Fournier and Grey, 2000: 27). CMS tend to marginalize, or to see as obsolete, those forms of resistance such as civil disobedience or labour organizing which are associated with critical theory in its Marxist forms. Similarly, there has been little coverage of activist campaigns which address diversity issues from the bottom up, working from outside or across organisations (for one example see Foldy & Creed, 1999).

CMS do not necessarily pay attention to diversity issues such as gender and ethnicity. For instance, Alvesson and Willmott's (1992) collection reviewing CMS makes only token mention of feminism as part of the CMS analytic framework (Gephardt, 1993), in spite of the long-running 'socialist/feminist' battles in which feminists have insisted that patriarchy must be included along with capitalism in critical analysis. 'Race' issues in both the First World (Nkomo, 1992) and the Third World (Prasad & Mills, 1997) have been accorded only a small place on the critical agenda.

Post-structuralism

As the discussion above shows, 'post-structuralism' is frequently included with the contemporary notion of the critical in OMS. The term 'post-structuralism' is used in this chapter to indicate a stream of intellectual critique which has challenged the idea that there is a single 'grand narrative' (Lyotard, 1984) that can explain the fundamental truth about a given situation, or that essential underlying structures of power (such as patriarchy or the class system) can be identified. Instead, post-structuralist writers set out to interrogate what is 'known' in order to disrupt the power relations of knowledge. The version of post-structuralism presented in this chapter is primarily a feminist one, in which issues of difference are central (Gheradi, 2003).

The key intellectual tool for post-structuralism is discourse analysis, but it should not be assumed that the word 'discourse' always signifies post-structuralist work.

There is now a very wide range of discourse analytic work in OMS, most of it neither post-structuralist nor critical in the sense of 'critical theory' (Prichard, Jones & Stablein, 2004). From a post-structuralist perspective, discourses or 'discursive formations' can be seen as consisting of language, knowledge, identity and practices, and the power relations within and between them. By showing how identities are discursively constructed, discourse analysis opens up identities to challenge. What can be described as 'a discourse' is arbitrary: it depends on the writer's theoretical base and object of study. In this chapter we refer to 'diversity' as a language, not as a discourse. We follow Foucault's notion of discourses or 'discursive formations' as macro-patterns within which power struggles are played out, such as discourses of 'business' or of 'social justice'. As Stoler points out, 'a shared vocabulary' on a topic such as 'race' can be '[infused] with different political meanings' as a function of its 'strategic mobility' (Stoler, 1995: 13). Terms such as 'black', 'white' or 'civil rights' work differently as they move around into different discursive settings. We take 'diversity' as the 'shared vocabulary' that we are exploring, and look at how it works as it circulates in different discursive contexts. In organizational theory and practice, diversity is framed in phrases such as 'workplace diversity', 'managing diversity' and 'workforce diversity' and linked to terms such as 'Equal Employment Opportunities' (EEOs) and Affirmative Action (AA). The meaning and political import of these terms can be very different depending on where you stand between the margins and centre of power at a given moment: as a social justice activist; as a manager, or perhaps both at different moments.

Identity and Agency

Feminist post-structuralist writers have been particularly concerned with the central concepts of 'same' (equal, identical) and 'different' (defined in contrast to an other) and with the power relationships and types of knowledge by which certain bodies are allocated certain identities: for example, man/woman; black/ white. An interest in the processes of identity creation leads to questions such as: How is the identity of 'woman' created in social practices? What effects does it have in various sites, such as workplace and home? Who gets to be the authoritative person, the one who 'knows' what this difference is and means? What are other possible identities that are suppressed or marginalized? Butler's (1990) book *Gender trouble* articulated the feminist post-structuralist debates of the late 1980s and early 1990s, when feminists encountered the post-structuralist legacy of European writers such as Derrida and Foucault (Benhabib, Butler, Cornell & Fraser, 1995; Nicholson, 1990; Weedon, 1987). Drawing on a critique of structural analyses, and sceptical of unifying biological or cultural categories of gender, they argued that gender is not an essential difference, but one that is constituted in discursive processes. The work of post-structuralist feminists is to create 'gender trouble', to interrupt and to question assumptions about gender boundaries, whether in the academic literatures or in everyday life. While Butler's work has slowly made its way into OMS, the feminist post-structuralist debates are less well known, yet they are valuable to understanding diversity issues. These debates focus on key questions of identity and agency.

In terms of identity, feminists have debated the political effects of destabilising identity categories such as men/women. Some ask: how is feminist theory and practice possible if you cannot make claims of behalf of a category of 'women'? Feminist post-structuralist writers argue that identity itself is a political category that establishes particular sets of power relations. For instance, claims made in the name of 'women' can actually suppress difference within the category. When white feminists set out to represent 'women' and their political interests, it quickly became obvious that there can be no universal category of 'women' which transcends differences of ethnicity and class, and that the attempt to create and enforce one will, in itself, reinforce those power relations which feminists may be setting out to change (Fuss, 1989; Holvino, 2003; Scott, 1988). The writings of black women, women of colour and indigenous women (Awatere, 1984; Lorde, 1984; Moraga & Anzaldua, 1983) similarly put pressure on claims to the shared political interests of 'women', and these are congruent with post-structuralist understandings of other identity categories in 'diversity' such as 'race' (Nkomo, 1992).

The concept of 'workplace diversity' assumes processes of identity categorization in which various types of 'diverse' identities are identified in order to be managed. Various writers in organizational diversity have identified the issue of collective vs. individual identity as central to the discursive uses of diversity (Liff, 1997; Nkomo & Cox, 1996), as various readings sometimes emphasize the commonalities of a group (as in designated EEO groups), and sometimes their individual differences (as in the idea that everyone is 'diverse' in some way). Feminist post-structuralism provides some analytic tools to look critically at these categorization processes and their power effects. These identity categories do not have to be abandoned, but should always be regarded sceptically (Riley, 1988).

This post-structuralist understanding of 'discourse' is associated with debates about agency – the capacity to act. Post-structuralist writers such as Butler (1995a; 1995b) have argued that the concept of a rational and free agent is theoretically untenable, and that discourse itself creates our sense of agency, depending on our historical and cultural situation. The question of agency is vitally important on a practical level for advocates of workplace diversity, and feminist post-structuralist writers have argued that getting an understanding of the various discourses that constitute your own subjectivity – ideas, emotions, sense of identity – can help you to be effective in action. For instance, Australian feminist writer Anna Yeatman has argued that feminist practitioners are most effective when they are able to 'understand how discursive practices operate, how they distribute power and constitute power, and how discursive interventions are possible. This will apply no less to their own discursive practices … as to those of others' (Yeatman, 1990: 160).

Post-structuralism has been described here as a form of intellectual critique, which sets out to do certain types of critical work. We want here to compare it briefly with the term 'post-modernism', which readers will frequently come across in the literature. It must be acknowledged immediately that there is no universally accepted distinction between the two terms. 'Postmodernism' is a much broader term, which can refer in a very general way to cultural phenomena occurring at this point in history ('after' modernism), and can also address issues of knowledge, diversity and power (Chia, 2003; Nicholson, 1990). The risk of the term 'postmodernism' is that it can be so broad as to be a very blunt instrument: it can be too easy to say that postmodernism means that we live in an era where identities are unstable and all differences are accepted. As Fournier has put it, there is 'something disturbing about having all otherness flattened into a play of differences that can be included as various degrees of the same … In this respect, the "post-modern" celebration of differences and diversity … merely brings in more differences to be turned into more of the same' (Fournier, 2002: 80–1). Similarly, post-structuralist and postmodern perspectives can be conflated under what Nealon has called a 'platitudinous social constructionism' whereby everything is 'socially constructed' but the processes and effects are not specified (Nealon, 1994).

TEXTS AS TALKING POINTS: CRITIQUE AND ITS BOUNDARIES

In this section we take two key texts as talking points. Both are rich texts which open up key issues for considering resistance and recuperation in relation to diversity. We take these as exemplary of certain issues, rather than as exemplary of the whole body of work of the various authors. In considering these pieces we take into account their rhetorical purposes. For instance, Humphries and Grice's (1995) paper is a polemical piece which addresses diversity scholars, challenging them from a strong critical analysis of global capitalism which contrasts strongly with the 'managing diversity' mainstream literature. By contrast, the Meyerson and Scully paper (1995) addresses general organizational studies and managerial audiences. We weave our discussions of these papers with propositions about how they can be related to the threads of critical theory and post-structuralism, making connections with the wider literature of workplace diversity as we go.

The first, Humphries and Grice's 'Equal, employment opportunity and the management of diversity: a global discourse of assimilation?' (1995), argues from a critical perspective that 'the management of diversity' is a seductive but ultimately exploitative phenomenon. It exemplifies, and is an early precursor of, a developing body of critical writing on 'managing diversity' in the organizational literature (Lorbiecki & Jack, 2000). We use this paper to do some groundwork on how critical and post-structuralist debates on diversity have played out in the last 15 years or so. The second text, Meyerson and Scully's 'Tempered radicalism and the politics of ambivalence and change' (1995), is a variant of a range of influential work published by Meyerson and various colleagues which addresses various audiences, both managerial and scholarly. It specifically espouses and engages with an organizational change stance, and is a test of the limits of what can be described as 'critical' work on diversity.

Humphries and Grice: Diversity as a Global Discourse of Assimilation

Humphries and Grice have taken on the issues of recuperation and resistance in their 1995 paper. They mark out the emergence of 'the management of diversity' in management theory and practice from the early 1990s, and argue that what they call the 'discourse' of diversity is no more than the seductive veneer of a fundamentally assimilationist capitalism. They argue that 'no adequate theory of social justice can be formulated without a concurrent analysis of the implications of globalizing capitalist practices' (Humphries & Grice, 1995: 31).

Social justice and the 'business case'

Humphries and Grice make a number of important critical moves. First, they acknowledge that concerns for social justice and resistance to what they call 'patterns of occupational segregation ... based on gender, race or other human characteristics' have driven early interventions such as EEO and AA (Humphries & Grice, 1995: 17), and they put these interventions in the context of historical processes – in this case the 'globalising capitalist economy' (1995: 30). By separating 'the discourse of equity' (1995: 31) from the 'pragmatic turn' of managerialism (1995: 18) they put back into the picture what many contemporary accounts of 'diversity' have erased – the history of resistance to 'occupational segregation', and the ethical frameworks that were earlier mobilized to address it. They see these early political and social frameworks as being gradually replaced by the 'discourse' of 'the management of diversity', so that diversity is no longer seen as an issue of 'moral reasons pertaining to equity and fairness' (1995: 31).

They identify the point at which 'the business case' for workforce diversity (Konrad, 2003) in many instances completely covers over and renders obsolete other accounts of organizational diversity. Writers from countries like New Zealand, Australia and the United Kingdom have noted that the local concept of 'Equal Employment Opportunities' has been specifically replaced or overlapped by the introduced US language of 'managing diversity', signalling a shift from equity to diversity (Jones, 2004; Liff, 1997; 1999; Sinclair, 2000). Some US-based writers have argued that the 'business case' for 'diversity' has from its origins foreclosed on the possibilities for fundamental change for those in the margins by creating a 'cognitive "iron cage"' where business objectives are taken as given (Litvin, 2002: 160).

Capitalism and globalization

Humphries and Grice's analysis steps back from the organization as a site of enquiry. They locate the shift from equity to diversity within managerialist discourses of global capitalism. 'Managerialism' here refers to the perspective taken by most management studies literature, which privileges the position and perspective of managers as defined by the 'strategic' discourse of the organizations in which they work (Knights & Morgan, 1991). Humphries and Grice oppose 'an *appearance* of concern with fairness, equality of opportunity and empowerment' to 'the economic argument *underlying* the discourse' (italics added). Locating this 'economic argument' within the logic of capitalism, 'managing diversity' is seen as a form of neo-racism, 'an attempt to maintain as many vestiges of … past exclusion as possible' (Humphries & Grice, 1995: 22). Concerns for justice for citizens from diverse social groups are subsumed under the agenda of capitalism. In particular Humphries and Grice argue that 'the new [global] hierarchy of privilege' consists of 'core, peripheral and unemployed workers' and that attention to a kind of individualized diversity distracts us from this more significant development, where marginalized communities in the First and Third Worlds are related to the peripheries of capitalism, where no 'managing diversity' programmes apply (1995: 30).

This argument reframes managerial accounts of diversity by demonstrating the political effects typically masked in HRM approaches to diversity. These approaches are inseparable from 'the parallel ascendancy of liberal labour policies' (1995: 30), policies based on 'social Darwinism' and 'market justice' (1995: 31), and emphasize individual identity, not membership of social groups with shared political interests which could mobilize around issues of social justice. Like other critics of 'diversity' in corporate culture, Humphries and Grice locate it within broader struggles over identity, linked in turn to HRM strategies of binding valued employees to the organization, while minimizing their resistance to organizational practices (Kersten, 2000; Ogbor, 2001). Ogbor (2001) describes 'managing diversity' programmes as an ideological response which is designed to contain social inequalities – that is, to resist resistance and to co-opt potential challenges to this inequality. As Willmott puts it: 'Cultural diversity is dissolved in the acid bath of the core corporate values' (1993: 534).

Key to this argument are two concepts of identity (individual versus group) and two opposed narratives: one of moral and political concerns with 'fairness' and equity; and one of global capitalism, linked to the exploitative tendencies of the HRM model. The seminal 'managing diversity' text was *Beyond race and gender: Unleashing the power of your total workforce by managing diversity* (Thomas, 1991), written by an African American, Roosevelt Thomas, to address perceived problems with the US AA model. By the early 1990s resistance to this model was such that Thomas believed a new one was needed to sidestep the backlash while continuing to make progress against racism. The 'individualism' associated by Humphries and Grice with 'managing diversity' is signalled in the book by a specific move *away* from identifying disadvantaged groups, and towards 'the many ways employees are different and the many ways they are alike' (Thomas, 1991: 12):

> Diversity includes everyone; it is not something that is defined by race or gender. It extends to age, personal and corporate background, education, function, and personality. It includes life-style, sexual preference, geographic origin, tenure with the organization ... and management or nonmanagement. (Thomas, 1991: 11)

In this scenario no group has special status, no difference matters more than any other, and 'everyone will benefit' (Thomas, 1991: 168). In particular, distinctions between advantaged and disadvantaged are erased, and the focus 'includes white males' (1991: 28). Thomas defines 'managing diversity' as 'a comprehensive managerial process for developing an environment that works for all employees' (1991: 10). This is a strategy that takes managerial power as given, that attempts to set up a win/win situation by avoiding political claims based on group identities.

A post-structuralist critique of Humphries and Grice

We now go on to critique Humphries and Grice's critical argument from a post-structuralist perspective. Our critique does not oppose but rather adds to their argument by painting a more complex picture. Their critical claims are based on 'grand narratives' (Lyotard, 1984). First, a reading of 'diversity' is given based on the grand narrative of a globalizing capitalist discourse. By reducing all practices of 'managing diversity' to exploitation, this argument effectively forecloses on other readings. It discounts the agency and effectiveness of marginalized groups in introducing diversity issues into organizational language. By comparison, a post-structuralist approach would focus on the specific historical and cultural aspects of power relations in a given setting. For instance, in the New Zealand private sector situation, where HRM tends not to be highly professionalized, there is a situation of what Nkomo and Cox call 'unmanaged diversity' (1996: 343). In such a situation there is little or no explicit employment policy of any kind, certainly no policy of EEO or of 'managing diversity' and no discursive opening for discussing equality except where legislation covers areas such as discrimination and sexual harassment. In this context HRM discourse can provide new openings for discussing issues of difference and power. For instance, in a study of the implications of HRM discourse for trade unions, Austrin (1994) has proposed that HRM provides new 'contexts of talk' in which new speaking positions are created. He sees these new contexts as an opportunity for unions, enabling 'new strategies of both managerial discipline and union resistance' (1994: 268), and compares this situation with one in which union women created new 'contexts of talk' within union discourse to open up issues of gender at work. Humphries and Grice acknowledge that 'managing diversity' policies may provide greater access into the new global labour markets for some, but their emphasis is on a fundamental inequity in that system. In contrast, in a post-structuralist view, there is no single story of power, and no discursive formation works in a totalizing way.

The next foundation of Humphries and Grice's claims is a narrative of 'fairness' and equity. It is from this position that Humphries and Grice present their critique of 'diversity' and its fundamental economic truths. A post-structuralist account would reject the idea that there is a single 'truth' that can be unmasked, because any single claim to truth inevitably marginalizes other claims (as white feminism does when it claims the 'truth' about gender, and as do marxian class-based explanations which exclude gender). In addressing issues of power and difference it is necessary to be very cautious about representation: who one is speaking *about* and *for* (Gunew, 1994). By contrast a post-structuralist approach to diversity emphasizes organizing around 'local allegiances' – a strategy which allows the dismantling of 'universal models' which 'confirm the old power structures' (Gunew & Yeatman, 1993: xiv). For example, Jones (2004) presents different readings of 'managing diversity' produced by several differently positioned groups in New Zealand workplaces: trade unionists; Pakeha (white) EEO practitioners; indigenous (Maori) and non-indigenous (Pacific Island) ethnic minorities. The different ethnic groups read 'diversity' differently depending on where they saw themselves as positioned in local ethnic politics: the Maori speakers strongly resisted being categorized as just another ethnic minority, while Pacific Island workers saw the concept of 'diversity' as opening up a wider range of possibilities than the binary Pakeha/Maori difference. In another take on workplace power relationships, the EEO practitioners defended the 'equal opportunity' agenda against the idea of 'managing diversity', while the unionists tended to see both EEO and 'managing diversity' practices as dominated by exploitative HRM perspectives.

The Humphries and Grice piece specifically warns against complicity with the discourse of globalization in the hope of equity. By contrast, feminist post-structuralism provides reflexive analyses which assume that complicity is an inevitable aspect of operating politically in discursive contexts – and focuses instead on analysing its complex and unpredictable effects in a given situation. It takes a reflexive approach to 'indicate the types of discourse from which particular feminist questions come, and to locate them socially and institutionally. Most important of all, it can explain the implications for feminism of these other discourses' (Weedon, 1987: 22). This version of post-structuralism emphasizes its ability to generate strategic political analysis. Social justice agendas must not be abandoned, but must be scrutinized differently. Gunew summarizes the situation as follows:

> Working for social justice is not necessarily at odds with a commitment to critical theory 'even' in its post-modern variants. It is necessary to state this in the face of consistent critiques which suggest that social justice issues inevitably translate into firmly entrenched binary positions, which are hierarchically positioned and involve mutual homogenization and reductionism ... This is not to deny the fact that political manoeuvrings sometimes set these categories against each other ... But this does not mean that

we have to accept the terms of such manipulations. *If we have a specific role as intellectuals it is precisely that of scrutinising and, if need be, redefining the conceptual terms of these debates.* (1993: 1; italics added)

In this spirit we move on to consider the recent influential work of Meyerson and her colleagues on 'tempered radicalism'.

Meyerson and Scully: The Politics of Ambivalence and Change

In our discussion of CMS, we pointed out that CMS typically do not move out of the 'armchair' (Meyerson & Kolb, 2000). One rationale given for this lack of praxis is that 'action' is associated with managerialist demands for constant instrumental problem-solving action (Fournier & Grey, 2000). By contrast, much of the literature on workplace diversity invites the reader to engage with an activist or change-oriented stance that is not simply managerialist, but which is linked to social justice movements and their agendas. The complicated relationships between these justice agendas and managerialist strategies provide very challenging problems which test our formulations of critical and post-structuralist approaches. To simplify: resistance can be read *both* ways – as 'bottom-up' action by marginalized groups and as 'top-down' responses by dominant groups resisting change. Even this binary framing of the issue is too simplistic – power and resistance are inextricably linked, and can work in all directions (Knights & Vurdubakis, 1994: 177) – but it serves to distinguish some of the problems faced by 'diversity' activists and their academic colleagues as they struggle to analyse and intervene in change processes.

Diversity and organizational change

For this discussion we focus on Meyerson and Scully's 'Tempered radicalism and the politics of ambivalence and change' (1995), using this work as a talking point to discuss notions of resistance and recuperation in relation to 'managing diversity'. We have chosen this paper because it considers possibilities for workplace activism through an exploration of 'tempered radicals' (TRs) – 'individuals who identify with and are committed to their organizations, and are also committed to a cause, community, or ideology that is fundamentally different from, and possibly at odds with the dominant culture of their organization' (Meyerson & Scully, 1995: 586). We read Meyerson & Scully (1995) alongside related papers which locate the change model of TRs within workplace diversity concerns. Meyerson and colleagues published a group of papers as a 'Symposium: Beyond armchair feminism' in 2000 (Meyerson & Kolb, 2000), aiming to put their theories of gender and change into workplace practice through experimental consulting projects. In addition we draw on Meyerson and Fletcher's 'A modest manifesto for shattering the glass ceiling', written for a management audience (2000), and on

Meyerson's book, *Tempered Radicals* (2001). Because Meyerson is an author in all the related papers we discuss here, we will refer to the authors as 'Meyerson and colleagues' when referring to this body of work as a whole.

Meyerson and colleagues' work shares some perspectives with post-structuralist approaches. First, they avoid a 'grand narrative' approach to equity. With their main focus on 'gender discrimination' in corporate environments, they argue that the 'revolutionary' approach of the 1960s, 1970s and 1980s is no longer a viable strategy for change. They argue instead for a 'small-wins' approach of incremental change that is not labelled with an equity agenda (Meyerson & Fletcher, 2000; Meyerson & Scully, 1995). This approach, like Thomas's introduction of 'managing diversity' (Thomas, 1991), is intended on a strategic level to avoid backlash. It acknowledges that the language of equity now occupies a place in organizational discourse where it is no longer gaining traction. Their proposition could be seen in the context of recent feminist post-structuralist work which stresses the 'fluidity of and permeability of definitions, boundaries and polarities' (Martin & Collinson, 2002: 258), and argues that 'it is possible to be a kind of feminist itinerant, moving across discourses, planting different kinds of seeds among different audiences' (Sinclair, 2000: 241). Could the work of Myerson and colleagues be a test case of this approach? Second, in the notion of the TR, Meyerson and colleagues address the issues of corporate culture, identity and resistance raised in our discussion of critical theory. Finally, in moving out of the 'armchair' of theory, Meyerson and colleagues have explored the complexities of resistance and recuperation in specific organizational situations.

The dual agenda

The term 'tempered radical' signals a strategy of achieving radical change in organizations by adopting non-threatening change practices and minimizing explicit references to the 'radical rhetoric' of justice and diversity (Meyerson & Fletcher, 2000). The premise of this concept is that it is possible to serve a dual agenda: to 'advance … equity perspectives while simultaneously serving the organization's instrumental goals' (Ely & Meyerson, 2000: 591). 'Ambivalence' is a key concept in tempered radicalism: TRs are 'radicals' because they challenge the status quo, both through their intentional acts and also just by 'being who they are, people who do not fit perfectly' (Meyerson & Scully, 1995: 586). But at the same time they are 'tempered' because they 'seek moderation' – 'they experience tensions between the status quo and alternatives, which can fuel organizational transformation' (1995: 586). Meyerson and Scully specifically bracket off the question of 'whether the tempered radical ultimately wins the battle for change' (1995: 587). Although some examples in their paper address 'diversity' issues, the specific social change agenda that these 'radicals' may be espousing is left open.

Prasad's 'historical investigation of the discourse of difference in the United States' (Prasad, 2001) provides a useful analytic framework within which to locate Meyerson and colleagues' work. Prasad points out that the developing discourse of diversity positions the subjects, objects and sites of change differently over time. In this context, Meyerson and colleagues' work can be seen as relating to a period where 'the business case' is dominant, and so the locus of change is the organization – not broader social movements such as the women's movement, nor wider international frameworks such as the human rights discourse. This focus forecloses other possibilities for action, and frames 'tempered radicalism' as individual and organizational. Even where the possibility of collective action is mentioned (Meyerson & Fletcher, 2000), all change initiatives must be subsumed within the pre-given strategic frameworks of the organization to which the tempered radical is ultimately not only accountable but loyal (Meyerson & Scully, 1995). This approach is very different from the critical proposition raised by Humphries and Grice (1995), that the politics of diversity inevitably brings company and community loyalties into conflict. In arguing that change benefits both men and women, Meyerson and colleagues (Meyerson & Fletcher, 2000) treat the inequality of women as more of a residual technical problem than as a pattern of power relations which continues to bring huge advantages to many men.

Diversity and resistance

The work of Myerson and colleagues is intriguing because it engages with organizational change and the possibilities of agency that are created when individuals experience tensions between 'diverse' subjectivities and organizational discourses – described by Meyerson and Scully as 'ambivalence'. But in talking about an individualized 'ambivalence' out of political context, they avoid the complex issues related to the discursive construction of the 'resistant' individual (Clegg, 1994), and the sense of agency which triggers the desire and possibility of change in individuals from marginalized groups (Findlay & Newton, 1998; Hollway, 1991). A critical post-structuralist approach can explore this dilemma further by describing practitioners as discursively constituted in corporate discourse, but at the same time capable of reflecting on their own discursive positionings in the process of critique (Yeatman, 1990). Discourse analytic work like Prasad's, which locates organizational politics within larger historical and cultural discursive formations (Prasad, 2001), is one kind of resource for such reflection. Another possibility is to carry out a more micro-level discourse analysis which considers how practitioners such as HRM managers are themselves positioned when they engage with the rhetoric of diversity: such an analysis can show how 'diverse' identities are created or challenged in the organizational processes of 'managing diversity' (Zanoni & Janssens, 2003). By showing how identities and change agendas are discursively created, such analyses disrupt our assumptions and, paradoxically, by showing the limits to our agency, can indicate how we can shift them. As philosopher Jean Grimshaw has remarked, feminists have become increasingly aware of the fact that 'nothing is innocent, that apparently "liberatory" ideals can only too easily be recuperated or undermined by that against which they seem to be struggling' (Grimshaw, 1993: 68–9). It is not a simple matter to distinguish when and how such recuperation is occurring.

We have shown that the work of Meyerson and colleagues raises a number of interesting questions in terms of resistance and recuperation. One of the most interesting ones is the one that Meyerson and Scully bracket out – does the TR approach work? In their 'Beyond armchair feminism' work, Meyerson and colleagues describe their experience of working as organizational consultants who pursued a dual agenda of gender equity and improved organizational performance. Their experience was that the 'gender narrative' got lost (Ely & Meyerson, 2000) – that technical rationality and social change did not in fact work side by side. Meyerson and colleagues do not ask or explain what is the source of the 'gender narrative' referred to here – who defines it, and within what agenda? Such a 'gender narrative', or analysis of difference and power, must be explicitly considered and debated if workplace diversity is to resist corporate power (whether or not political interventions are openly named in organizational contexts). As scholars and as activists, we must constantly return to considering our theoretical framework for change.

CONTINUING TO THEORIZE WORKPLACE DIVERSITY

In this chapter we have theorized workplace diversity through the lens of critical theory and post-structuralism – sometimes distinguishing these two perspectives, sometimes combining them. In discussing aspects of exemplary texts we have focused on the ways that power can be recuperated by dominant groups, through processes of assimilating workplace diversity into corporate discourse. We have singled out identity and agency as key theoretical concepts: 'identity' questioning the ways that people are represented as different or 'diverse' individuals, or members of 'diverse' groups; 'agency' as the capacity that people have to act, individually or collectively. These two concepts are strongly intertwined, as inherent in identities are varying possibilities of agency; and agency can enable people to question or resist the identities available to them.

At the beginning of the chapter we suggested that the 'business case' rhetoric of 'workplace diversity' can act like a Trojan horse: on the outside are the HRM arguments, on the inside is a passion for justice and, for the marginalized, a drive for empowerment. This 'dual agenda' is a tricky business. There is a constant risk that social justice agendas will become subservient to profit, that dominant groups will find ways to stay dominant regardless of EEO policies, and that key struggles over exploitation will take place out of sight in 'outsourced' workplaces around the world. On the other hand, workplace diversity struggles are necessary to bring social change into workplaces – and workplace diversity with a broader social agenda can create organizations as sites of wider social change.

These possibilities create strategic problems for 'diversity' change agents, especially where they enter the rhetoric of business to argue the case of diversity.

Clarity about agendas is critical to success, and requires an analysis that separates a business or organizational agenda from a social change agenda, so the two agendas can be evaluated against each other. What theoretical texts can do is to help organizational activists to clarify their own agendas, to make sense of the discursive contexts in which they find themselves. The development of such a critical analysis requires the ability to link global, social and organizational frames, as well as to observe and describe tactics which work. The explicit political agenda is usually missing from discussions of workplace diversity – perhaps an indication of how the academic literature is itself complicit with a taken-for-granted business case. Theorists and practitioners of workplace diversity should draw on a range of theoretical frames consistent with their own explicit social and political agendas, and relevant to their local conditions.

We have some suggestions for developing the theorization of workplace diversity. One well-established strategy for this in CMS is to turn to the European philosophers that we have cited as the basis for post-structuralist theory. Recently, for instance, the contribution of Bourdieu (e.g. 1993; 2001) to theories of gender has become influential in social theory (Adkins, 2003), and his arguments about social change and the development of a critical reflexive stance could be very useful in the discussions of activism covered in this chapter (e.g. Fowler & Wilson, 2004). But while critical and post-structuralist critiques open the door for diverse voices and knowledges, and for new understandings of diversity, the reiterative use of these theoretical sources has the ironic effect of reinforcing European and mostly masculine perspectives. It also reinforces the split between the philosophical and the activist in CMS. More important, we need more diverse voices – not just in the 'diversity' literature, but in organizational studies as a whole. As several authors have pointed out, in spite of exhortations to include 'more theories, voices and politics' (Townsley, 2003: 617), not much has changed in the last decade, even in CMS (see also Boje & Rosile, 1994; Calás & Smircich, 2003; Ferguson, 1994). This needed change goes to the heart of what we accept as management knowledge. As Nkomo pointed out in 1992 in respect to 'race', if even this single aspect of diversity could be positioned as central to the ways that we think about organizations, organizational theory would shift on its axis. The same shift could occur if differences such as sexuality, age or disability were moved from the margins to the centre of organization theory. Such a shift means more than just adding workplace diversity to the already established business agenda. Bringing in more diverse voices will involve changes in the ways that the discipline is organized – and diversity is resisted in academic hierarchies as it is in other organizational contexts. Meanwhile workplace diversity scholars can help create a shift in the literature by setting out to address a wider range of material on workplace diversity topics, deliberately reading and writing in sources from outside the Anglo-American West; and going outside the usual boundaries of management or organizational studies to read and write in theorists of difference and equality. A decade ago feminist scholar Trinh Minh-ha laid down this challenge:

How to really deal with the difficulties and complexities of difference, not just the difference between cultures but *the difference that questions a whole system of truth and representation* and allows each case of marginalisation to be dealt with as a unique case without losing sight of what it may share with others. (Trinh Minh-ha, 1994: 15; italics added)

In responding to this challenge, a critical post-structuralist account of workplace diversity must engage with differences within and between 'diverse' groups; with the historical and cultural specifics of a much wider range of 'diversities'; and with a diversity of political agendas within organizational and management studies.

NOTES

Thanks to the editors and especially to Judith Pringle for affirmation and for asking good questions.

1 Aotearoa is the name used to signify the Maori identity of 'New Zealand'.

REFERENCES

Adkins, L. (2003). Reflexivity: Freedom or habit of gender? *Theory, Culture & Society, 20*(6), 21–42.

Alvesson, M. (1987). *Organization theory and technocratic consciousness: rationality, ideology, and quality of work.* Berlin: W. De Gruyter.

Alvesson, M., & Deetz, S. (1996). Postmodernism and critical approaches to organizational studies: In S. R. Clegg, C. Hardy & W. Nord (Eds), *Handbook of organization studies.* (pp. 191–217). London: Sage.

Alvesson, M., & Deetz, S. (1999). Critical theory and postmodernism: Approaches to organizational studies. In S. Clegg & C. Hardy (Eds), *Studying organization: Theory and method.* (pp. 185–211). London: Sage.

Alvesson, M., & Willmott, H. (Eds) (1992). *Critical management studies.* Newbury Park, CA: Sage.

Austrin, T. (1994). Positioning resistance and resisting position: Human resource management and the politics of appraisal and grievance hearing. In J. Jermier, D. Knights & W. Nord (Eds), *Resistance and power in organizations* (pp. 199–218). New York: Routledge.

Awatere, D. (1984). *Maori sovereignty.* Auckland: Broadsheet.

Benhabib, S., Butler, B., Cornell, D., & Fraser, N. (1995). *Feminist contentions: A philosophical exchange.* New York: Routledge.

Best, S., & Kellner, D. (1991). *Postmodern theory: Critical interrogations.* London: Macmillan.

Boje, D., & Rosile, G. A. (1994). Diversities, differences and author's voices. *Journal of Organizational Change Management, 7*(6), 8–17.

Bourdieu, P. (1993). *The field of cultural production.* Cambridge: Polity.

Bourdieu, P. (2001). *Masculine domination.* Cambridge: Polity.

Butler, J. (1990). *Gender trouble: Feminism and the subversion of identity*. Routledge, London.

Butler, J. (1995a). Contingent foundations. In S. Benhabib et al., *Feminist contentions: A philosophical exchange* (pp. 35–58). New York: Routledge.

Butler, J. (1995b). For a careful reading. In S. Benhabib et al., *Feminist contentions: A philosophical exchange* (pp. 127–43). New York: Routledge.

Calás, M., & Smircich, L. (Eds) (1995). *Critical perspectives on organization and management theory*. Aldershot: Dartmouth.

Calás, M., & Smircich, L. (Eds) (1997). *Postmodern management theory*. Aldershot: Dartmouth.

Calás, M., & Smircich, L. (2002). Introduction. Symposium: On Critical Management Studies. *Organization*, 9(3), 363.

Calás, M., & Smircich, L. (2003). At home from Mars to Somalia: Recounting organizational studies. In H. Tsoukas & C. Knudsen (Eds), *The Oxford handbook of organization theory* (pp. 596–606). Oxford: Oxford University Press.

Chia, R. (2003). Organization theory as a postmodern science. In H. Tsoukas & C. Knudsen (Eds), *The Oxford handbook of organization theory* (pp. 114–39). Oxford: Oxford University Press.

Clegg, S. (1994). Power relations and the constitution of the resistant subject. In J. Jermier, D. Knights & W. Nord (Eds), *Resistance and power in organizations* (pp. 274–325). London: Routledge.

CMIG (2004). Critical Management Studies Interest Group of the Academy of Management. http://aom.pace.edu/cms/About/Domain.htm.

Cox, T. (1994). A comment on the language of diversity. *Organization*, 1(1), 51–8.

Ely, R., & Meyerson, D. (2000). Advancing gender equity in organizations. *Organization*, 7(4), 589–608.

Ferguson, K. (1994). On bringing more theory, more voices and more politics to the study of organization. *Organization*, 1(1), 81–99.

Findlay, P., & Newton, T. (1998). Re-framing Foucault: The case of performance appraisal. In A. McKinlay & K. Starkey (Eds), *Managing Foucault* (pp. 211–29). London: Sage.

Foldy, E., & Creed, W. E. (1999). Action learning, fragmentation, and the interaction of single-, double-, and triple-loop change: A case of gay and lesbian workplace advocacy. *Journal of Applied Behavioral Science*, 35, 207–27.

Foucault, M. (1984). On the genealogy of ethics: Overview of work in progress, In P. Rabinow (Ed.), *Foucault: A reader* (pp. 340–72). New York: Pantheon Books.

Foucault, M. (1991). Questions of method. In G. Burchell et al. (Eds), *The Foucault effect: Studies in governmentality* (pp. 73–86). Brighton: Harvester/Wheatsheaf.

Fournier, V. (2002). Keeping the veil of otherness: Practising disconnection. In B. Czarniawska and H. Hopfl (Eds), *Casting the other: The production and maintenance of inequalities in work organizations* (pp. 68–88). London: Routledge.

Fournier, V. & Grey, C. (2000). At the critical moment: Conditions and prospects for critical Management studies. *Human Relations*, 53(1), 7–32.

Fowler, B., & Wilson, F. (2004). Women architects and their discontents, *Sociology*, 38(1), 101–19.

Fuss, D. (1989). *Essentially speaking: Feminism, nature and difference*. New York: Routledge.

Gephardt, R. (1993). Review of Alvesson and Willmott, 1992. *Academy of Management Review*, 18(4), 798–803.

Gheradi, S. (2003). Feminist theory and organization theory. In H. Tsoukas & C. Knudsen (Eds), *The Oxford handbook of organization theory* (pp. 210–36). Oxford: Oxford University Press.

Grimshaw, J. (1993). Practices of freedom. In C. Ramazanoglu (Ed.), *Up against Foucault: Explorations of some tensions between Foucault and feminism* (pp. 51–72). London: Routledge.

Gunew, S. (1993). Multicultural multiplicities: US, Canada, Australia, *Meanjin,* Spring, 447–59.

Gunew, S. (1994). Playing centre field: Representation and cultural difference. In P. Fuery (Ed.), *Representation, discourse and desire: Contemporary Australian culture and critical theory* (pp. 86–98). Melbourne: Longman Cheshire.

Gunew, S., & Yeatman, A. (1993). Introduction. In S. Gunew & A. Yeatman (Eds), *Feminism and the politics of difference* (pp. xiii–xxv). Wellington: Bridget Williams Books.

Habermas, J. (1972). *Knowledge and human interests.* Boston: Beacon Press.

Hollway, W. (1991). *Work psychology and organizational behaviour: Managing the individual at work.* London: Sage.

Holvino, E. (2003). Complicating gender: The simultaneity of race, gender, and class in organization change(ing). In R. Ely, E. Foldy & M. Scully (Eds), *Reader in gender, work and organization* (pp. 87–98). Malden, MA: Blackwell.

Humphries, M., & Grice, S. (1995). Equal employment opportunity and the management of diversity: A global discourse of assimilation? *Journal of Organizational Change Management, 8*(5),17–32.

Jones, D. (2004). 'Screwing diversity out of the workers'? Three readings of the vocabulary of 'managing diversity'. *Journal of Organizational Change Management, 17*(3), 281–91.

Jones, D., Pringle, J., & Shepherd, D. (2000). 'Managing diversity' meets Aotearoa/New Zealand. *Personnel Review, 29*(3), 364–80.

Kersten, A. (2000) Diversity management: Dialogue, dialectics and diversion. *Journal of Organizational Change Management, 13*(3), 235–48.

Knights, D., & Morgan, G. (1991). Corporate strategy, organizations, and subjectivity: A critique. *Organization Studies, 12*(2), 251–73.

Knights, D., & Vurdubakis, T. (1994). Foucault, power, resistance, and all that. In J. Jermier, D. Knights & W. Nord (Eds), *Resistance and power in organizations* (pp. 167–98). London: Routledge.

Konrad, A. (2003). Defining the domain of workplace diversity scholarship. *Group & Organizational Management, 28*(1), 4–17.

Liff, S. (1997). Two routes to managing diversity: Individual differences or social group characteristics? *Employee Relations, 19*(1), 11–23.

Liff, S. (1999). Diversity and equal opportunities: Room for a compromise? *Human Resource Management Journal, 9*(1), 65–76.

Linstead, S. (Ed.) (2003). *Organization theory and postmodern thought.* London: Sage.

Litvin, D. (2002). The business case for diversity and the 'iron cage', In B. Czarniawka, & H. Höpfl (Eds), *Casting the Other: the production and maintenance of inequalities in work organizations* (pp. 160–84). London: Routledge.

Lorbiecki, A., & Jack, G. (2000). Critical turns in the evolution of diversity management. *British Journal of Management, 11*(Special issue), S17–31.

Lorde, A. (1984). *Sister outsider: Essays and speeches.* Trumansburg, NY: Crossing Press.

Lyotard, J. (1984). *The postmodern condition: A report on knowledge.* Minneapolis: University of Minnesota Press.

Manhire, B. (1991). The Milky Way Bar. In *The Milky Way Bar.* Wellington: Victoria University Press. http://www.city-gallery.org.nz/mainsite/FurtherInformation25.html.

Martin, P., & Collinson, D. (2002). 'Over the pond and across the water': Developing the field of 'gendered organizations'. *Gender, Work & Organization, 9*(3), 244–65.

Marx, K. ([1867–1895] 1992). *Capital: A critique of political economy.* First published in 3 vols. 1867–1895. Reprint edition. Harmondsworth: Penguin Books.

Meyerson, D. (2001). *Tempered radicals: How people use difference to inspire change at work*. Boston, MA: Harvard Business School Press.

Meyerson, D., & Fletcher, J. (2000). A modest manifesto for shattering the glass ceiling. *Harvard Business Review*, Jan–Feb, 127–36.

Meyerson, D., & Kolb, D. (2000). Beyond armchair feminism: Applying feminist organization theory to organizational change. *Organization, 7*(4), 553–71.

Meyerson, D., & Scully, M. (1995). Tempered radicalism and the politics of ambivalence and change. *Organization Science, 6*(5), 585–600.

Moraga, C., & Anzaldua, G. (Eds) (1983). *This bridge called my back : writings by radical women of color.* 2nd ed. New York: Kitchen Table, Women of Color Press.

Nealon, J. (1994). 'Review of Butler, Judith: Bodies that matter: On the discursive limits of 'sex'. *Postmodern Culture, 5*(1): http://muse.juh.edu/journals/postmodern_culture/index. html.

Nicholson, L. (Ed.) (1990). *Feminism/postmodernism.* New York: Routledge.

Nkomo, S. (1992). The emperor has no clothes: Rewriting 'race in organizations'. *Academy of Management Review, 17*(3), 487–513.

Nkomo, S., & Cox, T. Jr, (1996). Diverse identities in organizations. In S. Clegg, C. Hardy & W. Nord (Eds), *Handbook of organizational studies* (pp. 338–56). London: Sage.

Ogbor, J. (2001). Critical theory and the hegemony of corporate culture. *Journal of Organizational Change Management, 14*(6), 590–608.

Poster, M. (1989). *Critical theory and post-structuralism: In search of a context.* Ithaca, NY: Cornell University Press.

Prasad, A. (2001). Understanding workplace empowerment as inclusion: A historical investigation of the discourse of difference in the United States. *Journal of Applied Behavioral Science, 37*(10), 51–69.

Prasad, P., & Mills, A. (1997). From showcase to shadow: Understanding the dilemmas of managing workplace diversity. In P. Prasad, A. Mills, M. Elmes, & A. Prasad (Eds), *Managing the organizational melting pot: Dilemmas of workplace diversity* (pp. 3–27). Thousand Oaks, CA: Sage.

Prichard, C., Jones, D., & Stablein, R. (2004). Doing discourse analysis. In D., Grant, and C. Hardy, (Eds), *Handbook of organizational discourse analysis* (pp. 213–36). London: Sage.

Riley, D. (1988). *Am I that name? Feminism and the category of 'Women' in history.* London: Macmillan.

Rose, N. (1988). Calculable minds and manageable individuals. *History of the Human Sciences, 1*(2), 179–200.

Scott, J. (1988). Deconstructing equality – versus – difference: Or the uses of post-structuralist theory for feminism. *Feminist Studies, 14*(1), 33–50.

Sinclair, A. (2000). Women within diversity: Risks and possibilities. *Women in Management Review. 15*(5/6), 237–41.

Stablein, R. E., & Nord, W. R. (1985). Practical and emancipatory interests in organizational symbolism. *Journal of Management, 11*, 13–28.

Stoler, A. (1995). *Race and the education of desire: Foucault's 'History of Sexuality' and the colonial order of things.* London: Duke University Press.

Thomas, R. (1991) *Beyond race and gender: Unleashing the power of your total workforce by managing diversity.* New York: AMACOM.

Townsley, N. (2003). Review article: Looking back, looking forward. Mapping the Gendered Theories, Voices and Politics of Organization. *Organization, 10*(3), 617–39.

Trinh, Minh-ha (1994). Strategies of displacement for women, natives and their others: Intra-views with Trinh T. Minh-ha. *Women's Studies Journal, 10*(1), 5–25.

Weedon, C. (1987). *Feminist practice and post-structuralist theory.* London: Basil Blackwell.

Willmott, H. (1993). Strength is ignorance, slavery is freedom: Managing culture in modern organizations. *Journal of Management Studies, 30*(4), 515–52.

Willmott, H. (2003). Organization theory as a critical science. In H. Tsoukas & C. Knudsen (Eds), *The Oxford handbook of organization theory* (pp. 88–111). Oxford: Oxford University Press.

Yeatman, A. (1990). *Bureaucrats, femocrats, technocrats: Essays on the contemporary Australian state*. Sydney: Allen and Unwin.

Zanoni, P. & Janssens, M., (2003). Deconstructing difference: The rhetoric of Human Resource managers' diversity discourses. *Organization Studies, 25*(1), 55–74.

7

Diversity

The Cultural Logic Of Global Capital?

RAZA MIR, ALI MIR AND DIANA J. WONG

> In the cab-ride from the Rockefeller Center to Wall Street, as a South Asian taxi driver drives a South Asian stockbroker to work, the Plexiglas partition serves as a fundamental dividing line. Behind the partition sits the subject of globalization, while in front, driving the cab, is the historical subject of imperialism.[1]

The above quote by an activist–academic from New York stubbornly brings to the surface the submerged contestations of workplace diversity in the global terrain. The imagery is quite evocative. Two South Asians in a small enclosed space thousands of miles away from their birthplaces. Yet, while one subject visualizes a life that has been liberated from spatial constraints, the other experiences a sense of having been uprooted by economic upheaval, negotiating a bewildering and culturally alienating terrain in search of economic survival. There may be other complications submerged within the encounter. Perhaps the stockbroker has already acquired US citizenship, while the taxi driver is an undocumented alien without any institutional access. Perhaps the stockbroker has a family in the United States, while the taxi driver has left his family back home. While both the occupants of the cab are part of the US workforce, South Asians in the West, perhaps speakers of a common language, etc., there is no theory available that would ever be able to fold their experiences into a common framework of diversity.

One can immediately discern three important issues being raised by this quote:

1 National or regional identity is not an effective category to analyze global diversity. Even in relatively similar identity groups living and working in geographic proximity, there are workers (South Asian immigrant taxi drivers) and workers (South Asian immigrant stockbrokers), each with very different experiences of their work and their careers. Our discipline is quite well equipped to deal with the dilemmas of the stockbroker, but perhaps less so when it comes to the taxi driver.

2 Likewise, globalization itself is not as easy to represent in monolithic categories. One person's experience of the liberation associated with global consumption must necessarily be contrasted with another subject's experience of imperialism.

3 The category of economic class never ceases to be fundamental in the analysis of the relations of production that bind human beings into economic and cultural networks. Class transcends other identity groupings, and simultaneously offers problems and possibilities for theorizing a different global order than is usually observed in our discipline.

Thus, while analyzing the relationship between globalization and diversity, one must be extra careful not to fall prey to the seductive pulls of fixed categories. Unfortunately, our discipline has not had a distinguished history of avoiding these pulls and pitfalls. Most management research on workplace diversity has traditionally focused on the instrumental realities of revenue appropriation such as designing global new product teams (Sivakumar & Nakata, 2003), dealing with environments characterized by multilingual workforces (Teboul, 2002), analyzing and comparing managerial and HR practices in different countries (Dedoussis, 2004), training employees to work in countries with lesser understood cultures (Anwar & Chaker, 2003), effective team building using a multinational task force (Govindarajan & Gupta, 2001), and differences in accounting systems in different nations (Salter & Niswander, 1995). In the United States, the profound psychological impact of the 9/11 attacks has led to a greater focus on the security implications of global diversity, especially the impact of terrorism and threats of terrorism on HR practices (Kondrasuk, 2004). The hegemonic influence of Hofstede's classification of national culture (Bing, 2004) has led mainstream international management researchers to operate under the blithe assumption that national culture is *the* unit of analysis to probe for difference, and that archetypal country-level categories can offer an adequate enough roadmap to the analysis of difference (Beyer & Trice, 1991).

The reality, of course, is a bit more complex. Cultures have a way of eluding the straitjackets of national boundaries, sometimes bleeding across nations (Anderson, 1991), and sometimes fragmenting within the national space (DiMaggio, 1997). The workforce across the world has become more international than we had ever imagined. Now, studies in workplace diversity will have to deal with new issues such as outsourcing (Clott, 2004), migration (Mir, Mathew & Mir, 2000), international legal constraints (Hu, 2004), refugees (Keane, 2004), and in the theoretical realm, the rapidly unraveling of the dominant discourses of globalization (Banerjee & Linstead, 2001).

In this chapter, we would like to discuss the implications of this internationalization of work and the workforce on the ways in which we theorize and represent workplace diversity. Our thesis is that issues of workplace diversity in the global terrain cannot be divorced from issues of power and privilege, nor can they be shoe-horned into simplistic models. An understanding of global workplace diversity must necessarily be textured, multi-layered and context intensive. We seek to achieve two circumscribed objectives in this chapter. First, we try to marshal information about the global 'space' so as to problematize the manner in which the global workforce has been represented in the dominant literature on diversity. Second, we use this information to suggest an alternative way in which globalization needs to be theorized if we are to make our theories of diversity inclusive of the true heterogeneity that the global workforce represents. To that end, the rest of this chapter comprises four sections. In the first section, we briefly review the intersection between the literature on workplace diversity and the international management literature, pointing to the discursive and ideological character of this nexus. In the second section, we discuss the phenomenon of the internationalization of the economic sphere, in terms of the dispersal of economic activity and the migration of humanity across the world, and its implications. Here, we pay special attention to the changing terrain of global workplaces in terms of the spatial reorganization of work as well as a parallel reconfiguration of global labor. In the third section, we focus our attention on the theoretical term globalization. Here, we analyze how organizational theory has relied upon a relatively inadequate model of globalization. We offer ways in which we can deepen this representation by overlaying it with a variety of contextual insights. The final section comprises a discussion on the implications of the new formations of labor and work on future research on global diversity.

WRITING GLOBAL DIVERSITY: IDEOLOGY AND DISCOURSE

> There is a sense in which rapid economic progress is impossible without painful adjustments. Ancient philosophies have to be scrapped; old social institutions have to disintegrate; bonds of caste, creed and race have to burst; and large numbers of persons who cannot keep up with progress will have to have their expectations of a comfortable life frustrated. (United Nations Department of Economic Affairs, 1951)[2]

The above quote from the UN office in the 1950s offers a clear example of an *ideology* and a *discourse* at work. The 1950s were a period when the promise of 'development' was produced in the Third World, where a certain form of modernity was being touted as the harbinger of the pure 'present', one that could only be achieved through a radical, violent departure from the past (Berman, 1987). International regimes such as the World Bank offered a millenarian vision of revolutionary changes in the lives of people, and were willing to take drastic measures on behalf of the poor countries of the world, even resorting to violence (in collaboration with local elites) in the name of progress. Development became a *mantra* that was impossible to oppose from a rational perspective, and its pre-scriptions were isomorphically replicated across a number of countries. By the time this way of thinking unraveled, it was very late, and many of the initiatives taken unilaterally by 'experts' on behalf of poorer nations in the name of 'devel-opment' had brought untold misery (Illich, 1981).

In this example, we do not wish to focus on an analysis of development initia-tives, or on the motives of those who thrust them on the poor nations. We are con-cerned with the apparatus that was brought to bear to ensure that (a specific form of) development became hegemonic for well over half a century. We contend that this hegemony resulted precisely because the concept was presented through the rhetorical gestures of *ideology* and *discourse*.

We define ideology as a process by dominant social groups in which commu-nities and societies control oppressed groups with a minimum of conflict, through recourse to a putative 'common sense'. This common sense is produced through the management of a framework of symbols and values that legitimize the current order (Althusser, 1972). An ideology functions to pass off the narrow interest of a section of community as the interest of the community at large. Likewise, a dis-course, simply put, is a text that carries with it the power of institutional consent (Foucault, 1983). Discursive processes further legitimize an ideology not only by presenting it as being of paramount importance to social well-being, but by presenting counter-arguments as trivial, puny and self-interested. A discourse insinuates itself in mundane and quotidian social practices, and takes on a common-place character, thereby becoming hard to refute and dispute. For example, in the 1950s, to oppose development was to be against progress, against change, against the possibility that everybody would eventually have plenty to eat. Through the management of a variety of symbols, dominant groups including the World Bank were able to link the aspirations of the people with their own narrowly focused agenda (Escobar, 1994).

In a similar manner, we find that mainstream research on global diversity involves a certain celebratory narrative of the multicultural workplace, as a space where multiple subjectivities will find themselves plugged into a world of serene consumption. In the process, researchers confine their analysis only to those elements of the workforce who are potential beneficiaries of globalization, and extrapolate their experience to the population at large. For example, managers working in multinational corporations but affiliated with a certain nation may be studied and their concerns could be attributed to the entire workforce of that nation. Such research would involve the utilization of certain 'commonplace' analytical tools (such as Hofstede's framework, for example). All theorists and empirical researchers are encouraged in (and rewarded for) using these standard-ized templates of analysis (Baskerville, 2003). Eventually, constructs like the

Hofstede framework begin to approach the status of a truth. Based on such research, certain sedimented assumptions about the nature of global diversity become hegemonic (such as the notion that globalization primarily entails the consumption of global products). Disputing these assumptions in mainstream business press or academe then becomes an energy-consuming exercise, much like swimming against the tide. In this chapter, we seek to offer a counter-discourse, one that brings out the points of view of those subjectivities who have been left out of the research on the global aspects of workplace diversity.

Several of the chapters in this book have provided very compelling analyses of the literature on workplace diversity. It is not our intention to revisit that terrain. However, in order to anchor our own understanding of globalization in the terrain that constitutes organizational theory, it would perhaps be useful to identify a few important moments in the literature, and offer a reference point to our subsequent discussion on globalization.

Johnston and Parker (1987) forcefully brought diversity into the limelight in the US business world with their *Workforce 2000* report. Despite the forward-sounding title, the report only confirmed what practicing managers knew all along, that the workplace was hopelessly muddied from a perspective of gender, ethnicity, race and, increasingly, national origin. However, the report did have the effect of igniting an entire subfield in the organization studies literature, which focused on the multicultural organization. In many ways, studies of diversity and multiculturalism (Carnevale & Stone, 1994; Cox & Blake, 1991; Norton & Fox, 1997; Tsui, Egan, & O'Reilly, 1992) became popular because they offered ana-lytical categories that were less fractious and potentially divisive than, say, race. Parallel to this economic activity, an entire *diversity industry* emerged in the prac-titioner field (MacDonald, 1993), involving 'training videos, multiculturalism workshops, cultural sensitivity seminars, diversity audits and so on' (Prasad & Mills, 1997: 4). The field was now imbued with the twin desirable features of academic acceptability and professional lucre.

It was not as if the diversity literature or its concomitant organizational practices were not criticized. Theorists and researchers offered several analyses of the inadequacy of diversity training (Caudron, 1999; Flynn, 1998; McKee & Schor, 1999), and the fact that it created more problems than it solved (Hemphill & Haines, 1997). More significantly, people referred to the sedimented racism that underlay organizational structures and practices (Goldberg, 1993; Oliver & Shapiro, 1995; Van Dijk, 1993), and even implicated diversity training in further-ing such racism (Cavanaugh, 1997). However, such ideas never reached the main-stream, and continued to be parceled out as fringe literature, while the dominant discussion on diversity remained focused on national differences in behavior (Graen & Hui, 1996), the effect of intercultural differences on work and business (Harris & Kumra, 2000; Zakaria, 2000), and the discussion of specific benign organizational practices such as international transfers (Frey-Ridgway, 1997).

While much of the diversity literature focused on the domestic terrain, it was only a matter of time before the international management theorists found it useful as a theoretical appendage for Hofstede's wildly popular framework for the analysis of national cultures (Hofstede, 1980). In the main, the category of choice of choice for analyzing global diversity remained national identity. For example, in a 2001 article titled 'Building an Effective Global Team' published in the *Sloan Management Review*, Govindarajan and Gupta (2001: 64) ask: 'What if some team members come from highly individualized cultures such as the US and Britain, and others from highly collectivized cultures, like Venezuela and Japan?' Here, national identity is collapsed into a single category. In the imaginary generated by international diversity management literature, the political, geographic and economic space of the world is divided, parceled and territorialized into nation states. This creates and reaffirms this particular kind of ('Hofstedian') cultural aggregation.

Such a unitary understanding of global diversity must be contextualized against the fact that the terrain of international management remained anchored in the US cultural sphere, defining diversity as difference, and as divergence (Wong-MingJi & Mir, 1997). In many ways, the literature of global diversity also took on an *ideological* and *discursive* character.

As an empirical hook into the topic, let us consider the July 2004 issue of *Fortune* magazine, which reported its annual list of 500 corporations, noting that most of its members derived over 50% of their revenues from foreign operations (Fortune, 2004). Topping the list was Walmart with annual sales in excess of $260 billion. Interestingly, Walmart did not even have a single store outside the United States till 1990. In a highly appreciative case study, Hill (2003: 3–4) notes that by cleverly leveraging the global economy including supply chain management, Walmart reached a position whereby it had over 1300 stores and 305,000 'associates' (its euphemism for employees) outside of the United States in 2002, generating revenues in excess of $35 billion. The case is meant of course to extol the ability of Walmart, explicitly to succeed in a competitive environment, and, implicitly, to tap into a win–win situation in the global marketplace.

In a counter-ideological and counter-discursive framing of this situation, we must first acknowledge and, if necessary, highlight alternative elements of Walmart's 'international' presence. For example, it is a well-known fact that Walmart has been accused of taking advantage of the precarious situation of illegal immigrants in the United States to reduce its labor cost, employing them at sub-minimum-wage levels with no benefits.[3] Lesser known is its reputation for eventually bankrupting its international suppliers (Fishman, 2003). Walmart's presence in local communities as well as international markets is viewed with alarm not only by competitors, but also by the workforce in the region who fear the eventual erosion of their hard-fought pay and benefits. Some of these may be disputed allegations, but nevertheless they need to find space in the making of a balanced case about Walmart. In a similar vein, our chapter attempts to offer some counterpoints to the celebratory discourse of global diversity, both as a counterweight and as an attempt to address an important 'lack' in the literature. If we highlight the negative impacts of globalization on workplace diversity, it is only to address an imbalance that we have observed that pulls our discipline in the celebratory direction.

In the next section, we move into an analysis of the various internationalized elements of today's workplace. Our contention here is that the internationalization of economic operations must be understood at different levels, and from the perspective of different groups, in order to provide a meaningful analysis of workplace diversity.

THE GLOBAL WORKPLACE

> Globalization in its modern form is a process based less on the proliferation of computers than on the proliferation of proletarians. (Coates, 2000: 256)

When defined as a tendency of human activity to transcend the artificial boundaries of the nation state, globalization takes on the status of a tautology. Of course, human activity has become more international in a variety of spheres including the economic. We deal every day with the powerful images associated with globalization. Most prominent are those that relate to the internationalization of markets, as evidenced by global products such as Visa credit cards and Coca-Cola beverages. Likewise, the internationalization of production is in evidence every time we look under the collars of the garments we wear, where the 'Made in ...' sign is suffixed by a dazzling variety of nation states.

Less visible but vital to this version of the transnational workplace are the global economic regimes that underpin it. The global stock market sends billions of dollars across the world in a matter of a few keystrokes. Older protective barriers set in place to shield sovereign economies from global capital have been eroded, with the help of institutions such as the World Trade Organization (WTO) and its predecessor, the General Agreement on Tariffs and Trade (GATT), aided in great measure by the leverage exerted on debtor nations by the International Monetary Fund (IMF) and the World Bank. International trade embargos have softened recalcitrant nation states into submission, and the absence of the countervailing power of the Soviet Bloc has ensured the dominance of the neoliberal economic order. Consequently, measured global trade interestingly constituted 140% of measured world output in 2002 (Hill, 2003: 11).

At the macro level, two key drivers of the new international workplace/marketplace are technology and policy. Technology spurred global shift through the emergence of 'space-shrinking' advances in transportation (containerization, air freight) and communications (satellites, electronic media and the Internet). While space-shrinking technologies made the internationalization of economic activity possible, changes in manufacturing technology (computer-aided design, minimum efficient-scale plants) made such internalization inevitable (Dicken, 2003: 85–121).

At the policy level, the impetus to internationalize has been relentless. The *World Investment Report* of 2002 documented that of the nearly 1400 national laws concerning foreign direct investment that were amended in a variety of nations between 1991 and 2001, over 90% of them made such investment easier for the foreign bodies (United Nations, 2002a). Regional integration continued at a rapid pace with the euro emerging as a common currency for 12 nation states in 2002, while other regimes like the Andean Pact and Mercosur in South America, and ASEAN and SAARC in Asia, gained strength (Hill, 2003: 266–97). More recently, the trade representatives of 34 nations of North, South and Central America got together in November 2003 to put the finishing touches of the Free Trade Association of America (FTAA), an integrated economic zone in the tradition of NAFTA. Activists representing a rainbow of groups such as environment, labor and consumer rights provided a feisty counterpoint to the utopian arguments of 'free trade'.[4] The FTAA is not yet finalized, but given recent world trends, it appears quite inevitable.

Opposition to the rhetoric of 'free trade' and globalization is primarily based on issues of differential access to its benefits and varied experiences of the phenomenon itself. For example, while it is evident that access to communications media is an important antecedent to benefiting from the economic largesse of globalization, the countries of the 'Third World' find themselves looking at the wrong end of a worsening digital divide. In 2000, South Asian countries enjoyed 0.14 Internet hosts per 1000 citizens, compared to 1131 Internet hosts per 1000 citizens of the United States. For every 10 people in the United States, there were four PCs available in 2000, while there were only three PCs per 100 citizens of Latin America (Dicken, 2003: 103). As an illustration of the varied experiences of globalization by different groups, even in the United States, the lowest 10% of the workforce saw their real wages drop 20% between 1980 and 1995, while the top tiers have achieved substantial growth (Mander & Goldsmith, 1997). In summary, one can say that while the tendencies of global economic activity to internationalize cannot be denied, its impact on different people across the world has been decidedly mixed.

Global Labor

In his analysis of the relationship between globalization and labor, Munck (2002) suggests that the new era of globalization represents a second 'great transformation', in the same way Polanyi had theorized the great transformation created by the Industrial Revolution (Polanyi, 1957). Munck identifies two elements of this transformation as they relate to labor. The first, 'deterritorialization', is produced by the tendencies of capital to free itself from the constraints of geographic space. Karl Marx had referred to this concept as the 'annihilation of space by time', and indeed it appears that through a variety of maneuvers, geographic space has been rendered less salient (though never irrelevant) by corporations. The second tendency created by globalization is 'Brazilianization', or the spread of Third World-like work patterns into the industrial North. More and more, we are seeing the emergence of a contingent labor economy in the industrialized rich nations, where a workforce relies on increasingly temporary and precarious work. In effect, the patterns of employment that were once associated with the Third World have come to haunt the West (Beck, 2001).

Related to these two concepts, one can divide the global workforce into two groups: the migrants, and the recipients of globally mobile work. The migrant is propelled to the West in search of employment. While a small section of the migrant workforce does end up in highly skilled employment routines (Mahroum, 2000), a large majority of migrants inhabit the space of Brazilianization. The recipient of globally mobile work (outsourcing) also becomes an integral part of the global economy, albeit while fixed in space in the Third World. Similar to migrants, workers in the outsourcing economy constitute an economic spectrum, ranging from highly skilled workers to those who suffer the exploitative drudgery of sweatshops. An effective analysis of global diversity therefore must necessarily consider all these subjectivities, rather than confining itself to the elite among each category.

Global Migrants

In the period between 1985 and 2000, the global workforce grew from 1.6 billion to 2.8 billion, with over 2.1 billion coming from 'developing countries'. The labor pool in Third World nations grew at an annual rate of 2.1%, as compared to a growth rate of 0.5% in OECD countries (Munck, 2002: 7). At the turn of the millennium, 175 million people, comprising almost 3% of the world population, could be classified as international migrants (IOM, 2003). The patterns of migratory mobility reveal that a substantial number of these migrants had moved within Third World nations. However, the industrialized nations of the world had benefited most from the migration of highly skilled labor; for example, in 1999, the United States received 370,000 skilled workers (United Nations, 2002b).

These descriptive statistics increasingly point to the emergence of an internationally diverse workforce. Despite heavy natural and institutionally mandated restrictions on labor mobility, people have managed to pollinate the world with their own cultural and physical presence. Moreover, the increasing mobility of work across national boundaries has ensured that corporations operate in multiple national and cultural environments, bringing issues of workplace diversity to the forefront of international management as well.

Most studies of globalization often tend to confine their analysis to macro trends in the economy, rarely bringing their gaze to the level of people. Globalization does produce diversity, but also at the level of people. In the United States, a cursory look at the labor force reveals that it is characterized by a US domestic reliance on Filipina nurses, Mexican chili pickers, South Asian cab drivers, Chinese garment workers, Bangladeshi restaurant workers, East Asians assembling computer hardware at home in Silicon Valley, Venezuelan daycare workers, and a variety of women of multiple races who perform unpaid labor at home. Each one of them has an economic story to tell, some of which are narrated as theory, while others remained confined to more informal channels, as folk tales and anecdotes. Our contention is that a good theory of workplace diversity will find the room to represent all such stories within its framework.

Local Workers in the Global Economy

While one can map a number of historical and personal contingencies that led to the presence of international migrants on foreign soil, one could overlay those stories with those of a variety of workers in different parts of the world, whose labor contributes to the global economy, but who remain fixed in their own geographic space. In fact, it is indeed one of the most curious artifacts of the new globalization that the increasing mobility of capital (albeit along fixed circuits) is accompanied by an incarceration of labor within the boundaries of a nation state, circumscribed by documents such as the passport. The state technologies for controlling international migration defining the distinction between 'legal' and 'illegal' may seem timeless now, but the reality is that they were produced less than two centuries ago (Mongia, 1999).

Of late, the relative immobility of labor and the technology-led liberation of work from its moorings have led to the emergence of the interesting phenomenon of outsourcing (or its new name, 'offshoring') (Swann, 2004). There are a number of global viewpoints on outsourcing, each armed with wildly differing conclusions. On one hand, we have wildly optimistic studies such as a 2003 study by the McKinsey Global Institute which sought to demonstrate that offshoring creates wealth for the country sending jobs abroad (e.g. the United States) as well as the recipient nation (e.g. India). The study concluded that 'for every dollar of corporate spending outsourced to India, the US economy captures more than three-quarters of the benefit and gains as much as $1.14 in return. Far from being a zero-sum game, offshoring creates mutual economic benefit.'[5] On the other hand, we have more circumspect analyses suggesting that offshoring causes a modest decline in US jobs, around 5–9% of all job losses in the United States being attributable to offshoring[6] (Webb, 2004). Among more serious allegations is the impact of offshoring on labor practices. For instance, an economic model generated by the US labor groups contended that there was a direct relationship between the repression of worker rights in China and the reduced manufacturing costs of goods made there.[7]

While there is dispute about the impact of offshoring, there is no doubting that it is an exponentially growing sector with an emerging diverse labor force. To take a specific example, the IT sector in India generated offshoring revenues of $12.2 billion in 2003–4, a 35% increase over 2002–3.[8] Such offshoring not only creates a new element to global diversity, but brings with it a new set of concerns and issues (Mir et al., 2000) that research on global diversity must come to grips with in order to remain relevant to current concerns of working people.

In this section, we have attempted to underscore the completely heterogeneous nature of international economic growth, especially in its differential impact upon different people and subjectivities. In the next section, we address the theoretical formulation of 'globalization', subjecting it to critical scrutiny and suggesting ways in which it can be made more inclusive of the heterogeneity we have just described.

GLOBALIZATION: INTERROGATING A SLIPPERY CONSTRUCT

'Globalisation' is only a word, in some key respects a misleading word. We could simply say 'Empire'. (Aijaz Ahmad, 2000)

In the above section, we addressed the issue of the multiple ways in which economic activity was being internationalized. Had such activity been termed 'globalization', there would be hardly any cause to dispute it. However, the term globalization has itself taken on a variety of discursive and ideological meanings. It is used to define world commerce not only in goods and services, but in the commerce of ideas, symbols, meanings and cultures. It is used as a stick to beat earlier formulations of collective identity. For example, it has been exuberantly deployed to herald the death of nation states and to approve all manners of geographic expansion by multinational corporations. Ohmae (1995: cover) suggests that 'today's economy is genuinely borderless. Information, capital, and innovation flow all across the world at top speed, enabled by technology and fueled by consumers' desire for access to the best and least expensive products'. It is very difficult not to see how global citizenship is defined here by one's status as a consumer. Theses such as this are constantly being deployed by the executives of multinational corporations to decry any attempts by nation states to regulate the nature of capital and product flows across national barriers.

Likewise, globalization has been approvingly cited as an agent by which the 'symbolic' is being liberated from the 'territorial'. In other words, a symbol (say the United States) can be experienced without actually having to enter its territorial space (perhaps by eating a hamburger at a McDonald's outlet in Taipei, or watching a Hollywood movie in Brasilia). Similar breathless hype comes from Friedman[9] (1999), who celebrates globalization as the force that will provide access to the disadvantaged people of the world. 'The new era of globalization,' Friedman declares, 'is turbocharged'. For Friedman, the 'Lexus' version of globalization will eventually rein in the 'olive tree' version of fixity in time, space and culture, very much like the 'pure present' that would help achieve a radical departure, even a violent break from the past.

Other theorists have been more circumspect. Some point to the fact that the economy is not globalized, but merely an international economy which still responds to national policies (Hirst & Thompson, 1996). Others visualize a dynamic relationship between the multinational corporation and the state (Dicken, 2003: 274–313). Despite the fact that 51 of the 100 largest economies in the world are corporations, and that the top 500 multinational corporations (MNCs) account for nearly 70% of the worldwide trade,[10] their ability to ride roughshod over national sovereignty is still not a foregone conclusion. However, recent excesses by MNCs against sovereign nations, and by nation states in the name of security concerns, but in the backdrop of the looming interests of MNCs, have prompted critiques by theorists like Ahmad who find globalization to be little more than a euphemism for the conquest of the poor nations of the world by the West in general and the United States in particular, a form of imperialistic recolonization. In an equally damning analysis, Banerjee and Linstead (2001: 684) define globalization as a rhetoric that is tailored to respond to 'public criticisms on the dismantling of social institutions, redundancies or plant closing'. To them, the talk of an emerging globalization thus becomes the ideological arm of privatization, wealth concentration, neoliberal ingress of MNCs into Third World nations, and of global capitalism in general. After all, it is not as if the growth and spread of international corporate activity has contributed in any measure to world employment. In fact, through the combined use of technology and the threat of flight, corporations have also been able to control the labor force far more efficiently than in the past. Between 1980 and 1995, the asset base of MNCs increased sevenfold to $ 4 trillion, while their labor pool shrank by 7% (Klein, 2000).

It is not our intention to provide a critical analysis of globalization. The term has been celebrated by Friedman (1999) and Ohmae (1995), analyzed in a circumspect manner by Dicken (2003) and Hirst and Thompson (1996), and been critiqued by Munck (2002) and Sassen (1999). Banerjee and Linstead (2001) have cast their critique of globalization within the boundaries of organizational theory. Reference to these and several other texts on globalization will provide the reader with an adequate if bewildering spectrum of analyses.

Our limited task in the rest of this section is to highlight the manner in which the deployment of the term 'globalization' has the potential to affect the discussion on global diversity. To flesh out the nature of this impact, we suggest that two issues need to be considered: the effect of globalization on labor and the emerging global underclass, and the role played by the concept in the creation of the discourse of multiculturalism and diversity. Our brief contention here is that a variety of different labor experiences do not find expression in the dominant representations of the term globalization, and that the differential experiences of globalization by different identity are sought to be elided and smoothened over by recourse to new cultural formulations like multiculturalism and diversity, which function less as foundation and more as façade.

Globalization and Labor

Almost 4 billion people in the world can be classified as workers, or as members of the global labor class; 175 million of them labor as international immigrants, and a large number of the labor force are either directly or indirectly plugged into the global economy. Moreover, decisions taken in the name of globalization impact a large percentage of the world's working class. For instance, one of the ways in which the term 'globalization' has been deployed has been through the rhetoric of 'free trade'. However, labor analysis and critics of the neoliberal paradigm have contended that free trade is a conceptual argument that has been deployed primarily to oppose worker-friendly activities like trade unionism and local regulations to protect domestic economic activity by sovereign nations, and to remove social protection from labor rights (Munck, 2002: 11). In the absence or the relative weakening of countervailing labor forces like unions, the purveyors of global capitalism have resorted to deploying the term 'globalization' to reduce their moral obligations to the workforce.

In a recent comprehensive report on the state of labor in the global economy, the International Labor Organization[11] (ILO) recognized the difficulties associated with freedom of association and collective bargaining in a globalizing economy. The ILO recognized that organizing and bargaining in the global economy should involve not only unions, but groups of workers facing barriers to organizing, public sector employees, agricultural workers, workers in export processing zones, migrant workers and domestic workers. Challenges to labor rights arose partly from the threat of exit deployed by MNCs against countries, and the perceived inability to organize workers in the informal economy.

Slowly but surely, however, the voice of collective labor is again moving far beyond the boundary of the organized trade union. The recent collaborations between trade unions and labor groups in the informal sector, while presenting a countervailing response to forces of globalization, at the November 1999 meetings of the World Trade Organization in Seattle (Thomas, 2000) as well as the November 2003 meetings in Miami to finalize the proposed FTAA, should be seen as an attempt by unified labor groups to wrest some agency from the forces of globalization. Ironically, labor groups that had been fragmented in space and divided by ethnicity and national origin are now uniting in resistance against the forces of corporate globalization by engaging in a little 'globalization from below' (Brecher, Costello & Smith, 2000).

Globalization, Multiculturalism and Diversity

As a consequence of the international spread of economic activity, we increasingly contend with the phenomenon of people of multiple ethnicities and identities finding themselves in shared social spaces. In a variety of global firms, the workforce is drawn from different races, cultures and nationalities. Such diversity is readily theorized in the literature. But similar ethnic heterogeneity exists in a variety of places, be they grape farms in California, printer assembly units in Malaysia, apparel factories in the *maquiladoras* of Northern Mexico, among taxi drivers in Chicago, the souvenir sellers by the Eiffel Tower in Paris or the weavers of prayer rugs and Shiite religious artifacts in Karbala, Iraq.

It becomes desirable then for such groups to create for themselves a multicultural identity, one that neither denies differences nor engages in any discrimination. In many organic communities, such multiculturalism is taken for granted. Boundaries of identity are constantly being negotiated and exist in a state of flux. There are several examples of a homegrown multiculturalism that emerges within multiethnic communities.

However, one notices that in the bureaucratized realm of capitalist organizations, multiculturalism has functioned less as foundation and more as façade, dressing up an organizational monoculturalism (Prasad & Mills, 1997). Jacoby (1994) has observed that in the absence of any meaningful ceding of power by dominant groups, routines of multiculturalism and diversity have been transformed into buzzwords and talking points, sometimes signifying everything, and sometimes denoting nothing.

Multiculturalism and diversity have been deployed by MNCs as a Trojan horse to wage hegemony on behalf of an agenda of economic neoliberalism, and to solicit customers from among ethnic minorities (see Banerjee & Linstead, 2001: 703, for a critique of 'multicultural' symbols of consumption such as the Benetton advertisements). As early as 1997, Zizek had seen through the ideology of multi-culturalism, terming it 'the cultural logic of multinational capitalism' in a landmark article to which the title of this piece pays mimetic obeisance. In his characteris-tically forthright formulation, Zizek contends that the ideology of liberalism suggests that this age marks the end of 'immature' political passions (such as class struggle) and entering a 'mature' pragmatic universe of rational administra-tion and negotiated consensus. However, this very liberatory moment is marked by the re-emergence of hateful racism. Multiculturalism has been deployed by the liberal project, therefore, to elide 'the contemporary "postmodern" racism (that) is the *symptom* of the multiculturalist late capitalism, (and that a critique of multiculturalism can) bring to the light the inherent contradiction of the liberal-democratic ideological project' (Zizek, 1997: 28–9). Likewise, Hall (1991) has also critiqued the inability of multiculturalism to challenge racialized power rela-tionships in economic and social systems while speaking loftily of difference. The same can be said about the lip service paid to the concept of global diversity: that unless it is armed with a transformative agenda, all it will end up doing is to create a spectacle, an 'exotica of difference' (Hall, 1991).

One way in which the routines of global diversity and multiculturalism represent themselves is by the adoption by the 'core' of artifacts that belong to the 'periphery'. These artifacts could be theories (yoga and eastern mysticism), products (herbal remedies), fashions (bindis and henna), food (ethnic restaurants), music (reggae) and architecture (Trump Taj Mahal). Thus, it appears that theory and culture travel not from the core to the periphery but in reverse. But we increasingly observe that even when the margins do return to the metropole, they do so in an exoticized and commodified form, as parodying a diverse world, while still heralding a 'triumphal metropolitan nationalism' (Spivak, 2000). Unless our theories of diversity and multi-culturalism challenge such monoculturalism and metropolitan nationalism, they will remain little more than alibis against charges of racism and apologies for the rapacious ingress of global capitalism into the periphery.

CONCLUSION: WE ARE THE (Mc)WORLD

We have sought to accomplish three interrelated objectives thus far in the chapter:

1 We have suggested that while economic activity in the world has indeed become more internationalized, much more so in the recent past, the trajecto-ries of this internationalization are manifold and various, and several of them are not utopian. Internationalization produces mobility as well as incarcera-tion, plentitude as well as scarcity, wealth as well as wretchedness.
2 As if piggybacking on this internationalization, the term *globalization* offers a more completed theoretical formulation. We contend that this term comes with a lot of baggage that needs to be examined before it is embraced. We have

examined the mainstream theoretical discourse on globalization, and suggested that it needs to be deepened in order to address the concerns of a variety of subjects who experience it more as imperialism than anything liberatory.

3   Finally, our limited survey of the analytical tropes used in the theory and research of global workplace diversity suggests that they are static and inadequate in the main, and may even have ideological overtones. Our challenge as organizational theorists, then, is to produce a more inclusive analysis of global diversity: one that does not shy away from a critique of the role played by global corporations and institutions, and does not obscure some of the negative consequences of global shift.

Where then, should future studies of global workplace diversity concentrate their attention in order to be more sensitive to issues of multiplicity, history, context and class? In conclusion, we would like to offer five future theoretical issues that, if incorporated in our analysis, will go a long way in addressing the lacks that populate our literature on global diversity: circuits of labor, circuits of capital, the transformation of work, the persistence of nation states, and everyday resistances in the global workplace. In the globalized and diverse workplace, these issues represent challenges to our field, which need to be addressed if we are to retain a sense of effectiveness and currency.

Circuits of Labor

The quote at the beginning of this chapter suggested that labor enters the global realm through multiple circuits. Our literature and analysis should develop a greater curiosity about the process through which globalization produces diversity. The simple linear circuit of *globalization = porous nation state boundaries = people moving here and there* must necessarily be deepened. What are the ways in which capital seeks to control the mobility of labor? What are the ways in which labor subverts these controls (Peck, 1996)? What identity groups then constitute migrant labor in different countries? In what ways are their experiences unique, and in what ways can they be generalized into a larger analysis of the relationship between globalization and labor (Munck, 2002)?

We would like to recommend the use of postcolonial theory as an important theoretical lens to analyze global diversity (see Prasad, 2003, for an overview of postcolonial theory and its applicability to organizational analysis). Postcolonial theory has the advantage of being able to deal simultaneously with issues of economic and cultural difference, of exploitation as well as representation. Through postcolonial analysis, we can bring to the surface the histories of colonialism and imperialism that underlie a variety of issues that are of importance to global diversity. The presence of Algerians and Moroccans in France, Turks in Germany, South Asians and Afro-Carribeans in the UK, Vietnamese and Filipinos in the United States, is no accident, but a process that is related to the visible hand of colonial expansion in the recent past. What will the future bring for the diasporas of

Afghanistan, Iraq, Somalia and Sudan, among others? In effect, the study of global circuits of labor is in many ways a true study of empire (Hardt & Negri, 2001).

Circuits of Capital

While the assumption of ultra-mobile global capital has some grounding in reality, the parallel reality is that global capital too moves only in fixed circuits (Sassen, 1999). What, then, is the role of capital in producing a variety of industrial spaces and enclaves for the furtherance of globalization (such as the newly industrializing nations of South East Asia), while consigning others (such as sub-Saharan Africa) into the shadows of global capitalism (Dicken, 2003: 507–24)?

Likewise, we must remember that while the literature on globalization appears to take for granted the fact that globalization results in workplace diversity, it is relatively shy about accepting the other side of the coin: that globalization is also simultaneously a process of homogenization. In other words, when capital moves overseas, it seeks to recreate the local in the image of the dominant global (MTV, Hollywood). Theory and culture always travel along a gradient that is parallel to the gradient of capital flows, that is from the core to the periphery.

It is important, in our view, for organizational theorists to grapple with these issues, especially as they relate to global diversity. What is the role played by foreign direct investments in generating a specific trajectory of diversity? Does the capricious and fragmented nature of capital mobility produce different experiences of diversity for different people? What is the impact of cultural homogenization on issues relating to workplace diversity? Each of these issues assumes great salience in our research as the circuits of capital get more established.

The Transformation of Work

Technology-led (and policy-furthered) initiatives like business process outsourcing have a huge impact on labor struggles in both the industrialized nations as well as the 'recipient' nations of outsourcing. To take the example of a single country, recent analyses by the McKinsey Corporation[12] have estimated that the business process outsourcing sector in India grew by 60% in 2003. From the perspective of the US labor market in services, this is alarming news, despite soothing prognostications by policy-makers to the contrary. One would perhaps think that the Indian labor market should view this news with great optimism. However, it must be remembered that revenues from outsourcing are notoriously fickle, as analysis from other industries like apparel and footwear have shown (Gereffi, 2002). Despite their classification as 'foreign direct investment (FDI)', outsourcing investments have proven to be as fickle as 'foreign portfolio investments', which may be defined as frictionless and heavily contingent investments into a nation's economy through the stock market (Stallings, 1995). Likewise, it has been argued that multinationals in a variety of industries have produced a race to the bottom among poorer nations of the world who are desperate for FDI inflows (Rosen, 2002). In the long run, it appears that the only beneficiaries of the new international division of labor are the MNCs themselves.

What are the impacts of outsourcing in particular, and the mobility of work in general, on the dynamics of workplace diversity? This too is a very important empirical and theoretical question that needs to be addressed to imbue the literature with contemporaneity.

The Persistence of Nation States

Many theorists who study the international integrations emerging in the world are quick to offer predictions about the emergence of a unitary global economy and the subsequent weakening, or even the eventual dissolution of the nation state (Ohmae, 1995). The reality of course is that the more globalized the world becomes, the more dependent transnational institutions (including corporations and international regimes like the WTO) become on the nation state, to secure intellectual and other property rights, to maintain law and order, and to provide facilities conducive to business (Dicken, 2003: 122–63). At the same time, international regimes are deployed to twist the arm of the nation state into self-weakening moves such as the reduction of corporate taxes, lifting tariffs that might have provided protection to local infant industries and reduced government involvement in industry. Ultimately, these pressures push the nation state simultaneously into a position of prominence as well as a position of diminished strength in its ability to wield its sovereign authority. This may also have adverse security implications (as weakened nation states are unable to control the emergence of anti-social activities, some of which may have global implications). Moreover, there is a distressing tendency for weakened nation states to fall prey to undemocratic upheavals. Such upheavals (and new undemocratic regimes) are then subsequently accepted by the global community, in the name of safeguarding strategic interests such as corporate FDIs in the said country. Such a policy has dangerous long-term implications. Corporations have a rather sorry record in terms of their interventions in the sovereign running of nations, and have been known to manipulate foreign policies of powerful nations with disastrous effect (Barnet & Cavanaugh, 1995). The challenge for the international community from an institutional point of view is to foster an international governance regime that facilitates international exchange while still remaining fair to the sovereignty of nation states as well as the aspirations of a variety of subnational groups who are important if under-represented stakeholders in the global economy.

What is the effect of the weakened/important nation state on issues of global diversity? How will the shifting features of the nation state impact global labor? Will nation states be able to find ways to manage the twin pressures of needing to maintain law and order and reducing the social safety net that affords them hegemonic acceptance in the eyes of their citizenry? These issues carry great relevance in our field, and need to be researched and enveloped into our theories of global diversity.

Everyday Resistances in the Global Workplace

In their analysis of subtle struggles in workplaces characterized by the dominance of management over earlier labor formulations such as unions, Prasad and Prasad (1998) discuss the manner in which open confrontations are reduced, and replaced by 'subtle subversions', by acts of 'disengagement' and 'ambiguous accommodations'. Labor, it appears, improvises too in its struggle against the hegemony of global capital.

The position of the global migrant is in many ways similarly compromised by a variety of barriers to overt resistance, such as documents, immigration status, the matter of foreign-ness and cultural alienation. How, then, do disenfranchised international workers express their opposition to repugnant work practices?

Theorists of global diversity must pay special attention to the fact that in the absence of any real power, the responses of the foreign worker to exploitative work practices may take forms that are subtler, even irrational. Resistance to work practices under such circumstances often takes on a more passive, 'routine' dimension (Scott, 1985). Likewise, when a foreign corporation enters a poor country and seeks to establish a proletarianized workforce, the response of workers is similarly subtle and beyond the pale of traditional analysis. In a landmark study of the response of Malaysian women to the discipline introduced by MNCs, Ong (1987) documents how workers in modern organizational settings may play out their resistance through the invocation of ghosts, spirits, legends and religious deities. Studies of subtler forms of resistance to global capital would go a long way in imbuing the literature on workplace diversity with meaning.

By addressing these concerns in our theory and research, we will truly be able to avoid the pitfall of theorizing purely from the point of view of the liberated, *uber-globalized* subject whose agency and pleasure will be represented as the experiences of international workers at large. We have argued that the study of workplace diversity, especially in the global terrain, should take on a wider mandate. Be it the invisible history of colonialism or the current mandate of neoliberalism, the case of the accidental migrant or the case of the global worker incarcerated in local space, the subject of globalization or the subject of imperialism, unless we attempt to represent at least some of these diverse realities in our theory and research, we will only end up with a theory of global diversity that is little more than an ideological reaffirmation of the logic of global capitalism. Surely we can do much better.

NOTES

1 Quoted in Mathew (2005).

2 Quoted in Escobar (1994: 3).

3 http://www.cnn.com/2003/LAW/11/09/walmart.arrests.ap. Illegal immigrants arrested in raids sue Wal-Mart (accessed 6 June 2005).

4 See http://www.stopftaa.org. Stop the FTAA (accessed 6 June 2005).

5 http://www.mckinsey.com/knowledge/mgi/rp/offshoring. McKinsey & Company – Offshoring (accessed 6 June 2005).

6 See study at: http://www.bls.gov/news.release/reloc.toc.htm. Extended mass layoffs associated with domestic and overseas relocations, first quarter, 2004 (accessed 6 June 2005).

7 http://www.union-network.org/unitelecom.nsf/0/2A2D3A6E196A2508C1256EC300 35380B?OpenDocument. UNI Telecom President tells World Bank conference that out-sourcing is a threat to sustainable development (accessed 6 June 2005).

8 http://nasscom.org/artdisplay.asp?cat_id=314. Indian software and services exports (accessed 6 June 2005).

9 Both the Ohmae and Friedman quotes are cited in Dicken (2003: 11).

10 http://www.gatt.org/trastat_e.html. WTO: trade liberalisation statistics (accessed 6 June 2005).

11 http://www.ilo.org/dyn/declaris/DECLARATIONWEB.DOWNLOAD_BLOB? Var_ DocumentID=2502. Organizing for social justice (accessed 6 June 2005).

12 *Asia Times* (14 February 2003), archived at: http://www.atimes.com/atimes/South_ Asia/EB14Df06.html. India's outsourcing tipped to grow 60% (accessed 6 June 2005).

REFERENCES

Ahmad, A. (2000). Globalisation: A society of aliens? *Frontline*, *17*(20), 31–3.

Althusser, L. (1972). *Lenin and philosophy and other essays.* London: New Left Books.

Anderson, B. (1991). *Imagined communities: Reflections on the origin and spread of nationalism.* New York: New Left Books.

Anwar, S. A., & Chaker, M. N. (2003). Globalisation of corporate America and its impli-cations for management styles in an Arabian cultural context. *International Journal of Management*, *20*(1), 43–55.

Banerjee, S. B., & Linstead, S. (2001). Globalization, multiculturalism and other fictions: Colonialism for the new millennium? *Organization*, 8(4), 711–50.

Barnet, R., & Cavanaugh, P. (1995). *Global dreams: Imperial corporations and the new world order.* New York: Simon & Schuster Adult Publishing Group.

Baskerville, R. F. (2003). Hofstede never studied culture. *Accounting, Organizations and Society*, 28(1), 1–21.

Beck, U. (2001). *The brave new world of work.* Cambridge: Polity.

Berman, M. (1987). *All that is solid melts into air: The experience of modernity.* Hammondsworth: Penguin.

Beyer, J., & Trice, H. (1991). Cultural leadership in organizations. *Organizational Science*, 2(2), 1–23.

Bing, J. W. (2004). Hofstede's consequences: The impact of his work on consulting and business practices. *Academy of Management Executive*, *18*(1), 80–5.

Brecher, J., Costello, T., & Smith, B. (2000). *Globalization from below: The power of solidarity.* Boston: South End Press.

Carnevale, A. P., & Stone, S. C. (1994). Diversity: Beyond the golden rule. *Training and Development*, *48*(10), 22–39.

Caudron, S. (1999). Diversity watch. *Black Enterprise*, 29, 91–4.

Cavanaugh, J. M. (1997). (In)corporating the other? Managing the politics of workplace dif-ference. In P. Prasad, A. J. Mills, M. Elmes & A. Prasad (Eds), *Managing the organizational melting pot: Dilemmas of workplace diversity* (pp. 31–53). Thousand Oaks, CA: Sage.

Clott, C. B. (2004). Perspectives on global outsourcing and the changing nature of work. *Business and Society Review*, *109*(2), 153–70.

Coates, D. (2000). *Models of capitalism.* Cambridge: Polity.

Cox, T. H., & Blake, S. (1991). Managing cultural diversity: Implications for organizational competitiveness. *Academy of Management Executive*, 5(3), 45–56.

Dedoussis, E. (2004). A cross-cultural comparison of organizational culture: Evidence from universities in the Arab world and Japan. *Cross Cultural Management*, 11(1), 15–34.

Dicken, P. (2003). *Global shift: Reshaping the global economic map in the 21st century.* New York: Guilford.

DiMaggio, P. (1997). Culture and cognition. *Annual Review of Sociology*, 23, 263–87.

Escobar, A. (1994). *Encountering development.* Princeton, NJ: Princeton University Press.

Fishman, C. (2003). The Wal-Mart you don't know. *Fast Company*, 77, 68–72.

Flynn, G. (1998). White males see diversity's other side. *Workforce*, 78(2), 52–6.

Fortune (2004). Who's on top? The 2004 global 500. *Fortune* (19 July 2004).

Foucault, M. (1983). The order of discourse. In M. J. Shapiro (Ed.), *Language and politics* (pp.112–27). New York: New York University Press.

Frey-Ridgway, S. (1997). The cultural dimension of international business. *Collection Building*, 16(1), 12–23.

Friedman, T. (1999). *The lexus and the olive tree: Understanding globalization.* New York: Knopf.

Gereffi, G. (2002). Outsourcing and changing patterns of international competition in the apparel commodity chain. Paper presented at the Conference on Responding to globalization: Societies, groups, and individuals, Boulder, Colorado. Archived at: http://www.colorado.edu/IBS/PEC/gadconf/papers/gereffi.html.

Goldberg, D. T. (1993). *Racist culture: Philosophy and the politics of meaning.* Cambridge, MA: Blackwell.

Govindarajan, V., & Gupta, A. K. (2001). Building an effective global business team. *Sloan Management Review*, 42(4), 63–71.

Graen, G., & Hui, C. (1996). Managing changes in globalizing business: How to manage cross-cultural business partners. *Journal of Organizational Change Management*, 9(3), 25–44.

Hall, S. (1991). The local and the global: Globalization and ethnicity. In A. D. King (Ed.), *Culture, globalization and the world system.* London: Macmillan.

Hardt, T., & Negri, A. (2001). *Empire.* Cambridge, MA: Harvard University Press.

Harris, H., & Kumra, S. (2000). International manager development: Cross-cultural training in highly diverse environments. *Journal of Management Development*, 19(7), 602–14.

Hemphill, H., & Haines, R. (1997). *Discrimination, harassment and the failure of diversity training: What to do now.* Westport, CT: Quorum Books.

Hill, C. (2003). *International business: Competing in the global marketplace.* New York: McGraw-Hill Irwin.

Hirst, P., & Thompson, G. (1996). *Globalisation in question.* Cambridge: Polity.

Hofstede, G. (1980). *Culture's consequences: Comparing values, behaviors, institutions, and organizations across nations.* London: Sage.

Hu, J. (2004). The role of international law in the development of WTO law. *Journal of International Economic Law*, 7(1), 143–56.

Illich, V. I. (1981). The delinking of peace and government. *Gandhi Marg*, 3, 257–65.

IOM (2003). *World Migration 2003 – Managing migration: Challenges and responses for people on the move.* Geneva: IOM.

Jacoby, R. (1994). *Dogmatic wisdom: How the culture wars divert education and distract America.* New York: Doubleday.

Johnston, W. B. & Parker, A. E. (1987). *Workforce 2000: Work and workers for the 21st century.* Washington, DC: US Department of Labour.

Keane, D. (2004). The environmental causes and consequences of migration: A search for the meaning of 'environmental refugees'. *Georgetown International Environmental Law Review*, 16(2), 209–23.

Klein, N. (2000). *No space, no choice, no jobs, no logo: Taking aim at the brand bullies.* New York: Picador.

Kondrasuk, J. N. (2004). The effects of 9/11 and terrorism on human resource management: Recovery, reconsideration, and renewal. *Employee Responsibilities and Rights Journal, 16*(1), 25–44.

MacDonald, H. (1993). The diversity industry. *The New Republic*, 5 July, 22–5.

Mahroum, S. (2000). Highly skilled globetrotters: Mapping the international migration of human capital. *R & D Management, 30*(1), 23–31.

Mander, J., & Goldsmith, E. (1997). *The case against the global economy: And for a turn toward the local.* San Francisco: The Sierra Book Club.

Mathew, B. (2005). *Taxi! Cabs and capitalism in New York City.* New York: The New Press.

McKee, A., & Schor, S. (1999). Confronting prejudice and stereotypes: A teaching model. *Performance Improvement Quarterly, 12*(1), 181–99.

Mir, A., Mathew, B., & Mir, R. (2000). The codes of migration: The contours of the global software labor market. *Cultural Dynamics, 12*(1), 5–34.

Mongia, R. (1999). Race, nationality, mobility: A history of the passport. *Public Culture, 11*(3), 527–56.

Munck, R. (2002). *Globalisation and labour: The new great transformation.* London: Zed Books.

Norton, J. R., & Fox, R. E. (1997). *The change equation: Capitalizing on diversity for effective organizational change.* Washington, DC: American Psychological Association.

Ohmae, K. (1995). *The end of the nation-state: The rise of regional economies.* New York: Free Press.

Oliver, M., & and Shapiro, T. (1995). *Black wealth/white wealth: A new perspective on racial inequality.* New York: Routledge.

Ong, A. (1987). *Spirits of resistance and capitalist discipline: Factory women in Malaysia.* Albany, NY: State University of New York Press.

Peck, J. (1996). Work-place: The social regulation of labor markets. New York: Guilford Press.

Polanyi, K. (1957). *The great transformation. The political and economic origins of our time.* Boston: Beacon Press.

Prasad, A. (2003). *Postcolonial theory and organizational analysis: A critical engagement.* Basingstoke: Palgrave Macmillan.

Prasad, A., & Prasad, P. (1998). Everyday struggles at the workplace: The nature and implications of routine resistance in contemporary organizations. *Research in the Sociology of Organizations, 15*, 225–57.

Prasad, P., & Mills, A. J. (1997). From showcase to shadow: Understanding the dilemmas of managing workplace diversity. In P. Prasad, A. J. Mills, M. Elmes & A. Prasad (Eds), *Managing the organizational melting pot: Dilemmas of workplace diversity* (pp. 3–30). Thousand Oaks, CA: Sage.

Rosen, E. (2002). *Making sweatshops: The globalization of the U.S. apparel industry.* Berkeley, CA: University of California Press.

Salter, S. B., & Niswander, F. (1995). Cultural influence on the development of accounting systems internationally: A test of Gray's (1988) theory. *Journal of International Business Studies, 26*(2), 379–97.

Sassen, S. (1999). *Globalization and its discontents: Essays on the new mobility of people and money.* New York: The New Press.

Scott, J. C. (1985). *Weapons of the weak: Everyday forms of peasant resistance.* New Haven, CT: Yale University Press.

Sivakumar, K., & Nakata, C. (2003). Designing global new product teams: Optimizing the effects of national culture on new product development. *International Marketing Review, 20*(4), 397–445.

Spivak, G. (2000). Keynote address: Narratives for a new millennium conference. February: Adelaide, Australia.

Stallings, B. (1995). *Global change, regional response: The new international context of development.* New York: Cambridge University Press.

Swann, C. (2004). Economists enter war of words on outsourcing. *Financial Times*, 8 April, 8.

Teboul, J. C. (2002). Case study: The language dilemma. *Management Communication Quarterly*, *15*(4), 603–8.

Thomas, J. (2000). *Battle in Seattle: The story behind and beyond the WTO demonstrations*. Golden, CO: Fulcrum Books.

Tsui, A. S., Egan, T. D., & O'Reilly, C. A. (1992). Being different: Relational demography and organizational attachment. *Administrative Science Quarterly*, *37*, 549–79.

United Nations (2002a). *World investment report 2002*. New York and Geneva: United Nations.

United Nations (2002b). *Activities of the United Nations Statistics Division on international migration*. New York: United Nations Statistics Division.

Van Dijk, T. A. (1993). Introduction: The reality of racism. In T. A. Van Dijk (Ed.), *Elite Discourse and Racism* (pp. 1–17). Newbury Park, CA: Sage.

Webb, C. (2004). What outsourcing problem? *Washington Post* (11 June 2004): http://www.washingtonpost.com/wp-dyn/articles/A33998-2004Jun11.html.

Wong-MingJi, D., & Mir, A. (1997). How international is international management? Provincialism, parochialism, and the problematic of global diversity. In P. Prasad, A. J. Mills, M. Elmes & A. Prasad (Eds), *Managing the organizational melting pot: Dilemmas of workplace diversity* (pp. 340–65). Thousand Oaks, CA: Sage.

Zakaria, N. (2000). The effects of cross-cultural training on the acculturation process of the global workforce. *International Journal of Manpower*, *21*(6), 492–510.

Zizek, S. (1997). Multiculturalism, or the cultural logic of multinational capitalism. *New Left Review*, *225*, 28–51.

Part II

METHODS FOR STUDYING
WORKPLACE DIVERSITY

8

What Is Diversity and How Should It Be Measured?

DAVID A. HARRISON AND HOCK-PENG SIN

As organizations continue to be more diverse in the sociological and psychological characteristics of their workforces (Nemetz & Christensen, 1996; Offermann & Gowing, 1990), there continues to be a strong need to understand how diversity impacts individual and team processes and outcomes in the workplace. Indeed, diversity in work units has become an indisputably important topic in organizational science. Several reviews of work group research have also emphasized the relevance and importance of diversity for team effectiveness (e.g. Guzzo & Shea, 1992; West, Borrill & Unsworth, 1998; Williams & O'Reilly, 1998). The number of articles published has grown almost exponentially over the past two decades. Given this trend, it is obvious that diversity is commanding a great deal of research attention. That attention is one of the reasons for this handbook.

Given that diversity is an increasingly vital and pervasive topic, one would expect an increasingly consensual paradigm or set of conventions in the way it is studied. However, a close look at the literature suggests that it is not the case; even in research on work team diversity, there is no favored or dominant (set of) approach(es). This is not meant to suggest that a hegemony of a particular diversity theory or favored research strategy, such as a laboratory experiment or an ethnographic field study, would be beneficial. It is meant to suggest that some consistency in the *conceptual and empirical meaning ascribed to diversity* might be. Below, we examine three dimensions of this inconsistency.

INCONSISTENCIES IN DIVERSITY RESEARCH

Diversity has often been studied in an indeterminate manner; that is, the substantive meaning or constitutive definition of diversity often is not clearly specified. In their review, Milliken and Martins (1996) attempted to clarify this and suggested that various forms of work group diversity (observable traits such as demographic characteristics; unobservable traits such as personality and values; and functional characteristics, such as knowledge, skills and organizational experience) might be differentially related to group processes and outcomes (see also Harrison, Price & Bell, 1998; Lawrence, 1997; Pelled, 1996). Also, more recent works suggest that different 'levels' of diversity (e.g. surface versus deep) might be relevant and important depending on the amount of within-team social interaction (Harrison, Price, Gavin & Florey, 2002) or on the phase of the work group innovation process (e.g. Farr, Sin & Tesluk, 2003). Hence, there is a need for diversity researchers to be explicit about the substantive meaning or type of diversity being examined.

In addition, a variety of variables (e.g. age, sex, race, tenure, education, etc.) have been included as manifesting within-team diversity often using similar theory to justify the close examination of different variables across studies. The choice of different diversity variables in different contexts (i.e. inclusion or exclusion of one form of diversity versus another) has not been clearly articulated. In addition, different empirical indices might be used by different researchers to index the same team diversity variable. To illustrate the lack of consensus in the meaning and measures of team diversity variables, we briefly review and summarize three recent articles by Chatman and Flynn (2001), Colquitt, Noe and Jackson (2002) and Klein, Conn, Smith and Sorra (2001) (see Table 8.1).

In their first study, Chatman and Flynn (2001) investigated the effect of demographic heterogeneity on cooperative norms and effectiveness in teams. The demographic variables included were sex, race and national citizenship. Following Tsui, Egan, and O'Reilly (1992), *individual distances* were computed for each variable, regardless of underlying metric. Next, the authors summed across all three variables (sex, race, national citizenship) to yield an overall score on individual-level relational distances, which were used to test the individual-level hypotheses. Finally, team-level demographic diversity was computed via the coefficient of variation (Allison, 1978) by using the individual relational demographic scores within each team – a kind of repacked diversity at the team level of the interpersonal distances at the individual level (see also Tsui et al., 1992).

Colquitt et al. (2002) examined the effect of demographic diversity on climate level and climate strength for procedural justice. To assess team diversity, they adapted and used Campion et al.'s (1993) team heterogeneity measure. Team members were asked to rate, using a five-point scale, the *perceived diversity* of the team along three dimensions: sex, race and age. Team-level (demographic) diversity was then computed by averaging across those three ratings and across the members within each team.

Klein et al. (2001) studied the relationship between team demographic heterogeneity and variability in members' perceptions of the work environment. Several

TABLE 8.1 *In-depth examples of diverse ways of defining and assessing team demographic diversity*

Articles	Chatman & Flynn (2001)	Colquitt et al. (2002)	Klein et al. (2001)
Constitutive definition	None given	None given	None given
Demographic variables	Sex, race and citizenship	Sex, race and age	Sex, age, plant tenure, pay and education (race dropped due to lack of variability)
Actual vs. perceived	Actual	Perceived	Actual
Indices used	• Euclidean distance computed at the individual level for each variable • Sum across all three variables to yield individual level relational demography • Team-level demographic diversity computed via coefficient of variation by using the individual relational demographic scores within each team	• Used Campion, Medsker and Higg's (1993) team heterogeneity measure • Team members rated the perceived diversity of the team along the three dimensions • Team-level demographic diversity computed by averaging across those three ratings and members within each team	• Coefficient of variation computed at the team level age, plant tenure, level of pay and level of education • Blau's index was used to compute gender heterogeneity at the team level
Remarks	Global index across all three variables	Global index on perceived diversity across all three variables	Each demographic variable treated separately during analyses

demographic variables were assessed: sex, age, tenure, pay level, educational level and race. The coefficient of variation (Allison, 1978) was used as a measure of heterogeneity at the team level for age, tenure, pay level and education level. Blau's index (1977) was used to measure gender heterogeneity at the team level. Race heterogeneity was dropped due to a lack of between-group variability.

While these three sets of researchers studied different substantive topics, they all included diversity-related predictors for some team-level outcome. Despite the same umbrella term of team demographic diversity or heterogeneity, there are four important points that highlight the lack of consensus in team diversity research (see Table 8.1). First, only sex and race were included in all three studies (although it was eventually excised from the last study). Even as easily measured *demographic* variables, age, tenure, education level and national citizenship were not consistently assessed across the three studies. This demonstrates the lack of consistency in the types of, or even the number of, easily observed or social category variables included in team diversity research. *Psychological* forms of diversity are even more thinly and unevenly spread in their application (e.g. Jehn, Northcraft, & Neale, 1999; note that psychological diversity, in the form of within-group agreement, was arguably an outcome variable in both the Colquitt et al. and Klein et al. studies).

Second, Chatman and Flynn (2001) and Klein et al. (2001) assessed what might be termed a team's *actual* diversity whereas Colquitt et al. (2002) measured a team's *perceived* diversity. We believe that this difference has both theoretical and measurement implications (Riordan, 2000). Third, the way that team-level diversity was computed from individual-level measures varied substantially across the three studies. Chatman and Flynn (2001) first computed individual-level relational distance, and then derived team-level diversity using the coefficient of variation in the distances themselves. In contrast, Klein et al. (2001) used the coefficient of variation for variables with ordinal, interval or ratio metrics but Blau's index for nominal variables. Fourth and finally, both Chatman and Flynn (2001) and Colquitt et al. (2002) derived an omnibus (across variables) diversity index whereas Klein et al. (2001) computed team-level diversity for each demographic variable. In our opinion, this is a crucial distinction as it begs the question of whether diversity is a global or facet-specific construct.

These differences are even more noteworthy given that all of the three papers ostensibly studied 'diversity' consequences and were published in top journals at roughly the same time. In view of these divergent approaches to the meaning of diversity, one might ask whether the generally weak and discrepant results of studies that looked at similar diversity phenomena (Webber & Donahue, 2000) might be a function of differences in constitutive (actual versus perceived, global versus specific, and so on) or operational definitions (different indices used). While there is a preference and value in methodological triangulation in research (McGrath, 1982), divergent approaches to the meaning of team diversity research might have complicated interpretations of results in a way that researchers have not yet recognized.

Hence, the purpose of our chapter is (1) to constructively review how scholars have studied diversity thus far in both constitutive and operational definitions, (2) to critically compare approaches, and (3) to make recommendations about measurement for future diversity research. Our working supposition is that diversity research might make more cumulative progress if there were greater agreement about the meaning and measurement of diversity variables, or at least, an explicit statement of assumptions about the meanings and measures a researcher plans to use. In pursuing the purposes noted above, it is important to note that diversity has been studied at various levels of analyses: societal (Marsch, 2002), organizational (e.g. Boeker, 1997), work group (e.g. Harrison et al., 2002) and dyadic (e.g. Tsui et al., 1992). There have also been many investigations of diversity training (e.g. Rynes & Rosen, 1995). In the present chapter, we tend to focus on team and group diversity. Hence, we will not address diversity research conducted at other levels, research pertaining to diversity training, and reactions or management techniques about diversity. Such topics are covered in other chapters of the current handbook.

WHAT IS DIVERSITY?
CONSTITUTIVE DEFINITIONS

As with any construct enjoying burgeoning popularity and therefore widespread application in research, the term 'diversity' often goes under a variety of perhaps confusing guises or definitions (Ragins & Gonzalez, 2003; Williams & O'Reilly, 1998). An abbreviated but not exhaustive list of substituting or overlapping terms includes 'dispersion', 'inequality', 'within-group variability', '(dis)agreement', 'consensus', 'heterogeneity', 'homogeneity', 'deviation', 'difference', 'distance', 'relational demography', 'sharedness' and more. Before moving to what we hope is a broadly inclusive but still helpful characterization of the meaning of diversity as a construct, it is important to review why an unambiguous constitutive definition is necessary (Locke, 2003).

Necessity and Nature of Constitutive Definitions

If knowledge about diversity is to press forward, its status as a social science *construct* needs to be clarified. Constructs are abstractions or ideas that help to organize a domain of study; to do so they must initially be defined conceptually or *constitutively* (Kerlinger, 1990). Constructs can manifest themselves in different operationalizations or measures but the abstraction should remain the same. That is, the first step that social scientists are urged to take in the hypothetico-deductive approach to any research topic is to clearly state the nature of their constructs: to stipulate their meaning (Runkel & McGrath, 1972). As such, constitutive definitions state the 'what' of constructs; theories in which they are embedded state the 'why'. Clear constitutive definitions or stipulated meanings are critical for ensuring comparability of findings (Schwab, 1980), and for cumulating and making sense of the pattern of findings across studies (Hunter & Schmidt, 1990; Stone-Romero, 1994).

Constitutive definitions are the foundation for every stage of research that follows, at least in positivistic or post-positivistic epistemologies. Still, as with any realm of science, a constitutive definition of diversity is, to a large degree, arbitrary (sometimes the names are even arbitrary, as in the 'charm' attribute of a quark; for an opposing perspective arguing that some definitions are more reflective of reality than others, see Locke, 2003). One cannot argue about the construct validity of a constitutive definition, or use data to support or refute it. One can argue about how useful the definition is, by referring to the amount of nascent agreement scientists have regarding its stipulated meaning, by noting its overlap and distinction relative to constitutive definitions of other constructs, and by evaluating the degree to which those definitions support the logic, processes and goals of scientific inquiry (e.g. analysis and synthesis; description, prediction, understanding and control). Armed with a solid constitutive definition of diversity, one can then argue about the validity of particular operational definitions (see Allison, 1978).

The history and present state of diversity and diversity-like constructs, however, is not one that rests on sharply stated constitutive definitions such as those forwarded by Blau (1977). Instead, the term 'diversity' and ideas swirling around it have sometimes been appropriated from the fields of biology or population ecology (as 'species diversity', more of which is commonly thought of as representing a healthier ecosystem). The term 'diversity' has also been borrowed from political speech and popular usage, where it is usually summoned to refer to ethnic background or sex. The latter was strongly propelled by summaries of labor demographic trends in the United States during the 1980s, including Johnston & Packer's (1987) *Workforce 2000*. In other words, strong stipulative meanings generally have not been a priori considerations in the earlier decades of exploratory studies of diversity. Those studies preceded full-blown models of what diversity's effects might be (e.g. Elsass & Graves, 1997; Jackson, May & Whitney, 1995; Milliken & Martins, 1996). And, some researchers – including ourselves (e.g. Harrison et al., 1998) – have not offered any constitutive definition for diversity itself.

An Inclusive Constitutive Definition

To help generate some consensus, comparability and cumulation of results on an issue for which variation in opinions has not been particularly helpful, we there-fore propose our own definition. Diversity is the *collective amount of differences among members within a social unit*. We use the term 'collective' rather than 'total', for example, because there are a variety of meaningful ways to aggregate differences (average distance, total discrepancies, etc.), and we wanted to directly signal diversity as being a collective construct (see below; Morgeson & Hofmann, 1999). Yet, the diversity construct in this definition is still an amount that could be indexed on a unipolar continuum. One can reasonably talk about having more or less of it across teams, groups and other social units. When all members of such a social unit are identical to one another on *all* continua, there is zero diver-sity, which is almost assuredly impossible (see also Konrad, 2003). However, it is possible that there could be zero diversity on a subset of continua that a researcher defines as being relevant in a particular context.

We believe this definition has a number of strengths, including its breadth of inclusiveness for many of the terms in current use listed above (Elsass & Graves, 1997; Jackson et al., 1995; Milliken & Martins, 1996; Williams & O'Reilly, 1998). It is unique from those terms and it is explicitly *relational*. Each of the forms of demographic heterogeneity, variation, perception or (dis)agreement reviewed in the three studies above could be cast as special cases or specific forms of diversity. However, the mean level of procedural justice climate (Colquitt et al., 2002) would and should not be considered a form of diversity. In fact, the mean or location of any team-level variable would not serve as a diversity indicator.

Another, related question is if diversity could include collective differences on *any* variable whatsoever. From our definition, it could. However, we would encourage researchers to stay within the realm of demographics, skills, abilities, cognitive styles, perceptual orientations, personality dimensions, values, attitudes and beliefs that are germane to group functioning given a specific research con-text and theoretical orientation toward teams (Harrison et al., 1998; Pelled, 1996). Preferences for types of chocolate are unlikely to be germane in most teams; they may be central to functioning in the top management team at Hershey Foods. A final definitional boundary might deal with whether or not diversity is marked only by 'standing characteristics' of the group members, which is a set of psychological or demographic attributes that endures throughout the tenure of the team. Under such a stipulation, the only change that could occur in diversity would have to occur by the loss or gain of team members (e.g. Arrow & McGrath, 1993). Perhaps this assumption has become an implicit part of diversity research in management, as we could find no research tracking within-team changes in diversity over time *for teams with stable membership.*

Under the definition given above, diversity is a construct that has meaning only with respect to a particular 'meso' range of units of study (Klein & Kozlowski, 2002), and as such, it provides a bridge between micro and macro areas of organizational science. That is, it is obvious that an individual him- or herself cannot have diversity under this definition. At the other end of the spectrum, our diversity definition does not preclude talking about the diversity of large social collectives, including whole organizations, industries or workforces, although we limit our discussion in this chapter to teams and groups.

The definition above also allows for a variety of differences, actual or perceived, on any number of demographic or psychological variables. As long as a variable has at least nominal measurement properties, such as a set of numbers used to indicate classifications of ethnic background, then differences are preserved. In that sense, the definition captures the categorical notion of diversity implicit in the general question 'who is different from whom?' Sex is one diversity variable that falls under this notion. The definition also captures a continuous, distance-based diversity implicit in the general question 'to what extent are people different?' Degree of masculinity–femininity fits this more metric question. Finally, the definition would also support joint forms of diversity, as the demographic fault lines discussed by Lau and Murnighan (1998). However, as we recommend later, those faultlines or multiple forms of difference are better treated as multivariate distributions rather than sums of presumably unrelated demographic or psychological distances.

Points of Distinction from Blau and Others

Readers familiar with a sociological tradition might hasten to point out that several of the terms we listed earlier, including 'diversity' itself, were originally and clearly defined by Blau (1977). His use of the term presaged almost all of the current work in management, and he distinguished 'diversity' from 'heterogeneity.' For him, diversity reflected vertical or hierarchical differences, and 'inequality' was a particular operationalization of those status differences: 'diversity refers to the great number of different statuses among which a population is distributed. It is the graduated-parameter equivalent of heterogeneity. Its minimum is when all persons occupy the same status; its maximum is when every person occupies a different status' (p. 276). Under Blau's definition, diversity is only meaningful for variables that, at the least, rank-order individuals or subgroups on some ladder of relative standing – usually in the form of wealth, education, position or another indication of social power. 'Inequality' is a related term for Blau, but he takes it a step further: 'it is the average difference in relative standing, specifically the mean status distance in a population divided by twice the mean status, for any criterion of status' (p. 277). Because Blau formulates it as a distance, inequality would therefore be defined only in terms of interval or ratio-level data, in differences that have metric properties.

It is difficult to oppose this and the rest of his internally coherent set of definitions, as Blau's (1977) work is easily the most seminal and influential in the area. However, we believe the predominant use of 'diversity' in the current literature, as well as in this handbook, conveys a less restrictive, less status-driven definition. The closest kin in Blau's work to the definition we propose above might be his use of the term 'heterogeneity', which is more or less status-free: 'the distribution of population among many groups, defined by the probability that two randomly chosen persons do not belong to the same group' (p. 276). Taken together, his use of all three terms might compose our definition of diversity. And, under our constitutive definition, his derivation of various empirical indices can still help researchers with operation definitions of diversity for nominal, ordinal and interval data (using his formulas for heterogeneity, diversity and inequality, respectively; see the section on *operational definitions* below).

Dimensions of Diversity

Can a single number reflect a team's overall or global diversity? Despite the generality of our definition, we would answer that question with a fairly emphatic 'no'. Presuming that one has measured *the* diversity of a social unit means presuming that all possible differences among team members, on all possible variables, have been assessed and aggregated. We believe that would be impossible. But, if it were possible, it would still be imprudent. The (mainly psychometric or statistical) logic underlying such aggregation assumes either a latent or emergent construct based on positive correlations among its constituent elements (Harrison, 2002). Nothing is gained empirically by having a composite (Diversity = diversity[A] + diversity[B] + diversity[C]) in which the parts have no relationship to one another, as any empirical connection of an antecedent or outcome to the composite simply masks holding an identical strength of connection to each of its uncorrelated parts (i.e. mandating the same strength of weights on diversity[A], diversity[B] and diversity[C] when forming the composite; Edwards, 2001).

For instance, if one wanted to create a 'total demographic diversity' index, reflective measurement logic would require that diversity in ethnicity, age, sex, and so on would be related to one another; more or greater differences along one dimension should speak to more or greater differences along the others. The composite would then represent the shared or overlapping components of the diversity variables. However, a quick trip through the correlation matrices of recent diversity articles suggests that this is rarely the case. In the three running examples we have used in this chapter, the amount of shared variance across various diversity variables was generally quite low. In Klein et al. (2001: 8), the correlations between tenure, age, pay, education and gender variability ranged from -0.14 to 0.26 and only the pay and gender variability correlation was statistically significant. In Chatman and Flynn (2001: 965), the correlations between the participants' citizenship, race and sex ranged from -0.19 to 0.21 and -0.05 to 0.15 in study 1 and 2, respectively. Finally, in Colquitt et al. (2001), although the team demographic diversity was a global composite of the perceived diversity in age, race and gender, no reliability estimate was reported. More importantly, there is often no conceptual basis for expecting different dimensions of diversity to be significantly correlated with each other (e.g. why should there be more women in one ethnic group than in another?). Perhaps a better approach, and one that corresponds more directly to theoretical notions about the simultaneous or cumulative outflow of diversity variables having independent or even joint effects on the same outcomes (Lau & Murnighan, 1998), would be to treat them as a multivariate set rather than adding them together to reach a less meaningful total score.

Hence, we contend that diversity is meaningful only when it is more narrowly defined or dimensionalized. Diversity as a viable construct in research needs to be accompanied by some adjective or modifier: ethnic diversity, sex diversity, age diversity, cognitive ability diversity, educational background diversity, Protestant work ethic diversity, and so on. And, in all such cases, it is still sensible to talk about having a *collective amount of differences among members.* However, a meaningful composite might be made for 'organizational status diversity' as long as this is theoretically relevant, and the components of the composite – perhaps tenure diversity, educational attainment diversity, job level diversity and pay-level diversity – had positive correlations with one another. Even then, a case could be made for standardizing and aggregating these variables at the individual level to create a psychometrically tractable 'organizational status' variable for individual team members, and then computing one of the indices detailed below can be used to represent status diversity within the team.

In terms of dimensionalizing diversity, more abstract constructs have already begun to percolate through the literature. For example, various groups of researchers have proposed 'surface' versus 'deep' diversity levels, which might alternatively be cast as 'demographic' versus 'psychological', or 'visible' versus 'invisible' (Harrison et al., 1998; 2002; Jackson et al., 1995; Milliken & Martins, 1996). McGrath, Berdahl and Arrow (1995) divided diversity of team composition variables into three sets: (1) personality, demographics and traits (PDT), (2) values, beliefs and attitudes (VBA), and (3) knowledge, skills and abilities (KSA). The last might well be part of the bifurcation of diversity variables for Pelled (1996), who proposed that the important categories of diversity variables are task-relevant versus irrelevant.

Two things are notable about these higher-level distinctions in forms of diversity. First, they are all defined in such a way that creating a broader composite from them would not be particularly meaningful. Mashing all possible surface-level or demographic characteristics together into one overall index would create the same kinds of conceptual and empirical problems we documented earlier (i.e. assuming a latent construct for which every variable is a strictly and equally valid indicator). Perhaps more subtly, it is also unlikely that an expansive sampling of VBA components would form a coherent set. However, if the VBA were directed at the team members' goals or tasks, there is a good chance the patterns of diversity would coalesce (Harrison et al., 2002).

Second, diversity research has moved beyond a reliance on relational demography. Theorizing about diversity constructs has now come to more fully embrace psychological variables (e.g. Barrick, Stewart, Neubert & Mount, 1998; Barsade, Ward, Turner & Sonnenfeld, 2000; Neumann, Wagner & Christiansen, 1999), in some cases rediscovering 40-year-old research programs (e.g. Hoffman, 1959; Hoffman & Maier, 1961; Newcomb, 1961). As researchers push the edge of the psychological diversity envelope, other questions about the constitutive (and operational) definitions of diversity need to be answered.

Diversity of Perceptions and Perceptions of Diversity

One such question deals with the appropriate place of perceptions in diversity research (see also Riordan, 2000). An instigating reason for this stream of research in management was that elemental, demographic data points were less likely than psychological variables to be tainted by percept–percept bias or common methods variance (Pfeffer, 1983). When are such perceptions reasonable to add to the diversity mix?

As with most answers in the social sciences – it depends. Our constitutive definition of diversity suggests that studying perceptions is not only reasonable, it is necessary, *if those perceptions form the pivotal dimension for diversity's effects* (for an opposing viewpoint, see Konrad, 2003). For example, when studying juries, top management teams, or other groups responsible for bringing in and collectively processing complex social information, the diversity of particular perceptions (guilt or innocence; diagnosticity of a competitor's move) is the engine that might drive both conflict and creativity, turnover and top performance (e.g. Hinsz, Tindale & Vollrath, 1997). Still, under these circumstances and others (Harrison et al., 1998), the nature of what is being studied might be regarded as *actual* diversity of perceptions: measured originally at the individual level, and then collected as inter-individual differences to form a diversity measure at the team level.

In contrast, perceptions of diversity would seem to hold a more tenuous place in this research domain. On one hand, theory might prescribe that members cognitively process the collective amount of differences within their teams, and those cognitions are shared before affecting team-level outcomes (Riordan, 2000). That is, perceived diversity *is* the constitutively defined construct of interest (Harrison et al., 2002). On the other hand, more studies are appearing that use perceptions of diversity as proxy measures for actual diversity, especially for psychological variables (Jehn et al., 1999); sometimes they include disagreement (i.e. diversity of perceptions of diversity(!): Kilduff, Angelmar & Mehra, 2000). There is no clear evidence suggesting that such perceptions are consistently valid (e.g. Beyer et al., 1997; Harrison et al., 2002). There is clear evidence suggesting that perceptions of, or peer reports of, the variation in psychological variables held by others can be plagued by systematic biases of contamination (Harrison et al., 2002) and deficiency (Park & Judd, 1990; Park, Ryan & Judd, 1992; Quattrone & Jones, 1980). Perceptions of diversity are not yet substitutable for diversity of perceptions.

TABLE 8.2   Variety of investigations and application diversity indices in recent published research

	Articles	Diversity variables and indexes used	Outcome (social)	Outcome (task)
Demographic diversity	Harrison et al. (1998)	Age (CV), sex (Blau), ethnicity (Blau)	Social integration	
	Earley & Mosakowski (2000, Study 3)	Nationality (trichotomous categorization)	Satisfaction	Project performance
	Timmerman (2000)	Age (CV) and race (Blau)		Basketball and baseball performance
	Jehn et al. (1999)	Social category diversity (aggregate of sex and gender diversity via Teachman/entropy index)	Conflict and morale	Task performance
	Pelled et al. (1999)	Age (CV), tenure (CV), gender (Teachman), and race (Teachman)	Emotional conflict	Cognitive task performance
Psychological diversity	Harrison et al. (2002)	Conscientiousness (SD), values (SD), task meaningfulness (SD) and outcome importance (SD)	Social integration	Task performance
	Barrick et al. (1998)	Personality (variance)	Cohesiveness and viability	
	Jehn et al. (1997)	Values (coefficient alpha of organizational culture profile, treating members as *items*)	Task and relationship conflict	
	Barsade et al. (2000)	Affectivity (SD)	Task and relationship conflict and cooperativeness	Task performance (logged annual market-adjusted return)
	Neuman et al. (1999)	Personality (variance)		Task performance

HOW SHOULD DIVERSITY BE MEASURED? OPERATIONAL DEFINITIONS

While the stipulated meanings inherent in constitutive definitions are necessary and important, the next crucial step requires investigators to develop *operational* definitions or measurements for their constitutively defined constructs. Only after operational definitions have been developed can researchers empirically examine relationships of their focal construct with a proposed network of other constructs, and thereby come to conclusions about their nomological meaning(s). In team diversity research, there is no such widely used or accepted measurement, at least in way that researchers are accustomed to. Table 8.2 shows a tremendous variety of indices and applications in the diversity literature. In fact, we argue that no

TABLE 8.3   Properties of commonly used operational definitions of diversity

Index	Formula	Theoretical min/max	Operational min/max	Assumed scale level of X
Coefficient of variation[1]	$\sqrt{[\Sigma(X_i - X_{mean})^2/N]}$	0 to +∞	0 to $\sqrt{(N-1)}$	Ratio
Gini[1]	$(\Sigma|X_i - X_j|)/2 \times N^2 \times X_{mean}$	0 to +1	0 to $1-(1/N)$	Ratio
Standard deviation	$\sqrt{[\Sigma(X_i - X_{mean})^2/N]}$	0 to +∞	0 to $(b-a)/2$	Interval
Blau	$1 - \Sigma p_k^2$	0 to 1	0 to $(K-1)/K$	Categorical/ordinal
Teachman/ Shannon/entropy	$-(\Sigma p_k \times \ln(p_k))$	0 to +∞	0 to $-1 \times \ln(1/K)$	Categorical/ordinal
Euclidean distance:				
Individual level	$\sqrt{[\Sigma(X_i - X_j)^2/N]}$	0 to +1	0 to $\sqrt{[(N-1)/N]}$	Categorical/ordinal
		0 to +∞	0 to $\sqrt{[(N-1)(b-a)^2/N]}$	Interval
Team level (mean)	$\Sigma\sqrt{[\Sigma(X_i - X_j)^2/N]}/N$	0 to +1	$\sqrt{[(K-1)/K]}$	Categorical/ordinal
		0 to +∞	$(b-a)/\sqrt{(2)}$	Interval

[1]We are assuming non-negative raw values in the Computation CV and Gini indices

such universal instrument could be meaningfully constructed because diversity should be studied in a dimensionalized approach and not in global terms.

Almost all diversity indices are derived from distributional, compositional or relative properties of individuals (which maps squarely to the constitutive definition given above; see also Ragins & Gonzalez, 2003). For example, researchers interested in team demographic diversity will assess team member's attributes such as sex, race, age, etc., and compute a team-level diversity value via one or more diversity indices (e.g. Klein et al., 2001). Similarly, researchers who study psychological diversity (or deep-level diversity) might derive a team-level measure based on each team member's attitudes (e.g. Harrison et al., 1998), personality (e.g. Barrick et al., 1998) or values (Barsade et al., 2000). Thus, researchers first need to assess the individual-level attributes using measures that fit their theoretical argument. Then they need to compute the team diversity based on these individual-level measures using the most appropriate collective index. We review some of the most commonly used diversity indices next, noting their computation and features in Table 8.3.

Coefficient of Variation

Williams and O'Reilly (1998) commented that the coefficient of variation (CV; Allison, 1978) is one of the most commonly used indices for team-level demographic diversity research. The computational formula is essentially the within-group standard deviation (SD) divided by the group mean (see Table 8.3) for any variable on which team members might differ, X. Theoretically, CV can range from zero to positive infinity. The minimum value of 0 occurs when there is no variability within the group; that is, all team members have the same value of the measured attribute. As the variability within a group gets larger, and/or the mean gets smaller, CV approaches positive infinity.

While there is no theoretical upper bound for CV, operationally the values of CV are bounded when the X_i observations do not take negative values. In that case, the minimum is still zero but the maximum is $\sqrt{(N-1)}$ where N is the number of members in the team. This maximum occurs when all but one of the team members have a level of X_i that is equal to zero. For example, in a four-person team in which three members scored 0 and the remaining member scored 8, the standard deviation and the mean would be 3.46 and 2, respectively. Hence the value of CV is 3.46/2 = 1.73, which is also the square root of (4−1). Using another four-person team as an extreme example, where three members scored 0 and the remaining member scored 100, the standard deviation and the mean would be 43.30 and 25, yielding a CV of 1.73 (again the square root of (4−1)). Note that this maximum CV is obtained regardless of what the sole non-zero value might be. A sharply skewed distribution within a team shows a larger CV than a bimodal distribution.

It is crucial to note that this maximum, and hence *the interpretation of the CV, is substantially different from that obtained using other common diversity measures*. In essence, CV reflects the extreme lopsidedness of a distribution, but in a unidirectional or asymmetric way. As the relative gap grows between a smaller subset of elites at the top of a distribution and a larger subset of the great unwashed at the bottom, CV goes up. That makes it similar to an industry or market concentration ratio, where the maximum occurs when one firm has a monopoly (hence the original use of CV as a measure of *in*equality; Blau, 1977). However, if the distribution were flipped – few at the bottom, many at the top – CV goes down. This asymmetry occurs because the mean in the denominator is small in the former case and large in the latter. Other diversity measures, such as the standard deviation or the average Euclidian distance are symmetric. They would reflect the same level of diversity whether the minority is on the top or the bottom of the distribution.

Furthering this market- or commodity-based metaphor, the maximum possible CV occurs when there is one person at the top point of some continuum, and $n-1$ persons at the bottom, *with the bottom representing a zero amount*. Under such a condition, the elite person 'owns' all the resources or non-zero numerical amounts in the distribution, and everyone else 'owns' nothing. On the other hand, when the bottom of the distribution is a positive number, maximum CV is no longer the square root of $n-1$. In the example given above, with three members in a four-person team at 0, and the fourth member at 8, CV was 1.73. When the metric is shifted only slightly, with three members at 1, and the fourth member at 9, CV is substantially less: 1.15. When the metric is shifted dramatically, with three members at 100, and the fourth member at 108, CV is only 0.03.

This demonstration brings up some related, but crucial and little-known consequences of relying on CV to index diversity within a team. First, referring back to Allison (1978), Bedeian and Mossholder (2000) concluded that CV is meaningful and appropriate as a diversity index *only* when X_i has a ratio-level property. There is a fixed origin of measurement (zero point) and the variable values are all non-negative, such as for age, tenure or pay (but *not* for most psychological variables). The basis of this assumption is the division by the mean in the CV formula. To make a meaningful product or division of two variables, the level of measurement of the two variables must be a ratio (Schmidt, 1973). Second, CV's division by the mean carries with it an assumption that teams with higher average levels of X_i need *proportionally* higher levels of variation within themselves to be regarded as equally diverse as teams with lower means on X_i. For example, a work team with members who have an average age of 25 will be regarded as *twice* as diverse a team with an average age of 50, even though their within-team standard deviations are identical. A related point is that as the lower bound gets larger (e.g. minimum age in one organization being 20 while the other is 35), one needs greater spread to obtain the same value of CV. Third and most ominously, the asymmetric nature of CV might lead researchers to markedly different research conclusions than those who use symmetric diversity indices, as we implied earlier. Given what CV is sensitive to, it might be more useful as an index for studies of dominant coalitions or upper-echelon minorities than for diversity in general. In fact, although CV is widely popular and might be highly positively correlated with other diversity indices in many contexts, its weaknesses perhaps outweigh its strengths for using it in diversity research, unless the theoretical construct under investigation is explicitly characterized by power, status or some distribution of scarce and valued resources.

Gini Index

The Gini index is used less often in organizational behavior or human resources research than in strategy and organization theory. Its computational formula is the sum of all pairwise absolute differences between team (or upper-echelon) members on variable X, divided by $(2 \times N^2 \times X_{mean})$; see Table 8.3. Theoretically, the Gini index can range from zero to positive one. The minimum value of 0 occurs when there is no variability within the group; that is, all team members have the same value of the measured attribute. Operationally (with the range of X_i numbers and team sizes a diversity researcher might encounter in real data), the minimum value of Gini is still zero but the maximum is $1-(1/N)$ where N is the number of members in the team. Similar to CV, this maximum occurs when all but one of the team members have a value of 0 for X_i. For example, in a team of four where three members scored 0 and one member scored 8, the sum of all pairwise absolute differences and the mean would be 48 and 2, respectively. Hence the value of Gini is 0.75 (i.e. $48/(2 \times 2 \times 4^2)$). Similar to the computation of CV, the maximum value of Gini happens when the 'top' person gets *everything* and everyone else gets *nothing* (i.e. zeros). The lowest value should be non-negative (at least zero) for computation of CV and Gini to be meaningful and for the indices to retain their unipolar nature. Thus, Gini is also only appropriate for data that has ratio-level properties (Kimura, 1994).

The similarities between CV and Gini reflect that both come from the same family of inequality measures defined by Allison (1978: 870): $I = [(1/2N^2\Sigma|X_i-$

$X_j|q)^{1/q}]/X_{mean}$. The I in this formula is equivalent to CV when the exponent q equals 2. When q equals 1, I is equivalent to Gini. The Gini index might be chosen if researchers prefer their diversity measures to follow a common metric – in this case, ranging from 0 to 1 rather than 0 to infinity. Still, it shares the same shortcomings as CV (because it comes from the same family of measures), and would seem to have common-metric advantages only relative to CV.

Standard Deviation

The within-group standard deviation (SD) has also widely been used in team diversity research (e.g. Bedeian & Mossholder, 2000; Harrison et al., 2002). It has an advantage of not being an increasing function of team size; larger Ns do not create larger diversity scores if one uses the standard deviation. It is on the same metric as the original variable X, and is therefore somewhat easier to interpret than its square: the variance (e.g. Barrick et al., 1998). Note that when computing within-group SD, as well as CV above, one is interested in characteristics of the sample (the team) and not a larger population. In other words, the observed distribution of values for X_i in the team is the actual distribution of interest and it is not taken to be an approximation or estimate of a population parameter. Therefore, as presented in Table 8.3, the denominator of the formula for SD should be N and not $(N-1)$ as most researchers compute in other circumstances. Theoretically, SD can range from zero to positive infinity. The minimum value of 0 occurs when there is no variability within the group (i.e. all team members have the same X_i value).

Operationally, however, the values of SD are bounded by the numerical endpoints of the scale used, say a for the lower endpoint (the lowest value any individual can get) and b for the upper endpoint (the highest value). The smallest standard deviation is still zero when all the team members are stacked at exactly the same location. However, SD is at its maximum when the distribution of scores is as bimodal as possible, with half the team members stacked at a and the other half at b. Then, the SD equals $(b-a)/2$. For example, if a researcher used a seven-point (i.e. 1 to 7) scale to measure the individual team member's attribute, maximum team diversity occurs when half of the team members scored '1' and the other half scored '7'. In this case the SD will be 3 (i.e. $(7-1)/2$), regardless of the size of the team. Accordingly, the maximum values of SD for a five-point and nine-point scale would be 2 and 4, respectively.

We note that this exploration of the maximum of SD also has crucial substantive implications. If a researcher uses SD, he or she is considering a state of *balanced but bitterly opposed factions* (if X is a psychological value or attitude) or *utterly bipolar subgroups* (if X is a metric demographic variable such as age) *as most diverse*. Coalitions of team members that hold three or more positions on a particular continuum will be less diverse on that continuum than if they held only two positions. Similarly, an unbalanced set of two positions held by members within a group would be less diverse than a balanced one (if the coalitions were an equal distance apart in those two situations).

Finally, as in its use for other statistical purposes, SD also does not require ratio-level original data as do CV and the Gini index. The SD is an appropriate index when the data has at least interval-level properties. It is also possible and reasonable to compute and use SD for dichotomous (but not multi-category or ordinal) variables, where it is maximized when half the team members hold X_i values of 0 and half hold values of 1.

Blau's Index

Moving to operational definitions of categorical diversity variables, Blau's index (Blau, 1977) is one of the most widely used (e.g. Klein et al., 2001; Timmerman, 2000). The computational formula is $1-\Sigma_{pk}^2$, where p is the proportion of team members in the kth category. Theoretically, the values of Blau's index can range from zero to positive one. The minimum value of 0 occurs when everyone within the group belong to the same category (e.g. all team members are males). As team membership spreads across more categories, the value of Blau's index approaches positive one. That is, Blau's index is maximized when equal portions of a team are part of each possible X_k category. Note that this creates an identical maximum for dichotomous data (50% females and 50% males) as one would get using SD.

Operationally, however, the values of Blau's index are bound by the number of categories. The minimum is still zero but the maximum is $(K-1)/K$ where K is the total number of categories. For the balanced group of males and females mentioned above, sex diversity according to Blau's index will be 0.5 (i.e. $(2-1)/2$). However, with variables that have more categories (larger K), the maximum value of Blau's index is higher. For variables with 5 and 10 categories, the maximum would be 0.8 and 0.9, respectively. Hence, even though Blau's index is supposedly on the same 0–1 metric regardless of the (categorical) diversity dimension in question, scores are not comparable when the number of categories is not the same across dimensions.

Another little-known and lesser-used feature of Blau's index is its application to ordinal and interval-level data. Note that distances (beyond a 0 = same and 1 = different classification) are meaningless when Blau's index is used. However, if one's notion of maximum diversity on an interval-level variable is that everyone holds a different, discrete position on the continuum (say, each member of a seven-person group marks 1, 2, ..., or 7 on a seven-point task satisfaction item – which is the uniform distribution used by others such as James, Demaree & Wolf, 1984, as expected diversity or disagreement), Blau's index fits the bill. It is *not* maximized when teams are split widely on an interval-level variable.

Teachman/Shannon/Entropy Index

Many researchers have also used the Teachman index (Teachman, 1980), sometimes referred to as the entropy index, to compute team diversity for categorical variables (e.g. Jehn et al., 1999; Pelled et al., 1999). Although it is widely known as the Teachman index, he only reviewed and adopted its original development by Shannon (1948). The computational formula is $-\Sigma_{pk} \times I_n(p_k)$, where p is again the proportion of team members in the kth category. Theoretically, the values of Teachman's index can range from zero to positive infinity; that maximum distinguishes it from Blau's index. The minimum value of 0 occurs when everyone within the group belongs to the same category (e.g. all team members are males). As team membership spreads more evenly and across more categories, the value of Teachman's index gets larger.

As with Blau's index, however, the values of Teachman's index are bounded by the number of categories: K. The minimum is still zero but the maximum is $-1 \times I_n \times (1/K)$. For example, if the variable of interest is sex, which has only two categories, maximum team diversity occurs when half of the team members are males and the other half are females. Sex diversity according to Teachman's index will be 0.69 (i.e. $-1 \times I_n (0.5)$). The maximum values of Teachman's index for variables with 5 and 10 categories would be 1.61 and 2.30, respectively. Accordingly, Teachman's index for sex cannot be readily compared to the same index for ethnicity or functional background as the latter variables likely have more categories in organizational groups.

Euclidean Distance

Operational definitions of diversity based on Euclidean distances have been widely used in studies of relational demography (e.g. Tsui et al., 1992; Tsui & O'Reilly, 1989). However, it is important to recognize that the distance itself is an *individual-level* value; there is a distance for each member of the team. A Euclidean distance index sums how different an individual is in relation to all other individuals within a team. We broach it here not only because of its wide use, but because it has been used as a building block for team-level measures.

The computational formula for a Euclidean distance is $\sqrt{[\Sigma(X_i - X_j)^2/N]}$, which is the square root of the mean squared differences between person i and all others in the team. The index has been used for both categorical and continuous variables (e.g. Tsui et al., 1992). For categorical variables, the values of Euclidean index can theoretically range from zero to positive one, but the pairwise distances themselves can only be $X_i - X_j = 0$ or 1. The minimum value of zero occurs when the individual is the same as everyone else in the team, and, hence, all individuals in the team have the same zero distance from one another (e.g. all African Americans). As with some of the other diversity indices, however, the upper bound depends on team size. The maximum is $\sqrt{[(N-1)/N]}$, where N is the number of team members. For example, when a person is the only minority in a five-member group, the value of his or her Euclidean distance is 0.89 (i.e. $\sqrt{(4/5)}$). Hence, the maximum possible value of Euclidean index approaches positive one as the number of team members gets infinitely large. Therefore, the Euclidean index is not comparable across teams of different sizes, although comparability is improved as team sizes increases. The reason is demonstrated above as different team sizes have different maximum values.

For continuous variables, the values of Euclidean index can theoretically range from zero to positive infinity. Operationally, however, the upper bound is $\sqrt{[(N-1)(b-a)^2/N]}$, where N is the number of team members and a and b are the lower and upper endpoints of the scale used, as introduced earlier. For example, if a researcher used a seven-point (i.e. 1 to 7) scale, the maximum Euclidean distance value for a member in a four-person team occurs when the target team member scored '1' and the other three members scored '7'. In this case the value of Euclidean distance will be 5.20 (i.e. $\sqrt{[(4-1)(7-1)^2/4]}$; the same distance will occur when the target person scored 7 and the rest scored 1. That is, Euclidean distances are symmetric. The maximum possible value of individual Euclidean distance approaches infinity as the endpoints of the measurement scale and/or the number of team members get infinitely large.

A team-level diversity measure based on individual-level Euclidean distances is relatively straightforward. One can merely compute the mean of all members' Euclidean values within the team (e.g. Edwards, Klein, Shipp & Lim, 2003). For a continuous variable, the maximum value of this team-level, average distance will be $(b-a)/\sqrt{(2)}$. It is instructive to note the close similarity of this maximum to that of the SD: $(b-a)/2$. Indeed, an average Euclidean distance will also show maximum diversity at the same point and under the same conditions as SD, when two equally sized subgroups are situated at opposing poles of the distribution (even for dichotomous data) of the diversity variable X.

The formula simplifies for categorical variables, for which the maximum value of team diversity will be $\sqrt{(K-1/K)}$, where K is the total number of categories. Again, it is instructive to note the close similarity of this maximum to that of Blau's index: $(K-1)/K$. For example, if the variable is sex, which has only two categories, maximum team diversity occurs when half of the team members are males and the other half females. In this case, every team member's individual Euclidean distance is 0.71, and the team level diversity is also 0.71 (i.e. $\sqrt{(0.5)}$). Accordingly, the maximum values of team diversity increase as K increases; for variables with 5 and 10 categories, the maximum value of the team-level average Euclidean distance would be 0.89 and 0.95, respectively. Thus, for categorical variables, Euclidean distances are not comparable across dimensions of diversity that have different numbers of categories.

Within-Group (Dis)Agreement

Within-group agreement (R_{wg}; James et al., 1984; Lindell, Brandt, & Whitney, 1999) has become a popular research tool for justifying the aggregation of individual-level measures as indicators of group-level properties. That is, a high level of within-group agreement serves as an indication that there is enough shared perception among team members to justify aggregation of individual responses to represent a team-level concept; it represents the collective *lack* of differences within a team. According to George (1990), r_{wg} values of 0.70 or above demonstrate an acceptable level of consensus within a group. While r_{wg}, to our knowledge, has not been used as an index for team diversity per se, we have decided to discuss it here because it could legitimately and fruitfully be used to represent a substantive construct of group dispersion (see Chan, 1998, for discussion).

Two formulas have generally been used to derive r_{wg}. The original formula (James et al., 1984) is $r_{wg} = \{M[1-(\text{mean}_s^2/\sigma_{null}^2)]\}/\{M[1-(\text{mean}_s^2/\sigma_{null}^2)] + \text{mean}_s^2/\sigma_{null}^2\}$, where M is the number of items, and mean_s^2 is the item-wise variance across team members, which is then averaged over items. In addition, σ_{null}^2 is the variance of the null distribution (expected differences among team members when there is only random response or when there is no real agreement). Choosing this null distribution depends on what researchers assume would have been a completely stochastic process (i.e. respondents have no information to offer and are simply making marks on a scale or giving random responses to questions). If one assumes that any answer is equally as attractive as any other answer under such condition, the 'pile' of answers would be flat or uniform over all the answer options. This null is also called a uniform distribution, and the expected variance is $\sigma_{null}^2 = (K^2 - 1)/12$, where K is the number of different response options (K would be 5 on a Likert-type response format). While James et al. (1984) originally presented r_{wg} as a reliability coefficient, it has been clarified that r_{wg} is in fact an agreement index (James et al., 1993; Kozlowski & Hattrup, 1992). Taking note of this fact, Lindell et al. (1999) argued that the Spearman–Brown reliability correction (for multiple items) has been inappropriately applied when computing r_{wg}, and they proposed an alternative formula: $r_{wg}^* = 1-(\text{mean}_s^2/\sigma_{null}^2)$.

Essentially, both r_{wg} and r_{wg}^* are calculated based on a function of the observed variance within a group relative to an assumed null distribution (often the uniform/rectangular distribution). Theoretically, the values of r_{wg} can range from negative to positive infinity (see Lindell et al., 1999, for a discussion), which is the reason James et al. (1984) advised resetting all estimates of r_{wg} outside the range of 0 and 1 to zero (obtained values above one indicate an anomalous condition in which observed variance is much greater than expected variance from the null distribution). The values of r_{wg}^* range from −1 to +1 when the response categories (K) ranged from 2 to 5 (Lindell et al., 1999). Otherwise the lower bound will be beyond −1 when $K > 5$ (i.e. six-point response scales and above).

Applications to studies of diversity would be most likely with psychological or survey data, with limited response options. Rather than work with r_{wg} and r_{wg}^* at face value, however, researchers could reverse them and consider them indices of disagreement or diversity ($d_{wg} = 1 - r_{wg}$; perhaps less useful for $1 - r_{wg}^*$). That is, they could represent the collective amount of differences within a group, relative to what might be expect on the basis of chance. The term 'relative' is part of what distinguishes this type of index from the others. While CV and Gini evaluate differences relative to the mean of the within-group distribution, $1-r_{wg}$ or $1-r_{wg}^*$ evaluate differences relative to a pre-specified distributional shape.

TABLE 8.4   *Properties of effective diversity indices*

Properties	CV	Gini	SD	Blau	Teachman	Euclidean (mean)	Reverse r_{wg}	Reverse r_{wg}^{*}
Zero represents diversity or complete homogeneity	Y	Y	Y	Y	Y	Y	Y	N^2
Larger number means greater diversity	N^1	N^1	Y	Y	Y	Y	Y	Y
No negative values exist	Y	Y	Y	Y	Y	Y	N^3	N^2
The maximum asymptotes at a particular value	N^4	Y	N^4	Y	N^4	N^4	N^4	Y

[1]Larger numbers mean maximum inequality, which may or may not correspond with the researchers' definition of diversity.

[2]When maximum disagreement is used as the assumed null distribution in the computation, zero represents no diversity for reverse r_{wg}^{*}; also, r_{wg}^{*} will not yield negative values.

[3]Reverse r_{wg} has no negative values after the resetting procedure recommended by James et al. (1984)

[4]Theoretically, these indices do not have an upper bound, operationally, however, they all asymptote at a particular value as specified in Table 8.2.

WHICH IS BEST? MATCHING CONSTITUTIVE AND OPERATIONAL DEFINITIONS

Properties of an Effective Diversity Index

Having forwarded a general constitutive definition and reviewed some of the most commonly used operational definitions, one might wonder which diversity index is the best. The first and probably biggest key for proper use is to have an index that matches appropriately with the scale level of the variable studied. For example, Blau's index should be used only for categorical variables. In this section (see also Table 8.4), we evaluate the indices according to some of the main properties we believe to be important for an effective diversity index, one in which the meaning is clear and comparable to other findings, and one that corresponds to our constitutive definition of diversity as a *collective amount of differences among members within a social unit*.

First, to make intuitive sense, a value of *zero should represent no diversity or complete homogeneity*. This will aid interpretation because the numerical value corresponds to the underlying or substantive meaning of the construct. As presented in Table 8.4, all the indices discussed above, except r_{wg} and r_{wg}^{*}, satisfy this criterion. That is, the numerical value of each of the indices is zero when all the team members belong to the same category or possess the same level of the diversity attribute in question. For r_{wg}, it was first developed as an agreement index and zero actually represented complete disagreement. Hence, to use it as a diversity index, it might be advisable to reverse the r_{wg} such that zero now represents total agreement or no diversity. For r_{wg}^{*}, reversing alone does not work because the values still range from −1 to +1. Instead, researchers who are considering using reverse r_{wg}^* should also consider using maximum disagreement (i.e. ratings are equally distributed between the upper and lower extremes of the response scale; or square of maximum SD in Table 8.3: $(b-a)^2/4$) as the assumed null distribution when computing r_{wg}^* (see Lindell et al., 1999). With maximum disagreement as the denominator, the values of reverse r_{wg}^* will range from 0 to +1 and zero will represent total agreement or no diversity.

Second, to aid interpretation, *larger numerical values should mean greater diversity*. All the indices listed above satisfy this criterion in general. However, interpreting CV and Gini in this regard may be more complicated than it appears. Strictly speaking, these two indices were developed as narrower measures of inequality of resource allocations and not what is now more broadly thought of as *diversity* per se (Allison, 1978). This is evident from the fact that the maximum value for these two indices occurs when all except one person have a value of zero on the diversity variable in question. Hence, despite the popularity of these indices (especially CV), we question their blanket appropriateness for team diversity research. Instead, we make the recommendations below. We do believe it is important to control for the mean level of a variable before examining the effect of its diversity – because the two can be correlated – but this can be done through the use of a covariate in regression.

Researchers need to *explicitly specify their theoretical beliefs about what the highest possible level of diversity means*. This chapter demarcates three possible sets of such beliefs regarding what a *maximum* collective amount of difference entails. It could mean that one person reigns over all the rest of the members in a social unit, creating a strongly positively skewed distribution. In such a case CV and Gini are the most appropriate indices (as long as the data are ratio-level), with the latter theoretically bounded by one. Another meaning of maximum diversity is that a social unit contains subgroups occupying opposite endpoints of some continuum. Under this meaning, the distribution of the diversity variable would be symmetric and bimodal, and SD or average Euclidean distance would be the index of choice for at least interval-level data. A third meaning of maximum diversity might be that each social unit member takes a different category value, or is equally spaced from each of the contiguous members. Under those conditions, the distribution is uniform and amodal; Blau's or Teachman's index would suffice for any type of data, even though the former was built especially for nominal classifications.

Third, diversity is a unipolar construct, in that it ranges from zero to large amounts. In other words, negative diversity is meaningless and good diversity index *should not have negative values*. In general, all the indices above satisfied this criterion. For r_{wg}, it is possible to attain negative values and researchers need to reset values outside the range of 0 and +1 to zero, as recommended by James et al. (1984). To avoid negative values as well as to have meaningful zero value mentioned earlier, maximum disagreement should be used as the assumed null distribution when computing r_{wg}^* (see Lindell et al., 1999).

Finally, the maximum value of a good diversity index should *asymptote at a particular value*. That is, the value should not be unbounded. While indices such as CV, Teachman's, Euclidean distance and r_{wg} can yield positive values that are infinitely large, for practical purposes they are all bounded as well. It may be possible to put all diversity indices on a similar 0 to 1 metric via dividing them by their maximum listed in Table 8.3. This would reduce the inflating effects of group size, for example, on CV. However, the strength of this transformation would seem to be especially severe for those indices with a theoretical (but not operational) maximum of positive infinity, restricting their likely empirical range to something much less than the other indices.

CONCLUSION

All indications, including the publishing of this handbook, point to dramatic growth in research on diversity in organizations. Part of the purpose for the current chapter is to facilitate a parallel *maturation* of that research. Such maturation, we believe, comes from cumulativeness of findings, and an emerging consensus among scholars about what theories and methods do and do not remain viable in the area. We are not suggesting that diversity research should suppress its own internal diversity of ideas and approaches, which in many ways can be healthy. Indeed, questions about simple demographic differences have been elaborated and extended to address complex psychological and even perceived differences. However, we do believe that more would be understood about diversity phenomena if researchers paid more attention to constitutive definitions, perhaps adopting an overarching one such as proposed in this chapter – without assuming a single, omnibus level of diversity that represents all possible salient differences among work unit members. Just as importantly, choices of indices for operationalizing diversity should be made in full recognition of their often strikingly unique properties. We hope the current chapter has clarified those properties and helped to make such choices more informed.

REFERENCES

Allison, P. D. (1978). Measures of inequality. *American Sociological Review*, *43*, 865–80.

Arrow, H., & McGrath, J. E. (1993). How member change and continuity affects small group structure, process, and performance. *Small Group Research, 24*, 334–61.

Barrick, M. R., Stewart, G. L., Neubert, M. J., & Mount, M. K. (1998). Relating member ability and personality to work-team processes and team effectiveness. *Journal of Applied Psychology, 83*, 377–91.

Barsade, S. G., Ward, A. J., Turner, J. D. F., & Sonnenfeld, J. (2000). To your heart's content: A model of affective diversity in top management teams. *Administrative Science Quarterly, 45*, 802–36.

Bedeian, A. G., & Mossholder, K. W. (2000). On the use of the coefficient of variation as a measure of diversity. *Organizational Research Methods, 3*, 285–97.

Beyer, J. M., Chattopadhyay, P., George, E., Glick, W. H., Ogilvie, D. T., & Pugliese, D. (1997). The selective perception of managers revisited. *Academy of Management Journal, 40*, 716–37.

Blau, P. M. (1977). *Inequality and heterogeneity*. New York: Free Press.

Boeker, W. (1997). Strategic change: The influence of managerial characteristics and organizational growth. *Academy of Management Journal, 40*, 152–70.

Campion, M. A., Medsker, G. J., & Higgs, A. C. (1993). Relations between work group characteristics and effectiveness: Implications for designing effective work groups. *Personnel Psychology, 46*, 823–50.

Chan, D. (1998). Functional relations among constructs in the same content domain at different levels of analysis: A typology of composition models. *Journal of Applied Psychology, 83*, 234–46.

Chatman, J. A., & Flynn, F. J. (2001). The influence of demographic heterogeneity on the emergence and consequences of cooperative norms in work teams. *Academy of Management Journal, 44*, 956–74.

Colquitt, J. A., Noe, R. A., & Jackson, C. L. (2002). Justice in teams: Antecedents and consequents of procedural justice climate. *Personnel Psychology, 55*, 83–109.

Earley, P. C., & Mosakowski, E. (2000). Creating hybrid team cultures: An empirical test of transnational team functioning. *Academy of Management Journal, 43*, 26–49.

Edwards, J. R. (2001). Multidimensional constructs in organizational behavior research: An integrative analytical framework. *Organizational Research Methods, 4*, 144–92.

Edwards, J. R., Klein, K. J., Shipp, A. J., & Lim, B. C. (2003). The study of dispersion in organizational behavior research: An analytical framework using distributional moments. Paper presented at the 18th Annual Meeting of the Society for Industrial and Organizational Psychology, Orlando, Florida.

Elsass, P. M., & Graves, L. M. (1997). Demographic diversity in decision-making groups: The experiences of women and people of color. *Academy of Management Review, 22*, 946–73.

Farr, J. L., Sin, H. P., & Tesluk, P. E. (2003). Knowledge management processes and work group innovation. In L. V. Shavinina (Ed.), *International handbook of innovation* (pp. 574–86). Amsterdam: Elsevier Science.

George, J. M. (1990). Personality, affect, and behavior in groups. *Journal of Applied Psychology, 75*, 107–16.

Guzzo, R. A., & Shea, G. P. (1992). Group performance and intergroup relations in organizations. In M. D. Dunnette & L. M. Hough (Eds), *Handbook of industrial and organizational psychology* (Vol. 3, pp. 269–313). Palo Alto, CA: Consulting Psychologists Press.

Harrison, D. A. (2002). Meaning and measurement of work role withdrawal: Current controversies and future fallout under changing technology. In M. Koslowsky & M. Krausz (Eds), *Voluntary employee withdrawal and inattendance: A current perspective* (pp. 95–132). London: Plenum.

Harrison, D. A., Price, K. H., & Bell, M. P. (1998). Beyond relational demography: Time and the effects of surface- and deep-level diversity on work group cohesion. *Academy of Management Journal, 41*, 96–107.

Harrison, D. A., Price, K. H., Gavin, J. H., & Florey, A. T. (2002). Time, teams, and task performance: Changing effects of surface- and deep-level diversity on group functioning. *Academy of Management Journal, 45*, 1029–45.

Hinsz, V. B., Tindale, R. S., & Vollrath, D. A. (1997). The emerging conceptualization of groups as information processors. *Psychological Bulletin, 121*, 43–64.

Hoffman, L. R. (1959). Homogeneity of member personality and its effect on group problem-solving. *Journal of Abnormal and Social Psychology, 58*, 27–32.

Hoffman, L. R., & Maier, N. (1961). Quality and acceptance of problem solutions by members of homogeneous and heterogeneous groups. *Journal of Abnormal and Social Psychology, 62*, 401–7.

Hunter, J. E., & Schmidt, F. L. (1990). *Methods of meta-analysis: Correcting error and bias in research findings*. Thousand Oaks, CA: Sage.

Jackson, S. E., May, K. E., & Whitney, K. (1995). Understanding the dynamics of diversity in decision-making teams. In R. A. Guzzo & E. Salas (Eds), *Team decision-making effectiveness in organizations* (pp. 204–61). San Francisco: Jossey-Bass.

James, L. R., Demaree, R. G., & Wolf, G. (1984). Estimating within-group interrater reliability with and without response bias. *Journal of Applied Psychology, 69*, 85–98.

James, L. R., Demaree, R. G., & Wolf, G. (1993). r_{wg}: An assessment of within-group interrater agreement. *Journal of Applied Psychology, 78*, 306–9.

Jehn, K. A., Chadwick, C., & Thatcher, S. M. B. (1997). To agree or not to agree: The effects of value congruence, individual demographic dissimilarity, and conflict on workgroup outcomes. *International Journal of Conflict Management, 8*, 287–305.

Jehn, K. A., Northcraft, G. B., & Neale, M. A. (1999). Why differences make a difference: A field study of diversity, conflict, and performance in workgroups. *Administrative Science Quarterly, 44*, 741–63.

Johnston, W. B., & Packer, A. E. (1987). *Workforce 2000: Work and workers for the 21st century*. Indianapolis: Hudson Institute.

Kerlinger, F. N. (1990). *Foundations of behavioral research*. Toronto: Harcourt-Brace.

Kilduff, M., Angelmar, R., & Mehra, A. (2000). Top management-team diversity and firm performance: Examining the role of cognitions. *Organization Science, 11*, 21–34.

Kimura, K. (1994). A micro-macro linkage in the measurement of inequality: Another look at the GINI coefficient. *Quality and Quantity, 28*, 83–97.

Klein, K. J., Conn, A. B., Smith, D. B., & Sorra, J. S. (2001). Is everyone in agreement? An exploration of within-group agreement in employee perceptions of the work environment. *Journal of Applied Psychology, 86*, 3–16.

Klein, K. J. & Kozlowski, S. W. J. (2002). *Multilevel theory, research, and methods in organizations: Foundations, extensions, and new directions*. San Francisco: Jossey-Bass.

Konrad, A. M. (2003). Special issue introduction: Defining the domain of workplace diversity scholarship. *Group & Organization Management, 28*, 4–17.

Kozlowski, S. W. J., & Hattrup, K. (1992). A disagreement about within-group agreement: Disentangling issues of consistency versus consensus. *Journal of Applied Psychology, 77*, 161–7.

Lau, D. C., & Murnighan, J. K. (1998). Demographic diversity and faultlines: The compositional dynamics of organizational groups. *Academy of Management Review, 23*, 325–40.

Lawrence, B. S. (1997). The black box of organizational demography. *Organization Science, 8*, 1–22.

Lindell, M. K., Brandt, C. J., & Whitney, D. J. (1999). A revised index of interrater agreement for multi-item ratings of a single target. *Applied Psychological Measurement. 23*, 127–35.

Locke, E. A. (2003). Good definitions: The epistemological foundation of scientific progress. In J. Greenberg (Ed.), *Organizational behavior: The state of the science* (pp. 415–44). Mahwah, NJ: Erlbaum.

Marsch, J. B. T. (2002). Cultural diversity as human capital. *Communication and Cognition, 35*, 37–49.

McGrath, J. E. (1982). Dilemmatics: The study of research choices and dilemmas. In J. E. McGrath, J. Martin, & R. A. Kulka (Eds), *Judgment calls in research* (pp. 69–102). Beverly Hills, CA: Sage.

McGrath, J. E., Berdahl, J. L., & Arrow, H. (1995). Traits, expectations, culture, and clout: The dynamics of diversity in work groups. In S. E. Jackson & M. N. Ruderman (Eds), *Diversity in work teams: Research paradigms for a changing workplace* (pp. 17–45). Washington, DC: American Psychological Association.

Milliken, F., & Martins, L. (1996). Searching for common threads: Understanding the multiple effects of diversity in organizational groups. *Academy of Management Review*, *21*, 402–33.

Morgeson, F. P., & Hofmann, D. A. (1999). The structure and function of collective constructs: Implications for multilevel research and theory development. *Academy of Management Review*, *24*, 249–65.

Nemetz, P. L., & Christensen, S. L. (1996). The challenge of cultural diversity: Harnessing a diversity of views to understand multiculturalism. *Academy of Management Review*, *21*, 434–62.

Neuman, G. A., Wagner, S. H., & Christiansen, N. D. (1999). The relationship between work-team personality composition and the job performance of teams. *Group & Organization Management*, *24*, 28–46.

Newcomb, T. M. (1961). *The acquaintance process*. New York: Holt, Rinehart & Winston.

Offermann, L. R., & Gowing, M. K. (1990). Organizations of the future: Changes and challenges. *American Psychologist*, *45*, 95–108.

Park, B., & Judd, C. M. (1990). Measures and models of perceived group variability. *Journal of Personality and Social Psychology*, *42*, 1051–68.

Park, B., Ryan, C. S., & Judd, C. M. (1992). Role of meaningful sub-groups in explaining differences in perceived variability for in-groups and out-groups. *Journal of Personality and Social Psychology*, *63*, 553–67.

Pelled, L. H. (1996). Demographic diversity, conflict, and work group outcomes: An intervening process theory. *Organization Science*, *6*, 207–29.

Pelled, L. H., Eisenhardt, K. M., & Xin, K. R. (1999). Exploring the black box: An analysis of work group diversity, conflict, and performance. *Administrative Science Quarterly*, *44*, 1–28.

Pfeffer, J. (1983). Organizational demography. In L. L. Cummings & B. M. Staw (Eds), *Research in organizational behavior* (Vol. 5, pp. 299–357). Greenwich, CT: JAI Press.

Quattrone, G. A., & Jones, E. E. (1980). The perception of variability within ingroups and outgroups: Implications for the law of small numbers. *Journal of Personality and Social Psychology*, *13*, 269–77.

Ragins, B. R., & Gonzalez, J. A. (2003). Understanding diversity in organizations: Getting a grip on a slippery construct. In J. Greenberg (Ed.), *Organizational behavior: The state of the science* (pp. 125–63). Mahwah, NJ: Erlbaum.

Riordan, C. M. (2000). Relational demography within groups: Past developments, contradictions, and new directions. In G. R. Ferris (Ed.), *Research in personnel and human resources management* (Vol. 19, pp. 131–73). Greenwich, CT: JAI Press.

Runkel, P. J., & McGrath, J. E. (1972). *Research on human behavior: A systematic guide to method*. New York: Holt, Rinehart & Winston.

Rynes, S., & Rosen, B. (1995). A field survey of factors affecting the adoption and perceived success of diversity training. *Personnel Psychology*, *48*, 247–70.

Schmidt, F. L. (1973). Implications of a measurement problem for expectancy theory research. *Organizational Behavior and Human Decision Processes*, *10*, 243–51.

Schwab, D. P. (1980). Construct validity in organizational behavior. In L. L. Cummings & B. M. Staw (Eds), *Research in organizational behavior* (Vol. 2, pp. 3–43). Greenwich, CT: JAI Press.

Shannon, C. (1948). A mathematical theory of communications. *Bell System Technical Journal*, *27*, 397–423, 623–56.

Stone-Romero, E. F. (1994). Construct validity issues in organizational behavior research. In J. Greenberg (Ed.), *Organizational behavior: The state of the science* (pp. 155–80). Hillsdale, NJ: Erlbaum.

Teachman, J. D. (1980). Analysis of population diversity. *Sociological Methods and Research*, *8*, 341–62.

Timmerman, T. A. (2000). Racial diversity, age diversity, interdependence, and team performance. *Small Group Research, 31,* 592–606.

Tsui, A. S., Egan, T. D., & O'Reilly, C. (1992). Being different: Relational demography and organizational attachment. *Administrative Science Quarterly, 37,* 549–79.

Tsui, A. S., & O'Reilly, C. (1989). Beyond simple demographic effects: The importance of relational demography in supervisor-subordinate dyads. *Academy of Management Journal, 32,* 402–23.

Webber, S. S., & Donahue, L. (2001). Impact of highly and less job related diversity on work group cohesion and performance: A meta analysis. *Journal of Management, 27,* 141–62.

West, M. A., Borrill, C. S., & Unsworth, K. L. (1998). Team effectiveness in organizations. In C. I. Cooper & I. T. Robertson (Eds), *International Review of Industrial and Organizational Psychology* (Vol. 13, pp. 1–48). Chichester: Wiley.

Williams, K., & O'Reilly, C. (1998). Demography and diversity in organizations: A review of 40 years of research. In B. M. Staw & L. L. Cummings (Eds), *Research in organizational behavior* (Vol. 20, pp. 77–140). Greenwich, CT: JAI Press.

9

Feminist Qualitative Research and Workplace Diversity

AMY THURLOW, ALBERT J. MILLS AND JEAN HELMS MILLS

In this chapter we discuss the value and application of feminist qualitative research to the study of workplace diversity. Broadly defined, qualitative research is characterized as a methodology designed to illicit insights into the *meanings* and *understandings* that people associate with social relationships and events (O'Neill, 1995). In contrast to quantitative methods, qualitative methods:

> focus on interpretation rather than quantification; an emphasis on subjectivity rather than objectivity; flexibility in the process of conducting research; an orientation towards process rather than outcome; a concern with context – regarding behavior and situation as inextricably linked in forming experience; and finally, an explicit recognition of the impact of research process on the research situation. (Cassell & Symon, 1994, quoted in Brewerton & Millward, 2001: 12)

The value of qualitative research to the study of workplace diversity can be illustrated through analysis of two strongly related concepts – systemic discrimination and organizational culture. The term 'systemic discrimination' was coined by the Abella Commission (1984), a Canadian Royal Commission, chaired by Judge Rosalie Abella, that was charged with examining equity in employment. Through extensive collection and marshalling of statistics the Abella Commission was able to make a powerful case for legislation to address palpable discrimination against four designated groups – 'women, native people, disabled persons, and visible minorities'

(Abella, 1984: v). At the heart of the argument was strong evidence of systemic patterns of discrimination arising out of 'a disparately negative impact that flows from … the nature of systems designed for a homogeneous constituency [i.e. white able-bodied males]; and [...] practices based on stereotypical characteristics ascribed to an individual because of the characteristics ascribed to the group of which he or she is a member' (Abella, 1984: 9–10). The consequent legislation provided an important framework for judging the extent of, and steps taken to reduce, systemic discrimination across government agencies and government-funded organizations in the private sector. While the report provided the incentive to reduce systemic discrimination through legislative action, it did not ultimately explain how systemic discrimination develops, is maintained, and can be changed over time. That is where a qualitative research strategy can be vital in identifying the deep-rooted factors that shape and solidify discriminatory notions of organizational reality.

In recent years a number of feminist researchers have been drawn to the notion of organizational culture as a heuristic for exploring ways that discriminatory practices are formed. Many of these studies seek to identify not only the quantifiable imbalances in employment practices (Morgan, 1988; Wicks & Bradshaw, 2002) but the influence of such things as values (Wicks & Bradshaw, 2002), sensemaking processes (Helms Mills & Mills, 2000), symbolism (Gherardi, 1995), identity work (Thomas & Davies, 2002), corporate representations (Benschop & Meihuizen, 2002), and notions of masculinity (Collinson & Hearn, 1994), femininity (Wolf, 2002) and sexual orientation (Hearn & Parkin, 1987). The value in all these approaches is that by gaining insights into how discrimination develops and is maintained we can also develop appropriate change strategies.

So far we have given the impression that there are unitary approaches to qualitative research and feminism. Neither is the case. The qualitative research approach of any given researcher will be influenced by his or her underlying view of reality (ontology), ways of knowing (epistemology) and broad sociopolitical orientation (Burrell & Morgan, 1979). Although feminists share a common goal of working towards 'the political, economic, spiritual, sexual, and social equality of women' (The Wise Woman, 1982, 4: 2, 7, quoted in Kramarae & Treichler, 1985: 161), they also differ in their ontological and epistemological perspectives (Calás & Smircich, 1992; 1996). Thus, for example, feminist scholars from within a 'women in management' perspective may be more inclined to adopt positivist methods, including qualitative techniques that ultimately rely on quantification (e.g. counts of particular observed behaviors) rather than a concern with deep-rooted understanding. For example, Kanter's (1977) now classic study of gender at work consisted of a number of quantitative measures, including the outcome of 'some observations of women's leadership in organizations', involving 'a variety of coding schemes in meetings, including variations on Bale's "Interaction Process Analysis"' (p. 299). When, on the other hand, Ferguson (1984) set out to interview women in bureaucratic settings she made no 'claims to have selected a representative sample', pointing out that her 'interviews do not represent a statistically valid or reliable population and are not statistically generalizable' (p. xi). The essential difference between these feminists in their approach to qualitative methods is due, in large part, to their epistemological orientations, glimpsed in Kanter's intellectual debt to Karl Marx, Adam Smith and Peter Drucker, and Ferguson's intellectual debt to Michel Foucault.

In focusing on *feminist* qualitative research our aim is not to suggest that it is the best and only way to study workplace diversity: clearly there are a number other perspectives – including postcolonialist (Prasad & Prasad, 2002), racio-ethnic (Cox, 1990), post-structuralist (Morgan & Knights, 1991), Marxist (Clegg & Dunkerley, 1980), and others – that have made an important contribution to this field. We do, however, contend that feminism is a particularly appropriate approach to the study of workplace diversity given its historical preoccupation with gender, *difference* and *otherness*. We will engage with the strengths and limitations of the feminist approach later in the chapter.

THE FEMINIST PROJECT

The feminist project has developed through generations of social movement aimed at 'women's liberation' and has profound implications for research. In seeking to challenge the sexist character and structure of social life, feminists fundamentally challenge the dominant positivist viewpoint of research as objective, value free and non-political. In short, feminist research, in contrast to mainstream research, is *consciously* informed by a wider project (e.g. the betterment of women, women's liberation) that precedes any research activity. As such the feminist project influences the type of research activity that is undertaken, the questions asked and the desired outcomes. For example, when Kanter (1977: xi) set out to study 'how consciousness and behavior are formed by positions in organizations' she was 'motivated by [her] involvement in the women's movement to seek understanding of the fate of women as well as men in organizations'. And she set out to 'further the cause of equality for women in organizations' (Kanter, 1977: 291). This led her to raise questions about the relationship between gender and management, power, and opportunity.

Some feminist research, however, arises out of a 'broader' enquiry in which unexpected developments encourage a feminist turn. Cockburn's (1991: 3) study of male dominance and technological change 'began as a study of the human impact of technological change [before becoming] a study in the making and remaking of men [and] about the uses to which men put work and technology in maintaining their power over women'. In this case the unfolding meanings of the workplace spoke to Cockburn's feminism and helped to change the direction of the research.

On the surface this seems to suggest that feminist research differs from other research in terms of political agenda. Yes and no. Yes, feminist researchers do share a broad political agenda of change. That agenda, however, is by no means uniform in its strategies or desired outcomes. Liberal feminists, for example, may strive for greater numbers of women in positions of power and authority at work, while Marxist feminists may be more focused on the defeat of capitalist forms of organization and a revolutionary restructuring of society (Calás & Smircich, 1996). No, feminist research is not the only approach that is informed by preconceived notions, nor the only approach that engages in/with organizational politics. It can be argued that all research is biased and political in its start point (Hollway, 1989; Reed, 1978). Take for example research on organizational culture. This focus of interest has been explored in hundreds of books and articles since the late 1970s (Kieser, 1997) and it is fair to say that, in large part, they have concerned themselves with the relationship between organizational culture and business outcomes – including motivation, productivity, organizational growth, productivity, etc. (Hofstede, Neuijen, Ohavy & Sanders, 1990; Ouchi, 1981; Pascale & Athos, 1981; Peters & Waterman, 1982; Schein, 1985). These studies share a common goal of assisting organizational managers to improve 'bottom-line' performance, and that goal (which is rarely problematized) shapes the type of research questions asked.

Schein (1985) captures the profound differences between mainstream and feminist research in his contrast between, what he terms, ethnographic and clinical studies of organizational culture. He argues that the ethnographic perspective is detached, bringing to any research project 'a set of concepts or models that motivated the research in the first place'. The groups being studied 'are often willing to participate but usually have no particular stake in the *intellectual issues* that may have motivated the study' (Schein, 1985: 21; our emphasis). The clinical perspective, on the other hand, is 'one where the group members are clients who have their own interests as the prime motivator for the involvement of the "outsider", often labeled "consultant"' (Schein, 1985: 21–2). In contrast, feminist research assumes neither that groups are willing to participate as subjects nor that the researcher is merely intellectually curious and thus disinterested as in the ethnographic perspective. In any number of feminist studies of workplace diversity the *way* people are studied (the methods involved) is seen as part of the broader problem of addressing discriminatory practices (cf. Acker & van Houten, 1974). As we saw from the research commentaries of Kanter and Cockburn above, feminist researchers are far from disinterested in the focus of study and it outcomes. Nor do feminist researchers assume that research questions that serve the intellectual interests of the researcher and/or those who 'are paying' for the research (Schein, 1985: 21), namely organizational managers, are disinterested or unbiased. As numerous feminist researchers have indicated, almost all mainstream studies of organizational culture have neglected, if not downright ignored, gender and the potential effects of culture manipulation on the women and men involved (Aaltio, Mills & Helms Mills, 2002).

Feminist studies of organizational culture are more likely to set out with an examination of the impact of organizational culture on women's employability (Morgan, 1988), sense of self and self-worth (Katila & Merilainen, 2002), discrimination at work (Wicks & Bradshaw, 2002), or strategies of organizational change towards great equity (Marshall, 1993).

FEMINIST PHILOSOPHIES AND METHODOLOGICAL CHOICE

As we argued earlier, while there is a shared agenda of the betterment of womankind, feminists differ on a number of issues, including the definitions and understanding of central terms, strategies and outcomes. Thus, there are various feminist approaches to workplace diversity, reflecting the diversity of thought that underlies the different feminisms. Calás and Smircich (1996), for example, delineate a range of feminist theories that include liberal, Marxist, radical, socialist, post-structuralist, (post)colonial and psycho-analytic. This typology of feminisms is, for the most part, built around the broad political agenda that each perspective is thought to characterize, but there are other differences both within and beyond these boundaries that reflect ontological and epistemological differences (cf. Burrell & Morgan, 1979).

Each feminist perspective informs not only the research agenda but also how it is studied and the questions asked; in short, the methods used to study workplace diversity. Liberal feminists, for example, view women as essentially different from men but argue that those differences have been made too much of in workplace hiring and promotion to the detriment of women (cf. Henning & Jardin, 1977). This ontological view of women facilitates the study of workplace discrimination through statistical analysis of the extent to which women are excluded from certain organizations, occupations, industries and job positions. Schein (1973), for example, provided valuable insights into the relationship between the attitudes of male managers to women and management as an important variable in the relative exclusion of women from management positions. She did this by getting a number of male managers to respond to a series of affect terms which they were asked to relate to their understanding of women, men and leadership. The results indicated that the managers assigned similar affect terms to the notion of men and to leader but very different affect terms to the notion of women. Post-structuralist feminists, on the other hand, 'question the very stability of such cultural categories as gender' (Calás & Smircich, 1992: 226), focusing on 'the discursive nature of "social reality" and "subjectivity", and its inessential nature' (Calás & Smircich, 1996: 244). An excellent example of how feminist philosophy shapes the way that things are studied comes from Humphreys' (1994) account of different approaches to women's history. She argues that there are various feminist historiographies (or methods of studying history), including history by women, history about women and the history of conceptions gender. The first approach reflects an underlying philosophy of 'women's voice', seeking change by adding female voices to the narratives of history. The second approach is similar to the liberal feminist perspective, focusing on 'including women in the historical record', seeking change by revealing the contribution of women. The third approach owes more to feminist social constructionist approaches, focusing on how cultural features contribute to the social construction of 'women' and 'men'.

FEMINIST QUALITATIVE METHODS IN ACTION

According to Reinharz and Davidman (1992: 327), 'there is no single "feminist way" to do research'. The choice of qualitative or quantitative, and of positivist or anti-positivist qualitative, methods is rooted in ontological/epistemological preferences more than broad political agendas. Liberal feminism, for example, has been characterized as engaging in a 'stream of research [that] is strongly influenced by experimental and behaviorist psychology' (Calás & Smircich, 1996: 223). This research is heavily influenced by a predilection for realist/positivist views of reality. Nonetheless, this view of reality is not restricted to liberal feminism (but encompasses elements of socialist and Marxist feminism), nor does it describe liberal feminism as a whole. Some liberal feminists, for example, engage in quantitative research to establish statistical differences between men and women in the workplace, in terms of job level, hiring rates, opinions, etc. (e.g. Morrison, White & Van Elsor, 1987) but they may also engage in (positivist) qualitative research in an effort to understand how the people involved feel about discrimination at work (cf. Harriman, 1985). On the other hand, the prospects of quantitative research diminish among those feminists who reject realist and positivist notions of reality, including post-structuralist and interpretivist feminists, who are more defined by their ontological preference than their political agenda. In short, while the use of quantitative methods is an option among some feminist perspectives, we may find evidence of a qualitative research approach in every feminist perspective.

RESEARCH TECHNIQUES IN CONTEXT

In this section, for reasons of space, we will explore selected techniques of qualitative research.

Kicking over the Traces: Content Analysis, Discourse Analysis and Historiography

In studying workplace diversity it is not always possible or necessary to speak to or observe members of an organization. It depends on the specific purpose of the study and the researcher's theoretical framework. Materialist feminists, for example, may be primarily interested in (re)constructing histories of women (cf. Rowbotham, 1974) and other so-called minorities through the collection of archival materials and content analysis of existing accounts. Feminist post-structuralists may use discourse analysis to deconstruct the understandings that we bring to and make sense of a particular organizational context. Feminist historiographic accounts and/or content analysis may be used to develop an understanding of the context in which workplace diversity is enacted, or to deconstruct observations and interviews.

Content analysis

An example of the first type of approach is that of Acker and van Houten (1974), who analyzed the readings, diaries and notes of the original Hawthorne Studies researchers from a feminist perspective. By analyzing what the original researchers had to say, how they said it, what they included and what they excluded, Acker and van Houten (1974) were able to draw attention to the potential sex dynamics that may have influenced management practice at the Hawthorne works and the process of management research of those who developed the Hawthorne Studies.

Other forms of content analysis include work by Benshop and Meihuizen (2002) who deconstruct text and photographic material from the annual reports of a number of companies – revealing the gendered character of corporate presentation. See also the work of Helms Mills (2005), who examines representations of diversity through three major periods of organizational change in the annual reports of a utility company.

Discourse analysis

Calás (1992) used discourse analysis in her study of the representation of Hispanic women in US organizational scholarship. In this study, she reviews various texts found in Western organization studies and deconstructs the dominant discourse that refers to Hispanic women. By asking particular questions – 'How are these discourses constituted? How are they similar to already constituted organizational discourses? How would these constructions impede the appearance of "the different"?' – she offers an intervention into the reproduction of this emerging identity (Calás, 1992: 203). In the discussion that follows, Calás analyzes the concepts in the text in the categories of time, race and voice and from comparative epistemological perspectives. This methodology offers insight into the developing 'knowledge-about-Hispanic-women' being produced in organizational scholarship.

Historiography

Mills' study of race and gender in British Airways over time (Mills, 1994; 1995; 1996) is an example of a social constructionist feminist approach to history. Mills set out to uncover 'how the cultural features of an organization contribute to the social construction of "womanhood" or "manhood"' (Mills, 2002: 292) and notions of race and ethnicity. The research included textual analysis of 'cultural traces' reflected in 'corporate memories' developed by those in privileged positions (e.g. managers, editors, corporate accountants, marketing personnel, film producers) and for specific ends, as well as interviews with some of the mean and women who had worked for the company over a period of time.

Crossing the Boundaries: Narrative Analysis, Life Histories and Discourse Analysis

While some methods of analysis focus on the traces of enacted agency (i.e. past actions), other feminist methods attempt to capture the sensemaking processes in action through such things as narrative analysis, discourse analysis and life histories.

Narrative analysis

This is a process of gathering and analyzing narratives and interpreting meaning from these. For example, Olsson's (2000) study of women managers' narratives of gender in the context of organizational archetypes looks at the role of organizational myths and stories in the definition of leadership as heroic masculinism.

The study involved women business students who also held management positions at various levels and studied at a New Zealand university. The sample of 26 stories was coded and analyzed on the bases of recurring themes. Attitudes towards women managers are discussed in three interrelated categories: invisibility, sexuality and stereotypes. Through an analysis of the themes represented in the women's stories, the researcher is able to identify modern myths of management and create space for the introduction of a women's archetype of leadership excellence. The study concluded that:

> The women managers' stories in this study 'break the silence' and expand official organizational myths to provide vibrant assertions of women's experiences. In parodic inversions of heroic masculinism represented in the Ulysses quest, these stories reveal that the 'monsters' and trials of women's career journeys, are not to do with their competencies or abilities, but rather to do with stereotyped attitudes encountered along the way. The stories also suggest a distinctive female archetype of women as leaders. (Olsson, 2000: 302)

Discourse analysis

Hardy (2001: 26) describes discourse as 'the practices of talking and writing ... which bring objects into being through the production, dissemination, and consumption of texts'. Dick and Cassell (2002) employ a technique of discourse analysis to focus on the issue of resistance to diversity initiatives in a British police force. They introduce their methodology with a discussion of the problems they see as inherent in research methods, which speak on behalf of subordinated groups. As a result, their approach was to facilitate non-directive and open-ended interviews/conversations. Unlike Calás's post-structuralist approach, Dick and Cassell use Potter and Wetherell's (1987) concept of 'interpretive repertories' to identify discourses that police officers used to construct their accounts of promotion and sexual harassment. The technique:

> involves a close examination of the vocabulary used when talking about a specific issue (i.e. promotion or sexual harassment) and the development of appropriate labels to

describe this vocabulary. [Dick and Cassell] used the method of constant comparisons, taken from grounded theory (Glaser & Strauss, 1967) to achieve this aim. [They] identified and made extracts of each occasion when ourselves or the participants had spoken about promotion and sexual harassment. [They] then compared each extract with every other, looking for similarities and differences in the ideas articulated in the extracts. This enabled [them] to identify two dominant interpretive repertoires (discourses). (Dick & Cassell, 2002: 961)

The authors then examined each discourse through Fairclough's (1992) three dimensions of analysis – text, discourse practice and social practice. This analysis leads the authors to argue for a 'far more critical and theoretical approach to the management of diversity' (Dick & Cassell, 2002: 973).

Life histories

The life history method is a presentation of 'the experiences and definitions held by one person, one group, or one organization as this person, group or organization interprets those experiences' (Denzin, 1970: 220). 'Data for life histories can come from private documents such as diaries, letters or taped accounts, or from public records such as autobiographies, television or newspaper stories, minutes of meetings, doctors' records and the like' (Kirby & McKenna, 1989: 81). The challenge in using this methodology, as with other methods of textual analysis, is usually one of access to complete documentation.

Kirby and McKenna (1989: 82) outline the following process used in the life history research approach:

1 List the landmarks or milestones in the person's life.
2 Gather material by interviewing, library searches and so on.
3 Reconstruct the experiences of the individual by filling in a chronological account of his or her experiences.
4 Detail the reconstruction with information available from others and/or by incorporating parallel life histories.
5 Repeat steps 2–4 until, as much as possible, the life history takes shape as a relatively complete accounting of the individual's life experience.

Cotterill and Letherby (1993) offer an interesting discussion of the importance of personal biographies as a tool in feminist research. Contributing to the debate on the role of the experience of the researcher in feminist qualitative research, Cotterill and Letherby (1993: 67) discuss the importance of the biography and the challenges involved in including the researcher's autobiography at the publication stage. They conclude not only that the process of research using personal biographies is important in a retrospective sense, as a historical perspective, but that the research experience 'also alters the personal biographies of the future for all those involved'.

Bell and Nkomo (1992) argue that a life history approach is useful for understanding the experiences that influence women's career choices and opportunities. They contend that such an approach allows the researcher to move beyond universal notions of women by taking into account 'the interactive layers, role and expectations as well as the contexts in which their lives are embedded' (p. 245). In this way we are forced to acknowledge 'the differing experiences of women due to their gender, racial-ethnic, and class identities. And [to take] into account women's lives from a holistic perspective rather than compartmentalizing their lives' (p. 236).

Living with the Results: Interviews, Observations and Ethnographies

Some research methods are designed to directly engage with the members of an organization; these can range from interviews and observations to more extensive ethnographic study.

Interviews

Interviews in feminist qualitative research can take a number of forms. They may appear as conversations, structured interview settings, focus group interactions, sharing of information through storytelling, etc. The concept of the 'long interview' as an open-ended and relatively unstructured approach to gathering information is a key component in much qualitative research. As advocated by McCracken (1988: 9), 'the long interview is one of the most powerful methods in the qualitative armory. For certain descriptive and analytic purposes, no instrument of inquiry is more revealing.'

However, there is some debate among researchers as to the role of the interviewer and, to some extent, the role of the participant in the interview, whatever its form. McCracken (1988) describes the role of the interviewer as one that is benign, accepting and curious. He suggests that the interviewer should present as neutral to sympathetic and even the body language of the interviewer should appear benign. He suggests that interviewers appear 'slightly dim and too agreeable' rather than risk upsetting the atmosphere of safety for the respondent (McCracken, 1988: 38).

This perspective is quite different from that of a number of feminist researchers who view the interview process more as a sharing of information than a search for 'truth', which may or may not be withheld by participants. Kirby and McKenna (1989), for example, argue that the form of the interview should be defined by the interviewer and the participant together. The participant should be seen as more than just data and the interviewer as more than just the vehicle for gathering this data. Interviews that are described as 'non-exploitative' are considered to be a guided conversation where the interviewer and the participant both share information and contribute to the research (Kirby & McKenna, 1989: 66).

In their description of the elements of interview research, Kirby and McKenna (1989) emphasize the fact that both the researcher and the participant should get what they want and need out of the experiences. The interview is described more as an interactive process of information sharing than the traditional, quantitative interview, which would be much more structured with a very limited role for the researcher.

On the other hand, there are those feminist researchers who do see merit in searching for truth rather than a process of sharing. Kanter's (1977) study of corporate leaders, for example, set out to probe the extent to which workplace discrimination relied more on 'the nature of organization' rather then individual men and women (p. 291).

Although the interview format is to be unstructured in the feminist qualitative approach, Kirby and McKenna (1989: 74) contend that there is still a need for clear and well-conceived questions:

> the basis of all interviews is the question ... You must transform your research focus from one research question into many specific questions that will help you, the interviewer, stay close to the research focus and help the participant respond to questions about her or his own experience in an insightful and thoughtful way. The way in which you word the questions, the order in which you ask them and what the participant thinks you might be seeking are components of the interview process.

The application of these questions, and the involvement of the participant in the process, allows feminist qualitative researchers the opportunity to explore the subjective experience of those involved in a more profound way. For example, in Lee's (2002) study of gendered workplace bullying in the British Civil Service, feminist qualitative research exposed the gender dynamics of bullying and uncovered a more complex relationship between gender and bullying than had been offered in previous analysis. Her qualitative methodology, which involved 50 semi-structured interviews with male and female workers who had been exposed to bullying, provided insight that challenged previous work in this area. Earlier studies into bullying had been conducted from a quantitative perspective, and concluded that because men and women had both been exposed to bullying in the workplace, it was not a gender-related issue (i.e. Adams, 1992). Lee's (2002) feminist qualitative approach offered a more in-depth analysis of the impact of gender on bullying, finding that bullying was experienced differently by men and women and it could be a gendered experience for workers. This analysis problematized the absence of a gender analysis in the existing workplace bullying discourse (Lee, 2000: 227).

Aaltio (2002: 201–2), however, suggests 'gender issues sometimes disappear when a researcher tries to capture them by means of interviews', because the interviewee's 'talk and stories are not merely unique to the individual, but they take place within gendered cultural contexts'. To deal with this she argues for a process of 'shadowing' where 'we read gendered processes from material in which gender (notions of women and men) is not explicitly mentioned' (Aaltio, 2002: 201). This can involve examination of not only what is said, but also the organizational culture in which the interview takes place.

Observation

There are various forms of observation in qualitative research but we shall deal with three here – observation, participant observation and ethnography. Observation is in many ways the most straightforward when it involves someone who is known to be a researcher spending time observing certain activities and making notes. For example, to understand the impact of organizational structure on discrimination Kanter (1977: 299) 'watched meetings of two professional women's leadership training programs, a task force at a church, an innovative parochial school, an "alternative" service organization, and a traditional service organization. [She] took field notes and used a variety of coding schemes in meetings.' Pollert (1981) also used observation (and a series of informal interviews) to detail the factory lives of women workers in a Bristol (UK) tobacco company. She initially attempted to engage in participant observation by getting a job at the factory but this met with resistance from the trade union. Thus, she did not have to make a secret of the fact she was a researcher. This suited Pollert (1981: 6) because she 'did not have much chance of learning how to do the work (weighing, for example) in a short period of time, and because adroit enough to talk, observe, or think about anything except keeping up'.

Nonetheless, because observations can encourage people to be on their best (less obviously gendered) behaviour some researchers prefer participant observation in which 'the observer participates in the daily life of the people under study, either openly in the role of researcher or covertly in some disguised role' (Becker & Geer, 1957: 28). As a form of gaining access to people's ongoing sensemaking or accounts of reality this has proven a useful but troubling approach for feminist researchers (Breeman, Guberman, Fournier, Gervais & Lamoureux, 2003). For one thing, participant observation may hide as much as it reveals through the influence of the gendered relations and expectations in which they occur (Brayton, 2004). For example, the needs of the feminist researcher to have access to participants can come into conflict with the cultural expectations of women's role. As Warren (1988: 13) explains, 'the fieldworker's initial reception by the host society is a reflection of cultural contextualization of the fieldworker's characteristics, which include marital status, age, physical appearance, presence and number of children, and ethnic, racial, class, or national differences as well as gender'.

These factors can be even more problematic in ethnographic research where the researcher attempts to become embedded in a particular organizational community over time.

Ethnography

Arguing for a 'gendered perspective to cultures' to uncover resistance to organizational change, Shepheard and Pringle (2004: 160) undertook an ethnographic study of a US company operating in New Zealand. The case study was designed to illuminate 'the gendered nature of organizational cultures and more importantly the gendered nature of resistance to specific attempts to change the organizational culture' (p. 164). The study involved a 12-month investigation that included interviews, discussions, observations and analysis of corporate documents. In this way, argue Shepheard and Pringle (2004: 164), the combination of techniques used over a longish period of time allowed them to 'discern layers of meaning from a close reading of participants' "short stories"'.

Being Feminist: Autoethnography, the Self in Research and Techniques of the Self

Stanley and Wise (1983: 165) advocate a recognition of the fact that 'personal, direct experience, underlies all behaviours and actions'. As a result, the requirement for generalizability and external validity required in the quantitative approach is less important in qualitative research. The focus here is on a more profound understanding of the experiences of individuals, rather than a large-scale study of a particular demographic group. This has led a number of feminist researchers to examine the role of the self in qualitative research.

Autoethnography

A recent example of autoethnicity can be found in the work of Hearn (2004). Attempting to provide insights on the processes of gendering, Hearn found himself reflecting on his own experiences and how they could help to illuminate the linkages between 'men, gender, sexuality, violence, organizations, management, and multiple social divisions' (Hearn, 2004: 40). To that end, focusing on his involvement in a university hiring process – as the candidate – he developed 'a reflexive composite methodology, combining participatory action research, documentary analysis, critical life history, memory work and autoethnography' (Hearn, 2004: 40). Through this approach Hearn develops insights into the gendering of organizational processes but in a way that 'raises complex uncertainties about the nature of knowledges and the relations of Ones to Others' (Hearn, 2004: 60) .

The self in feminist research

Katila and Merilainen (2002: 185) argue that 'placing self in the centre of research – that is, seeing self both as the subject and the object of research – can be a meaningful and fruitful strategy' for dealing with 'discriminative organizational cultures'. At the heart of this strategy has been the generation of data 'based on naturally occurring conversations, some of which we [they wrote down] on site, and some of which [they] recorded from memory afterwards' and the utilization of 'any and all situationally available techniques to gather data' (p. 188). Reflecting on their strategy, Katila and Merilainen (2002) are aware of the dangers that their work will be seen as biased – that they would be seen as 'too intimately involved with the organization under study and its members to be able to distance [themselves] from the field' (p. 192). Their answer is that 'there are no essential differences between the subjects and objects of knowledge' (p. 193). They conclude, by 'reporting on our identity work as female academics in a male-dominated academic community, we have been able to highlight the gendered nature of academic work in general, and the difficulties women face in constructing their professional identity in particular' (p. 197).

Techniques of the self

In a similar vein Brewis (2004) puts herself in focus, drawing on Foucault's notion of techniques of the self to her 'being-in-the-world' (p. 24). In fact, the study is fourfold:

> first, to outline the ways in which we moderns are enjoined to interpret ourselves ...; second, to describe the price [she] has paid for [her] own 'truths' of 'self'; third, to review [her] efforts to change how [she thinks] about what happens to [her]; and, fourth, to suggest that, although we might be 'free' to make alterations in this regard, these alterations are by no means easy nor are they passports to a better way of life. (pp. 37–8)

In her brave attempt at critical self-analysis Brewis leaves us with powerful insights into the related problems of identity work, organizational discourse and resistance.

Deconstructing the Social Constructions: Deconstruction

Finally, at the end of the day, we need to make sense of what we have studied. How we do that will largely depend on which feminist approach we have taken in the first place. Making sense of data may be as simple as 'writing up' the 'results' through to what post-structuralists call 'deconstruction'. To end this section, and with full apologies to the many feminist approaches that we have not been able to cover, we take a brief look at deconstruction – and only one (post-structuralist) variant at that.

Deconstruction

This is another approach applied to textual analysis and it asserts that there is no one true account of the world. Therefore, only partially objective truths can be created as all language creates a discourse that will, at the same time, include some voices and exclude others.

Martin's (1990) study of organizational taboos used a deconstruction of an excerpt from a speech given by a corporate CEO. In response to a question about the company's concern for the well-being of women employees with children, the CEO told a story, by way of example. Martin introduces her methodology by saying 'I deconstruct and reconstruct this story from a feminist viewpoint, examining what it says, what it does not say, and what it might have said. This analysis highlights suppressed gender conflicts implicit in this story and shows how apparently well-intentioned organizational practices can reify, rather than alleviate, gender inequalities' (Martin, 1990: 339).

And the Underprivileged Methods

Due to the limits of time and space we have only focused on some of the techniques of feminist study leaving out of account several other important methodologies, including symbolic interactionism (Hall, 2003), hermeneutics (Code, 2003), feminist standpoint theory (Harding, 2004), feminist materialism (Kuhn & Wolpe, 1978), postcolonialism (Prasad, Mills, Elmes & Prasad, 1997) and a rich variety of postmodernist and post-structuralist feminist research (Olesen, 1994).

CHALLENGES IN USING THESE METHODOLOGIES

The application of feminist qualitative research methodology is not without its limitations. The major criticisms of this perspective are similar to those leveled at qualitative research in general. These include; the role of the researcher and subject, research bias, ethical practice, validity and credibility. As Fielding (1999) points out, 'Qualitative methods have lately enjoyed enhanced legitimacy and are increasingly used in academic and applied social research. Yet the field is marked by controversy about virtually every key tenet of qualitative inquiry, from matters of epistemology to purely practical matters of relations with research subjects.'

In response to the question of research bias and research subjectivity, feminist qualitative researchers would argue that bias is a misplaced term (Olesen, 1994: 165). The researcher's experience and involvement in the research process are seen as resources, rather than 'problems' to be overcome in the research process. The challenge for researchers is to recognize and reflect upon their involvement in the process so that their views may be an appropriately attributed part of the research.

CONCLUSION

The feminist approach to qualitative research offers a unique response to current criticisms of workplace diversity initiatives. A reliance on quantitative, ethnocentric research over the past decade has failed to illuminate the underlying problems with diversity management, be it as a program, field of research or paradigm. More recently, a feminist critique of the state of workplace diversity has offered some insight into the fundamental issues that need be addressed if diversity management is to succeed. These include the potential of backlash towards marginalized groups, a lack of definitional clarity of the term diversity management, and a 'watering down' of diversity issues to that of affirmative action programs. Feminist qualitative research techniques offer an opportunity for researchers to begin to address issues of relationships, power and oppression within organizations by providing a more profound understanding of the experience of individuals within organizations.

As in any research program, researchers must define their research objectives and identify data accordingly. Feminist qualitative researchers must also justify this 'alternative' research methodology to the dominant paradigm. In the end, however, the challenge for feminist qualitative researchers may be a question of how to represent their research as well as how to conduct it. Although a feminist perspective may help to provide a wider audience for diversity research, there are many organizations that prefer to leave issues of diversity to the human resources department. Feminist qualitative research provides a critique of this practice, and contributes to the growing understanding of the limitations of traditional organizational practices with regards to marginalized groups. The fundamental goals of feminist and diversity research are to facilitate change and provide opportunities for representation of marginalized groups and individuals. If these goals are to be realized, researchers in these perspectives must work together with postmodern and critical researchers who are theorizing organizational power.

At the same time, if diversity initiatives are to be meaningful in contemporary organizations, researchers must recognize the environment in which workplace diversity research takes place. It can be argued that to discount organizational structures as they currently exist is unrealistic. 'Critique is a valuable way of exposing the negative outcomes of organizations but of itself it will not lead to change' (Mills, 1998: 297). We would encourage critical organizational theorists to incorporate the insights gained through mainstream management theory, and build on that knowledge to effect organizational change.

Finally, we want to return to the point that we introduced at the beginning of this chapter, that feminist qualitative research is a useful way of generating insights into workplace diversity. We have argued that qualitative research need not be seen as an alternative to quantitative research and can even be complementary, but it depends on which feminist perspective you take and your respective understanding of qualitative and quantitative research. We have also attempted to provide various examples where feminist research has attempted to deal with issues of gender, race, ethnicity and class. Nonetheless, we are cognizant that some may ask: how can a perspective that is women centered adequately deal with the broader issues of diversity, which has come to stand for race/ethnicity, sexual orientation, disability and age, as well as gender? There are four answers to this question that, we hope, will provide an appropriate conclusion to this chapter:

1 As we have argued above, feminism draws attention to difference and otherness, serving as a method for exposing how the social construction of organizational life and of knowledge per se contributes to different subjectivities and associated outcomes.

2 Workplace diversity is a highly problematic term that has served to open up debate on workplace discrimination while simultaneously constraining it by problematizing everyone except the able-bodied white and heterosexual male. In the process various, sometime contradictory, political struggles have been reduced to a single issue of diversity (Prasad & Mills, 1997). Thus, arguably, we need to search not for an artificially designed method that mirrors the call for understanding workplace diversity, but for multiple perspectives that are based on the specific struggles of the different constituencies involved.

3 Feminism makes an important contribution to insights into/or the deconstruction of workplace diversity not by subsuming its political focus on women's liberation under a broader umbrella, but by continuing to stress the problematic of gender discrimination.

4 To us, this means that feminism has much to offer workplace diversity research where it is able to deal with issues of race, ethnicity, class, sexual orientation and age while continuing to focus on the contribution of those insights to addressing gender discrimination at work.

REFERENCES

Aaltio, I. (2002). Interviewing female managers: Presentations of the gendered selves in contexts. In I. Aaltio & A. J. Mills (Eds), *Gender, identity and the culture of organizations* (pp. 201–18). London: Routledge.

Aaltio, I., Mills, A. J., & Helms Mills, J. C. (2002). Exploring gendered organizational cultures. *Culture and Organization, 8*(2), 77–9.

Abella, R. S. (1984). *Equity in employment. A Royal Commission report.* Ottawa: Ministry of Supply and Services Canada.

Acker, J., & van Houten, D. R. (1974). Differential recruitment and control: The sex structuring of organizations. *Administrative Science Quarterly, 9*(2), 152–63.

Adams, A. (1992). *Bullying at work.* London: Virago.

Becker, H. S., & Geer, B. (1957). Participant observation and interviewing: A comparison? *Human Organization, XVI,* 28–32.

Bell, E., & Nkomo, S. (1992). Re-visioning women managers' lives. In A. J. Mills & P. Tancred (Eds), *Gendering organizational analysis* (pp. 235–47). Newbury Park, CA: Sage.

Benschop, Y., & Meihuizen, H. E. (2002). Reporting gender: Representations of gender in financial and annual reports. In I. Aaltio & A. J. Mills (Eds), *Gender, identity and the culture of organizations* (pp. 160–84). London: Routledge.

Brayton, J. (2004). What makes feminist research feminist? The structure of feminist research within the social sciences: http://www.unb.ca/web/PAR-L/win/feminmethod.htm (Retrieved 22 May 2005).

Breeman, J., Guberman, N., Fournier, D., Gervais, L., & Lamoureux, J. (2003). Are the movement's organizations open to the movement's members? A study of democratic practices in women's groups in Québéc. *New Feminist Research, 30*(1–2), 101–24.

Brewerton, P., & Millward, L. (2001). *Organizational research methods.* London: Sage.

Brewis, J. (2004). Refusing to be 'me'. In R. Thomas, A. J. Mills & J. Helms Mills (Eds), *Identity politics at work: Resisting gender, gendering resistance* (pp. 23–39). London: Routledge.

Burrell, G., & Morgan, G. (1979). *Sociological paradigms and organizational analysis.* London: Heinemann.

Calás, M. (1992). An/other silent voice? Representing 'Hispanic Woman' in organizational texts. In A. J. Mills & P. Tancred (Eds), *Gendering organizational analysis* (pp. 201–21). London: Sage.

Calás, M. B., & Smircich, L. (1992). Using the 'F' word: Feminist theories and the social consequences of organizational research. In A. J. Mills & P. Tancred (Eds), *Gendering organizational analysis* (pp. 222–34). Newbury Park, CA: Sage.

Calás, M. B., & Smircich, L. (1996). From 'The Woman's' point of view: Feminist approaches to organization studies. In S. R. Clegg, C. Hardy & W. R. Nord (Eds), *Handbook of organization studies* (pp. 218–57). London: Sage.

Clegg, S., & Dunkerley, D. (1980). *Organization, class and control.* London: Routledge & Kegan Paul.

Cockburn, C. (1991). *Brothers: Male dominance and technological change.* London: Pluto Press.

Code, L. (2003). *Feminist interpretations of Hans-Georg Gadamer.* University Park, PA: Pennsylvania State University Press.

Collinson, D., & Hearn, J. (1994). Naming men as men: Implications for work, organization and management. *Gender, Work & Organization, 1*(1), 2–22.

Cotterill, P., & Letherby, G. (1993). Weaving stories: Personal auto/biographies in feminist research. *Journal of the British Sociological Association, 27*(1), 67–80.

Cox, T. H., Jr (1990). Problems with organizational research on race and ethnicity issues. *Journal of Applied Behavioral Sciences, 26,* 5–23.

Denzin, N. (1970). *The Research Act: A Theoretical Introduction to Sociological Methods.* Chicago, IL: Aldine.

Dick, P., & Cassell, C. (2002). Barriers to managing diversity in a UK constabulary: The role of discourse. *Journal of Management Studies, 39*(7), 953–76.

Fairclough, N. (1992). *Discourse and social change.* Cambridge: Polity.

Ferguson, K. E. (1984). *The feminist case against bureaucracy.* Philadelphia, PA: Temple University Press.

Fielding, N. (1999). The norm and the text: Denzin and Lincoln's handbooks of qualitative method. *British Journal of Sociology, 50*(3), 525.

Gherardi, S. (1995). *Gender, symbolism, and organizational culture.* London: Sage.

Glaser, B. G., & Strauss, A. L. (1967). *The discovery of grounded theory: Strategies for qualitative research.* Chicago: Aldine.

Hall, J. (2003). Analyzing women's roles through graphic representation of narratives. *Western Journal of Nursing Research, 25*(5), 492–508.

Harding, S. G. (2004). *The feminist standpoint theory reader: intellectual and political controversies.* New York: Routledge.

Hardy, C. (2001). Researching organizational discourse. *International Studies of Management and Organization, 31*(3), 25–47.

Harriman, A. (1985). *Women/men, management.* New York: Praeger.

Hearn, J. (2004). Personal resistance through persistence to organizational resistance through distance. In R. Thomas, A. J. Mills & J. Helms Mills (Eds), *Identity politics at work: Resisting gender, gendering resistance* (pp. 40–63). London: Routledge.

Hearn, J., & Parkin, P. W. (1987). *'Sex' at 'Work': The power and paradox of organizational sexuality.* Brighton: Wheatsheaf.

Helms Mills, J. (2005). Representations of diversity and organizational change in a North American utility company. *Gender, Work & Organization, 12*(3), 242–69.

Helms Mills, J. C., & Mills, A. J. (2000). Rules, sensemaking, formative contexts and discourse in the gendering of organizational culture. In N. M. Ashkanasy, C. P. M. Wilderom & M. F. Peterson (Eds), *Handbook of organizational culture and climate* (pp. 55–70). Thousand Oaks, CA: Sage.

Henning, M., & Jardin, A. (1977). *The managerial woman.* New York: Anchor/Doubleday.

Hofstede, G., Neuijen, B., Ohavy, D. D., & Sanders, G. (1990). Measuring organizational culture: A qualitative and quantitative study across twenty cases. *Administrative Science Quarterly, 35*(2).

Hollway, W. (1989). *Subjectivity and method in psychology: gender, meaning and science.* London: Sage.

Humphreys, S. (1994). What is women's history? In J. Gardiner (Ed.), *What is history today?* (pp. 87–9). London: Macmillan.

Kanter, R. M. (1977). *Men and women of the corporation.* New York: Basic Books.

Katila, S., & Merilainen, S. (2002). Self in research: Hopelessly entangled in the gendered organizational culture. In I. Aaltio & A. J. Mills (Eds), *Gender, identity and the culture of organizations* (pp. 185–200). London: Routledge.

Kieser, A. (1997). Rhetoric and myth in management fashion. *Organization*, 4(1), 49–74.

Kirby, S. L., & McKenna, K. (1989). *Experience, research, social change: Methods from the margins*. Toronto: Garamond.

Kramarae, C., & Treichler, P. A. (1985). *A feminist dictionary*. London: Pandora Press.

Kuhn, A., & Wolpe, A. (1978). *Feminism and materialism: Women and modes of production*. London: Routledge & Kegan Paul.

Lee, D. (2002). Gendered workplace bullying in the restructured UK civil service. *Personnel Review*, 31(1/2), 205–28.

Marshall, J. (1993). Patterns of cultural awareness as coping strategies for women managers. In S. E. Kahn & B. C. Long (Eds), *Work, women and coping: A multidisciplinary approach to workplace stress* (pp. 90–110). Montreal: McGill–Queen's University Press.

Martin, J. (1990). Deconstructing organizational taboos: The suppression of gender conflict in organizations. *Organization Science*, 1(4), 339–60.

McCracken, G. D. (1988). *The long interview*. Newbury Park, CA: Sage.

Mills, A. J. (1994). The gendering of organizational culture: Social and organizational discourses in the making of British Airways. In M. DesRosiers (Ed.), *Proceedings of the Administrative Sciences Association of Canada, Women in Management Division* (Vol. 15, pp. 11–20). Halifax, Nova Scotia: Administrative Sciences Association of Canada.

Mills, A. J. (1995). Man/aging subjectivity, silencing diversity: Organizational imagery in the airline industry – the case of British Airways. *Organization*, 2(2), 243–69.

Mills, A. J. (1996). Corporate image, gendered subjects and the company newsletter – the changing faces of British Airways. In G. Palmer & S. Clegg (Eds), *Constituting management: Markets, meanings and identities* (pp. 191–211). Berlin: de Gruyter.

Mills, A. J. (1998). Toward an agenda of radical organizing: Introduction to the special issue. *Canadian Review of Sociology and Anthropology*, 35(3), 281.

Mills, A. J. (2002). Studying the gendering of organizational culture over time: Concerns, issues and strategies. *Gender, Work & Organization*, 9(3), 286–307.

Morgan, G., & Knights, D. (1991). Gendering jobs: Corporate strategies, managerial control and dynamics of job segregation. *Work, Employment & Society*, 5(2), 181–200.

Morgan, N. (1988). *The equality game: Women in the federal public service (1908–1987)*. Ottawa: Canadian Advisory Council on the Status of Women.

Morrison, A., White, R., & Van Elsor, E. (1987). *Breaking the glass ceiling*. Reading, MA: Addison-Wesley.

Olesen, V. (1994). Feminisms and models of qualitative research. In N. K. Denzin and Y. L. Lincoln (Eds), *Handbook of qualitative research* (pp. 158–74). Thousnad Oaks, CA: Sage.

Olsson, S. (2000). Acknowledging the female archetype: Women managers' narratives of gender. *Women in Management Review*, 15(5/6), 296–306.

O'Neill, B. (1995). The gender gap: Re-evaluating theory and methods. In S. Burt & L. Code (Eds), *Changing methods: Feminists transforming practice* (pp. 327–56). Peterborough, Ontario: Broadview Press.

Ouchi, W. (1981). *Theory Z*. Reading, MA: Addison-Wesley.

Pascale, R. T., & Athos, A. G. (1981). *The art of Japanese management: Applications for American executives*. New York: Simon & Schuster.

Peters, T., & Waterman, R. (1982). *In search of excellence – Lessons from America's best run companies*. New York: Warner Communications.

Pollert, A. (1981). *Girls, wives, factory lives*. London: Macmillan.

Potter, J., & Wetherell, M. (1987). *Discourse and social psychology: Beyond attitudes and behaviour*. London: Sage.

Prasad, A., & Prasad, P. (2002). Otherness at large: Identity and difference in the new globalized organizational landscape. In I. Aaltio & A. J. Mills (Eds), *Gender, identity and the culture of organizations* (pp. 57–71). London: Routledge.

Prasad, P., & Mills, A. J. (1997). From showcase to shadow: Understanding the dilemmas of managing workplace diversity. In P. Prasad, A. J. Mills, M. Elmes & A. Prasad (Eds),

Managing the organizational melting pot: Dilemmas of workplace diversity (pp. 3–27). Thousand Oaks, CA: Sage.

Prasad, P., Mills, A. J., Elmes, M., & Prasad, P. (Eds) (1997). *Managing the organizational melting pot: Dilemmas of workplace diversity*. Thousand Oaks, CA: Sage.

Reed, E. (1978). *Sexism and science*. London: Pathfinder.

Reinharz, S., & Davidman, L. (1992). *Feminist methods in social research*. New York: Oxford University Press.

Rowbotham, S. (1974). *Hidden from history: Rediscovering women in history from the seventeenth century to the present*. New York: Pantheon.

Schein, E. H. (1985). *Organizational culture and leadership*. San Francisco: Jossey-Bass.

Schein, V. E. (1973). The relationship between sex role stereotypes and requisite management characteristics among female managers. *Journal of Applied Psychology, 57*, 89–105.

Shepheard, D. M., & Pringle, J. K. (2004). Resistance to organizational culture change. A gendered analysis. In R. Thomas, A. J. Mills & J. Helms Mills (Eds), *Identity politics at work: resisting gender, gendering resistance* (pp. 160–76). London: Routledge.

Stanley, L., & Wise, S. (1983). *Breaking out: Feminist consciousness and feminist research*. London: Routledge & Kegan Paul.

Thomas, R., & Davies, A. (2002). Gender and the new public management. *Gender, Work & Organization, 9*(4), 372–96.

Warren, C. A. B. (1988). *Gender issues in field research*. Newbury Park, CA: Sage.

Wicks, D., & Bradshaw, P. (2002). Gendered value foundations that reproduce discrimination and inhibit organizational change. In I. Aaltio & A. J. Mills (Eds), *Gender, identity and the culture of organizations* (pp. 137–59). London: Routledge.

Wolf, N. (2002). *The beauty myth: How images of beauty are used against women*. New York: Perennial.

10

Measures for Quantitative Diversity Scholarship

DONNA CHROBOT-MASON, ALISON M. KONRAD
AND FRANK LINNEHAN[1]

The field of diversity scholarship has grown dramatically since the appearance of *Workforce 2000: Work and workers in the 21st century* (Johnston & Packer, 1987), the Hudson Institute publication that firmly established workplace diversity scholarship as a management subfield. In the last two decades, management and organizational scholars have used concepts previously established within the fields of psychology and sociology to address research questions arising from the acknowledgement that multiple social identity groups increasingly work together within organizational contexts. Through this work, scholars have extended disciplinary understandings of diversity-related concepts by crossing levels of analysis and adding an understanding of organizations as systems that was largely absent from research grounded in purely psychological or sociological perspectives.

As the field has matured, a need has arisen to improve the quality of the research by enhancing the reliability and validity of measurement. The purpose of this chapter is to provide an overview of the best measures we found in a broad review of the extant quantitative literature. On the basis of our review, we have generated five tables presenting reliability and validity information. Due to space considerations, we are only able to cover five research domains: social identification, diversity readiness and resistance, discrimination and harassment, organization practices, and organization climate. We offer this chapter as a resource identifying the most reliable and valid measures for a variety of research questions as well as identifying areas where further measurement development is warranted.

SOCIAL IDENTIFICATION

Assessing social identification is a critical step for moving research beyond surface categorizations of people into demographic categories. Recognizing the variation within demographic groups, measures of social identification attempt to capture individual differences in the meanings and level of importance individuals attach to their identity group memberships.

Early measures of identification with identity groups focused on gender (see Table 10.1). The Bem Sex-Role Inventory (BSRI, Bem, 1974) and the Personal Attributes Questionnaire (PAQ, Spence & Helmreich, 1978) were developed to assess the extent to which women and men considered themselves to hold traits associated with masculinity and femininity. A meta-analysis examining 63 samples of undergraduate student responses to the BSRI and the PAQ (Twenge, 1997a) showed that women's masculinity scores have risen over time and that the difference between women's and men's self-reported masculinity has become smaller. The PAQ showed smaller changes over time than the BSRI did, and Twenge argues that the PAQ is preferable to the BSRI due to the inclusion of some socially undesirable items in the BSRI femininity index that are not included in the PAQ femininity index.

Several measures have been developed within the field of counseling psychology to assess racial and ethnic identity development. In general, these measures attempt to determine an individual's stage of development in achieving a healthy racial identity. There is an extensive body of both theoretical and empirical literature that spans across three decades but a thorough review of this literature is beyond the scope of this chapter. However, we wish to make some recommendations to organizational researchers and practitioners as to how such measures might prove useful within the work context.

The Black and White Racial Identity Attitude Scales (Helms, 1990) are still considered to be the benchmark measures of racial identity and have been used as a model for the development of other identity scales to assess female identity and gay/lesbian identity (Downing & Roush, 1985; Walters & Simoni, 1993). However, these measures have been strongly criticized for their psychometric limitations, the focus on whites' attitudes toward blacks and vice versa to the exclusion of the individuals' attitudes and affect toward their own racial group, and due to the fact that many items now appear outdated. Although the Oklahoma Racial Attitudes Scale - Preliminary Form (ORAS-P, Choney & Behrens, 1996) measure attempts to address some of these concerns, it is still considered to be in the developmental stages and its use may also be limited for organizational researchers and practitioners. However, we do agree with Kirkland and Regan (1997) who suggest that such measures may be useful diagnostic tools as a precursor to the implementation of organizational diversity interventions such as diversity training programs. These measures, along with others that we will discuss next, may allow the trainee to evaluate him- or herself with respect to readiness for training and general comfort level with diversity.

TABLE 10.1

Social identification

Study/measures	Validation sample	Reliability evidence[1]	Validity evidence
Bem (1974) Bem Sex-Role Inventory (BSRI) (20 masculine and 20 feminine items)	100 students; 444 male; 279 female	Masculinity = 0.86 (both samples), femininity = 0.80 to 0.82 Four-week test–retest reliability for both masculinity and femininity = 0.90	The self-descriptions of males and females in Bem's original study differed significantly on the two dimensions of masculinity and femininity in the predicted direction Self-descriptions on the BSRI showed a small to moderate positive correlation with social desirability bias in Bem's original study See also: Blanchard-Fields et al. (1994), Holt & Ellis (1998), Konrad & Harris (2002)
Button (2004) Identity management strategies (29 items constituting 3 subscales: counterfeiting, avoiding and integrating)	423 adults	Counterfeiting = 0.80 Avoiding = 0.86 Integrating = 0.90	The three-factor structure was replicated for both gay men and lesbians None of the three factors was significantly correlated with social desirability bias
Choney & Behrens (1996) Oklahoma Racial Attitudes Scale Preliminary Form (ORAS-P) (50 items with 7 subscales)	249 white students (45% male)	(0.72 to 0.82), except for the three-item scale which was 0.68. Test–retest (0.46 to 0.76)	Pope-Davis, Vandiver & Stone (1999) compared the WRIAS and the ORAS-P. The two scales overlapped on two factors (degree of racial comfort and attitudes toward racial equality). Only the WRIAS loaded on the attitudes of racial curiosity factor and only the ORAS-P loaded on the unachieved racial attitudes factor
Douthitt et al. (1999) Diversity of Life Experiences (DOLE) (26 items)	209 students (55% male, 89% Caucasian)	Total scale = 0.74	Evidence for convergent and discriminant validity is presented
Dunbar (1997) The Personal Dimensions of Difference Scale (10 demographic items, 21 items to assess 3 subscales)	791 (37% white, 68% men); 744 (33% men, 39% white)	(0.59 to 0.89) Test–retest (0.69 to 0.79)	Positively correlated with the WRIAS and subjective well-being

(Continued)

TABLE 10.1 (Continued)

Social identification

Study/measures	Validation sample	Reliability evidence[1]	Validity evidence
Helms (1990) Black Racial Identity Attitude Scale (RIAS-B) and White Racial Identity Attitude Scale (WRIAS) (50 items for each scale)			An extensive body of literature exists on the use and validation of the RIAS-B, including: • Ponterotto & Wise (1987) • Helms & Carter (1991) • Carter (1996) • Pope-Davis & Ottavi (1994) • Neville et al. (1996) • Brown et al. (1996)
Luhtanen & Crocker (1992) Collective Self-Esteem Scale (16 items with 4 subscales). Subscales include: membership esteem, public collective self-esteem, private collective self-esteem, and importance to identity	887 students (49% male, 91% white); 83 students (65% female, 14.5% non-white); 180 students (70% female, 11% non-white)	Total scale (0.85) Subscales (0.73 to 0.85) Test–retest = 0.68	Collective self-esteem was moderately correlated with self-esteem but not related to social desirability
Phinney (1997) Multigroup Ethnic Identity Measure (MEIM) (23 items with 4 subscales and 3 background questions)	417 HS (44% male, 95% racial minority); 136 college students (35% male, 17% white)	Overall scale (0.81) for high school students; subscales (0.69 to 0.75) Overall scale (0.90) for college students; subscales (0.74 to 0.86)	Phinney (1992; 1997) reports a positive relationship between ethnic identity and self-esteem, and that racial/ethnic minorities and women score higher than whites and men Ponterotto et al. (2003) reviewed 12 studies using the MEIM and collected additional data from 219 high school students to conduct a confirmatory factor analysis. They found two subscales (ethnic identity and other-group orientation) to be distinct, have satisfactory internal consistency, and moderate support for construct and criterion-related validity See the following for more information: Lee et al. (2001) Spencer et al. (2000), Worrell (2000), Yancey et al. (2001)

(Continued)

TABLE 10.1 (Continued)

Social identification

Study/measures	Validation sample	Reliability evidence[1]	Validity evidence
Spence & Helmreich (1978; 1979; 1980)			
Personal Attributes Questionnaire (PAQ) (55-item long form, 16- or 24-item short forms)	1769 HS; 715 college students	8-item masculinity short form = 0.85 8-item femininity short form = 0.82	Considered more desirable for women Males scored higher on self-reports of masculinity while females scored higher on femininity Correlations of the masculinity and femininity subscales with social desirability bias range from 0.08 to 0.36
Tropp & Wright (2001)			
In-group in the Self (IIS) measure Pictorial measure (Venn-like diagrams) to assess the level to which the other is included in the self	74 white women; 176 Latinos (34% male); 88 students; 154 students	Test–retest (0.76)	Strongly correlated with both cognitive and relational variables associated with in-group identification, and with other measures of in-group identity

[1]Reliability estimates are Cronbach's alphas unless otherwise indicated.

The Multigroup Ethnic Identity Measure (MEIM, Phinney, 1992) is a measure of ethnic identity achievement and differs from the RIAS and WRIAS in that it is intended to be applicable for all ethnic groups and attempts to measure attitudes and behaviors associated with one's own ethnic group rather than another group. There is sufficient evidence to support the psychometric properties of this scale; however, most of the studies conducted to date have been within the field of counseling or clinical psychology and with adolescent groups. Thus, its use with adult populations within the work context is yet to be tested. However, organizational researchers have recently begun to use the MEIM with promising results. Kim and Gelfand (2003) found some support that ethnic identity moderates the impact of recruitment brochures on recruitment outcomes. Chrobot-Mason (2004) found that manager and employee ethnic identity interacted to impact employee perceptions of managerial support. Finally, Linnehan, Chrobot-Mason and Konrad (2002) found support for the relationship between ethnic identity and intentions to behave in support of diversity goals and values.

Measures have also been established to assess an individual's identity strength, based on the premise that members of the same social identity group will vary widely with respect to the strength with which they identify with a particular group. Although there are others, we present just two in our review. The Luhtanen and Crocker (1992) scale, particularly the subscale Importance to Identity, has been widely used in the psychology literature to assess the salience and importance a particular social identity holds for individuals. The Dunbar (1997) measure is not as well established, but still holds promise as a concise measure of identity strength and perceptions of empowerment. Tropp and Wright (2001) developed a pictorial measure of identity strength to assess the extent to which a particular group is included in the individual's definition of self.

These measures may be useful within an organizational setting as another self-diagnostic tool to initiate discussions during diversity training workshops about the importance of race and other social identities for some individuals. They may also be used to assess the relative importance of particular social identities for a group of employees in order to determine the resistance or support for various diversity interventions or programs intended to facilitate the development of certain demographic groups within the organization.

A recent development in this literature has been the assessment of identity management strategies among lesbians and gays. Button's (2004) measure assesses three possibilities: counterfeiting, avoiding and integrating. He replicated the three-factor structure for both lesbians and gays and showed that none of the three factors were correlated with social desirability bias.

DIVERSITY READINESS AND RESISTANCE

Although the need to measure employee resistance or acceptance of diversity programs and diversity itself has been recognized by diversity scholars for decades, only a handful of measures exist for this purpose. The Diversity of Life Experiences (DOLE) scale is a biodata instrument designed to assess background experiences with diversity and preference for diversity and new experiences. Miville et al. (1999) developed a promising Likert-format measure to assess attitudes and acceptance of diversity. It was developed to assist counselors and is based on the premise that an awareness of peoples' likenesses and differences is critical to effectively interact with diverse clients. Although the Universal Diverse Orientation (UDO) measure has not been widely used within the organizational context, we believe it could be useful for placement or as a self-diagnostic tool to determine fit for a position requiring work with or leadership of a diverse group of employees.

A number of researchers have written about the need to assess and develop diversity or multicultural skills for managers who work in a diverse setting and lead multicultural workgroups (Chrobot-Mason, 2003; Offerman & Phan, 2002; Thomas, 1998). However, very little empirical work has yet been done in this area leaving this a rich area for future research. Another goal for future work in this area is the creation of tools to assess the development of organizations with respect to diversity practices, policies and climate. Ely and Thomas (2001) and Chrobot-Mason and Thomas (2002) propose that, similar to individuals, organizations differ with respect to their level of development and readiness for diversity. Future research is needed to adequately measure organizational readiness for diversity and measure the organizations' progress following diversity interventions.

Scholars have developed a variety of measures of attitudes toward different demographic groups. Numerous sexism and racism indices exist, and other authors have created reliable and valid indices of attitudes toward gays (Herek, 1984; 1987; 1994) and heavy-set people (Crandall, 1994) (see Table 10.2). Researchers may find these individual difference indicators useful for distinguishing among members of the same demographic group in order to develop better predictions of behavior in diverse workplaces. Organizational practitioners may find these measures of readiness for, or resistance to, diversity useful for needs assessment prior to the introduction of a diversity initiative as well as evaluation of the effectiveness of diversity interventions.

Sexism

Historically, the first measures of attitudes toward specific demographic groups to be developed focused on sexism, and Spence and Helmreich (1972) were the first to develop a measure of sexism, which they called the Attitudes toward Women Scale (AWS). The Sex-Role Egalitarianism Scale (SRES, Beere et al., 1984; King & King, 1990; 1997) is an updated version of the AWS. Two 25-item short forms with excellent psychometric properties exist assessing five content areas: marital, parental, employment, social and educational. The measure is proprietary and must be attained from Sigma Assessment Systems, Inc. (at time of printing, the short forms were available in Canada for CDN$50 for 25).

TABLE 10.2

Diversity readiness and resistance

Study/measures	Validation sample	Reliability evidence[1]	Validity evidence
Beere et al. (1984) King & King (1990; 1997) Sex-Role Egalitarianism Scale (SRES) (2 95-item long forms (B & K) 25-item short forms (BB & KK) assessing 5 content areas: marital, parental, employment, social and educational	530; 252 and 608 college students; 115	Long forms: Total scale = 0.97 Average of 0.87 for 5 subscales Test–retest = 0.88 to 0.91 for total, and averaged 0.85 for the 5 subscales Short forms: Total scale = 0.92 to 0.94 Test–retest reliability = 0.88 for both forms	Women showed more egalitarian scores than men in several studies Several studies have shown moderate to strong correlations between traditional scores on the SRES and approval of the use of violence in domestic disputes Several studies have shown strong positive correlations with the Attitudes toward Women Scale (Spence & Helmreich, 1972) Several studies have shown that correlations with social desirability bias are minimal
Crandall (1994) Antifat Attitudes Questionnaire (AFA) (26 items)	Students: 251 1114; 26; 30; 42; 2406	Three factors: Dislike of fat people = 0.84 Fear of becoming fat = 0.79 Fat is due to lack of willpower = 0.66	Men scored higher than women on dislike of fat people, while women scored considerably higher than men on fear of becoming fat Dislike of fat and willpower but not fear of fat were positively predicted by several conceptually relevant ideological indices More socially desirability answers were given on the Modern Racism Scale than on the AFA
Dunton & Fazio (1997) Motivation to Control Prejudiced Reactions (17 items)	418 and 429 community participants	Total scale = 0.74 to 0.81	Two-factor structure replicated across 3 separate samples High scores on Factor 1 of this measure were negatively associated with scores on the Modern Racism Scale High scores on Factor 1 of this measure were associated with a reduced link between an unobtrusive measure of racism and scores on the Modern Racism Scale

(Continued)

TABLE 10.2 (Continued)

Diversity readiness and resistance

Study/measures	Validation sample	Reliability evidence[1]	Validity evidence
Glick & Fiske (1996) Ambivalent Sexism Inventory (ASI) (22 items comprising two 11-item subscales assessing Hostile and Benevolent Sexism)	Students: 833; 171 937; 85 Community: 144; 112	Glick & Fiske (1996) Hostile = 0.80 to 0.92; Benevolent = 0.73 to 0.85 Masser & Abrams (1999) 2 samples of 395 + 491 UG students + 153 adult employees Hostile = 0.75 to 0.88 Benevolent = 0.61 to 0.83	Men scored higher than women on both dimensions in 5 of the 6 studies; in Study 6, men scored higher than women on hostile sexism only Hostile and benevolent sexism were moderately positively correlated with the Attitudes toward Women Scale (Spence & Helmreich, 1972), Old Fashioned Sexism, and Rape Myth Acceptance (Burt, 1980) Study 2 showed hostile and benevolent sexism scores were significantly correlated with Paulhus's (1988) impression management measure Glick & Fiske (1997) found that hostile sexism was more strongly correlated with the Modern Sexism Scale (Swim et al., 1995) than benevolent sexism was Masser & Abrams (1999) replicated the two-factor structure, found that men showed higher scores than women, and found that hostile sexism was negatively associated with attitudes toward women's rights Glick et al. (2000) validated the factor structure in 19 countries and linked the inventory to an objective measure of societal gender inequality
Greenwald et al. (1998) Implicit Associations Test (IAT) (response latencies in 50 computer trials)	Students: 32; 32; 26	None	Findings in Experiment 1 indicate that short 10-item versions of the IAT may be as effective for measuring implicit attitudes as 50-item versions Error rates were positively correlated with response latencies, indicating greater difficulty in making the counter-stereotypical associations Large discrepancies in response latencies between stereotypical and counter-stereotypical associations, indicating greater difficulty in making the counter-stereotypical association The effect sizes detected by the IAT are substantially larger than is possible with explicit self-report measures

(Continued)

TABLE 10.2 (Continued)

Diversity readiness and resistance

Study/measures	Validation sample	Reliability evidence[1]	Validity evidence
Herek (1984; 1994) Attitudes Toward Lesbians and Gay Men Scale (ATLG) (20 items comprising 2 10-item subscales assessing attitudes toward lesbians (ATL) and attitudes toward gay men (ATG))	Students: 437; 469; 368; 110 405; 36 community members; 960 adults	Total scale = 0.90 to 0.96 ATL = 0.77 to 0.92 ATG = 0.89 to 0.92 Three week test-retest reliability = 0.90 for the total scale, 0.84 for ATL and 0.83 for ATG	Responses to 64 questions about lesbians or gay men taken from previous studies indicated that a unidimensional factor structure representing condemnation or tolerance explained most of the variance Heterosexual women showed significantly more positive attitudes toward lesbians and gay men than heterosexual men did Herek (1987) found that UG students whose essays indicated positive attitudes toward lesbians or gay men showed considerably higher (positive) scores on the ATL and the ATG In multiple samples, negative attitudes on ATL and ATG were correlated with more traditional sex role attitudes, adherence to a fundamentalist religious tradition, less contact and less positive contact with lesbians or gay men
Linnehan et al. (2003) See also: Linnehan et al. (2002) Diversity Attitudes, Subjective Norms, and Behavioral Intentions (15 behavioral intentions, 13 possible outcomes of behavior for attitudes, 2 referent groups for subjective norms)	326; 176 college students	5 behavioral intention factors: 0.72 to 0.86 5 attitude factors: 0.85 to 0.88 5 subjective norms: 0.71 to 0.84	The 5-factor structure for the behavioral intention items found in Sample 1 was confirmed with CFA on Sample 2 Virtually all of the associations between the 5 behavioral intentions, attitudes, and subjective norms were significant in regression equations in both samples Linnehan et al. (2002) found support for the validity and reliability of a similar set of measures among employees
McConahay (1986) Modern Racism Scale (7 items)	879; 709 white adults	Total scale = 0.82	Modern Racism items formed a separate factor from Old-Fashioned Racism items in 3 independent samples Modern Racism factor strongly positively correlated with Old-Fashioned Racism in all 3 samples (rs = 0.58 to 0.66) The Modern Racism Scale was less reactive to experimenter race effects Participants with higher Modern Racism scores were more likely to discriminate in a hiring preference experiment

(Continued)

TABLE 10.2 (Continued)

Diversity readiness and resistance

Study/measures	Validation sample	Reliability evidence[1]	Validity evidence
Miville et al. (1999)			
Universal-Diverse Orientation (UDO) (45 items)	Students: 93 whites (72% male); 111 (70% male, 70% white); 153 (35% female, 53% white); 135 African Americans (71% female)	Test–retest = 0.94 Alpha ranged from 0.89 to 0.95	Evidence of convergent and discriminant validity presented by the authors Thompson et al. (2002) found that UDO was related to one of the Big Five Personality traits (Openness to Experience) in counselor trainees
Neville et al. (2000)			
Color-Blind Racial Attitudes Scale (CoBRAS) (20 items)	1100 college students and adults	Total scale = 0.84 to 0.91 Racial Privilege subscale = 0.71 to 0.83 Institutional Discrimination subscale = 0.73 to 0.81 Blatant Racial Issues subscale = 0.70 to 0.76 Test–retest reliability = 0.68 for total scale, 0.80 for Racial Privilege and Institutional Discrimination subscales, and 0.34 for Blatant Racial Issues Scale	CFA supported the 3-factor structure in independent samples Moderate to strong positive correlations with the Quick Discrimination Index, Modern Racism Scale and Global Belief in a Just World Total scale and two of the three subscales not significantly correlated with social desirability (Blatant Racial Issues Scale showed a significant correlation of 0.20) Women scored lower than men, but whites did not consistently score lower than Latinos or African Americans (high scores indicated more color-blind attitudes)
Ponterotto et al. (1995)			
Quick Discrimination Index (QDI) (30 items)	875 participants	Total scale = 0.88 Factor 1 (general multicultural attitudes) = 0.80 to 0.85 Factor 2 (personal interaction with racial diversity) = 0.83, Factor 3 (women's equality) = 0.65 to 0.76 Test–retest reliability = 0.82 to 0.96 for Factor 1, 0.65 to 0.87 for Factor	CFA confirmed the 3-factor structure in an independent sample Moderate positive correlations with the New Racism Scale and the Multicultural Counseling Awareness Scale Not significantly correlated with social desirability bias Women scored higher than men and people of color scored higher than whites (high scores indicated greater acceptance of diversity and greater support for women's equality)

(Continued)

TABLE 10.2 (Continued)

Diversity readiness and resistance

Study/measures	Validation sample	Reliability evidence[1]	Validity evidence
Swim et al. (1995) Old-Fashioned and Modern Sexism (5 items assessing Old-Fashioned Sexism, 8 items assessing Modern Sexism)	Students: 638; 788	Old-Fashioned Sexism = 0.65 to 0.66 Modern Sexism = 0.75 to 0.84 Campbell et al. (1997) reported an alpha of 0.65 for the Modern Sexism scale	Old-Fashioned and Modern Sexism constituted two separate factors in factor analysis in Study 1 CFA replicated the 2-factor structure in Study 2 Both factors showed small to moderate negative correlations with humanitarian values Respondents with higher sexism scores were more likely to overestimate the representation of women in male-dominated jobs Modern Sexism scores predicted a variety of voting and employment attitudes but Old-Fashioned Sexism did not Campbell et al. (1997) found Modern Sexism was uncorrelated with social desirability bias
Terrell & Terrell (1981) Cultural Mistrust Index (CMI) (48 items assessing 4 domains: education and training, interpersonal relations, business and work, politics and Law)	Students: 172	Test-retest = 0.86	Respondents who reported experiencing more racial discrimination scored more highly on the CMI (total scale) Items correlating significantly with a Social Desirability measure were eliminated
Tougas et al. (1995) Neosexism scale (11 items)	Students: 130	Total scale = 0.76 to 0.78 Test-retest = 0.84 Campbell et al. (1997) = 0.81 Masser & Abrams (1999) = 0.62 to 0.85	Neosexism was a stronger negative predictor of support for affirmative action for women than Old-Fashioned Sexism in Study 1 Neosexism predicted rejection of affirmative action for women and low evaluation of women's qualifications in Study 2 Campbell et al. (1997) replicated the unidimensional factor structure and argued that the neo-sexism scale's psychometric performance was superior to that of the Modern Sexism Scale (Swim et al., 1995) Masser & Abrams (1999) replicated the unidimensional factor structure, found that men showed higher scores than women, and found that neosexism was negatively associated with attitudes toward women's rights

[1]Reliability estimates are Cronbach's alphas unless otherwise indicated.

Other updated sexism indices include Glick and Fiske's (1996) ambivalent sexism inventory, Swim et al.'s (1995) modern sexism measure, and Tougas et al.'s (1995) neosexism scale. Although the psychometric properties of the SRES are superior to all of these measures, all three of them show adequate reliability and validity for meeting commonly accepted standards for academic research. Additionally, the ambivalent sexism inventory has been validated cross-culturally, and national averages on this measure have been associated with objective measures of gender inequality (Glick et al., 2000).

Racism

A large number of racism indices have been developed. McConahay's (1986) seven-item Modern Racism Scale is most commonly used by researchers and shows acceptable psychometric properties as well as behavioral evidence for validity. Two recent attempts to improve upon the Modern Racism Scale include Ponterotto et al.'s (1995) Quick Discrimination Index (QDI) and Neville et al.'s (2000) Color-Blind Racial Attitudes Scale (CoBRAS). The Multicultural Attitudes and Interaction with Racial Diversity subscales of the QDI show good psychometric properties, but we recommend researchers use the SRES or Neosexism index instead of the Women's Equality subscale of the QDI. Likewise, the Racial Privilege and Institutional Discrimination subscales of the CoBRAS show good psychometric properties, but the Blatant Racial Issues Scale does not. More research assessing the reliability and validity of the CoBRAS and QDI would be welcome, and researchers may be interested in the conceptual content and specific antecedents and outcomes of the more reliable subscales of these measures.

Most racism measures focus on the views of the dominant majority. Terrell and Terrell (1981) created the Cultural Mistrust Inventory (CMI), which assesses attitudes of oppressed minorities toward the dominant racial group in four domains: education, interpersonal relations, business and work, and politics and law. Although the measure showed strong test–retest reliability, the CMI needs further validation.

Openness to Diversity

Milville et al.'s (1999) Universal Diverse Orientation and Linnehan et al.'s (2003) measure of diversity attitudes, subjective norms and behavioral intentions are broader instruments designed to capture general openness toward diversity rather than attitudes toward any specific group. As such, these measures might be useful accompaniments to organizational interventions designed to address diversity in general. Millville et al.'s measure converged with the Big Five Personality Trait of Openness to Experience (Thompson et al., 2002). Linnehan et al.'s (2003) approach is based on the theory of reasoned action, and both attitudes and subjective norms predicted behavioral intentions in both a student sample and an employee sample (Linnehan et al., 2002).

Implicit Associations Test

Self-report indicators of readiness for diversity pose concerns regarding social desirability bias. Dunton and Fazio (1997) created a measure of the Motivation to Control Prejudiced Reactions specifically to assess the impression management people engage in as they attempt to hide their prejudices toward members of other demographic groups. They demonstrated that this measure was negatively associated with scores on the Modern Racism Scale (McConahay, 1986), indicating that measure's reactivity to social desirability bias.

One method that shows promise for overcoming this issue is the Implicit Associations Test (IAT, Greenwald et al., 1998). The IAT presents respondents with 50 computer trials during which they are asked to press a key indicating whether a set of words represents something good or bad. In each trial, a word is paired with a picture. The length of time between presentation of the word and the respondent's keystroke, or latency, is measured. Response latency is compared when 'good' and 'bad' words are paired with pictures of different demographic groups. The extent to which a respondent shows a long (short) latency when pairing a 'good' (bad) word with a particular demographic group compared to another group over 50 trials is thought to be an indicator of an unconscious and automatic prejudiced reaction. A considerable body of research shows that response latencies are longer for counter-stereotypical associations than for stereotypical associations (for a meta-analysis, see Poehlman, Uhlmann, Greenwald & Banaji, 2004). Additionally and importantly, effect sizes indicating the extent to which people stereotype are considerably larger when assessed with the IAT than is observed with explicit self-report measures.

The IAT is cumbersome to use compared to a typical survey format, and for this reason it is likely unsuitable for many organizational applications. Greenwald et al. (1998), however, present evidence suggesting that 10 computer trials may be just as effective as 50 for assessing automatic stereotyping, and scholarly research may benefit from the enhanced ability to detect subconscious biases offered by this type of instrument.

DISCRIMINATION AND HARASSMENT

Measures of discrimination and harassment assess participants' perceptions of their organizational experiences (Table 10.3). Organizational practitioners may find these measures useful for needs assessment and for evaluating the effectiveness of diversity interventions. Organizational researchers may find these measures useful for capturing somewhat proximal outcomes of diversity that have been linked with more distal outcomes of satisfaction, commitment, strain and withdrawal.

Several measures of sexual harassment exist, but the Sexual Experiences Questionnaire (SEQ) has by far the best evidence for reliability and validity

TABLE 10.3

Discrimination and harassment

Study/measures	Validation sample	Reliability evidence[1]	Validity evidence
Cortina et al. (2001) Workplace Incivility Scale (WIS) (7 items)	1167 employees	Total scale = 0.89	CFA supported the unidimensional factor structure Strong (r = −0.59) negative correlation with the Perception of Fair Interpersonal Treatment Scale (Donovan et al., 1998) Regression indicated a variety of dimensions of job satisfaction were negatively associated with WIS Regression indicated job withdrawal and distress were positively associated with WIS
Fitzgerald et al. (1988; 1995) Sexual Experiences Questionnaire (SEQ) (18 items assessing the three dimensions of gender harassment, unwanted sexual attention and sexual coercion)	Students: 1395; 1205 Female faculty: 307	Total scale = 0.86 to 0.92 Two-week test–retest stability (for 46 UG students) = 0.86 Split-half reliability coefficients for 5 subscales = 0.62 to 0.86, averaging 0.75	The 5 dimensions were based on content analysis of a survey of college women Factor analysis supported the existence of 3 factors: gender harassment, unwanted sexual attention and sexual coercion, confirmed across two settings (workplace and students) and cultures (the US and Brazil) All but 3 items were significantly positively correlated with the criterion item, 'I have been sexually harassed' Average item–criterion correlations were smallest for gender harassment and largest for sexual coercion, indicating consistency with the different levels of sexual harassment (sexual assault showed little variation) Gender harassment and seductive behavior were more common than more serious forms of harassment Men showed lower scores than women Female students showed lower scores than female faculty
James et al. (1994a) Workplace Prejudice/ Discrimination Inventory (15 items)	89 minority; 46	Study 1: (0.90) – 16 items Study 2: (0.93) – 15 items	Items developed based on social identity theory Evidence for both convergent and discriminant validity reported Evidence for criterion-related validity reported as well Study 1: women and older adults reported more discrimination Study 2: work units with a history of discrimination complaints scored higher

(Continued)

TABLE 10.3 (Continued)

Discrimination and harassment

Study/measures	Validation sample	Reliability evidence[1]	Validity evidence
			James et al. (1994b) found that high scores on this index were associated with higher blood pressure in a sample of 89 employees of color
Sanchez & Brock (1996)			
Perceived workplace discrimination (10 items)	139 Hispanic	Total scale = 0.87	2 judges independently assessed the relevance of the items to the construct
			A unidimensional factor structure was obtained and confirmed with CFA
			Regression analysis indicated the perceived discrimination index was negatively associated with organizational commitment and job satisfaction while being positively associated with work tension
Schneider et al. (2000)			
Ethnic Harassment Experiences Scale (EHE) (7 items assessing two factors: exclusion and verbal harassment)	Students: 127; 50; 361 Employees: 110	Exclusion = 0.47 to 0.88 Verbal harassment = 0.74 to 0.82	CFA confirmed the 2-factor structure for both white and Hispanic participants
			Exclusion and verbal harassment interacted to lead to increased post-traumatic stress among school district employees
			Exclusion and verbal harassment interacted to result in poorer health and lower life satisfaction among graduate students

[1]Reliability estimates are Cronboch's alphas unless otherwise indicated.

(Fitzgerald et al., 1988). The SEQ's 18 items assess the three dimensions of gender harassment, unwanted sexual attention and sexual coercion. Cortina (2001) developed a version of the SEQ specifically for Latinas and presents evidence for reliability and validity.

Of the four measures of experienced prejudice, discrimination and incivility, James et al.'s (1994a) measure has the strongest evidence for validity, predicting both complaint behavior and blood pressure. Cortina et al.'s (2001) Workplace Incivility Scale shows promise as an efficient (seven-item) unidimensional measure assessing negative workplace experiences.

ORGANIZATIONAL PRACTICES

Equal Employment Opportunities/Diversity

This research focuses on the relation between the presence of human resource structures and such outcomes as workforce composition, pay equity and the advancement of members of historically marginalized groups in organizations (see Table 10.4). The methodological challenge facing researchers in this area has been to create valid, usable measures from the countless human resource and equal opportunity practices in organizations today. It is common practice among researchers working in this area to generate summative or mean-based indices of these HR procedures and structures to create their measures. Scales are often created from these indices based on such factors as their intended objectives and type. This latter approach is seen in the work of Leck and her associates in their studies of the effects of Canada's Employment Equity Act on a large sample of Canadian employers (Leck, 2002; Leck & Saunders, 1992; 1996; Leck et al., 1995).

Examples of researchers who have used summative and mean-based indices include Konrad and Linnehan (1995) who created structural indices based on the focus of HR procedures. Since these scales were created by taking the mean of the number of practices present in the organization, this study used the proportion of the particular practices in each of the 138 employers in their sample. This same method of creating scales, based on the presence of certain benefits in an organization, was also used by Konrad et al. (2003) in their study of the relation between employer benefits and an organization's retention of former welfare clients. Evidence of scale reliability using this method is found in Moore et al. (2001) which used a proportional scale of 14 HRM practices that promote gender equity.

Despite their common usage, both proportional and summative-based indices of organizational practices have significant limitations. These limitations are similar to those pointed out by Cappelli and Neumark (1999) in their review of research on 'high-performance' work practices, which focuses on the relation between these work practices and organizational performance. As pointed out by Cappelli and Neumark (1999), the presence of organizational practices, whether

TABLE 10.4

Organizational Practices

Study/measures	Validation sample	Reliability evidence[1]	Validity evidence
Elvira & Graham (2002) Formalized compensation (3: total compensation base pay and merit pay raise) Less formalized compensation (1-incentive bonus)	8259 firms	None	Higher proportion of women in a job: the lower the total compensation and base salary, the lower the likelihood of receiving an incentive bonus, and the lower the incentive bonus earnings. Negative earnings effects from sex composition were greatest for bonus earnings, less for base salary and no effect on merit pay raises

French (2001)
Firm schema:
  Classical
  Anti-discrimination
  Affirmative action
Gender diversity (multiple)
	1976 firms	Range from 0.48 to 0.85	EFA, CFA and cluster analyses used to validate schema
			Firms categorized in gender diversity and classical approaches had lower percentages of women managers than companies using the affirmative action approach

Goodman et al. (2003) Firm's emphasis on promotion and development of employees (8 items)	228 firms	0.78	Significant, positive relation with likelihood of women in top management positions
Goodstein (1994) Child care benefits (9 items) Child care costs (2 items) Employer knowledge (5 items)	1239 firms	0.84 (child care benefits) 0.96 (child care costs) 0.91 (employer knowledge)	Large firms more likely than small firms to pursue responsive strategies Percentage of female employees positively related to responsive strategies Child care benefits positively related to acquiescence and compromise strategy, negatively related to defiance approach Employer knowledge positively related to acquiescence and compromise approaches See also: Ingram & Simons (1995)
Goodstein (1995) Elder care benefits (summative index of 17 benefits)	407 firms	None	Number of other employer-provided benefits and importance of elder care benefits to employee productivity were both positively and significantly related to number of elder care benefits

(Continued)

TABLE 10.4 (Continued)

Organizational Practices			
Study/measures	Validation sample	Reliability evidence[1]	Validity evidence
Importance to productivity (1 item) Costs as barrier (1 item) Other work–family practices (15 items)			
Holzer & Neumark (2000a; 2000b) Use of AA in recruiting and hiring (1 item for each)	3200 firms	None	Using AA in recruitment was related to number of recruitment methods used, and the number of black female and Hispanic job applicants Using AA in hiring was related to lower levels of educational attainment of new hires, but performance ratings and compensation for white females and black employees in firms that used AA in hiring were comparable with those of other workers
Konrad et al. (2003) Benefit scales: Financial/health (6 benefits (presence/absence)) Family friendly (18 benefits)	561 females	0.87 (financial health) 0.78 (family friendly)	Financial/health benefits positively related to retention of welfare-to-work program participants Family-friendly benefit scale was not related to retention
Konrad & Linnehan (1995) HRM practices (119 items) Identity-blind structures (63 items) Identity-conscious structures (54 items)	138 firms	0.88 (identity blind) 0.93 (identity conscious)	Independent raters categorized structures Identity-conscious scale significantly related to the level of the highest ranking woman in the organization and the percentage of people of color in management Identity-blind structures were not significantly related to any diversity-related outcomes
Konrad & Mangel (2000) Work/life index (WLI) (19 work/life activities)	195 firms	0.77	Employers employing a larger percentage of women developed more work/life programs Firms employing a larger percentage of women showed a stronger relationship between extensiveness of work/life programs and productivity

(Continued)

TABLE 10.4 *(Continued)*

Organizational Practices

Study/measures	Validation sample	Reliability evidence[1]	Validity evidence
Leck & Saunders (1992)			
Employment Equity Program (EEP): Formalization (5 items) Comprehensiveness (3 items) Support (2 items)	294 firms	0.84 (formalization) 0.90 (comprehensiveness) 0.65 (support)	Significant correlations between both EEP formalization and comprehensiveness with more representative hiring of women in management and non-management. EEP support was correlated with more representative hiring of women in non-management jobs. See also: Leck et al., 1995 (added 'effectiveness' measure) and Leck and Saunders (1996)
Moore et al. (2001)			
HRM, gender equity programs Summative index (14 items)	196 firms	0.87	Not related to the percentage of women in the organizations' hierarchy
Osterman (1995)			
Work–family program index (9 work–family practices)	875 firms	0.75	Percentage of female employees positively related to w–f programs Firms seeking to implement high-commitment work systems are more likely to put into place w–f programs Analyses controlled for presence of other benefits
Perry-Smith, & Blum (2000)			
Work–family policies (8 items)	527 firms	Three factors: leave policies, traditional dependent care and less traditional dependent care	Used cluster analysis to validate four categories of organizations: (1) low on all policies; (2) leaves and less traditional; (3) leaves and traditional; (4) high on all w–f policies
Reskin & McBrier (2000)			
Recruitment through: Personal network (1 item) Open method (1 item) Formalization of personnel practices (8 items)	516 firms	None	Use of open recruiting methods was related to the percentage of women holding managerial jobs The interaction of formalization with organizational size was positively related to the percentage of women holding managerial jobs. The size of the negative effect of formalization on the proportion of males holding managerial jobs depended upon the size of the firm

[1]Reliability estimates are Cronbach's alphas unless otherwise indicated.

they be identified as 'high performance' or those relating to workforce diversity, does not guarantee that the practices are applied consistently or at all throughout the organization, thus limiting the researcher's ability to make causal inferences between the practices and the diversity-related outcomes. Very few of the studies we reviewed addressed this possibility or identified this as a limitation of the research. We urge future researchers to enhance their measures beyond the mere existence of diversity-related practices in organizations, to ascertain if, and to what degree, these practices are both understood by employees and enforced by the management of the workplaces being studied.

The implementation date of the practices is another factor which is often omitted by researchers studying the relation between diversity-related organizational structures and relevant outcomes such as gender and racial composition of a firm's workforce. For example, it is highly unlikely that an affirmative action plan that was only recently introduced into an organization and focuses on the long-term recruitment and advancement of members of historically marginalized groups will have any impact on that group's representation in the workforce or in the hierarchy of the firm in the near term. As such, in addition to using the number of practices in organizations as a measure in this type of research, it is also important to identify their date of implementation, since the co-existence of these practices with outcomes of interest provides little evidence of causality between the practice and these outcomes. This emphasizes the importance of more multi-organizational and longitudinal studies.

Another measurement issue yet to be fully addressed by many researchers focusing on organizational practices is assessing the relative weight or importance of each practice. Implicit in the development of additive or proportional measures is the assumption that each practice is of equal importance to the employees of the firm and to the outcomes being measured. For example, in Konrad and Linnehan's 1995 study, the practices 'members of protected groups are specially targeted to receive management development training' and 'an Equal Employment Policy exists' are given equal weight in the calculation of their scale of identity-conscious structures. It seems highly likely, however, that the impact of these two practices would be different for some of the outcomes on which this study focused.

French (2001) took an evolutionary step in extending measurement of organizational practices by differentiating firm practices in her study of the relation of organizational structures and gender equity in 1976 Australian companies. Through cluster analysis of 58 practices, French (2001) created a categorization schema and four equity profiles, based upon the type of organizational structures in place.

Other studies focusing on organizational practices and workforce diversity have used what must be considered even less valid measures of HR structures than summative or proportional indices, often out of necessity. Given the nature of this type of research it is surprising that this does not happen more often, since persuading companies to respond to surveys is challenging and response rates, which are often inversely related to survey length, can be low. Perhaps the most extensive studies in the United States exploring the relation between organizational practices and workforce diversity are those of Holzer and Neumark (2000a;

2000b). These studies used data from 3200 employers in four major metropolitan areas in the United States to examine the diversity-related outcomes of the use of affirmative action (AA). In contradiction to the extensive nature of their sample, the key measures used in these studies were single-item questions, (1) if the firm used AA in recruitment (referring to the last hire for a position) and (2) if AA was used in the hiring decision

Unfortunately, other studies have also had to rely on single-item measures of firm practices. Elvira and Graham (2002) measure the degree of formalization in compensation as three separate single-item measures: the amount of total compensation, base salary and merit pay raises. Similarly, Reskin and McBrier (2000) use a single item to measure the extent to which a firm used open recruitment methods, which they defined as sources such as: job posting, advertising or using employment agencies to recruit applicants. In their study, firms that used any of these methods 'frequently' were coded a 2, firms that used any of the methods 'sometimes' were coded a 1, and firms that never used any of these methods a 0. By reducing this measure to a single item, it is difficult to differentiate which recruitment method may be most strongly related to the outcome they studied; that is, the proportion of the firm's managers and administrators who are male (and female). In addition, similar to other scales based on Likert-type response options, one cannot be sure that each responding firm used the same definition of the scale anchors, 'never, sometimes and frequently'.

Finally, there are studies that have explored the relation of certain organizational characteristics and diversity-related outcomes, which did not include a measure or count of specific HR practices. In a study of organizational characteristics that are related to the proportion of women in top management positions, Goodman et al. (2003) created an eight-item scale measuring the firm's emphasis on promotion and development of employees of both management and non-management employees.

Work–Family Practices

While scales for equal employment opportunity and diversity practices have usually been used as independent variables by researchers, what differentiates the research focusing on work family practices is the evolution from studies using the measures as dependent variables to those using these scales as explanatory variables. In the former studies (e.g. Goodstein, 1994; 1995; Ingram & Simons, 1995; Osterman, 1995) researchers use strategic management theory to predict the presence of work–family practices in organizations, while researchers taking the latter strategy (e.g. Konrad & Mangel, 2000; Perry-Smith & Blum, 2000) explore the relation between the presence of these practices and organizational outcomes.

Regardless of the research focus, however, work–family practice scales have often been created in a manner similar to that used in the equal employment and diversity practice studies. For example, Osterman (1995) created a summative work–family practice index by adding the number of work–family practices that were present in the organizations from a list of eight work–family practices. Konrad and Mangel (2000) used a similar approach, but asked firm respondents to select from a list of 19 work–life initiatives.

Similar to French (2001), some of the studies focusing on work–family practices have also developed schema to categorize organizations based on the presence of certain work–family related benefits. Goodstein (1994; 1995) developed a categorization scheme to classify organizations into four groups, depending upon the presence or absence of certain dependent care or elder care benefits. These groups represented responses to pressures to adopt these benefits and ranged from acquiescence and compromise to avoidance and defiance. A similar approach to categorizing organizations was also taken by Ingram and Simons (1995) and Perry-Smith and Blum (2000).

While the sum of the evidence from these studies offers encouragement to organizations contemplating implementing work–family practices, the interpretation of the results is limited by measurement issues. As mentioned, the mere presence of an organizational practice may not be closely related to its use, as sometimes employees may be discouraged from using such practices by their employers. Additionally, researchers must continue to work on identifying the universe of organizational practices, as past studies have collected data on as few as 8 and as many as 19 practices. Should other practices be considered? What are they? Should only formal programs be included in these studies? These are questions for future research.

ORGANIZATIONAL CLIMATE

Although diversity scholars have consistently called for theoretically strong, psychometrically sound quantitative measures to assess diversity and evaluate the impact of diversity initiatives, there has been surprisingly little work done in this area. A 2002 review of five instruments to assess workplace discrimination, prejudice and diversity concludes that 'the conceptualization, development, and validation of workplace diversity measures are in the preliminary stages of research' (Burkard, Boticki & Madson, 2002: 356). We agree with this assessment based on our own review of existing measures and, in general, would advise caution in using any of the existing measures described in Table 10.5. We were unable to locate any published measure that was grounded in theory, had reasonable evidence for strong reliability and validity using multiple and diverse samples, and could be used in a variety of organizational settings.

Many have argued that the diversity climate construct is multi-dimensional, and that the absence of blatant prejudice and discrimination does not in and of itself equate to a positive work environment for diverse employees. This review of existing diversity climate measures reveals that researchers are conceptualizing diversity climate as the following: (1) the existence of practices and policies to support diversity and/or provide opportunities for traditionally less advantaged

TABLE 10.5

Organizational climate

Study/measures	Validation sample	Reliability evidence[1]	Validity evidence
Bergman (2003) Women Workplace Culture Questionnaire (WWC) (24 items total, 4 factors)	446 females	Subscales 0.71 to 0.87	Grounded theory approach to developing items Employees working in male-dominated organizations suffered more from gender-related attitudes than those working in female-dominated organizations Significant correlations between factors and health, psychosocial stress and work satisfaction
Block et al. (1995) Reactions to Interracial Situations at Work Questionnaire Equality (3 items) Discrimination (3 items) Reverse discrimination (6 items) Tokenism (2 items) Affirmative action (4 items) Organizational interventions (4 items) Management interventions (4 items) Personal interventions (4 items) Comfort interacting with black people at work (4 items) Comfort interacting with black people socially (6 items) (41 items; 12 subscales)	98 white MBA students (76% male)	Range from 0.57 to 0.87	Respondents with the highest level of white racial identity development had the most positive reactions to interracial situations at work
Chrobot-Mason & Aramovich (2004) Positive Climate for Diversity (32 items, 6 factors)	1731 public service employees (70% men, 81% white)	Ranged from 0.86 to 0.71	Item development based on Taylor Cox's (1991) model of a multicultural workplace Evidence for overall model fit for racial and gender subgroups Related to perceptions of climate for innovation, empowerment and turnover intentions

(Continued)

TABLE 10.5 (Continued)

Organizational climate

Study/measures	Validation sample	Reliability evidence[1]	Validity evidence
Ellis & Sonnenfeld (1994) Items to assess employee perspectives on race and gender relations in the firm (4 items – race and gender relations; 4 items – benefits of training program)	922 employees	None	Respondents exposed to the training were more likely to perceive that leaders of the firm valued diversity
Germano et al. (2003) Inclusion measure (11 items)	244 students (55% Caucasian)		Goodness-of-fit statistics reported as well as validation evidence
Hegarty & Dalton (1995) Organizational Diversity Inventory (ODI) (20 items, 5 factors)	450 managers (46% female)	Subscales 0.64 to 0.80	Managers completing MBA program developed items Cross-validation indicates good fit indices for GFI, AGFI, CFI, IFI No information provided about the racial/ethnic composition of the sample
Hicks-Clarke & Iles (2000) Positive Climate for Diversity Scale: Policy support (yes/no existence of diversity practices and policies) (6 items) Equity recognition comprised three scales: (1) organizational justice (8 items), support for diversity (5 items) and recognition for diversity (5 items) taken from Kossek & Zonia (1993)	272 managers	0.66 to 0.84	Positive relationships found between climate and organizational commitment, job satisfaction and career commitment.
Hulin et al. (1996) Organizational Tolerance for Sexual Harassment Inventory (OTSHI) (18 items)	263 students, 1156 employees	Total scale = 0.95 to 0.96	Women in both samples considered their organizations to be more tolerant of sexual harassment than men In the public utility, OTSHI scores were lower in units that had been targeted for sexual harassment intervention and were positively correlated with employees' reports of sexual harassment (rs ranged from 0.19 to 0.45) Two subsequent research studies have shown the OTSHI to be a positive predictor of employee-reported incidents of sexual harassment (Bulger, 2001; Fitzgerald et al., 1997)

(Continued)

TABLE 10.5 *(Continued)*

Organizational climate

Study/measures	Validation sample	Reliability evidence[1]	Validity evidence
Kossek & Zonia (1993)	775 (46% minority women, 43% minority men)	Ranged from 0.70 to 0.90	Scale development and validation was not the primary purpose of the article
Diversity climate			
Value efforts to promote diversity			The greater the ratio of women in a unit, the more favorable diversity activities were viewed.
Attitudes toward qualifications of racio-ethnic minorities			
Attitudes toward women's qualifications			Positive relationship found between units whose allocation of resources to minorities was perceived as insufficient and attitudes that value diversity and favorable perceptions of the qualifications of minorities
Department support for women			
Department support for racio-ethnic minorities			
(20 items; 4 factors)			
Kossek, et al. (1996)	775 faculty (84% white, 52% male)	Ranged from 0.69 to 0.89	Gender, gender dissimilarity, race and race dissimilarity were significant predictors of perceptions of diversity climate
Diversity climate			
Attitudes toward employer efforts to promote diversity (8 items)			
Commitment of administration to diversity (5 items)			
Fairness of organization (5 items)			
Work group support of multiculturalism (6 items)			
Qualifications of women and minorities scales (5 items)			
Equality of support for racio-ethnic minorities and women (3 items each)			
Perceived work group mix (5 items)			
Professional and social interaction with diverse members (6 items) (10 scales)			
Montei et al. (1996)	67 students (93% white, 66% female); 349 municipal employees; 279 students (52% male, 82% white)	Ranged from 0.71 to 0.90	Study 2: correlation with Marlowe Crowne Social Desirability Scale non-significant
Attitudes Toward Diversity Scale (ATDS)			
Attitudes toward coworkers who are a minority (30 items)			Study 2: Confirmatory factor analysis supported 3-factor model
Attitudes toward having a supervisor who is a minority			
Attitudes toward the hiring and promotion of minorities			
Mor Barak et al. (1998)	2686 employees (37% female, 64% Caucasian)	from 0.71 to 0.86	Item contributors included HR managers, project and mid-level managers, line workers
Diversity Perceptions Scale			
Organizational fairness			Items were pre-tested twice with a diverse sample of company workers
Organizational inclusion			
Personal value for diversity			Caucasian men perceived the organization as more fair and inclusive than women or racial minorities
Personal comfort with diversity			
(16 items; 4 factors)			Women and racial minorities saw more value in and felt more comfortable with diversity than Caucasian men

[1]Reliability estimates are Cronbach's alphas unless otherwise indicated.

employees, (2) perceptions of organizational and leader support for diversity, (3) perceptions of the existence of bias, discrimination and prejudice, and (4) perceptions and overall evaluation of the experience of being a dominant/non-dominant group member within the organization.

Although no single scale seems to adequately measure all four of these dimensions, the Workplace Prejudice/Discrimination Inventory by James (1994a) was developed based on theory and preliminary evidence suggests strong psychometric qualities. We would recommend that researchers and practitioners who intend to assess the existence of these negative aspects of diversity climate consider the WPDI. Recently, this scale was used to measure workplace discrimination for gay and lesbian employees (Ragins & Cornwell, 2001). The work of Kossek and Zonia (1993) and Kossek et al. (1996) is a strong example of the utility of assessing diversity climate when evaluating the impact of diversity interventions and representation. However, because the items are specifically designed to assess a university context, the measure will not be generalizable to other organizational settings unless the original items are drastically modified, in which case reliability and validity indices must be re-evaluated.

Future research holds promise for the development of theoretically based and psychometrically sound instruments that assess multiple dimensions of the organizational climate for diversity and link climate to important organizational outcome variables. For example, Chrobot-Mason and Aramovich (2004) recently presented their research findings on the development and validation of a six-factor measure of diversity climate based on Taylor Cox's (1991) model of a multicultural work environment. Germano et al. (2003) are also in the preliminary stages of developing a measure of inclusion and have begun to examine the antecedents and consequences of inclusion within a diverse organization.

As research and practice in the area of organizational diversity moves beyond counting the number of employees within each racial category and the number of EEO complaints, and moves toward the assessment of more subjective measures such as employee perceptions of the extent to which they can 'be themselves at work', we anticipate the development of stronger and more comprehensive measures of diversity climate and culture.

CONCLUSION

In this chapter, we have provided an overview of diversity-related measures ranging from those at the individual level, such as social identification and attitudes toward diversity, to the organizational level, such as diversity-related HR practices and organizational climate. In our summary of the measures' psychometric strengths and weaknesses we, unfortunately, have often concluded that the degree to which many of the variables accurately and reliably measure their underlying constructs is limited. As these limitations apply to our own work in this field, we are fully aware that a diversity scholar's search for psychometrically sound measures is often hindered by many factors, including social desirability, and changing social norms and taboos. Perhaps this is why the implicit association test is so promising to many scholars today, as it attempts to circumvent many of these obstacles.

Despite these challenges, we urge diversity scholars to continue to develop new ways to measure these very important constructs, continually improving their validity and reliability. For us, this work is much too visible and far too important to be associated with scholarly efforts that are anything less than rigorous.

NOTE

1 The authors are listed alphabetically. All contributed equally to the chapter.

REFERENCES

Beere, C. A., King, D. W., Beere, D. B., & King, L. A. (1984). The sex-role egalitarianism scale: A measure of attitudes toward equality between the sexes. *Sex Roles*, *10*, 563–76.

Bem, S. L. (1974). The measurement of psychological androgyny. *Journal of Consulting and Clinical Psychology*, *42*(2), 155–62.

Bergman, B. (2003). The validation of the women workplace culture questionnaire: Gender-related stress and health for Swedish working women. *Sex Roles*, *49*(5/6), 287–97.

Blanchard-Fields, F., Suhrer-Roussel, L., & Hertzog, C. (1994). A confirmatory factor analysis of the Bem Sex Role Inventory: Old questions, new answers. *Sex Roles*, *30*, 423–57.

Block, C. J., Roberson, L., & Neuger, D. A. (1995). White racial identity theory: A framework for understanding reactions toward interracial situations in organizations. *Journal of Vocational Behavior*, *47*, 71–188.

Brown, S. P., Parham, T. A., & Yonker, R. (1996). Influence of a cross-cultural training course on racial identity attitudes of white women and men: Preliminary perspectives. *Journal of Counseling & Development*, *74*, 510–16.

Bulger, C. A. (2001). Union resources and union tolerance as moderators of relationships with sexual harassment. *Sex Roles*, *45*, 723–41.

Burkard, A. W., Boticki, M. A., & Madson, M. B. (2002). Workplace discrimination, prejudice, and diversity measurement: A review of instrumentation. *Journal of Career Assessment*, *10*(3), 343–61.

Burt, M. R. (1980). Cultural myths and support for rape. *Journal of Personality and Social Psychology*, *38*, 217–30.

Button, S. B. (2004). Identity management strategies utilized by lesbian and gay employees. *Group & Organization Management*, *29*, 470–94.

Campbell, B., Schellenberg, E. G., & Senn, C. Y. (1997). Evaluating measures of contemporary sexism. *Psychology of Women Quarterly*, *21*, 89–102.

Cappelli, P. & Neumark, D. (1999). *Do 'high performance' work practices improve establishment-level outcomes?* (Working Paper No. 7374). Cambridge, MA: National Bureau of Economic Research.

Carter, R. T. (1996). Exploring the complexity of racial identity attitude measures. In G. R. Sodowsky & J. C. Impara (Eds), *Multicultural assessment in counseling and clinical psychology* (pp. 193–223). Lincoln, NE: Buros Institute of Mental Measurements.

Choney, S. K., & Behrens, J. T. (1996). Development of the Oklahoma racial attitudes scale preliminary form (ORAS-P). *Multicultural Assessment in Counseling and Clinical Psychology*, pp. 225–40.

Chrobot-Mason, D. (2003). Developing multicultural competence for managers: Same old leadership skills or something new? *The Psychologist-Manager Journal*, 6(2), 5–20.

Chrobot-Mason, D. (2004). Managing racial differences: The role of majority managers' ethnic identity development on minority employee perceptions of support. *Group & Organization Management*, 29, 5–31.

Chrobot-Mason, D., & Aramovich, N. (2004). Employee perceptions of an affirming climate for diversity and its link to attitudinal outcomes: A comparison of racial and gender groups. Paper presented at the Annual Meeting of the Academy of Management, New Orleans, LA.

Chrobot-Mason, D., & Thomas, K. M. (2002). Minority employees in majority organizations: The intersection of individual and organizational racial identity in the workplace. *Human Resource Development Review*, 1(3), 323–44.

Cortina, L. M. (2001). Assessing sexual harassment among Latinas: Development of an instrument. *Cultural Diversity & Ethnic Minority Psychology*, 7, 164–81.

Cortina, L. M., Magley, V. J., Williams, J. H., & Langhout, R. D. (2001). Incivility in the workplace: Incidence and impact. *Journal of Occupational Health Psychology*, 6, 64–80.

Cox, T., Jr (1991). The multicultural organization. *Academy of Management Executive*, 5, 34–47.

Crandall, C. S. (1994). Prejudice against fat people: Ideology and self-interest. *Journal of Personality and Social Psychology*, 66, 882–94.

Donovan, M. A., Drasgow, F., & Munson, L. J. (1998). The perceptions of fair interpersonal treatment scale: Development and validation of a measure of interpersonal treatment in the workplace. *Journal of Applied Psychology*, 83, 683–92.

Douthitt, S. S., Eby, L. T., & Simon, S. A. (1999). Diversity of life experiences: The development and validation of a biographical measure of receptiveness to dissimilar others. *International Journal of Selection and Assessment*, 7, 112–25.

Downing, N. E., & Roush, K. L. (1985). From passive acceptance to active commitment: A model of feminist identity development for women. *The Counseling Psychologist*, 13, 695–709.

Dunbar, E. (1997). The personal dimensions of difference scale: Measuring multi-group identity with four ethnic groups. *International Journal of Intercultural Relations*, 21(1), 1–28.

Dunton, B. C. & Fazio, R. H. (1997). An individual difference measure of motivation to control prejudiced reactions. *Personality and Social Psychology Bulletin*, 23, 316–26.

Ellis, C., & Sonnenfeld, J. A. (1994). Diverse approaches to managing diversity. *Human Resource Management*, 33(Spring), 79–109.

Elvira, M. M., & Graham, M. E. (2002). Not just a formality: Pay system formalization and sex-related earnings effects. *Organization Science*, 13, 601–17.

Ely, R. J., & Thomas, D. A. (2001). Cultural diversity at work: The effects of diversity perspectives on work group processes and outcomes. *Administrative Science Quarterly*, 46, 229–73.

Fitzgerald, L. F., Drasgow, F., Hulin, C. L., Gelfand, M. J., & Magley, V. J. (1997). Antecedents and consequences of sexual harassment in organizations: A test of an integrated model. *Journal of Applied Psychology*, 82(4), 578–89.

Fitzgerald, L. F., Gelfand, M. J., & Drasgow, F. (1995). Measuring sexual harassment: Theoretical and psychometric advances. *Basic and Applied Social Psychology*, 17, 425–45.

Fitzgerald, L. F., Shullman, S. L., Gold, Y., Ormerod, M., & Weitzman, L. (1988). The incidence and dimensions of sexual harassment in academia and the workplace. *Journal of Vocational Behavior*, 32, 152–75.

French, E. (2001). Approaches to equity management and their relationship to women in management. *British Journal of Management, 13*, 267–85.

Germano, L. M., Major, D. A., Fletcher, T. D., Clarke, S. M., & Cardenas, R. A. (2003). Belonging and contributing: Validation of an Inclusion Measure. Paper presented at the 81st Annual Meeting of the Virginia Academy of Science, Charlottesville, VA.

Glick, P., & Fiske, S. T. (1996). The ambivalent sexism inventory: Differentiating hostile and benevolent sexism. *Journal of Personality and Social Psychology, 70*, 491–512.

Glick, P., & Fiske, S. T. (1997). Hostile and benevolent sexism: Measuring ambivalent sexist attitudes toward women. *Psychology of Women Quarterly, 21*, 119–35.

Glick, P., Fiske, S. T., Mladinic, A., Saiz, J. L., Abrams, D., Masser, B., Adetoun, B., Osagie, J. E., Akande, A., Alao, A., Brunner, A., Willemsen, T. M., Chipeta, K., Dardenne, B., Dijksterhuis, A., Wigboldus, D., Eckes, T., Six-Materna, I., Expósito, F., Moya, M., Foddy, M., Kim, H., Lameiras, M., Sotelo, M. J., Mucchi-Faina, A., Romani, M., Sakalli, N., Udegbe, B., Yamamoto, M., Ui, M., Ferreira, M. C., & López, W. L. (2000). Beyond prejudice as simple antipathy: Hostile and benevolent sexism across countries. *Journal of Personality and Social Psychology, 79*, 763–75.

Goodman, J. S., Fields, D. L., & Blum, T. C. (2003). Cracks in the glass ceiling: In what kinds of organizations do women make it to the top? *Group & Organization Management, 28*(4), 475–501.

Goodstein, J. D. (1994). Institutional pressures and strategic responsiveness: Employer involvement in work-family issues. *Academy of Management Journal, 37*, 350–82.

Goodstein, J. D. (1995). Employer involvement in eldercare: An organizational adaptation perspective. *Academy of Management Journal, 38*, 1657–71.

Greenwald, A. G., McGhee, D. E., & Schwartz, J. L. K. (1998). Measuring individual differences in implicit cognition: The Implicit Association Test. *Journal of Personality and Social Psychology, 74*, 1464–80.

Hegarty, W. H., & Dalton, D. R. (1995). Development and psychometric properties of the organizational diversity inventory (ODI). *Educational and Psychological Measurement, 55*(6), 1047–52.

Helms, J. E. (1990). *Black and white racial identity: Theory, research, and practice.* Westport, CT: Greenwood Press.

Helms, J. E., & Carter, R. T. (1991). Relationships of white and black racial identity attitudes and demographic similarity to counselor preferences. *Journal of Counseling Psychology, 38*(4), 446–57.

Herek, G. M. (1984). Attitudes towards lesbians and gay men: A factor-analytic study. *Journal of Homosexuality, 10*, 39–51.

Herek, G. M. (1987). Can functions be measured? A new perspective on the functional approach to attitudes. *Social Psychology Quarterly, 50*, 285–303.

Herek, G. M. (1994). Assessing attitudes toward lesbians and gay men: A review of empirical research with the ATLG scale. In B. Greene & G. M. Herek (Eds), *Lesbian and gay psychology: Theory, research, and clinical applications* (pp. 206–28). Thousand Oaks, CA: Sage.

Hicks-Clarke, D., & Iles, P. (2000). Climate for diversity and its effects on career and organizational attitudes and perceptions. *Personnel Review, 29*(3), 324–45.

Holt, C. L., & Ellis, J. B. (1998). Assessing the current validity of the Bem Sex-Role Inventory. *Sex Roles, 39*, 929–41.

Holzer, H. J., & Neumark, D. (2000a). What does affirmative action do? *Industrial and Labor Relations Review, 53*, 240–71.

Holzer, H. J. & Neumark, D. (2000b). Assessing affirmative action. *Journal of Economic Literature, 38*, 483–568.

Hulin, C. L., Fitzgerald, L. F., & Drasgow, F. (1996). Organizational influences on sexual harassment: Perspectives, frontiers, and response strategies. In M. Stockdale (Ed.), *Sexual harassment in the workplace* (Vol. 5, pp. 127–50). Thousand Oaks, CA: Sage.

Ingram, P., & Simons, T. (1995). Institutional and resource dependence determinants of responsiveness to work-family issues. *Academy of Management Journal, 38,* 1466–82.

James, K., Lovato, C., & Cropanzano, R. (1994a). Correlational and known-group comparison validation of a workplace prejudice/discrimination inventory. *Journal of Applied Social Psychology, 24*(17), 1573–92.

James, K., Lovato, C., & Khoo, G. (1994b). Social identity correlates of minority workers' health. *Academy of Management Journal, 37,* 383–96.

Johnston, W. B., & Packer, A. H. (1987). *Workforce 2000: Work and workers in the 21st century.* Indianapolis, IN: Hudson Institute.

Kim, S. S., & Gelfand, M. J. (2003). The influence of ethnic identity on perceptions or organizational recruitment. *Journal of Vocational Behavior, 63,* 396–416.

King, L. A., & King, D. W. (1990). Abbreviated measures of sex-role egalitarian attitudes. *Sex Roles, 23,* 659–73.

King, L. A., & King, D. W. (1997). Sex-role egalitarianism scale. *Psychology of Women Quarterly, 21,* 71–87.

Kirkland, S. E., & Regan, A. M. (1997). Organizational racial diversity training. *Racial identity theory: Applications to individual, group, and organizational interventions* (pp. 159–75). Mahwah, NJ: Lawrence Erlbaum Associates.

Konrad, A. M., Deckop, J., & Perlmutter, F. D. (2003). *Employer human resource practices and job retention of former welfare clients.* Philadelphia, PA: Temple University, Center for Public Policy.

Konrad, A. M., & Harris, C. (2002). Desirability of the Bem Sex-Role Inventory items for women and men: A comparison between African Americans and European Americans. *Sex Roles, 47,* 259–71.

Konrad, A. M., & Linnehan, F. (1995). Formalized HRM structures: Coordinating equal employment opportunity or concealing organizational practices? *Academy of Management Journal, 38,* 787–820.

Konrad, A. M., & Mangel, R. (2000). The impact of work-life programs on firm productivity. *Strategic Management Journal, 21,* 1225–37.

Kossek, E. E., & Zonia, S. S. (1993). Assessing diversity climate: A field study of reactions to employer efforts to promote diversity. *Journal of Organizational Behavior, 14,* 61–81.

Kossek, E. E., Zonia, S. S., & Young, W. (1996). The limitations of organizational demography: Can diversity climate be enhanced in the absence of teamwork? In M. N. Ruderman, M. W. Hughes-James & S. E. Jackson (Eds), *Selected research on work team diversity* (pp. 121–50). Washington, DC: American Psychological Association.

Leck, J. D. (2002). Making employment equity programs work for women. *Canadian Public Policy, 28,* S85–100.

Leck, J. D., & Saunders, D. M. (1992). Hiring women: The effect of Canada's employment equity act. *Canadian Public Policy, 18,* 203–21.

Leck, J. D., & Saunders, D. M. (1996). Achieving diversity in the workplace: Canada's employment equity act and members of visible minorities. *International Journal of Public Administration, 19,* 299–322.

Leck, J. D., St Onge, S., & LaLancette, I. (1995). Wage gap changes among organizations subject to the employment equity act. *Canadian Public Policy, 21,* 387–401.

Lee, R. M., Falbo, T., Doh, H. S., & Park, S. Y. (2001). The Korean diasporic experience: Measuring ethnic identity in the United States and China. *Cultural Diversity & Ethnic Minority Psychology, 7*(3), 207–16.

Linnehan, F., Chrobot-Mason, D., & Konrad, A. M. (2002). The importance of ethnic identity to attitudes, subjective norms and behavioral intentions toward diversity. Paper presented at the Annual Meeting of the Academy of Management, August, Denver, CO.

Linnehan, F., Konrad, A. M., Reitman, F., Greenhalgh, A., & London, M. (2003). Behavioral goals for a diverse organization: The effects of attitudes, social norms, and racial identity for Asian Americans and Whites. *Journal of Applied Social Psychology, 33,* 1331–59.

Luhtanen, R., & Crocker, J. (1992). A collective self-esteem scale: Self-evaluation of one's social identity. *Personality and Social Psychology Bulletin, 18*(5), 302–18.

Masser, B., & Abrams, D. (1999). Contemporary sexism: The relationships among hostility, benevolence, and neosexism. *Psychology of Women Quarterly, 23,* 503–17.

McConahay, J. B. (1986). Modern racism, ambivalence, and the Modern Racism Scale. In J. F. Dovidio & S. L. Gaertner (Eds), *Prejudice, discrimination, and racism* (pp. 91–125). New York: Academic Press.

Miville, M. L., Gelso, C. J., Pannu, R., Liu, W., Touradji, P., Holloway, P., & Fuertes, J. (1999). Appreciating similarities and valuing differences: The Miville-Guzman Universality-Diversity Scale. *Journal of Counseling Psychology, 46*(3), 291–307.

Moore, M. E., Parkhouse, B. L., & Konrad, A. M. (2001). Women in sport management: Advancing the representation through HRM structures. *Women in Management Review, 16*(2), 51–61.

Montei, M. S., Adams, G. A., & Eggers, L. M. (1996). Validity of scores on the attitudes toward diversity scale (ATDS). *Educational and Psychological Measurement, 56*(2), 293–303.

Mor Barak, M. E., Cherin, D. A., & Berkman, S. (1998). Organizational and personal dimensions in diversity climate: Ethnic and gender differences in employee perceptions. *Management and Behavioral Science, 34*(1), 82–104.

Neville, H. A., Heppner, M. J., Louie, C. E., Thompson, C. E., Brooks, L., & Baker, C. E. (1996). The impact of multicultural training on white racial identity attitudes and therapy competencies. *Professional Psychology: Research and Practice, 27*(1), 83–9.

Neville, H. A., Lilly, R., Duran, G., Lee, R. M. & Browne, L. (2000). Construction and initial validation of the Color-Blind Racial Attitudes Scale (CoBRAS). *Journal of Counseling Psychology, 47,* 59–70.

Offermann, L. R., & Phan, L. U. (2002). Culturally intelligent leadership for a diverse world. In R. E. Riggio, S. E. Murphy & F. J. Pirozzolo (Eds), *Multiple intelligences and leadership* (pp. 187–214). Mahwah, NJ: Lawrence Erlbaum Associates.

Osterman, P. (1995). Work-family programs and the employment relationship. *Administrative Science Quarterly, 40,* 681–700.

Paulhus, D. L. (1988). *Assessing self-deception and impression management in self-reports: The Balanced Inventory of Desirable Responding* Vancouver: University of British Columbia.

Perry-Smith, J. E., & Blum, T. C. (2000). Work-family human resource bundles and perceived organizational performance. *Academy of Management Journal, 43,* 1107–17.

Phinney, J. S. (1992). The multigroup ethnic identity measure. *Journal of Adolescent Research, 7,* 156–76.

Phinney, J. S. (1993). A three-stage model of ethnic identity development in adolescence. In M. E. Bernal & G. P. Knight (Eds), *Ethnic Identity* (Chapter 5, pp. 61–79). Albany, NY: University of New York Press.

Phinney, J. S., Cantu, C. L., & Kurtz, D. A. (1997). Ethnic and American identity as predictors of self-esteem among African-American, Latino, and White adolescents. *Journal of Youth and Adolescence, 26*(2), 165–85.

Poehlman, T. A., Uhlmann, E., Greenwald, A. G., & Banaji, M. R. (2004). Understanding and using the Implicit Association Test: Meta-analysis of predictive validity. Unpublished manuscript. Available from M. R. Banaji, Department of Psychology, Harvard University, 33 Kirkland Street, Cambridge, MA 02138.

Ponterotto, J. G., Burkard, A., Reiger, B. P., & Grieger, I. (1995). Development and initial validation of the Quick Discrimination Index (QDI). *Educational and Psychological Measurement, 55,* 1016–31.

Ponterotto, J. G., & Wise, S. L. (1987). Construct validity study of the racial identity attitude scale. *Journal of Counseling Psychology, 34*(2), 218–23.

Ponterotto, J. G., Gretchen, D., Utsey, S. O., Stracuzzi, T., & Saya, R., Jr (2003). The multigroup ethnic identity measure (MEIM): Psychometric view and further validity testing. *Educational and Psychological Measurement, 63*, 502–15.

Pope-Davis, D. B., & Ottavi, T. M. (1994). The relationship between racism and racial identity among white Americans: A replication and extension. *Journal of Counseling & Development, 72*(January/February), 293–97.

Pope-Davis, D. B., Vandiver, B. J., & Stone, G. L. (1999). White racial identity attitude development: A psychometric examination of two instruments. *Journal of Counseling Psychology, 46*, 70–9.

Ragins, B. R., & Cornwell, J. M. (2001). Pink triangles: Antecedents and consequences of perceived workplace discrimination against gay and lesbian employees. *Journal of Applied Psychology, 86*(6), 1244–61.

Reskin, B. F., & McBrier, D. B. (2000). Why not ascription? Organizations' employment of male and female managers. *American Sociological Review, 65*, 210–33.

Sanchez, J. I., & Brock, P. (1996). Outcomes of perceived discrimination among Hispanic employees: Is diversity management a luxury or a necessity? *Academy of Management Journal, 39*, 704–19.

Schneider, K. T., Hitlan, R. T., & Radhakrishnan, P. (2000). An examination of the nature and correlates of ethnic harassment experiences in multiple contexts. *Journal of Applied Psychology, 85*, 3–12.

Spence, J. T., & Helmreich, R. L. (1972). The Attitudes Toward Women Scale: An objective instrument to measure attitudes toward the rights and roles of women in contemporary society. *JSAS Catalog of Selected Documents in Psychology, 2*, 667–8.

Spence, J. T., & Helmreich, R. L. (1978). *Masculinity and femininity: Their psychological dimensions, correlates, and antecedents.* Austin, TX: University of Texas Press.

Spence, J. T., & Helmreich, R. L. (1979). Comparison of masculine and feminine personality attributes and sex-role attitudes across age groups. *Developmental Psychology, 15*, 583–4.

Spence, J. T., & Helmreich, R. L. (1980). Masculine instrumentality and feminine expressiveness: Their relationships with sex role attitudes and behaviors. *Psychology of Women Quarterly, 5*, 147–63.

Spencer, M. S., Icard, L. D., Harachi, T. W., Catalano, R. F., & Oxford, M. (2000). Ethnic identity among monoracial and multiracial early adolescents. *Journal of Early Adolescence, 20*(4), 365–87.

Swim, J. K., Aikin, K. J., Hall, W. S., & Hunter, B. A. (1995). Sexism and racism: Old-fashioned and modern prejudices. *Journal of Personality and Social Psychology, 68*(2), 199–214.

Terrell, F., & Terrell, S. (1981). An inventory to measure cultural mistrust among blacks. *Western Journal of Black Studies, 5*(3), 180–4.

Thomas, K. M. (1998). Psychological readiness for multicultural leadership. *Management Development Forum, 1*(2), 99–112.

Thompson, R. L., Brossart, D. F., Carlozzi, A. F., & Miville, M. L. (2002). Five-factor model (Big Five) personality traits and universal-diverse orientation in counselor trainees. *Journal of Psychology: Interdisciplinary & Applied, 136*(5), 561–72.

Tougas, F., Brown, R., Beaton, A. M., & Joly, S. (1995). Neosexism: Plus ça change, plus c'est pareil. *Personality and Social Psychology Bulletin, 21*, 842–9.

Tropp, L. R., & Wright, S. C. (2001). Ingroup identification as the inclusion of ingroup in the self. *Society for Personality and Social Psychology, Inc., 27*(5), 585–600.

Twenge, J. M. (1997a). Changes in masculine and feminine traits over time: A meta-analysis. *Sex Roles, 36*, 305–25.

Twenge, J. M. (1997b). Attitudes toward women, 1970–1995: A meta-analysis. *Psychology of Women Quarterly, 21*, 35–51.

Walters, K. L., & Simoni, J. M. (1993). Lesbian and gay male group identity attitudes and self-esteem: Implications for counseling. *Journal of Counseling Psychology, 40*, 94–9.

Worrell, F. C. (2000). A validity study of scores on the multigroup ethnic identity measure based on a sample of academically talented adolescents. *Educational & Psychological Measurement, 60*(3), 439–47.

Yancey, A. K., Aneshensel, C. S., & Driscoll, A. K. (2001). The assessment of ethnic identity in a diverse urban youth population. *Journal of Black Psychology, 27*(2), 190–208.

Part III

DIMENSIONS OF WORKPLACE DIVERSITY

11

Of Small Steps and the Longing for Giant Leaps

Research on the Intersection of Sex and Gender within Workplaces and Organizations

YVONNE BENSCHOP

The story of sex and gender in the workplace as a field of scholarly research begins with second-wave feminism which provided the impetus to question women's positions in society. Second-wave feminism was a very active phase in the women's movement, in which women's unease and dissatisfaction with their domestic roles as stay-at-home wives and mothers were articulated and translated into demands for equal pay, equal education, child care and free contraception. Discontent with the sexual division of labor lies at the beginning of a steady flow of studies concerning men and women at work and in organizations. Since then, the boundaries of the domain have been explored enthusiastically from various disciplines, angles and theoretical lenses. The result is a broad variety of issues studied: from occupational segregation to sexual harassment and from work–family arrangements to the feminization of management. The asymmetries between the sexes have been substantially documented. Horizontal sex segregation – the division of men and women within different professions – vertical sex segregation, the under-representation of women in the higher hierarchical levels in the organization and the continuing wage gap between men and women are persistent symptoms of the inequalities in women's and men's labor positions that continue to exist worldwide.

This is not to say that we have not come a long way. Seen from a historical perspective, one might be able to tell wonderful stories of the progress made. Indeed, compared to their grandmothers and mothers, many women today have a lot more options available to engage in various forms of paid work. An international comparison of 56 countries in Africa, the Americas, Asia and Europe shows a modest decline in industrial and occupational sex segregation in the majority of the cases (Jacobs & Lim, 1995). Virtually all occupations are open to women, and some women have risen to the top of organizations and boards of directors. Historians might say that the glass is half full here. Yet, a lot still needs to be accomplished. The over-representation of women among the lowest-paid, lowest-grade workers seems to be present at all times and in all places. Although sex discrimination may take different forms and shapes in different contexts, the systematic gender order (Gherardi, 1995) always values the masculine over the feminine, not the other way around. From this dominant perspective, the glass seems to hold only a few drops of water.

Over the past 35 years, sex and gender in combination with work and organization have emerged as a research area, fueled by conceptual developments in women/gender studies. Roughly, the interest started in the late 1960s and first centered on the notion 'women and work', to document and explain patterns of women's employment. Serious challenges were made to the silencing, misrepresentation and absence of women in studies on work and organization. Simultaneously, legislation was developed in nations such as the UK, the United States and the Netherlands to counteract sex discrimination, and legislative action was undertaken to ensure equal employment opportunities (Benschop, Brouns & de Bruijn, 1998; Hakim, 1996; Reskin, 1998). In the 1980s, an increasing number of working women made profound changes in the workforce, and many women acquired credentials to follow careers in management positions. During this time, the attention gradually shifted to the concept of 'gender and organization'. Gender and organization entailed a move beyond the identification of sex differences in order to question the meanings of those differences, to study how they constitute organizations and how they are (re)produced by organizational (power) processes (see for instance Mills & Tancred, 1992). At the same time, as public opinion began to shift, questions arose concerning the desirability and necessity of preferential treatment for women and support for equal opportunity policies decreased (Lorber, 1994). Since the 1990s, another conceptual change has been occurring, one that promises to break with categorical thinking in terms of men and women, masculine and feminine. Inspired by the critique of black feminists, Eastern European feminists and so-called 'Third World' feminists on the domination of white, middle-class themes and issues, a differentiation between women has been summoned to do justice to the variation in women's experiences and positions. The intersections of gender with other identity categories, such as ethnicity, nationality and social class, and their functioning as parallel and interlocking systems have become the central focus of analysis (Collins, 1993). The various intersections are sometimes summarized under the heading of diversity. Yet, intersectionality and diversity can, but do not necessarily, coincide, because some broad perspectives of diversity embrace all differences and shy away from the underlying power processes that are central to the intersections of core identity categories (Crenshaw, 1997). This chapter will illustrate how this increasingly theoretical and conceptual complexity has made its mark on the research done in this area.

In this chapter, I present a selective overview of the research on sex and gender in the context of work and organizations. As this area of research has mushroomed, it is impossible to cover it comprehensively within the boundaries of a single chapter. I restrict my discussion to the terrain of labor in formal organizations. Although the accent is mainly on the research which has been carried out in organization studies and in sociological studies of work, studies rooted in other disciplines are also discussed since this is typically an interdisciplinary research area. The chapter intends to (1) illustrate the broad spectrum of issues studied, (2) discuss the theoretical underpinnings, and (3) review the contributions to the existing knowledge in this field. Since the chapter is also intended to provide an introduction for newcomers, I include seminal works, but also discuss less well-known writings and prioritize recent work not yet covered by other overviews. I am indebted to these earlier overviews (especially Alvesson & Billing, 1997, Calás & Smircich, 1996; Powel & Graves, 2003). Their extensive coverage of the research on women in management and leadership has helped me limit my discussion of this well-researched and reviewed area. Another pressing concern that should be noted is that much of the research is Eurocentric and Anglocentric. Due to the domination of the English language in the sciences in general, studies conducted in other languages have been largely excluded. As a scholar's fluency in English and the quality of his or her work do not necessarily coincide, this probably deprives us of many valuable voices, insights and contexts. On a related note, Western cultural essentialism poses Western problems as universal problems. In the research on sex, gender, work and organization this entails a preoccupation with authority, careers and part-time work; in other words, with the values and interests of white, middle-class women, excluding questions and realities relevant to women on the margins (see also Mohanty, Russo & Torres, 1991; Prasad & Prasad, 2002). This chapter reflects those restrictions in so far that it merely addresses Western European, North American and similar countries. It only discusses research published in English and in Dutch, with a particular emphasis on the British and United States writings that dominate the field, although an effort has been made to include work from scholars of other nationalities.

The chapter begins with a discussion of the central concepts of sex and gender, addressing the meaning and scope of both concepts, their relation to one another, and the way in which scholars use them as descriptive and analytical categories in the context of work and organizations. Then, two major debates in women's/ gender studies – the public–private divide and the equality/difference debate – and their spin-off in the context of work and organization are discussed. In the next section, three major research lines are identified. These research lines highlight the functioning of the labor market, individual choices of women, and gendered organizational processes and practices respectively. The chapter ends with the elaboration of some major trends and challenges to the field.

CONCEPTUALIZING SEX, GENDER AND POWER

The terms sex and gender have caused – and are still causing – conceptual confusion both in everyday usage and in research. The first author to make a conceptual distinction between sex and gender was Oakley (1972: 58), who stated that 'Sex' is a biological term: 'gender' a psychological and cultural one. In this view, sex principally allows only two categories: 'men' and 'women' and refers to the biological differences between the sexes, whereas the notion of gender calls attention to the socio-cultural meanings of these differences and of the more abstract notions of masculinity and femininity. Femininity and masculinity are not fixed, binary oppositions. Their meanings are socially constructed, multiple and variable in different contexts. The distinction between the two notions is important because it makes it possible to show that it is not the small biological difference that is so significant, but the importance ascribed to that difference in society that accounts for its major impact (Schwarzer, 1976). However, the presentation of sex as a biology-based phenomenon and gender as a sociocultural-based phenomenon (Gentile, 1993) is itself contested (Deaux, 1993; Unger & Crawford, 1993). Many authors today favor a more nuanced understanding of the terms, arguing that sex emerges from a complex interaction of biological and socio-cultural factors, and is as much a social construction as gender is. Despite these established epistemological complexities, it is my opinion that a distinction between sex and gender is useful as an analytical position in the context of work and organization. The term sex can be reserved to indicate and describe women and men in organizations, whereas the term gender can be used to go beyond the descriptive to the analysis of the meanings of distinctions between women and men, femininity and masculinity.

Scott provides an important dimension to the conceptualization of gender. She states that 'gender is a constitutive element of social relationships based on perceived differences between the sexes and gender is a primary way of signifying relationships of power' (Scott, 1986: 94). These two elements – gender as a regulatory principle in the social relations of men and women, and the connection between gender and power – have become the central influences in the knowledge production on gender issues.

The relationship between gender and power has always been the *raison d'être* of feminist theorizing, questioning and challenging patterns of male domination and female subordination in different contexts (Davis, 1991). As Moi (1989: 101) puts it: 'Feminism is about the need to reconceptualize power, understand it differently, see the creative potential in power.' Gender inequalities are complex and call for a specific conception of power that maneuvers between two dilemmas. The first occurs when structural forces are seen as the main cause of gender inequalities, because that reduces actors to 'structural dopes', unable to act against what the structure imposes on them. The second dilemma occurs when individual actions are seen as the cause of inequalities; holding women accountable for their positions easily leads to blaming-the-victim. Hence, the reciprocity of structure and action (Giddens, 1984) is central to the analysis of the relation between gender and power. Furthermore, gender intersects with other power relations such as manager/employee and mentor/protégé, and the relations between men and women are also influenced by other social identities like ethnicity, class and age. This questions the relative importance of gender in relations between the sexes in specific contexts and results in a plea for plurality.

The notion of gender enables the identification of subtle forms of sex discrimination, since sex discrimination is not restricted to positions of women and men, but is also related to seemingly gender neutral phenomena such as labor markets, politics and organizations. In the late 1980s, complex notions of gender have been developed, which differentiate between several layers or dimensions that are analytically distinct but in reality always interwoven. Harding's (1986) distinction between institutions, symbols and identities has been the most influential model in the field. Institutions and organizations are the first dimension. Assumptions about men and women, masculinity and femininity are embedded in the design and structuring of organizations. Institutions have a gender identity: the military, for instance, is inherently masculine whereas a daycare centre is associated with femininity. The second, symbolical dimension contains dichotomous and sometimes subtle images and norms about masculinity and femininity. The production of gender symbols occurs when pairs of concepts are constructed as oppositions (rational/emotional, dark/light, hard/soft) and one concept gets associated with masculinity, the other with femininity. A typical example is the masculine connotation of the top manager and the feminine connotation of the secretary. The last dimension is concerned with gender as a primary structuring principle in the ascribed and subjective identities of people. Ideas and values of what it takes to be male or female influence how men and women identify themselves and are identified by others.

Acker (1990; 1992) specified this layered model of gender in four sets of gendered processes in organizations. The first set is the production of gender divisions in organization structures. Gender segregation is reproduced in the composition of work processes, jobs and hierarchies and in allocation processes like recruitment and selection and career planning. The second set of gendered processes involves symbolic representations of masculinity and femininity in organization cultures. Symbols, images, rules, conventions and values direct, maintain or sometimes challenge gender divisions. Stereotypes are strong gender images, as many female managers who have been mistaken for secretaries or male nurses who have been confused with doctors will know. The third set concerns the social interaction processes that constitute organizational activities. Gender plays a part in the interactions at different levels. Interactions between managers and employees, between colleagues and between workers and customers are also interactions between men and women, women and women and men and men. The fourth and final set of gendering processes concerns the identity of organization members as gendered persons. The reproduction of gender distinctions in organizations takes place through the identity of organization members, through their opinions, experiences and expressions in relation to the gendered division of labor and expectations of 'gender-appropriate' organizational behavior. Acker's four sets of processes have become an influential framework, guiding many studies on gender in organizations, as we shall see in the overview of research. The interrelation of different processes is also illustrated by two of the major debates in women's/gender studies that are discussed in the following section.

MAJOR DEBATES

Public–private Divide

Going back to archaic ideas of male hunters and female gatherers, this debate evolves around the division of men and women over separate spheres of life. Anthropologists argue that the public sphere of politics, power and work is reserved for men, the private sphere of reproduction, household and family is the domain and responsibility of women (Rosaldo, 1980). The domination of men and subordination of women stems from the hierarchical order of these spheres, for the public is valued over the private and women are excluded from the public sphere. The debate focuses on three issues: the separation of the two spheres, the strict division of the sexes over the spheres and the exclusive location of power in the public sphere (Brouns, 1995). It is argued that the two spheres are not separate but intrinsically connected. Governments for instance are public institutions per se, intervening in private relationships between women and men through matrimonial laws and regulations. Also, feminists call for a revaluation of the private sphere, claiming that certain power positions can and should be derived from running a household and raising the next generation. An influential contribution to the debate is made by Fraser (1989) who further refines the public and the private into four spheres: the family, economy, government and public sphere. She argues that implicit ideas of masculinity and femininity underlie these spheres, and that women and men take up different positions in those spheres: women feature predominantly as clients and consumers, while men are presented as citizens and employees.

The public–private divide is no longer prominent on the agenda as more and more women have entered the labor market in recent decades. Yet, the increased participation of women in employment is not accompanied by a comparable increase in the participation of men in household tasks and care-taking. In that respect, current issues around work/life balance (Den Dulk, 2001; Drew, Emerek & Mahon, 1998; Frederiksen-Goldsen & Scharlach, 2001; Hochschild, 1997; Lewis & Lewis, 1996) can be understood as a redefinition of the public–private debate. The combination of work and family life is often recognized as one of the most pressing issues in the field of sex, gender, work and organization and has become a vast and ever-expanding terrain of research. Work and family are rarely seen as separate domains anymore; the premise of mutual dependence of the two is widely recognized. Several theoretical perspectives are used to understand the interrelation of work and family, of which spillover theory and conflict theory are the most dominant (Parasuraman & Greenhaus, 2002). Spillover theory postulates that effect, attitude and behavior from one domain also apply to the other domain, for instance the greater the satisfaction with family life, the greater the satisfaction with work is. Studies on conflict consistently report that the work situation has a negative effect on private life more often than the other way around (Geurts, Haris, Demerouti, Dickkers & Kompier, 2002). From an organizational perspective, work–family conflicts are questioned through notions like the 'ideal worker' (Acker, 1992; see also below under the research line on gendering organizations) to comment on the problematic reduction of workers to employees, and the 'mommy track' (Benschop & Doorewaard, 1998a; Lorber, 1994) that indicates that women with children are derailed to jobs open to flexible work arrangements, which are predictably the lower-paid, lower-prestige jobs. There is also a growing body of literature on the family-responsive policies or work/life balance programs that organizations are developing to facilitate their employees in managing the interface between paid work and other activities in life (De Cieri, Holmes, Abbott & Pettit, 2005; Glass & Finley, 2002; Konrad & Mangel, 2000). Usually, these policies or arrangements come down to flexible working time, leave opportunities and child care provisions. As they are often directed at women, there is a danger that they reproduce ideological stereotypes of motherhood being incompatible with career commitment and advancement, reinforcing the traditional sex-specific public–private divide.

Equal or Different?

The second major debate in women/gender studies revolves around the question whether women are the same or different as men. Advocates of the difference perspective see women as essentially different from men and strive for a revaluation of the feminine. The argument goes that women have a special contribution to make to organizations; their different experiences, values, behavior, feeling and thinking provide them with complementary qualifications much needed in organizations. Fletcher (1994) speaks of women's relational skills and their privileging of openness and connection. In contrast, the perspective of equality states that women are principally equal to men. Differences between the sexes are due to discrimination and prejudice against women. These differences will disappear as soon as women and men receive equal treatment. The equality perspective appeals to our sense of justice and fairness in its call for equal opportunities for all. The central claim is that there are no real or significant differences in ability, qualification or work orientation that would account for the promotion and wage gaps (Reskin & Padavic, 1994). Another, more recent, argument in this perspective is more managerial than moral in nature and has become known as the 'business case for gender equality' (Dickens, 1999). Not using the full potential of female employees is castigated as inefficient, uneconomic and an organizational waste.

Both 'equality' and 'difference' are problematic and complex notions (Webb, 1997) that are often conceptually confused when societal inequalities between women and men are mistaken for 'natural' differences between the sexes (Komter, 1990). Brouns (1993: 34–5) shows how sameness of women and men easily leads to the undervaluation of social differences and inequalities. The claim that men and women are the same implicitly reinforces the male norm constructing women as deviant and lagging behind. Difference is just as problematic as it presupposes fundamental differences between women and men, and reduces the differences to the essence or nature of 'Woman' and 'Man'. Furthermore, this notion of difference is suspect because it is always utilized to keep women in subordinate positions. Yet Scott (1988: 43) states: 'Feminists can not give up 'difference': it has been our most creative analytic tool. We cannot give up equality, at least as long as we want to speak to the principles and values of our political system.' The dilemma disappears with the acknowledgement that the recognition of material inequalities is not the same as the revaluation of the feminine and that difference and sameness are only relative to each other (Liff & Wacjman, 1996). As Cockburn (1991) argues, men and women are both the same *and* different.

In the context of work and organization, specific societal inequalities concerning labor positions are at stake. I argue that a normative judgment on the ontological difference or sameness of women and men is irrelevant in this context. Such a judgment does not contribute to the explanation of inequalities in work and organization for it can be used either way. An argumentation that appeals to difference can be used to justify the division of labor between the sexes: women are different and hence should do different things. But on grounds of the same difference, the division of labor between the sexes can be questioned by reasoning that women have their own contribution to make and should be incorporated in the labor process.

One area that is illustrative of the equality/difference debate in the context of work and organization is the controversial issue of sex differences in leadership styles. The 'crucial difference' camp argues that female leaders and managers exceed their male counterparts in people-orientated, democratic and web-like styles of leadership (Helgesen, 1990; Rosener, 1990). The 'no difference' camp observes similarities in the way men and women lead and attributes different leadership styles of men and women to situational factors, or gender differences in status or power (Klenke, 1993; Powell, 1999). The vast amount of research on sex differences in leadership styles is compressed in two meta-analyses. Both Eagly and Johnson's (1990) overview of 162 studies done between 1961 and 1987 and Van Engen and Willemsen's (2000) coverage of 26 studies in the period 1987–2000 show that evidence for sex differences in leadership behavior is mixed and that leadership is a contextual phenomenon. Evidence for sex differences is found in the sense that women tend to democratic and participative leadership styles; other styles do not show sex differences. Evidence against sex differences is found in studies conducted in organizations, because female and male leaders do not differ there. In contrast, in laboratory studies more task-oriented styles for men and more interpersonally oriented styles for women are found. So, leadership styles are contingent upon the type of organization and upon the setting of the study. Van Engen and Willemsen argue against simple dichotomous schemes of leadership styles and their linkage to masculinity or femininity (see also Billing & Alvesson, 2000). All in all, the dispute continues, as no decisive answers are given and there is research support for the standpoints of both adversaries and advocates of sex differences.

The issue of leadership styles continues to be 'hot' as the newest insights (Eagly, Johannesen-Schmidt & Van Engen, 2003) show that women slightly exceed men in the transformational leadership styles that bear a positive relation to leaders' effectiveness. Transformative leaders are visionary, charismatic, inspirational people that nourish, stimulate and motivate subordinates to contribute to organizational goals. This leadership style fits well with contemporary organization concepts that appeal to autonomous, responsible workers who self-organize in teams and/or networks. A study in the British public sector (Maddock, 1999) explored how female managers work as innovative change agents creating alternative work practices and cultures that sustain participation. Despite the difficulties and oppositions these female managers encounter, they challenge their organizations and the traditional gender and power relations that work to frustrate innovation and conserve masculine-gendered cultures. So, these latest findings support the crucial difference perspective and ground contemporary claims that women are superior leaders.

After this discussion of two major debates and the research related to it, I will introduce the three research lines that guide the analysis of the research on sex, gender, work and organization in the next section.

THREE RESEARCH LINES

In this chapter, I distinguish three lines of research, which focus on different levels of analysis, contain different research topics and are largely informed by different theoretical approaches. The first research line documents the persistence of sex segregation at a macro level. The functioning of the external and internal labor market is considered the primary explanation for the unequal positions of the sexes. The second research line explains the unequal positions by micro-level factors external to the labor market, such as processes of socialization and individual choices of women. The third line of research takes the meso level of organizations as the main point to study the contributions that organizations make to the (re)production of gender. Of course, many issues (like occupational segregation) are typically multilevel phenomena and a lot of studies do not fall neatly in one of the research lines distinguished. I take the theoretical orientation of those studies as a guide for my discussion of them in one or the other research line.

Functioning of the Labor Market

In this line of research, authors try to explain differences in labor market positions of men and women. Various theoretical frameworks are used to understand issues like the wage gap and occupational segregation. Economic theories feature prominently in this research line. Large-scale surveys are the favored method, although case studies of internal labor markets are also conducted. Many studies document the increasing participation of women since the 1960s and the continuous labor market segregation in various contexts (e.g. Roos, 1985, for 12 industrialized countries; Crompton, 1997, for the UK, and also France, Norway, Russia and the Czech Republic).

Pay differentials between men and women attract considerable scholarly attention. It is a well-researched area; estimates of the wage gap have been published for many different countries at many different points in time. A meta-analysis of the international wage gap (Weichselbaumer & Winter-Ebmer, 2003) roughly reports a decline over time with raw wage differentials falling from around 65% in the 1960s to around 30% in the 1990s, due to the increased labor market productivity of females. The unexplained or discriminatory component of the wage gap that is not due to unequal productivities is not or only slightly declining, depending on the methodology used. Important as the wage gap may be as a symbol of gender inequality, it is a symptom and there are many different explanations in stock as this section illustrates.

Occupational sex segregation is another well-researched issue. Both the supply and the demand side of labor are examined from a variety of competing theoretical perspectives. With respect, to the supply side of labor, the economic neoclassical human capital theory relates people's personal capital (education, training, experience) to their labor positions (Becker, 1971). That men generally have better positions than women is explained by the investments men choose to make in themselves. The disproportionate representation of women in lower-skilled occupations is considered to be the effect of women's choices for those occupations and their concern for families. Human capital explanations are largely rebutted by feminist research. Roos (1985) compared the labor force behavior, occupational position and attainment patterns of American married and never-married women. She finds little support for the human capital explanation that marital responsibilities for family and childrearing account for women's disadvantaged positions, because women without those responsibilities do not fare much better. De Jong (1985) tried the explanatory power of human capital theory by studying matched pairs in a large Dutch bank. She found insufficient explanation for career differences between men and women. Women and men who had similar starting capital in terms of education and experience differed after five years, with women holding lower-level positions that were often not in the core business of the bank. So, processes on the demand side of the labor market need to be taken into account to explain these differences.

Examinations on the demand side of the labor market draw attention to institutional, socio-cultural and structural constraints that influence the behavior of employers and employees. One often-used theory regarding this demand side is the segmentation theory. In this perspective, the labor market is not a homogeneous whole, but comprises several labor markets or segments with specific rules and opportunities that function more or less separately. The primary segment contains attractive work, good pay, opportunities for advancement and good working conditions and is mostly populated by men. The secondary segment is characterized by less challenging work, lower pay and poorer working conditions and comprises many 'female jobs' (Barron & Norris, 1976). Studies on sex segregation and allocation processes point out how employers have an interest in these separate segments and adapt their recruitment practices accordingly (Crompton, 1997; Tijdens, 1989; Watts & Rich, 1993). The attractive primary segment is reserved for employees the organization needs, trusts and wants to invest in: these are mainly men. For the secondary segment with its relatively cheap, flexible and often temporary jobs, women are recruited. Women are considered less reliable workers because of family responsibilities and they are expected to prefer flexible work arrangements.

To understand the position of the relatively few women in the primary segment, Kanter's (1977) work is helpful. Her influential token theory deals with the consequences of numerical relations for work behavior. Kanter analyzes how women in a minority position (tokens) amongst male colleagues in a large US company have to cope with enhanced visibility, are seen as role models for their sex, evoke a sense of contrast with their male counterparts and are expected to assimilate to majority (male) ways. Ott's (1985) study of male nurses and female police officers in the Netherlands indicates that male tokens in the nursing profession profit from their visibility, whereas female tokens in the police force encounter barriers because of their exceptional position. Research on token women in top positions in the Dutch banking sector (Benschop & Doorewaard, 1998a) shows how women are still confronted with the higher demands that influence the quality of their work. But enhanced visibility can sometimes be advantageous, because women are noticed when they perform well and they can rise faster up the ladder than their male counterparts.

The persistent pattern of sex-specific staffing of separate labor market segments can be explained by statistical discrimination. From this perspective, it is rational for employers to discriminate against individuals on account of the perceived abilities and characteristics of the group they belong to, to avoid the costs they associate with the employment of that group (Anker, 1997). Evidence of statistical discrimination was found by Konrad and Cannings (1997) in their study of two large US firms, where women in management were viewed with suspicion and their commitment and competence were over-tested. It is also statistical discrimination when employers are reluctant to hire a woman in a management position because women cost organizations in terms of maternity leave, absenteeism and turnover. However, it should be noted here that employers' attitudes toward maternity at work are imbedded in cultural belief systems. There are considerable national differences in policies and expenditures for work–family arrangements: the family-based systems of countries like Germany, Austria and the Netherlands contrast with well-developed child care systems in countries like France, Sweden and Denmark (Plantenga & Hansen, 1999).

Feminists have developed alternative explanations for the economic and institutional perspectives on gender segregation in the labor market. Rooted in Marxist critiques on capitalism and critiquing Marxism for its failure to address patriarchy properly, dual-systems theory takes both women's oppression as workers under capitalism and their subordination as women under patriarchy into account to understand gender inequality in the labor market (Hartmann, 1981). Based on her empirical research into the contributions of trade unions to labor market segregation, Walby (1986) refines dual-systems theory by showing the tensions between capitalism and patriarchy. She argues that capitalist exploitation does not subsume male dominance and that a better understanding of patriarchy is needed. In her later work, she develops a concept of patriarchy as a system of social structures and practices, in which men dominate, oppress and exploit women (Walby, 1990: 20). Dual-systems theory and Walby's elaboration of it are contested for their overly deterministic and economistic orientation that fails to recognize how structures of domination are not only the medium but also the outcome of active agents (Collinson, Knights & Collinson, 1990: 44).

An alternative feminist framework that does leave room for agency is queuing theory, which distinguishes between labor queues, the ranking of possible workers by employers, and job queues, the worker's ranking of jobs (Reskin & Roos, 1990). Queuing theory focuses attention on how the interaction of employers' preferences for workers (determined by human capital and discriminatory considerations) and workers' preferences for jobs determines labor market outcomes (Rich, 1995: 361). Case studies on the feminization of male occupations in the United States, like pharmacists, insurance adjusters and examiners and bus drivers (Reskin & Roos, 1990), and clerical, banking occupations (Rich, 1995), show that labor queues are essentially gender queues.

In summary, this line of research allows for a better understanding of the contribution that the organization of work makes to the continuation of societal relations. The functioning of external and internal labor markets contributes to the inequality of the sexes. In separate segments of the labor market, the organization of work differs, demanding full-time availability and effort in the primary segment and allowing for part-time performance in the secondary segment only. The division of the sexes over those segments reinforces the dominant pattern of the breadwinner–care-taker model. Studies concerning women's positions in the primary segment do not refute this pattern either, for they suggest that women in management ranks are still tokens that have to adjust to majority rules.

The studies discussed here concentrate primarily on the functioning and organization of the external and internal labor market, but outside the labor market, their theoretical explanations are also ranging to individual choices. This brings us to the next line of research.

Women's Choices

This second line of research explains the differences between the sexes in work and organization by factors outside the work context. Social–psychological, individual-level theoretical approaches of women's choices in life and work are dominant. Men and their choices merely serve as contrast: how men's choices restrict women's choices (either as their partners or as their bosses and coworkers) often remains unseen. When it comes to research methods, the survey is the principal approach, but there are also studies that use qualitative interview data.

A popular explanation for the sexual division of labor is that of individual choice. In this view, women *choose* to be primarily responsible for care-taking and the household. They opt for low-grade and low-paid part-time jobs to be able to combine paid work with their responsibilities at home. Women do not choose the long hours and big salaries that come with the territory of top positions. Hakim (1996; 2000) has developed her controversial preference theory accordingly. She points at female heterogeneity in work orientations and, based on a substantial number of surveys in Europe and in the United States, distinguishes three work preferences. She asserts that some 20% of women prefer to stay at home (home-makers); some 20% of women prefer to engage in employment careers (career women) and the majority of women (adaptives) prefer to combine work and family without giving priority to either one. In contrast, men have only one pattern of continuous employment and no feasible alternative choices open to them. Hakim argues that the ideologies of the sexual division of labor and of sexual difference are the most effective mechanisms for the subordination of women and explicitly states that women are the main propagators of sex role ideologies and behaviors (1996: 202–11).

Hakim's work fits in a tradition where women's employment, work commitment and sexrole attitudes are analyzed as central issues against a background of sex socialization processes and the care of children. Preference theory harmonizes with human capital theory and rational choice explanations of women's economic behavior. Its assertions have met a lot of critique. Crompton and Harris (1998: 131) emphasize contextual and structural constraints. They call Hakim's micro-level approach voluntaristic and inadequate in its assumption of a level playing field, when material and power differentials between women and men are clear. Their interviews with women doctors and bankers in the UK, Norway, France, Russia and the Czech Republic illustrate how work orientations are much more complex, variable over the life cycle and multi-stranded than Hakim's rather static and simple approach can capture. More critique comes from Proctor and Padfield (1999) who use interview data with two groups of British, young, adult women: 'single workers' (single, childless and employed full time) and 'early mothers' (partnered mothers, part-time employed). They find that Hakim's threefold typology is not elaborated sufficiently as the category of 'adaptives' is a 'caricatured residual category', whereas the combination of work and family is the most significant category, both empirically and theoretically. Furthermore, they emphasize the interplay of agency and structure, as choices are never made in the abstract, and are dependent of social structural conditions and differences in opportunities. Finally, Fagan (2001) looks at survey data of working-time preferences in the UK and observes a diversity that cuts across simple gender distinctions with both men and women preferring more flexible arrangements. Apparently, gender differences in working-time preferences are often assumed or deduced from working-time patterns instead of empirically investigated. Fagan states that working-time status certainly is no indicator for work orientations as Hakim suggests, as this disregards the impact of the gender order and employers' segmentation practices.

All in all, the main critique point on the explanatory power of individual choice is that subjective choices and preferences are restricted by the influence of the social context, hegemonic power processes and power relations. The critique also exemplifies a clash of research paradigms and methodologies, for large-scale survey data typically cannot take into account the complexity and social embeddedness of choice processes that qualitative interviews can.

Besides choices between work and family, career choices per se are also an important topic in this research line. A central issue is horizontal sex segregation, or why women choose to work in daycare centers and men opt for construction work (to name a few stereotypes). Correll's (2001) study of early career decisions of American students shows that gender stereotypes constrain early career-relevant choices (like taking math) of women and men in two distinct ways. Gender stereotypes affect how others channel individuals into sex-specific activities and subsequent career trajectories. They also bias people's self-perceptions of their abilities and affect how individuals 'self-select' into occupational relevant activities. In their study of career preferences of young Israeli adults, Gati, Givon and Osipow (1995) find that the similarities between the sexes are manifold. The differences they do observe coincide with traditional patterns of males preferring business and technology orientations and females preferring social and humanistic orientations. Similar findings are reported in the meta-analysis of Konrad, Ritchie, Lie and Corrigall (2000), which shows relatively small sex differences in job attribute preferences in the United States. The observed different preferences for characteristics of jobs are generally consistent with gender roles and stereotypes (e.g. women attach greater importance to interpersonal relationships, men value earnings and power).

Konrad et al. note how many studies in this area lack a theoretical perspective guiding interpretations of the observed sex differences. That may account for the popularity of stereotypes and sex role socialization processes as explanations. The trouble is then that this type of research often reproduces stereotypes, when various activities and job characteristics are labeled and linked to dimensions of masculinity and femininity. Also, the attention for socialization processes seems to overcome an over-voluntaristic explanation, but only to arrive at a static and overdeterministic explanation that leaves little room for agency. For Reskin and Padavic (1994) sex role socialization explanations do not suffice because: 'far more influential than the messages we picked up 20 years earlier as children are the opportunities, rewards and punishments we encounter as adults' (p. 77).

Summarizing, the research in this line mainly questions positions and choices of women as a group and contrasts them with the choices men make. The accentuation and problematization of positions and behavior of women has a number of negative consequences: it exemplifies categorical thinking by activating and stressing sex differences and it does not do justice to similarities between the sexes or variation between women. Although a micro-level and psychological focus is eminent, there is a bundle of research, with a feminist signature, countering this focus and stressing the importance of contextual, structural and organizational constraints and the complexity of intertwined career and life choices. Conceptually, this entails a shift from sex differences toward gendering processes. That brings us to the following line of research.

Gendering Organizations

The third and last line of research discussed here typically focuses on the organizational level and studies the contributions that organizations make to the (re)production of gender. Although this line is informed by a various strands of feminism, social-constructivist and post-structural feminist frameworks (Calás & Smircich, 1996) prevail. Main issues concern the organization of gender and gendered cultures, and both material inequalities and discursive constructions are analyzed. Methodologically, the local and situated analyses of case studies and ethnographies constitute the favored approach in this line of research.

One central theme constitutes the underlying processes that account for the persistent structuring of organizations along gender lines. Acker's gendering processes (as discussed in the first section) and her concept of the gendered substructure of organization, or related notions like gender subtext, are used to examine constructions of gender in organizations. The processes of gendering are elaborated in organization concepts, organizational practices and jobs within organizations. For instance, classic concepts of organization theory such as Taylorism, bureaucracy, and contemporary concepts like team-based work that are generally presented as neutral, are analyzed as actually drawing upon and reinforcing gender divisions (Ferguson, 1984; Metcalfe & Linstead, 2003; Savage & Witz, 1992). Similar critiques are developed about human resource management models and practices that perpetuate rather than challenge gender inequalities. The rhetoric of HRM (the valuing of individual talent) seems compatible with gender equality, but the reality is that HR models are inherently gendered and HRM practices have different implications for women and men at work (Dickens, 1998; Truss, 1999).

A key element in the organization of gender is the notion of the abstract or 'ideal' worker (Acker, 1990; 1992). Organization concepts, organization structures and job descriptions contain rules and codes that prescribe workplace behavior and include abstract conceptions of workers. Characteristics of this abstract worker are full-time availability, mobility, high qualifications, a strong work orientation and no responsibilities in life other than the ones required by the organization. Although presented as neutral in organizational texts, these characteristics are normative and, in day-to-day reality, correspond to the assumed characteristics of male workers rather than to those of female workers. There is no such thing as 'the ideal worker', however; recently, differentiated notions of 'ideal workers' have been developed that vary across different models of work organization (Benschop & Doorewaard, 1998b) and across different gender orders and societal contexts (Tienari, Quack & Theobald, 2003).

The structuring of organizations along gender lines also takes place through the gender typing of jobs: the construction of masculine or feminine connotations of jobs and the accompanying norms of who is suitable to fulfill that job. The research in this area studies definition processes that cast socially important, professional and skilled jobs as masculine, as Cockburn's (1983) case studies in the London newspaper industry and Stivers' (1993) work on public administration illustrate.

Many studies address the deviances from gender-typed jobs by focusing on women in male-dominated occupations like science (*Gender, Work & Organization*, 2003: issue 2; Xie & Schauman, 2003), accounting (Oakes & Hammond, 1995), engineering (Evetts, 1996) and information and communication technology (Webster, 1996; 2004). Incidentally, there is attention paid to men in female-dominated jobs (Cross & Bagilhole, 2002). Constructions of work in female-dominated occupations are also the object of research as studies on secretaries (Pringle, 1988), teachers (Acker, 1989) and nurses (Lee-Treweek, 1997) illustrate.

Another stream of research takes a cultural perspective and looks at the gendering of organizational culture (Gherardi, 1995; Aaltio & Mills, 2002). As gender was originally defined as a cultural construct, there is a strong conceptual relation between gender and culture. While differentiated meanings of gender can be negotiated in specific organizational contexts, on the level of the symbolic gender order (Connell, 1987), dominant cultural prototypes of masculinity and femininity have greater stability. Qualitative case studies and ethnographies are favored approaches for empirical research in this area, as they allow for the local and situated accounts that illustrate the dynamics of gendering. For instance, Korvajärvi (2002) examines the dynamics of 'doing gender' (Gherardi, 1994; West & Zimmerman, 1987) in Finnish white-collar work organizations. She concludes that gendering processes are characterized by informalization and individualization, resulting in the confinement of gender in localities situated outside work organizations and preventing open debate about it. Similarly, Poggio (2000) studies the symbolic gender order in four cases of male-dominated organizations in Italy. She documents how women and men produce and negotiate gender cultures in traditional and more egalitarian organizations. Poggio notes how attempts to change these gender cultures should not target individuals but organizations, for organizations produce the symbolic order of gender. A final example of studies on gendered organization cultures is Mills' work on, among other things, the organizational imagery (1995) and corporate masculinity (1998) of British Airways. Mills demonstrates how airline companies influence popular culture with prominent and enduring images of idealized masculinity ('pilot', 'engineer') and femininity ('stewardess') (2002: 125).

As Mills' studies illustrate, the cultural approach to gender and organizations encompasses the analysis of organizational texts and discourses. Several studies have recognized the importance of corporate annual reports for the (re)production of gender inequality. The longitudinal study of General Motors' annual reports between 1917 and 1976 (Tinker & Neimark, 1987) regards these reports as ideological instruments that are vital parts in the perpetuation of traditional meanings of gender in organizations. The analysis of visual and textual representations of gender in Dutch annual reports (Benschop & Meihuizen, 2002) shows how these reports continue to present stereotypical images of powerful masculine managers and attractive feminine customers in a variation of the classic male breadwinner–female care-taker divide. Recently, a number of studies have employed discourse analysis to analyze the interrelation between gender and entrepreneurship. Ahl (2004) critically examines constructions of female entrepreneurs in research articles.

She explains how entrepreneurship with its potentially positive associations of self-actualization, autonomy and financial self-sufficiency is researched in relation to women in such a way that it constructs women as secondary and 'Other' (Ahl, 2004: p. 185). Similarly, Bruni, Gherardi and Poggio (2004) coin the term 'entrepreneur mentality' referring to the system of thinking about entrepreneurship, entrepreneurial practice and being an entrepreneur. The gender sub-text underlying the discourse of entrepreneur mentality, they argue, reproduces male experience and practice as the preferred normative value, leaving women with the position of the 'Other'.

Sexuality is another theme that has a direct reference to gendered organizational cultures and that has inspired a whole stream of research. Sexuality is a crucial element of gender and power relations in organizations (Hearn & Parkin, 1987). More specifically, organizations exist with and through norms and practices that are compulsory heterosexual (Hearn & Parkin, 2001: 16). Research into the area of sexuality in organizations is frequently about sexual harassment (e.g. Stockdale, 1996; Timmerman & Bajema, 2000), reflecting the association of sexuality at work with domination, sexism, subordination and oppression. Yet, sexuality at work is too complex and multifaceted to be reduced to a painful problem. On the other side of the spectrum, studies on romance, desire and erotic tension indicate the possibility of pleasurable sexual relations in the workplace, without failing to acknowledge the power processes involved (Brewis & Grey, 1994; Mainiero, 1989; Powell & Foley, 1998). Subtle practices of sexuality in organizations are difficult to study for obvious reasons of accessibility. To acknowledge that sexual attractiveness influences decision making in recruitment and selection processes, career prospects and performance evaluations goes against popular beliefs and widespread convictions that capacities and qualities are all that matter. Yet, case studies report how sexual attraction influences interactions with coworkers, supervisors and customers (Alvesson & Billing, 1997; Gherardi, 1995). Paradoxically, sexuality is sometimes mobilized as an organizational resource. This is obvious in service sector jobs like secretary, receptionist or airhostess, where sexual attractiveness, notably of female staff, is managed to appeal to supervisors and customers (Brewis & Linstead, 2000; Mills, 1997; Pringle, 1988).

Compared to the first two research lines, the research object shifts here from clear manifestations of sex and gender inequality to organizational processes (re)producing gender in various ways. The research in this last line substantiates the duality of gender and organization, treating gender and organization as mutually constitutive. Gender is part of organizing; it is an important element in the organization and division of labor. At the same time, organizations and work are elements in the shaping of gender relations. Even though inconsistencies, ambiguities and paradoxes are part of these gendering processes in organizations (Hearn, 1998), hegemonic masculinity and femininity reappear persistently in the research in this line.

Overlooking the three research lines, one is dazzled by the number of perspectives, theories, explanations and elaborations of the intersections of sex and gender with work and organizations. The different research lines highlight particular issues in particular ways. Manifestations of social inequalities in labor markets, individual choices of women and the deconstruction of organization processes (re)producing gender all add to our understanding of this field. Questions addressed in one line of research do not render questions asked in other lines obsolete. Nevertheless, this is evidently a complex field, where multiple meanings and conceptual contestations rule. Part of this can be attributed to the interdisciplinary character of the field that accounts for its infusion from many different angles, each with their own favored epistemologies and methodologies. Another part stems from the multiple facets of the field, and the many discussions within and between various subfields. Whole books have been written on topics that for reasons of brevity needed to be discussed here in a single paragraph. The productivity is impressive and continues rapidly.

What is clear is that our understanding of gender and organizations does not begin at the door of the office or factory. Work and living are interrelated. Sex segregation in the labor market is interwoven with responsibilities of women and men in the household. Individual motivations and ambitions are informed by societal expectations, perceptions of socio-structural situations and organizational opportunities. And gender is embedded in organizational processes and practices. It is also clear that the configuration of gender relations in organizations is subject to change only very slowly, hence interpretative repertoires of inequality and discrimination feature most prominently.

TRENDS AND CHALLENGES

The rich variation in epistemology, theoretical perspectives, scope and research topics gives a broad overview of possibly relevant factors and helps to build a multi-dimensional picture of this complex field. The discrepancies in the theoretical frameworks used result in strong debates in feminist organization studies and open up discussions with other disciplines studying work and organizations, rendering this a lively and dynamic field of study and practice. Yet, the accomplishments are often viewed with pessimism. Alvesson and Billing (1997: 225) warn against a 'ghettoization' of gender research, noting that it is an isolated and marginalized approach that so far has had limited influence on organization studies. In their opinion, the debates should not be limited to converts to feminism. They suggest that the way to proceed is to enrich organizational themes like innovation, learning, participation and transformation through the consideration of gender aspects, and to enable the investigation of intersections of gender with other organizational repertoires like organizational performance or quality of work. Although I agree with their fruitful suggestions for new lines of research, I am inclined to a more positive evaluation of the accomplishments in this field and challenge the overly modest disposition that values contributions to the mainstream over the development of the field itself. The research on sex and gender articulates and problematizes issues in the theory and practice of work and organizations that would otherwise be overlooked (cf. Calás and Smirich, 1996). Current thinking about social inequalities in the workplace would not stand where it is today if the issue had not been taken up by feminist research, and that is but one example. The more recent studies on workplace diversity have benefited enormously from the insights and conceptualizations of power processes, material inequalities and discursive practices developed in this field. New light is also shed on processes and practices of organizing. The contributions to the diversity at work discussion are manifold: research on sex and gender defined the facts and figures necessary to assess segregation in the workplace, enabling the monitoring of that segregation. It opened up the discussion of alternative work arrangements and work values, showed the cost of minority positions and abstract images of ideal workers and hence questioned the monolithic climate that hindered a diverse workforce. It has pointed to the different effects of HRM practices for women and men at work. The research on gender and leadership led to the valuing of women's styles of management. The huge literature on sexual harassment also contributed to the improvement of work relations, since it made male employees aware of appropriate behavior toward women. Furthermore, debates within feminist organization studies and between different strands of feminism can also be framed as necessary for a further sophistication of our understanding of the dynamics of gendering in organizations. We need the converted in feminism if we want to take this field further.

A major challenge for current research about gender and organization is parting with categorical thinking. In this field, gender is usually stressed as the fundamental structuring principle in organizations. Traditional and hierarchical gender structures are found time and again in empirical studies and they are such persistent materialities in organizations that they seem to hinder alternative interpretations of gender. Yet, not only many women, but also many men are ambivalent to those gender structures. Hence, the call for the examination of the multiplicity of gendered identities is increasing. We see the elaboration of this multiplicity taken up within studies on men and masculinities. A fast-growing body of research now interrogates social constructions of men and masculinities at work. Collinson and Hearn (1994), for instance, identify five organizational masculinities – authoritarianism, paternalism, entrepreneurialism, informalism and careerism – that are embedded in managerial discourses and practices. The multiplicity of masculinities enables scrutiny of relations between men, relations between men and women and relations between masculinities and femininities (Collinson & Hearn, 1996). As is the case with conceptualizations of gender, differentiated and variable conceptualizations of masculinities are accompanied by notions like hegemonic masculinity, expressing the stable or dominant form of masculinity that stems from deep-rooted unequal power relations between the sexes (Kimmel, 1987). Case studies on men and masculinities are conducted in a variety of empirical settings, ranging from inherently masculine organizations like NASA (Maier, 1997) and coal mines (Wicks, 2002), to organizations less univocally gendered like airlines (Mills, 1998) and insurance companies (Hodgson, 2003). Interesting questions can be posed about new definitions of organizational masculinity. Will those definitions reflect the identities of men who want to combine work and care (Brandth & Kvande, 2002), will they reflect the requirements of the 24-hour economy, emphasizing the need for availability and career commitment, or will they be able to capture the multiple gendered identities and subjectivities that exist simultaneously and shift according to context?

The call for differentiation goes further and questions emerge as to how fundamental gender is as an organizing principle. Gender interferes with other organizing principles and aspects of identity such as ethnicity, age, race, profession and socio-economical background. This interference calls attention to the relative meaning of gender in specific contexts. While the theoretical relevance of intersectionality (Collins, 1993) is widely recognized nowadays, few studies actually investigate how gender interacts with nationality, race, ethnicity and class in the workplace. A notable exception is Bell and Nkomo's (2001) comparative study of professional identities and career experiences of American black and white women. The life stories they collected of black and white women pioneering as female managers illustrate the separate paths these women went to carve out their identities as managers. Bell and Nkomo (2001: 164) give the example of the metaphor of breaking the glass ceiling that can only be used to describe white women's advancement in management ranks. Black women managers face non-transparent concrete walls they can only chip away at slowly or climb over, leaving the walls intact. Another exception constitutes Adib and Guerrier's (2003) article on the experiences of women in hotel work. The narratives of those women illustrate the complexity and ambiguity of women's construction and articulation of their identities at work. Gender intersects with race, ethnicity, nationality and class, not by adding up differences, but rather through contextual negotiations of shifting and simultaneous, fluid identities.

Another major challenge is posed by issues of globalization. The Eurocentrism and Anglocentrism noted earlier mean that this field of research has hitherto largely neglected the impact of postcolonial women's movements on work and organization, and also failed to recognize the organizational realities of 'Third World' women and their relations with 'First World' women. This body of literature in organization studies has not kept pace with the discussions of positions of women in the global economy that feature in disciplines like sociology, anthropology and political science. So, there is a lot to be learned from the increasing amount of research that questions how gender works in the world economic system. Enloe's (1989: 16) classic work unravels the complicated power processes that place men at the top of international hierarchies, but do not render women passive victims of the international politics of the multinationals in the banana, tourist or garment industries. She states that women of different classes and different ethnic groups make their own calculations in order to cope with or benefit from those industries and the international political system around them (1989: 198). Likewise, studies on women working in Mexican *maquiladoras* (Cravey, 1998), the garment sector in Bangladesh (Dannecker, 2000) and on Filipino women working as domestic servants abroad (Parreñas, 2002) show how women workers are exploited, often for the benefit of other women wearing the clothes and employing the nannies and maids. This research examines not only how hegemonic power relations privilege men and affluent women and sustain the exploitation of women workers, but also analyzes how women workers find ways to resist and subvert their exploitation (Ong, 1991).

Differentiated conceptualizations of gender can also help in thinking about how gender can be done differently in organizations. Now that so much effort has gone into understanding how gender is done in organizations, these insights might be taken one step further to suggest interventions in and transformations of the gendering processes. A consequence of the duality of gender and organizations is that to change gendering processes means to change organization processes. To do gender differently therefore requires fundamental innovations in organizations. These innovations may link up with contemporary transformations in organizations toward participation, networking and cooperation, but cannot be reduced to them. A gender perspective needs to be integrated in those transformations explicitly in order to initiate changes in the gendered character of organizational structures and cultures. What is needed in this respect is a framework that balances between counteracting systematic gender inequalities and revealing and appreciating variation and diversity in gender relations in organizations, without privileging one or the other. The development of such a framework that can contribute to doing gender differently is a major challenge for future work in the gender and organizations field and might be the giant leap longed for.

REFERENCES

Aaltio, I., & Mills, A. (2002). *Gender, identity and the culture of organizations*. London: Routledge.

Acker, J. (1990). Hierarchies, jobs, bodies: A theory of gendered organizations. *Gender & Society, 4*(2), 139–58.

Acker, J. (1992). Gendering organizational theory. In A. J. Mills & P. Tancred (Eds), *Gendering organizational analysis* (pp. 248–260). Newbury Park, CA: Sage.

Acker, S. (1989). *Teachers, gender and education*. London: Falmer.

Adib, A., & Guerrier, Y. (2003). The interlocking of gender with nationality, race, ethnicity and class: The narratives of women in hotel work. *Gender, Work & Organization, 10*(4), 413–32.

Ahl, H. (2004). *The scientific reproduction of gender inequality*. Malmö: Liber.

Alvesson, M., & Billing, Y. Due (1997). *Understanding gender and organizations*. London: Sage.

Anker, R. (1997). Theories of occupational segregation by sex: An overview. *International Labour Review, 136*(3), 315–40.

Barron, R. D., & Norris, G. M. (1976). Sexual divisions and the dual labor market. In D. L. Barker & S. Allen (Eds), *Dependence and exploitation in work and marriage* (pp. 47–69). London: Longman.

Becker, G. (1971). *The economics of discrimination*. Chicago: University of Chicago Press.

Bell, E., & Nkomo, S. (2001). *Our separate ways*. Boston: Harvard Business School Press.

Benschop, Y., Brouns, M., & de Bruijn, J. (1998). From inequality to pluriformity: Thinking about gender, work and organisations. In G. Evers, B. van Hees & J. Schippers

(Eds), *Work, Organisation and Labour in Dutch Society* (pp. 199–223). Dordrecht: Kluwer.

Benschop, Y., & Doorewaard, H. (1998a). Covered by equality: The gender subtext of organizations. *Organization Studies, 19*(5), 787–805.

Benschop, Y., & Doorewaard, H. (1998b). Six of one and half a dozen of the other: The gender subtext of Taylorism and team-based work. *Gender, Work & Organization, 5*(1), 5–18.

Benschop, Y., & Meihuizen, H. E. (2002). Keeping up gendered appearances: Representations of gender in financial annual reports. *Accounting, Organizations and Society, 27*, 611–36.

Billing, Y. Due, & Alvesson, M. (2000). Questioning the notion of feminine leadership: A critical perspective on the gender labeling of leadership. *Gender, Work & Organization, 7*(3), 144–57.

Brandth, B., & Kvande, E. (2002). Reflexive fathers: Negotiating parental leave and working life. *Gender, Work & Organization, 9*(2), 186–203.

Brewis, J., & Grey, C. (1994). Re-eroticizing the organization: An exegesis and critique. *Gender, Work & Organization, 1*(2), 67–82.

Brewis, J., & Linstead, S. (2000). *Sex, work and sex work: Eroticizing organization.* London: Routledge.

Brouns, M. (1993). *De homo-economicus als winkeldochter: Theorieën over arbeid, macht en sekse* (Theories of labor, power and sex). Amsterdam: SUA.

Brouns, M. (1995). Kernconcepten en debatten. In M. Brouns, M. Verloo & M. Grünell, *Vrouwenstudies in de jaren negentig* (Women's studies in the '90s, pp. 29–51). Bussum: Coutinho.

Bruni, A., Gherardi, S., & Poggio, B. (2004). Entrepreneur-mentality, gender and the study of women entrepreneurs. *Journal of Organizational Change Management, 17*(3), 256–68.

Calás, M. B., & Smircich, L. (1996). From 'The Woman's' point of view: Feminist approaches to organization studies. In S. Clegg, C. Hardy & W. Nord (Eds), *Handbook of organization studies* (pp. 218–57). London: Sage.

Cockburn, C. (1983). *Brothers. Male dominance and technological change.* London: Pluto.

Cockburn, C. (1991). *In the way of women: men's resistance to sex equality in organizations.* Ithaca, NY: IRL Press.

Collins, P. H. (1993). Towards a new vision: Race, class and gender as categories of analysis and connection. In P. H. Collins, *Race, sex, class, I* (pp. 25–46). Memphis, TE: University of Memphis, The Center of Research on Women.

Collinson, D., & Hearn, J. (1994). Naming men as men: Implications for work, organization and management. *Gender, Work & Organization, 1*(1), 2–22.

Collinson, D., & Hearn, J. (1996). *Men as managers, Managers as men.* London: Sage.

Collinson, D., Knights, D., & Collinson, M. (1990). *Managing to discriminate.* London: Routledge.

Connell, R.W. (1987). *Gender and power.* Stanford, CA: Stanford University Press.

Correll, S. (2001). Gender and the career choice process: The role of biased self-assessments. *American Journal of Sociology, 106*(6), 1691–730.

Cravey, A. (1998). *Women and work in Mexico's maquiladoras.* Lanham, MD: Rowan & Littlefield.

Crompton, R. (1997). *Women and work in modern Britain.* Oxford: Oxford University Press.

Crompton, R., & Harris, F. (1998). Explaining women's employment patterns: 'Orientations to work' revisited. *British Journal of Sociology, 49*(1), 118–36.

Cross, S., & Bagilhole, B. (2002). Girls' jobs for the boys? Men, masculinities and non-traditional occupations. *Gender, Work & Organization, 9*(2), 204–29.

Crenshaw, K. (1997). Intersectionality and identity politics: Learning from violence against women of color. In M. Shanley & U. Narayan, *Reconstructing political theory* (pp. 178–93). University Park, PA: Pennsylvania State University Press.

Dannecker, P. (2000). Collective action, organization building, and leadership: Women workers in the garment sector in Bangladesh. *Gender and Development, 8*(3), 31–9.

Davis, K. (1991). Critical sociology and gender relations. In K. Davis, M. Leijenaar & J. Oldersma (Eds), *The gender of power* (pp. 65–86). London: Sage.

Deaux, K. (1993). Commentary: Sorry, wrong number – A reply to Gentile's call. *Psychological Science, 4*, 125–6.

De Cieri, H., Holmes, B., Abbott, J., & Pettit, T. (2005). Achievements and challenges for work-life balance strategies in Australian organizations. *International Journal of Human Resource Management, 16*(1), 90–103.

Den Dulk, L. (2001). *Work-family arrangements in organizations.* Amsterdam: Rozenberg.

Dickens, L. (1998). What HRM means for gender equality. *Human Resource Management Journal, 8*(1), 23–40.

Dickens, L. (1999). Beyond the business case: A three-pronged approach to equality action. *Human Resource Management Journal, 9*(1), 9–19.

Drew, E., Emerek, R., & Mahon, E. (1998). *Women, work and the family in Europe.* London: Routledge.

Eagly, A. H., Johannesen-Schmidt, M. C., & Van Engen, M. L. (2003). Transformational, transactional, and laissez-fare leadership styles: A meta-analysis comparing women and men. *Psychological Bulletin, 129*(4), 569–91.

Eagly, A. H., & Johnson, B. T. (1990). Gender and leadership style: A meta-analysis. *Psychological Bulletin, 108*(2), 233–56.

Enloe, C. (1989). *Bananas, beaches & bases.* Berkeley, CA: University of California Press.

Evetts, J. (1996). *Gender and career in science and engineering.* Bristol: Taylor & Francis.

Fagan, C. (2001). Time, money and the gender order: Work orientations and working-time preferences in Britain. *Gender, Work & Organization, 8*(3), 239–65.

Ferguson, K. (1984). *The feminist case against bureaucracy.* Philadelphia: Temple University Press.

Fletcher, J. (1994). Castrating the female advantage: Feminist standpoint research and management science. *Journal of Management Inquiry, 3*(1), 74–82.

Fraser, N. (1989). *Unruly practices: Power, discourse and gender in contemporary social theory.* Oxford: Polity.

Frederiksen-Goldsen, K. I., & Scharlach, A. E. (2001). *Families and work. New directions in the twenty-first century.* Oxford: Oxford University Press.

Gati, I., Givon, M., & Osipow, S. H. (1995). Gender differences in career decision making: The content and structure of preferences. *Journal of Counseling Psychology, 42*(2), 204–16.

Gender, Work & Organization (2003). Special issue on gender and academe, *10*(2).

Gentile, D. A. (1993). Just what are sex and gender anyway? A call for a new terminilogical standard. *Psychological Science, 4*, 120–2.

Geurts, S., Haris, T., Demerouti, E., Dikkers, J., & Kompier, M. (2002). Reeks werk en privé. Waar werk en privé elkaar raken (Series work and private life: When work and private life meet). *Gedrag en Organisatie, 15*(3), 163–83.

Gherardi, S. (1994). The gender we think, the gender we do in our everyday organizational lives. *Human Relations, 47*(6), 591–610.

Gherardi, S. (1995). *Gender, symbolism and organizational culture.* London: Sage.

Giddens, A. (1984). *The constitution of society.* Cambridge: Polity.

Glass, J. L., & Finley, A. (2002). Coverage and effectiveness of family-responsive workplace policies. *Human Resource Management Review, 12*(3), 313–37.

Hakim, C. (1996). *Key issues in women's work.* London: Athlone.

Hakim, C. (2000). *Work-lifestyle choices in the 21st century: Preference theory.* Oxford: Oxford University Press.

Harding, S. (1986). *The science question in feminism.* Ithaca, NY: Cornell University Press.

Hartmann, H. (1981). The unhappy marriage of Marxism and feminism: Towards a more progressive union. In L. Sargent (Ed.), *Women and revolution* (pp. 1–41). Boston, MA: South End Press.

Hearn, J. (1998). On ambiguity, contradiction and paradox in gendered organizations. *Gender, Work & Organization*, 5(1), 1–4.

Hearn, J., & Parkin, W. (1987). *'Sex' at 'work'. The power and paradox of organisation sexuality*. New York: St Martin's Press.

Hearn, J., & Parkin, W. (2001). *Gender, sexuality and violence in organizations*. London: Sage.

Helgesen, S. (1990). *The female advantage*. New York: Doubleday Currency.

Hochschild, A. (1997). *The time bind*. New York: Metropolitan Books.

Hodgson, D. (2003). Taking it like a man: Masculinity, subjection, and resistance in the selling of life insurance. *Gender, Work & Organization*, 10(1), 1–21.

Jacobs, J. A., & Lim, S. T. (1995). Trends in occupational and industrial sex segregation in 56 countries, 1960-1980. In J. Jacobs (Ed.), *Gender inequality at work* (pp. 259–94). Thousand Oaks, CA: Sage.

Jong, A. de (1985). *De positie van vrouwen bij een grote bank*. (The position of women in a large bank). Rotterdam: Erasmus University.

Kanter, R. M. (1977). *Men and women of the corporation*. New York: Basic Books.

Kimmel, M. S. (1987). *Changing men*. Newbury Park, CA: Sage.

Klenke, K. (1993). Meta-analytic studies of leadership: Added insights or added paradoxes. *Current Psychology*, 12(4), 326–43.

Komter, A. (1990). *De macht van de dubbele moraal* (The power of the double standard). Amsterdam: Van Gennep.

Konrad, A. M., & Cannings, K. (1997). The effects of gender role congruence and statistical discrimination on managerial advancement. *Human Relations*, 50(10), 1305–28.

Konrad, A., & Mangel, R. (2000). The impact of work-life programs on firm productivity. *Strategic Management Journal*, 21, 1225–37.

Konrad, A. M., Ritchie, J. E., Lie, P., & Corrigall, E. (2000). Sex differences and similarities in job attribute preferences: A meta-analysis. *Psychological Bulletin*, 26(4), 593–641.

Korvajärvi, P. (2002). Locating gender neutrality in formal and informal aspects of organizational cultures. *Culture and Organization*, 8(2), 101–15.

Lee-Treweek, G. (1997). Women, resistance and care: An ethnographic study of nursing work. *Work, Employment & Society*, 11(1), 47–64.

Lewis, S., & Lewis, J. (Eds) (1996). *The work-family challenge*. London: Sage.

Liff, S., & Wajcman, J. (1996). 'Sameness' and 'difference' revisited: Which way forward for equal opportunity initiatives? *Journal of Management Studies*, 33(1), 79–95.

Lorber, J. (1994). Guarding the gates: The micropolitics of gender. In J. Lorber, *Paradoxes of gender* (pp. 225–52). New Haven, CT: Yale University Press.

Maddock, S. (1999). *Challenging women*. London: Sage.

Maier, M. (1997). 'We have to make a MANagement decision': Challenger and the dysfunctions of corporate masculinity. In P. Prasad, A. J. Mills, M. Elmes, & A. Prasad (Eds), *Managing the organizational melting pot: Dilemmas of workplace diversity* (pp. 226–54). Thousand Oaks, CA: Sage.

Mainiero, L. A. (1989). *Office romance: Love, power and sex in the workplace*. New York: Rawson Associates.

Metcalfe, B., & Linstead, A. (2003). Gendering teamwork: Re-writing the feminine. *Gender, Work & Organization*, 10(1), 94–119.

Mills, A. J. (1995). Man/aging subjectivity, silencing diversity: Organizational imagery in the airline industry – the case of British Airways. *Organization*, 2(2), 243–69.

Mills, A. J. (1997). Duelling discourses – desexualization versus eroticism in the corporate framing of female sexuality in the British airline industry 1945–1960. In P. Prasad et al. (Eds), *Managing the organizational melting pot* (pp. 171–98). Thousand Oaks, CA: Sage.

Mills, A. J. (1998). Cockpits, hangars, boys and galleys: Corporate masculinities and the development of British Airways. *Gender, Work & Organization*, 5(3), 172–88.

Mills, A. J. (2002). History/herstory: An introduction to the problems of studying the gendering of organizational culture over time. In I. Aaltio & A. J. Mills (Eds), *Gender, identity and the culture of organizations* (pp. 115–36). London: Routledge.

Mills, A. J. & Tancred, P. (Eds) (1992). *Gendering organizational analysis*. Newbury Park, CA: Sage.

Mohanty, C. T., Russo, A., & Torres, L. (1991). *Third world women and the politics of feminism*. Bloomington: Indiana University Press.

Moi, T. (1989). Patriarchal thought and the drive of knowledge. In T. Brennan (Ed.), *Between feminism and psychoanalysis* (pp. 4–10). London: Routledge.

Oakes, L., & Hammond, T. (1995). Biting the epistemological hand: Feminist perspectives on science and their implications for accounting research. *Critical Perspectives on Accounting*, 6(1), 49–75.

Oakley, A. (1972). *Sex, gender and society*. London: Temple Smith.

Ong, A. (1991). The gender and labor politics of postmodernity. *Annual Review of Anthropology*, 20, 279–309.

Ott, M. (1985). *Assepoesters en kroonprinsen: een onderzoek naar de minderheidspositie van agents en verplegers* (Cinderellas and crown princes: A study of the minority position of police officers and nurses). Amsterdam: SUA.

Parasuraman, S., & Greenhaus, J. H. (2002). Toward reducing some critical gaps in work-family research. *Human Resource Management Review*, 12, 299–312.

Parreñas, R. (2002). *Servants of globalization: Women, migration and domestic work*. Stanford, CA: Stanford University Press.

Plantenga, J., & Hansen, J. (1999). Assessing equal opportunities in the European Union. *International Labour Review*, 138(4), 351–79.

Poggio, B. (2000). Between bytes and bricks: Gender cultures in work contexts. *Economic and Industrial Democracy*, 21(3), 381–402.

Powell, G. N. (1999). *Handbook of gender and work*. Thousand Oaks, CA: Sage.

Powell, G. N., & Foley, S. (1998). Something to talk about: Romantic relationships in organizational settings. *Journal of Management*, 24(3), 421–48.

Powell, G. N., & Graves, L. M. (2003). *Women and men in management* (3rd edn). Thousand Oaks, CA: Sage.

Prasad, A., & Prasad, P. (2002). Otherness at large: Identity and difference in the new globalized organizational landscape. In I. Aaltio & A. J. Mills (Eds), *Gender, identity and the culture of organizations* (pp. 57–71). London: Routledge.

Pringle, R. (1988). *Secretaries talk*. London: Verso.

Proctor, I., & Padfield, M. (1999). Work orientations and women's work: A critique of Hakim's theory of the heterogeneity of women. *Gender, Work & Organization*, 6(3), 152–62.

Reskin, B. F. (1998). *The realities of affirmative action in employment*. Washington, DC: American Sociological Association.

Reskin, B., & Padavic, I. (1994). *Women and men at work*. Thousand Oaks, CA: Pine Forge Press.

Reskin, B. F., & Roos, P. A. (1990). *Job queues, gender queues*. Philadelphia: Temple University Press.

Rich, B. L. (1995). Explaining feminization in the US banking industry. *Sociological Perspectives*, 38(3), 357–80.

Roos, P. A. (1985). *Gender and work: A comparative analysis of industrial societies*. New York: State University of New York Press.

Rosaldo, M. Z. (1980). The use and abuse of anthropology: Reflections on feminism and cross-cultural understanding. *Signs*, 5(3), 389–417.

Rosener, J. D. (1990). Ways women lead: The command-and-control leadership style associated with men is not the only way to succeed. *Harvard Business Review*, 68(6), 119–25.

Savage, M., & Witz, A. (1992). *Gender and bureaucracy*. Oxford: Blackwell.

Schwarzer, A. (1976). *Der kleine Unterschied und seine grossen Folgen* (The small difference with the big consequences). Frankfurt am Main: Fischer.

Scott, J. (1986). Gender: A useful category of historical analysis. *American Historical Review*, 91(5), 1053–75.

Scott, J. (1988). Deconstructing equality-versus-difference. *Feminist Studies*, 14(1), 33–50.

Stivers, C. (1993). *Gender images in public administration*. Newbury Park, CA: Sage.

Stockdale, M. S. (Ed.) (1996). *Sexual harassment in the workplace*. Thousand Oaks, CA: Sage.

Tienari, J., Quack, S., & Theobald, H. (2003). Organizational reforms, 'ideal workers' and gender orders: A cross-societal comparison. *Organization Studies, 23*(2), 249–80.

Tijdens, K. (1989). *Automatisering en vrouwenarbeid* (Computerization and women's work). Utrecht: Jan van Arkel.

Timmerman, G., & Bajema, C. (2000). The impact of organizational culture on perceptions and experiences of sexual harassment. *Journal of Vocational Behavior, 57*(2), 188–205.

Tinker, T., & Neimark, M. (1987). The role of annual reports in gender and class contradictions at general motors 1917–1976. *Accounting, Organisations and Society, 12*(1), 71–88.

Truss, C. (1999). Human resource management: Gendered terrain? *International Journal of Human Resource Management, 10*(2), 180–200.

Unger, R. K., & Crawford, M. (1993). Commentary: Sex and gender – The troubled relationship between terms and concepts. *Psychological Science, 4*, 122–4.

Van Engen, M. L., & Willemsen, T. (2000). *Gender and leadership styles: A meta-analysis of research published in the 1990s*. Tilburg: WORC.

Walby, S. (1986). *Patriarchy at Work: patriarchal and capitalist relations in employment*. Cambridge: Polity.

Walby, S. (1990). *Theorizing patriarchy*. Oxford: Blackwell.

Watts, M., & Rich, J. (1993). Occupational sex segregation in Britain 1979–1989. *Cambridge Journal of Economics, 17*(2), 159–77.

Webb, J. (1997). The politics of equal opportunity. *Gender, Work & Organization, 4*(3), 159–67.

Webster, J. (1996). *Shaping Women's Work: Gender, employment and information technology*. London: Longman.

Webster, J. (2004). Digitising inequality: The cul-de-sac of women's work in European services. *New Technology, Work and Employment, 19*(3), 160–76.

Weichselbaumer, D., & Winter-Ebmer, R. (2003). *A meta-analysis of the international gender wage gap* (Discussion Paper No. 4127). London: Centre for Economic Policy Research: www.cepr.org/pubs/dps/DP4127.asp (Accessed 6 June 2005).

West, C., & Zimmerman, D. (1987). Doing gender. *Gender and Society, 1*(2), 125–51.

Wicks, D. (2002). Institutional bases of identity construction and reproduction: The case of underground coal mining. *Gender, Work & Organization, 9*(3), 308–37.

Xie, Y., & Schauman, K. A. (2003). *Women in science: career processes and outcomes*. Cambridge, MA: Harvard University Press.

12

Men, Masculinities and Workplace Diversity/Diversion

Power, Intersections and Contradictions

JEFF HEARN AND DAVID COLLINSON

In a recent research interview the chief HRM manager of a large global company that is prominent in favouring diversity management, rather than gender equality or equal opportunities as its management strategy, stated:

> We should aim at benefiting from diversity. There is not just the word 'diversity' but also the issue of gaining benefits. You are right that if we have total diversity it may lead nowhere, we will never arrive at the conclusion. One needs to have some realism here. To summarize the three main business reasons why we think diversity is important I would say that first, we want to encourage creativity in our organization. Second, we need to better understand our customers. And third, we want to have an inclusive working environment allowing us to expand our pool of potential recruits. Our staff should enjoy working for this company.

The interview continued:

> Q: What kind of gender policies do you have in your organization?
> A: I'm tempted to say that this conversation will be very short if we discuss this issue. Let me rephrase the question. Why would you have gender policies in the first place?
> Q: Well, what I'm asking is that …
> A: Yes, yes, but in our culture, everyone is equal and there isn't a need for such policies. Whether this is the reality, whether the practices promote equality is then another story. [Jabbing his finger at the woman interviewer] You shouldn't look at gender policies but practices. That's the real issue. (Hearn & Piekkari, 2005: 441)

Theories and practices of diversity, diversity in organizations and diversity management are ways of connecting different social relations with each other. Following the diverse social movements of the 1960s and 1970s, there has been a host of initiatives in diversity management in workplaces, many of them practical and policy in orientation (Esty, Griffin & Schorr-Hirsh, 1995; Kossek & Lobel, 1996; Loden & Rosener, 1991). These have often addressed how to 'manage' diversity rather than the impact of social movements on organizations. However, it remains an open question to what extent a focus on 'diversity', in its various forms, necessarily and specifically addresses gender relations in general and in particular, the gendering of men.

In this chapter we discuss the implications of gendering men and masculinities for the analysis of both diversity in organizations and management, and diversity management. The chapter approaches this task by way of the following main sections: 'diversity' in critical studies on men and masculinities; men, diversity and power; diverse genderings of men in workplaces and other organizations; men and diversity management; and concluding remarks.

'DIVERSITY' IN CRITICAL STUDIES ON MEN AND MASCULINITIES

Men can now be named as men: there is increasing recognition and analysis of men as gendered people, not genderless humans, classes, managers, workers, unemployed, etc. (Collinson & Hearn, 1994; Hanmer, 1990). Although naming men as gendered people may (or may not) seem obvious, there continues to be a massive avoidance of this in theory and practice – in organizations, managements, academe and elsewhere. The 'noticing' of men as gendered, in both theory and practice, has meant that previously taken-for-granted powers and authority of men, social practices of men and ways of being men can be considered much more problematic. While these gendered processes may not yet be much more negotiable, they can at least be recognized as more open to debate. Men and masculinities are more talked about than ever before, yet it is less clear what being a man is and how men will be in the future.

The gendering of men in contemporary societies has arisen from several sources and directions. First, there have been major gendered socio-economic changes at home, work and elsewhere impacting on men, so that men can no longer rely on their traditional authority being unchallenged. A crucial aspect of such change is the impact of feminism. Questions have been asked by feminists about all aspects of men and men's actions from feminist empirical studies of men (Cockburn, 1983; 1991), theoretical consolidations regarding men (hooks, 1984; O'Brien, 1981) to feminist (Friedman & Sarah, 1982) or mixed (Chapman & Rutherford, 1988; Hearn and Morgan, 1990) conferences on men. Various feminist initiatives focus on different aspects of men and suggest different analyses and ways forward for men (Gardiner, 2001; Schacht & Ewing, 1998; Segal, 1990).

Feminist theory and practice has increasingly highlighted the importance of diversity of women, and thus of men too.

Additionally, men have been named through gay movements and queer politics (Beemyn & Eliason, 1996; Plummer, 1981; 1992; Weeks, 1977/1990). While generalizing about these critiques is difficult, they emphasize the desirability of (some) men to each other, public recognition of men through same-sex desire, and the associated or implied critique of heterosexual men's practices. They both complement and sometimes conflict with some feminist analyses (Edwards, 1994), and also place diversity amongst men centre stage.

The focus on men and masculinities has also come from some men's explicit relations and responses to feminism (Brod, 1987; Connell, 1987; 1995; Digby, 2000; Hearn, 1987; 1992; Kimmel, Hearn & Connell, 2005). These include profeminist or anti-sexist responses, as well as work that is ambiguous in relation to feminism or even anti-feminist in perspective. Again men are shown to be diverse, both in terms of relations with feminism and in being or not being explicitly engaged in such relations. There is a further range of critical, more or less gendered perspectives that have directly or indirectly problematized men and masculinities. These include postcolonialism, critical race theory, post-structuralism, postmodernism, globalization and transnational studies, most of which stress diversities amongst men.

There are as many ways of studying men as there are versions of social science, ranging from analysis of masculine psychology to societal and structural analyses; from detailed ethnographies of men's activity and constructions of specific masculinities in specific discourses to analyses of men in global contexts. Our approach here argues for interdisciplinary Critical Studies on Men (CSM) (Hearn, 1997) that are historical, cultural, relational, materialist, deconstructive, anti-essentialist studies on men (Connell, Hearn & Kimmel, 2005). The notion of men is not to be essentialized and reified, or derived from a fixed, inner core or traits, as in some 'men's studies'. CSM are: on men; explicitly gendered; critical; by women and men, separately or together.

In CSM 'men' is seen as a social category, and distinctions are made between men, masculinities and men's practices, both individual and collective. CSM have brought the theorizing of men and masculinities into sharper relief, making them explicit objects of theory and critique. In critiquing sex role theory (Eichler, 1980), the pluralizing of masculinity to masculinities in the late 1970s and early 1980s has been an important advance. Increasingly, different masculinities are interrogated in the plural, not the singular – hegemonic, complicit, subordinated, marginalized, resistant. In a key article Carrigan, Connell and Lee (1985: 586) wrote:

> What emerges from this line of argument [on heterosexual–homosexual ranking of masculinity] is the very important concept of *hegemonic masculinity*, not as 'the male role', but as a particular variety of masculinity to which others – among them young and effeminate as well as homosexual men – are subordinated. It is particular groups of men, not men in general, who are oppressed within patriarchal sexual relations, and whose situations are related in different ways to the overall logic of the subordination of women to men. A consideration of homosexuality thus provides the beginnings of a dynamic conception of masculinity as a structure of social relations. (Emphasis in original)

A decade later in *Masculinities*, Connell (1995) discusses hegemonic masculinity in more depth. He notes that hegemonic masculinity is open to challenge and possible change, and now defines it slightly differently as:

> the configuration of gender practice which embodies the currently accepted answer to the problem of legitimacy of patriarchy, which guarantees (or is taken to guarantee) the dominant position of men and the subordination of women. (p. 77)

Hegemonic masculinity can thus be seen as a political category, an aspiration, that can never be fulfilled. Masculinity, hegemonic or not, comprises signs, practices and performances that obscure contradictions.

The concept of masculinities has been very important, even though commentators use the term differently, to serve several definite academic and political purposes. Perhaps above all, recent studies have foregrounded questions of power. There is lively current debate on the limitations not only of hegemonic masculinities (Collinson & Hearn, 2005), but also of the very idea of 'masculinities', including around the confusions of different usages of the term (Donaldson, 1993; Whitehead, 2001). The very concept of 'masculinity/masculinities' has been critiqued for its ethnocentrism, historical specificity, false causality, possible psychologism and conceptual vagueness (Hearn, 1996b; 2004). Thus it may be more precise to talk of men's individual and collective practices, or men's identities or discourses on or of men, rather than the gloss 'masculinities'.

There is also concern with more precise specifications of men's individual and collective practices within gendered globalizations or glocalizations. Recent critical research on men has moved towards more international, transnational and global perspectives, away from the focus on the Western world and individual nations, and towards the South and transnational processes (Cleaver, 2002; Connell, 1993; 1998; Morrell, 2001; Morrell & Swart, 2005; Ouzgane & Coleman, 1998; Pease & Pringle, 2001), as in such transnational categories as in 'global business masculinity' (Connell, 1998), and 'men of the world' (Hearn, 1996a).

MEN, POWER AND DIVERSITY
IN WORKPLACES

These general issues of men, power and diversity are relevant in analysing men and masculinities in workplaces, and diversity and diversity management. Diverse men and masculinities inhabit and are located in diverse organizations, from large corporates to small enterprises. Studies of masculinity have often underestimated the significance of organizations as sites for the production and reproduction of men's power and masculinities, even though workplace issues such as organizational control, decision making, remuneration and culture crucially reflect and reinforce masculine material discursive practices. Men and masculinities are formed and constructed in work processes of control, collaboration, innovation, competition, conformity, resistance and contradiction. As entrepreneurs, innovators, owners, board members, managers, supervisors, team leaders, administrators, trade unionists, service providers, manual workers and unemployed workers, men have been prominent in the formation, development and change of organizations.

Many studies have made explicit the gendering of men and masculinities in workplaces. Emphasizing paid work as a central source of men's identity, status and power, feminist organizational studies have demonstrated how 'most organizations are saturated with masculine values' (Burton, 1991: 3). They have critically analysed the centrality of masculine models of lifetime, full-time, continuous employment and shown how masculine assumptions are embedded in organizational structures, cultures and practices. For many men, employment provides resources and symbolic benefits that mutually reinforce their power and authority at 'work' and 'home'. Men have been shown to exercise control over women, through job segregation, discrimination, pay inequities and harassment.

Organizational studies focusing on men include those on relations of bureaucracy, men and masculinities (Bologh, 1990; Morgan, 1996); transformations in managerial masculinities (Roper, 1991; 1994); the continuing numerical dominance of men, especially at the highest levels (Davidson & Burke, 2000; Vinnicombe, 2000); managerial identity formation processes (Kerfoot & Knights, 1993); and masculine models, stereotypes and symbols in management. Men, especially in mixed working situations, like other 'members of dominant and status identity groups typically display more aggressive nonverbal behaviours, speak more often, interrupt others more often, state more commands and have more opportunity to influence' (Merrill-Sands et al., 2003: 334).[1]

In our own work on men and masculinities we have explored historical relations of men and management in reproducing patriarchies (Collinson & Hearn, 1996a; Hearn, Kovalainen & Tallberg, 2002); reconceptualizing management–labour relations as interrelations of masculinities (Collinson, 1992); men managers' routine discrimination against women in selection (Collinson, Knights & Collinson, 1990; Hearn & Collinson, 1998) and (mis)management of sexual harassment cases (Collinson & Collinson, 1989); and the possibility of men's non-oppressive, even profeminist management and leadership (Hearn, 1989; 1994). Men at work can also be understood in terms of their domestic situation. For example, some men managers can be seen as working fathers distancing themselves from children and family (Collinson & Hearn, 1994). Such strategies may seem to show corporate commitment, yet reinforce gendered stresses in families, with their own gender power relations (Collinson & Collinson, 1997, 2004).

Among many areas of current debate, three interrelated questions have particularly preoccupied researchers concerned to examine gendered power relations and dominant masculinities in the workplace: the concept of patriarchy; unities and differences between men and between masculinities; and men's subjectivities. In each case, there are tensions between generalizations about and diversities within men and masculinity.

Masculinities operate in contexts of *patriarchy* or patriarchal relations. Patriarchy is understood in this context as men's structural dominance in society. The development of a dynamic conception of masculinities can be understood as part of the feminist and gendered critique of a monolithic conception of patriarchy (Rowbotham, 1979). The notion of masculinities fits well with the move to more differentiated, historically specific analyses of patriarchy (Hearn, 1987; 1992; Walby, 1986; 1990).

Masculinities are not fixed, but may shift over time and place. The focus on multiple masculinities helps in examining the shifting nature of asymmetrical power relations not only between men and women, but also between men in workplaces. Gendered power relations can simultaneously both change yet remain broadly the same. Just as a major issue within feminism has been the relation of commonalities and differences between women, so men can be analysed in terms of *unities and differences*, within patriarchy. In organizations there are tensions between the collective power of men and differentiations amongst men (Collinson & Hearn, 1994; Hearn & Collinson, 1993). Men's gender relations intersect with other social divisions, such as age, class, ethnicity; men's gender power relations are complex, contradictory and diverse. This is exemplified by Barrett's (1996) study of US Navy officers which shows how multiple masculinities co-exist in one organization: aviators emphasized masculinity as risk taking; surface warfare officers prioritized endurance; supply officers prided themselves on technical rationality. The Navy reproduces a dominant masculinity with multiple forms, valuing toughness, perseverance, aggressiveness, rugged heterosexuality, unemotional logic, stoic refusal to complain. Women and gay men serve as the differentiated others, against which heterosexual men construct, project, differentiate and display gendered identity.

The analytical importance of multiplicity and diversity has become clear in studies on the ambiguous, discontinuous, fragmented nature of gendered *selves*, *subjectivities, identities* and *sexualities* within asymmetrical power relations (Kondo, 1990). Difference and its construction, such as by age, class, sexuality, ethnicity, occupation, are important in reproducing gendered asymmetrical power between men and between men and women. Many men seem to be preoccupied with creating and maintaining masculine identities, gendered power and status at work (Collinson, 1992; Willis, 1977). Men's search to construct such identities may draw on organizational resources, discourses and practices. Masculine selves are constantly negotiated and reconstructed in routine workplace interaction through processes of identification and differentiation. These identities may be threatened by factors such as class divisions, unemployment, technology, equal opportunity policies (Cockburn, 1991). At the same time, a recurrent feature of hegemonic and multiple masculinities at work is intense competition between men, partly fuelled by desire to display dominance and validate identity. Yet competitive cultures and practices may render the search for dominance highly precarious, by reproducing material and symbolic insecurities competition sought to overcome. The search to secure clearly defined, coherent identities may, paradoxically, reinforce rather than resolve insecurity (Collinson, 1992).

DIVERSE GENDERINGS OF MEN AND MASCULINITIES IN WORKPLACES

Analysis of men and masculinities in workplaces sheds light on the diverse nature of power relations there (Collinson & Hearn, 2000). Distinctions between hegemonic, complicit and subordinated masculinities suggest that some masculinities (e.g. white, middle-class, middle-aged, heterosexual, Christian, able-bodied) often dominate others (e.g. working-class or gay masculinities). These former masculinities tend to predominate, at least ideologically, in powerful organizational and managerial positions, while others are subordinated. Although many groups of men at work have been researched, some forms of diversity amongst men, such as age and disability, remain underexplored. The diversity of masculinities is partly shaped by different forms and sites of work and masculinity (Collinson & Hearn, 1996b), varying by, for example, industry, class, organizational type.

Home and Work

Although our focus is on organizational workplaces, it is important not to neglect the home as a workplace, and men's continued low participation in domestic work. Feminist studies have highlighted unpaid domestic labour as an important site of gendered work and of men's domination of women. The home is still often not seen as a workplace at all, with domestic tasks unacknowledged as work. Constructions, definitions and understandings of work are both material and ideological: what work is considered to be – in both everyday life and research – is gendered and contested. In this chapter our focus is on organizational workplaces, whilst seeking to be aware of the connections of work in organizations and work at home. In many ways organizational workplaces are built upon unpaid domestic labor (Hearn, 1987; O'Brien, 1981). Gender domination *within* organizations is paralleled by the dominant gender valuing of the public sphere *over* the domestic sphere; there is thus a double gendered domination in dominant constructions of organizations.

Dominant masculinities in the home complement, often in difficult and contradictory ways, the masculinities of employment. On the one hand, the geographical separation of paid work and domestic life may reinforce specific masculinities at home and in the public workplace. On the other hand, for some men, paid work may take over the house and home, via constructions around life vocation, relations with technology, working long hours or maximizing earnings. The erosion of the private sphere by employment is likely to increase with new technologies and corporate attempts to reduce costs. For many managerial and professional workers employed by 'greedy organizations', more demands are being made on domestic time and space. In demonstrating men's obsession with computers in a Cambridge high-tech company, Massey (1993) discussed how paid work dominates space, time and interaction at home. Even when wives persuaded husbands to spend more time with children, the most usual outcome was that games were played by fathers and children on home computers. However, simple associations of dominant masculinities and technology are problematized, with the greater embeddedness of new technologies in both women's and men's everyday lives (Heiskanen & Hearn, 2004).

Class, Status, Hierarchy and Occupation

Initially, critical empirical research on men and masculinities in organizations tended to concentrate on those in subordinate positions, particularly working-class and manual workers. Cockburn's (1983) study of printers reveals how manual skills can be defined as highly masculine (also see Morgan, 2005; Tolson, 1977). Working-class masculinities and masculine solidarities are subject to growing challenge with global economic restructuring (Blum, 2000). Collinson (1988; 1992; 2000) examines how men manual workers construct organizational counter-cultures and working-class masculine identities based on the negation of 'others', such as management (as effeminate and ignorant about the processes of production), office workers (as unproductive 'pen pushers') and women (as manipulative and exploitative). The complex amalgam of resistance, compliance and consent comprising shopfloor sub/counter-cultures is frequently expressed in highly masculine discourses and practices. Collinson shows how class inequalities, cultures and identities are reproduced in routine work practices, reinforcing and structuring masculinities. In workplaces that treat manual workers as 'second class', such men may redefine their identity and dignity within work counter-culture through highly masculine values of being the breadwinner, 'being practical', 'having common sense', 'honesty' and 'independence'. Office work is seen as limiting freedom and masculine identity. While supervisors and managers may take their work home and 'worry about it' in their 'free time', shopfloor workers try to keep a strict separation between 'public' and 'private' life.

Office work has often been ignored as a site of masculinities. Women's clerical work is still not only undervalued but frequently reflects stereotypical 'home-maker' tasks. Men, by contrast, are often employed in relatively well-paid, high-discretion positions that sometimes reflect and reinforce an inflated status as organizational 'breadwinners'. Male-dominated professions and technical occupations such as computer specialists, lawyers and academics are frequently characterized by highly masculine values and assumptions. For example, in insurance sales, men often elevate and exaggerate their organizational contribution to reinforce their power, status and identity at work (Collinson et al., 1990). Despite the work drawing on mental rather than manual skills, masculine mystique abounds. The task is described as a heroic drama in which 'intrepid', 'valiant' men venture into the 'dangerous' world of finance and 'against the odds' return with new business. Men in selling frequently construct an image of self-control and resilience to 'take the knocks' in the aggressive market. Such masculine class images impact on selection criteria resulting in the exclusion of women. Yet closer analysis reveals that this masculine imagery may be misleading. Much work consists of establishing long-term 'business relationships' with intermediaries and agents who recommend services to customers; nurturing this business requires interpersonal skills. After-sales service is central in the sales process, and women working in offices are often key in resolving clients' difficulties to retain product loyalty.

In most workplaces, industries and countries men dominate management. Yet it is managers who exercise formal power in workplaces and men who frequently exercise power over women. Mainstream and more critical management theory, ideology and practice neglect these issues. While various masculinities shape managerial practices, managerial practices also impact on specific masculinities. Pervasive, dominant managerial masculinities take the form of different workplace control practices, such as authoritarianism, careerism, paternalism, entrepreneurialism (Collinson & Hearn, 1994). Kerfoot and Knights (1993) contend that paternalism and strategic management are concrete manifestations of historically shifting forms of masculinity. Arguing that these managerial approaches both reflect and reinforce 'discourses of masculinism', they suggest that 'paternalistic masculinity' and 'competitive masculinity' have the effect of privileging men vis-à-vis women, ranking some men above others, and maintaining as dominant certain forms and practices of masculinity. Managerial masculinities might thus be understood as form(s) of (different) hegemonic masculinities.[2]

Managerial masculinities are also hegemonic within organizations in the sense that those in senior positions enjoy comparatively high salaries and other remuneration packages through secretarial support, share options, company cars, pensions, holiday entitlements and other benefits. Even when they are dismissed, senior managers may receive substantial 'golden handshakes', and poor performance does not seem to prevent re-employment in other managerial positions. On the other hand, there is also some movement towards a 'proletarianization' and reduced security for managers, particularly those in the middle grades, as a result of delayering and business process reengineering.

Sexualities

In addition to diversities by class, status, hierarchy and occupation, other sources of diversity amongst men and masculinities, such as by sexuality, are gaining attention. While many organizations are constructed as asexual (though heteronormative) sites of rationality, they can also be deconstructed as sites of sexuality (Hearn & Parkin, 1995). Indeed heterosexuality and heterosexual men are often the unspoken category in organizational analysis and diversity thinking. Kimmel (1993) contends that 'homophobia' and men's fear of other men is the 'animating condition of the dominant definition of masculinity in America'[3] (p. 135). Bird (1996) argues that through male homosocial, heterosexual interactions, hegemonic masculinity is maintained as the norm to which men are accountable. Male homosociality combines emotional detachment, competitiveness and viewing women as sexual objects, and thus perpetuates hegemonic masculinity, which suppresses subordinate masculinity and reproduces a pecking order among men. Interestingly, the pervasiveness of heterosexuality and homosociability is not contradictory; rather homosociability is often used by hegemonic heterosexual men to exclude others and to reproduce their like.

Men's heterosexuality is often understandable in terms of relations between men (sometimes homosocial relations), as is clear in their use of pin-ups and pornography in workplaces. Images of 'women' are displayed or viewed on screens as signs for contact between men, just as 'women' may figure as currency of conversation, jokes and putdowns in men's socializing (Cockburn, 1983; Collinson, 1988). 'Individual' harassments of women can also sometimes be seen as exchanges between men. Two major, apparently contradictory, aspects to such sexual dynamics in organizations are: pervasiveness and dominance of men's heterosexuality (Collinson & Collinson, 1989); and pervasiveness and dominance of men's homosociability, namely preferring same-gender company and spaces (Hearn, 1985; 1992; Kanter, 1977). The contradiction of these aspects operates in, for example, horseplay, often by and between heterosexually identified men, parodying homosexuality.

Studies have reported on the marginalization and subordination of gay men. Empirical studies in the 1970s and 1980s focused on lesbians' and gay men's experiences in organizations, particularly, though not only, experiences of discrimination and violation (e.g. Bell & Weinberg, 1978; Saghir & Robins, 1973; Schneider, 1984). These were often initially part of campaigns or other political interventions (Beer, Jeffrey & Munyard, 1983; Campaign for Homosexual Equality, 1981; Taylor, 1986). Various studies have examined the more specific experiences of lesbians and gay men in business (Signorile, 1993; Woods & Lucas, 1993), the public sector (Humphries, 2000; Skelton, 1999), the police (Burke, 1993), and the military (Cammermeyer, 1995; Hall, 1995). On the other hand, the UK Gay and Lesbian Census (ID Research, 2001) found that while 15% of lesbians and gay men in the workplace who responded believe their sexuality has hindered their job prospects, a surprisingly large number (43%) had managerial roles. These figures are not fully representative, and do not take account of individuals not 'out' at work.

Racialization, Ethnicity, Culture and Transnationalization

It is often the case that it is those who are subordinated, who are made 'other', who are initially recognized in explicit relation to the social division in question; for example, ethnic minority men, men of colour and black men. There is a large research and policy literature on discrimination against such men compared with ethnic majority or white men. Numerous studies have highlighted racism in organizational and workplace contexts. Research from the Higher Education Statistics Agency shows that black and Asian graduates are twice as likely as white graduates to be unemployed six months after leaving university. Compared with their white counterparts, black and Asian graduates are less successful at all stages of the recruitment process, from the initial application and interview through to job offer (*First Destinations of Students* ..., 2000/01). Two out of every five black and Asian police officers in the UK have made some form of complaint about racism in the force (Blackstock & Rees, 1998). Travis (1998) has reported on problems of racism in the British Home Office with managers accused of engaging in bullying, racist banter, victimization of black staff and discrimination in recruitment and promotion. Racial oppressions and discriminations bring negative health effects (Krieger & Sidney, 1996; Landrine & Klonoff, 1997). 'Accumulations of microaggressions' can affect the self-confidence and self-respect of those targeted (Benokraitis, 1998: 8–10).

The intersection of racial and ethnic disadvantage with gender and masculinities produces complex dynamics. Men's experience of ethnic and racial subordination may contradict their gender advantage relative to women of similar ethnicity or racialization (Edmondson Bell & Nkomo, 2001; McGuire & Reskin, 1993). Men's experience of social subordination may challenge forms of masculinity that assume privilege. Similar contradictions may persist in workplaces in the relations of ethnic minority men, men of colour and black men to white and ethnic majority women, who may be their organizational supervisors and managers. At the same time, there are gradually growing numbers of ethnic minority men, black men and men of colour entering supervision and management, especially lower and middle management in some sectors and countries. All these 'relative marginalizations' by ethnicity and racialization may be compounded by class, nationality, language, religion and other diversities, discriminations and oppressions.

As with heterosexual masculinities, and indeed in some senses men and masculinities more generally, forms of whiteness and white masculinities are characteristically left invisible, taken for granted, assumed but unstated – an absent but present privilege (McIntosh, 1990).[4] Future work needs to extend this focus on diversity; for example, to analyse and critique white masculinities at work, and how they intersect with age, class, nationality and nationalism, racism and racialization, religion, and so on – in effect to deconstruct the dominant (Hearn, 1996a; 2004). Postcolonialism in its many forms challenges unified white Western male positionality. Accordingly, categories of white men, WHAM (White, Heterosexual Able-bodied Men), need to be part of analysis (Hearn & Collinson, 1994).

Multiple workplace masculinities may also be shaped by national and regional cultures. Woodward (1996) reveals how international organizations like the European Commission are gendered bureaucracies with the 'male' norm as dominant and include masculine practices of resistance to female leadership. With the globalization of management, men and masculinities on management in organizations are likely to impact even more. Connell (2001) has critically analysed the form of transnational business masculinity that is increasingly hegemonic and directly connected to patterns of world trade and communication dominated by the West and the global 'North', as opposed to the 'South'.

EVALUATION AND CRITIQUES OF MULTIPLE MASCULINITIES

The term 'multiple masculinities' has become an important concept in exploring the pervasive, diverse and shifting character of men's hegemonic power, culture and identity in workplaces. This emphasis on diversity explores how certain masculinities usually predominate and are privileged in organizations, but they can also take various forms at different times in multiple organizations producing different organizational effects. This term helps to show how organizational and gendered power relations can shift in detail whilst simultaneously remaining asymmetrical in overall structure. It addresses how diverse subjectivities interact with power relations in ambiguous, contradictory or paradoxical ways. Nevertheless, there are a number of possible difficulties with a multiple masculinities approach to diversity.

First, the meaning of 'hegemonic masculinity/multiple masculinities' remains somewhat unclear, vague and imprecise, lacking in definition. Second, the emphasis upon difference and pluralized masculinities could become a new, and perhaps more sophisticated, way of excluding women, of losing women from analysis and politics (Collinson & Hearn, 1994). Third, the term 'multiple masculinities' has been criticized for being merely descriptive of various 'types'. Indeed a focus on difference may collapse into a taxonomy of masculinities and a list of objectified categories of men. Such categorization fails to address either men's lived social experience, or the fluidity, shifting and changing character of all social relations, identities and practices (Kondo, 1990). A fourth criticism is that it presents an overly negative orientation towards men in the workplace (Alvesson & Billing, 1997). We do not agree with this, as discussed elsewhere (Collinson & Hearn, 2005).

A fifth critique, outlined by MacInnes (1998), is that we are witnessing 'the end of masculinity'. For him, masculinity is becoming obsolete in describing contemporary social structures and processes. Against this, an interest in subjectivities in relation to power asymmetries can enhance analysis of workplace power relations by highlighting processes through which structures are negotiated, reproduced and resisted. Finally, notions of 'hegemonic' and 'multiple' masculinity/ies can be criticized for oversimplifying workplace power relations and neglecting their simultaneous, countervailing and contradictory character. Different social divisions cut across asymmetrical power relations in multiple, mutually reinforcing or counterposing ways. Rarely can complex organizational power relations be reduced solely to issues of gender; but equally the neglect of gender, men and masculinity often renders critical analyses of power relations fundamentally flawed.

Thus when applying notions of 'hegemonic' or 'multiple' masculinities to workplaces, their meanings are not always obvious. Masculinities can carry internal contradictions confirming or undermining power and identity. Men often collaborate, cooperate and identify with one another, reinforcing a shared unity;

at the same time, relations between men can be characterized by conflict, competition and self-differentiation, serving to intensify differences and divisions between men. Understanding men and masculinities at work involves examining interconnections between structures and subjectivities. Considering multiple sources of identity and their tensions can assist analysis of cross-cutting power relations in accounts of hegemonic/multiple masculinities that recognize ambiguity and contradiction. Although we acknowledge the validity of several concerns noted above in relation to hegemonic and multiple masculinities, developing sophisticated understandings of workplaces remains pressing – equally in organizational and managerial practice and policy, and in diversity management.

DIVERSITY MANAGEMENT, GENDER EQUALITY AND EQUAL OPPORTUNITIES POLICY

Current debates on diversity and diversity management in organizations and indeed problematizations of diversity need to conceptualize men. Most mainstream approaches to international and transnational management, that one might think are centrally about diversity, are silent on conceptualizing men (Bartlett & Ghoshal, 2000; Holden, 2002; Punnett & Shenkar, 2004; cf. Hearn, 2005). Gender analysis is often absent from mainstream texts and when it is introduced, it is often in a very limited way. For example, discussions of gender in international human resource management are sometimes reduced to questions of women as expatriates (Dowling & Welch, 2004; Harris, 2004; Harzing & Van Ruysseveldt, 2004).

Similarly, studies of diversity frequently neglect issues of power and identity. Foldy (2002) reveals the importance of workplace power dynamics for understanding diversity. She shows how power relations influence identity construction in the context of diversity training, affinity groups and mentoring programmes. Foldy suggests that organizations play a particularly important part in shaping workplace identity by classifying, categorizing, distributing and acculturating individuals and groups. Diversity programmes directly address identity issues and identity in turn is a key site for the reproduction of power relations. On the one hand, by opening up the terrain of identity, diversity programmes invite the possibility of creative change and resistance. Extra-organizational identities like race or gender can be a source of resistance to existing power relations. But diversity programmes that seek to 'empower' employees may also be designed to harness and incorporate the very identities that can otherwise be the basis of resistance in organisations. Foldy's focus on the fundamentally interwoven nature of power, identity and diversity can be usefully developed by a closer analysis of men and masculinity.

To move beyond the mainstream silence, neglect and very partial approach to a wider understanding of diversity, diversity management, HRM, IHRM, and issues of power and superordination more generally, involves analysing men as a social group. Such enquiry includes differences amongst men and their interrelations. Such contradictory diversities regarding men impact upon both the identities of organizational members and organizational cultures. In this sense, diversity management can be understood as part of gendered management, and part of the contradictions within. This involves the simultaneous deconstruction of men/masculinities and management in the context of patriarchy. As managers, men's control and authority may be more contradictory and heterogeneous than it often appears. Delayering and intensification of managerial work may problematize the view that management constitutes the clearest form of hegemonic masculinity (Collinson & Collinson, 1997; 2004). The hierarchical, gendered power of men managers is by no means homogeneous, monolithic or inevitable. Power relations are complex and shifting, sometimes mutually reinforcing, on other occasions cross-cutting with countervailing and contradictory effects.

First, there are contradictions arising from the various divisions and differences within management itself, in terms of hierarchical, spatial and functional differentiations, and tensions between formulation of corporate policy and its implementation. Strategic solutions to management's control problem may compete and be fragmented. Diversity management can be part of these internal divisions and contradictions.

Second, management is set within complex tensions between ownership and control, technological and social relations. Alongside antagonistic relations between capital and labour is a co-existing and contradictory interdependence limiting managerial power. Employers' contradictory demands for both dependable yet disposable workers result in changing emphases, first, upon managerial prerogative and coercion (Scientific Management), and, second, upon worker cooperation and consent (Human Relations) as product and labour market conditions shift. Diversity management is generally understandable as part of the latter strategy. Yet neither of these two strategies can fully reconcile the contradiction between control and coordination in the capital–labour relation. Management control is constrained by its contradictory relationship with labour, and is also highly gendered. Diversity management can also be understood as part of the gendered construction and operation of management, indeed increasingly mainstream management. This involves diversity management being developed as part of (strategic) HRM, alongside and often in distinction from the 'main mission' of supposedly agendered strategic corporate management.

Third, there are contradictions between different men and masculinities. Management differentiates men, both between managers and non-managers, and between different types of managers. Managerial masculinities might be understood as forms of hegemonic masculinity. Contradictions may exist between hegemonic managerial authority and diverse managerial masculinities, as well as between ambitious male managers seeking to purchase their career progress at others' cost. Again diversity management can be implicated in such diverse ways of being men. Differences within and amongst management, men and masculinities may be intertwined with other social differences, such as age, class, ethnicity, locality, nationality, religion.

These interwoven contradictions highlight the complex conditions, processes and consequences of managerial control in the workplace. They question conventional assumptions regarding managerial power and reveal the analytical importance of similarities and differences between men, masculinities and managements. Equally, they consider how the power of 'men as managers' and 'managers as men' is circumscribed in various ways. Yet despite the contradictory conditions and consequences of the exercise of gendered, hierarchical power, men managers' preoccupation with control over both women and labour continues to characterize many routine workplace practices, including diversity management.

In these various complex ways, diversity management can, at one level, be conceptualized as a men's/managerial project. It can be used to downplay gender and men's gender power (as illustrated by the quotation at the beginning of this chapter), and a means of diversion from gender relations by focusing on a 'diversity' that can mean everything, anything or nothing. In another sense, diversity management and programmes might be seen as a contradictory gender project, both incorporating gender and other social divisions into mainstream agendas, and having the potential to be fundamentally deconstructive and threatening to men's hegemonic power. As with multiculturalism (McLaren, 1994), there are various ways of both promoting and conceptualizing diversity management that are less or more challenging to existing power structures, including gender power (Prasad & Mills, 1997; Prasad, Mills, Elmers & Prasad, 1997). And just as Okin (1997) asked, 'Is multiculturalism bad for women?', so we might add 'Is multiculturalism – or diversity – good for men?' – that is, in obscuring men's power and promoting men's dominant interests.

The various approaches to diversity include those based on cognitive-functional, cultural or social differences (Merrill-Sands et al., 2000; 2003). Furthermore, variations in the theory and practice of diversity management overlap with variations in the theory and practice of gender and equality interventions. Thomas and Ely's (1996)[5] and Kirton and Greene's (2000)[6] discussions of alternative, more or less radical approaches to diversity and their possible limitations resonate with Fletcher and Ely's (2003) and Kolb, Fletcher, Meyerson, Merrill-Sands & Ely's (2003) fourfold framework of 'fixing the women', 'celebrating differences', 'creating equal opportunities' and 'revising work culture' that presents various forms of more or less fundamental engagements with gender arrangements (Ely & Foldy, 2003).[7]

Crucially, in these various frameworks there are questions of who constructs 'diversity'? Who defines diversity? Who decides? And which forms of diversity are legitimate (Cockburn, 1991)? This can be seen as part of the interrogation of dominant organizational cultures as part of the long agenda of equal opportunities. It necessitates attention to categories of white men, such as WHAM (white, heterosexual able-bodied men), in analysis and policy. Importantly, one of the most fundamental forms of diversity within organizations arises from hierarchical power differences there, and the diversities amongst men in those hierarchies. Such entrenched diversities are often missing from debates on diversity management.

We can also ask which men and what specific masculinities are favoured and disfavoured in diversity programmes – in their setting up, management and control, and their implementation, consumption and effects. These implications clearly affect both women and men in the organizations concerned. Diversity management and programmes may also provide space for the development of further paradoxes around men and differential forms of power. An example would be the enactment of some men's racism against other men. These contradictions can also be reproduced in the detailed structure and practices of diversity management and diversity programmes, such as the discriminatory practice of asking training programme participants to speak on behalf of a subordinated category, such as 'black people', to which they happen to belong.

Men's power is partly maintained through their commonalities with each other. Typically, men are bound together, not necessarily consciously, by shared interests and meanings, sexuality, socio-economic power and representational privileging. Men's collective power persists partly through the assumption of hegemonic forms of men and masculinities, often white, heterosexual, able-bodied, as the primary form, to the relative exclusion of subordinated men and masculinities. If multiplicity, multiculturalism and diversity amongst men and masculinities are emphasized then there is a danger that other social divisions and power inequalities in organizations are excluded from analysis. There is also a danger that inequalities will only be perceived in terms of some men's disadvantage and with it a failure to appreciate the complexities of these divisions and inequalities. Indeed one of the most fundamental forms of diversity that exists within organizations arises from hierarchical power differences within organizations, and the diversities amongst men in those organizational hierarchies. These entrenched diversities are indeed often missing from debates on diversity and diversity management.

Moreover, hegemonic, subordinated and diverse masculinities change over time, can be shaped by underlying ambiguities, differ according to age, class, ethnicity and other social divisions, and may be central in reproducing these other social divisions. Intersections of gender (men) and other diversities of age, class, culture, disability, religion, language, ethnicity, race, sexuality, are vital to analyse. Yet, an emphasis upon multiplicity in the diversity management project ought not to degenerate into a pluralism that gives insufficient attention to structured patterns of gendered power and inequality. While attention to diversity is certainly needed, this should not be at the expense of retaining the focus on the structured asymmetrical relations of power between men and women. As Cockburn (1991) wrote, a focus upon multiple masculinities should not 'deflect attention from the consistency in men's domination of women at systemic and organizational levels, from the continuation of material, structured inequalities and power imbalances between the sexes' (p. 225). The challenge is to maintain this double focus on difference without neglecting gender and other structural powers (Foldy & Creed, 1999; Holvino, 2001).

CONCLUDING REMARKS

While hegemonic masculinity and multiple masculinities are useful and important concepts in the critical analysis of gender and diversity in the workplace, theoretical and empirical work is necessary to develop these ideas. Several conceptual and theoretical problems remain unresolved within these debates, including the conceptualization of 'masculinity/ies', the ways in which masculinities relate to other elements of power, culture and subjectivity; while recognizing a multiplicity of masculinities, there is a need to retain a focus upon the asymmetrical nature of gendered power relations. A complex view of power as material and discursive helps to explain lived contradictions 'within' different 'types of masculinity' and men themselves as embodied sites of power. This perspective suggests a critical view on diversity management, with a focus on identity as a disruptive contested site, with men and masculinities (or even hegemonic masculinity) thus frequently characterized by contradictions.

These developments may be located more broadly within recent debates on globalization, postcolonialism and men's practices (Banerjee & Linstead, 2001; Holvino, 2003). Focusing on men throws some doubt on the more ambitious claims of globalization theses, not only in their frequently non-gendered analysis but more specifically in the implicit convergence often assumed amongst men and masculinities (Hearn & Parkin, 2001). Transnational and global studies of men continue to show the divergences amongst men, and between women and men. On the one hand, there are privileged global businessmen; on the other hand, non-privileged migrant men with relatively less power. Diversity management needs to engage with these diversities, between privilege and non-privilege, gender, regional location, class and other social divisions. A more far-reaching and structural implication of globalization and postcolonial perspectives is that the growing impact of global Western corporations creates further forms of 'diversity' and inequality between and within regions, localities and genders that are rarely addressed in debates on diversity and diversity management. This is a further, much greater challenge for theory and intervention on men, gender relations and diversity. To do this necessitates deconstructing the dominant at local and global levels (Hearn, 1996a).

Analysis of the changing shape of workplaces, organizations and management is needed. With changing forms of organizing across time, space, cyberspace and cybertime, traditional notions of organizations as relatively geographically isolated in a particular place, are increasingly problematic. Similarly, the notion of organization in relation to transnationalism, globalization, localization and new information and communication technologies is becoming progressively more complex. Organizational workplaces increasingly involve transnational organizations, interorganizational relations, networks, network organizations, net-organizations and virtual organizations. Such historical conditions create many more possible positions of power and diversity for men and masculinities, and hence ways for men, organizations and managements to be reciprocally formed, in a late modern, globalizing and diverging world.

We have reviewed here the gendered diversity of men and masculinities in workplaces. Our approach seeks to challenge men's taken-for-granted dominant power, masculinities and practices in workplaces in general and diversity management in particular. A broad understanding of diversity, diversity management,

HRM and IHRM, and power and superordination needs to address, critique and deconstruct men and masculinities as men as a social group or social category, as differences and their interrelations. This social group includes those forms of diversity of men that arise from hierarchical power differences within work-places, and the diversities amongst men in those positions and hierarchies. Attention to such entrenched diversities is indeed rare in debates on diversity and diversity management. To confront these genderings of men could facilitate less coercive, less divisive workplaces and work practices, fundamental rethinking of the social organization of the gender and domestic division of labour, and transformation of 'men' at 'work'.

NOTES

We are grateful to Alexander Fleishmann and Judith Pringle for comments on earlier drafts of this chapter.

1 Citing Canney Davison and Ward (1999) and Sessa and Jackson (1995).

2 There are many ways in which the authority and status of managers can signify 'men' and vice versa. Cultural processes of signification include the size and position of personal offices; office furniture; the display of pictures and plants; the use or control of computers and other equipment; and the choice of clothing. While business suits appear to have a transnational significance, their particular style, cut and cost are important, not least as a means of managing impressions through 'power dressing' (Collier, 1998; Feldman & Klich, 1991). The colour and style of shirts, braces, shoes, socks and ties (Gibbings, 1990) can carry embodied, context-specific meanings that may reflect and reinforce their organizational hegemony.

3 America here means the United States.

4 Cited in Merrill-Sands et al. (2003: 334–5).

5 Thomas and Ely outline three paradigms: discrimination-and-fairness; access-and-legitimacy; and learning-and-effectiveness.

6 Kirton and Greene discuss liberal (fair equal opportunity, positive action or strong positive action), radical and managing diversity equality initiatives.

7 They also build on similar earlier debates on the long and short agendas of equal opportunities (Cockburn, 1989; Jewson & Mason, 1986).

REFERENCES

Alvesson, M., & Billing, Y. Due (1997). *Understanding gender and organizations.* London: Sage.

Banerjee, S. B., & Linstead, S. (2001). Globalization, multiculturalism and other fictions: Colonialism for the new millenium? *Organization, 8*(4), 683–722.

Barrett, F. (1996). The organizational construction of hegemonic masculinity: The case of the U.S. Navy, *Gender, Work & Organization, 3*(3), 129–42.

Bartlett, C. A., & Ghoshal, S. (2000). *Transnational management: Text, cases and read-ings in cross-border management* (3rd edn). Boston: McGraw-Hill.

Beemyn, B., & Eliason, M. (Eds) (1996). *Queer studies: A lesbian, gay, bisexual and transgender anthology.* New York: New York University Press.

Beer, C. R., Jeffrey, R., & Munyard, T. (1983). *Gay workers: Trade unions and the law.* London: NCCL.

Bell, A. P., & Weinberg, M. S. (1978). *Homosexualities: A study of diversity among men and women.* New York: Simon and Schuster.

Benokraitis, N. J. (1998). *Subtle sexism.* Thousand Oaks, CA: Sage.

Bird, S. (1996). Welcome to the men's club: Homosociality and the maintenance of hegemonic masculinity, *Gender and Society, 10,* 120–32.

Blackstock, C., & Rees, P. (1998). Racism rife in police force, say black police. *Independent on Sunday,* 26 April: 5.

Blum, J. A. (2000). Degradation without deskilling: Twenty-five years in the San Francisco shipyards. In M. Burawoy, J. A. Blum, S. George, Z. Gille, T. Gowan, L. Haney, M. Klawiter, S. H. Lopez, S. Ó. Riain & M. Thayer (Eds), *Global ethnography: Forces, connections and imaginations in a postmodern world* (pp. 106–36). Berkeley, CA: University of California Press.

Bologh, R. W. (1990). *Love or greatness? Max Weber and masculine thinking – A feminist inquiry.* London: Unwin Hyman.

Brod, H. (Ed.) (1987). *The making of masculinities. The new men's studies.* London and Boston: Allen and Unwin.

Burke, M. E. (1993). *Coming out of the blue: British police officers talk about their lives in 'The Job' as lesbians, gays and bisexuals.* London and New York: Cassell.

Burton, C. (1991). *The promise and the price.* Sydney: Allen and Unwin.

Cammermeyer, M. (1995). *Serving in silence.* Harmondsworth: Penguin.

Campaign for Homosexual Equality (1981). *What about the gay workers?* London: CHE.

Canney Davison, S., & Ward, K. (1999). *Leading international teams.* London: McGraw-Hill.

Carrigan, T., Connell, R. W., & Lee, J. (1985). Toward a new sociology of masculinity. *Theory and Society, 14*(5), 551–604.

Chapman, R., & Rutherford, J. (Eds) (1988). *Male order: Unwrapping masculinity.* London: Lawrence and Wishart.

Cleaver, F. (Ed.) (2002). *Masculinities matter! Men, gender and development.* London and New York: Zed Books.

Cockburn, C. K. (1983). *Brothers.* London: Pluto.

Cockburn, C. K. (1989). Equal opportunities: The short and long agendas. *Industrial Relations Journal, 20*(3), 213–25.

Cockburn, C. K. (1991). *In the way of women: Men's resistance to sex equality in organizations.* London: Macmillan.

Collier, R. (1998). 'Nutty professors,' 'men in suits' and 'new entrepreneurs': Corporeality, subjectivity and change in the law school and legal practice. *Social & Legal Studies, 7*(1), 27–53.

Collinson, D. L. (1988). Engineering humour: Masculinity, joking and conflict in shop floor relations. *Organization Studies, 9*(2), 181–99.

Collinson, D. L. (1992). *Managing the shopfloor: Subjectivity, masculinity and workplace culture.* Berlin: Walter de Gruyter.

Collinson, D. L. (2000). Strategies of resistance: Power, knowledge and subjectivity in the workplace. In K. Grint (Ed.), *Work and society: A reader* (pp. 163–98). Cambridge, Mass.: Polity.

Collinson, D. L., & Collinson, M. (1989). Sexuality in the workplace: The domination of men's sexuality. In J. Hearn, D. Sheppard, P. Tancred-Sheriff & G. Burrell (Eds), *The sexuality of organization* (pp. 91–109). London and Newbury Park, CA: Sage.

Collinson, D. L., & Collinson, M. (1997). Delayering managers: Time-space surveillance and its gendered effects. *Organization, 4*(3), 373–405.

Collinson, D. L., & Hearn, J. (1994). Naming men as men: Implications for work, organization and management. *Gender, Work & Organization, 1*(1), 2–22.

Collinson, D. L., & Hearn, J. (Eds) (1996a). *Men as managers, Managers as men.* London: Sage.

Collinson, D. L., & Hearn, J. (1996b). 'Men' at 'work': Multiple masculinities in multiple workplaces. In M. Mac an Ghaill (Ed.), *Understanding masculinities: social relations and cultural areas* (pp. 61–76). London: Open University.

Collinson, D. L., & Hearn, J. (2000). Critical research studies on men, masculinities and managements. In M. J. Davidson & R. J. Burke (Eds), *Women in management: Current research issues. Volume II* (pp. 263–78). London: Paul Chapman/Sage.

Collinson, D. L., & Hearn, J. (2005). Men and masculinities in work, organizations and management. In M. Kimmel, J. Hearn & R. W. Connell (Eds), *Handbook of studies on men and masculinities* (pp. 289–310). Thousand Oaks, CA: Sage.

Collinson, D. L., Knights, D., & Collinson, M. (1990). *Managing to discriminate*. London: Routledge.

Collinson, M., & Collinson, D. L. (2004). The power of time: Leadership, management and gender. In C. F. Epstein and A. L. Kalleberg (Eds), *Rethinking time at work* (pp. 219–46). Chicago: Chicago University Press.

Connell, R. W. (1987). *Gender and power*. Cambridge: Polity.

Connell, R. W. (1993). The big picture: Masculinities in recent world history. *Theory and Society*, *22*(5), 597–623.

Connell, R. W. (1995). *Masculinities*. Cambridge: Polity.

Connell, R. W. (1998). Globalization and masculinities. *Men and Masculinities*, *1*(1), 3–23.

Connell, R. W. (2001). Masculinity politics on a world scale. In S. Whitehead & F. Barrett (Eds), *The masculinities reader* (pp. 369–74). Cambridge, MA: Polity.

Connell, R. W., Hearn, J., & Kimmel, M. (2005). Introduction. In M. Kimmel, J. Hearn & R. W. Connell (Eds), *Handbook of studies on men and masculinities* (pp. 1–12). Thousand Oaks, CA: Sage.

Davidson, M., & Burke, R. (Eds) (2000). *Women in management: Current research issues. Volume II*. London: Sage.

Digby, T. (Ed.) (2000). *Men doing feminism*. New York: Routledge.

Donaldson, M. (1993). What is hegemonic masculinity? *Theory and Society*, *22*(5), 643–57.

Dowling, P. J., & Welch, D. E. (2004). *International human resource management: Managing people in a multinational context* (4th edn). London: Thomson.

Edmondson Bell, E. L., & Nkomo, S. M. (2001). *Our separate ways: Black and white women and the struggle for professional identity*. Boston, MA: Harvard Business School Press.

Edwards, T. (1994). *Erotics and politics*. London and New York: Routledge.

Eichler, M. (1980). *The double standard: A feminist critique of feminist social science*. London: Croom Helm.

Ely, R. J., & Foldy, E. G. (2003). Diversity: Overview. In R. Ely, E. Foldy & M. Scully (Eds), *Reader in gender, work and organization* (pp. 321–6). Oxford and New York: Blackwell.

Esty, K., Griffin, R., & Schorr-Hirsh, M. (1995). *Workplace diversity: A manager's guide to solving problems and turning diversity into a competitive advantage*. Avon, MA: Adams Media Corporation.

Feldman, D., & Klich, N. (1991). Impression management and career strategies. In R. Giacalone & P. Rosenfeld (Eds), *Applied impression management* (pp. 67–80). Newbury Park, CA: Sage.

First Destinations of Students Leaving Higher Education Institutions 2000/01 (2001). London: Higher Education Statistics Agency. Available online at: www.hesa.ac.uk/press/pn59/pn59.htm (Retrieved 16 May 2005).

Fletcher, J. K., & Ely, R. J. (2003). Introducing gender: Overview. In R. Ely, E. Foldy & M. Scully (Eds), *Reader in gender, work and organization* (pp. 3–9). Oxford and New York: Blackwell.

Foldy, E. G. (2002). 'Managing' diversity: Identity and power in organizations. In I. Aaltio & A. Mills (Eds), *Gender, identities and the culture of organizations* (pp. 92–112). London and New York: Routledge.

Foldy, E. G., & Creed, W. E. D. (1999). Action learning, fragmentation, and the interaction of single-, double-, and triple-loop change: A case of gay and lesbian workplace advocacy. *Journal of Applied Behavioral Science*, 35(2), 207–27.

Friedman, S., & Sarah, E. (Eds) (1982). *On the problem of men*. London: Women's Press.

Gardiner, J. K. (Ed.) (2001). *Masculinity studies and feminist theory*. New York: Columbia University Press.

Gibbings, S. (1990). *The tie: Trends and traditions*. London: Studio Editions.

Hall, E. (1995). *We can't even march straight*. London: Vintage.

Hanmer, J. (1990). Men, power and the exploitation of women. In J. Hearn & D. Morgan (Eds), *Men, masculinities and social theory* (pp. 21–42). London and New York: Unwin Hyman/Routledge.

Harris, H. (2004). Women's role in international management. In A. -W. Harzing & J. Van Ruysseveldt (Eds), *International human resource management* (pp. 357–86). London: Sage.

Harzing, A.-W., & Van Ruysseveldt, J. (Eds) (2004). *International human resource management* (2nd edn). London: Sage.

Hearn, J. (1985). Men's sexuality at work. In A. Metcalf & M. Humphries (Eds), *The sexuality of men* (pp. 110–28). London: Pluto.

Hearn, J. (1987). *The gender of oppression: Men, masculinity and the critique of Marxism*. Brighton: Wheatsheaf.

Hearn, J. (Ed.) (1989). Men, masculinities and leadership: Changing patterns and new initiatives. Special Issue, *Equal Opportunities International*, 8, 1.

Hearn, J. (1992). *Men in the public eye: The construction and deconstruction of public men and public patriarchies*. London and New York: Routledge.

Hearn, J. (1994). Changing men and changing managements: Social change, social research and social action. In M. J. Davidson & R. Burke (Eds), *Women in management – Current research issues* (pp. 192–209). London: Paul Chapman.

Hearn, J. (1996a). Deconstructing the dominant: Making the one(s) the other(s), *Organization*, 3(4), 611–26.

Hearn, J. (1996b). Is masculinity dead? A critique of the concept of masculinity/masculinities. In M. Mac an Ghaill (Ed.), *Understanding masculinities: Social relations and cultural arenas* (pp. 202–17). Buckingham: Open University Press.

Hearn, J. (1997). The implications of critical studies on men. *NORA. Nordic Journal of Women's Studies*, 5(1), 48–60.

Hearn, J. (2004). From hegemonic masculinity to the hegemony of men. *Feminist Theory*, 5(1), 97–120.

Hearn, J. (2005). Tracking 'the transnational': Studying transnational organizations and managements, and the management of cohesion. *Culture and Organization*, 10(4), 273–90.

Hearn, J., & Collinson, D. L. (1994). Theorizing unities and differences between men and between masculinities. In H. Brod & M. Kaufman (Eds), *Theorizing masculinities* (pp. 97–118). Newbury Park, CA: Sage.

Hearn, J., & Collinson, D. L. (1998). Men, masculinities, managements and organisational culture. *Zeitschrift für Personal Forschung*, 12(1), 210–22.

Hearn, J., Kovalainen, A., & Tallberg, T. (2002). *Gender Divisions and Gender Policies in Top Finnish Corporations* (Research Report 57). Helsinki: Swedish School of Economics and Business Administration.

Hearn, J., & Morgan, D. H. J. (Eds) (1990). *Men, masculinities and social theory*. London and Boston: Unwin Hyman.

Hearn, J., & Parkin, W. (1995). *'Sex' at 'Work': The power and paradox of organisation sexuality, revised and updated*. London and New York: Prentice Hall/Harvester Wheatsheaf.

Hearn, J., & Parkin, W. (2001). *Gender, sexuality and violence in organizations: The unspoken forces of organization violations*. London: Sage.

Hearn, J., & Piekkari, R. (2005). Gendered leaderships and leaderships on gender policy: National context, corporate structures, and chief human resources managers in transnational corporations. *Leadership*, 1(4), 429–54.

Heiskanen, T., & Hearn, J. (Eds) (2004). *Information society and the workplace: Spaces, boundaries and agency.* Routledge, London.

Holden, N. J. (2002). *Cross-cultural management: A knowledge management perspective.* Harlow: Financial Times Prentice Hall.

Holvino, E. (2001). *Working Paper No. 14.* Boston, MA: Center for Gender in Organizations, Simmons School of Management.

Holvino, E. (2003). Complicating gender: The simultaneity of race, gender and class in organization change(ing). In R. Ely, E. Foldy & M. Scully (Eds), *Reader in gender, work and organization* (pp. 3–9). Oxford and New York: Blackwell.

hooks, b. (1984). *Feminist theory: From margin to center.* Boston, MA: South End Press.

Humphries, J. (2000). Organizing sexualities, organization inequalities: Lesbians and gay men in public service occupations. *Gender, Work & Organization, 6*(3), 134–51.

ID Research (2001). *Gay and lesbian census.* London: ID Research.

Jewson, N., & Mason, D. (1986). The theory and practice of equal opportunities policies: liberal and radical approaches. *Sociological Review, 34*(2), 307–34.

Kanter, R. M. (1977). *Men and women of the corporation.* New York: Basic Books.

Kerfoot, D., & Knights, D. (1993). Management masculinity and manipulation: From paternalism to corporate strategy in financial services in Britain. *Journal of Management Studies, 30*(4), 659–79.

Kimmel, M. S. (1993). Masculinity as homophobia: Fear, shame, and silence in the construction of gender identity. In H. Brod & M. Kaufman (Eds), *Theorizing masculinities* (pp. 119–41). Newbury Park, CA, and London: Sage.

Kimmel, M., Hearn, J., & Connell, R. W. (Eds) (2005). *Handbook of studies on men and masculinities.* Thousand Oaks, CA: Sage.

Kirton, G., & Greene, A. M. (2000). *The dynamics of managing diversity.* Oxford: Butterworth–Heinemann (2nd edn, 2004).

Kolb, D., Fletcher, J. K., Meyerson, D. E., Merrill-Sands, D., & Ely, R. J. (2003). Making change: A framework for promoting gender equity in organizations. In R. Ely, M. Scully & E. Foldy (Eds), *Reader in gender, work and organization* (pp. 10–15). Oxford and New York: Blackwell.

Kondo, D. (1990). *Crafting selves: Power, gender and discourses of identity in a Japanese workplace.* Chicago: University of Chicago Press.

Kossek, E. E., & Lobel, S. (Eds) (1996). *Managing diversity: Human resources strategies for transforming the workplace.* Oxford: Blackwell.

Krieger, N., & Sidney, S. (1996). Racial discrimination and blood pressure: The CARDIA study of young Black and White adults. *American Journal of Public Health, 86*(10), 1370–78.

Landrine, H., & Klonoff, E. A. (1997). *Discrimination against women: Prevalence, consequences, remedies.* Thousand Oaks, CA: Sage.

Loden, M., & Rosener, J. B. (1991). *Workforce America! Managing employee diversity as a vital resource.* Homewood, IL: Business One Irwin.

MacInnes, J. (1998). *The end of masculinity.* Buckingham: Open University Press.

Massey, D. (1993). Scientists, transcendence and the home/work boundary. In J. Wadjman (Ed.), *Organization, gender and power* (Warwick Papers in Industrial Relations, 48, pp. 17–25). Warwick: University of Warwick.

McLaren, P. (1994). Whiter terror and oppositional agency: Towards a critical multiculturalism. In D. T. Goldberg (Ed.), *Multiculturalism: A critical reader* (pp. 45–74). Malden, MA: Blackwell.

McGuire, G., & Reskin, B. F. (1993). Authority hierarchies at work: The impacts of race and sex. *Gender and Society, 7*(4), 487–507.

McIntosh, P. (1990). White privilege: Unpacking the invisible knapsack. *Independent School,* Winter, 31–4.

Merrill-Sands, D. and Holvino, E. with Cummings, J. (2000). *Working Paper #11,* Boston: Center for Gender in Organizations, Simmons School of Management.

Merrill-Sands, D. and Holvino, E. with Cummings, J. (2003). Working with diversity: A focus on global organizations. In R. Ely, E. Foldy & M. Scully (Eds), *Reader in gender, work and organization* (pp. 327–42). Oxford and New York: Blackwell.

Morgan, D. H. J. (1996). The gender of bureaucracy. In D. L. Collinson & J. Hearn (Eds), *Men as managers, managers as men* (pp. 43–60). London: Sage.

Morgan, D. H. J. (2005). Class and masculinity. In M. Kimmel, J. Hearn & R. W. Connell (Eds), *Handbook of studies on men and masculinities* (pp. 165–177). Thousand Oaks, CA: Sage.

Morrell, R. (Ed.) (2001). *Changing men in Southern Africa.* London: Zed Books.

Morrell, R., & Swart, S. (2005). Men in the Third World: Postcolonial perspectives on masculinity. In M. Kimmel, J. Hearn & R. W. Connell (Eds), *Handbook of studies on men and masculinities* (pp. 90–113). Thousand Oaks, CA: Sage.

O'Brien, M. (1981). *The politics of reproduction.* London: Routledge & Kegan Paul.

Okin, S. M. (1997) Is multiculturalism good for women? *Boston Review, 22*(5), 25–8.

Ouzgane, L., & Coleman, D. (1998). Postcolonial masculinities: Introduction. *Jouvert: A Journal of Postcolonial Studies, 2*(1): http://social.chass.ncsu.edu/jouvert/v2i1/con21. htm (Retrieved 10 December 2003).

Pease, B., & Pringle, K. (Eds) (2001). *A man's world: Changing men's practices in a globalized world.* London: Zed Books.

Plummer, K. (Ed.) (1981). *The making of the modern homosexual.* London: Hutchinson.

Plummer, K. (Ed.) (1992). *Modern homosexualities.* London: Routledge.

Prasad, P., & Mills, A. J. (1997). From showcase to shadow: Understanding the dilemmas of managing workplace diversity. In P. Prasad, A. J. Mills, M. Elmes & A. Prasad (Eds), *Managing the organizational melting pot: Dilemmas of workplace diversity* (pp. 3–18). Thousand Oaks, CA: Sage.

Prasad, P., Mills, A. J., Elmes, M., & Prasad, A. (Eds) (1997). *Managing the organizational melting pot: Dilemmas of workplace diversity.* Thousand Oaks, CA: Sage.

Punnett, B. J., & Shenkar, O. (Eds) (2004). *Handbook for international management research* (2nd edn). Ann Arbor: University of Michigan Press.

Roper, M. R. (1991). Yesterday's model: Product fetishism and the British company men 1945–85. In M. R. Roper & J. Tosh (Eds), *Manful assertions: Masculinities in Britain since 1800* (pp. 190–211). London and New York: Routledge.

Roper, M. R. (1994). *Masculinity and the British organization man since 1945.* Oxford: Oxford University Press.

Rowbotham, S. (1979). The trouble with 'patriarchy'. *New Statesman, 98,* 970.

Saghir, M. T., & Robins, E. (1973). *Male and female homosexualities: A comprehensive investigation.* Baltimore, MD: Williams and Wilkins.

Schacht, S. P., & Ewing, D. W. (Eds) (1998). *Feminism and men: Reconstructing gender relations.* New York: New York University Press.

Schneider, B. E. (1984). The office affair: Myth and reality for heterosexual and lesbian women workers. *Sociological Perspectives, 27*(4), 443–64.

Segal, L. (1990). *Slow motion: Changing men, changing masculinities.* London: Virago.

Sessa, V., & Jackson, S. (1995). Diversity in decision-making teams: All differences are not created equal. In M. Chemers, S. Oskamp & M. Costanzo (Eds), *Diversity in organizations: New perspectives for a changing workplace* (pp. 133–56). London: Sage.

Signorile, M. (1993). *Queer in America: Sex, the media and the closets of power.* New York: Anchor.

Skelton, A. (1999). The inclusive university? A case study of the experiences of gay and bisexual higher educators in the UK. In P. Fogelberg, J. Hearn, L. Husu & T. Mankkinen (Eds), *Hard work in the academy* (pp. 190–209). Helsinki: Helsinki University Press.

Taylor, N. (Ed.) (1986). *All in a day's work: A report on anti-lesbian discrimination in employment and unemployment in London.* London: Lesbian Employment Rights.

Thomas, D. A., & Ely, R. J. (1996). Making differences matter: A new paradigm for managing diversity. *Harvard Business Review,* September/October, 79–90.

Tolson, A. (1977). *The limits of masculinity.* London: Tavistock.

Travis, A. (1998). Straw acts on racism in Home Office. *Guardian*, 24 August, 7.

Vinnicombe, S. (2000). The position of women in management in Europe. In M. Davidson and R. Burke (Eds), *Women in management: Current research issues: Volume II* (pp. 9–25). London: Sage.

Walby, S. (1986). *Patriarchy at work.* Cambridge: Polity.

Walby, S. (1990). *Theorizing patriarchy.* Oxford: Blackwell.

Weeks, J. (1977). *Coming out: Homosexual politics in Britain, from the nineteenth century to the present.* London: Quartet (rev. edn 1990).

Whitehead, S. (2001). Man: The invisible gendered subject? In S. Whitehead & F. Barrett (Eds), *The masculinities reader* (pp. 351–68). Cambridge, MA: Polity.

Willis, P. (1977). Learning to Labour. London: Saxon House.

Woods, J. D., & Lucas, J. H. (1993). *The corporate closet: The professional lives of gay men in America.* New York: Free Press.

Woodward, A. E. (1996). Multinational masculinities and European bureaucracies. In D. L. Collinson & J. Hearn (Eds), *Men as managers, Managers as men* (pp. 167–85). London: Sage.

13

Race and Ethnicity in Organizations

KAREN L. PROUDFORD AND STELLA NKOMO

The study of race in organizations, especially in the United States, has followed an interesting trajectory. In a comprehensive review of 20 journals, Cox and Nkomo (1990) wrote of 'invisible men and women', referring to the limited research on the experience of racial and ethnic minorities in organizations. Nkomo (1992) made an analogy to the *Emperor Has No Clothes* fairy tale to underscore the general inattention to race in organization studies and the limited ways in which race had been studied by organizational scholars. For this chapter we reviewed the same journals listed by Cox and Nkomo (1990), focusing on articles published in 1995 and thereafter (see Table 13.1). In addition, we searched widely for other relevant work published in books or journals not listed in the table.[1] Our goal was to offer a comprehensive overview of how race in organizations has been studied since 1995 and beyond.

Since the Cox and Nkomo (1990) and Nkomo (1992) articles, research on race in organizations has increased. To fully appreciate the trajectory of the study of race and ethnicity in organizations, the first part of this chapter explores the concepts as well as the theoretical orientations found within the broader sociological and psychological literature. It is the latter two disciplines that have dominated the social scientific study of race and ethnicity. Next, we offer a summary of the research, framed within a significant shift we noted in the way researchers have approached the topic: first, as a single factor; second, in conjunction with other relevant demographic variables; and third, as subordinate to the multifaceted notion of diversity. The coverage of the research in this chapter is primarily in the United States context, but has been supplemented by a wider view where the literature was

TABLE 13.1   *List of journals selected for review*

Academy of Management Journal
Academy of Management Review
Administrative Science Quarterly
American Journal of Psychology
American Journal of Sociology
California Management Review
Decision Sciences
Human Relations
Industrial and Labor Relations Review
Journal of Applied Behavioral Science
Journal of Applied Psychology
Journal of Business
Journal of Management Studies
Journal of Occupational Psychology
Management Science
Organization Behavior and Human Decision Processes
Personnel Psychology
Public Personnel Management
Social Forces
Social Science Quarterly

available and appropriate. Finally, we discuss the implications of our review for the future study of race in contemporary organizations.

THE CONCEPT OF RACE

As a concept, race has had a long and contested history. This history can best be understood by excavating its past. While such an undertaking could occupy its own volume, Banton (1998) offers a useful history of racial theories as falling into three major phases. In the first phase, race was conceptualized as lineage. Banton argues that the origins of the idea of race first appeared in the early eighteenth century in the work of the scientist Linnaeus. Natural historians, in their efforts to collect, describe and classify specimens, unfortunately used the word race to account for differences among humans, including skin color (Banton, 1998). Banton points out scientists used race to designate a group of people, but they could equally well have used some other word. In other words, race had no analytical value. At that point in history there was no idea of race. It is only the next phase when genealogists confronted the evidence of evolution in nature and the unequal development of human societies that a race explanation gained currency. Starting with the work of Cuvier, there was increasing sympathy for the view that the differences in human societies could be attributable to physical causes and biological inheritance. Race came to signify a permanent category of humans equivalent to species categorization; hence, the birth of different 'races' – European or white; African or black; Chinese or yellow; South Asian or brown; and Native American or red (Banton, 2001). These distinctions deepened to validate a hierarchy of races with the white race unquestionably superior to the black, brown, yellow and red 'races'.

It would be many years before the primacy of the biological argument was dethroned. During the third phase, biological explanations were superseded by more powerful explanations, which recognize race as a social construction. Banton (1998) argues that powerful explanations can be made to understand differences among people and the concept of race is not needed. Montagu (1997) has referred to what he calls the fallacy of race. He asserts that 'race is one of the most dangerous myths of our time, and one of the most tragic' (Montagu, 1997: 41). According to Montagu (1997), race does not correspond to any biological referent and racial categories are so arbitrary as to be meaningless. Technically, there is no such thing as race. Yet, the concept has not disappeared. Some scholars suggest the problem may be the lack of a separate term like gender which distinguishes it from sex (Montagu, 1997). In a social constructionist view, race does exist, not for biological reasons but for social reasons. Race is a social creation – a social construction – that divides and categorizes individuals by phenotypical markers such as skin color supposedly signifying underlying essential differences. The problem is that the everyday man or woman believes race exists – that it is immutable. Today scholars define race as a social construction by which individuals and groups are classified by others, are assigned labels, and/or assign labels to themselves (Thomas & Dyall, 1999). This definition underscores that one's race is not objective but subjective. It can be assigned by others or assumed by self-definition.

THE CONCEPT OF ETHNICITY

The meaning of ethnicity is no less fraught with conflict than the concept of race. There are two scholarly positions on the meaning of ethnicity. Some scholars do not view it as a distinctive concept. These scholars use race and ethnicity interchangeably. Accordingly, a group can simultaneously be racial and ethnic. For example, Cox (1993) proposed the term racio-ethnicity to capture the idea that groups may be constituted as both racial and ethnic. Other scholars argue that ethnicity should supersede and even replace the concept of race. In their analysis, race is not a viable concept given recent biological evidence to the contrary. These scholars position ethnicity as a broader concept, distinct from race. An ethnic group is thus defined as a set of people who share a common cultural background that is often embedded in language and religion. For instance, the basic social anthropological model of ethnicity found in the work of Jenkins (1997: 13) offered the following propositions about the meaning of ethnicity:

Ethnicity is about cultural differentiation;
Ethnicity is concerned with culture—shared meaning but it is also rooted in, and the outcome of social interaction;
Ethnicity is no more fixed than the culture of which it is a component, or the situations in which it is produced and reproduced;
Ethnicity is both collective and individual, externalized in social interaction and internalized in personal self-identification.

Jenkins (1997) points out that although 'race' is an allotrope of ethnicity, they both are somewhat different social phenomena. Ethnicity is said to be ubiquitous while 'race' is not (Jenkins, 1997: 167). Scholars go on to confuse the issue by pointing out that a common culture may be associated with certain common biological characteristics, such as skin color, but it need not be (Fraser & Burchell, 2001). For example, the English, Scots and Welsh can be described as having a similar 'race' but are typically viewed as three distinctive cultural groups. Yet, we know this too is a contentious issue. One need only look at the debates in England about who can be English and whether or not the children of immigrants from the Caribbean and other countries can be English. Another example highlights the problem. African Americans in the United States are often referred to as a racial group while Hispanics are referred to as an ethnic group. As Yanow (2003) points out, although race and ethnicity are often used to refer to different things, they are also used interchangeably.

What scholars do agree upon is that race and ethnicity are socially constructed concepts. They are human inventions, created for social and political purposes (Yanow, 2003). Conceptualizations of ethnicity also emphasize its subjectivity. For example, psychologists have developed theories to explain racial/ethnic identity formation. Ethnic identity theory, also referred to as racial identity theory, focuses on the processes by which individuals develop a racial identity (Helms & Piper, 1994). Theories of racio-ethnic identity formation have also been developed for specific racioethnic groups. For example, Helms (1990) proposed a stage model of identity development for whites. Cross (1991) developed a model he calls 'Nigrescene' to capture racial identity development of blacks.

While the distinctiveness of the concepts is debatable, what is clear is that 'race' and ethnicity are both consequential in everyday experience and historically both have been organizing principles for domination, oppression and even genocide (Jenkins, 1997). If one takes a turn around the world, the evidence of the significance of these concepts is overwhelming. Horrific tragedies from the Holocaust to the genocidal slaughter in Rwanda, Serbia and Darfur (Sudan) are all rooted in so-called ethnic or racial difference. Persistent racial and ethnic prejudices exist in almost every part of the world. It is hard to find a society where some group has not been classified as the 'Other' on the basis of ethnicity or 'race' (Sidanius & Pratto, 1999). Indeed many of the theories used to understand race have also been used to understand the effects of ethnicity in society.

DOMINANT THEORETICAL FRAMEWORKS

One of the most dominant theoretical approaches has been the field of intergroup relations. Intergroup relations is a very broad term which covers a number of related theoretical perspectives. Sherif (1966) defined intergroup relations as the relations between two or more groups and their respective members. Prejudice and discrimination are the most commonly studied aspects of intergroup relations

(Nkomo, 1992). Prejudice is generally defined as a negative attitude toward a social group and members of that group, usually based upon a faulty and inflexible generalization or stereotype (Fiske, 1998). Discrimination refers to overt behavior toward a group and its members. It includes verbal and non-verbal acts, whether intended or unintended. Most theorists distinguish between discrimination at the individual level and institutional level (Dovidio, Brigham, Johnson & Gaertner, 1996). The former refers to actions carried out by individuals based on negative attitudes; for example, a manager may not hire Hispanics for middle management positions because of a belief that Hispanics are less competent than whites. Institutional discrimination pertains to institutional norms, practices and policies which help to create or perpetuate sets of advantages or privileges for dominant group members to the exclusion or unequal access of subordinate groups. Racism has been used to describe a combination of prejudice and discrimination which has become institutionalized in an organization or society (Fraser & Burchell, 2001).

The study of intergroup relations has evolved from personality-based explanation for prejudice and discrimination to explanations dominated by cognitive theoretical perspectives. The psychodynamic theory of the authoritarian personality formulated by Adorno and his colleagues (1950) postulated that prejudice was due to personality differences. Individuals who scored high on authoritarianism displayed more prejudicial attitudes. Inconsistent results led to skepticism concerning authoritarian personality as a predictor of prejudice (Pettigrew, 1958).

Currently, particularly in the United States, cognitive processes have dominated social psychology explanations for race prejudice and discrimination. Modern social psychology cognitive theories for explaining prejudice include social identity theory, social categorization theory and attribution theory. The phenomenological approach of social identity and social categorization theory postulates that individuals depend on social group (e.g. men, women, blacks, whites, etc.) membership for their identity, and they tend to strive for a positively valued social identity (Tajfel, 1981). The evaluation of one's own group is determined with reference to specific other groups through social comparisons in terms of value-laden attributes and characteristics. In other words, the need for positive self-esteem leads to prejudice. Categorization and cognitive biases result in stereotypes and the mere categorization of persons into in-group and out-group membership is sufficient to affect interpersonal perceptions of behavior (Guinote & Fiske, 2003). Within this theoretical perspective, the solution to prejudice is a reduction in the salience of group boundaries. Social attribution theory refers to how members of different social groups explain the behavior, outcomes of behavior and the social conditions that characterize members of their own group (in-group) and other (the out-group) social groups (Tajfel, 1981). Individuals who are members of the in-group tend to see out-group members as more similar to one another and may think of them in stereotyped terms or evaluate them negatively (see Kulik & Bainbridge, this volume, for a detailed explanation of psychological perspectives on diversity).

ALTERNATIVE THEORETICAL PARADIGMS

Beginning in the late 1980s, a number of additional perspectives on race and ethnicity have arisen. These include theories of modern racism, everyday racism, social dominance theory, black feminist theory, critical race theory, postcolonial theory, and the postmodern approaches rooted in the fields of culture studies and difference. Theoretical controversy centers on the dominance of cognitive approaches (individual level of analyses) to the neglect of structural and institutional influences (Fiske, 1998). Some scholars argue for an approach that combines cognitive and structural elements of prejudice. They argue that the idea of race has never existed outside of a framework of group interest (Essed, 1991). Research also suggests that there are contradictions in the way individuals hold prejudiced attitudes and their subsequent behavior. Several scholars have proposed constructs that capture new forms of racism and the persistence of prejudice. These constructs include symbolic racism, everyday racism, modern racism and aversive racism (Dovidio & Gaertner, 1986; 1998; Pettigrew & Meertens, 1995). Yet, other perspectives suggest race must be understood in relation to other systems of exclusion, marginalization and oppression. All of these perspectives counter the view that racism is an individual problem and attempt to explain it within broader social relations. These paradigms offer a critical analysis of the concept of race and call for greater attention to structure, power and context in understanding its effect in societies and organizations. We offer a brief overview of each of these perspectives.

Dovidio and Gaertner (1986; 1998) identify a new form of racial prejudice, referred to as aversive racism, which is composed of a blend of anti-black affect and the traditional moral values embodied in the Protestant ethic and egalitarian beliefs. Their work demonstrates how prejudices and racism persist in covert forms within society in general. In a similar vein, Essed (1991) developed the concept of everyday racism to acknowledge the macro (structural) properties of racism as well as the micro inequities perpetuating the system. In her work, everyday racism is:

> defined as a process in which (a) socialized racist notions are integrated into meanings that make practices immediately definable and manageable, (b) practices with racist implications become in themselves familiar and repetitive, (c) underlying racial and ethnic relations are actualized and reinforced through these routine or familiar practices in everyday situations. (Essed & Goldberg, 2002: 190)

Omi and Winant's (1986) theory of racial formation is consistent with Essed's approach. They define racial formation as:

> the process by which social, economic, and political forces determine the content and importance of racial categories, and by which they are in turn shaped by racial meanings. Crucial to this formulation is the treatment of race as a central axis of social relations which cannot be subsumed or reduced to some broader category of conception. (Omi & Winant, 1986: 61–2)

Social dominance theory (SDT) as formulated by Sidanius and Pratto (1999) has been most critical of social identity theory for understanding race and ethnic relations and the persistence of inequality in society. Sidanius and Pratto (1999) argue that social inequality exists in essentially all modern societies and appears to be rather self-sustaining. They explain this phenomenon through the concept of social dominance orientation (SDO). SDT holds that structural inequality reproduces and reinforces itself through a psychological mechanism known as SDO. According to this perspective, SDO is a very general individual differences orientation expressing the value that people place on non-egalitarian and hierarchically structured relationships among social groups (Sidanius & Pratto, 1999: 61). In other words, individuals with a high SDO favor inequality, while those with a low SDO do not. Cross-cultural research has demonstrated that higher-status racio-ethnic groups have greater SDO. In the United States, the relatively high racio-ethnic groups of European and Asian Americans have greater SDO than Latinos and African Americans, whereas in Israel the higher-status Ashkenazim have higher levels of SDO than the Mizrachim (Levin, Sidanius, Rabinowitz & Federico, 1998).

Black feminist theory and feminist anti-racist theories argue for a perspective recognizing the interrelationship between race and other forms of domination. Within these perspectives, race and gender are defined as 'interlocking categories', as 'intersecting systems', as 'interdependent systems', as 'indivisible categories', or as 'interrelated axes of social structure'. Employing the notion of intersectionality, scholars within this tradition assert that race and gender are not experienced as separate or additive but as linked and simultaneous (Acker, 1999; Glenn, 1999; hooks, 1984). While race and gender are seen as distinctive systems of oppression, they are theorized as part of one overarching structure of domination. Andersen and Hill Collins (1995) view race, class and gender as interrelated axes of social structure within a more generalized matrix of domination. Similarly, Hill Collins (1990) refers to this as the social relations of domination. In other words, people are oppressed and social hierarchy is maintained by a number of other bases besides these two – class, ethnicity, sexuality, age and physical ability. The ideological underpinnings of this matrix are a belief in domination and a belief in notions of superiority and inferiority.

Critical race theory (CRT) emanated from the work of legal scholars who argue that the civil rights movement in the United States had stalled and the old approaches of amicus briefs, marches and litigation were yielding smaller returns when confronting subtler manifestations of *de facto* discrimination. One of the organizing principles of CRT is that racism is an ordinary and fundamental part of American society, not an aberration that can be readily remedied by law (Bell, 1997). Another cornerstone is the belief that culture constructs its own social reality in its own self-interest. Critical race theorists point to how 'stock stories' about institutional practices can result in unintended benefits for the white majority. Stock stories justify the world as it is by 'perpetuating the distribution of rights, privileges and opportunity established under a regime of uncontested white supremacy' (Crenshaw, Gotanda, Peller & Thomas, 1995: xxix).

Postcolonial theory has also emerged as a significant alternative to traditional approaches to the study of race and ethnicity. This work highlights the complex processes of racial and gender identification experienced by the colonized during colonial and postcolonial periods (Back & Solomos, 2000). Scholars have demonstrated the way in which colonialism and hegemony helped to construct colonized people as the 'Other' (Bhabha, 2000; Mohanty, 2000; Parry, 1998; Said, 1978). Cultural studies scholars emphasized the need to examine race as a social and political relation (e.g. Hall, 1980; Morley & Chen, 1996).

Recently, other scholars have called for the very abandonment of the race construct and have labeled it a spurious and empty ideological construct (Gilroy, 1998; 2000). Gilroy (1998: 839) offers an analysis of the substantive problems with the idea that people conceptualize and act upon racial difference. He argues that racism would be better countered if scholars made a more consistent effort to de-nature and de-ontologize 'race'. According to Alexander and Alleyne (2002), the study of race appears to be at a conceptual impasse. They argue: 'the debates on race and ethnicity have coalesced around two opposing poles, both encapsulated in the notion of "difference"; on the one hand, appearing in the ethnicity-rich guise of a pluralist cultural difference and, on the other, as a theory-bound and increasingly ethereal "politics of difference"' (Alexander & Alleyne, 2002: 543). The former approach is criticized as a reification of essentialist ideals of experience and multiculturalism, while the latter is seen as ignoring structural inequalities in favor of a focus on postmodernist abstract fragmented identities. Frustration rests with the observation that despite a proliferation of academic theory, racism continues to prevail in society. In sum, the terrain of the study of race has become more complex and contested. Surely this development has major implications for how organization studies scholars approach the study of race in the twenty-first century.

In the next section, we summarize the empirical research on race, with particular attention to work completed since 1995. Our review outlines research focused on (1) the impact of race on relevant organizational processes and outcomes, (2) the interaction effects of race and other demographic variables on behavior, and (3) the influence of diversity, with race as one component among many, on organizational life.

THE IMPACT OF RACE IN ORGANIZATIONS

A review of the empirical work since 1995 reveals partial movement in the directions set by Cox and Nkomo (1990) and Nkomo (1992) and a new set of challenges for researchers in this area. There is now a growing body of empirical evidence supporting and detailing the impact of race. Some work follows from a long tradition in the sociological and psychological literatures. Research has shown persistence of disparities in rates of employment (Fairlie & Sundstrom, 1999; Western & Pettit, 2000), wages, earnings and pay (Anderson and Shapiro, 1996; Barnum, Liden & DiTomaso, 1995; Durden and Gaynor, 1998; Holzer, 1998; Juhn, 2003), personnel assessment/test taking (Arthur, Edwards & Barrett, 2002; Schmit & Ryan, 1997), measures of managerial competence (Goldstein, Yusko & Nicolopoulos, 2001), cognitive ability (Roth, Bevier, Bobko, Switzer &

Tyler, 2001) and promotion (Baldi & McBrier, 1997). Research in organizational behavior has also found that race affects the composition and quality of one's social network. Ibarra (1995) found that minority group members tend to have more racially diverse network ties. They were less likely than whites to believe that their networks would bring additional access to career opportunities.

In a continuation of the long stream of research on rater–ratee effects, Mount, Hazucha, Holt and Sytsma (1995) and Mount, Sytsma, Hazucha and Holt (1997) found that race affects performance ratings. Black raters rated blacks higher than they rated whites; they also rated black and white managers higher than their white counterparts did. Stoll, Raphael and Holzer (2004) also find race effects in their study of hiring decisions. They examine data from 1992 to 1994 and find that black hiring officers are more likely to hire blacks than are white hiring officers. The tendency of blacks to hire blacks may be counterbalanced by subtle forms of racism practiced by whites. Brief, Dietz, Cohen, Pugh and Vaslow (2000) find that whites who have racist attitudes may feel authorized to discriminate against black applicants if given a 'business justification' by a person whom they view as having legitimate authority. This type of obedience behavior is not surprising. Brief et al.'s subjects were all white undergraduates, though, making it difficult to reach conclusions about the implications of such findings.

Shenhav and Haberfeld (1992) studied 117 privately owned firms in the Detroit area and have some interesting findings about the impact of race on earnings. They found that 'white workers in "black-type" firms are "penalized" when the number of blacks employed reaches a certain proportion of the work force. Black workers, however, are not affected by working in black-type firms' (p. 137). They suggest partial support for the labeling perspective under institutional theory (DiMaggio & Powell, 1983) – whites are negatively affected but blacks are not when the work has been labeled as black.

Taken together, these findings support Wilkinson's (1995) assertion that 'race remains a principal determinant of social organization, affecting every aspect of employment, educational opportunity, health, and justice' (p. 168).

BEYOND BLACK AND WHITE

Our review also reveals a more inclusive and complex view of race. For example, in prior years, research on Asian Americans was practically non-existent. One reason for the lack of observable interest is that organizational scholars may believe 'that Asians Americans are too successful to be considered a disadvantaged minority group' (Cheng, 1997: 278). This 'model minority' view has framed the issue of identity for Asian Americans and is one that some researchers are attempting to view in a more balanced way (Thatchenkery & Cheng, 1997). Asian Americans are viewed as having 'high educational attainment, high median family income, low crime rates, a lack of juvenile delinquency, and a lack of mental illness' (Cheng, 1997: 278). It is not clear, however, that these have translated into gains for them in the workplace. Cheng reports that Asian Americans have attained higher levels of education but do not see a proportional increase in earnings. Friedman and Krackhardt (1997) have found that they are excluded from the social networks needed to successfully advance in companies. The Cheng (1997) and Thatchenkery and Cheng (1997) pieces (see also Oyserman & Sakamoto, 1997) may open pathways to new, more complex research.

Sanchez and Brock (1996) found that perceived discrimination among Hispanics had impacted levels of organizational commitment, satisfaction and tension. Employees who grew up in the United States, were Cuban and had high-income jobs were less likely to feel the effects of perceived discrimination. Nonetheless, the authors suggest that managers pay close attention to the possibility of differential treatment.

Researchers have also begun to investigate the notion of race itself. There is a burgeoning literature that deviates from a long-standing tradition of treating race as synonymous with 'black' and instead acknowledges 'whiteness' as a racial category (e.g. Chesler, 2001; Grimes, 2001). In addition, categorization processes are becoming more complex as individuals begin to question which 'box to check' when asked about race. More people are identifying themselves as biracial (Korgen, 1998; Rockquemore & Brunsma, 2002). Hispanics are sometimes viewed as having the option of selecting from several racial identities, while Asian Americans may eventually consider themselves white (Yancey, 2003). Kirnan, Bragger, Brecher and Johnson (2001) also suggest that choosing a race is not an easy question. They found that individuals asked to identify their race were influenced by the categories presented. Proximity to the United States may also exert influence on how one identifies by race. Landale and Oropesa (2002) found that mainland and island Puerto Ricans typically identify their race as Puerto Rican. The choices of those who do not, however, are quite different. Puerto Ricans in the United States identified themselves as Hispanic/Latino, Hispanic American or American, while those in Puerto Rico identified as white, black or *trigueña* (mixed race).

RACE AND GENDER

One of the most significant shifts in this body of research is the inclusion of gender in analyses on race (and vice versa). In fact, literature which addresses race alone is rapidly disappearing. For example, there is now an expanding literature dealing with black women. Researchers have been noting the absence of gender in research on race (e.g. Bell, Denton & Nkomo, 1993; Bell & Nkomo, 2001; Blake, 1999; Hill Collins, 1986, 1991; Ferdman, 1999; Proudford & Thomas, 1996). Parker and ogilvie (1996) studied the leadership strategies of African American women and outline ways in which those strategies are influenced by culture, race and gender. Bell (1990) describes the life of black women as 'bicultural' because they must navigate two sets of boundaries in order to be successful in organizations. Denton (1990) discusses the importance of supportive relationships in helping black women meet the challenges of organizational life (see also Slevin & Wingrove, 1998). Bhavnani and Coyle (2000) examined the experiences of black and ethnic minority women in the UK. Booysen (2001) reported on the differences in the cultural orientations of black and white women managers in South Africa, while Thomas, Proudford and Cader (1999) examined the role of women of color as "outsiders within" (Hill Collins, 1986) on a global level. They suggest that women of color who occupy influential positions may be more likely than white women to adopt informal, less threatening roles in order to thwart efforts to challenge their formal authority. There is also evidence of difference in earnings among Mexican, black and white women (Antecol & Bedard, 2002), with those of Mexican and black women lagging the earnings of white women.

Sociologists, whose research centers on structural inequality and stratification, have also incorporated gender in their analyses. Cotter, Hermsen and Vanneman (1999) note that:

> [t]he additive and independent character of racial and gender inequalities implies that white women are economically disadvantaged relative to white men because they are women; however, white women's earnings inequality is not as great as that [of] African American and Hispanic women due to the benefits that accrue to white women from their membership in the dominant racial/ethnic group. (p. 453)

Similarly, Cohen's (1998) analysis of individual and metropolitan area data determined that a larger black population was associated with lower earnings for black men and women and higher earnings for whites. Cohen's results are consistent with the crowding hypothesis supposition that occupational segregation coupled with a high proportion of minority workers depresses minority wages (Bergmann, 1974), as is Gittleman and Howell's (1995) finding, from studying jobs across the United States, that 'black and Hispanic men were more concentrated in the worst jobs in 1990 than a decade earlier'.

Mirchandani (2003) examined the racial and gendered nature of emotion work through an analysis of the experiences of an ethnically diverse group of female small-business owners in Canada. She found that immigration histories, racial backgrounds and class resources often affect the nature of the emotion work which women do as part of their paid work. McGuire (2002) offers an in-depth analysis of the effects of gender and race on informal networks and inequality. She supplements research findings about employer bias by noting that coworkers may also use gender as basis for the unequal distribution of resources and rewards.

Influential work on promotion to top management positions has been carried out by Powell and Butterfield (1994; 1997; 2002), who examine promotion to top management. Powell and Butterfield (1997) studied one department in a federal government agency with a small number of people of color – nevertheless, they found that race had an indirect, though not a direct effect, on promotion. They conclude that '[i]deal promotion practices do not guarantee that minority employees will fare as well as other employees when promotion decisions are made for top management positions' (p. 126). Rather, one's status as an insider or outsider and one's work experience, which differed by race, influenced the decisions. Powell and Butterfield (2002) complemented the initial study and its gender counterpart (Powell & Butterfield, 1994) by examining the effects of race and gender on decisions to refer and select a diverse set of applicants for top management positions. They found that the race and gender composition of the selection panel did impact its decisions. Race and gender also moderate the relationship between mobility and compensation (Brett & Stroh, 1997; Dreher & Cox, 2000).

Cotter, Hernsen, Ovadia and Vanneman (2001) found a glass ceiling effect for women but not for minority men. They note that, 'While African American men are less likely than white men to achieve each of the earnings benchmarks, the gap does not grow larger later in their careers, nor is it especially stronger at high earnings levels' than at low earnings levels' (p. 671). Interestingly, they conclude that 'glass ceilings appear to be a phenomenon of gender stratification' (p. 671), though the effect on African American women warrants further exploration. Their findings contradict, as those of Bell et al. (1993) do, the notion of the 'double advantage' and support what Davidson (1997) has called the 'concrete ceiling' barring black women from reaching the highest levels of organizations.

Researchers are also using multi-phase studies to conduct research on race and gender. One notable example is Cianni and Romberger (1995) who employed group interviews and a survey in order to examine perceptions that whites, blacks, Hispanics and Asians (the small number of Native Americans prevented them from inclusion) had about access to opportunities for development and advancement. The qualitative data yielded rich insights. For example, while white men viewed training opportunities as rewards for having performed, white women reported not being offered these opportunities. Hispanic women were offered training but were not considered for promotions. Asian men and women indicated that they had access to technical training, but not management training (consistent with Cheng, 1997). Hispanic and black men both were uncertain of the value that training or other development opportunities held in terms of facilitating their advancement, and black women viewed themselves as being altogether disconnected from such opportunities.

RACE IN THE CONTEXT OF DIVERSITY

Equally, if not more, important than the inclusion of gender in analyses on race is the shift in focus from race to diversity. In these studies, which gained influence during the 1990s, race is combined with other demographic categories, such as gender and age, to determine the impact of each, separately and taken together, on relevant organizational outcomes. Pfeffer's (1981; 1983) organizational demography model was the first to point to the importance of age, gender, tenure and other demographic variables and link them to organizational processes and outcomes, which laid the foundation for research that simultaneously addresses multiple demographic variables. Tsui, Egan and O'Reilly (1992), for example, found that diversity was associated with lower levels of attachment among group members. The negative effects were larger for whites and men than for non-whites and women, leading Tsui et al. to suggest that more research is needed about the reactions majority group members have to the presence of minorities.

By the late 1990s, diversity was an accepted term in the organizational literature. This changed the focus from the affirmative action framework characterizing earlier studies that focused on giving all people access to opportunities to the notion of managing diversity, which promises increased efficiency, respect for contributions of all employees, and opportunities for organizational learning (Thomas & Ely, 1996). Bond and Pyle (1998) suggest that for organizations to effectively manage diversity, there will have to be basic, fundamental changes in organizational practices, values and processes. This emphasis on respect for the individual has perhaps led to research interest in the perceptions of the various groups. Mor Barak, Cherin and Berkman (1998), for example, use social identity theory, intergroup relations and organizational demography to develop hypotheses about the perceptions whites have about the diversity climate, which includes individuals' views and prejudices as well as organizational policies and procedures. A strength of the study is its attention to the interaction of race and gender; however, it lacks theoretical focus. They found that whites viewed the organization as being more fair and inclusive than did minorities, particularly African Americans. By contrast, minorities were more comfortable with diversity than whites (see also Kossek & Zonia, 1993)

Diversity is also a central theme in the conflict literature, which has its roots in group behavior and social identity theory. Jehn, Northcraft and Neale (1999) find that demographic dissimilarity in groups often leads to process losses. This confirms prior research indicating that people prefer to be with their like peers, especially when the group is in the minority (Mehra, Kilduff & Brass, 1998). Group members have difficulty resolving tensions and strains associated with race, gender and the like, and may view them as a distraction from the central task. Other research has shown, however, the importance of making a distinction between surface and deep-level diversity, or diversity in demographics versus diversity in assumptions, beliefs and values. Harrison, Price and Bell (1998) found that dissimilar values had a stronger negative impact on groups than demographic dissimilarity.

IMPLICATIONS

This review of the empirical work on race reveals some progress since Cox and Nkomo's (1990) article. What is encouraging is that researchers are able to obtain more data about this controversial, and sometimes volatile, topic. That, we expect, will continue, allowing researchers greater access to the kinds of data that yield answers to the most pressing research questions. What leaves the body of work unsatisfying at present is that we are left where we started: we still know *that* differences exist, but little about the mechanisms that perpetuate and sustain those differences and, consequently, how to eradicate the negative consequences of racial differences in organizations.

Here, we outline some conclusions about the state of the empirical research and suggestions for the future. First, empirical work still suffers from a lack of theoretical focus. Some theoretical frameworks, though promising, have not been refined for years (e.g. embedded intergroup relations as per Alderfer, 1977; 1987) providing a weak foundation on which to test hypotheses. Rather, it appears that a sense of urgency driven largely by anticipated demographic trends precipitated and shaped research questions and focus. Authors explain the results in some of the studies (e.g. Mor Barak et al., 1998) using multiple theories, with no further guidance as to why one theory might prove more powerful than the other. In addition, there is no theoretical distinction made between the types of diversity; such distinctions are critically important if the current move toward simultaneously examining multiple demographic variables continues.

Cox and Nkomo (1990) called for a complicated view of diversity and Brickson (2000) reconceptualizes identity as 'multifaceted, dynamic and influenced by multiple forces'. Proudford (1998) questions the assumption that bias, discrimination, tensions and strains originate where they appear and calls for more expansive conceptual frameworks that consider context and dynamics associated with race. For example, Smith and Elliott (2002) find that the composition of the work group has an impact on the race of the supervisor – a finding that goes beyond traditional notions of selection that focus on the race of the selection officer and the applicant. But such studies are the exception. The predominance of social cognition theories which focus on in-group/out-group difference without attention to disproportionately adverse consequences faced by some groups also constrains our understanding of race in organizations. This conceptual frame is consistent with the methodology used in some studies of diversity which treat all differences, including gender, race, age, tenure with the organization and functional specialty, as identical (e.g. Harrison et al., 1998; Harrison, Price, Govin & Florey, 2002; Pelled, Eisenhavelf & Xin, 1999). Some studies even combine all these dimensions to create a 'diversity' score along which all dimensions are weighted equally (e.g. Chatman, Polzer, Barsacle & Neale, 1998; Jehn et al., 1999). Conceptual frames that acknowledged the influence of social structural characteristics would indicate that methods must consider each dimension in a way that is consistent with historical patterns of inclusion and exclusion, power and privilege in the society (e.g. Martins, Milliken, Wiesenfeld & Salgado, 2003). Thoughtful consideration of the distinct, and often disproportionate, impact of these patterns is often given in the interpretation of the findings. We would suggest, however, that their influence be more directly and fully investigated.

Linnehan and Konrad (1999) write cogently about the shift to diversity. They assert that '[d]iversity initiatives are being pulled away, however, from the original mission of improving the career opportunities and work climate experienced by historically excluded demographic groups' (p. 399) and that being inclusive in terms of inviting and valuing the unique contributions of a number of different groups is not necessarily compatible with correcting past and present inequalities. They suggest four problematic themes in the literature: first, the notion of diversity shifts the focus from inequality; second, an emphasis on diversity sidesteps issues of prejudice and discrimination; third, some authors go to great lengths to distinguish between diversity and affirmative action, even so far as to suggest a shift from one to the other (e.g. Thomas, 1990); and fourth, diversity programs may fail to interrupt, challenge or question the status quo. Linnehan and Konrad (1999) suggest a consideration of intergroup power relations and make a cogent argument for a focus on reducing intergroup inequality. In their view, cultural differences intertwine with power differentials in a way that breeds and sustains inequality.

As we noted in the first part of this chapter, modern racism, black feminist theory, critical race theory, postcolonial theory, postmodern and critical approaches, and social dominance theory have had less influence on the theoretical frameworks used by organizational scholars to study race and ethnicity. They offer considerable promise, however, for unpacking the historical, cultural, social and political context within which racial dynamics are enacted. For example, Bell and Nkomo (2001) use black feminist theory to understand the experience of black women managers and recent research has employed the constructs of modern racism, aversive racism and everyday racism (see e.g. Deitch, Barsky, Butz, Brief, Chan & Bradley 2004; Dipboye & Halverson, 2004). A. Prasad (this volume) has offered an overview of postcolonial theory and its relevance to organization studies. We believe organizational scholars need to expand their approaches to incorporate these frameworks. For instance, postcolonial theory may be particularly useful for understanding race and ethnicity in other regions of the world, especially those with a different history than the United States, while critical race theory may be helpful in analyzing race and corrective measures like affirmative action.

Theoretical divergence, coupled with the sense of urgency, has led researchers in a number of different directions. Some research ties diversity to organizational performance (e.g. Richard, 2000), perhaps in response to the business case requirement from companies. Though there is evidence that racial diversity can be related to firm performance, we find it curious that there should be such an interest. Perhaps this interest is related to linking race and diversity to organizational change (e.g. Grimes, 2001; Kossek, Markel & McHugh, 2003) as researchers assert that fundamental organizational change will have to occur in order to improve experiences and chances for minority groups. For example, Chesler, Crowfoot and Bryant (1978) suggested some time ago that training regarding the acquisition and utilization of power may help alleviate group conflict in organizations. Zane (2002) notes that the acceptance of diversity, with its attendant positive consequences, may be intertwined with an organization's capacity for facilitating meaningful dialogue within and across identity and organizational groups.

Second, the empirical work is constrained by research design and methodology. Few major studies are based on longitudinal data despite theorists' assertions that the operation of race in organizational life is a dynamic process (see as notable exceptions Harrison et al., 1998; 2002). We are limited by our inability to capture and test those dynamics. Moreover, empirical studies continue to rely most heavily on samples of management personnel, though one can learn about management by surveying those who are not in management. Though significant progress has been made, non-whites continue to be heavily under-represented in the management ranks, making small sample sizes a problem. There is also clearly a preference for quantitative methodology. Ethnographic and other qualitative approaches may help to examine the often complex and subtle nature of race and ethnicity in organizations. We would also encourage scholars to incorporate critical discourse analysis and rhetorical analyses as approaches particularly suitable for interrogating the ontology of race and ethnicity in organizations (Zanoni & Janssens, 2004).

Lastly, we note that the research has been dominated by North American perspectives, particularly that of the United States. We searched journals that might contain studies of race and ethnicity in non-US contexts. These journals included: *Organization Studies, Asia Pacific Journal of Management, Personnel Review, Journal of Management Studies* and the *British Journal of Management* for the period 1995–2004. Only two articles from that period surfaced. While we do not maintain our search was exhaustive, it underscores the need for caution in assuming that the current body of work on race and ethnicity in organization provides a basis for understanding these issues in other parts of the world. For example, Jones, Pringle and Shepherd (2000) in their research in Aotearoa/New Zealand, show that diversity based on the demographics and dominant cultural assumptions of the United States fails to address and may, in fact, obscure key local 'diversity issues'.

The last decade of research on race bears out Cox and Nkomo's (1990) and Nkomo's (1992) assertions that organizational processes are not race neutral. Future work will either continue to shed light on the impact of race or once again shield it as the research focus shifts to diversity.

NOTE

1 We searched the following electronic databases: ABI/INFORM Global, EBSCO, EMERALD, SWETS and INGENTA for the period 1995–2004.

REFERENCES

Acker, J. (1999). Rewriting class, race and gender: Problems in feminist thinking. In M. M. Ferree, J. Lorber & B. B. Hess (Eds), *Revisioning gender*. Thousand Oaks, CA: Sage.

Adorno, T. W., Frenkel-Brunswick, E., Levinson, D. J., & Sanford, R. N. (1950). *The authoritarian personality*. New York: Harper.

Alderfer, C. (1977). Group and intergroup relations. In J.R. Hackman & J. L. Suttle (Eds), *Improving life at work* (pp. 227–96). Santa Monica, CA: Goodyear.

Alderfer, C. (1987). An intergroup perspective on group dynamics. In J. Lorsch (Ed.), *Handbook of organizational behavior* (pp. 190–220). Englewood Cliffs, NJ: Prentice Hall.

Alexander, C., & Alleyne, B. (2002). Introduction: Framing difference: racial and ethnic studies in twenty-first century Britain. *Ethnic and Racial Studies*, 25(4), 541–51.

Anderson, D., & Shapiro, D. (1996). Racial differences in access to high-paying jobs and the wage gap between blacks and whites. *Industrial and Labor Relations Review*, *49*(2), 273–86.

Andersen, M. L., & Hill Collins, P. (1995). *Race, class and gender*. Belmont, MA: Wadsworth.

Antecol, H., & Bedard, K. (2002). The relative earnings of young Mexican, black and white women. *Industrial and Labor Relations Review*, *56*(1), 122–35.

Arthur, W., Edwards, B., & Barrett, G. (2002). Multiple-choice and constructed response tests of ability: Race-based subgroup performance differences on alternative pencil-and-paper test formats. *Personnel Psychology*, *55*(4), 985–1009.

Back, L., & Solomos, J. (2000). *Theories of race and racism*. London: Routledge.

Baldi, S., & McBrier, D. (1997). Do the determinants of promotion differ for blacks and whites? Evidence from the U.S. labor market. *Work and Occupations*, *24*(4), 478–97.

Banton, M. (1998). *Racial theories*. Cambridge, Cambridge University Press.

Banton, M. (2001). Progress in ethnic and racial studies. *Ethnic and Racial Studies*, *24*(2), 173–94.

Barnum, P., Liden, R., & DiTomaso, N. (1995). Double jeopardy for women and minorities: Pay differences with age. *Academy of Management Journal*, *38*(3), 863–80.

Barth, F. (1969). *Ethnic groups and boundaries: The social organization of cultural difference*. Oslo: Universitetsforlaget.

Bhabha, H. K. (2000). Race, time and the revision of modernity. In L. Back & J. Solomos (Eds), *Theories of race and racism* (pp. 354–68). London: Routledge.

Bhavnani, R., & Coyle, A. (2000). Black and ethnic minority women managers in the UK – continuity or change. In M. Davidson & R. Burke (Eds), *Women in management: current research issues* (Vol. II). London: Sage.

Bell, D. (1997). Foreword. In A. K. Wing (Ed.), *Critical race feminism: A reader*. New York: New York University Press.

Bell, E., Denton, T., & Nkomo, S. M. (1993). Women of color in management: Towards an inclusive analysis. In E. Fagenson (Ed.), *Women in management: Trends, perspectives and challenges* (pp. 105–30). Newbury Park, CA: Sage.

Bell, E. J., & Nkomo, S. M. (2001). *Our separate ways: Black and white women and the struggle for professional identity*. Boston, MA: Harvard Business School Press.

Bell, E. L. J. (1990). The bicultural life experience of career-oriented black women. *Journal of Organizational Behavior*, *11*(6), 459–77.

Bergmann, B. (1974). Occupational segregation, wages and profits when employers discriminate by race and sex. *Eastern Economic Journal*, *1*, 103–10.

Blake, S. (1999). At the crossroad of race and gender: Lessons from the mentoring experiences of professional Black women. In A. Murrell, F. Crosby & R. Ely (Eds), *Mentoring dilemmas: Developmental relationships in multicultural organizations*. Mahwah, NJ: Lawrence Erlbaum.

Bond, M., & Pyle, J. (1998). Diversity dilemmas at work. *Journal of Management Inquiry*, *7*(3), 252–69.

Booysen, L. (2001). The duality of South African leadership: Afrocentric or eurocentric? *South African Journal of Labour Relations*, Spring/Summer, 36–63.

Brett, J., & Stroh, L. (1997). Jumping ship: Who benefits from an external labor market career strategy? *Journal of Applied Psychology*, *82*(3), 331–41.

Brickson, S. (2000). The impact of identity orientation on individual and organizational outcomes in demographically diverse settings. *Academy of Management Review*, *25*(1), 82–101.

Brief, A., Dietz, J., Cohen, R. R., Pugh, S. D., & Vaslow, J. (2000). Just doing business: Modern racism and obedience to authority as explanations for employment discrimination. *Organizational Behavior and Human Decision Processes*, *81*(1), 72–97.

Chatman, J., Polzer, J., Barsade, S., & Neale, M. (1998). Being different yet feeling similar: The influence of demographic composition and organizational culture on work processes and outcomes. *Administrative Science Quarterly, 43*(4), 749–80.

Cheng, C. (1997). Are Asian American employees a model minority or just a minority? *Journal of Applied Behavioral Science, 33*(3), 277–90.

Chesler, M. (2001). The charge to the white male brigade. *Journal of Applied Behavioral Science, 37*(3), 299–304.

Chesler, M., Crowfoot, J., & Bryant, B. (1978). Power training: An alternative path to conflict management. *California Management Review, 21*(2), 84–90.

Cianni, M., & Romberger, B. (1995). Perceived racial, ethnic, and gender differences in access to developmental experiences. *Group & Organization Management, 20*(4), 440–59.

Cohen, P. (1998). Black concentration effects on black-white and gender inequality: Multilevel analysis for U.S. metropolitan areas. *Social Forces, 77*(1), 207–29.

Cotter, D. A., Hermsen, J. M., Ovadia, S., & Vanneman, R. (2001). The glass ceiling effect. *Social Forces, 80*(2), 655–81.

Cotter, D. A., Hermsen, J. M., & Vanneman, R. (1999). Systems of gender, race, and class inequality: Multilevel analyses. *Social Forces, 78*(2), 433–60.

Cox, T. (1993). Problems with research by organizational scholars on issues of race and ethnicity. *Journal of Applied Behavioral Sciences, 26*(1), 5–23.

Cox, T., & Nkomo, S. (1990). Invisible men and women: A status report on race as a variable in organization behavior research. *Journal of Organizational Behavior, 11*(6), 419–31.

Crenshaw, K., Gotanda, N., Peller, G., & Thomas, K. (Eds) (1995). *Critical race theory: The key writings that formed the movement.* New York: The New Press.

Cross, W. E. J. (1991). *Shades of black: Diversity in African-American identity.* Philadelphia: Temple University Press.

Davidson, M. J. (1997). *The black and ethnic minority woman manager: Cracking the concrete ceiling.* London: Sage.

Deitch, E. A., Barsky, A., Butz, R. M., Brief, A. P., Chan, S., & Bradley, J. C. (2004). Subtle yet significant: The existence and impact of everyday racial discrimination in the workplace. *Human Relations, 56*(11), 1299–1324.

Denton, T. C. (1990). Bonding and supportive relationships among black professional women: Rituals of restoration. *Journal of Organizational Behavior, 11*(6), 447–57.

DiMaggio, P., & Powell, W. (1983). The iron cage revisited: Institutional isomorphism and collective rationality in organizational fields. *American Sociological Review, 48*(2), 147–60.

Dipboye, R. L., & Halverson, S. K. (2004). Subtle (and not so subtle) discrimination in organizations. In R. W. Griffin & A. O. Leary-Kelly (Eds), *The dark side of organizational behavior* (pp. 131–58). San Francisco: Jossey-Bass.

Dovidio, J. F., Brigham, J. C., Johnson, T. T., & Gaertner, S. L. (1996). Stereotyping, prejudice and discrimination: Another look. In N. Macrae, C. Stangor & M. Hewstone (Eds), *Stereotypes and stereotyping* (pp. 276–319). New York: Guilford.

Dovidio, J., & Gaertner, S. L. (1986). Prejudice, discrimination, and racism: Historical trends and contemporary approaches. In J. F. Dovidio & S. L. Gaertner (Eds), *Prejudice, discrimination, and racism* (pp. 1–34). Orlando, FL: Academic Press.

Dovidio, J., & Gaertner, S. L. (1998). On the nature of contemporary prejudice: The causes, consequences and challenges of aversive racism. In J. Eberhardt & S. Fiske (Eds), *Confronting racism: the problem and the response* (pp. 3–32). Newbury Park, CA: Sage.

Dreher, G., & Cox, T. (2000). Labor market mobility and cash compensation: The moderating effects of race and gender. *Academy of Management Journal, 43*(5), 890–900.

Durden, G., & Gaynor, P. (1998). More on the cost of being other than white and male: Measurement of race, ethnic, and gender effects on yearly earnings. *American Journal of Economics and Sociology, 57*(1), 95–103.

Essed, P. (1991). *Understanding everyday racism: an interdisciplinary theory*. London: Sage.

Essed, P., & Goldberg, D. T. (Eds) (2002). *Race critical theories*. Oxford: Blackwell.

Fairlie, R. W., & Sundstrom, W. A. (1999). The emergence, persistence, and recent widening of the racial unemployment gap. *Industrial and Labor Relations Review*, *52*(2), 252–70.

Ferdman, B. (1999). The color and culture of gender in organizations: Attending to race and ethnicity. In G. Powell (Ed.), *Handbook of gender & work*. Thousand Oaks, CA: Sage.

Fiske, S. T. (1998). Stereotyping, prejudice and discrimination. In D. T. Gilbert, S. T. Fiske & G. Lindzey (Eds), *The handbook of social psychology* (4th edn, Vol. 1, pp. 357–411). Oxford: Oxford University Press.

Fraser, C., & Burchell, B. (2001). *Introducing social psychology*. Cambridge: Polity.

Friedman, R., & Krackhardt, D. (1997). Social capital and career mobility: A structural theory of lower returns to education for Asian employees. *Journal of Applied Behavioral Science*, *33*(3), 316–34.

Gilroy, P. (1998). Race ends here. *Ethnic and Racial Studies*, *21*(5), 838–47.

Gilroy, P. (2000). *Between camps: Nations, cultures and the allure of race*. London: Penguin.

Gittleman, M., & Howell, D. (1995). Changes in the structure and quality of jobs in the United States: Effects by race and gender, 1973–1990. *Industrial and Labor Relations Review*, *48*(3), 420–40.

Glenn, E. N. (1999). The social construction and institutionalization of gender and race: An integrative framework. In M. Ferree, J. Lorber & B. Hess (Eds), *Revisioning gender* (pp. 3–43). Thousand Oaks, CA: Sage.

Goldstein, H. D. W., Yusko, K. P., & Nicolopoulos, V. (2001). Exploring black-white sub-group difference of managerial competencies. *Personnel Psychology*, *54*(4), 783–807.

Grimes, D. (2001). Putting our own house in order: Whiteness, change and organization studies. *Journal of Organizational Change Management*, *14*(2), 132–49.

Guinote, A., & Fiske, S. (2003). Being in the outgroup territory increases stereotypic perceptions of outgroups: Situational sources of category activation. *Group Processes and Intergroup Relations*, *6*(4), 323–32.

Hall, S. (1980). Race articulation and societies structured in dominance. In *UNESCO sociological theories: Race and colonialism*. Paris: UNESCO.

Harrison, D. A., Price, K. H., & Bell, M. P. (1998). Beyond relational demography: Time and the effects of surface- and deep-level diversity on work group cohesion. *Academy of Management Journal*, *41*(1), 96–107.

Harrison, D. A., Price, K. H., Gavin, J. H., & Florey, A. T. (2002). Time, teams, and task performance: Changing effects of surface- and deep-level diversity on group functioning. *Academy of Management Journal*, *45*(5), 1029–45.

Helms, J. E. (1990). *Black and white racial identity*. Westport, CT: Greenwood Press.

Helms, J. E., & Piper, R. E. (1994). Implications of racial identity theory for vocational psychology. *Journal of Vocational Behavior*, *44*, 124–38.

Hill Collins, P. (1986). Learning from the outsider within: The sociological significance of black feminist thought. *Social Problems*, *33*(6), 14–32.

Hill Collins, P. (1990). *Black feminist thought: Knowledge, consciousness, and the politics of empowerment*. New York: Routledge.

Holzer, H. (1998). Employer skill demands and labor market outcomes of blacks and women. *Industrial and Labor Relations Review*, *52*(1), 82–98.

hooks, b. (1984). *Feminist theory: From margin to center*. Boston, MA: South End Press.

Ibarra, H. (1995). Race, opportunity, and diversity of social circles in managerial networks. *Academy of Management Journal*, *38*(3), 673–703.

Jehn, K. A., Northcraft, G. B., & Neale, M. A. (1999). Why differences make a difference: A field study of diversity, conflict and performance in work groups. *Administrative Science Quarterly*, *44*(4), 741–63.

Jenkins, R. (1997). *Rethinking ethnicity: Arguments and explorations*. London, Sage.

Jones, D., Pringle, J., & Shepherd, D. (2000). Managing diversity meets Aotearoa/ New Zealand. *Personnel Review, 29*(3), 364–80.

Juhn, C. (2003). Labor market dropouts and trends in the wages of black and white men. *Industrial and Labour Relations Review, 56*(4), 643–62.

Kirnan, J., Bragger, J. D., Brecher, E., & Johnson, E., (2001). What race am I? The need for standardization in race question wording. *Public Personnel Management, 30*(2), 211–20.

Korgen, K. O. (1998). *From black to biracial: Transforming racial identity among Americans.* Westport, CT: Praeger.

Kossek, E., Markel, K., & McHugh, P. (2003). Increasing diversity as an HRM strategy. *Journal of Organizational Change Management, 16*(3), 328–52.

Kossek, E., & Zonia, S. (1993). Assessing diversity climate: A field study of reactions to employer efforts to promote diversity. *Journal of Organizational Behavior, 14*(1), 61–81.

Landale, N. S., & Oropesa, R. S. (2002). White, black, or Puerto Rican? Racial self-identification among mainland and island Puerto Ricans. *Social Forces, 81*(1), 231–54.

Levin, S., Sidanius, J., Rabinowitz, J. & Federico, C. (1998). Ethnic identity, legitimizing ideologies, and social status: A matter of ideological asymmetry. *Political Psychology, 19*(2), 373–404.

Linnehan, F., & Konrad, A. (1999). Diluting diversity: Implications for intergroup inequality in organizations. *Journal of Management Inquiry, 8*(4), 399–414.

Martins, L. L., Milliken, F. J., Wiesenfeld, B. M., & Salgado, S. R. (2003). Racioethnic diversity and group members' experiences: The role of the racioethnic diversity of the organizational context. *Group & Organization Management, 28*(1), 75–106.

McGuire, G. M. (2002). Gender, race, and the shadow structure: A study of informal networks and inequality in a work organization. *Gender and Society, 16*(3), 303–22.

Mehra, A., Kilduff, M., & Brass, D. (1998). The social networks of high and low self-monitors: Implications for workplace performance. *Administrative Science Quarterly, 46*(1), 121–46.

Mirchandani, K. (2003). Challenging racial silences in studies of emotion work: Contributions from anti-racist feminist theory. *Organization Studies, 24*(5), 720–42.

Mohanty, C. (2000). Under western eyes: Feminist scholarship and colonial discourses. In L. Back & J. Solomos (Eds), *Theories of race and racism* (pp. 302–23). London: Routledge.

Montagu, A. (1997). *Man's most dangerous myth: The fallacy of race* (6th edn, abridged student edn). Walnut Creek, CA: AltaMira Press.

Mor Barak, M., Cherin, D., & Berkman, S. (1998). Organizational and personal dimensions in diversity climate: Ethnic and gender differences in employee perceptions. *Journal of Applied Behavioral Science, 34*(1), 82–104.

Morley, D., & Chen, K. H. (Eds) (1996). *Stuart Hall: Critical dialogues in cultural studies.* London: Routledge.

Mount, M., Hazucha, J. F., Holt, K., & Sytsma, M. (1995). Rater-ratee effects in performance ratings of managers. *Academy of Management Journal, Best Paper Proceedings,* 141–5.

Mount, M., Sytsma, M., Hazucha, J. F., & Holt, K. (1997). Rater-ratee race effects in developmental performance ratings for managers. *Personnel Psychology, 50*(1), 51–69.

Nkomo, S. (1992). The emperor has no clothes: Rewriting 'race in organizations'. *Academy of Management Review, 17*(3), 487–513.

Nkomo, S.M., & Cox, T. (1996). Diverse identities in organizations. In S. R. Clegg, C. Hardy & W. R. Nord (Eds), *Handbook of organization studies* (pp. 338–56). London: Sage.

Omi, M., & Winant, H. (1986). *Racial formation in the United States: From the 1960s to the 1980s.* New York: Routledge.

Oyserman, D., & Sakamoto, I. (1997). Being Asian American: Identity, cultural constructs, and stereotype perception. *Journal of Applied Behavioral Science, 33*(4), 435–53.

Parker, P., & ogilvie, dt (1996). Gender, culture, and leadership: Toward a culturally distinct model of African-American women executives' leadership strategies. *Leadership Quarterly, 7*(2), 189–214.

Parry, B. (1998). *Delusions and discoveries: Studies on India in the British imagination 1880–1930*. London: Verso.

Pelled, L. H., Eisenhardt, K., & Xin, K. R. (1999). Exploring the black box: An analysis of work group diversity, conflict, and performance. *Administrative Science Quarterly*, *44*(1), 1–28.

Pettigrew, T. (1958). Personality and socio-cultural factors in intergroup attitudes: A cross-national comparison. *Journal of Conflict Resolution*, *2*(1), 29–42.

Pettigrew, T., & Meertens, R. (1995). Subtle and blatant prejudice in western Europe. *European Journal of Social Psychology*, *25*(1), 57–76.

Pfeffer, J. (1981). *Power in organizations*. Marshfield, MA: Pitman.

Pfeffer, J. (1983). Organizational demography. In L. L. Cummings & B.M. Staw (Eds), *Research in organizational behavior* Vol. 5 (pp. 299–357). Greenwich, CT: JAI Press.

Powell, G. N., & Butterfield, D. A. (1994). Investigating the 'glass ceiling' phenomenon: An empirical study of actual promotions to top management. *Academy of Management Journal*, *37*(1), 68–86.

Powell, G. N., & Butterfield, D. A. (1997). Effect of race on promotions to top management in a federal department. *Academy of Management Journal*, *40*(1), 112–28.

Powell, G. N., and Butterfield, D. A. (2002). Exploring the influence of decision makers' race and gender on actual promotions to top management. *Personnel Psychology*, *55*(2), 397–428.

Proudford, K. L. (1998). Notes on the intra-group origins of inter-group conflict in organizations: Black-white relations as an exemplar. *Journal of Labor and Employment Law*, *1*(2), 615–37.

Proudford, K. L., & Thomas, K. (1999). The organizational outsider within. *Journal of Career Development*, *26*(1), 3–5.

Richard, O. C. (2000). Racial diversity, business strategy, and firm performance, *Academy of Management Journal*, *43*(2), 164–77.

Rockquemore, K. A., & Brunsma, D. L. (2002). *Beyond black: Biracial identity in America*. Thousand Oaks, CA: Sage.

Roth, P. L., Bevier, C. A., Bobko, P., Switzer, F., & Tyler, P. (2001). Ethnic group differences in the cognitive ability in employment and educational settings: A meta-analysis. *Personnel Psychology*, *54*(2), 297–330.

Said, E. (1978). *Orientalism*. Harmondsworth: Penguin.

Sanchez, J. I., & Brock, P. (1996). Outcomes of perceived discrimination among Hispanic employees: Is diversity management a luxury or necessity? *Academy of Management Journal*, *39*(3), 704–19.

Schmit, M. J., & Ryan, A. M. (1997). Applicant withdrawal: The role of test-taking attitudes and racial differences. *Personnel Psychology*, *50*(4), 855–76.

Shenhav, Y., & Haberfeld, Y. (1992). Organizational demography and inequality. *Social Forces*, *71*(1), 123–43.

Sherif, M. (1966). *In common predicament: Social psychology of intergroup conflict and cooperation*. Boston: Houghton-Mifflin.

Sidanius, J., & Pratto, F. (1999). *Social dominance: An intergroup theory of social hierarchy and oppression*. Cambridge: Cambridge University Press.

Slevin, K., & Wingrove, C. R. (1998). *From stumbling blocks to stepping stones: The life experiences of fifty professional African-American women*. New York: New York University Press.

Smith, R. A., & Elliott, J. R. (2002). Does ethnic concentration influence employees' access to authority? An examination of contemporary urban markets. *Social Forces*, *81*(1), 255–78.

Stoll, M. A., Raphael, S., & Holzer, H. (2004). Black job applicants and the hiring officer's race. *Industrial and Labor Relations Review*, *57*(2), 267–87.

Tajfel, H. (1981). *Human groups and social categories: Studies in social psychology*. Cambridge and New York: Cambridge University Press.

Thatchenkery, T., & Cheng, C. (1997). Seeing beneath the surface to appreciate what 'is': A call for a balanced inquiry and consciousness raising regarding Asian Americans in organizations. *Journal of Applied Behavioral Science, 33*(3), 397–406.

Thomas, D., & Dyall, L. (1999). Culture, ethnicity, and sport management: A New Zealand perspective. *Sport Management Review, 2*(2), 115–32.

Thomas, D., & Ely, R. (1996). Making differences matter: A new paradigm for managing diversity. *Harvard Business Review, 74*(5), 79–90.

Thomas, K., Proudford, K. L., & Cader, J. (1999). Global outsiders within: Informal roles of women of colour. *International Review of Women and Leadership, 5*(2), 14–25.

Thomas, R. R. (1990). From affirmative action to affirming diversity. *Harvard Business Review, 68*(3), 107–17.

Tsui, A. S., Egan, T., & O'Reilly, C. (1992). Being different: Relational demography and organizational attachment. *Administrative Science Quarterly, 37*(4), 549–79.

Western, B., & Pettit, B. (2000). Incarceration and racial inequality in men's employment. *Industrial and Labour Relations Review, 54*(1), 3–16.

Wilkinson, D. (1995). Gender and social inequality: The prevailing significance of race. *Daedalus, 124*(1), 167–78.

Yancey, G. (2003). *Who is white? Latinos, Asians, and the new black/nonblack divide.* Boulder, CO: Lynne Rienner.

Yanow, D. (2003). *Constructing 'race' and 'ethnicity' in America: category-making in public policy and administration.* Armonk, NY: M.E. Sharpe.

Zane, N. (2002). The glass ceiling is the floor my boss walks on: Leadership challenges in managing diversity. *Journal of Applied Behavioral Science, 38*(3), 334–54.

Zanoni, P., & Janssens, M. (2004). Deconstructing difference: The rhetoric of human resource managers' diversity discourses. *Organization Studies, 25*(1), 55–74.

14

Age and Ageism in Organizations

A Review and Consideration of National Culture

ELISSA L. PERRY AND JENNIFER D. PARLAMIS

When people exchange information about important life events (e.g. getting married, having a child, being promoted, retiring), they often talk or ask about the age of the individuals involved. This reflects the fact that age is a primary dimension upon which people categorize and perceive others (Brewer, 1988). In fact, societies use age universally to make distinctions among their members (Keith, 1982). Research suggests that people use a variety of age-related cues to differentiate among individuals from early childhood (Montepare & Zebrowitz, 1998). Focusing on age in the context of person perception is a relatively automatic process, occurring outside the conscious awareness of the perceiver (Perdue & Gurtman, 1990). All of this suggests that age information may be a salient basis upon which a variety of social judgments including those related to employment are made.

Issues related to age and aging have become increasingly important as evidence for the aging of populations and labor forces in the industrialized world mounts. The percentage of older people in the population is expected to grow, particularly in the industrialized nations of the world (Atchley, 2000; Forteza & Prieto, 1994). For example, by 2050, it is estimated that 20% of the total population of Americans (79 million) will be 65 or older. In addition, most of Europe and Japan have a relatively high proportion of older people in their population and labor force (Patrickson & Hartmann, 1995; Robson, 2001). Based on 1995 data, it is projected that by 2020, the proportion of individuals 65 years and older in the populations of European countries such as Denmark, Finland, Sweden, Germany and France will be approximately 17–22% and in Japan the percentage could be as high as 25% (Elkin, 2001). Individuals 65 years and older will comprise a relatively smaller but still sizeable proportion of the populations of such countries as Australia, New Zealand and Canada (approximately 15–17%) (Elkin, 2001). Walker (1999) acknowledged the importance of this demographic trend and noted, 'It is not an overstatement to say that the impact of population aging on employment and the labor market is one of the most pressing issues confronting European societies' (p. 367), and that age discrimination in employment is an increasingly important part of Europe's policy agenda. For example, there have been a number of demonstrations in Europe protesting government efforts to make tax payers contribute more by staying in the workforce longer. These efforts are the result of pressures that aging populations are placing on pension plans (Rice-Oxley, 2003).

The primacy of age as a basis for social perception, and the aging of workforces worldwide, suggest that it is important to consider the role of age and aging in organizations. The current chapter has two primary purposes. First, we provide a selective review of the literature related to age and aging in organizations. We focus primarily, but not exclusively, on literature written since previous reviews (e.g. Hansson, Dekoekkoek, Neece & Patterson, 1997; Lawrence, 1996a; Perry, 1997) were conducted (1995 to the present) and attempt to take a greater international focus. However, it is important to note that our literature search was conducted in the United States. Although we made strong attempts to identify research conducted in other countries, we could not access literature and research that were not written in English. We organize our review around the various stages of the employment relationship (recruitment and selection; performance and evaluation; training and career development; exit from the organization) and highlight current research related to each stage of employment. Second, we review the limited cross-cultural research exploring the role and impact of age in organizations that has been conducted. We argue that the role of culture in understanding issues of age and aging in organizations has been understudied and underdeveloped in the literature. We conclude the chapter with a discussion of directions for future research and theoretical development.

LITERATURE REVIEW

Age Stereotypes

To understand the role of age and ageism in organizations, it is important to distinguish between attitudes toward and beliefs individuals have about older people, behavior toward older people, and institutional practices and policies as they relate to older people (Wilkinson & Ferraro, 2001). Much of the research exploring the content of older worker stereotypes in the United States is dated but suggests that people often hold negative and inaccurate beliefs about older workers. For example, older individuals have been perceived as less effective (O'Connell & Rotter, 1979), less active and energetic (Kogan & Shelton, 1960;

Levin, 1988), resistant to change, less creative, less trainable (Rosen & Jerdee, 1976b; 1977), more opinionated (Craft, Doctors, Shkop & Benecki, 1979), and having less performance capacity, potential for development and interpersonal skills (Crew, 1984; Rosen & Jerdee, 1976a). However, there is also evidence that beliefs about older workers are not always negative (Kite & Wagner, 2002). For example, older workers are often perceived to be more reliable and dependable (Rosen & Jerdee, 1976a).

There appear to be three trends in recent research related to age stereotypes. First, research is accumulating on the content of stereotypes in a variety of countries (e.g. Gibson, Zerbe & Franken, 1993; Gray & McGregor, 2003; Johansson, 2003; Lyon & Pollard, 1997; Singer, 1986; Smith, 2001; Steinberg, Donald, Najman & Skerman, 1996; Taylor & Walker, 1994; Warr & Pennington, 1993). For example, in a study of Canadian personnel managers, Gibson et al. (1993) found that older workers were perceived as more stable, experienced and having more individual initiative than younger workers. In contrast, younger workers were perceived as having greater potential for development than older workers. In a survey of respondents from New Zealand, Smith (2001) found evidence of negative stereotypes regarding older employees' interest in training and their ability to adapt to change and learn new skills. However, older workers were perceived to be more reliable, have greater interpersonal skills, have more useful experience and be more loyal. In a study of personnel managers and directors, Taylor and Walker (1994) reported that although employers appear to be developing more positive attitudes about older workers, they still perceive the latter as harder to train and as having difficulty adapting to new technology. In addition, there are some attempts to compare older worker stereotypes across countries (Chiu, Chan, Snape & Redman, 2001; Levy & Langer, 1994; Smith, 2001). For example, Chiu et al. (2001) compared and found some differences in the age-related stereotypes of individuals in Hong Kong and the UK. Similarly, Smith (2001) found both similarities and differences in the attitudes people held toward older non-managerial employees in New Zealand and the UK. Our review of this literature suggests that older worker stereotypes are ubiquitous and share a number of similarities across a variety of countries. While older workers are generally perceived as more dependable and stable, they are also perceived as more difficult to train, less adaptable and slower to learn.

A second trend in age stereotype research includes calls for and the beginning of explorations into economic dimensions of age-related stereotypes and perceptions (Finkelstein & Burke, 1998; Finkelstein, Higgins & Clancy, 2000). For example, Finkelstein and Burke (1998) found that older individuals were perceived as less economically beneficial. This is consistent with a survey of UK managers conducted by Arrowsmith and McGoldrick (1996) which found that 50% of those surveyed believed that older workers are more costly to employ. Finally, a survey of New Zealand employers found that only 25.5% of respondents indicated that older workers were more likely to offer a better return on investment (Gray & McGregor, 2003).

A third trend in the age stereotype research is a continued exploration of the effects of contextual factors (e.g. individual, organizational, decision-related) on attitudes toward older workers and older worker stereotypes (Chiu et al., 2001;

Finkelstein, Burke & Raju, 1995; Hassell & Perrewe, 1995). For example, Chiu et al. (2001) examined the extent to which organizational factors (organizational size, type of industry, having an equal opportunity policy that specifically refer-enced age) influenced attitudes that people held about older workers. They found that only one organizational factor, the existence of an ageism policy, influenced older worker stereotypes. The presence of age discrimination policies was signif-icantly associated with more positive beliefs about the adaptability of older work-ers and marginally associated with more favorable attitudes about providing older workers training. Hassell and Perrewe (1995) explored the effects of interactions with older workers, rater's supervisory status and age on beliefs about older workers. They found that younger workers' interactions with older workers significantly and positively affected their beliefs about older workers. Moreover, older supervisors had more negative beliefs about older workers than younger supervisors. Much of the existing research has focused on individual-level factors, particularly the role of rater age. The study by Chiu et al. (2001) represents one of the few research efforts that considers the influence of contextual variables at multiple and higher levels of analysis (country, organization).

We have identified three trends in the age stereotype literature: exploration of age stereotypes across multiple countries; study into economic dimensions of age-related stereotypes and perceptions; and continued exploration of the effects of contextual factors on age-related attitudes and stereotypes. The majority of the research we cite has taken one of two methodological approaches. One approach presents raters (college students, employees) with hypothetical person profiles and asks them to describe the individuals in the profiles using traits or character-istics and/or make employment decisions about these individuals. This research typically manipulates the age of the target and compares evaluations of older and younger hypothetical individuals (e.g. Kogan & Shelton, 1960; Rosen & Jerdee, 1976b; 1977). Age has been treated as both a within- and between-subjects factor in this research. The second approach asks raters (primarily non-student samples) to describe older and younger individuals (e.g. using lists of traits). These studies do not manipulate the age of hypothetical employees or applicants. Direct com-parisons of older and younger workers are often made in this research (Gibson et al., 1993; Lyon & Pollard, 1997).

Age stereotypes may underlie attitudes about, behaviors toward and organiza-tional policies and practices that affect older workers. Next, we review research that explores the role of age in employment decisions, organizational behavior, and organizational policies and practices related to various stages of the employ-ment relationship (recruitment and selection, training and career development, performance evaluations and exits from the organization).

Age, Recruitment and Selection

Sullivan and Duplaga (1997) noted that studies on the effects of age on employ-ment decisions have consistently found a bias in favor of younger applicants. Relatively few respondents to surveys report targeting older workers in recruitment

(Robson, 2001). Moreover, there is some evidence that older job searchers face more obstacles than younger job searchers. For example, older job searchers take longer to find jobs and take pay cuts when they find them (Simon, 1996). Although a review of the literature exploring the role of age in access discrimination appeared toward the end of the 1990s (Perry, 1997), relatively little US-based research has been conducted since that time (see Bendick, Brown & Wall, 1999, for an exception). Bendick et al. (1999) found that older confederates applying for real entry-level sales and management jobs received less favorable responses from employers 41.2% of the time compared to younger and equally qualified confederates. In her review, Perry (1997) observed that while early research focused on the main effects of age on selection decisions, later research considered the role of contextual factors in selection decisions (Perry, 1997).

A contextual variable that has received significant research attention is the nature of the job for which applicants apply. A number of studies have examined whether older applicants are evaluated more positively for jobs that are perceived to be 'old-typed', while younger applicants are evaluated more positively for jobs perceived to be 'young-typed' (Cleveland, Festa & Montgomery, 1988; Perry, 1994; Perry & Bourhis, 1998; Perry, Kulik, & Bourhis, 1996). These studies have primarily relied on lab experimental methodologies using student samples, and focused on a relatively narrow range of jobs. This research has not found consistent evidence for the hypothesized age by job interaction. Perry (1997) speculated that this may be due to the fact that the age by job interaction is moderated by other factors (e.g. rater age bias) which when unmeasured obscure results. In addition, earlier research, for the most part, failed to consider the possibility that the age by job interaction is asymmetric. However, research finds that older applicants applying for young-typed and typically less prestigious jobs may be penalized more than young applicants applying for old-typed and more prestigious jobs (Perry et al., 1996).

Recent research has considered contextual variables in addition to job stereotypes that may moderate the effect of age on selection decisions (e.g. Finkelstein & Burke, 1998; Perry et al., 1996). For example, based on social cognition and social identity theories, Finkelstein and Burke (1998) developed hypotheses about the effects of rater age, age salience, job-relevant information and age identity on the likelihood of being interviewed. Among a sample of managers who were asked to evaluate an older and younger hypothetical applicant, the researchers found that older applicants were less likely to be given an interview than equally qualified younger applicants. They also found evidence for an unpredicted interaction between rater age and age identity in the low age salience condition. For raters higher in age identity, as rater age increased, likelihood to interview ratings for both older and younger targets were higher. For raters lower in age identity, ratings decreased with rater age. In addition to exploring an interaction between age and job stereotypes, Perry et al. (1996) studied the role of raters' age bias and the extent to which raters were cognitively busy on their selection decisions regarding hypothetical applicants. They found that age congruence effects (applicant age × job age-type) were stronger when raters were biased against older workers. In addition an applicant age × age bias × cognitive busyness interaction was found. The differential evaluation of older and younger applicants resulting from high rater bias was greater in the busy compared to the non-busy condition as predicted. When low-bias subjects were not cognitively busy they evaluated the older and younger applicants comparably as expected. However, contrary to expectation, low-bias subjects evaluated the old applicant more favorably than the young applicant when they were cognitively busy.

We have two overall observations about recent US-based research exploring the role of age in recruitment and selection. First, relatively little field research has been conducted (Perry, 1997). Second, much of the recent research that has been conducted has relied on social cognition and social identity theories to make predictions about the context in which age discrimination in selection is most likely. This may explain the limited attention given to organizational and environmental factors that may play a role in age discrimination. Both observations suggest the importance of future research employing multiple and diverse methodologies and exploring a broader range of contextual factors.

In contrast to US-based research, relatively little experimental research exploring the effects of age on recruitment and selection has been conducted outside the United States (for exceptions see Gringart & Helmes, 2001; Singer & Sewell, 1988; van Beek, Koopmans & van Praag, 1997). An exception is a study by van Beek et al. (1997) which manipulated attributes (including age) of fictitious job applicants and studied the effects on Dutch managers' selection-related judgments. They found significantly lower preferences for older compared to equally capable younger applicants. The majority of recruitment and selection research that has been undertaken outside the United States has involved large-scale descriptive surveys of personnel and line managers' attitudes about older workers and reports about employers' policies toward older workers (Taylor & Walker, 1993; 1998). For example, Taylor and Walker (1993; 1994) conducted a mail survey of 500 personnel managers and directors in the UK in 1991. Forty-three percent of this sample considered age to be an important factor in the recruitment of employees. Fifteen percent of the sample reported that they specified maximum recruiting ages in advertisements for jobs. In addition, a majority of respondents indicated that individuals 60 years of age were too old to recruit. Taylor and Walker (1998) further explored this data to assess whether attitudes regarding older workers were related to respondents' reports that their organization was interested in recruiting more older people. They found that respondents who believed that older people wanted to train and had 'a lot of mileage left in them' were more likely to report that their organization was seeking to recruit more older people. The authors concluded that managers' attitudes are associated with employment practices that directly affect older workers.

In 2000, the London-based Chartered Institute of Personnel and Development sponsored a large, nationally representative phone survey of 1004 adults designed to study self-reported experiences of age discrimination (Compton-Edwards, 2001). Respondents reported that they faced age discrimination in recruitment because of recruitment advertisements which indicated an age limit (12% of respondents in paid work) or recruiters who perceived them to be too old (10% of respondents aged 45–54). A 1995 survey of organizations across 15 EU countries suggested that relatively few organizations across Europe target individuals over

50 in recruitment. The percentage of employers increasing their numbers of older recruits varied somewhat across countries (Parsons & Mayne, 2001). Norway, the exception, reported the highest percentage of employers (approximately 40%) increasing recruitment of workers over 50. Approximately 10% of employers in the UK, Switzerland, France and Ireland reported increasing the number of older recruits, while even smaller percentages reported doing so in the remaining EU countries. Finally, Steinberg et al. (1996) found that a small minority of Australian executives favored recruiting individuals aged 45 and older.

Age, Performance and Performance Evaluation

Research on age and job performance in the workplace has traditionally focused on actual declines in physical and mental abilities as a function of age and the role of stereotypes in performance evaluations of older workers (Liden, Stilwell & Ferris, 1996). Warr (1994) concluded that, 'The overall finding from more than 100 research investigations is that there is no significant difference between the job performance of older and younger workers' (p. 309). In addition, Warr (1994) noted that differences within age groups typically exceed average differences across them. Although the majority of studies that have been conducted have assessed performance using supervisors' ratings, a number of studies have explored actual job performance. A review of the latter indicates that job performance typically increases up to the age of 44 then continues to increase, plateaus or declines slightly (Warr, 1994). The lack of an *overall* relationship between age and job performance may be explained by the fact that although age is related to declines (e.g. response speed, working memory), these may be offset by other factors (e.g. experience) and they are likely to occur after the age at which people retire from the workforce (Greller & Simpson, 1999; Warr, 1994).

Recent studies have considered the role of context in the age–performance relationship to a greater extent. A number of studies exploring issues of age and job performance have relied on theories of organizational demography (Liden et al., 1996; Pelled, Eisenhardt & Xin, 1999; Tsui, Porter & Egan, 2002; Webber & Donahue, 2001). Research exploring the effects of demographic background on work behaviors and attitudes takes a compositional or relational demographic as compared to a categorical approach (Tsui et al., 2002). While a categorical approach explores the direct effects of an individual's age on job performance, a compositional approach considers the demographic make-up of a group and a relational demographic approach considers the relative demographics of an individual and the group or an individual and another individual. Both compositional and relational demographic approaches argue that demographic similarity leads to attraction and favorable treatment whereas dissimilarity results in less favorable perceptions and treatment (Tsui et al., 2002).

Organizational demography research (compositional and relational) has studied age as one of a number of demographic factors. For example, Webber and Donahue (2001) conducted a meta-analysis exploring the effects of work group demographic diversity on cohesion and work performance. They suggested that while work group diversity on some demographic dimensions (e.g. functional background) is likely to be relevant to the work group's task and therefore to positively influence group performance, other demographic dimensions such as age are less relevant to group tasks and are expected to have little influence on group performance. Results revealed that there was no overall relationship between demographic dimensions that were less job related (including age) and work group performance. Although there is some evidence that age similarity influences group processes (e.g. emotional conflict), these processes tend to have little effect on work group performance (Pelled et al., 1999).

Other researchers have explored the effects of demographic similarity between supervisors and subordinates on task performance and extra-role behavior (e.g. Liden et al., 1996; Perry, Kulik & Zhou, 1999; Shore, Cleveland & Goldberg, 2003; Tsui & O'Reilly, 1989; Tsui et al., 2002) primarily using field study methodology. For example, Liden et al. (1996) explored the effects of the age of sales representatives and their supervisors on both objective (e.g. average number of calls to retail outlets per day) and subjective measures (supervisors' ratings) of performance. They found that older employees performed better than younger employees on objective and subjective performance measures and subordinates of older supervisors outperformed subordinates of younger supervisors on objective performance measures. However, age similarity did not significantly predict objective or subjective performance ratings. Tsui and O'Reilly (1989) similarly found no evidence that the age similarity of supervisors and subordinates positively influenced performance ratings.

Some researchers have suggested that in some cases age dissimilarities between supervisors and subordinates may have positive effects on job performance and extra-role behaviors (e.g. Perry et al., 1999; Tsui et al., 2002). They argue that based on social/relational norms and the status associated with age, supervisors are expected to be older than their subordinates. Therefore, only certain age differences (when subordinates are older than their supervisors) are expected to have negative consequences for work performance. For example, Tsui et al. (2002) found that age similarity between supervisors and subordinates was positively associated with task performance (supervisor ratings) and extra-role behaviors (e.g. helping others; helping the organization). However, additional analyses revealed that subordinates who were older than their supervisors were rated lower on task performance and extra-role behaviors than subordinates who were younger or similar in age to their supervisors. In contrast, Perry et al. (1999) found that subordinates who were older than their immediate supervisors engaged in citizenship behaviors more frequently than subordinates who were younger than their immediate supervisors. Finally, Shore et al. (2003) found a significant interaction between employee and manager age on job performance. However, the pattern of this interaction differed depending on whether job performance was evaluated by employees or managers. Thus, while compositional demography research tends to find little support for the effects of age on performance, relational demography research has found some but inconsistent effects.

In contrast to demography research which directly explores the dynamics of age contexts, Cleveland and Shore (1992) studied the effects of person and context-oriented definitions of age on individuals' performance ratings and promotability. For example, they found that employees' perceptions of their age relative to their work group interacted with their chronological age to significantly influence managers' ratings of employees' performance. Specifically, chronologically older workers in younger work groups were given the highest ratings, while chronologically older workers in older work groups were given the lowest ratings. Finally, some primarily field study research has emphasized the role of age norms in performance ratings (e.g. Lawrence, 1988; 1996b; Saks & Waldman, 1998). This research suggests that there are age norms associated with jobs and that those who deviate from these norms may be vulnerable to rating bias. Age norms serve as a context that influences judgments about individuals.

While there appears to be some research attention to the relationship between age and performance, our review of more recent literature supports Clapham and Fulford's (1997) observation that 'there is a dearth of empirical research addressing the specific relationship between age and promotability' (p. 374; see Shore et al., 2003, for an exception). Based on a survey of employees and managers in a large multinational firm, Shore et al. (2003) found interactions between manager and employee chronological age consistently predicted performance and promotability. For example, younger mangers evaluated younger employees more highly on potential and promotability than older employees, while older managers evaluated older and younger employees similarly.

Relatively little recent research outside the United States has explored issues related to age and job performance. A study by Saba, Guerin and Wils (1998) found that the extent to which Canadian professionals, 50 years and older, perceived that their organization allowed them to meet their expectations regarding a variety of work conditions (e.g. by providing opportunities for promotion and a supportive environment), positively influenced self-reported work performance. In addition, research from the UK finds evidence of age stereotypes that would seem to have particular relevance for performance judgments (Taylor & Walker, 1994; Warr & Pennington, 1993). For example, there is evidence that older workers are perceived as more effective (e.g. more productive and reliable) but less adaptable (e.g. more inflexible) than younger workers (Taylor & Walker, 1994; Warr & Pennington, 1993).

Age, Training and Career Development

In today's rapidly changing workplace, continuous training and development are essential for organizational competitiveness. Those who do not update their skills may experience negative career consequences. Against this backdrop, there is evidence that older workers receive less formal training and career counseling than younger workers (Cleveland & Shore, 1992; Frazis, Gittleman & Joyce, 1998; Mirvis & Hall, 1996; Maurer & Rafuse, 2001). However, as Maurer and Rafuse (2001) pointed out, it is difficult to determine whether age differences are the result of employers' differential treatment of older workers or older workers' self-determined behavior.

Age differences in training may be due to differential access provided by employers. Some suggest that differential training access and treatment represents bias against older workers (Mirvis & Hall, 1996). As noted earlier, older workers are often perceived as less receptive to new ideas, less innovative, less future oriented, resistant to change and harder to train than younger individuals (Levin, 1988; Rosen & Jerdee, 1976a; 1976b; 1977). In a study of MBAs, Greller (2000) found evidence of age norms suggesting that people are expected to be less concerned with the development of new skills as they age. These stereotypes and age norms may play a role in the training gap (Mirvis & Hall, 1996). Relatively little empirical research has assessed the extent to which differential treatment contributes to age differences in training access (Maurer & Rafuse, 2001). However, a laboratory study conducted by Dedrick and Dobbins (1991) found that, following poor job performance, training was rated as more appropriate for younger compared to older subordinates. Further, there is some evidence that companies report spending more money on training younger than older workers (Barth, McNaught & Rizzi, 1993) and older workers may be given more routine job assignments which in turn provide fewer opportunities for development (Salthouse & Maurer, 1996).

It is important to note that some argue that employers' provision of younger workers with greater opportunities for training and development than older workers is not a function of bias. Human capital theory proposes that there are both higher opportunity costs of investing in training and shorter time horizons over which to reap the benefits of training investments in older workers. Therefore, this theory suggests that decisions to provide younger rather than older workers with greater opportunities and resources for training reflects rational and not biased decision making. However, some authors have called into question a number of the basic assumptions of human capital theory (e.g. Greller & Simpson, 1999) and find evidence that is not entirely consistent with this theory (Simpson, Greller & Stroh, 2002). Evidence that turnover among older workers is low, that the life of skills tends to be short, and that younger workers in fact tend to leave or to be poached by competitors (Gray & McGregor, 2003), calls into question the professed inability of employers to recoup their investment in training older workers. This type of research may help us determine the extent to which training outcomes are based on biased versus rational decisions.

A second explanation for differences in access to training experienced by older and younger workers is that employees are less inclined to participate in training and development activities as they get older (Salthouse & Maurer, 1996; Schabracq, 1994). Human capital theory suggests that older employees have disincentives to invest in their own training for the same reasons that employers do. Consistent with this, using archival data, Simpson et al. (2002) found that participation in general skills training declined with age. However, they also found that older workers were more likely to participate in training targeting the development of focused occupational skills (e.g. targeted career and job-related courses) than younger workers, suggesting that current economic models may be too simplistic. Motivation is an important factor influencing whether individuals update their skills (Sterns & Dorsett, 1994). However, negative stereotypes may reduce older workers' confidence and motivation to participate in training and development opportunities and take on challenging work assignments. Some authors have suggested that organizational factors may also influence individuals' willingness to engage in development activities (Salthouse & Maurer, 1996; Sterns & Dorsett, 1994).

Ultimately, older workers' participation in training and career development activities may be a function of both individual and organizational factors (Salthouse & Maurer, 1996; Sterns & Dorsett, 1994). For example, in a theoretical paper, Maurer (2001) suggested that self-efficacy for development of career-relevant skills influences voluntary participation in training and development activities. Further, organizational-level factors (e.g. supervisory support, availability of training and development resources) and individual-level factors (e.g. anxiety and health) may adversely affect key antecedents (e.g. mastery experiences, physiological influences) of self-efficacy with increasing age. Exploring these relationships is a useful direction for future research.

Another topic of interest in the literature is the relationship between age and job-related training performance. A meta-analysis by Kubeck, Delp, Haslett and McDaniel (1996) found that, in general, older individuals showed less mastery of training material, completed the final training task more slowly, and took longer to complete the training program than younger individuals. A more recent meta-analysis (Callahan, Kiker & Cross, 2003), focusing on older learners, found that both the instructional method used (e.g. lecture, modeling, active participation) and instructional factors (e.g. self-pacing, trainee group size) influenced older learners' training performance. Specifically, the use of lecture, modeling and active participation methods positively improved the training performance of older learners. In addition, training that occurred in smaller groups or that allowed for self-pacing was also positively associated with training performance. Evidence of age differences in training performance has led to suggestions for developing training programs (e.g. longer training times) that may be beneficial to all workers, particularly older workers (Sterns & Doverspike, 1989). However, organizations tend not to adjust their training as a function of trainee age (Barth et al., 1993; Mirvis & Hall, 1996).

Hall and Mirvis (1995) noted that more attention has been given to training older workers than longer-term career development issues. It is widely observed that traditional linear models of career development where individuals are expected to move through a sequence of predictable career stages are obsolete (Sullivan, 1999). More contemporary conceptions of careers emphasize the importance of individual differences, changing circumstances and continuous learning (Hall & Mirvis, 1995; Sterns & Miklos, 1995). More attention to this area is important as some have observed that in the context of current demographic changes, careers will mostly likely be extended raising issues about how best to facilitate this process (Greller & Simpson, 1999).

We found limited recent research on issues related to age and training outside of the United States. However, several surveys have been conducted primarily in the UK, exploring respondents' attitudes about age and training and organizational practices related to training. One survey of MBA students in the UK found that students held negative views about older workers' ability to learn quickly, grasp new ideas and their interest in training (Lyon & Pollard, 1997). Similarly, a large survey of personnel directors and managers by Taylor and Walker (1994) found that a significant portion of employers agreed that older workers were less trainable than younger workers. In a survey of UK managers by Arrowsmith and McGoldrick (1996), 38% reported that there were age barriers related to training. Finally, Gray and McGregor

(2003) found that 32.5% of New Zealand employers and 23.6% of employees aged 55 and over agreed that older workers were more likely to be less willing to train.

Consistent with US-based research, research conducted outside of the United States also reveals that there are fewer training opportunities for older compared to younger workers. For example, a study of Dutch supervisors found that older employees tended to hold jobs in which there were fewer opportunities for learning and development (Boerlijst, 1994). In addition, older employees received less training than younger employees. Taylor and Walker (1994) reported that 13% of UK respondents did not train management past the age of 50 and that 17% did not train other staff past the age of 50. Similarly, in their study of UK managers, Arrowsmith and McGoldrick (1996) found that 40% of those aged 55 and older reported receiving no training within the previous 12 months compared to 18% of those under 35 years of age. In separate surveys of New Zealand employers and employees aged 55 and older respectively, Gray and McGregor (2003) reported a gap between what employers espoused and what employees reported they received with respect to training opportunities. Finally, Dixon (2003) noted that there is a negative relationship between age and participation in job-related training, but that age differences are relatively modest. As was the case in the US literature, relatively little research outside the United States has explored issues of career development and age specifically. An exception to this is Saba et al.'s (1998) study of senior Canadian public sector professionals that suggests that organizations' training and career development practices may influence the extent to which older individuals feel their work aspirations can be achieved in their current organization. These latter perceptions can in turn affect job outcomes such as job satisfaction and organizational commitment.

Age and Exits from the Organization

There are a number of ways in which employees exit organizations. Three in particular have received considerable research attention in recent years: voluntary turnover; involuntary turnover (e.g. layoffs/downsizing); and retirement. In his review of the literature, Warr (1994) concluded that voluntary turnover is lower among older compared to younger workers. However, a meta-analysis conducted by Healy, Lehman and McDaniel (1995) found that the relationship between age and voluntary turnover was small and near zero. In contrast to this evidence, many have suggested and found that older workers are likely to be targeted in downsizings and layoffs due to negative older worker stereotypes (e.g. older workers are less adaptable to change), the fact that they tend to occupy mid-level positions that are often the focus of downsizing, and due to slow company growth (Mirvis & Hall, 1996; Sterns & Gray, 1999). Based on a study conducted by *Money Magazine*, Simon (1996) reported that more than 16% of 55–64 year old workers were downsized or laid off between 1991 and 1993, an increase of 5% from the early 1980s. In contrast, the percentage of workers aged 20–24 decreased from 19% in the early 1980s to less than 16% between 1991 and 1993. In addition, displaced older workers took longer to find jobs and those finding jobs often had to take reductions in pay. Similarly, Chan and Stevens (2001) found that job loss (i.e. involuntary separations) at age 50 or older significantly reduced the future employment probabilities of older workers.

While early research in the United States focused on the relationship between age and individual turnover, more recent research has begun to consider the role of contextual factors at both the individual and group levels of analysis. For example, organizational demography research has explored the effect of age context on turnover. Demography researchers suggest that differences in age may result in communication difficulties and conflict, lower social integration and therefore increased turnover (Williams & O'Reilly, 1998). In a review of diversity research, Milliken and Martins (1996) concluded that turnover rates are higher in groups that are more dissimilar in terms of age. In addition, individuals who are different from their group members on age are more likely to turnover. Later reviews of the demography literature (Riordan, 2000; Williams & O'Reilly, 1998) confirmed that age dissimilarity is positively related to turnover behavior and intentions. Additional research has explored how age may interact with a variety of situational variables (e.g. employment status, pay and work values, reward systems) to influence exit behavior (Finegold, Mohrman & Spreitzer, 2002; Riordan, Griffith & Weatherly, 2003). For example, Finegold et al. (2002) found that satisfaction with job security was more strongly related to older than younger workers' desire to remain in their companies. In addition, satisfaction with opportunities to develop technical skills and pay linked to individuals' performance had a stronger negative relationship with willingness to change companies for those under 30 relative to those over 45. However, the authors noted that while the effects of age are statistically significant, they are small. Together this research suggests that the relationship between age and turnover behavior may vary as a function of situational factors.

There is a significant amount of research exploring retirement issues in the United States. Research, for example, has explored the factors that influence retirement decisions. Factors identified as important to the retirement decision include: pension plan incentives, financial status, health status, job difficulty and spouses' retirement status (Hansson et al., 1997; Yeatts, Folts & Knapp, 1999). Two issues that have received increasing attention are trends toward early retirement and increasingly blurred exits from the workforce.

First, there is a trend toward early retirement (Han & Moen, 1999; Sterns & Gray, 1999). Consistent with this, there is evidence that people plan to retire earlier than perceived retirement age norms (Sterns & Gray, 1999). A significant negative implication of this trend, along with the aging of the workforce, is cost pressure placed on government-funded retirement systems (e.g. Social Security). As a result, US policy has focused on ways to increase the time older workers can spend in the workforce and reduce obstacles that make it difficult for older workers to be employed (Robson, 2001). The decision to retire is complex and influenced by a variety of personal and environmental factors (Sterns & Gray, 1999). Hansson et al. (1997) suggested that what is currently needed is an integration of current findings and theoretical perspectives.

Second, there is an increasing tendency toward 'blurred' rather than 'crisp' exits from the workforce (Han & Moen, 1999; Hansson et al., 1997; Sterns & Gray, 1999). Individuals are increasingly likely to exit and reenter the workforce with no clear-cut transition to retirement. Transitions to retirement may involve bridge jobs, either related or unrelated to the individual's previous career, that help employees make a gradual transition to retirement (Greller & Stroh, 1995). Education and financial situation are most predictive of postretirement employment (Han & Moen, 1999). However, there is evidence that late career job changes have negative consequences on compensation and job status (Greller & Simpson, 1999). Older workers appear to desire phased retirement and there appears to be some, albeit small, movement on the part of employers to provide it (e.g. chances to transfer to less demanding jobs) (Mirvis & Hall, 1996; Robson, 2001).

The majority of recent research exploring the relationship between age and organizational exits outside of the United States provides evidence that older workers are more likely than younger workers to be targeted for redundancy and focuses on trends toward early retirement. First, several researchers in the UK observed that older workers were more likely than younger workers to be made redundant in the late 1970s and early 1980s (Walker & Taylor, 1993). In addition, the negative impact of redundancy was greater for older than younger workers. Walker and Taylor (1993) suggested that employer attitudes played a significant role in these redundancy decisions and were reinforced by public policy that encouraged redundancy among older workers. In a more recent survey, 58% of managers indicated that they employed downsizing strategies targeting older workers and 54% indicated that older employees would be more likely to be made redundant in their organizations because of their age (Arrowsmith & McGoldrick, 1996). It is important to note that the existence of age discrimination laws in the United States and their current absence in the UK would make it difficult to employ similar research methodologies in the United States. Arrowsmith and McGoldrick's (1996) findings are consistent with Patrickson and Hartmann's (1995) observation that older workers in Australia were more likely to be targeted for redundancies during the spate of downsizings that occurred in the late 1980s and early 1990s.

The overwhelming majority of recent research and writing outside of the United States documents and discusses the trend toward early retirement and the implications of this trend for public policy (Kilbom, 1999). In their survey of personnel directors and managers in the UK, Taylor and Walker (1994) found little evidence that male respondents worked past the state pension age of 65 years. Much discussion has been given to how public policy in many European countries traditionally supported early retirement (e.g. Parsons & Mayne, 2001; Taylor, 2001; Taylor & Walker, 1997; Van Dalen & Henkens, 2002; Walker & Taylor, 1993). However, in light of the aging of the workforce and reduction in the number of younger entrants, governmental policies across Europe and elsewhere are increasingly changing to encourage older workers to remain in or reenter the workforce (Parsons & Mayne, 2001; Robson, 2001; Taylor, 2001; Taylor & Walker, 1997; Walker & Taylor, 1993; Weber, Whitting, Sidaway & Moore, 1997). For example, a number of countries have made eligibility for early retirement more difficult, increased retirement age (Germany, Japan, New Zealand, Ireland, United States), provided financial incentives to employers who employ older workers (e.g. France, Germany), and experimented with delayed retirement (Kilbom, 1999; Taylor, 2001). These changes are largely driven by concerns about cost pressures on public pensions and retirement funds (Parsons & Mayne, 2001). Many authors discuss the effects of current public policies and make suggestions for policy changes (e.g. encourage the use of gradual retirement schemes). For example, Van Dalen and Henkens (2002) explored the extent to which two different early-retirement policies (traditional versus more actuarially neutral) might influence the age at which Dutch respondents' retire. The traditional scheme was one that encouraged early retirement with most firms fixing the early-retirement age at 60 and providing up to 80% of the gross wage, whereas the newer early-retirement scheme was intended to discourage early exit from the organization by equating time accumulated at work with the retirement payout.

Some authors have noted that trends toward early retirement have been supported not only by public policy, but by organizational policies and the expectations and attitudes of many older employees themselves (Kilbom, 1999; Parsons & Mayne, 2001). Organizational policies may not support recent governmental attempts to increase the work life of older employees (Clark & Ogawa, 1996; Van Dalen & Henkens, 2002). There is little evidence that employers are taking steps to encourage later retirement and may actually prefer retirement at lower ages (Taylor & Walker, 1994; Weber et al., 1997). For example, despite government pressures, Japanese firms have been reluctant to increase mandatory retirement ages due to concerns about the costs of employing older workers (Clark & Ogawa, 1996). Moreover, Taylor and Walker (1994) reported that more than two-fifths of respondents had voluntary early-retirement systems in place. In a study of Dutch supervisors, Henkens (2000) reported that a third indicated that they wanted all of their older subordinates to stop working upon reaching early-retirement age (60 years). In addition, some research has explored factors (respondent age, job requirements, organizational context, and expectations about older workers' performance) that may influence peoples' perceptions about appropriate retirement ages (Henkens, 2000; Joulain, Mullet, Lecomte & Prevost, 2000).

There is also evidence that older workers seem to prefer early retirement. Most Dutch organizations use 60 as their minimum age of retirement. However, a study of Dutch residents indicated a preference to retire at an average age of 58.6 years if they could choose their retirement date freely (Van Dalen & Henkens, 2002). Research in Europe and Japan finds that in addition to external factors (e.g. public pension plan, wage system), internal factors (e.g. health status, financial security, family status) also influence older workers' retirement decisions (Watanabe-Muraoka, Kawasaki & Sato, 1998; Weber et al., 1997).

THE IMPORTANCE OF CULTURE

A trend that we found across the literatures that we reviewed is an increasing tendency to consider the role of context in the relationship between age and employment outcomes and behaviors. National culture is a contextual variable that has, to date, received relatively little attention. Culture is the 'collective programming of the mind that distinguishes the members of one group or category of people from another' (Hofstede, 2001: 9). These collective values or norms of a society are part of the environment in which organizations exist and manifest themselves in organizational practices and policies. There are two reasons why we believe more international and cross-cultural research is needed. First, Parsons and Mayne (2001) observed that international research on aging has been sparse and has not systematically studied age-related issues across countries. In addition, the research that has been conducted relies heavily on the US experience. Relatedly, despite evidence that the status of older people varies across cultures (Cox, 1990), there is little cross-cultural research exploring issues of aging in organizations. Kite and Wagner (2002) observed that 'a comprehensive understanding of culture's influence on attitudes toward ageing and older adults is lacking' (p. 152). Second, the limited research we found comparing age effects across countries suggests that there are potentially important similarities as well as differences in how age influences employment attitudes and outcomes. For example, Tsui et al. (2002) speculated that norms surrounding age may be more salient in cultures that place greater value on the elderly with different implications for the effect of age on workplace attitudes and behaviors.

As a result of the relatively little cross-cultural research comparing attitudes about, behaviors toward and organizational policies regarding older workers conducted, there is minimal information about the relative standing of any given country on these factors. Furthermore, to date, a narrow range of countries has been studied and cumulative knowledge about the cross-cultural effects of age on any given criterion is limited. Many of the cross-cultural studies we identified used the United States or UK as a point of comparison with other countries. Therefore, we focus our review using the UK and United States as benchmarks.

Cultural Comparisons Relative to the United States

Levy and Langer (1994) compared the attitudes of Americans and citizens of mainland China about aging. Chinese participants in their study had more favorable attitudes about aging than American participants. The authors suggested that China has a long and strong tradition of honoring its elders. Pelled and Xin (2000) studied the extent to which age similarity between supervisors and subordinates influenced the quality of supervisor–subordinate relationships in the United States and Mexico. The authors suggested that relational age norms are quite strong in Mexico and that workers expect those in positions of power to be older than those in lower positions of power. In addition, they noted that older individuals command respect in Mexico. This suggests that violations of age norms (subordinates older than their supervisors) should result in more negative consequences in Mexico than in the United States. Consistent with this, they found age similarity had a stronger negative effect in Mexico than in the United States. In other words, when expected differences in age did not occur, the quaity of the relationship between supervisors and subordinates suffered. The quality of the relationship between supervisors and subordinates is likely to have implications for a number of employment outcomes including job performance and turnover intentions (Gerstner & Day, 1997). The authors also observed that relational demography effects accounted for more variance in the US than in the Mexican sample.

Farh, Tsui, Xin and Cheng (1998) studied the effects of age similarity in supervisor–subordinate dyads in Taiwan. The authors indicated that predicting age effects is difficult. China has strong relational age norms and age is accorded special status and respect. Thus, positive reactions of a younger supervisor toward an older and respected subordinate may contrast with the negative effect an older subordinate experiences in a relatively lower-status position. Although they did not directly compare age effects in China and the United States, they concluded that their results differed from the typical pattern found in the United States. Specifically, they found no effect for age similarity on performance, organizational commitment or trust in supervisor. They suggested that this may be because demographic variables, including age, are less important in some cultures than others. Their research suggested that particularistic ties that involve interpersonal relationships between individuals (e.g. being a relative, having the same ancestral origin) may be a more important basis than demographic variables for social identification and attraction between employees in China.

Cultural Comparisons Relative to the UK

Smith (2001) reported that although there were similarities in attitudes held toward older individuals, respondents from New Zealand tended to have more positive attitudes than respondents from the UK. Interestingly, New Zealand has more legislative protections in place for older workers than the UK. Not surprisingly, results also indicated that New Zealand respondents were more likely to prefer legislation against age discrimination than UK respondents. Chiu et al. (2001) compared age stereotypes of respondents in Hong Kong and the UK. They did not make a prediction about the effect of country on age stereotypes because they suggested that complex dynamics may be at work. While Hong Kong puts less emphasis on individual rights, it also has a strong tradition of respecting the elderly. Although UK respondents did not have uniformly more positive stereotypes than Hong Kong respondents, the researchers concluded that, overall, Hong Kong respondents were more prone to age discrimination than were UK respondents. For example, Hong Kong respondents were more likely to believe that younger workers should be given priority with respect to training opportunities, and more UK (47%) than Hong Kong respondents (10%) indicated that employees did not experience age discrimination in the region where they worked. Finally, Johansson (2003) assessed younger people's perceptions and experiences of older employees in the UK and Sweden. Although they did not seem to be interested in directly comparing the attitudes of respondents across the two countries (and would have difficulty doing so given their small sample size), they concluded that attitudes across the two countries were very similar.

Parsons and Mayne (2001) reported the results of a large-scale survey conducted across 15 countries. Their primary focus was comparing UK employers' human resource policies and practices with those of employers in other countries. For example, they indicated that a greater percentage of employers in Norway reported increasing their number of older recruits and used flexible working time as a method to recruit and retain older workers than in the UK. In addition, a greater percentage of French than UK employers introduced phased retirement to support the recruitment and retention of older workers.

Finally, in their cross-cultural study, Chiu et al. (2001) found that only 13% of respondents in their Hong Kong sample reported that they worked for an organization that had an age discrimination policy compared to 43% of respondents in the UK sample. Moreover, the presence of age discrimination policies was associated with more positive beliefs about older workers.

Additional Studies

In addition to the research comparing particular countries to the UK or United States, Weber et al. (1997) provided a qualitative review of governmental and organizational policies and practices across four European countries: France, Germany, Spain and Sweden. They concluded that although employers in all four countries seem to prefer the use of early-retirement and redundancy policies to manage their workforces, this is less the case in Sweden than in the other three countries. In addition, there was some evidence that employer policies in Sweden, relative to the other three countries, are more supportive of development opportunities that are open to all employees.

In his review of the literature exploring the relationship between age and job performance, Warr (1994) cited studies from both the UK and the United States which indicated that the relationship between age and job performance is nonexistent. This research suggests that the age–job performance relationship appears to be similar across the UK and the United States. However, a number of authors report that employers in the UK continue to use age information in their job advertisements (Taylor & Walker, 1993) and employees report experiencing age discrimination in recruitment because of age limits in job advertisements (Compton-Edwards, 2001). The use of age limits in job advertisements in the United States is prohibited by legislation protecting older workers' rights. The UK currently has no formal legislation protecting the rights of older workers (Chiu et al., 2001). Thus, there are likely to be fewer organizational and governmental policies protecting older workers in the UK relative to the United States.

The limited cross-cultural and international research that has explored the role of age and ageism in organizations suggests that culture may be a relevant contextual factor. Specifically, the relationship between age and a number of employment processes and outcomes may differ as a function of cultural, historical, legal, economic and political factors that differ in important ways across countries. Future theoretical and empirical research is necessary to develop and test a framework for understanding how the role of age in employment may differ across countries. This may be valuable in light of increasing globalization and the aging of a number of populations worldwide.

DISCUSSION

Our review of the literature suggests that older worker stereotypes are ubiquitous and share a number of similarities across a variety of countries. Older workers are consistently perceived as more dependable and reliable, more difficult to train and less adaptable. However, despite significant overlap in the content of older worker stereotypes across countries, there appear to be some differences in the favorability of attitudes toward older workers across countries (e.g. Chiu et al., 2001; Smith, 2001).

While US-based research has traditionally relied more on experimental than field methodologies, research in other countries has tended to use large-scale surveys to study issues surrounding age, recruitment and selection. However, research in the United States and abroad finds consistent evidence that older workers face more obstacles in recruitment and selection than younger workers (e.g. Sullivan & Duplaga, 1997; Taylor & Walker, 1993). Research, particularly in the United States, currently seems focused on exploring the contexts in which biases against older workers in recruitment and selection are most likely to operate.

Both US- and internationally based research finds little to no overall relationship between age and job performance (Warr, 1994). However, recent research in the United States suggests that it may be important to consider the role of age context in performance evaluations. Specifically, some age differences between supervisors and subordinates may have negative implications for subordinates' performance ratings (Shore et al., 2003; Tsui et al., 2002).

There is consistent evidence in the United States and abroad that older workers generally receive less training than younger workers (Boerlijst, 1994; Cleveland & Shore, 1992; Frazis et al., 1998; Taylor & Walker, 1994). What is unclear are the reasons for these differences. Some authors have suggested that it is important to explore not only individual-level factors such as age, but factors correlated with age as well as organizational factors (Maurer, 2001; Sterns & Dorsett, 1994). US-based research has also found consistent evidence of a negative relationship between age and job-related training performance (Kubeck et al., 1996).

While there is little evidence that age is significantly related to voluntary turnover (Healy et al., 1995), there is some evidence that older workers are likely targets in layoffs and downsizings in the United States and abroad (Patrickson & Hartmann, 1995; Simon, 1996; Walker & Taylor, 1993). In addition, US research has more recently considered the role that age context (e.g. age distribution of the work group) plays in turnover behavior and intentions (Milliken & Martins, 1996; Riordan, 2000). A great deal of attention has been given to issues related to the trend toward early retirement found in the United States and many industrialized countries. Much of this research focuses on factors influencing retirement decisions and policy issues.

Implications for Theory and Research

Based on our review of the literature we make three general observations and discuss their implications for future research and theoretical development. First, there is no single theoretical framework that has been proposed to explain the role of age in employment outcomes and behavior. This is most likely a function of the fact that the role of age in organizations has been studied across a number of disciplines (e.g. psychology, sociology, economics, gerontology) that have often applied different theories to understand different outcomes and behaviors at different levels of analysis. As a result, it is difficult to have a complete understanding of how age operates in the workplace. For example, age stereotypes and age norms are often studied by researchers in different disciplines (psychologists versus sociologists), applying different although related theoretical frameworks. We call for a more systematic theoretical integration of knowledge across disciplines in order to advance our understanding of the role age plays in organizations. A tighter theoretical framework may also contribute to a more systematic approach to studying age-related topics.

Second, there is a trend, particularly in US-based research, to explore the contexts in which age plays a greater and lesser role in employment outcomes. For example, based on our review, research finds that organizational factors (e.g. anti-age discrimination policies) may influence attitudes about older workers; the nature of jobs (e.g. age-typing) may influence selection decisions; age norms and the relative age of supervisors and subordinates may influence subordinates' performance ratings and the latter may also influence extra-role behaviors; and age dissimilarity of a group may influence turnover behavior. To date, national culture as context has received little attention in the literature.

As a result of the limited cross-cultural research conducted, it is difficult to make any firm conclusions about the role culture plays in organizational age effects. We suggest that there is a need for more cross-cultural research in order to obtain a fuller understanding of the influence of culture on age and ageism in organizations. In addition to relatively stable cultural values, future research and theory should also consider features of countries that may have more variable and short-term effects on the role of age in organizations. For example, current economic conditions (e.g. labor shortages) and political situations may influence the role that age plays in employment decisions. We also encourage cross-cultural studies of countries that have received relatively little attention to date. For example, unlike many modern industrialized countries, population aging is not viewed as a problem in a number of Middle Eastern countries where birth rates are relatively high (Turner & Lichtenstein, 2002). It may be particularly informative to study the role of age in these countries compared to those experiencing rapid aging of their workforces. Countries are likely to differ in the relative importance they place on age in society. For example, research by Farh et al. (1998) suggested that age information may be more important in US than Chinese organizations. A theoretical framework is needed to better understand and predict the role of age and ageism across cultures. We also encourage researchers to expand the set of criteria that they explore, while at the same time conducting a sufficient amount of research on each criterion so that more definitive conclusions can be drawn.

Third, research tends to address individual biases (e.g. age, gender, race) in isolation (Cleveland & Hollman, 1991) and our review focused on the role of age in employment processes and outcomes. However, individuals are simultaneously members of multiple demographic categories (e.g. age, race, gender, ethnicity). There is evidence that an individual's age may interact with his or her other demographic characteristics to influence employment outcomes (e.g. Duncan & Loretto, 2004; Goldberg, Finkelstein, Perry & Konrad, 2004; Gringart & Helmes, 2001; Perry, 1997). For example, Gringart and Helmes found evidence of actual age discrimination in hiring against older Australians with older women experiencing the most discrimination. Consistent with this, a survey of employees in a UK financial services firm found women were more likely than men to experience ageist attitudes across all ages (Duncan & Loretto, 2004). Results of this study also revealed that women may be perceived as older earlier in their careers and be perceived to experience performance declines at a younger age relative to men. The authors observed that little is known about how age interacts with gender to influence employment outcomes. We suggest that future research and theoretical development are necessary to begin to understand how and when age interacts with other demographic characteristics of individuals (in addition to gender) to influence employment outcomes.

Age-related issues have received a great deal of attention in the popular press and some academic literature due to the aging of workforces and concerns about the effect of retirement on public pensions across a number of countries. However, despite this interest, it is remarkable how much we still do not understand about the role that age plays in organizational life and how this role may vary across countries.

REFERENCES

Arrowsmith, J., & McGoldrick, A. (1996). *Breaking the barriers: A survey of managers' attitudes to age and employment*. London: The Institute of Management.

Atchley, R. C. (2000). *Social forces and aging: An introduction to social gerontology* (9th edn). Belmont, CA: Wadsworth Thomson Learning.

Barth, M. C., McNaught, W., & Rizzi, P. (1993). Corporations and the aging workforce. In P. H. Mirvis (Ed.), *Building the competitive workforce: Investing in human capital for corporate success* (pp. 156–99). New York: Wiley.

Bendick, M., Jr, Brown, L. E., & Wall, K. (1999). No foot in the door: An experimental study of employment discrimination against older workers. *Journal of Aging & Social Policy, 10*(4), 5–23.

Boerlijst, J. (1994). The neglect of growth and development of employees over 40 in organizations: A managerial and training problem. In J. Snel & R. Cremer (Eds), *Work and aging: A European perspective* (pp. 251–71). London: Taylor & Francis.

Brewer, M. B. (1988). A dual process model of impression formation. In T. K. Srull & R. S. Wyer, Jr (Eds), *Advances in social cognition, Volume I* (pp. 1–36). Hillsdale, NJ: Lawrence Erlbaum Associates.

Callahan, J. S., Kiker, D. S., & Cross, T. (2003). Does method matter? A meta-analysis of the effects of training method on older learner training performance. *Journal of Management*, *29*(5), 663–80.

Chan, S., & Stevens, A. H. (2001). Job loss and employment patterns of older workers. *Journal of Labor Economics*, *19*(2), 484–521.

Chiu, W. C. K., Chan, A. W., Snape, E. & Redman, T. (2001). Age stereotypes and discriminatory attitudes towards older workers: An East-West comparison. *Human Relations*, *54*(5), 629–61.

Clapham, M. M., & Fulford, M. D. (1997). Age bias in assessment center ratings. *Journal of Managerial Issues*, *9*(3), 373–87.

Clark, R. L., & Ogawa, N. (1996). Human resource policies and older workers in Japan. *The Gerontologist*, *36*(5), 627–37.

Cleveland, J. N., Festa, R. M., & Montgomery, L. (1988). Applicant pool composition and job perceptions: Impact on decisions regarding an older applicant. *Journal of Vocational Behavior*, *32*, 112–25.

Cleveland, J. N., & Hollman, G. (1991). Context and discrimination in personnel decisions: Direct and mediated approaches. In J. R. Meindl, R. L. Cardy, & S. Puffer (Eds), *Advances in information processing in organizations* (Vol. 4, pp. 223–38). Greenwich, CT: JAI Press.

Cleveland, J. N., & Shore, L. M. (1992). Self- and supervisory perspectives on age and work attitudes and performance. *Journal of Applied Psychology*, *77*, 469–84.

Compton-Edwards, M. (2001). *Age discrimination at work: Survey report* (February). London: Chartered Institute of Personnel and Development.

Cox, H. G. (1990). Roles for aged individuals in post-industrial societies. *International Journal of Aging and Human Development*, *30*(1), 55–62.

Craft, J. A., Doctors, S. I., Shkop, Y. M., & Benecki, T. J. (1979). Simulated management perceptions, hiring decisions, and age. *Aging and Work*, *3*, 95–102.

Crew, J. C. (1984). Age stereotypes as a function of race. *Academy of Management Journal*, *27*(2), 431–5.

Dedrick, E. J., & Dobbins, G. H. (1991). The influence of subordinate age on managerial actions: An attributional analysis. *Journal of Organizational Behavior*, *12*, 367–77.

Dixon, S. (2003). Implications of population ageing for the labour market. *Labour Market Trends*, *111*(2), 67–76.

Duncan, C., & Loretto, W. (2004). Never the right age? Gender and age-based discrimination in employment. *Gender, Work & Organization*, *11*, 95–115.

Elkin, G. (2001). Ageism in the 'Quarter Acre Pavlova Paradise' – will she be right? In I. Glover, & M. Branine (Eds), *Ageism in Work and Employment* (pp. 255–67). Burlington, VT: Ashgate Publishing.

Farh, J., Tsui, A. S., Xin, K., & Cheng, B. (1998). The influence of relational demography and guanxi: The Chinese case. *Organization Science*, *9*(4), 471–88.

Finegold, D., Mohrman, S., & Spreitzer, G. M. (2002). Age effects on the predictors of technical workers' commitment and willingness to turnover. *Journal of Organizational Behavior*, *23*, 655–74.

Finkelstein, L. M., & Burke, M. J. (1998). Age stereotyping at work: The role of rater and contextual factors on evaluations of job applicants. *Journal of General Psychology*, *125*, 317–45.

Finkelstein, L. M., Burke, M. J., & Raju, N. S. (1995). Age discrimination in simulated employment contexts: An integrative analysis. *Journal of Applied Psychology*, *80*, 652–63.

Finkelstein, L. M., Higgins, K. D., & Clancy, M. (2000). Justifications for ratings of old and young job applicants: An exploratory content analysis. *Experimental Aging Research*, *26*, 263–83.

Forteza, J. A., & Prieto, J. M. (1994). Aging and work behavior. In M. Dunnette, L. Hough & H. Triandis (Eds), *Handbook of industrial organizational psychology* (Vol. 4, pp. 447–83). Palo Alto, CA: Consulting Psychologists.

Frazis, H., Gittleman, M., & Joyce, M. (1998). *Determinants of training: An analysis using both employer and employee characteristics.* Washington, DC: Bureau of Labor Statistics.

Gerstner, C. R., & Day, D. V. (1997). Meta-analytic review of leader-member exchange theory: Correlates and construct issues. *Journal of Applied Psychology, 82,* 827–44.

Gibson, K. J., Zerbe, W. J., & Franken, R. E. (1993). The influence of rater and ratee age on judgments of work-related attributes. *Journal of Psychology, 127,* 271–80.

Goldberg, C., Finkelstein, L. M., Perry, E. L., & Konrad, A. M. (2004). Job and industry fit: The effects of age and gender matches on career progress outcomes. *Journal of Organizational Behavior, 25,* 807–29.

Gray, L., & McGregor, J. (2003). Human resource development and older workers: Stereotypes in New Zealand. *Asia Pacific Journal of Human Resources, 41*(3), 338–53.

Greller, M. M. (2000). Age norms and career motivation. *International Journal of Aging and Human Development, 50*(3), 215–26.

Greller, M. M., & Simpson, P. (1999). In search of late career: A review of contemporary social science research applicable to the understanding of late career. *Human Resource Management Review, 9,* 309–47.

Greller, M. M., & Stroh, L. K. (1995). Careers in midlife and beyond: A fallow field in need of sustenance. *Journal of Vocational Behavior, 47,* 232–47.

Gringart, E., & Helmes, E. (2001). Age discrimination in hiring practices against older adults in Western Australia: The case of accounting assistants. *Australasian Journal of Ageing, 20,* 23–8.

Hall, D. T., & Mirvis, P. H. (1995). The new career contract: Developing the whole person at midlife and beyond. *Journal of Vocational Behavior, 47,* 269–89.

Han, S., & Moen, P. (1999). Clocking out: Temporal patterning of retirement. *American Journal of Sociology, 105*(1), 191–236.

Hansson, R. O., Dekoekkoek, P. D., Neece, W. M., & Patterson, D. W. (1997). Successful aging at work: Annual review, 1992–1996: The older worker and transitions to retirement. *Journal of Vocational Behavior, 51,* 202–33.

Hassell, B. L., & Perrewe, P. L. (1995). An examination of beliefs about older workers: Do stereotypes still exist? *Journal of Organizational Behavior, 16,* 457–68.

Healy, M. C., Lehman, M., & McDaniel, M. (1995). Age and voluntary turnover: A quantitative review. *Personnel Psychology, 48,* 335–44.

Henkens, K. (2000). Supervisors' attitudes about the early retirement of subordinates. *Journal of Applied Social Psychology, 30,* 833–52.

Hofstede, G. (2001). *Culture's consequences: Comparing values, behaviors, institutions and organizational across nations* (2nd edn). Thousand Oaks, CA: Sage.

Johansson, I. (2003). Intergenerational relations at work in Sweden and the UK. In M. Kumashiro, T. Cox, W. Goedhard & J. Ilmarinen (Eds), *Aging and work* (pp. 143–52). London: Taylor & Francis.

Joulain, M., Mullet, E., Lecomte, C., & Prevost, R. (2000). Perception of 'appropriate' age for retirement among young adults, middle-aged adults, and elderly people. *International Journal of Aging and Human Development, 50*(1), 73–84.

Keith, J. (1982). *Old people as people: Social and cultural influences on aging and old age.* Boston, MA: Little, Brown.

Kilbom, A. (1999). Evidence-based programs for the prevention of early exit from work. *Experimental Aging Research, 25,* 291–9.

Kite, M. E., & Wagner, L. S. (2002). Attitudes toward older adults. In T. D. Nelson (Ed.), *Ageism: Stereotyping and prejudice against older persons* (pp. 129–61). Cambridge, MA: MIT Press.

Kogan, N., & Shelton, F. (1960). Differential cue value of age and occupation in impression formation. *Psychological Reports, 7,* 203–16.

Kubeck, J. E., Delp, N. D., Haslett, T. K., & McDaniel, M. A. (1996). Does job-related training performance decline with age? *Psychology and Aging, 11,* 92–107.

Lawrence, B. S. (1988). New wrinkles in the theory of age: Demography, norms, and performance ratings. *Academy of Management Journal, 31*, 309–37.

Lawrence, B. S. (1996a). Interest and indifference: The role of age in the organizational sciences. *Research in Personnel and Human Resource Management, 14*, 1–59.

Lawrence, B. S. (1996b). Organizational age norms: Why is it so hard to know one when you see one? *The Gerontologist, 36*(2), 209–20.

Levin, W. C. (1988). Age stereotyping: College student evaluations. *Research on Aging, 10*, 134–48.

Levy, B., & Langer, E. (1994). Aging free from negative stereotypes: Successful memory in China and among the American deaf. *Journal of Personality and Social Psychology, 66*, 989–97.

Liden, R., Stilwell, D., & Ferris, G. (1996). The effects of supervisor and subordinate age on objective performance and subjective performance ratings. *Human Relations, 49*, 327–47.

Lyon, P., & Pollard, D. (1997). Perceptions of the older employee: Is anything really changing? *Personnel Review, 26*, 245–57.

Maurer, T. J. (2001). Career-relevant learning and development, worker age, and beliefs about self-efficacy for development. *Journal of Management, 27*, 123–40.

Maurer, T. J., & Rafuse, N. E. (2001). Learning, not litigating: Managing employee development and avoiding claims of age discrimination. *Academy of Management Executive, 15*(4), 110–21.

Milliken, F. J., & Martins, L. L. (1996). Searching for common threads: Understanding the multiple effects of diversity in organizational groups. *Academy of Management Review, 21*, 402–33.

Mirvis, P. H., & Hall, D. T. (1996). Career development for the older worker. In D. T. Hall (Ed.), *The career is dead – long live the career: A relational approach to careers* (pp. 278–96). San Francisco: Jossey-Bass.

Montepare, J. M., & Zebrowitz, L. A. (1998). Person perception comes of age: The salience and significance of age in social judgments. *Advances in Experimental Social Psychology, 30*, 93–161.

O'Connell, A. N., & Rotter, N. G. (1979). The influence of stimulus age and sex on person perception. *Journal of Gerontology, 34*, 220–8.

Parsons, D., & Mayne, L. (2001). Ageism and work in the EU: A comparative review of corporate innovation and practice. In I. Glover, & M. Branine (Eds), *Ageism in work and employment* (pp. 237–53). Burlington, VT: Ashgate Publishing.

Patrickson, M., & Hartmann, L. (1995). Australia's ageing population: Implications for human resource management. *International Journal of Manpower, 16*, 34–47.

Pelled, L. H., Eisenhardt, K. M., & Xin, K. R. (1999). Exploring the black box: An analysis of work group diversity, conflict, and performance. *Administrative Science Quarterly, 44*, 1–28.

Pelled, L. H., & Xin, K. R. (2000). Relational demography and relationship quality in two cultures. *Organization Studies, 21*(6), 1077–94.

Perdue, C. W., & Gurtman, M. B. (1990). Evidence for the automaticity of ageism. *Journal of Experimental Social Psychology, 26*, 199–216.

Perry, E. L. (1994). A prototype matching approach to understanding the role of applicant gender and age in the evaluation of job applicants. *Journal of Applied Social Psychology, 24*, 1433–73.

Perry, E. L. (1997). A cognitive approach to understanding discrimination: A closer look at applicant gender and age. *Research in Personnel and Human Resource Management, 15*, 175–240.

Perry, E. L., & Bourhis, A. C. (1998). A closer look at the role of applicant age in selection decisions. *Journal of Applied Social Psychology, 28*, 1670–97.

Perry, E. L., & Kulik, C. T., & Bourhis, A. C. (1996). Moderating effects of personal and contextual factors in age discrimination. *Journal of Applied Psychology, 81*, 628–47.

Perry, E. L., Kulik, C. T., & Zhou, J. (1999). A closer look at the effects of subordinate-supervisor age differences. *Journal of Organizational Behavior*, *20*, 341–57.

Rice-Oxley, M. (2003). Europe balks at reforms pushing retirement age back. *Christian Science Monitor*, 16 May, 7.

Riordan, C. M. (2000). Relational demography within groups: Past developments, contradictions, and new directions. *Research in Personnel and Human Resource Management*, *19*, 131–73.

Riordan, C. M., Griffith, R. W., & Weatherly, E. W. (2003). Age and work-related outcomes: The moderating effects of status characteristics. *Journal of Applied Social Psychology*, *33*, 37–57.

Robson, W. B. P., & British–North American Committee (2001). *Aging populations and the workforce: Challenges for employers*. Winnipeg, Manitoba: Printcrafters.

Rosen, B., & Jerdee, T. (1976a). The influence of age stereotypes on managerial decisions. *Journal of Applied Psychology*, *61*(4), 428–32.

Rosen, B., & Jerdee, T. (1976b). The nature of job-related age stereotypes. *Journal of Applied Psychology*, *61*, 180–3.

Rosen, B., & Jerdee, T. (1977). Too old or not too old. *Harvard Business Review*, *55*(6), 85–105.

Saba, T., Guerin, G., & Wils, T. (1998). Managing older professionals in public agencies in Quebec. *Public Productivity & Management Review*, *22*(1), 15–34.

Saks, A. M., & Waldman, D. A. (1998). The relationship between age and job performance evaluations for entry-level professionals. *Journal of Organizational Behavior*, *19*, 409–19.

Salthouse, T. A., & Maurer, T. J. (1996). Aging, job performance, and career development. In J. Birren & K. Schaie (Eds), *Handbook of the psychology of aging* (4th edn, pp. 353–64). San Diego, CA: Academic Press.

Schabracq, M. J. (1994). Motivational and cultural factors underlying dysfunctioning of older employees. In J. Snel & R. Cremer (Eds), *Work and aging: A European perspective* (pp. 235–49). London: Taylor & Francis.

Shore, L. M., Cleveland, J. N., & Goldberg, C. B. (2003). Work attitudes and decisions as a function of manager age and employee age. *Journal of Applied Psychology*, *88*, 529–37.

Simon, R. (1996). Too damn old. *Money*, *25*(7), 118–25.

Simpson, P .A., Greller, M. M., & Stroh, L. K. (2002). Variations in human capital investment activity by age. *Journal of Vocational Behavior*, *61*, 109–38.

Singer, M. S. (1986). Age stereotypes as a function of profession. *Journal of Social Psychology*, *126*, 691–2.

Singer, M., & Sewell, C. (1988). Age stereotyping and the age bias effect in selection interviews. *New Zealand Journal of Business*, *10*, 37–47.

Smith, D. J. (2001). Old enough to know better: Age stereotypes in New Zealand. In I. Glover and M. Branine (Eds), *Ageism in work and employment* (pp. 219–35). Aldershot: Ashgate Publishing.

Steinberg, M., Donald, K., Najman, J., & Skerman, H. (1996). Attitudes of employees and employers towards older workers in a climate of anti-discrimination. *Australian Journal on Ageing*, *15*(4), 154–8.

Sterns, H. L., & Dorsett, J. G. (1994). Career development: A life span issue. *Experimental Aging Research*, *20*, 257–64.

Sterns, H. L., & Doverspike, D. (1989). Aging and the training and learning process. In I. Goldstein (Ed.), *Training and development in organizations* (pp. 299–333). San Francisco: Jossey-Bass.

Sterns, H. L., & Gray, J. H. (1999). Work, leisure, and retirement. In J. C. Cavanaugh & S. K. Whitbourne (Eds), *Gerontology: An interdisciplinary perspective* (pp. 355–90). New York: Oxford University Press.

Sterns, H. L., & Miklos, S. M. (1995). The aging worker in a changing environment: Organization and individual issues. *Journal of Vocational Behavior*, *47*, 248–68.

Sullivan, S. E. (1999). The changing nature of careers: A review and research agenda. *Journal of Management*, 25, 457–84.

Sullivan, S. E., & Duplaga, E. A. (1997). Recruiting and retaining older workers for the new millennium. *Business Horizons*, 40(6), 65–9.

Taylor, P. (2001). Older workers and the cult of youth: Ageism in public policy. In I. Glover, & M. Branine (Eds), *Ageism in work and employment* (pp. 271–83). Burlington, VT: Ashgate Publishing.

Taylor, P., & Walker, A. (1993). Employers and older workers. *Employment Gazette*, 101, 371–8.

Taylor, P., & Walker, A. (1994). The ageing workforce: Employers' attitudes towards older people. *Work, Employment and Society*, 8(4), 569–91.

Taylor, P., & Walker, A. (1997). Age discrimination and public policy. *Personnel Review*, 26, 307–18.

Taylor, P., & Walker, A. (1998). Employers and older workers: Attitudes and employment practices. *Ageing and Society*, 18, 641–58.

Tsui, A. S., & O'Reilly, C. A. (1989). Beyond simple demographic effects: The importance of relational demography in superior-subordinate dyads. *Academy of Management Journal*, 32, 402–23.

Tsui, A. S., Porter, L. W., & Egan, T. D. (2002). When both similarities and dissimilarities matter: Extending the concept of relational demography. *Human Relations*, 55, 899–929.

Turner, J., & Lichtenstein, J. H. (2002). Social Security in the Middle East: A brief review. *Journal of Aging and Social Policy*, 14(1), 115–24.

van Beek, K. W. H., Koopmans, C. C., & van Praag, B. M. S. (1997). Shopping at the labour market: A real tale of fiction. *European Economic Review*, 41, 295–317.

Van Dalen, H. P., & Henkens, K. (2002). Early-retirement reform: Can it and will it work? *Ageing & Society*, 22, 209–31.

Walker, A. (1999). Combating age discrimination at the workplace. *Experimental Aging Research*, 25, 367–77.

Walker, A., & Taylor, P. (1993). Ageism versus productive aging: the challenge of age discrimination in the labor market. In S. Bass, F. Caro, & Y. Chen (Eds), *Achieving a productive aging society* (pp. 61–79). London: Auburn House.

Warr, P. (1994). Age and job performance. In J. Snel & R. Cremer (Eds), *Work and aging: A European perspective* (pp. 309–22). London: Taylor & Francis.

Warr, P., & Pennington, J. (1993). Views about age discrimination and older workers. In P. Taylor, A. Walker, B. Casey & H. Metcalf (Eds), *Age and employment: Policies, attitudes, and practices* (pp. 75–106). London: Institute of Personnel Management.

Watanabe-Muraoka, A. M., Kawasaki, T., & Sato, S. (1998). Vocational behavior of the Japanese in late adulthood: Focusing on those in the retirement process. *Journal of Vocational Behavior*, 52, 300–11.

Webber, S. S., & Donahue, L. M. (2001). Impact of highly and less job-related diversity on work group cohesion and performance: A meta-analysis. *Journal of Management*, 27, 141–62.

Weber, T., Whitting, G., Sidaway, J., & Moore, J. (1997). Employment policies and practices towards older workers: France, Germany, Spain and Sweden. *Labour Market Trends*, 105(4), 143–8.

Wilkinson, J. A., & Ferraro, K. F. (2001). Thirty years of ageism research. In T. D. Nelson (Ed.), *Ageism: Stereotyping and prejudice against older persons* (pp. 339–58). Cambridge, MA: MIT Press.

Williams, K. Y., & O'Reilly, C. A., III (1998). Demography and diversity in organizations: A review of 40 years of research. *Research in Organizational Behavior*, 20, 77–140.

Yeatts, D. E., Folts, W. E., & Knapp, J. (1999). Older worker's adaptation to a changing workplace: Employment issues for the 21st century. *Educational Gerontology*, 25, 331–47.

15

Seven Conversations about the Same Thing

Homophobia and Heterosexism in the Workplace

W. E. DOUGLAS CREED

Early in the summer of 2003, a member of the Academy of Management family – an informal group of lesbian, gay, bisexual, and transgender (LGBT) members of the AoM – sent a message to the group's listserv.[1] A key word search of the index of papers accepted for presentation at the 2003 annual meetings showed that the number of papers dealing with LGBT workplace issues had increased from 3 in 2002 to 13 in 2003. That this was something of a cause for celebration reflects how very little there has been in the mainstream scholarly management literature about workplace homophobia and heterosexism.

Due to this acknowledged dearth (Ragins & Wiethoff, 2005), this chapter will serve less as a review piece and more as a framing of intellectual 'conversations' that are emerging or need to happen in the organizational literature. In framing these conversations, I also draw on the work of cultural historians, social psychologists, sociologists, and scholars and practitioners in social work, psychiatry, clinical psychology, counseling psychology and education, and on actual conversations with several management scholars interested in the issues of diversity and sexual prejudice in the workplace. Neither exhaustive, nor fully representative of the diverse existing work across the many disciplines cited above, these conversations are offered as a jumping-off point – or as part of the coming-out process for mainstream research in management.

Below I begin by considering the principal analytical concepts used in social scientific inquiries into the nature of prejudice against lesbian and gay people. These culturally contingent constructs challenge us not only in terms of how we frame a question and at what levels of analysis we work, but also in terms of where we choose to come down in a meaning-making contest that has been described as a culture war (Hunter, 1991). Organizational scholars studying homophobia and heterosexism should at all times maintain a concern for how these phenomena operate across levels of analysis even as they focus their research at a single level of analysis. I then present six other areas of research where organizational scholars could make valuable contributions by joining the conversation.

CONVERSATION 1: A ROSE BY ANY OTHER NAME – HOMOPHOBIA, HETEROSEXISM OR SEXUAL PREJUDICE

The term *homophobia* became a staple of late twentieth century political discourse (Wickberg, 2000). First appearing in print in 1969, homophobia was coined by psychologist George Weinberg (1972) to describe both heterosexual dread of close contact with homosexuals and gay peoples' own self-loathing or 'internalized homophobia'. Since 1972 various definitions of the term have included not just an aversion to gay people, their culture and their lifestyles, but also an irrational fear of homosexuality, and behaviors or actions stemming from this aversion or fear (Herek, 2004).

When coined, the term represented a conceptual revolution, as homophobia was positioned to 'supplant homosexuality as the sickness in need of a cure' (Wickberg, 2000: 47). Until 1973, homosexuality was officially listed as a diagnosable mental illness by the American Psychiatric Association (LeVay, 1996). This 'expert' framing gave credibility to the classification of LGBT people as abnormal, mired gay folk in scientifically endorsed self-images that they were unhealthy, deviant and perverted (Herman, 1995), and left them vulnerable to all manner of damaging therapies (Duberman, 1991). This reversal of diagnostic terms challenged the mental health establishment's scientizing and legitimation of a prejudice. At the same time, it implicitly located the problem of anti-gay prejudice at the individual level – as a psychological problem, albeit one with social consequences. This became the basis for critique on both analytical and political grounds. Some faulted homophobia for depicting sexual prejudice as a matter of individual psychology, even pathology, analytically disconnected from the ideology and historical institutions of persecution that reinforce the prejudice (Herek, 2000). Social conservatives rejected it because they saw abhorrence for homosexuality not as a phobia but as a moral stance backed by millennia of sacred teachings.

As an alternative, *heterosexism* emerged as a description of 'an ideological system that denies, denigrates, and stigmatizes any nonheterosexual form of behavior, identity, relationship, or community' (Herek, 1990). Although homophobia has remained the term of choice to describe anti-homosexual prejudice (Wickberg, 2000) and its popular use has expanded to refer to both individual and societal phenomena, scholars have typically used homophobia to refer to individual attitudes and behaviors, while using heterosexism to refer to higher-level phenomena such as institutions of oppression (Herek, 2000). One conceptual advantage of heterosexism is that it highlights the possibility of parallels between anti-gay prejudice and other culturally pervasive prejudices such as sexism, racism and anti-Semitism (Herek, 2004).

The Distinctiveness of Homophobia and Heterosexism?

The nature of these parallels and what if anything is distinctive about prejudice against homosexual people remain important questions, however. According to Young-Bruehl (2002), early research on prejudice assumed that all prejudices are alike – a combined manifestation of authoritarianism and ethnocentrism. This perspective is reflected today in the 'common roots' view that racism, sexism and heterosexism arise from the same social, political, and cultural foundations (Herek, 1990; Ragins, Cornwell, & Miller, 2003). An alternative view holds that prejudices differ because people have need of different types of prejudices: 'different targets of prejudice … serve different purposes. … prejudices are like mechanisms of defense against groups constructed differently via projection and then experienced differently as sources of anxiety and threat' (Young-Bruehl, 2002: 267) This framing of prejudices as purposeful defense mechanisms – analogous to the psycho-analytical concept of ego defenses – points to the need for us to consider the differences in the organizational uses served by heterosexism, sexism, and racism at the individual, group, organizational, interorganizational field and institutional levels.

Beyond asking what may be the distinctive uses of anti-gay prejudice, scholars point to other distinctive attributes. According to Young-Bruehl (1996), anti-gay prejudice is unique among the four principal prejudices (sexism, racism, anti-Semitism and heterosexism) because it alone manifests each of what she sees as the three theoretical sub-types of prejudice: obsessional, hysterical and narcissistic prejudice. Gay people have been constructed as: conspiring enemies bent on the destruction of straight people and society (an obsessional prejudice); other and threatening – 'clannish and dangerous "like" Jews, sexually obsessed and predatory "like" people of color' (Fone, 2000: 6) (a hysterical prejudice); and intolerably different (a narcissistic prejudice) because gay men are not real men, and lesbians are 'women who "do what men do—they compete for women"' (Young-Bruehl, 1996: 36ff., cited in Fone, 2000: 6). This makes anti-gay prejudice very versatile, able to accommodate a greater spectrum of the psychosocial needs for prejudice than other isms.

Some scholars also point to three other purportedly distinctive features of heterosexism. First, heterosexism may have an unparalleled affective component, a heterosexual fear of being, becoming or being perceived as gay (Herek, 1984). The relative invisibility of gay people and their capacity to pass as straight fuels this fear by enabling speculation and suspicion about sexual orientation. In contrast, Ragins et al. (2003) argue that individuals are not usually afraid of becoming or being taken for a person of another race or gender. Second, the invisibility of sexual orientation makes its stigma contagious, in a form of guilt by association known as a 'courtesy stigma' (Goffman, 1963; Herek & Capitanio, 1996). According to Ragins et al. (2003) stigma by association on the basis of race or gender is probably rare in modern organizations. Third, homophobia and heterosexism involve complex social constructions that historically have demonized gay individuals as inherently flawed and abhorrent on religious grounds (Fone, 2000; Herman, 1997). While historically, both racism and sexism have been justified on religious grounds, Ragins et al. argue that today's politically mobilized, religiously based heterosexism has no or few direct analogues in modern racism and sexism. While each of these features may be operative in organizations, how peculiar they are to heterosexism is a matter of debate. For example, it is not difficult to imagine situations in which some people are still afraid of being taken for a person of another ethnicity, where religious prejudice can still employ the concept of the morally abhorrent infidel, and people of one race could be stigmatized for associating with people of another.

Sexual Prejudice and Heterosexism – a Functional Approach

The conceptual expansion of homophobia in popular usage has led Herek to propose that psychological inquiry will be better served by a more fine-grained analytical term:

> *sexual prejudice* refers to all negative attitudes based on sexual orientation, whether the target is homosexual, bisexual, or heterosexual … [It] encompasses heterosexuals' negative attitudes toward: (a) homosexual behavior; (b) people with a homosexual orientation; and (c) communities of gay, lesbian, and bisexual people. Like other types of prejudice, sexual prejudice has three principal features: It is an attitude (i.e. an evaluation or judgment); it is directed at a social group and its members; and it is negative, involving hostility or dislike. (Herek, 2000: 20)

The advantages of this conceptualization, according to Herek, are: first, it is a descriptive term, free of the a priori assumptions regarding origins, dynamics and underlying motivations that might be inferred from *homophobia*; second, it makes explicit the link between the study of anti-gay attitudes and the tradition of social psychological research on prejudice; and third, as a construct, *sexual prejudice* 'does not require value judgments that anti-gay attitudes are inherently irrational or evil' (Herek, 2000: 20).

This last point may set off alarm bells for people who believe anti-gay prejudice is inherently evil, but it alerts us to two critical questions. One concerns the ways this prejudice is not irrational for the beneficiaries of institutionalized hetero-sexist privilege. The other concerns the cultural roots for the moral construction of heterosexism and gay identity. Both concerns point to the need to contextualize our scientific constructs in the history of the patterned social construction of people with same-sex orientations as other, deficient, evil and threatening. We need to attend particularly to how this history informs the symbolic signi-ficance people with anti-gay prejudices attach to their beliefs and actions (Herman, 1997).

In this vein, Herek (1984) has argued for a functional approach to understand-ing sexual prejudice that clearly resonates with Young-Bruehl's conception of prejudices as social defense mechanisms. The fundamental assumption of Herek's approach is that 'people hold and express particular attitudes because they derive psychological benefit from doing so' (Herek, 2004). An additional assumption important for this discussion is that attitudes are dynamic. Situational factors affect the relative salience of different psychological needs, thereby affecting the degree to which an attitude or prejudice is functional or dysfunctional in a particular situation.[2]

According to Herek, heterosexuals' attitudes toward lesbian and gay people and homosexuality fill four principal psychological functions, one experiential and three symbolic.[3] First, when serving an *experiential function*, attitudes pro-vide interpretive frames for making sense of past experiences of direct contact with gay people 'by helping the individual fit those interactions into a larger world view, one that is organized primarily in terms of the individual's own self interest' (Herek, 2004).[4] When serving an experiential function, a heterosexual's positive or negative attitudes are based on prior pleasant or unpleasant experi-ences of particular gay and lesbian people.

Absent prior contact, however, gays and lesbians are primarily symbols for heterosexuals and attitudes toward symbols serve functions other than making sensible past experience. Herek points to three functions that serve symbolic pur-poses, including bolstering self-esteem, strengthening bonds with others who hold similar attitudes, and relieving anxiety over unconscious conflicts. More specifically, a *value-expressive function* fosters the heterosexual's affirmation of beliefs and values closely linked to his or her self-concept and can increase self-esteem. A *social-expressive* function strengthens the heterosexual's sense of membership in a particular group and facilitates getting love and approval from important others such family and peers. An *ego-defensive* function alleviates anxiety stemming from unconscious conflicts such as those pertaining to sexuality or gender identity/performance.

Importantly, these motivations for and functions of sexual prejudice operating at the individual level are linked to heterosexism operating at higher levels of analysis. Heterosexist ideology is the mother of all situational factors that deter-mine the psychological salience of sexual prejudice for the individual.

A particular manifestation of sexual prejudice can serve one or more of these functions only when the individual's psychological needs converge with the culture's ideology about homosexuality. Antigay prejudice can be value-expressive only when an individual's self-concept is closely tied to values that also have become socially defined as antithetical to homosexuality. It can be social-expressive only insofar as an individual strongly needs to be accepted by members of a social group that rejects gay people or homosexuality. It can be defensive only when lesbians and gay men are culturally defined in a way that links them to an individual's own psychological conflicts. (Herek, 2004).

The connection across levels of analysis suggests that understanding and combating prejudice requires understanding the psychological, social and institutional functions prejudicial ideologies and actions play (Sears, 1997).

In drawing on this functional approach, two points warrant highlighting for our thinking about sexual prejudice in organizations and workplaces. First, for sexual prejudice to be a psychologically beneficial attitude for the individual, it needs to converge with cultural ideologies of heterosexism and available social constructions of homosexuality. Sexual prejudice is dynamic and its functionality situational. The psychological benefits cannot arise or persist in an ideological, political or psychosocial vacuum. This suggests that to study heterosexism in organizations we need to consider those aspects of organizations, as situations, that are likely to affect the salience of sexual prejudice. In addition, we need to consider those social constructions of homosexuality and of LGBT people that remain available within organizations' cultural context, ready to provide the oxygen.

The protean nature of anti-gay prejudice noted by Young-Bruehl suggests that a wide variety of social constructions are and will likely remain available for use in organizations, although waxing and waning in their currency. Fone (2000) identifies several forms of institutionalized homophobia that might still be serviceable in organizations even today. Building on a medieval Christian foundation that framed homosexuality in terms of sin and heresy, the Reformation witnessed the transformation of the sodomite as sinner into an amalgam of sinner, threat to social order, and enemy of the state; we see this demonology mirrored in twentieth century US history (Fone, 2000). After World War I exposed US soldiers to 'European decadence', what Fone calls a 'xenophobic strain of homophobia' depicted gay men as immasculine and un-American, 'conflating sexual difference with a betrayal of the nation's values' (2000: 385). Research on sexuality in the 1940s that presented homosexuality as more widespread than commonly believed and offered a somewhat more sympathetic view (especially Kinsey, Pomeroy & Martin's (1948) research on male sexual behavior) triggered virulent editorial attacks in *Time* and *Newsweek* depicting gays as degenerate and dangerous. These were harbingers of the 1950s' depiction of the homosexual as political menace during the era of Senator Joseph McCarthy.[5] It was in response to this 'state-sponsored homophobia' – spilling from an anti-communist hysteria into a witch-hunt for homosexual employees in the Dept. of State and other areas of government – that organized gay opposition to workplace discrimination first arose in the United States (Fone, 2000: 414).

How enduring and serviceable such negative constructions of gayness are in modern organizations deserves research. However, research into a dominant group's social construction of a historically stigmatized group can be very difficult due to modern social proscriptions of blatant prejudice (Dovidio & Gaertner, 1986). One approach could be using frame analysis (Creed, Langstraat & Scully, 2002) to look at organizational contests over non-discrimination policy. In contests over the legitimacy of a controversial policy, each side frames its case to invoke powerfully resonant 'deeper cultural themes and counterthemes on behalf of one's preferred frame and to neutralize the potential resonances of the most important rival frames' (Gamson, 1998: 74). Ironically, because cultural themes and counterthemes share many assumptions, 'whenever one [theme] is invoked, the other [countertheme] is always present in latent form, ready to be activated' (Gamson, 1998: 74). Even if policy contests are where both positive and negative social constructions are most likely to become visible, it does not follow that each type of construction will be equally discernible, especially in an era that drives many expressions of prejudice underground. Researchers may have to do the counterintuitive, looking for latent negative constructions in the advocates' positive framings.

CONVERSATION 2: WHAT ARE THE REALITIES OF ANTI-LGBT PREJUDICE IN THE WORKPLACE?

LGBT invisibility has long allowed the realities of anti-gay prejudice to go unrecognized. Fear of job discrimination leads many LGBT people to mask their identities in the hope of averting the worst consequences of sexual prejudice (Woods, 1994). This alone would be enough to cause the underreporting of discrimination. However, the advent of visible LGBT communities making justice claims in both organizations and the broader society has led some to dispute the reality of anti-LGBT workplace discrimination for political reasons. For example, the Family Research Council, a leading opponent of LGBT civil rights, argues that homosexuals do not need civil rights protections because most homosexuals cannot honestly report that they have been discriminated against and, as a group, homosexuals are economically privileged, politically powerful and have undue influence on the media (Creed, Scully & Austin, 2002).[6]

Research in this area shows such depictions to be inaccurate (Croteau, 1996; Van Den Bergh, 1999). While much of this work has been in the popular business press (Day & Schoenrade, 2000), scholarly research done in the late 1970s and 1980s indicates that a majority of gays and lesbians would expect to experience workplace discrimination if their orientation were known, including harassment, ostracism, job loss and physical violence (Levine, 1979; Levine & Leonard, 1984). One would hope that that has changed in the last 25 years, but whether, where, why and how much it has changed are all open empirical questions.

Organizational scholars could approach these questions through a combination of historical and contemporaneous research. For example, archival material and historical accounts of the establishing of gay and lesbian professional associations in such professions as psychiatry, psychology, medicine, law and academe provide a picture of the professional and workplace concerns that motivated organizing (e.g. D'Emilio, 1992). Content analysis of these accounts, along with retrospective data from early movement participants, could provide the background against which to study the concerns and experience of current members of these professions.

Economist Lee Badgett has played a key role in documenting some of the economic realities of LGBT experience, including debunking politically motivated claims by conservatives that gays and lesbians constitute an economic elite not in need of workplace protection. She has found that, controlling for education and experience, gays, lesbians and bisexuals have lower incomes than their straight counterparts (Badgett, 1995). Nonetheless, groups like the proponents of Colorado's Amendment 2, the Family Research Institute and opponents of gays and lesbians in the military continue to advance anti-gay political causes through the use of 'bad science in the service of stigma' (Herek, 1998; Pietrzyk, 1994).[7] This bad science, according to scholarly critics including the APA and ASA, can rely on a disregard for scientific method, a misrepresentation and distortion of scientific literature, and the violation of professional ethical principles (Herek, 2004). So, while this direction for research is more descriptive than theory based, methodologically rigorous studies that stand up to challenges regarding their validity and bias could nonetheless advance significantly our understanding by documenting the nature, scope and trends over time of anti-gay workplace discrimination.

CONVERSATION 3: WORKING OUT – THE DETERMINANTS AND CONSEQUENCES OF WORKPLACE DISCLOSURE DECISIONS

Despite the fragmented and atheoretical nature of most research on LGBT workplace experience (Ragins & Cornwell, 2001), the issues of self-disclosure and non-disclosure – their motivations, means and consequences – are unifying themes. There are many reasons for this. The first is developmental: 'the disclosure and integration of sexual identity into all social roles, including the role of worker, has been conceptualized as the apex of identity development for gay and lesbian individuals and as essential to psychosocial adjustment and general psychological well-being' (Rostosky & Riggle, 2002: 411). Second, passing requires complex stratagems, making the management of others' knowledge of one's sexual identity almost a career in itself (Woods, 1994). The emotional, psychological and spiritual costs are great, making nondisclosure a source of stress in itself, with various work and life consequences (DiPlacido, 1998). A third reason is activist. Coming out of the closet is seen as essential to combating homophobia and heterosexism, first, because contact with and education about the experiences of LGBT people are seen as antidotes to demonizing myths and ignorance (Bridgewater, 1997; Sears, 1997), and, second, because being open and self-affirming are seen as acts of resistance against systems of heterosexist oppression.

Coming out is perhaps the *sin qua non* of LGBT emancipation, but it also increases the likelihood of being the target of discrimination. Existing research shows that fear of workplace discrimination leads many LGBT people to feel the need to remain closeted or to pass as heterosexual to avoid harassment, pay discrimination, firings and the denial of promotions (Badgett, 1996; 2001). Thus, in the workplace, LGBTs exist with the tension between wanting the benefits of disclosure – greater personal authenticity, political and social empowerment, more open and potentially more productive relationships with colleagues, and freedom from the need to devote untold energy to passing and the related fear of discovery – and fearing its possible costs (Griffith & Hebl, 2002). As a result, in any organizational setting where LGBT employees anticipate some risk, they routinely grapple with the decision of whether and how to claim their identities. Each and every work relationship may entail a new and potentially difficult disclosure (Creed & Scully, 2000). Consequently, researchers have conceptualized coming out as a 'recurring, rational decision-making process that [LGBT] individuals undertake each time they encounter new persons and new situations and that requires the assessment of the potential benefits and costs' (Rostosky & Riggle, 2002: 411).

Given the theoretical importance of coming out, several organizational scholars have studied the factors affecting LGBT employees' decision-making process and the impact of being closeted or out on several key organizational outcomes (Chrobot-Mason, Button & DiClementi, 2001; Ostfeld & Jehn, 1998). In a study of gay men, Shallenberg (1994) found the most common motivations for disclosure in the workplace were making a statement about 'who I am', investing in meaningful relationships, and 'mak[ing] a political statement out of a sense of responsibility to the community' (p. 31). Other research points to such factors as lower levels of internalized homophobia (Rostosky & Riggle, 2002), coping resources (Chung, 2001), a non-heterosexist organizational climate (Bieschke & Matthews, 1996), top management support (Day & Schoenrade, 2000), the presence of non-discrimination policies in one's own and in one's partner's workplace (these factors operate independently because of the risk of stigma by association) (Rostosky & Riggle, 2002), the presence of supportive LGBT employee and community networks, commitment to equality for LGBT people, and the instrumentality of self-disclosure in mobilizing support for policy initiatives (Creed & Scully, 2000) as all effecting the likelihood of disclosure. Ragins et al. (2003) find that team composition plays a role: regardless of gender or race, all LGBT people with supervisors of the same race are more likely to be out, while LGBT people in work teams composed primarily of men, that are not racial balanced, or have male supervisors, report experiencing more homophobia and discrimination (two factors that moderate disclosure decisions). Ragins et al. also find important within-group differences, including that gay people of color are less likely to disclose than their white counterparts.

As this catalogue of findings shows, important research in this area is proceeding at the individual, group, organizational and interorganizational level. In one of the first attempts at integration, Ragins & Cornwell (2001) draw on Jones's (1972) model of institutional racism to construct a multilevel framework for the integration of current organizational theories, commonly used in the study of diversity, as they apply to the antecedents and consequences of workplace sexual prejudice. They consider the impact of: (1) macro societal practices, such as existence of local and state protective legislation; (2) meso-level factors, such as organizational culture and human resource policies and practices; and (3) micro-level factors such as work group composition (Kanter, 1977) and supervisor/subordinate relational demography (Riordan, 2000) on a theoretical mediator, the LGBT employee's subjective perception of workplace discrimination, and its impact on several outcomes. These include willingness to disclose one's sexual identity and such traditional outcomes of interest as job satisfaction, organizational commitment, self-esteem, career commitment and turnover intensions, as well as promotions and compensation. Clearly, the greatest long-term benefit we can hope for from this effort is that it sets the bar higher for organizational behavior scholars by calling for research on the impact of heterosexism that crosses several levels of analysis. Their most interesting findings, however, unfold at the level of symbolic communication and concern the impact of organizational culture and practices. For example, the inviting of same-sex partners to company social events carried special symbolic significance for LGBT employees and, not surprisingly, was a strong predictor of lower levels of perceived discrimination. This points to an important direction for future research. At a time when organizations routinely and not always believably espouse valuing diversity, what gestures or actions actually signal to organizational members that prejudiced attitudes are unwelcome and that diversity is valued? Why is the symbolic significance of these gestures so great? What does this say about the underlying cultural discourses of heterosexism and LGBT inferiority? (Research identifying the significance both purveyors and opponents of sexual prejudice attach to particular actions, symbols or institutions is also another way of addressing the issue, discussed earlier, of what negative constructions of gayness persist in modern organization.) And how do these signals affect LGBT employees' willingness to sell the issue of greater inclusion and non-discrimination (Dutton, Ashford, Lawrence & Miner-Rubino, 2002)?

Based on these precedents, in addition to more research on coming out, it is easy to envision future research on the effects of being out and of the experience of greater or lesser degrees of inclusion, acceptance, respect, hostility or discrimination on such outcomes as satisfaction (Ellis & Riggle, 1995), commitment, well-being (Driscoll, Kelley & Fassinger, 1996), communication, group integration, helping behavior, the ability to contribute, turnover, etc. Research could also consider the impact of different types of heterosexist discrimination, ranging from overt to covert discrimination, and the question of aversive or modern discrimination (Ragins & Wiethoff, 2005). In aversive discrimination, as a result of modern social prescriptions against blatant prejudice, prejudiced individuals can espouse values of inclusion and fairness and believe themselves to be free of prejudice, because recognizing one's prejudices is an aversive experience (Dovidio & Gaertner, 1986). Their unconscious prejudices can lead to subtle enactments such as physical distancing, discriminatory work and team assignments, and negative decisions regarding hiring, performance appraisal and promotion (C. Wiethoff, personal communication).

This catalogue of possible research topics should not mask the great diversity among people who share a vulnerability to sexual prejudice. While I have used the more inclusive LGBT as a category, clearly gay, lesbian, bisexual and transgender people may also have significantly different workplace experiences and concerns (Chung, 2003). How each of these groups experiences sexual prejudice in the workplace and the impact on their disclosure decisions and identity claiming processes warrants research. These experiences are also likely to be affected by the intersection of multiple identities. For example, Holvino (2001) proposes that race, ethnicity, class, sexual orientation, gender, age, disability and nationality reflect simultaneous social construction processes operating at multiple levels. At the levels of individual and group identities, these dimensions of difference produce reproduce particular identities that define how individuals come to see themselves and how others see them. At the levels of institutional and social practice, they define the systems of stratification embedded in organizational structures and ways of working – thereby reproducing inequality and privilege along various axes of difference. The simultaneity of identities is likely to affect workplace enactments of identity and interactions (Foldy, 2003) and ways of making justice claims (Creed, 2003; Creed & Scully, 2000).

Clearly, an extended conversation on the dynamics of coming and being out in the workplace holds promise, but I offer a caveat pertaining to the acknowledged fragmented and atheoretical nature of the research. Some of this research has yet to get beyond tautological overarching arguments – *either* that the freer organizations and work units are of sexual prejudice, the lower one's subjective experience of discrimination and the more positive one's attitude and performance, *or* the more heterosexist and hostile the workplace, the greater the LGBT individual's felt injustice, fear of discrimination and unwillingness to be open. Both of these arguments would seem to go without saying since it is difficult to imagine either set of conditions leading to alternative outcomes. Move on fast. My recommendation would be for scholars working at the individual and group levels of analysis to explore how contextualizing their work in higher-level cultural and socio-political theories might add greater coherence and weight to their work.

CONVERSATION 4: LAVENDER COLLAR JUNGLE – HOMOPHOBIA, CAREERS, AND THE PROFESSIONS

Research on the links between homophobia/heterosexism and the professions has proceeded on two main fronts. One pertains to the impact of sexual prejudice on

LGBTs' career concerns and choices and on their career adjustment, actualization and trajectories. The other front pertains to the impact of anti-gay prejudice on professional proficiency. Anti-gay activists see the professions, especially teaching, as contested terrain, where what is at risk is the normalization of the 'homosexual lifestyle', the well-being of children, and even the survival of the nation, for example, the danger of having gays in the military or gays with security clearances (Herek, 1990). In contrast, scholars working from the implicit position of acceptance and equality see homophobia as a threat to professionalism and as a source of professional dysfunction, particularly in the helping professions.

Professional Proficiency

The growing body of work looking at the consequences for competent performance of unexplored homophobia among clinical social workers can serve as the conceptual model for research on other professions (e.g. Berkman & Zinberg, 1997; Gramick, 1983). A social worker's unexamined homophobia can affect his or her treatment of an LGBT client through biasing a diagnosis, undermining the creation of an appropriate treatment plan or influencing key mechanisms of the treatment (such as transference and counter-transference). Heterosexism can also affect the training of social workers and other types of therapists by impeding systematic consideration in the curriculum of LGBT concerns that are relevant to client services (Cramer, 1997) or by making it difficult for LGBT educators to come out or offer their experiences and expertise as resources for their students (Cain, 1996). Russell and Greenhouse (1997) offer a case study of how 'homonegativity' – in the form of a heterosexual female supervisor and a lesbian therapist failing to address the latter's sexual orientation – interfered with the supervisory relationship itself, which is central to practical clinical training. Avoiding the topic of sexual orientation also led to the omission of information critical to designing the client's treatment plan. Such concerns over proficiency with culturally diverse client populations has led to an ongoing transformation of many helping professions, including the articulation of a variety of guidelines for working with particular social identity groups. (See Chung, 2003, for a discussion and adaptation of APA guidelines for proficiency with multicultural and LGBT populations to career counseling.)

This focus on anti-gay prejudice as a source of professional dysfunction – which echoes the diagnostic reversal behind the coining of *homophobia* – provides a fruitful model for exploring the consequences of homophobia for the performance of a variety of professions and organizational roles. While it is still common to hear allegations that LGBT people are unsuitability for some professions, for example, the military, teaching, the ministry, it is far less common to see any treatment of the ways homophobic people are professionally dysfunctional (the popular film, *Philadelphia*, with its depiction of homophobic attorneys is perhaps the exception that proves the rule). It is easy to imagine valuable research on homophobia as an impediment to effective performance in a variety of roles, including strategic marketing, human resources (Hebl, Foster, Mannix & Dovidio, 2002), management, customer contact, and mentoring and supervisory functions in a variety of professional settings. In addition, there is need for research on the effectiveness of particular strategies for combating homophobia in particular professions, such as law enforcement, medicine, journalism and teaching (e.g. Sears & Williams, 1997).

Contested Terrain: The Symbolic Significance of Homophobia across Professions

The impact of homophobia on professional performance also points to two other importance questions. One concerns the variance in institutionalized homophobia across professions. The other concerns the symbolic significance of professionalization and of certain professions in particular in the organizational world.

Regarding variance across the professions, such variance demands scientific explanation if we are to understand the functions and consequences of homophobia in the organizational world. Some of the research in this area is relatively mainstream, given it still deals with homophobia. Certain industries or functions are apparently particularly heterosexist. For example, being gay in sales is reportedly a problem because sales 'is the most male-dominated, locker-room industry this side of working on the railroad' (Adams & Vasilakis, 1996). Private sector and trade unions have been slower than public sector unions in responding to sexual diversity issues (Hunt & Rayside, 2002). Other research in this area is quite provocative. For example, Belkin (2001) argues that military homophobia remains strong and resists change because of an 'organizational shame' rooted in the fact that organizational norms and routines, as they intersect with the identity formation processes of young recruits, foster same-sex desire and practices. By defining what constitutes and proscribing gayness, the military constructs boundary conditions that protect straight service people from negative self-definitions despite occasional same-sex behaviors. Thus, institutionalized homophobia 'allows the military to conceal itself as a site that generates same-sex practices and gay identities and permits heterosexual service members who have same-sex sex to understand themselves as normal' (Belkin, 2001: 106). (See Ponger, 1999, for an analysis of homophobia in professional sports.)

Professions vary not only in their degree of institutionalized homophobia, but also in their symbolic significance. Institutional theorists have pointed to professionalization as a mechanism both of institution building (DiMaggio, 1991) and of the creation and diffusion of normative practices within and across organizational fields (DiMaggio & Powell, 1983). The success of openly LGBT professionals, particularly in professions associated with the healthy functioning of society, implicitly and explicitly challenges constructions of reality that demonize LGBT people. So, we might speculate that LGBT advances in certain professions will continue to be highly contested, for example, the ongoing battle over the recent election of an openly gay Episcopal bishop in the Diocese of New Hampshire.

Thus, we need research on the symbolic meaning of LGBT acceptance in particular professions and the implications of such visible advances for the maintaining or dismantling of cultural heterosexism.

Clearly, such research could also extend to explorations of the histories of LGBT interest groups within the professions. For example, Taylor and Raeburn (1995) have written of the history of the gay and lesbian caucus within the ASA. More research could be done on the history and dynamics of grassroots efforts to combat homophobia by LGBT groups within other professional domains and associations, for example, medicine, journalism, the law, psychology and the ministry. Comparative work on how the experiences of these professional groups are different and why would also be valuable.

Discrimination, Gay Career Decision Making and Coping Strategies

A number of counseling psychologists have conducted research on the career decision making of LGBT individuals. At the heart of this work is the idea that life and career are so interrelated that career planning and counseling interventions must flow from the total life experience (Croteau & Hedstrom, 1993). Experiences of stereotyping, gay stigma and prejudice can be especially relevant to understanding LGBT careers because they can affect vocational self-concepts, world views, career decisions and vocational adjustment (Chung, 2003). Most existing assessment and intervention techniques, and models of career choice and development, have not systematically considered sexual orientation as a factor (Croteau & Thiel, 1993; Dunkle, 1996), so one key objective of this stream of research has been exploring and correcting for the inadequacies resulting from this heterosexist bias (Croteau, Anderson, DiStefano & Kampa-Kokesch, 2000).

For example, Chung (1995) has looked beyond the common individual-level predictors used in career assessment, such as personality and interest measures, to environmental factors that enter into LGBT persons' decision making, for example, manifest degree of tolerance for LGBT people in the profession. Because coming out is a recurring process, for LGBT individuals it remains a factor as they move across jobs, teams or organizations. Thus, Chung (2001) considers the factors affecting successful navigation of one's vocational path. He offers multi-dimensional frameworks for conceptualizing discrimination (formal vs. informal, potential vs. encountered and perceived vs. real) and coping strategies, which are subdivided into vocational choice strategies (self-employment, job tracking and risk taking), and work adjustment or discrimination management strategies (quitting, silence, social support, and confrontation). Two issues should make coping strategies of special interest to organizational scholars. First, there is the idea that LGBTs self-select into job tracks with employers of choice where they expect more affirmation. Second, they likely adjust their levels of work and organizational commitment to compensate for experiences of inequity and discrimination or to manage knowledge of their identities. Both of these coping strategies have implications for human resource management and organizational effectiveness.

Homophobia and heterosexism do not affect the careers of only LGBT people, however, as research on heterosexual male teachers suggests. Classrooms, like other workplaces, are arenas for the enactment of identity, including gender and sexual identity. Heterosexual men in teaching often have particular challenges in enacting their male, heterosexual identities because the profession has histori- cally been gendered as female. As a consequence, many men use homophobic discourses (as well as sexist and power-inflected discourses) to enact their hetero- sexual male identities in the classroom, with potentially ill consequences for LGBT and heterosexual students alike (Francis & Skelton, 2001). For people entering other professions historically dominated by members of the other gender, the challenges associated with the social construction of identity are likely to make these professional settings arenas for discourses of homophobia and hetero- sexism. This suggests that – in line with a functional approach to understanding sexual prejudice – such settings may be especially valuable research sites for understanding the distinctive organizational uses for homophobia (Jome & Tokar, 1998). The obverse may also be true. Professions that have remained male or female dominated likewise may provide good arenas for studying the modern organizational functions of homophobia.

CONVERSATION 5: WHAT ARE THE EFFECTIVE WAYS OF COMBATING HETEROSEXISM AND HOMOPHOBIA IN THE WORKPLACE?

Many LGBT scholars and their allies have not wanted simply to study homopho- bia and its consequence per se, but rather have been concerned with understand- ing ways of combating it successfully. In terms of this conversation, research at the micro level has drawn principally on social psychological concerns, while research at the macro-sociological level has drawn on neo-institutionalist and social movement theories.

Changing Individuals' Workplace Behaviors

One example of such explicitly and avowedly activist scholarship is the edited volume *Overcoming Heterosexism and Homophobia: Strategies that Work* (Sears & Williams, 1997). Most of the approaches presented are based on the application of social psychological theories – regarding prejudice, communication and the different norms and needs of ethnic, racial, and professional communities – to the design of actual interventions, for example, self-disclosure and training programs. In general, many of these strategies emphasize the need for the intervention to be tailored so as to address both the psychosocial need sexual prejudice fills for the change target and the cultural norms and location of the audience (professional, organizational and/or social identity group culture). For example, Stewart (1997) argues that sexual orientation training for law enforcement agencies must address subcultural norms that disdain sensitivity training and the impact on officers' identity formation of police stereotypes regarding hypermasculinity, authoritarianism, bigotry and cynicism. Accordingly, Stewart argues that effective professional training needs to be: (1) comprehensible, in the sense that it starts where the students are in their understandings of gender, sexuality and their professions; (2) meaningful or relevant to the professional subculture; (3) modeled, in the sense that the teachers need to be enough of the culture to be worthy of emulation; and (4) authentic, in the sense that the training is directly applicable to the professional's role and identity. Entirely theoretically sound, these four characteristics have had only limited empirical testing in the context of anti-homophobia training across professions.

In reality, there is surprisingly little research on the effectiveness of many of the popular approaches – such as LGBT speaker panels, diversity training programs and other workplace interventions – in changing workplace place behaviors or individuals' beliefs (Croteau & Kusek, 1992; Emert & Mulburn, 1997). Clearly, organizational scholars interested in organizational culture, identity and change could all pursue important research using sexual diversity training as the topic. Ragins and Cornwell (2001) point out that we actually know little about how organizations develop cultures that are accepting or even affirming of LGBT people (Button, 2001). Their question – are the processes like those for developing respect for other forms of diversity or are organizations that accept sexual orientation 'more "highly evolved" with respect to diversity' (Ragins & Cornwell, 2001: 1256)? – suggests how research on organizational approaches to heterosexism could extend our knowledge of the relative efficacy of different perspectives on diversity (Ely & Thomas, 2001). Perhaps scholars who apply single-, double- and triple-loop action learning methods to ethical problems in organizations (Nielsen, 1996) have a special contribution to make in this area due to the ways in which anti-heterosexism interventions challenge individual, organizational and underlying cultural assumptions (Foldy & Creed, 1999).

Workplace Activism and the Transformation of the Workplace

At a more macro level, research on anti-homophobia work has focused on the ways in which the LGBT civil rights movement has entered corporations in the form of LGBT employee groups and mobilized advocates of equitable treatment. Raeburn (2004) offers a very valuable historical perspective on the rise and growth of an organized LGBT movement in the Fortune 1000 over the last 25 years. She identifies three distinct periods of patterned employee group formations:

a slow rise in new organizing (1978–89); a period of rapid growth (1990–4); and a slackening in new foundings (1995–8). She finds this ebb and flow of social movement activity linked to shifts in the broader socio-political context (McAdam, McCarthy & Zald, 1996). For example, early workplace organizing emerged in response to anti-gay initiatives by the New Right in the 1970s, for example, Anita Bryant's campaign to repeal a gay rights ordinance in Dade County. Growth in the early 1990s reflects in part the response to 'suddenly imposed grievances' (Walsh, 1981, quoted in Raeburn, 2004), including Colorado's Amendment Two (a statewide ballot initiative banning municipalities from passing local civil rights protection for LGBT people) and the institutionalization of the military closet in the form of the 'don't ask, don't tell' policy.

Perhaps most importantly in terms of organizational scholars' efforts to understand processes of change in an interorganizational field (DiMaggio & Powell, 1983), Raeburn points to effects of the AIDS epidemic – a flourishing of grassroots service organizations in the LGBT community and the more radical translation and reincorporation of tactics used at the zenith of gay liberation in the early 1970s by groups like ACT UP (AIDS Coalition to Unleash Power). (The Internet also emerged as a tool, with Digital Queers, ahead of the curve for Internet organizing, announcing in the early 1990s: 'We're here. We're queer. We've got email.') Together, these factors led to a sudden expansion in the movement's strategic repertoire and organizational resources across the entire spectrum of organizing. At the same time, Raeburn notes, the more radical tenor of groups like ACT UP created a 'radical flank effect' (Haines, 1988) that made the professional approaches of workplace activists less threatening to corporate elites. This rich picture of interorganizational resource building and the penetration of movement activity into corporations offers a compelling explanation for why the majority of corporations that adopted gay-positive policies such as domestic partner benefits did so only after mobilized groups of LGBT employees exerted pressure.

Working within the same neo-institutionalist/social movements frameworks, Creed and Scully, and their colleagues, complement this sweeping historical picture with analysis that looks at the dynamics of micromobilization, the social psychological processes by which people are transformed into agents able to challenge the status quo (Gamson, 1992). They show how workplace activists animate at the micro level the sort of organizational political process presented by Raeburn through focusing on: the techniques and strategies of workplace advocacy (Scully, Creed & Ventresca, 2005); the framing of arguments and legitimations for policy proposals (Creed, Scully & Austin, 2002; Creed, Langstraat & Scully, 2002); the enactment of marginalized identities in the interest of affecting acceptance and change (Creed, 2003; Creed & Scully, 2000); and the workings of interorganizational networks (Scully et al., 2005). This work emphasizes the roles of: the personalizing of the political as the basis for mobilization and advocacy, a process that creates agents even while mobilizing them; the ways LGBT workplace advocates create and diffuse repertoires of action within and across employee networks, tailoring them to their organizational cultures and local discourses; and the adaptation of broader cultural frames, such as civil rights, in the legitimation of workplace justice claims and the construction of a shared identity (Scully & Creed, 2005).

Research on the impact of movement activity also appears in the industrial relations literature. Hunt and his colleagues offer comparative perspectives on the historical role of organized labor in advancing the cause of workplace equity for LGBT people (Hunt, 1999; Hunt & Rayside, 2002), showing some of the surprising ways in which public sector unions in Canada in particular have been at the forefront of anti-homophobia change in the workplace.

Organizational homophobia remains a major challenge, both for organized labor in the United States (Krupat & McCreery, 1999) and for corporate America. Taken together, these streams of research point to the need to better understand the factors affecting the empowerment of LGBT people as individual employees, as members of employee groups and as unionists. The uneven success of workplace advocacy, strategies, and techniques for combating workplace homophobia suggest that scholars could focus on the ways in which professional norms, industry, class structure, culture (at the national, organizational, team and social identity group levels), and changing socio-political dynamics affect the efficacy of anti-homophobia interventions.

CONVERSATION 6: WHAT ARE THE IMPLICATIONS OF CULTURAL EMBEDDEDNESS FOR ORGANIZATION RESEARCH ON HETEROSEXISM AND HOMOPHOBIA?

Many of these conversations have already suggested that understanding individual workplace experiences and organizational practices hinges in part on our ability to understand the larger institutional context in which they are embedded. For example, earlier conversations have pointed to heterosexism as a feature of the institutional environment, to deeper cultural discourses as a determinant of the symbolic significance individuals assign to organizations' cultural practices and gestures, to gendered professions as a mechanism for perpetuating heterosexist discourse, and to social movements as conduits for repertoires of action and the mobilization of resources. Homophobia, LGBT authenticity and resistance are all embedded in higher-level cultural phenomena. In this conversation, I would like to pose more direct questions about the implications for organizational research of this embeddedness.

As conversation 1 suggests, anti-gay prejudice has deep roots in Western culture, but even in the West, cultural differences seem to matter a great deal when it comes to how and to what degree heterosexism manifests itself. Consider this juxtaposition. Exit polls from the November 2004 elections in the United States showed a concern for 'moral values' was a decisive factor in George W. Bush's reelection. People all along the political spectrum took this as code for opposition to same-sex marriage, which had emerged as an election-year issue. In contrast, since early 2004 same-sex marriage has fast been becoming the norm across the Canadian provinces and is expected to pass in the Spanish parliament in early 2005 despite intense Vatican opposition.

For organizational researchers, this contrast should trigger special attention to how cultural and ideological forces appear to be sustaining heterosexist institutions and organizational practices in some countries and dismantling them in others. Unlike many prejudices, in some countries, heterosexism continues to enjoy the support of many powerful members and institutions of society. For example, United States Supreme Court Justice Antonin Scalia, in his dissent in *Lawrence & Garner* v. *Texas* (which overturned the Texas anti-sodomy law and expanded the right to privacy under the United States Constitution), chided the court majority for deciding that the moral disapprobation of homosexual conduct does not constitute a legitimate state interest (Supreme Court of the United States, June 26, 2003, Dissent 1, pp. 20–1). While the court decision itself opens the door for further constitutional challenges to state-sponsored discrimination against LGBT people, Scalia's dissent reflects the institutional strength of anti-gay sentiment in the United States.

In 2003, the Vatican also increased its pressure on Catholic politicians worldwide by instructing them to oppose, as a matter of faith, changes in laws that might legitimate same-sex relationships. To vote in favor of such a law would be 'harmful to the common good' and 'gravely immoral' (Congregation for the Doctrine of the Faith, 2003: 5). (This appears to be having little impact on Spanish and Canadian politicians.)

Both Scalia's and the Vatican's positions share a common feature of defenses of heterosexism – the depiction of anti-gay discrimination as morally valid and essential to preserving social order.

> Some homophobes contend that … homophobia, rather than being a form of bigotry or intolerance, ratifies the values of society and of the institutions that constitute and govern it. Th[eir] appeal to Scripture, law, and centuries of custom reinterprets the history of persecution as a history of the proper application of justice and the maintenance of morality, virtue, and civic order against a subversive form of sexual conduct and an equally dangerous sexual species. (Fone, 2000: 420)

The claim that anti-gay persecution is essential for preserving morality and civic order should alert organizational researchers to the questions of how an emancipated LGBT culture continues to be more or less threatening in different cultural settings and, if we accept a functional perspective, how anti-gay prejudice continues to serve a need for different cultural collectives. Notwithstanding the (perhaps improbable) possibility of a growing gay-affirming sensibility among the global managerial elite, it is difficult to imagine that organizations and organizational scholarship can be insulated from their larger societies' varying needs for anti-gay prejudice or from the ways in which many organizational practices reproduce heteronormitivity (Gonzalez, 1999).

The need for anti-gay prejudice seems to be remaining strong in some powerful circles in the United States. Prasad suggests that the persistence of American homophobia stems in part from the need to preserve cultural myths that 'enshrine [masculine] archetypes such as the Calvinist and the Cowboy, thereby leaving little space for sexual diversity of any kind' (personal communication). The concern for organizational scholars is how these myths and the related ideologies of self-reliance, detachment, impersonality, superiority and male dominance actually imprint contemporary United States organizations and marginalize minorities, women and LGBT people, 'whose cultural values and lifestyles come into repeated conflict' with these cultural codes (Prasad, 1997).

Bronski (1998), in an analysis that focuses on the American experience, argues that anti-gay prejudice is perhaps inescapable. Building on a Freudian analysis regarding the tension between pleasure and social order (Freud, 1961a; 1961b), Bronski argues that gay culture cannot avoid being antagonistic to heterosexist cultural structures.

> Homosexuality offers a clear critique of the ideology of heterosexuality … It challenges accepted ideas about sexual activity, gender roles, relationships, marriage, family, work, and child rearing. Most important, it offers an unstinting vision that liberates sex from the burden of reproduction and places pleasure at the center of sexual activity. (Bronski, 1998: 13)

In effect, Bronski argues, the full acceptance of gay culture runs counter to deep cultural beliefs about the role of sexual sublimation in the work ethic and the diversion of energy toward other social goals. While heterosexual people are attracted by gay culture's creativity and freedom of self-expression, at some level, a visible gay culture, with its relative rejection of sexual sublimation, is the straight world's worst fear.[8]

How applicable Bronski's analysis is across national cultures is open to debate, but it points to an important question. Given the power and tenacity of institutionalized heterosexism in which organizations are embedded, is a workplace free of sexual prejudice imaginable? If not, then all research on LGBT workplace experience would need to consider the institutional constraints imposed by heterosexist ideology and all action would need to be viewed critically in terms of its role in sustaining or resisting heterosexist ideological hegemony. Today, many scholars are likely to interpret the adopting of domestic partner benefits and other gay-friendly workplace policies by more and more United States corporations as evidence of widespread social change. A serious intellectual embrace of the cultural embeddedness of these policy changes means we must ask if LGBT advances in the workplace are bellwethers and the seeds of greater social transformation, aberrations or something in between. If we take for granted that heterosexism is powerfully institutionalized, we should scrutinize apparent advances in organizational tolerance and remain aware of the dynamics of aversive prejudice, covert discrimination and other mechanisms that can perpetuate sexual prejudice.

Embeddedness and Theory

To the degree that the study of heterosexism and homophobia in organizations unfolds under the rubric of managing diversity, it will remain in the theoretical mainstream and scholars are likely to employ theories that treat difference as a problem to deal with in the interest of organizational effectiveness – or perhaps even workplace justice (Gonzalez, 1999; Prasad & Mills, 1997). This can be practical, and appropriate as well, since it enhances the validity of such research in the field. The explicit treatment of sexuality in organizations has not had a long history of acceptance in many academic circles (Burrell & Hearn, 1989) and framing the issues of LGBT workplace experiences in terms of mainstream theoretical questions stands to increase acceptance of these topics. Much of the literature reviewed here is situated in this broad theoretical framework. The embeddedness of our academic careers means that pragmatic concerns like publishing or perishing will shape the ways the study of heterosexism in organizations unfolds. The risk to us as scholars is that pragmatism can encourage us to remain uncritical of the ways in which mainstream organizational theory can reproduce hegemony. For example, in an effort to queer organizational theory, Gonzalez argues that mainstream research on diversity is 'part of a discourse whose main interest is to control and manipulate', through reconstituting ideological structures that 'keep oppressed peoples in conditions of subordination' (Gonzalez, 1999: 4).

No one familiar with neo-institutionalist organizational theory can have read this chapter and not have long since had me pegged theoretically. I advocate the use of any theory that enables critical attention to the ways in which institutionalized belief systems shape meaning and identity, privilege and marginality, and power and the possibility of resistance, but I prefer neo-institutionalist approaches because of their social constructionist focus on historical context, belief-systems and language. This has colored my readings and the style of argumentation in this chapter and I hope has won some of you over to exploring this perspective.

But any theoretical stance that fosters an iconoclastic approach to understanding organizational phenomena and interrogates how organizations advance definitions of normal and 'put people in their place' will do (Hall, 2003: 13). For some, queer theories would seem a natural fit. (I am not an expert and it is beyond my power and the purpose of this chapter to explain queer theories.) At first, I doubted their relevance because few organizational scholars or LGBT employees are challenging 'compulsory heterosexuality' (Rich, 1980); LGBT employees' concerns are usually more concrete – freedom from discrimination, the well-being of their families. However, queer theories have all of the desirable features of institutionalist approaches: 'historizing and "deconstructing" are ways of differently imagining our future as well as understanding our past' (Hall, 2003: 46). Queering organizational theory opens up discussion of how contemporary ways of organizing and organizational theorizing reproduce hegemonic heterosexism and engender various forms of oppression (Gonzalez, 1999). What's not to like about that?

CONVERSATION 7: OUT ON THE BUSINESS SCHOOL FACULTY – WHAT WILL OUR OWN EXPERIENCES OF HETEROSEXISM BE?

The past few years have witnessed the coalescence of a small but increasingly active group of LGBT management scholars in the AoM, many of whom are out of the closet in the workplace and a few of whom are conducting work on LGBT workplace issues. It certainly cannot be an accident of fate that gay and lesbian management scholars are later to the table than scholars in the ASA and the APA, each of which has had LGBT caucuses since 1974. It is probably safe to say that many business schools will not be amenable places for conducting research on heterosexism in organizations. Management scholars have to contend with the fact that it is a more conservative discipline than psychology or social work and more pragmatic discipline than sociology. What should LGBT management scholars expect?

Research on the formation and history of the Lesbian and Gay Caucus of the ASA shows that being an openly gay, lesbian and bisexual (GLB) scholar has its consequences (Taylor & Raeburn, 1995). Based on survey data collected in 1982 and 1992, GLB sociologists whose scholarly work focused on gay issues or who were active politically on gay issues ('activist' scholars) experienced more negative career outcomes than either out scholars whose work or behavior was not seen as activist or GLB scholars who were more or less closeted. These outcomes included discrimination in hiring, bias in tenure and promotion, exclusion from social and professional networks, harassment in their departments and their classrooms, and devaluation of scholarly work on lesbian and gay topics. Academics confronting homophobia in other disciplines encounter similar problems (Buckridge et al., 1998; McNarron, 1997).

So as I reflect on the emergence of the AoM Family and other academic groups and on my own career experiences, these questions and possible directions for research appear: (1) Why has the emergence of LGBT issues at the AoM been so far behind their emergence at the ASA or the APA? (2) If we as management scholars are hoping to open up research on workplace homophobia and heterosexism in particular, what light do we need to shine on the workplaces where management knowledge is created? (3) From a reflective inquiry perspective, what are our own concerns about workplace homophobia and the consequences for our own careers? How should these concerns inform our scholarship and our teaching? (4) What in fact are the consequences of studying LGBT issues for management scholars? (5) What strategies might be necessary so our work is not dismissible as narrow, frivolous, subjective, overly political or biased?

CONCLUSION: TO THE BARRICADES IN A CULTURAL WAR?

These conversations hold many challenges for organizational scholars. First, as the coining and subsequent critique of *homophobia* and the emergence of *heterosexism* as an alternative construct suggest, choosing among these analytical constructs has implications beyond important questions of levels of analysis and rigor. These concepts are the products of contested social construction processes about the very nature of anti-LGBT prejudice and about LGBT people either as threats to the social order or as worthy of freedom from prejudice. Our constructs and approaches for studying sexual prejudice can be fully but not solely scientific, since they reflect where we choose to come down in these meaning-making contests. To conduct research on anti-gay prejudice arguably constitutes participating in a culture war. Is it important for organizational scholars to consider the nature of these culture wars (Herman, 1997) as we study *homophobia* and *heterosexism* in the workplace because they are, in effect, fighting words.

Second, anti-gay prejudice operates at and across multiple levels of analysis. Individual-level prejudices converge with cultural ideologies of heterosexism. Individual resistance and enactments of identity reflect cultural- and movement-level schemas and repertoires of action. Sexual prejudice is dynamic, functionally situational and culturally embedded. This highlights the risks of conducting social science as usual, abstracting constructs from their ideological and sociopolitical contexts for analytical ease (Benson, 1977).

Third, in pointing to the embeddedness of organizations (and managerial scholarship) in a cultural context that continues to find uses for anti-gay prejudice, these conversations implicitly calls for a critical-historical and avowedly ethical stance that is uncommon in management research – a discipline that Van Maanen (1995) accuses of physics envy.

Research on heterosexism can draw on and contribute to a wide spectrum of organizational theories and empirical streams. But the evidence, ranging from the research on the experiences of GLB sociologists, to the dearth of research in the mainstream management literature, to the slow emergence of an LGBT caucus in the AoM, suggests both that to conduct such research could have negative consequences for researchers' careers and many LGBT scholars recognize those risks. For better or worse, choosing to do research on organizational heterosexism means that LGBT management scholars will live what they research.

NOTES

1 Today it is common to see lesbian, gay, bisexual and transgender strung together as if people with these diverse orientations shared a single social identity. Of course, they do not and the differences in their self-understandings and experiences in society and the workplace warrant careful study. What they do share is their being the objects of hetero-sexist prejudice. Thus LGBT is more a political label, meant to signal the greater inclusiveness of the 'gay liberation' and equal rights movement, than it is a scientific category. I support this inclusiveness. However, when I am discussing scientific literature with a more limited scope, I will use appropriately limited categories such as gay male or lesbian rather than LGBT.

2 Two other key assumptions are that different individuals can derive different benefits from apparently identical attitudes or prejudices, while for a single individual, various attitudes about different objects can serve distinct functions.

3 In this context, Herek writes explicitly about gay people and homosexuality, although we might speculate that these functions also underlie attitudes toward bisexuals and transgender people.

4 According to Herek, sexual prejudice can only serve as experiential when the heterosexual has had personal contact with gay men or lesbians.

5 The phrase 'commie pinko faggot' was still in use among high school boys in the 1970s as an uncritical lampooning of a far darker construction of homosexuals that reflects the ease with which anti-gay prejudice can be fused with other prejudices and cultural anxieties.

6 The Family Research Council enumerates the criteria for civil rights projections as a history of political powerlessness, economic deprivation and unchangeable characteristics.

7 It is the work of Paul Cameron, chairman of the Family Research Institute, that is considered by many to be the apotheosis of bad, homophobic science. Cameron, who has a PhD from the University of Colorado, was expelled in 1983 from the American Psychological Association. In 1985, the American Sociological Association adopted a resolution asserting that Cameron 'has consistently misinterpreted and misrepresented sociological research on sexuality, homosexuality, and lesbianism', noting that 'Dr. Paul Cameron has repeatedly campaigned for the abrogation of the civil rights of lesbians and gay men, substantiating his call on the basis of his distorted interpretation of this research.' (The final resolution was published in ASA Footnotes, Feb. 1987, p. 14.) Herek (1998), an expert on anti-gay prejudice at the University of California at Davis, has published an extensive critique of the research methods used in survey studies conducted in 1983 and 1984 which have served as the bases for most of Cameron's published work on the links between homosexuality and child molestation, public health, social disorder, sexually transmitted diseases and suitability for teaching. Herek identifies flaws, any one of which, he argues, would have been sufficient to cast doubts on the validity of any results. In a nutshell, these flaws focus on: (1) use of a narrow sample that does not justify Cameron's pattern of broad generalization; (2) the masking of a low response rate and other evidence that suggests the sample is not random and representative; (3) the use of subsamples too small to support his analyses and conclusions; (4) validity problems with the questionnaires stemming from respondents' inability or unwillingness to provide accurate responses (e.g. adults were asked to recall when school teachers, camp counselors and 34 other categories of adult authority figure made sexual advances toward them during their childhoods); (5) the absence of evidence that the data collection involved unbiased interviewers who were unaware of the studies' hypotheses and were trained to collect sensitive information from potential participants; and (6) the explicit publishing of researcher agenda and bias during the data collection (in one city the local

newspaper ran a story under the headline, 'Lincoln man: poll will help oppose gays'). Information about Cameron and Herek's analysis of the methodological flaws are available at:

http://psychology.ucdavis.edu/rainbow/html/facts_cameron.html and

http://psychology.ucdavis.edu/rainbow/html/facts_cameron_survey.html

8 According to Bronski, while the rejection of sublimation is the straight world's worst fear, this vision of liberation also makes the lives of LGBT people the straight world's 'best fantasy' because the freedoms of self-expression found in gay culture are enviable, titillating, exciting and creative. The world would be a better place, in Bronski's analysis, if straight people acted more like gay people.

REFERENCES

Adams, M., & Vasilakis, A. (1996). Selling out. *Sales and Marketing Management, 148*(10).

Badgett, L. (1995). The wage effects of sexual orientation discrimination. *Industrial and Labor Relations Review, 48*, 726–39.

Badgett, M. V. L. (1996). Employment and sexual orientation: Disclosure and discrimination in the workplace. In A. L. Ellis & E. D. B. Riggle (Eds), *Sexual identity on the job: Issues and services* (pp. 29–52). New York: Haworth Press.

Badgett, M. V. L. (2001). *Money, myths, and change: The economic lives of lesbians and gay men*. Chicago: University of Chicago Press.

Belkin, A. (2001). Breaking rank: Military homophobia and the production of queer practices and identities. *Georgetown Journal of Gender and the Law, 3*, 83–106.

Benson, J. K. (1977). Organizations: A dialectic view. *Administrative Science Quarterly, 22*, 1–21.

Berkman, C. S., & Zinberg, G. (1997). Homophobia and heterosexism in social workers. *Social Work, 42*, 319–32.

Bieschke, K. J., & Matthews, C. (1996). Career counselor attitudes and behaviors towards gay, lesbian, and bisexual clients. *Journal of Vocational Behavior, 48*, 243–55.

Bridgewater, D. (1997). Effective coming out: Self-disclosure strategies that reduce sexual identity bias. In J. T. Sears & W. L. Williams (Eds), *Overcoming heterosexism and homophobia: Strategies that work* (pp. 65–75). New York: Columbia University Press.

Bronski, M. (1998). *The pleasure principle: Sex, backlash, and the struggle for gay freedom*. New York: St Martin's Press.

Buckridge, S. O., CJ, Darby, K. M., Freeman, S., Hegarty, M. E., Mizell, C. A., Raeburn, N. C. & RN (1998). Being lesbian/gay/queer in the university. An e-mail conversation. *Journal of Women's History, 10*(1), 157–73.

Burrell, G. & Hearn, J. (1989). The sexuality of organization. In J. Hearn, D. Sheppard, P. Tencred-Sheriff and G. Burrell (Eds), *The Sexuality of Organization*. Thousand Oaks, CA: Sage.

Button, S. B. (2001). Organizational efforts to affirm sexual diversity: A cross-level examination. *Journal of Applied Psychology, 86*, 17–28.

Cain, R. (1996). Heterosexism and self-disclosure in the social work classroom. *Journal of Social Work Education, 32*(1), 65–77.

Chrobot-Mason, D., Button, S. B., & DiClementi, J. D. (2001). Sexual identity management strategies: An exploration of antecedents and consequences. *Sex Roles, 45*, 321–36.

Chung, Y. B. (1995). Career decision making of lesbian, gay, and bisexual individuals. *Career Development Quarterly, 44*, 178–90.

Chung, Y. B. (2001). Work discrimination and coping strategies: Conceptual frameworks for counseling lesbian, gay, and bisexual clients. *Career Development Quarterly*, *50*, 33–44.

Chung, Y. B. (2003). Ethical and professional issues in career assessment with lesbian, gay, and bisexual persons. *Journal of Career Assessment*, *11*, 96–112.

Congregation for the Doctrine of the Faith (2003). Considerations regarding proposals to give legal recognition to unions between homosexual persons, 3 June: www.vatican.va.

Cramer, E. (1997). Strategies for reducing social work students' homophobia. In J. T. Sears & W. L. Williams (Eds), *Overcoming heterosexism and homophobia: Strategies that work* (pp. 287–98). New York: Columbia University Press.

Creed, W. E. D. (2003). Voice lessons: Tempered radicals and the use of voice and silence. *Journal of Management Studies*, *40*(6), 1503–36.

Creed, W. E. D., Langstraat, J., & Scully, M. (2002). A picture of the frame: Frame analysis as technique and as politics. *Organizational Research Methods*, *5*(1), 34–55.

Creed, W. E. D. & Scully, M. A. (2000). Songs of ourselves: Employees' deployment of social identity in workplace encounters. *Journal of Management Inquiry*, *9*, 391–413.

Creed, W. E. D., Scully, M., & Austin, J. (2002). Clothes make the person: The tailoring of legitimating accounts and the social construction of identity. *Organization Science*, *13*(5), 475–96.

Croteau, J. M. (1996). Research on the work experiences of lesbian, gay and bisexual people: An integrative review of methodology and findings. *Journal of Vocational Behavior*, *48*, 195–209.

Croteau, J. M., Anderson, M. Z., DiStefano, T. M., & Kampa-Kokesch, S. (2000). Lesbian, gay, and bisexual vocational psychology: Reviewing foundations and planning construction. In R. M. Perez, K. A. DeBord & K. J. Bieschke (Eds), *Handbook of counseling and psychotherapy with lesbian, gay, and bisexual clients* (pp. 383–408). Washington, DC: American Psychological Association.

Croteau, J. M., & Hedstrom, S. M. (1993). Integrating communality and difference: The key to career counseling with lesbian women and gay men. *Career Development Quarterly*, *41*(3), 201–10.

Croteau, J. M., & Kusek, M. T. (1992). Gay and lesbian speaker panels: Implementation and research. *Journal of Counseling and Development*, *70*, 396–401.

Croteau, J. M., & Thiel, M. J. (1993). Integrating sexual orientation in career counseling: Acting to end a form of the personal-career dichotomy. *Career Development Quarterly*, *42*, 174–9.

D'Emilio, J. D. (1992). *Making trouble: Essays on gay history, politics, and the university.* New York: Routledge.

Day, N. E., & Schoenrade, P. (2000). The relationship among reported disclosure of sexual orientation, anti-discrimination policies, top management support and work attitudes of gay and lesbian employees. *Personnel Review*, *29*(3), 346–63.

DiMaggio, P. J. (1991). Constructing an organizational field as a professional project: U.S. Art Museum, 1920–1940. In W. W. Powell and P. J. DiMaggio (Eds), *The new institutionalism in organizational analysis* (pp. 267–92). Chicago: University of Chicago Press.

DiMaggio, P. J., & Powell, W. W. (1983). The iron cage revisited: Institutional isomorphism and collective rationality in organizational fields. *American Sociological Review*, *48*, 147–60.

DiPlacido, J. (1998). Minority stress among lesbians, gay men, and bisexuals: A consequence of heterosexism, homophobia, and stigmatization. In G. M. Herek (Ed.), *Stigma and sexual orientation: Understanding prejudice against lesbians, gay men, and bisexuals* (pp. 138–59). Thousand Oaks, CA: Sage.

Dovidio, J. F., & Gaertner, S. L. (Eds) (1986). *Prejudice, discrimination, and racism.* San Diego: Academic Press.

Driscoll, J. M., Kelley, F. A., & Fassinger, R. E. (1996). Lesbian identity and disclosure in the workplace: Relation to occupational stress and satisfaction. *Journal of Vocational Behavior, 48,* 229–42.

Duberman, M. (1991). *Cures: A Gay Man's Odyssey*. New York: Dutton.

Dunkle, J. H. (1996). Toward an integration of gay and lesbian identity development and Super's Life-span Approach. *Journal of Vocational Behavior: Special Vocational Issues of Lesbian Women and Gay Men, 48*(2), 149–59.

Dutton, J. E., Ashford, S. J., Lawrence, K. A., & Miner-Rubino, K. (2002). Red light, green light: Making sense of organizational context for issue selling. *Organization Science, 13*(4), 355–72.

Ellis, A. L., & Riggle, E. D. B. (1995). The relation of job satisfaction and degree of openness about one's sexual orientation for lesbians and gay men. *Journal of Homosexuality, 30,* 75–85.

Ely, R. J. & Thomas, D. A. (2001). Cultural diversity at work: The effects of diversity perspectives on work group processes and outcomes. *Administrative Science Quarterly, 46*(2), 229–73.

Emert, T., & Mulburn, L. (1997). Sensitive supervisors, prepared practicum, and 'queer' clients: A training model for beginning counselors. In J. T. Sears & W. L. Williams (Eds), *Overcoming heterosexism and homophobia: Strategies that work* (pp. 272–87). New York: Columbia University Press.

Foldy, E. G. (2003). Being all that you can be: Identity and interactions in organizations. Paper presented at the Annual Meeting of the Academy of Management, Seattle, WA.

Foldy, E. G., & Creed, W. E. D. (1999). Action learning, fragmentation, and the interaction of single, double, and triple loop change: A case of gay and lesbian workplace advocacy. *Journal of Applied Behavior Science, 35*(2), 207–27.

Fone, B. (2000). *Homophobia: A history*. New York: Metropolitan Books/Henry Holt.

Francis, B., & Skelton, C. (2001). Men teachers and the construction of heterosexual masculinity in the classroom. *Sex Education, 1*(1), 9–21.

Freud, S. (1961a). *Beyond the pleasure principle* (J. Strachey, Trans. and Ed.). New York: Norton.

Freud, S. (1961b). *Civilization and its discontents* (J. Strachey, Trans. and Ed.). New York: Norton.

Gamson, W. A. (1992). The social psychology of collective action. In. A. D. Morris and C. M. Mueller (Eds), *Frontiers in social movement theory* (pp. 53–76). New Haven, CT: Yale University Press.

Gamson, W. A. (1998). Social Movements and cultural change. In M. G. Guigni, D. McAdam and C. Tilly (Eds), *From Contingency to Democracy* (pp. 57–77). New York: Rowman & Littlefield Publishers.

Goffman, E. (1963). *Stigma: Notes on the management of spoiled identity*. New York: Simon & Schuster.

Gonzalez, C. (1999). Sexuality and organizational theorizing: A queer theory approach. Paper presented at the Academy of Management Meeting, Chicago, IL.

Gramick, J. (1983). Homophobia: A new challenge. *Social Work*, March–April, 137–41.

Griffith, K. H., & Hebl, M. R. (2002). The disclosure dilemma for gay men and lesbians: 'Coming Out' at work. *Journal of Applied Psychology, 87,* 1191–9.

Haines, H. H. (1988). *Black radicals and the civil rights movement, 1954–1970*. Knoxville: University of Tennessee Press.

Hall, D. E. (2003). *Queer theories*. New York: Palgrave Macmillan.

Hebl, M. R., Foster, J. B., Mannix, L. M., & Dovidio, J. F. (2002). Formal and interpersonal discrimination: A field study of bias toward homosexual applicants. *Personality and Social Psychology Bulletin, 28,* 815–25.

Herek, G. M. (1984). Beyond 'homophobia': A social psychological perspective on attitudes towards lesbians and gay men. *Journal of Homosexuality, 10,* 1–21.

Herek, G. M. (1990). Gay people and government security clearances: A social science perspective. *American Psychologist, 45*(9), 1035–42.

Herek, G. M. (1998). Bad science in the service of stigma: A critique of Cameron group's survey studies. In G. M. Herek (Ed.), *Stigma and sexual orientation: Understanding prejudice against lesbians, gay men, and bisexuals* (p. 255). Thousand Oaks, CA: Sage.

Herek, G. M. (2000). The psychology of sexual prejudice. *Current Directions in Psychological Science, 9*, 19–22.

Herek, G. M. (2004). Personal homepage. Dept. of Psychology, UC Davis: http://psychology.ucdavis.edu/rainbow/html/prej_defn.html and http://psychology.ucdavis.edu/rainbow/html/facts_cameron.html (Accessed August 2003 and January 2004).

Herek, G. M., & Capitanio, J. P. (1996). 'Some of my best friends': Intergroup contact, concealable stigma, and heterosexuals' attitudes toward gay men and lesbians. *Personality & Social Psychology Bulletin, 22*, 412–24.

Herman, D. (1997). *The antigay agenda: Orthodox vision and the Christian right.* Chicago: University of Chicago Press.

Herman, E. (1995). *Psychiatry, psychology, and homosexuality.* New York: Chelsea House.

Holvino, E. (2001). *Complicating gender: The simultaneity of race, gender, and class in organizational change(ing).* Center for Gender in Organizations Working Paper No. 14, Simmons School of Management, Boston, MA.

Hunt, G. (Ed.) (1999). *Laboring for rights: Unions and sexual diversity across nations.* Philadelphia: Temple University Press.

Hunt, G., & Rayside, D. (2002). Canadian labour and sexual diversity activism in comparative perspective. Paper presented at the Annual Conference of the Association of Industrial Relations Academics of Australia and New Zealand, Queentown, New Zealand. Available at: http://www.mngt.waikato.ac.nz/depts/sml/airaanz/old/conferce/queenstown2002/pdf/volume1/Hunt&RaysideRef-Canadian.pdf

Hunter, J. D. (1991). *Culture wars: The struggle to define America.* New York: Basic Books/Harper Collins.

Jome, L. M., & Tokar, D. M. (1998). Dimensions of masculinity and major choice traditionality. *Journal of Vocational Behavior, 52*, 120–34.

Jones, J. M. (1972). *Prejudice and racism.* Reading, MA: Addison-Wesley.

Kanter, R. M. (1977). *Men and women of the corporation.* New York: Basic Books.

Kinsey, A. C., Pomeroy, W. B., & Martin, C. E. (1948). *Sexual behavior in the human male.* Philadelphia: W. B. Saunders.

Krupat, K., & McCreery, P. (1999). Homophobia, labor's new frontier? A discussion with four labor leaders. *Social Text, 17*(4), 59–72.

LeVay, S. (1996). *Queer science: The use and abuse of research into homosexuality.* Cambridge, MA: MIT Press.

Levine, M. P. (1979). Employment discrimination against gay men. *International Review of Modern Sociology, 9*, 151–63.

Levine, M. P., & Leonard, R. (1984). Discrimination against lesbians in the work force. *Signs: Journal of Women in Culture and Society, 9*, 700–10.

McAdam, D., McCarthy, J. D., & Zald, M. N. (Eds) (1996). *Comparative perspectives on social movements: Political opportunities, mobilizing structures, and cultural framings.* New York: Cambridge University Press.

McNarron, T. A. H. (1997). *Poisoned ivy: Lesbian and gay academics confronting homophobia.* Philadelphia: Temple University Press.

Nielsen, R. (1996). *The politics of ethics: Methods for acting, learning, and sometimes fighting, with others in addressing ethical problems in organizational life.* New York: Oxford University Press.

Ostfeld, M., & Jehn, K. E. (1998). *The visibility decision-making model: The gay individual as social perceiver of power and safety in the organization* (Working Paper). The Wharton School of the University of Pennsylvania.

Pietrzyk, M. E. (1994). Queer science. *New Republic, 211*(14), 10–13.

Ponger, B. (1999). Outta my endzone: Sport and the territorial anus. *Journal of Sport & Social Issues, 23*(4), 373–89.

Prasad, P. (1997). The protestant ethic and the myths of frontier. In P. Prasad, A. Mille, M. Elmes & A. Prasad (Eds), *Managing the organizational melting pot: Dilemmas of workplace diversity*. Thousand Oaks, CA: Sage.

Prasad, P. & Mills, A. J. (1997). From showcase to shadow. In P. Prasad, A. J. Mills, M. Elmes & A. Prasad (Eds), *Managing the Organizational Melting Pot: Dilemmas of Workplace Diversity*. Thousand Oaks, CA: Sage.

Raeburn, N. (2004). *Inside out: The struggle for lesbian, gay, and bisexual rights in the workplace*. Minneapolis: The University of Minnesota Press.

Ragins, B. R., & Cornwell, J. M. (2001). Pink triangles: Antecedents and consequences of perceived workplace discrimination against gay and lesbian employees. *Journal of Applied Psychology, 86*, 1244–61.

Ragins, B. R., Cornwell, J. M., & Miller, J. S. (2003). Heterosexism in the workplace: Do race and gender matter? *Group & Organization Management, 28*, 45–74.

Ragins, B. R., & Wiethoff, C. (2005). Understanding Heterosexism at Work: The Straight Problem. In A. Collella & B. Dipboye, (Eds), *The psychological and organizational bases of discrimination at work*. San Francisco: Jossey-Bass.

Rich, A. (1980). Compulsory heterosexuality and lesbian existence. *Signs: Journal of Women in Culture and Society, 5*(4), 631–60.

Riordan, C. M. (2000). Relational demography within groups: Past developments, contradictions, and new directions. *Research in Personnel and Human Resource Management, 19*, 131–73.

Rostosky, S. S., & Riggle, E. D. B. (2002). 'Out' at work: The relation of actor and partner workplace policy and internalized homophobia to disclosure status. *Journal of Counseling Psychology, 49*(4), 411–19.

Russell, G. M., and Greenhouse, E. M. (1997). Homophobia in the supervisory relationship: An invisible intruder. *Psychoanalytic Review, 84*(1), 27–42.

Scully, M. & Creed, W. E. D. (2005). Subverting our stories of subversion. In G. Davis, D. McAdam, W. R. Scott & M. Zald (Eds), *Social Movements and Organizational Theory* (pp. 310–22). New York: Cambridge University Press.

Scully, M., Creed, W. E. D., & Ventresca, M. (2005). *More than switchpersons on the tracks of history: Situated agency & contested legitimacy during the diffusion of domestic partner benefits*. Working paper.

Sears, J. T. (1997). Thinking critically/intervening effectively about homophobia and heterosexism. In J. T. Sears & W. L. Williams (Eds), *Overcoming heterosexism and homophobia: Strategies that work* (pp. 13–48). New York: Columbia University Press.

Sears, J. T., & Williams, W. L. (Eds) (1997). *Overcoming heterosexism and homophobia: Strategies that work*. New York: Columbia University Press.

Shallenberg, D. (1994). Professional and openly gay: A narrative study of the experience. *Journal of Management Inquiry, 3*(2), 119–42.

Stewart, C. (1997). Sexual orientation training in law enforcement: A preliminary review of what works. In J. T. Sears & W. L. Williams (Eds), *Overcoming heterosexism and homophobia: Strategies that work* (pp. 326–38). New York: Columbia University Press.

Supreme Court of the United States (2003). Lawrence et al. v. Texas, No. 02–102. Dissent, June 26, pp. 20–1:

www.supremecourtus.gov/opinions/02pdf/02–102.pdf

Taylor, V., & Raeburn, N. (1995). Identity politics as high-risk activism: Career consequences for lesbian, gay, and bisexual sociologists. *Social Problems*, *42*(2), 252–73.

Van Den Bergh, N. (1999). Workplace problems and needs for lesbian and gay male employees: Implications for EAPs. *Employee Assistance Quarterly*, *15*, 21–60.

Van Maanen, J. (1995). Style as theory. *Organizational Science*, *6*(1), 133–43.

Weinberg, G. (1972). *Society and the healthy homosexual*. New York: St Martin's Press.

Wickberg, D. (2000). Homophobia: On the cultural history of an idea. *Critical Inquiry*, *27*, 42–57.

Woods, J. D. (1994). *Corporate closets: The professional lives of gay men in America*. New York: Free Press.

Young-Bruehl, E. (1996). *The anatomy of prejudices*. Cambridge, MA: Harvard University Press.

Young-Bruehl, E. (2002). Homophobias: A diagnostic and political manual. *Constellations*, *9*(2), 263–73.

16

The Influence of Disability
on Role-Taking in Organizations

EUGENE F. STONE-ROMERO, DIANNA L. STONE
AND KIMBERLY LUKASZEWSKI

Approximately one out of every five individuals in the United States has a disability, and it is anticipated that 30% of those without disabilities will become disabled during their working years (US Bureau of Census, 2000). Thus, people with disabilities (PWD) make up the largest minority group in the United States. However, they often have one of the lowest employment rates. For example, recent census data (US Bureau of Census, 2000) show that only 31.4% of PWD are employed, compared to 84.4% of people without disabilities (PWOD). In order to reduce this and other problems faced by PWD, the Americans with Disabilities Act (1990; ADA) was passed. Regrettably, since its passage, employment rates for PWD have actually declined (Stone & Williams, 1997). Furthermore, PWD are three times more likely to live below the poverty level than PWOD, and when they are employed they typically earn $10,000 less than PWOD because they are often segregated in low-paying dead-end jobs (US Bureau of Labor Statistics, 2004). Given these and related problems, it is clear that PWD have few opportunities to experience a fulfilling work life, and this may not only undermine their feelings of self-worth, but also help to perpetuate their stigmatization (Goffman, 1963; Mechanic, 1998).

Stereotypes about People with Disabilities

Although there are a number of reasons for the employment problems experienced by PWD, researchers have argued that stereotypes and associated stigmas may be key sources of such problems (Stone & Colella, 1996; Stone, Stone & Dipboye, 1992). For example, research suggests that employers are concerned that PWD may (1) not have the skills and abilities needed to perform their work, (2) increase the demands placed on supervisors (Peck & Kirkbride, 2001), (3) create inequity in the workplace because of needed accommodations (Colella, 2001), (4) increase health care costs, and (5) have low levels of emotional adjustment, as reflected in such indicators as bitterness, nervousness and depression (Fichten & Amsel, 1986). These views notwithstanding, research has shown consistently that many of these concerns are unfounded and PWD have many talents and skills that can add significant value in the workplace (Greenwood & Johnson, 1987). For example, research shows that PWD have lower turnover and absenteeism rates, and perform as well, if not better, than PWOD (Greenwood & Johnson, 1987). In addition, research indicates that although the training time for people with some types of disabilities (e.g. learning disabilities) is greater than that for PWOD, the long-term benefits of hiring PWD far outweigh the additional resources devoted to their training (Pooley & Bump, 1993). Similarly, health care costs do not rise when firms hire PWD, and the cost of most accommodations is extremely low (i.e. averages less than $50 per accommodation). Nevertheless, as noted below, PWD are often accorded out-group status in organizations and treated accordingly. That is, as out-group members they suffer diminished levels of distributive justice, procedural justice and interactional justice (Stone-Romero & Stone, 2005).

Paucity of Research on People with Disabilities in Organizations

Despite the growing number of PWD in the United States, relatively little research has focused on disability issues in the related fields of organizational behavior, human resource management, and industrial and organizational psychology (Colella & Stone, 2004; Stone & Colella, 1996). In addition, much of the theoretical work on disability issues has focused on such topics as cognitive biases (Stone & Colella, 1996; Stone et al., 1992), unfair discrimination (Colella & Stone, 2004) and reactions to requests for accommodation (Colella, 2001). Moreover, much of the research has been aimed at understanding the effects of disabilities on such personnel-related matters as (1) personnel selection (Bordieri, Drehmer & Comminel, 1988; Cesare, Tannenbaum & Dalessio, 1990; Christman & Slaten, 1991), (2) job assignment (Jones, 1997), and (3) performance evaluation (Colella, DeNisi & Varma, 1998; Czajka & DeNisi, 1988).

It is noteworthy that very little research has focused on possible differences between the work scripts (Shank & Abelson, 1977) and role conceptions of PWD and PWOD. However, to the extent that PWD operate on the basis of different work-related scripts or role conceptions than their role senders (i.e. individuals in their role set), problems may arise because their behavior may be inconsistent with extant expectations and norms (Katz & Kahn, 1978; Stone & Stone-Romero, 2004; Stone-Romero, Stone & Salas, 2003). Unfortunately, very little is known about this issue. However, in view of the growing numbers of PWD in US organizations, it is critical that we develop a better understanding of the just-noted issues.

Purposes of the Chapter

In view of the foregoing, the primary purposes of this chapter are to (1) consider the influence of disabilities on work-related scripts and the role-taking process in organizations, (2) describe the strategies that PWD can use to manage social interactions in organizations, and (3) detail reasons for interpersonal problems that may arise between PWD and PWOD in organizations. Our treatment of these issues relies on several perspectives, including script theory (Shank & Abelson, 1977), social identity theory (e.g. Tajfel, 1982; Turner, 1987), terror management theory (Solomon, Greenberg & Pyszczynski, 1991), theory and research on stigmas (e.g. Goffman, 1963; Jones et al., 1984), and Stone and Stone-Romero's (2004) revised version of the seminal role-taking model of Katz and Kahn (1978).

SCRIPTS AS A BASIS FOR ORGANIZATIONAL BEHAVIOR

The efficiency and effectiveness of organizations depends on their members exhibiting dependable role behavior (Katz & Kahn, 1978). However, it is impossible for organizations to specify all of the prescriptions and proscriptions associated with any given role. As a result, they rely on the anticipatory socialization of workers for jobs, including the learning of general scripts for work behavior. *Scripts* are plans or structures that specify appropriate sequences of behaviors and events in various contexts, including work organizations (Shank & Abelson, 1977). When a script is activated, individuals typically engage in the behaviors called for by it. Among the many examples of scripts are a server's script for taking a customer's food order in a restaurant, and a physician's script for performing an appendectomy.

Functions of Scripts

Scripts serve a number of important purposes in organizations. For example, they enable incumbents to behave in accordance with general role expectations. In addition, they allow incumbents to 'fill in the gaps' when information about appropriate behaviors (e.g. role expectations) is not specified explicitly. Thus, for instance, a restaurant manager does not have to tell a server to take a customer's food and drink orders in a restaurant. The server script informs the server of the required actions.

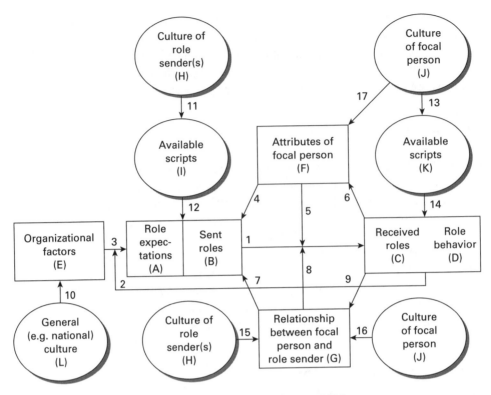

FIGURE 16.1   *The revised role-taking model (Stone & Stone-Romero, 2004)*

Differences in Work-related Scripts

As a result of differences in their life experiences and socialization processes, PWD often enter work organizations with somewhat different work-related scripts and expectations than PWOD. We comment on a number of script-related issues below in the section on the revised role-taking model.

Although there are many reasons why differences in work-related scripts of PWD and PWOD produce problems in organizations, a major reason is that encounters between incumbents with disabilities and role senders without disabilities open the door to considerably higher levels of anxiety among both incumbents and role senders. It stems from at least three sources. First, PWD may leave role senders uncertain about their ability to exhibit satisfactory role behavior. Second, consistent with terror management theory (Solomon et al., 1991), PWD may threaten the worldviews of role senders. For example, an incumbent with a disability may be inconsistent with the Darwinist view that only 'the fit should survive.' Third, some types of disabilities evoke negative emotional reactions in people, leading to interactions that are strained (Jones et al., 1984). We address these issues more fully below.

In view of this chapter's focus on role-taking, we consider the issue of work-related scripts within the context of a revised version of the seminal model of the role-taking developed by Katz and Kahn (1978). The revised role-taking model, shown in Figure 16.1, explicitly considers the influence of culture on the role-taking process (Stone & Stone-Romero, 2004). However, prior to describing the model, we consider three general issues: (1) the cultures of US organizations, (2) social identity theory, and (3) terror management theory and its implications for the treatment of PWD in work organizations.

THE CULTURES OF US ORGANIZATIONS

Consistent with Hofstede (1980), in this chapter the term culture refers to 'a set of collective, shared, learned values which represent a broad tendency to prefer certain states of affairs over others' (p. 25). Just as there are national cultures and subcultures, many organizations have unique cultures. For example, the culture of a research and development firm is likely to differ substantially from that of a metropolitan police department SWAT team or a US Army Ranger battalion.

Several researchers have argued that US organizations are dominated by European ideologies and values (e.g. Cox, 1993; Stone-Romero & Stone, 1998; Trice & Beyer, 1993). *Ideologies* are sets of shared, interrelated beliefs about how things work, what is worth having or doing, and how people should behave (Trice & Beyer, 1993). Thus, norms, values and scripts are all subsumed under the general rubric of ideologies.

Values of US Organizations

Trice and Beyer (1993) argue that US culture emphasizes such values as (1) rationality and depersonalization in decision making, (2) competitive achievement, (3) individualism and self-reliance, (4) the allocation of outcomes based on proportionality, (5) efficiency, and (6) standardized approaches to performing tasks. In the following subsections, we consider a subset of these values and their impact on organizational phenomena.

Competitive achievement

US organizations place a great deal of value on competitive achievement and their managers tend to be intolerant of poor performance, low levels of effort, or other signs of a lack of competitive achievement (Trice & Beyer, 1993). Workers are only hired and assured ongoing employment if they have both the motivation and ability to meet or exceed extant performance standards. As a result of these norms and values, role senders often develop expectations that employees will be highly competitive and will display high levels of performance on a consistent basis. Based on these and related expectations, role senders are likely to view PWD as unable to compete or meet requisite performance standards.

Individualism and self-reliance

Because of the value placed on individualism and self-reliance or self-sufficiency in US organizations, workers are expected to perform their roles independently, with little or no assistance from others (Jones et al., 1984; Trice & Beyer, 1993). One important corollary of this norm is that individuals should refrain from asking others for help or assistance. To the degree that individuals deviate from this norm, they run the risk of being viewed as unworthy by others, suffering blows to their esteem (Jones et al., 1984).

Interestingly, self-reliance is valued so highly in the United States that individuals who are not self-reliant (e.g. people who receive social assistance or welfare) are often the object of hostility and viewed as misfits (Hsu, 1961). For example, PWD who are perceived as being helpless are likely to be ostracized in organizations because their coworkers think that they are (1) unable to do their fair share of the work, (2) dependent on others, and (3) incapable of meeting performance standards unless granted special accommodations.

Proportionality

US culture stresses the allocation of resources on the basis of equity (i.e. proportionality; Leventhal, 1980). Thus, it is generally believed that people who make the greatest contributions to social systems should receive the greatest outcomes. Furthermore, perspectives on social justice (Leventhal, 1980) argue that individuals who fit the ideal prototype (e.g. young, male, attractive, physically fit) are: (1) accorded higher status than others in society, (2) viewed as providing greater inputs than others, and (3) believed to deserve greater outcomes than others. As a result, relative to PWD, role senders are likely to perceive that PWOD deserve greater levels of outcomes and, thus, are likely to provide them with commensurate levels of outcomes. At least one reason for this is role senders are likely to believe that PWD contribute fewer inputs to organizations and, therefore, actually deserve lesser outcomes than PWOD. In addition, on the basis of the belief that PWD are less capable than PWOD of doing work, supervisors may assign them to low-status jobs or to jobs that have little or no opportunities for advancement. See Stone-Romero and Stone (2005) for an extended discussion of the impact of out-group status on justice in organizational contexts.

Standardization

No doubt as one of the byproducts of bureaucracy theory, many US organizations have standardized practices (Katz & Kahn, 1978; March & Simon, 1958). The norm is that all employees should be treated alike, and no one should be given special treatment because it may give them a competitive advantage (Colella, 2001). Thus, role senders are unlikely to react positively to requests for accommodation from PWD. In addition, they are likely to resent or devalue PWD who request special accommodations in order to perform their jobs (Colella, 2001; Jones et al., 1984). Two glaring examples of this come from recent experiences of individuals who attempted to gain access to courthouses in southern US states. In 1996, George Lane, a paraplegic who showed up for a court appearance in Polk County, Tennessee, had to crawl up the steps of the courthouse, which had no wheelchair ramp or elevator. While doing so, court employees laughed at him (Braker, 2004). In 2004, Beverly Jones, a court reporter who was wheelchair bound, was unable to access a women's bathroom because it was on the second floor and she had no way of climbing the steps. Courthouse employees told her that no accommodation could be made for her (Fly, 2004).

Implications of Ideologies

As should be apparent from the above, the dominant culture in the United States is a key determinant of many of the factors that govern behavior in US organizations. Of particular importance here is that it has a profound influence on the way that PWD are treated in organizational contexts. Also serving to explain the treatment accorded to PWD in organizations are two theoretical perspectives from social psychology, i.e. social identity theory and terror management theory. We consider these next.

SOCIAL IDENTITY THEORY

Social identity theory posits that a person's social identity is a function of all of the identifications that they use in construing their views of the self (Tajfel, 1982; Turner, 1987). Stated somewhat differently, the social identity of an individual is based upon all of the social categories (e.g. groups) to which he or she belongs or is thought to belong. Thus, for example, one of the groups to which PWOD belong is the 'able-bodied'. Membership in this group often has important implications for the way in which PWD are viewed. More specifically, vis-à-vis PWOD, PWD are generally regarded as belonging to such out-groups as the blind, the paraplegic, the quadriplegic and the deaf.

Viewing PWD as out-group members is often functional for PWOD in that it enables them both to maintain and enhance their sense of self-esteem and to minimize the anxiety that arises in dealings with PWD (Solomon et al., 1991). For instance, PWOD can take pride in the fact that they have no disabling conditions that would interfere with normal activities (e.g. work, recreation). In addition, viewing PWD as out-group members leads PWOD to attend to and accentuate differences between themselves and PWD. To the degree that an individual is viewed as an outgroup member, he or she may be regarded as a threat to the well-being of in-group members. In addition, as is noted below, when PWOD work alongside PWD, there are likely to be strains in their interpersonal relations. Terror management theory (Solomon et al., 1991) provides an intriguing basis for understanding the basis of such strains.

TERROR MANAGEMENT THEORY

In this section we consider three general issues associated with terror management theory. More specifically, we cover (1) the basic propositions of the theory, (2) the implications of it for behavior in organizations, and (3) the strategies used by in-group members to deal with challenges to their worldviews posed by out-group members.

Basic Propositions of the Theory

Terror management theory (Solomon et al., 1991) posits that the mere existence of people who do not share our cultural beliefs or values is often threatening and anxiety evoking. The basic propositions of the theory are that: (1) people have an acute awareness of death and this is the basis of ongoing anxiety, (2) among the important desires that develop early in life are to be spared from death and experience minimal anxiety, (3) to relieve the terror associated with the prospect of death, people embrace world views that are culture specific, (4) these world views afford individuals with a sense of security and provide them with standards against which their behavior can be judged to be of value, thereby assuring them of some form of immortality through leaving an enduring mark on the world, (5) threats to such world views create anxiety because discrepant ideas imply that they may be wrong, and (6) these threats lead individuals to feel vulnerable, thus heightening their sense of mortality (Solomon et al., 1991).

Terror management theory supports the view that behavior that is considered to be highly appropriate in one cultural milieu may be viewed as quite inappropriate in another. For example, 'in corporate America, a ruggedly individualistic and competitive person is held in high regard. However, the same type of person would be utterly ostracized in many Native American cultures' (Solomon et al., 1991: 104). The same behavior would also be frowned upon in many other collective cultures (e.g. those of people indigenous to Tibet, Peru and Hawaii). What this implies is that scripts that are viewed as common and appropriate in some cultures may not be looked upon similarly in other cultures (Stone-Romero & Stone, 2002). As such, when PWOD deal with PWD in organizational contexts, assumed or actual differences in worldviews and scripts can lead PWOD to view PWD as outsiders who pose threats to their worldviews.

Implications for Role Taking in Organizations

In terms of the revised role-taking model described below, a person's worldview affects the degree to which they are viewed as a valuable or worthy person in a social system (e.g. an organization). Thus, encountering a worldview that is consonant with that of the dominant culture in an organization (e.g. that of PWOD) serves as an anxiety buffer (Solomon et al., 1991). However, when a person from the dominant culture encounters PWD, their worldview is threatened and their anxiety buffer may break down.

Strategies Used in Dealing With Out-group Members

In order to avoid or reduce threats to their worldview, members of the dominant culture are likely to take a number of steps. We consider several of them below.

Derogating out-group members

A frequently used strategy for dealing with members of out-groups (e.g. PWD) who are thought to not share the worldview of in-group members (e.g. PWOD) is to derogate them (Solomon et al., 1991). Doing so undermines the credibility of PWD and thus defuses the threat posed by their worldview. Consistent with this argument, a considerable body of research shows that PWD are frequently denigrated by PWOD (Goffman, 1963; Jones et al., 1984; Stone & Colella, 1996; Stone et al., 1992). In addition, social cognition research shows that in-group members tend to attribute negative traits to out-group members, and hold negative expectations about their behavior (e.g. Hamilton, 1981; Herman, Zanna & Higgins, 1986; Miller & Brewer, 1984; Tajfel, 1982). For example, in-group members attribute performance problems of PWD to their disabilities rather than to other factors (Jones et al., 1984).

A number of psychological factors may explain why PWD are denigrated by others including: (1) realistic threats to the existence of in-group members (e.g. PWD may transmit pathogens), (2) symbolic threats to the worldview of in-group members (e.g. PWD threaten beliefs in social Darwinism, meritocracy, distributive justice and self-sufficiency), (3) anxiety stemming from intergroup contact (e.g. interactions that result in discomfort for PWOD), and (4) negative stereotypes about out-group members (e.g. PWD) justify their subordination.

Exclusion from social systems

Another strategy that can be used to diminish the threat caused by out-group members is to exclude them from social systems. For example, research reveals that PWD are less likely to be hired in organizations than PWOD (Stone & Colella, 1996; Stone et al., 1992). In addition, relative to PWOD, PWD are offered fewer advancement opportunities, treated more disrespectfully and excluded more from informal social networks (Chima, 1998; 2002; Loo, 2001).

Research shows that PWOD are likely to experience considerable anxiety (e.g. that stemming from relational uncertainty) when interacting with PWD (Goffman, 1963; Jones et al., 1984). Thus, they often avoid interactions with these individuals (Jones et al., 1984; Stone & Colella, 1996). This is unfortunate because suitable forms of contact between PWD and PWOD may lessen contact-induced anxiety. For this to occur, the contact must result in PWOD recognizing that the scripts of PWD pose little or no threat to their well-being.

Assimilation of out-group members

Yet another strategy for dealing with individuals who do not share the worldview of the dominant culture is to require them to assimilate, i.e. adopt, the worldview of the dominant culture (Jones et al., 1984; Schneider, 1987; Solomon et al., 1991; Stone-Romero et al., 2003). For instance, most organizations use both post-hire socialization processes and reward and punishment systems to encourage the assimilation of individuals and motivate them to adopt a specific worldview (Hackman, 1976; 1992; Porter, Lawler & Hackman, 1975; Stone-Romero et al., 2003; Van Maanen, 1976). Consistent with this assimilation perspective, Schneider's (1987) ASA model suggests that acculturation processes are widely used in organizations to foster a desired culture. As a consequence, out-group members (e.g. individuals with disabilities or people who have a worldview that differs from the one that is prevalent in an organization) often encounter considerable difficulty, including distributive injustice, procedural injustice and interpersonal injustice (Stone-Romero & Stone, 2005).

THE REVISED ROLE-TAKING MODEL

We now describe elements in the revised role-taking model. In the process of doing so, we consider several issues that are of relevance to the plight of PWD in organizations (e.g. stigmas).

Culture and organizational factors

A considerable body of research supports the view that culture and its associated ideologies influence the way that organizations are structured and managed, affecting such organizational factors as their design, policies, practices, standards for role behavior and reward systems (e.g. Erez, 1994; Erez & Earley, 1993; Hofstede, 1980; 1991; Imai, 1986; Morishima, 1982; Ouchi, 1981; Stone & Stone-Romero, 2004; Stone-Romero et al., 2003; Trice & Beyer, 1993). Interestingly, ideologies are often non-conscious because they stem from beliefs that are ingrained so deeply and subconsciously that individuals within a culture are often unaware of their impact on beliefs, values, attitudes and behaviors. As is noted below, this has important implications for the role-taking process.

The revised role-taking model specifies that national culture (referred to hereinafter as culture) affects a host of organizational factors (e.g. design of jobs, nature of control systems, degree of hierarchy, division of labor). In turn, these influence the expectations of role senders. For example, because US culture values individualism and competitive achievement (Hofstede, 1980; 1991; Spence, 1985), organizational policies and practices in the United States tend to promote competition among workers (e.g. through the use of merit pay systems). The reward systems used by many universities are an excellent example of this. More specifically, raises, promotions, tenure, teaching loads and a host of other valued outcomes in many universities are allocated on the basis of highly competitive reward systems.

Culture and scripts of role senders

Consistent with social psychological theory and research, the revised role-taking model indicates that culture affects the attributes of role senders, including their beliefs, attitudes, values and personality (e.g. Markus & Kitayama, 1991; Triandis, 1994). Of particular importance to our analysis is the notion that culture influences both their work-related scripts and the expectations that they develop about a person in a focal role (i.e. focal person, FP). For instance, because US culture stresses self-reliance, role senders (e.g. a FP's supervisors, peers and subordinates) expect role incumbents to work independently, with little or no assistance from others.

Role expectations

Organizational factors and the scripts of role senders are the basis of the expectations that role senders develop about the FP. When the FP has a disability, role senders may develop relatively low expectations about his or her performance, which may be based upon the assumed relation between the disability and the capacity of the FP to meet the expectations of a given role (Hamilton, 1981; Jones et al., 1984). Thus, on the basis of extant stereotypes, role senders may believe that PWD are helpless, dependent on others, incapable of competing successfully with others (Fichten & Amsel, 1986) and incapable of meeting role expectations. Goffman (1963) provides a clear example of this in noting that 'a person with cerebral palsy may not only be seen as burdensome in face-to-face communication, but also may induce the feeling that he is questionable as a solitary task performer' (p. 50).

Stigmas

Role senders often have stereotype-based beliefs about PWD that differ from those of PWOD. As a result, the issue of stigmas merits consideration. In his seminal work on the management of spoiled identities, Goffman (1963) defined a stigma as a real or perceived discrepancy between a person's virtual and actual social identities. A *virtual social identity* represents what is expected of the individual in terms of various attributes (e.g. abilities, personality traits, etc.). It reflects what a person 'should be' within a given culture or society. In work organizations, role senders generally expect the FP to be free of disabilities, especially those that might have a bearing on his or her ability to perform.

An individual's *actual social identity* represents the way that he or she is actually perceived by others or is capable of being perceived. Thus, for example, a role sender might view a PWD as helpless, emotionally labile and incapable of performing his or her role-related obligations.

A person is *stigmatized* or *marked* when their actual social identity is negatively discrepant from their virtual social identity. PWD are often stigmatized on the basis of differing from what is considered 'normal' in society (Goffman, 1963; Jones et al., 1984). In addition, vis-à-vis the PWOD in-group, many PWD are regarded as out-group members.

The stigma notion is extremely important vis-à-vis the general issues considered by this chapter: A substantial amount of research shows that PWD are stigmatized in US society, and typically experience high levels of unfair discrimination in organizational contexts (Stone & Colella, 1996; Stone et al., 1992). For example, research shows that observers often view PWD as being unable to perform, incapable of competing with others, dependent, helpless, hypersensitive, depressed, distant, shy, unattractive, bitter, nervous, unhappy and submissive (Fichten & Amsel, 1986; Goffman, 1963; Jones et al., 1984; Makas, 1988). Thus, in work organizations, role set members (e.g. supervisors and peers) are likely to view PWD as incapable of fully meeting the requirements of their roles. In addition, they often expect that PWD will engage in self-limiting or self-handicapping behavior. Although some have argued that PWD have poor self-concepts and engage in self-limiting behavior (e.g. Crocker & Major, 1989; Jones, 1997), we believe that this is an unfortunate overgeneralization.

Role set members also may perceive that because of such factors as their depression, bitterness and defensiveness, PWD lack the emotional adjustment needed to interact effectively with their coworkers. As a result, PWD may experience such treatment-related discrimination problems as assignment to low-level jobs, segregation from coworkers, poor performance evaluations and lack of mentoring (Stone-Romero & Stone, 2005).

Regrettably, on the basis of invalid stereotypes, role set members may overgeneralize from a person's disability (Hamilton, 1981). That is, they may assume that a person with one type of disability has others (Jones et al., 1984; Stone et al., 1992). Thus, for example, people in wheelchairs often report that others raise their voices when talking to them because they assume that a person who is unable to walk also has hearing deficits.

Culture and reactions to PWD

Cultures vary in terms of normative standards and views about the ideal role incumbent. As a result, there are often cross-cultural differences in reactions to disabilities. For example, research shows that (1) Japanese children are more likely to show sympathy to a child in a wheelchair than American children (Crystal, Watanabe & Chen, 1999), (2) individuals from China are less likely to stigmatize those with Alzheimer's disease than Anglo-Americans (Hinton, Guo, Hillygus & Levkoff, 2000), (3) people in Islamic societies are less likely to view mental disorders as a stigma than individuals in Western cultures (Al-Issa, 2000), and (4) alcoholics are more likely to be ostracized in Middle Eastern than Western countries (Bush, White, Kai, Rankin & Bhopal, 2003). Regrettably, there is virtually no organizational research on cross-cultural differences in reactions to disability-related stigmas.

Sent roles

Having developed expectations, the role sender communicates them to the FP in the form of sent roles. These may be verbal and/or non-verbal in nature. Their overall purpose is to influence the FP's role behavior.

Given that all of the requirements of roles cannot be specified or communicated to role incumbents, role senders rely on the anticipatory socialization of the FP to behave in accordance with such requirements. However, because PWD often have different socialization experiences than PWOD (Goffman, 1963; Jones et al., 1984), role senders may not believe that PWD have had socialization experiences that were sufficient to prepare them for work roles. In addition, role senders may indirectly (subtly) or directly communicate the view that a FP's disability makes him or her less capable of performing at a criterion level than PWOD. As a consequence, the role sender may assign the FP to relatively low-level tasks.

Received roles

As a considerable amount of research in the communication literature demonstrates, sent messages are often inconsistent with received messages (see e.g. Katz & Kahn, 1978; Porter & Roberts, 1976). This has important implications for the role-taking process. More specifically, the roles communicated to the FP are typically not equivalent to the roles that he or she receives. In addition, role senders often communicate role expectations in an ambiguous manner. For example, because of the discomfort experienced in dealing with PWD, role senders may not clearly communicate their expectations to a FP with a disability. Moreover, the roles communicated by various senders may conflict with one another. Finally, as indicated below, the attributes of the FP may influence both the accuracy of received roles and subsequent role behavior.

Role behavior

Once the FP receives one or more sent roles, he or she manifests some degree of compliance with them. The level of compliance is dependent on such factors as situational constraints and his or her abilities, personality, understanding of received roles and conception of the role. For instance, a FP with a disability may view deviations from standardized work procedures as acceptable if they do not have a negative effect on performance.

Evaluations of role behavior

Having observed the FP's behavior, role senders then compare it to their expectations, both implicit and explicit. If a FP with a disability does not comply fully with role expectations then one or more role senders will evaluate his or her performance negatively. As noted below, this will affect interpersonal relations between the FP and the role senders.

Relationship between focal person and role senders

The FP's behavior will affect both his or her work performance and the quality of interpersonal relations between him or her and various role senders. For example, if a FP with a disability does not use standard work methods, role senders may evaluate the FP negatively, and liking for him or her may decrease. In addition, if the relationship between the role sender and the FP is strained, there is likely to be a discrepancy between the sent role and the received role. As a result of not getting along well with the role sender, the FP may not interpret the sent role in a veridical manner. Finally, the relationships between the FP and role senders will be influenced by the nature of their respective cultures. More specifically, a FP's disability is likely to have a more damaging effect on his or her relationship with the role sender in some cultures than in others (e.g. Castro, 1997; Crystal et al., 1999; DeAngelo, 2000; Hinton et al., 2000; Saetermoe, Scattone & Kim, 2001). For instance, traditional Mexican Americans are more likely than Anglo-Americans to view mental illness as a stigma (DeAngelo, 2000).

Effects of culture and scripts on interpersonal relations

The cultures and scripts of role senders and the FP affect their interpersonal relationship. Thus, for example, we posit that the greater the similarity of the work scripts of a FP and a role sender, the better will be their interpersonal relationship (Byrne, 1971; Solomon et al., 1991; Stone & Stone-Romero, 2004). One reason for this is that work script similarity will lead the role sender to believe that the FP will comply with role expectations. In addition, the greater the similarity of scripts, the lesser the anxiety produced by interactions between the FP and role senders (Solomon et al., 1991). However, because the work scripts of PWD and PWOD often differ from one another, interpersonal relations between PWD and role senders without disabilities are likely to be strained.

The results of research are consistent with the view that the degree of similarity between role senders and the FP affects interpersonal relationships between them. For example, social psychological research shows that similarity has a positive impact on such outcomes as affective reactions, interpersonal attraction and helping behavior (Byrne, 1971). In addition, research in organizational psychology shows that similarity (e.g. between job applicants and interviewers or between raters and ratees) has a positive effect on ratings of the ability of job applicants (Lin, Dobbins & Farh, 1992), hiring recommendations (Peters & Terborg, 1975), performance ratings (Pulakos & Wexley, 1983) and merit increases (Turban & Jones, 1988).

As is detailed below, the interpersonal relationship between a FP with a disability and a role sender who has no disability will be influenced by the way in which the FP manages information about his or her disability. For instance, the greater the degree to which the FP stresses his or her abilities (as opposed to disabilities) in dealings with the role sender, the more positive will be their relationship. In addition, the relationship will be more harmonious to the degree that the FP provides the role sender with individuating information that serves to disconfirm negative stereotypes about PWD. (These and other strategies for managing information are considered below in the section on specific strategies used in managing disabilities.)

However, when the scripts of a FP with a disability and a role sender without a disability differ, the FP will be (1) more likely to experience role conflict, role ambiguity and receive low performance evaluations, and (2) less likely to comply with role expectations and receive such positive outcomes as in-group status, pay raises, advancement opportunities and mentoring. Consistent with the just-noted arguments, research shows that relative to PWOD, PWD are more likely to experience both access discrimination and treatment discrimination (see e.g. Chima, 1998; 2002; Hosoda, Stone-Romero & Coats, 2003; Perry, Hendricks & Broadbent, 2000; Stone & Colella, 1996; Stone et al., 1992).

Attributes of the FP

Attributes of the FP refer to all of the individual difference variables that influence the propensity of the FP to think, act, feel and behave in various contexts. These include his or her motives, values, attitudes, preferences, abilities, skills and behavioral tendencies (Katz & Kahn, 1978). As Figure 16.1 indicates, these attributes influence several aspects of the role-taking process. We comment on three of them below.

First, the FP's attributes moderate the relation between sent roles and received roles. For example, if a FP with a disability believes that he or she is capable of performing the job, the FP may react negatively if role senders communicate low expectations about the FP's performance. In addition, in the interest of demonstrating that the low expectations are unwarranted, the FP may exert the effort needed to perform at a high level.

Second, attributes of the FP influence both role expectations and sent roles. For instance, a FP's disability may lead the role sender to develop low expectations about his or her performance, and the role sender may communicate these to the FP.

Third, attributes of the FP are influenced by his or her role-related experiences (e.g. Kahn, Wolfe, Quinn, Snoek & Rosenthal, 1964; Katz & Kahn, 1978; Kohn & Schooler, 1983; Link, Lennon & Dohrenwend, 1993). For example, if FPs with disabilities are consistently assigned to low-scope jobs, it is likely that their self-esteem and task-related self-efficacy will decline, and over time they may lose the ability to perform jobs of higher scope.

Disablement and personality

Disablement often has a profound impact on the FP's personality (e.g. self-concept, emotional adjustment, motivation). For example, it may have a negative impact on the FP's self-concept (Goffman, 1963; Jones et al., 1984). One reason for this is that research shows that an individual's self-concept is influenced by the degree to which he or she lives up to the norms and values of a culture (Kagan & Knight, 1979). Thus, to the extent that a FP's disability leads him or her to feel incapable of meeting the expectations of role senders, there may be negative effects on his or her esteem and expectancies of performing role-related tasks.

As Goffman (1963) and Jones et al. (1984) have noted, stigmatization may lead PWD to use a number of strategies for managing the actual or potential stigmatization stemming from disabilities of various types (see the section below on specific strategies used in managing disabilities). For example, a person with a hearing impairment may feign daydreaming rather than admit being hard of hearing. In addition, a person with low self-esteem may not perceive they are good enough to do challenging work, and, as a result, may not take advantage of promotion opportunities offered them (Jones, 1997). However, as noted below, not all reactions to disablement are negative. In particular, individuals who are high in resilience may develop a survivor identity and work tirelessly to demonstrate that they can succeed in spite of their disability (see the section below on factors that influence reactions to disablement).

Culture and attributes of the FP

To a considerable extent, the FP's attributes are a function of his or her experiences in life (Dohrenwend, 1975; 2000; Dohrenwend & Dohrenwend, 1974; Goffman, 1963; Jones et al., 1984; Kohn & Schooler, 1983), including those associated with childrearing and socialization processes (e.g. Markus & Kitayama, 1991; Triandis, 1994). This is an important issue because PWD often have had very different life experiences than PWOD. In part, these are a function of the nature of the FP's disability and the extent to which it leads PWOD to view him or her as an outgroup member. In addition, differences in experiences are the result of the means that the FP uses to cope with the problems stemming from his or her disability. PWD are often members of specific subcultures (e.g. people who are sight impaired, hearing impaired, paraplegic, alcohol dependent, morbidly obese) and their beliefs, attitudes and behaviors are affected by membership in them. As Goffman (1963) noted, 'members of a particular stigma category will have the tendency to come together into small social groups whose members all derive from the same category' (p. 23), and being in a category 'can function to dispose its members to group-formation and relationships' (p. 24). Similarly, Jones et al. (1984) observed that in order to avoid the discomfort produced by interacting with 'normals', stigmatized individuals often choose to interact with individuals who share their marks. For example, there are support groups to promote the interests of disabled war veterans. However, it deserves stressing that individuals with a given disability may not identify consistently with or affiliate regularly with others who have the same disability. Rather, they often engage in affiliation cycles in which the degree of contact with similar others increases and decreases over time (Goffman, 1963).

Culture of the FP and scripts

In accordance with extant research and theory (e.g. Markus & Kitayama, 1991), the revised role-taking model specifies that the culture of the FP influences the scripts that are available to him or her, including those that are relevant to the world of work (e.g. Imai, 1986; Morishima, 1982; Ouchi, 1981; Stone-Romero & Stone, 1998). Thus, in the absence of highly explicit role-related prescriptions and proscriptions, PWD may behave on the basis of very different scripts than those used by PWOD. One reason for this is that because of their disabilities, PWD often use creative or novel means for performing tasks. For example, a FP with severe vision impairment may avoid reading papers in front of coworkers because having to hold them very close to the face would accentuate his or her disability (Goffman, 1963). Nevertheless, for the reasons noted above, role senders without disabilities may perceive that work should be performed in a standardized fashion. In contrast, given their backgrounds and experiences, PWD may not perceive that standardized behavior is a prerequisite to meeting performance standards.

In part, the scripts that PWD use in various contexts are a function of the expectations and demands of others (Goffman, 1963; Jones et al., 1984). The way that PWD behave may be determined by the role-related expectations of both professionals (e.g. physicians, psychiatrists, rehabilitation specialists) and non-professionals (e.g. acquaintances, family members, role set members). Jones et al. (1984) refer to this as role acceptance. For example, although PWD may regard unsolicited offers of assistance as encroachments on their personal space or privacy, they are often taught to be gracious in accepting them. As noted by an individual with a crippling condition, 'people do not only expect you to play your part; they also expect you to know your place' (Carling, cited in Goffman, 1963: 120).

Differences in scripts

A number of differences in the work scripts and role expectations of incumbents with disabilities and role set members without disabilities are provided in Table 16.1. As noted above, because of these differences, several problems may arise when FPs with disabilities interact with role set members (e.g. supervisors or coworkers).

Job-related motivation and KSAOs

As is detailed below, PWD are typically highly motivated to meet or exceed performance standards. Moreover, they often regard themselves as having the knowledge, skills, abilities and other attributes (KSAOs) to meet such standards. However, role senders without disabilities may perceive PWD as lacking the relevant KSAOs, and thus as not being capable of performing at a criterion level. For example, a person with cerebral palsy noted: 'I was often bogged down by the medieval prejudices of the business world. Looking for a job was like standing before a firing squad. Employers were shocked that I had the gall to apply for a job' (Henrich & Kriegel, 1961, cited in Goffman, 1963: 34).

Some Consequences of Role-Related Problems

Clearly, differences between the scripts and behaviors of PWD and PWOD can lead to strains in social interactions. For example, such differences may elicit feelings of threat and contact-related anxiety (Solomon et al., 1991; Stephan, Ybarra & Bachman, 1999), increasing the odds of both interpersonal and intergroup conflict

TABLE 16.1   *Differences in work scripts and expectations of people with
disabilities and people without disabilities*

People with disabilities may:	People without disabilities may:
Not perceive they are disabled	Perceive person is disabled
Have a strong desire to achieve	Perceive person is not motivated to achieve
Use unique strategies for doing work	Believe there is one best way to perform job
Request accommodations that allow them to perform their work	Resent any requests for accommodations
Not be willing or able to participate in social events	Perceive person is anti-social or dislikes role set members
Strive to be self-reliant	Assume person is not self-reliant
Deemphasize their disability	Stress limitations posed by disability

in organizations. Regrettably, the same conflict may have dysfunctional consequences
for workers, work groups and organizations, and these consequences are likely to
be especially negative when PWD have worldviews that differ greatly from
the worldviews of organizations (Colella, 1996; Colella, DeNisi & Varma, 1997;
Colella et al., 1998; Stone & Colella, 1996; Stone et al., 1992).

Some Other Disability-Related Issues

The degree to which disabilities may influence the role-related activities of PWD
is a function of several factors. We deal with four of them here: (1) differences
between views about disabilities, (2) visibility of disabilities, (3) activities
affected by disabilities, and (4) views about accommodation for disabilities.

Differences in views about disabilities

There are often important differences between the views that PWD have about
themselves and the way they are viewed by others (Goffman, 1963; Jones et al.,
1984). For example, a disability may be much less important to the person with
it than it is to others. In this regard, research shows that many PWD do not view
themselves as disabled (Jones et al., 1984). This is illustrated vividly by Jeff
Dennis who had one of his legs amputated above the knee after suffering injuries
sustained while skydiving with the US Army's elite Golden Knights Parachute
Team (*Ohio Willow Wood*, undated). Through exceptional effort, he learned to
walk with a prosthetic limb and petitioned the US Army to return him to active
duty and jump status. Whereas many observers both within and outside of the
US Army viewed him as severely disabled, Dennis did not share this view. He
continues to skydive and provides instruction on it.

Note, in addition, that people who are born with deafness may not perceive that
they are disabled because they have not experienced sound, and do not compare
themselves to people who can hear (Jones et al., 1984; Vash, 1981). Likewise,
although individuals who are paralyzed may realize they cannot walk, they know
that they have other qualities (e.g. cognitive ability, creativity, interpersonal
skills) that render their inability to walk moot in many contexts. As a result, their
disability may be far less important to them than it is to others (Vash, 1981).

Visibility of the disability

When a person's disability is not readily apparent (i.e. hidden), they are stigmatizable or markable. The person is capable of being stigmatized or marked should the disability be revealed at some point in time. Interestingly, as long as a person's disability (e.g. AIDS) remains hidden, their interactions with others may not be seriously affected. Nevertheless, the stigmatizable person may be uncomfortable in dealings with others as a result of the fear that their disability may be revealed in the future.

In contrast to hidden disabilities, those that are visible often serve as a basis for the stigmatization of PWD. Unfortunately, although many such disabilities have little or no effect on a person's competence or performance in a given context, they may elicit negative affective reactions (e.g. feelings of discomfort, anxiety) in others (e.g. PWOD) and lead to strained social interactions (Bodenhausen, 1993; Goffman, 1963; Jones et al., 1984; Stone et al., 1992). As Jones et al. (1984) noted, 'most of us experience something ranging from vague uneasiness to extreme revulsion' (p. 226) in the presence of such individuals with such conditions as facial disfigurement, withered limbs, tumors or cerebral palsy. As a result, many PWD are shunned by others, including their coworkers.

Activities affected by the disability

Some disabilities are quite limiting in nature (e.g. quadriplegia), barring individuals from engaging in many forms of activity. However, others (e.g. heart disease) may only limit certain types of activity (e.g. strenuous physical work). However, the way that PWD are viewed by others is often stereotype driven. And, as a result of illusory correlation, observers may infer incorrectly that a disability that affects a person's capacity to perform one set of activities limits their ability to perform others. For example, because a woman with cerebral palsy had slurred speech and an awkward gait, an observer assumed that 'her mind ... did not function very well' (Jones et al., 1984: 159). In addition, people with congenital disabilities are often viewed as monsters, 'both mentally and physically' (Jones et al., 1984: 63).

Accommodation issues

Many PWD believe that it is acceptable to ask for accommodations that will enable them to perform in their organizational roles. However, PWOD may resent such requests on the basis of the belief that special treatment violates equity norms. Thus, equity-conscious role set members may resent any and all accommodations requested by incumbents with disabilities. This may result in conflict between PWD and their role senders.

Specific Strategies Used in Managing Disabilities

Goffman (1963) and Jones et al. (1984) described a number of strategies that individuals can use to manage their spoiled identities and minimize negative evaluations on the part of others. The general purpose of these strategies is to gain acceptance in social systems (e.g. work organizations). We describe several such strategies below. However, prior to doing so, we note three important points. First, several of these strategies overlap. Second, PWD may use more than one strategy for identity management purposes. Third, the fact that such strategies may be used by PWD does not imply that we advocate their use. At least one reason for this is that PWD should be evaluated on the basis of their capacity to perform role-related activities instead of on the basis of superficial attributes (e.g. disfigurement) or assumed ability deficits.

Correcting problems with disabilities that detract from attractiveness

In order to gain acceptance from others, PWD often use corrective strategies to disguise or correct appearance-related problems stemming from disabilities. For example, individuals with severe facial disfigurement associated with cleft palate often undergo plastic surgery (Stone et al., 1992).

Unattractiveness is an important stigma because of the implications that is has for social relations. As has been noted elsewhere, unattractiveness 'has its initial and prime effect during social situations, threatening the pleasure we might otherwise take in the company of its possessor' (Goffman, 1963: 50).

Correcting features that render individuals unattractive is very important in organizational contexts. One reason for this is that interactions with unattractive people lead to negative affective reactions (Bodenhausen, 1993; Goffman, 1963; Jones et al., 1984). For instance, research by Kurzban and Leary (2001) showed that disfigurement typically elicits feelings of disgust in others. They argued that this is a functional reaction, in that it cues observers that disfigured individuals are poor social exchange and/or courtship partners. In addition, because attractiveness is a sign of prestige in many societies, attractive individuals are assumed to contribute greater inputs to social systems than unattractive individuals (Leventhal, 1980). In accordance with this view, results of a recent meta-analysis of experimental research showed that attractiveness is positively correlated with the way individuals are viewed in organizational contexts. For example, relative to less attractive people, individuals who are more attractive are more likely to be hired, promoted, given positive performance evaluations and viewed as having the potential to succeed if hired (Hosoda et al., 2003).

Not surprisingly, research suggests that steps taken to increase attractiveness may help individuals lessen stigmatization and, thus, gain access to jobs (Stone et al., 1992). For example, research on obesity suggests that obese people are stigmatized because they are viewed as unattractive and lacking in self-control (Bell, McLaughlin & Sequeira, 2003). However, they can regain societal acceptance by losing weight. In addition, plastic surgeons often donate their services to individuals with facial disfigurements to increase the societal acceptance of such individuals.

Passing for normal through non-disclosure

Another strategy that can be used by PWD to gain acceptance is to not reveal or disclose hidden stigmas in the interest of passing for normal (Goffman, 1963).

Interestingly, people with disabilities appear to be keenly aware of societal norms and standards, and recognize that some types of disabilities are more likely to elicit negative reactions than are others (Stone & Colella, 1996). For example, research shows that individuals who have conditions that are perceived as threatening (e.g. mental illness, epilepsy), contagious (e.g. AIDS) or incurable (e.g. malignant forms of cancer) are more likely to be ostracized in society than are individuals with less stigmatizing conditions (e.g. diabetes, heart disease; Stone & Colella, 1996).

Unfortunately, research shows that people often believe that such conditions as cancer and physical disabilities are communicable or contagious (Jones et al., 1984). As a result, parents are reluctant to let their children interact with individuals who have these and other conditions. Not surprisingly, therefore, individuals with hidden disabilities may be highly motivated to keep information about them from others. By keeping the disability hidden, stigmatizable people can (1) pass for normal, (2) maintain positive interactions with others, and (3) gain valued outcomes in organizational contexts.

Interestingly, research shows that individuals are likely to conceal information about hidden stigmatizing conditions (e.g. AIDS; Vest, Vest, Perry & O'Brien, 1995), and are often unwilling to request accommodations for such conditions because the request will lead to the revelation of the condition and stigmatization (Baldridge & Veiga, 2001). In addition, research indicates that the use of a concealment strategy may be especially effective when the person has a disability that affects social interactions (e.g. epilepsy), but the same strategy may become problematic if the subsequent disclosure of the disability violates the expectations of others (Stone, 1986; Tagalakis, Amsel & Fichten, 1988).

Downplaying the relevance of the disability

Another strategy that PWD can use to gain acceptance is to admit they have a disability, but downplay its importance (Goffman, 1963). The purpose of this strategy is to modify others' beliefs and expectancies (e.g. about ability levels), and thus gain their acceptance. To the degree that the strategy succeeds, the increased contact between the stigmatized individual and others may result in the person being viewed in an individuated manner, as opposed to a member of a stigmatized group (Miller & Brewer, 1984).

High performance on the job

In organizational contexts, an important issue in evaluating PWD is the degree to which they are viewed as having the capacity to perform in a given role (e.g. Stone & Colella, 1996). Thus, they may exert high levels of effort over protracted periods of time in the interest of meeting or exceeding performance standards.

Although some research has directly assessed the effects of performance on observers' reactions to PWD, the results of it have been mixed (Colella et al., 1997; Krefting & Brief, 1976; Rose & Brief, 1979). In some cases the research shows that when PWD perform at high levels, others evaluate them positively (Florey & Harrison, 2000; Rose & Brief, 1979). However, in other cases research indicates that PWD are rated negatively regardless of their performance (Stone et al., 1992).

High performance in other areas

PWD can attempt to disconfirm stereotype-based expectancies about their ability by mastering activities that are typically not open to people who share their limitations. For example, a person with paraplegia may climb mountains in their free time to demonstrate that their disability is not as limiting as others view it.

Disidentifiers

PWD may use signs of various types as 'disidentifiers' for the purpose of casting doubt on the validity of stereotypes about them (Goffman, 1963). For example, an individual with Parkinson's disease may earn advanced educational degrees (e.g. PhD, MD, JD) or professional credentials (e.g. CPA) as a means of disconfirming negative stereotypes.

Acknowledging the disability

PWD may acknowledge their disabilities in order to reduce others' anxiety levels in social contexts (Goffman, 1963). As noted above, interactions with PWD often lead to discomfort on the part of PWOD that stems from the fact that PWOD are uncertain about what to say or do during such interactions. To decrease this uncertainty, PWD may describe the nature of their disability to others in the hopes of clarifying interaction norms, putting others at ease and showing they are emotionally detached from their conditions. Interestingly, research suggests that this strategy may be quite effective in some contexts (Stone & Colella, 1996). However, research in personnel selection contexts shows that the effectiveness of the same strategy depends on (1) the stage in the selection process at which the disability is revealed (Tagalakis et al., 1988), (2) the nature of the disability (Stone, 1986), and (3) the degree to which the disclosure is viewed as voluntary (Stone, Shetzer & Eggleston, 1986).

Stressing similarity on various attributes

PWD can increase liking on the part of others and gain their acceptance by stressing similarity to them on such attributes as interests, attitudes, opinions, hobbies and values. The general objective of doing this is to provide a basis for the PWD to be viewed in an individuated manner. In this regard, Goffman (1963) argues that people with stigmas often develop special social skills for moving past their initial devaluation in social interactions by revealing individuating information that serves such purposes as both 'pegging' their true identity and leading others to develop more positive views about their conduct, character and behavior. Identity pegs (e.g. disclosing positive information about the self) may allow PWD to lessen the discrepancy between their virtual and actual social identities. Although we know of no specific organizational research on the effectiveness of this strategy for PWD, as noted above, research in social psychology shows that perceived similarity is positively related to interpersonal attraction (Byrne, 1971).

Transcending disability victim status

PWD are often viewed as being preoccupied with and bitter about their victim status. Although some PWD may assume the role of victim, not all such people embrace this role. As noted above, many individuals with disabilities engage in activities aimed at demonstrating that, rather than being victims, they can perform successfully in many roles. One variable that influences the ability of PWD to distance themselves from the victim role is resiliency. In this regard, O'Leary and her colleagues (O'Leary, 1998; O'Leary & Ickovics, 1995) contend that when individuals are confronted by a challenge, they may respond in three ways (i.e. survive, recover or thrive). Individuals who are high in resiliency have the tendency to view negative experiences in a positive way (e.g. to see life's problems as challenges to be overcome).

Assuming that disability-related stressors are not overwhelming, PWD may use a number of adaptive strategies to deal with them. Their ability to do so is a function of numerous factors, one of which is life's experiences (e.g. socialization). For example, research on individuals with post-polio problems indicates that as children they experienced a very different environmental context than PWOD (Polio Post News, 2002). More specifically, they were (1) isolated and separated from families as a result of being in hospitals for great periods of time, (2) socialized to stress recovery and the achievement of challenging goals (e.g. use it or lose it), (3) instructed to overcome disabilities through hard work, (4) taught to be survivors who used whatever abilities they had, and (5) led to believe that the expression of emotions and self-pity was not only unacceptable, but was self-defeating. These socialization experiences had a dramatic impact on their self-identities, personalities and behaviors. For example, many individuals with post-polio have high needs for achievement and view themselves as survivors rather than victims. In addition, as a group, they have achieved relatively high levels of education, and many have had very successful professional careers. In short, as a result of their life's experiences, many such individuals have demonstrated their capacity to thrive in the face of adversity and have disconfirmed invalid stereotypes about members of their group (e.g. modified others' beliefs about their motivation, ability and personality).

It is important to recognize that a number of variables may moderate the relationship between stressors and their effects, including social support and socioeconomic status (O'Leary & Ickovics, 1995). For example, Ruggerio, Taylor and Lydon (1997) argue that social support often gives PWD the ability to cope with unfair discrimination and other types of stressors.

Factors that Influence Individuals' Reactions to Disablement

Research shows that reactions to disablement (including effects on personality and self-identity) vary across individuals. For example, research in rehabilitation psychology shows that a number of factors affect reactions to disablement, including (1) the impact of a disability on valued activities, (2) the time at which disablement occurs, (3) the cause of the disability, and (4) the rate of the disability's onset (Vash, 1981). We comment on these factors below.

Impact on valued activities

Research shows that individuals react more negatively to disabilities that limit the degree to which they can perform activities that are central to their self-identity (Vash, 1981). For example, a highly athletic person is likely to react more negatively to paralysis than someone who is less athletic (e.g. one who spends free time playing chess).

Time of disablement

Individuals who are disabled relatively late in life are more likely to react negatively and suffer blows to their self-concept than are people who are disabled relatively early in life. One reason for this is that PWD who have been disabled since birth do not feel the loss of a valued activity or ability. For instance, individuals who are deaf often do not perceive they are disabled, and report they prefer silence in their lives because a life with a multitude of sounds might be maddening.

Cause of disablement

The cause of a disability is an important determinant of how individuals respond to it. For example, people who are disabled as a result of an accident are prone to experience shame if they caused it, but are likely to experience anger if someone else was responsible for it.

Rate of the disability's onset

Whether the onset of a disability was sudden or prolonged affects the person's reactions to it (Jones et al., 1984). For instance, if a young adult suddenly develops multiple sclerosis at the age of 25 he or she is likely to react more negatively to it than will a person who has had arthritis for a protracted period.

CONCLUSIONS

We believe that our revised role-taking model has a number of important implications for research and practice vis-à-vis PWD. In terms of research, there is a paucity of studies that have dealt with the plight of PWD in organizations. Moreover, there are virtually no studies that have considered the way in which differences between the cultures of PWD and PWD affect the role-taking process. Thus, research is needed on this and related issues. We believe that our revised role-taking model affords a very useful framework for guiding such research. For instance, studies are needed to (1) determine how the work-related scripts of PWD differ from those of PWOD; (2) assess how relationships between PWD and PWOD are affected by their respective cultures; and (3) test for the moderating effect of the culture of PWD on the relation between sent roles and received roles.

With respect to practice, a number of recommendations stem from our revised role-taking model, especially from the view that PWD and PWOD often have different work-related scripts. First, role senders need to determine whether it is essential that all incumbents in given roles perform their duties in a standardized fashion. If an analysis suggests that standardized practices are not vital, then PWD should be allowed to meet the requirements of their roles in accordance with their own scripts. Second, role senders need to develop an understanding of the worldviews of PWD. By so doing, they should be able to avert a host of problems that may result from differences between their own worldviews and those of PWD. Third, PWD need to (1) recognize how differences in worldviews can interfere with their acceptance by role set members, (2) work proactively to convince them that the differences will not impede their role-related performance, and (3) provide individuating information to role set members. Fourth, as appropriate, role senders need to more fully communicate their expectations to PWD. As noted above, in most organizations only a subset of the requirements of any given role are codified and transmitted to role incumbents in a clear and comprehensive manner (e.g. in written form). Vaguely communicated expectations may be especially problematic if role senders make the unwarranted assumption that PWD have the same cultural backgrounds as PWOD. For example, PWD may 'fill in gaps' in communicated expectations with work-related scripts that are inconsistent with the expectations shared by PWOD. Thus, sent roles may need to vary as a function of the cultural background of the FP. To the extent that role senders do a better job of both formulating appropriate expectations and communicating them to PWD, the behavior of PWD should be increasingly consistent with the expectations. As a result, it may be possible to decrease the many role-related problems that PWD often encounter in organizations.

REFERENCES

Al-Issa, I. (2000). *Mental illness in the Islamic world*. Madison, CT: International Universities Press.

Americans With Disabilities Act of 1990. Public Law No. 101-336, 104 Stat. 328 (1990). 42 U.S.C.A. § 12101 *et seq.*

Baldridge, D. C., & Veiga, J. (2001). Toward a greater understanding of the willingness to request an accommodation: Can requesters' beliefs disable the Americans with Disabilities Act? *Academy of Management Review, 26*, 85–99.

Bell, M. P., McLaughlin, M. E., & Sequeira, J. M. (2003). Age, disability, and obesity: Similarities, differences, and common threads. In M. S. Stockdale & F. J. Crosby (Eds), *The psychology and management of workplace diversity* (pp. 191–205). Malden, MA: Blackwell.

Bodenhausen, G. V. (1993). Emotions, arousal, and stereotypic judgements: A heuristic model of affect and stereotyping. In D. M. Mackie & D. L. Hamilton (Eds), *Affect, cognition, and stereotyping: Interactive processes in group perception* (pp. 13–37). San Diego: Academic Press.

Bordieri, J. E., Drehmer, D. E., & Comninel, M. E. (1988). Attribution of responsibility and hiring recommendations for job applicants with low back pain. *Rehabilitation Counseling Bulletin, 32*, 140–8.

Braker, B. (2004). Put Scalia in a wheelchair: A disabled rights activist discusses the start of a landmark case on states' rights and what she sees as the Supreme Court's 'erosion' of the ADA. *Newsweek*, 14 January: keepmedia.com (Retrieved 26 August 2004).

Bush, J., White, M., Kai, J., Rankin, J., & Bhopal, R. (2003). Understanding influences on smoking in Bangladeshi and Pakistani adults. *British Medical Journal, 326*, 962–7.

Byrne, D. (1971). *The attraction paradigm.* New York: Academic Press.

Castro, A. (1997). Mexican-American values and their impact on mental health care. *Dissertation Abstracts International: Section B: The Sciences & Engineering, 57*(9–B), 5909.

Cesare, S. J., Tannenbaum, R. J., & Dalessio, A. (1990). Interviewers' decisions related to applicant handicap type and rater empathy. *Human Performance, 3*, 157–71.

Chima, F. (1998). Workplace and disabilities: Opinions on work, interpersonal, and intrapersonal factors. *Journal of Applied Rehabilitation Counseling, 29*, 31–7.

Chima, F. O. (2002). Employee assistance and human resources collaboration for improving employment and disabilities status. *Employee Assistance Quarterly, 17*, 79–94.

Christman, L. A., & Slaten, B. L. (1991). Attitudes toward people with disabilities and judgments of employment potential. *Perceptual and Motor Skills, 72*, 467–75.

Colella, A. (1996). The organizational socialization of employees with disabilities: Theory and research. In G. R. Ferris (Ed.), *Research in personnel and human resources management* (pp. 351–417). Greenwich, CT: JAI Press.

Colella, A. (2001). Coworker distributive fairness judgments of the workplace accommodation of employees with disabilities. *Academy of Management Review, 26*, 100–16.

Colella, A., DeNisi, A. S., & Varma, A. (1997). Appraising the performance of employees with disabilities: A review and model. *Human Resources Management Review, 7*, 27–53.

Colella, A., DeNisi, A. S., & Varma, A. (1998). The impact of ratee's disability on performance judgments and choice as partner: The role of disability–job fit stereotypes and interdependence of rewards. *Journal of Applied Psychology, 83*, 102–11.

Colella, A., & Stone, D. L. (2004). Workplace discrimination toward persons with disabilities: A call for some new research directions. In R. Dipboye & A. Colella (Eds), *The psychological and organizational bases of discrimination at work* (pp. 227–53). Mahwah, NJ: Lawrence Erlbaum.

Cox, T. (1993). *Cultural diversity in organizations: Theory, research, and practice.* San Francisco: Berrett-Koehler.

Crocker, J., & Major, B. (1989). Social stigma and self-esteem: The self-protective properties of stigma. *Psychological Review, 96*, 608–30.

Crystal, D. S., Watanabe, H., & Chen, R. S. (1999). Children's reactions to physical disability: A cross-national developmental study. *International Journal of Behavioral Development, 23*, 91–111.

Czajka, J. M., & DeNisi, A. S. (1988). Effects of emotional disability and clear performance standards on performance ratings. *Academy of Management Journal, 31*, 394–404.

DeAngelo, L. M. (2000). Stereotypes and stigmas: Biased attributions in matching older persons with drawings of viruses. *International Journal of Aging and Human Development, 51*, 143–54.

Dohrenwend, B. P. (1975). Sociocultural and social-psychological factors in the genesis of mental disorders. *Journal of Health and Social Behavior, 16*, 365–92.

Dohrenwend, B. P. (2000). The role of adversity and stress in psychopathology: Some evidence and its implications for theory and research. *Journal of Health and Social Behavior, 41*(March), 1–19.

Dohrenwend, B. P., & Dohrenwend, B. S. (1974). Social and cultural influences on psychopathology. *Annual Review of Psychology, 25*, 417–52.

Erez, M. (1994). Toward a model of cross-cultural industrial and organizational psychology. In H. C. Triandis, M. D. Dunnette, and L. M. Hough (Eds), *Handbook of industrial and organizational psychology* (2nd edn, Vol. 4, pp. 559–607). Palo Alto, CA: Consulting Psychologists Press.

Erez, M., & Earley, P. C. (1993). *Culture, self-identity, and work.* New York: Oxford University Press.

Fichten, C. S., & Amsel, R. (1986). Trait attributions about college students with a physical disability: Circumplex analyses and methodological issues. *Journal of Applied Social Psychology, 16*, 410–27.

Florey, A. T., & Harrison, D. (2000). Responses to informal accommodation requests from employees with disabilities: Multistudy evidence on willingness to comply. *Academy of Management Journal, 43*, 224–33.

Fly, C. (2004, August 26). Judge denies class-action status in disabled access case. *Williamson County Review Appeal.*

Goffman, E. (1963). *Stigma: Notes on the management of spoiled identity.* Englewood Cliffs, NJ: Prentice Hall.

Greenwood, R., & Johnson, V. A. (1987). Employee perspectives on workers with disabilities. *Journal of Rehabilitation, 53*, 37–45.

Hackman, J. R. (1976). Group influences on individuals. In M. Dunnette (Ed.), *Handbook of industrial and organizational psychology* (pp. 1455–1525). Chicago: Rand McNally.

Hackman, J. R. (1992). Group influences on individuals in organizations. In M. D. Dunnette & L. M. Hough (Eds), *Handbook of industrial and organizational psychology* (2nd edn, Vol. 3, pp. 199–267). Palo Alto, CA: Consulting Psychologists Press.

Hamilton, D. L. (1981). *Cognitive processes in stereotyping and intergroup behavior.* Hillsdale, NJ: Erlbaum.

Herman, C. P., Zanna, M. P., & Higgins, E. T. (1986). *Physical appearance, stigma, and social behavior: The Ontario symposium, Vol. 3.* Hillsdale, NJ: Lawrence Erlbaum.

Hinton, L., Guo, Z., Hillygus, J., & Levkoff, S. (2000). Working with culture: A qualitative analysis of barriers to the recruitment of Chinese-American family caregivers for dementia research. *Journal of Cross-Cultural Gerontology, 15*, 119–37.

Hofstede, G. (1980). *Culture's consequences: International differences in work-related values.* Beverly Hills, CA: Sage.

Hofstede, G. (1991). *Cultures and organizations: Software of the mind.* London: McGraw-Hill.

Hosoda, M., Stone-Romero, E. F., & Coats, G. (2003). The effects of physical attractiveness on job-related outcomes: A meta-analysis of experimental studies. *Personnel Psychology, 56*, 431–62.

Hsu, F. L. K. (1961). American core values and national character. In F. L. K. Hsu (Ed.), *Psychological anthropology: Approaches to culture and personality* (pp. 209–33). Homewood, IL: Dorsey.

Imai, M. (1986). *Kaizen: The key to Japan's competitive success.* New York: Random House.

Jones, E. E., Farina, A., Hastorf, A. H., Markus, H., Miller, D. T., Scott, R. A., & de French, R. (1984). *Social stigma: The psychology of marked relationships.* San Francisco: W. H. Freeman.

Jones, G. E. (1997). Advancement opportunity issues for persons with disabilities. *Human Resources Management Review, 7*, 55–76.

Kagan, S., & Knight, G. P. (1979). Cooperation-competition and self-esteem: A case of cultural revelation. *Journal of Cross-Cultural Psychology*, *10*, 457–67.

Kahn, R. L., Wolfe, D. M., Quinn, R. P., Snoek, J. D., & Rosenthal, R. A. (1964). *Organizational stress: Studies in role conflict and role ambiguity*. New York: Wiley.

Katz, D., & Kahn, R. (1978). *The social psychology of organizations* (2nd edn). New York: Wiley.

Kohn, M., & Schooler, C. (1983). *Work and personality: An inquiry into the impact of social stratification*. Norwood, NJ: Ablex.

Krefting, L. A., & Brief, A. P. (1976). The impact of applicant disability on evaluative judgment in the selection process. *Academy of Management Journal*, *19*, 675–80.

Kurzban, R., & Leary, M. R. (2001). Evolutionary origins of stigmatization: The functions of social exclusion. *Psychological Bulletin*, *127*, 187–208.

Leventhal, G. S. (1980). What should be done with equity theory? New approaches to studying fairness in social relationships. In K. J. Gergen, M. S. Greenberg & H. Willis (Eds), *Social exchange: Advances in theory and research* (pp. 27–55). New York: Plenum.

Lin, T. R., Dobbins, G., & Farh, J.-L. (1992). A field study of race and age similarity effects on interview ratings in conventional and structural interviews. *Journal of Applied Psychology*, *77*, 363–71.

Link, B. G., Lennon, M. C., & Dohrenwend, B. P. (1993). Socioeconomic status and depression: The role of occupations involving direction, control, and planning. *American Journal of Sociology*, *98*, 1351–87.

Loo, R. (2001). Attitudes of management undergraduates toward persons with disabilities: A need for change. *Rehabilitation Psychology*, *46*, 288–95.

Makas, E. (1988). Positive attitudes toward disabled people: Disabled and nondisabled persons' perspectives. *Journal of Social Issues*, *46*, 49–61.

March, J. G., & Simon, H. A. (1958). *Organizations*. New York: Wiley.

Markus, H. R., & Kitayama, S. (1991). Culture and the self: Implications for cognition, emotion, and motivation. *Psychological Review*, *98*, 224–53.

Mechanic, D. (1998). Cultural and organizational aspects of application of the Americans with Disabilities Act to persons with psychiatric disorders. *Milbank Quarterly*, *76*, 905.

Miller, N., & Brewer, M. B. (Eds) (1984). *Groups in contact: The psychology of desegregation*. Orlando, FL: Academic Press.

Morishima, M. (1982). *Why has Japan succeeded? Western technology and the Japanese ethos*. Bath: Cambridge University Press.

Ohio Willow Wood (undated). *Pathfinder amputee: Jeff Dennis*: http://www.owwco.com/Content/OWW/en-US/pdf/Newsletter/PM2000_Fall.pdf (Retrieved 26 August 2004).

O'Leary, V. E. (1998). Strength in the face of adversity: Individual social thriving. *Journal of Social Issues*, *54*, 425–47.

O'Leary, V. E., & Ickovics, J. R. (1995). Resilience and thriving in response to challenge: An opportunity for a paradigm shift in women's health. *Women's Health: Research on Gender, Behavior, and Policy*, *1*, 121–42.

Ouchi, W. C. (1981). *Theory Z*. Reading, MA: Addison-Wesley.

Peck, B., & Kirkbride, L. T. (2001). Why businesses don't employ people with disabilities. *Journal of Vocational Rehabilitation*, *16*, 71–5.

Perry, E. L., Hendricks, W., & Broadbent, E. (2000). An exploration of access and treatment discrimination and job satisfaction among college graduates with and without physical disabilities. *Human Relations*, *52*, 923–55.

Peters, L., & Terborg, J. R. (1975). The effects of temporal placement of unfavorable information and of attitude similarity on personnel selection decisions. *Organizational Behavior and Human Performance*, *13*, 279–93.

Polio Post News (2002). *The characteristics of people with post-polio*. Dunnellon, FL: Polio Post News.

Pooley, J. M., & Bump, E. A. (1993). The learning performance and cost effectiveness of mentally disabled workers. *Group & Organization Management, 18*, 88–23.

Porter, L. W., Lawler, E. E., & Hackman, J. R. (1975). *Behavior in organizations.* New York: McGraw-Hill.

Porter, L. W., & Roberts, K. H. (1976). Communication in organizations. In M. D. Dunnette (Ed.), *Handbook of industrial and organizational psychology* (pp. 1553–89). Chicago: Rand McNally.

Pulakos, E., & Wexley, K. N. (1983). The relationship among perceptual similarity, sex, and performance ratings in management subordinate dyads. *Academy of Management Journal, 26*, 129–39.

Rose, G., & Brief, A. (1979). Effects of handicap and job characteristics on selection evaluations. *Personnel Psychology, 32*, 385–92.

Ruggiero, K. M., Taylor, D. M., & Lydon, J. E. (1997). How disadvantaged group members cope with discrimination when they perceive that social support is available. *Journal of Applied Social Psychology, 27*, 1581–1600.

Saetermoe, C. L., Scattone, D., & Kim, K. H. (2001). Ethnicity and the stigma of disabilities. African-American, Latin-American or European-American counterparts. *Psychology & Health, 16*, 699–714.

Schneider, B. (1987). The people make the place. *Personnel Psychology, 40*, 437–53.

Shank, R., & Abelson, R. (1977). *Scripts, plans, goals, and understanding: An inquiry into human knowledge structures.* Hillsdale, NJ: Lawrence Erlbaum.

Solomon, S., Greenberg, J., & Pyszczynski, T. (1991). A terror management theory of social behavior: The psychological functions of self-esteem and cultural worldviews. In M. P. Zanna (Ed.), *Advances in experimental social psychology* (Vol. 24, pp. 93–159). San Francisco: Academic Press.

Spence, J. T. (1985). Achievement American style: The rewards and costs of individualism. *American Psychologist, 40*, 1285–95.

Stephan, W. G., Ybarra, O., & Bachman, G. (1999). Prejudice toward immigrants. *Journal of Applied Social Psychology, 29*, 2221–37.

Stone, D. L. (1986). *The effects of nondisclosure of physical handicaps on personnel selection.* Paper presented at the August meeting of the Academy of Management, Chicago.

Stone, D. L., & Colella, A. (1996). A model of factors affecting the treatment of disabled individuals in organizations. *Academy of Management Review, 21*, 352–401.

Stone, D. L., & Stone-Romero, E. F. (2004). The influence of culture on role-taking in culturally diverse organizations. In M. S. Stockdale & F. J. Crosby (Eds), *The psychology and management of workplace diversity* (pp. 78–99). Malden, MA: Blackwell.

Stone, D. L., & Williams, K. (1997). The impact of ADA on the selection process: Applicant and organizational issues. *Human Resources Management Review, 7*, 203–31.

Stone, E. F., Shetzer, L., & Eggleston, S. (1986). Effects of handicap type, handicap revelation mode, and interviewee on ratings of applicant suitability. Paper presented at the August meeting of the Academy of Management, Chicago.

Stone, E. F., Stone, D. L., & Dipboye, R. L. (1992). Stigmas in organizations: Race, handicaps, and physical attractiveness. In K. Kelley (Ed.), *Issues, theory, and research in industrial/organizational psychology* (pp. 385–457). Amsterdam: Elsevier Science.

Stone-Romero, E. F., & Stone, D. L. (1998). Religious and moral influences on work-related values and work quality. In D. Fedor & S. Ganoush (Eds), *Advances in the management of organizational quality* (Vol. 3, pp. 185–285). Greenwich, CT: JAI Press.

Stone-Romero, E. F., & Stone, D. L. (2002). Cross-cultural responses to feedback: Implications for individual, group, and organizational effectiveness. In G. R. Ferris & J. J. Martocchio (Eds), *Research in personnel and human resources management* (Vol. 21, pp. 275–331). Amsterdam: JAI Press.

Stone-Romero, E. F., & Stone, D. L. (2005). How do organizational justice concepts relate to discrimination and prejudice? In J. Greenberg & J. A. Colquitt (Eds), *Handbook of organizational justice* (pp. 439–67). Mahwah, NJ: Lawrence Erlbaum.

Stone-Romero, E. F., Stone, D. L., & Salas, E. (2003). The influence of culture on role conceptions and role behavior in organizations. *Applied Psychology: An International Review, 52*, 328–62.

Tagalakis, V., Amsel, R., & Fichten, C. S. (1988). Job interview strategies for people with a visible disability. *Journal of Applied Social Psychology, 18*, 520–32.

Tajfel, H. (Ed.) (1982). *Social identity and intergroup relations*. Cambridge: Cambridge University Press.

Triandis, H. C. (1994). *Culture and social behavior*. New York: McGraw-Hill.

Trice, H., & Beyer, J. (1993). *The cultures of work organizations*. Englewood Cliffs, NJ: Prentice Hall.

Turban, D. B., & Jones, A. P. (1988). Supervisor-subordinate similarity: Types, effects and mechanisms. *Journal of Applied Psychology, 73*, 228–34.

Turner, J. C. (1987). *Rediscovering the social group: A self-categorization theory*. Oxford: Basil Blackwell.

US Bureau of Census (2000). *2000 Census Report*: www.census.gov. (Retrieved 2003 1 August).

US Bureau of Labor Statistics (2004). *Labor Report*: www.bls.gov. (Retrieved 2004 22 August).

Vash, C. L. (1981). *The psychology of disability*. New York: Springer.

Vest, J. M., Vest, M. J., Perry, S. J., & O'Brien, P. P. (1995). Factors influencing managerial disclosure of AIDS health information to coworkers. *Journal of Applied Social Psychology, 12*, 1043–57.

Van Maanen, J. (1976). Breaking-in: Socialization to work. In R. Dubin (Ed.), *Handbook of work, organization, and society* (pp. 67–130). Chicago: Rand McNally.

17

Locating Class in Organizational Diversity Work

Class as Structure, Style and Process

MAUREEN A. SCULLY AND STACY BLAKE-BEARD

The topic of 'class' does not always make its way into the discussion of diversity nor into the formation of social identity-based caucuses in the workplace. Class sometimes enters covertly, with the awkward labels 'levelism' or 'statusism'. These labels divert attention toward local aspects of organizational hierarchy and away from the broader societal significance of class as deeply rooted and enduring stratification. In the United States, people often deny the existence of 'class' as a factor in life chances, because concepts like social mobility and equal opportunity are so strongly promulgated (if not always strongly believed when closer scrutiny is prompted). In a pilot of a survey with questions on how 'class background' affects promotion prospects in a company, respondents thought the questions meant what 'classes' they had taken, in school and on the job. They just did not know how to approach the question and the word 'class' (Scully, 1993). Even as Americans insist on ignorance about the topic of class, they turn out to be exquisitely attuned to detecting class, as Rainwater (1974) showed in a study in which participants viewed videos of people talking and correctly identified their income bracket from accent, style and a thousand nuanced indicators. There is a strong ambivalence about class in the United States. There is a denial born of the wish that we had equality of opportunity, even while there is a laser-sharp attention to class that filters how we react to one another and contributes to reproducing inequality. In this chapter, we will emphasize that class is a vital dimension of social identity, which has been a focal concept for organizational diversity, but moreover, following the critical tradition, class is a vital dimension of work and life in organizations, part of the very fibers of organization. Class is at once very much a dimension of diversity and unlike any other dimensions of diversity, because it prompts re-examination of many fundamental premises not just of organizations but of capitalism, meritocracy and distributive justice.

Social scientists have a myriad of approaches to class. Passionate political opinions can attach to treating 'class' in one way or another. We present three ways of thinking about class, distilled from research in sociology, political economy, anthropology and critical management studies: class as structure, class as style and class as process. We do not seek to pit these approaches against one another. Rather, we offer them as tools or frameworks that might be particularly relevant for researchers and practitioners concerned with diversity in organizations. For each approach to class, we open by examining its meaning, evolution and usefulness. We then offer three particular aspects of each approach that prompt questions or issues of special relevance for diversity in organizations. The questions arise throughout each section, and, for convenience, are summarized in Table 17.1. The class-as-structure approach receives the longest treatment, as it is historically antecedent and foundational to the other two approaches. Throughout this chapter, we emphasize that class is more than an individual trait (even more than a set or markers or a social identity) and must be understood as having a structural basis and having both material and political implications for members of all classes and for organizations.

CLASS AS STRUCTURE

Much of the work on class traces its origins to formulations from Marx (Marx, 1967; 1970; 1976; Marx & Engels, 1962), often embracing these origins but sometimes denying them. Marx never completed his treatment of class, but it can be derived from his works, which are typically cited as postulating two classes distinguished by their place in the system of production. Capitalists own the means of production. Laborers sell their commodified labor in return for a wage. Capitalists pay labor below the value of their contribution and thereby extract 'surplus value' or profit from the operations they own. Capitalists rationalize the production process and own the products. Laborers become alienated from the methods and results of their labor, as contrasted to craft-based production. Workers are also alienated from one another as the structures of production fragment jobs and supervision supplants collaboration (Gordon, Edwards & Reich, 1982). Even from this highly simplified depiction, it is evident where numerous frictions arise.

First, how do capitalists and laborers coexist? Capital and labor have conflicting interests (e.g. retaining more profits versus earning more wages, repressing

TABLE 17.1 *Summary of pressing questions that derive from the three approaches to class*

Approach to class	Issues with implications for diversity	Pressing questions for diversity work
Class as structure	Legitimation of inequality	How do we start and sustain conversations about inequality when the prevalent belief in meritocratic ideology legitimates inequality and chills the discussion?
	Class consciousness	How do we nurture class consciousness in the face of forces that mask class factors and fear dissent that may result from class consciousness?
	Class as 'outside' organizations	How do we bring class inside the organization, and not leave it as an external factor that organizations inherit?
Class as style	Accent, dress and manners	How do we surface awareness that certain aspects of dress and style that are taken for granted as business appropriate are not just characteristics of elites?
	Universal versus particular speech and reasoning styles	How do we foster an appreciation for the styles of reasoning and speech that the working class brings to organizations?
		How do we generate conversations across different class styles to learn from the best of each?
	Toward an appreciation of class differences	How do we keep the discussion of class grounded in the material reality of class inequality and not turn class into just another individual trait?
Class as process	Class as 'inside' organizations	How do we recognize the ways in which everyday organizational procedures reproduce class?
	Simultaneity	How do we see class as inextricably linked to other social identities in the lived experience of employees?
		How do we recognize that class is both like other social identities and distinct?
	Class as a process of mobilization	How do we use the dynamic aspect of class as a process to motivate change in organizations to make them more inclusive, just, diverse, effective, meaningful places to work?

conflict versus spurring system change). Labor process theory has explored specifically how these conflicts are manifested at the point of production, in everyday life on the shopfloor, or increasingly in service operations (e.g. Burawoy, 1980; Edwards, 1979). Capital seeks ways to control labor, and labor finds ways to resist control, which often triggers new modes of control and occasionally some labor-friendly changes; the dynamics of control and resistance persist. A hallmark of looking at organizational life through a class-as-structure lens is that conflict is always brewing – and can bubble to the surface despite efforts to contain it.

Second, who gets to decide how work gets done? Managers, on behalf of capitalists, see their role as providing oversight, planning and direction of activities toward broader goals. Coordination is an essential ingredient in organizations, even when labor gains more authority. For example, self-managing teams at Southwest Airlines did better if there was some formalized coordinator role (Hoffer Gittell, 2003). The cascade of rules and procedures down a bureaucracy can provide both guidance and some assurance of fair regularity (Adler &

Borys, 1996; Gouldner, 1954; Weber, 1978). The conventional management literature accepts and describes this role of management unproblematically. A critical approach surfaces the additional aspects of management that involve controlling, policing and disciplining labor such that workers' resistance is curbed and their labor produces returns for managers and owners. Not only is labor demeaned, but the tremendous body of tacit knowledge that workers possess is not respected nor tapped. Time-and-motion studies (famously introduced by Taylor, 1911) are seen from this perspective as primarily a form of control, not efficiency (Braverman, 1974); Taylor's approach persists today, for example, as housecleaners employed by a national chain are instructed to wipe countertops with circles only in one direction, never employing what they know about cleaning a house and leaving them fatigued from managerial moves that turn them into drones (Ehrenreich, 2001). Where the class divide maps onto a separation of 'conception' and 'execution' (Braverman, 1974), clashes over competence can arise. Managers summon technical experts to show that there are better methods. Employees use 'work to rule' resistance to show managers that following these methods hampers production and that workers' adaptations are the better methods. While some managerial coordination remains necessary, layers of gratuitous control over employees have built up, making work a place of boredom, fatigue and humiliation (e.g. Ehrenreich, 2001; Linder & Nygaard, 1998; Parker & Slaughter, 1988). Students at the University of California Berkeley studied the employees who cleaned their classrooms and supported university life and found that they suffered myriad 'minor indignities' as their dedication and contributions were ignored (Purser, Schalet & Sharone, 2004). Tensions between managers' and workers' notions of how best to run the workplace will simmer and sometimes boil over.

Third, where do managers, professionals and others fit into the stylized two-class depiction? Knowledge workers have an ambiguous class position (Ehrenreich & Ehrenreich, 1971), because they own their intellectual capital (like capitalists) and work for wages (like laborers). Are they capitalists, laborers or a third class? Marx acknowledged the existence of other class locations (e.g. landowners, intellectuals, state officials). But sometimes the robustness of the two-class model is questioned in the face of contemporary work roles, and then with that, the whole portrait of class-based conflict at work is dismissed as no longer relevant. But understanding the tensions produced by the aspects of class and control described above is a useful window onto precisely the challenges for emerging groups who seek to apply expertise and have meaningful work, such as, for example, skilled technicians in biotechnology companies (Barley & Bechky, 1994), who display a mix of class markers (wearing jeans, doing routine work, getting their hands dirty, holding PhDs, being courted for positions, etc.). These workers may be unlikely to experience themselves collectively as a class. Marsden (1997) shows that class structure is a useful starting point for understanding class as a process, treated below, and for tracing how the control regimes that are integral to the workplace make workers in a variety of class locations isolated and fungible in a way counter to the spirit of diversity, inclusivity and appreciation of differences. In organizations, class relations are often 'handled' by an industrial relations department or subgroup of human resource management and rarely intersect with the work of diversity. Understanding class as a dimension of diversity – but distinct from the American liberal idea that diversity is about removing biases to open the gates of individualistic opportunity – may provoke useful reframings of both class and diversity.

The concerns discussed above follow from understanding class as located in the structure of how organizations are governed and how work is organized. A class-based analysis of organizations, particularly one rooted in this structural approach, tends to be at odds with more traditional organizational behavior studies (Nord, 1974). These latter studies emphasize harmony rather than conflict, choice rather than constraint, and legitimate authority rather than control. A new trend toward 'positive' or 'appreciative' inquiry is at risk of smoothing away conflict and painting an incomplete portrait of work. The dominant view of organizations (versus the class-oriented critical view) tells a clear story of the legitimacy and general desirability of status quo class differences, in language so alluring and familiar it is unquestioned. The market allocates wages in a way that reflects the consensual social valuing of different jobs. Workers can change jobs if wages or conditions do not suit them. Managers have attained their position fairly through special expertise that they ply in a way that best builds commitment and enhances productivity. Their role as agents of shareholders is to maximize worker productivity.

A class-based analysis questions all these premises and often stirs up needed controversy. However, class-based analyses have been more rare than they were in the 1970s and into the 1980s. The fact that such analyses are dubbed 'critical' can marginalize them. Critical analyses are challenged as overly sensitive to detecting conflict and as too willing to use their hammer to see everything as a nail. In contrast, mainstream studies are seen as more balanced, affable, constructive and neutral in their stance. Offe (1985) challenges this neutrality with a simple compelling example of how the mainstream view is taken for granted in the very way that we frame workplace issues: we often hear of labor making a 'wage demand' (cranky, insistent, contentious labor), but we never hear conversely of capitalists or managers making a 'profit demand'.

A discourse that critiqued exorbitant salaries for top managers appeared in the business and popular press but did not translate into a movement that yielded changes. The dominant logic carries the ready rebuttal that these salaries must be paid to retain top talent, signal a certain corporate élan, and remain competitive (as explained by Bok, 1993, and Khurana, 2002). An example anchored in wage distribution is in the spirit of the class as structure perspective, in its insistence on keeping the material basis and implications of class in view. The wage gap is widening in the United States, which must be a factor as class enters the diversity domain (Bullock, 2004). US multinational companies are also exporting meritocratic logic and HR practices that might widen the gap worldwide.

The structural approach to class sets a tone and should undergird the class-as-style and class-as-process approaches. As we will do for each of the three approaches to class, we introduce some particular issues from the class-as-structure perspective that have special implications for bringing class into organizational diversity work. The three issues are: the legitimation of inequality by meritocratic ideology (which can chill discussion of class differences and remedies for inequality), class consciousness (which may be less crystallized than the collective aspect of other social identities) and class as 'outside' organizations (which exonerates organizations from attending to inequality).

The Legitimation of Inequality

Diversity trainers have noted that the prevalent belief in meritocracy can chill a discussion of how race or gender bias impede advancement opportunities. Affirmative action policies are meant to correct the opportunity structure where it departs from meritocracy, but they are sometimes taken themselves as departures from meritocracy by those who believe that the system is already working well. The belief in meritocracy is related to class in that it is the dominant ideology that legitimates stratification and stands as an alternative to a belief that class (or race or gender) are unfair biases. A meritocracy has three distinct features (Daniels, 1978). First, merit is a well-defined and measurable basis for selecting individuals for positions. Second, individuals have equal opportunity to develop and display their merits and thereby to advance. Third, the positions into which individuals are sorted through this contest come with appropriately different levels of reward, income and status.

In contrast, the class-based view of the opportunity structure contests each of these three premises. First, it seeks to show that merit is defined by elites to be those features that make them appear the most meritorious. For example, an educational degree might be a requirement for a job, thereby excluding people whose experience would make them qualified but whose class background did not direct them toward college. Markers of elite style, discussed in the next section, are sometimes elevated to markers of merit.

Second, family class background is argued to be a better predictor of 'who gets ahead' than individual merit. Class standing is transmitted intergenerationally; that is, parents' class is a good predictor of an individual's class. If all players stood equally at the starting line at birth, then inheritance should not be a strong predictor of outcome. Instead, empirical studies find that merit alone cannot explain inequality, but neither can class alone (e.g. Bowles & Gintis, 1973; Jencks et al., 1972; 1979). Of course, there are some banner cases of 'rags to riches', such as Iacocca's (1984) best-selling autobiography of his rise from car showroom floor to CEO, but any meritocracy needs only just enough permeability of elite ranks to justify the possibility that 'anyone can make it'. Aspirations for advancement are at once urged and cooled out (Brint & Karabel, 1989). The dominant pattern remains one where it is difficult to break out of the lower class. Notably, this process of 'making it' or upward mobility usually happens in organizations and is hinged to the procedures and politics of evaluation and promotion in the organization.

Third, the differential value to society of different jobs – and the concomitant differences in rewards – can be contested, although this critique of meritocratic premises is rendered least often. From a class-based perspective, the value of labor's contribution is emphasized. The wage gap between the highest- and lowest-paid positions is seen as the result of the power of those at the top to pay themselves handsomely (as recent scandals in the United States have revealed) and not a real reflection of differences in merit or societal value. The early case for meritocracy (Davis & Moore, 1966) was that there would be a societal consensus supporting stratification and higher wages for special jobs, such as neurosurgeons, pilots, bridge designers. Everyone in society benefits from these jobs attracting and rewarding the most meritorious. But while societal consensus might support differences that reward special excellence (a class-based critique does not imply simple egalitarianism), the current gap that has corporate leaders paid 420 times the wage of janitors, welders and secretaries is harder to justify with this early functionalist and consensual account of meritocracy.

There are discussions of how these two different views of inequality – meritocratic and class based – are promulgated, in addition to the empirical explorations of which is the better explanation of inequality in the United States. Theoretical work has long emphasized that the belief in meritocracy is promoted because it favors elites. Elites use 'autobiographical reasoning' to describe their positions as the outcome of hard work and ability, extrapolating from their own experiences. For example, the British director Michael Apted (Apted, 2004) has tracked a cohort of people from different classes since they were children in 1963, interviewing them every seven years to see how their highly class-based lives have unfolded. At age 21, a young man from an elite family talks into the camera to say that he can see through the premise of this project – that it will show his youthful privilege and now here he is at Oxford. However, he goes on to say, that misses the point. He has worked very hard, studied difficult subjects, pulled many an all-nighter. Indeed, in his case, hard work and success appear correlated. But one could say he is a bad 'intuitive scientist' to universalize from his case, because he has not considered the 'control experiments': people who work hard but do not get ahead, and people who get ahead despite no hard work (e.g. through inheritance or what is called, with surprising candor about class, 'unearned income'). He attempts to universalize from his experience of working hard to the conclusion that anyone who works hard can succeed. Marx and Engels (1970: 64) wrote that the ruling class 'is compelled, merely in order to carry through its aim, to represent its interest as the common interest of all the members of society …: it has to give its ideas the form of universality'. Weber (1978: 953) writes that 'every highly privileged group develops the myth of its natural superiority'.

Of course, there is a corollary to this meritocratic belief system, which is that those who have not fared well in a stratified social order are not meritorious, hard working, talented or vital contributors. The tenets of meritocracy hang together like a 'logical syllogism' (Huber & Form, 1973) and give a tenacious force to the meritocratic ideal. On the one hand, recent public debates in the United States over welfare reform betray a widespread belief in this 'blame the victim' approach to poverty (e.g. Katz, 1990; Ryan, 1971). On the other hand, a growing body of literature is showing how poor people work extremely hard and provide vital – and even intimate – services, such as domestic help and childrearing, but are doing so at not even subsistence wages (Chang, 2000; Ehrenreich & Hochschild, 2004; Parrenas, 2001). Census data (2000) show that lower-class workers get up and leave for work an hour earlier than their middle-class counterparts. Emerging 'living wage' campaigns (Luce, 2004) urge a recognition that class should not be a barrier to respect and a decent livelihood. The logic of meritocracy, however, makes people blame themselves – not structural obstacles – for being in a low class position (Della Fave, 1980).

Ultimately, what is at stake is the reproduction of inequality. Inequality will be persist if it goes uncontested. Meritocratic ideology serves as a bulwark against dissent, but one that can sometimes be transgressed.

Class Consciousness

Scholars have wondered for thousands of years why the many do not rise against the few where there is inequality. Dissent and change may require that working-class people come to understand their shared class position and how it limits their chances for interesting work, income, education for their children and even longevity. Meritocratic ideology and a focus on consumption divert the working class from taking this view (Goldthorpe, 1969; Mann, 1973). Narrow job classifications and a contest to move up locally within one's job ladder occupy people's energies at work (e.g. from Assembler I to Assembler II, not to Director of Manufacturing). Attention is shifted away from vertical inequality (Martin, 1982). The insight of labor process theory is to locate these dynamics of class in the workplace and not just in revolutions at the state level.

Some in the class-as-structure perspective would dispense with a role for ideology and class consciousness at all (Abercrombie, Hill & Turner, 1980), focusing instead on the importance of available resources and opportunities for dissent (McCarthy & Zald, 1977). Others see ideology and consciousness as parts of the structure and vital to both its perpetuation and its dismantling (e.g. Mann, 1970; Martin, Brickman & Murray, 1984; Sewell, 1985). Gouldner (1980) helpfully distinguishes 'two Marxisms'. In 'scientific Marxism', the progress toward revolutionary change is embedded in the structures and the contradictions that will eventually unravel capitalism. Conscious effort on the part of the oppressed class is not a necessary mechanism. In contrast, 'critical Marxism' requires that the working class identify with one another as a class, with a shared place in an oppressive structure and shared interests, in order to create radical change. Change toward *what* is not always clearly specified (Martin, Scully & Levitt, 1990) and is sometimes filled with utopian glances forward or backward (Jameson, 1982), because the status quo anchors and limits alternative visions. A dominant ideology may be one of several powerful hegemonic forces arrayed toward maintaining the status quo to benefit the most powerful, but workers (and not just an intellectual vanguard) will find the cracks in the armor and seize moments for resistance and change; focusing on these dynamics would usher in an entirely different approach to the nature and purposes of 'organizational strategy' (Levy, 2004).

These discussions may seem located miles above the workplace in the domain of grand theory, but they are necessary to orient workplace diversity programs that include class. Consciousness of shared interests may or may not sustain or change societies, but it does come into play in workplace practices. For example, consciousness of a shared social identity with collective concerns about equitable treatment – like race, gender or sexual orientation – is an emerging basis for the formation of employee groups or caucuses (Creed, this volume; Creed, Scully & Austin, 2002; Scully and Segal, 2002). These groups can be locations for 'micro-mobilization' (McAdam, 1988), where members shift their attributions away from individual merit or self-blame to make sense of inequalities they have experienced in the organization and come to recognize that their entire group may be facing biases. Increasingly called 'affinity groups', they are most recently emerging along the dimensions of age, disability and religion. Employee groups of this kind have not emerged on the dimension of class, perhaps because they follow the constructivist turn toward social identity as a performance rather than as a structural location; we discuss the nature and possibility of class-based employee groups in later sections.

Class as 'Outside' Organizations

Many organizations take class to be a broad societal factor that stands outside them and about which they really cannot do much. Hiring managers argue that they inherit applicants who are already affected by class background, such as differential schooling opportunities. They cannot single-handedly remedy inequalities that trace to kindergarten and even before. If they do see their organization as having tiers of people from different classes, it is because this is the labor pool that the market and the broader society present to them. A limitation of this view is that organizational leaders do not consider their own role in creating the class structure through their systems of classifying and rewarding jobs.

Wages are not just filtered through organizations by markets, but are produced by organizations and their logics and procedures for valuing positions and moving people among them. A considerable literature has examined how organizations are the site where social stratification is produced (Baron, 1984). Some structural properties that affect individuals' prospects for upward mobility, within and across classes, include: whether there are openings available in higher levels (Stewman & Konda, 1983; White, 1970), whether their job is linked to others in a ladder or a dead-end (e.g. Baron, Davis-Blake & Bielby, 1986), how those jobs and pathways are gendered (Reskin & Roos, 1991), whether an idiosyncratic job is created for them (Miner, 1987), and whether they have a spurt of early success that is propitious for later advancement (Rosenbaum, 1979). Research on the structural properties of advancement systems has its intellectual origins in correcting the meritocratic myth. It tries to show that inequality can result from differences in structures, not individual merits. Despite research findings that contradict meritocracy, the language of meritocracy is tenacious. Studies of structures do not tend to focus on what the occupants of these structures believe about their movement through these structures. Adding class to the learning-oriented work on diversity may surface these beliefs and help bring class back inside the organization. The perspectives of 'class as style' and 'class as process' bring class closer into the everyday experience of life in stratified organizations.

CLASS AS STYLE

Class is manifested in the United States and other countries by a variety of indicators. Systems of stratification persist, have meaning and shape social life when there are these subtle but detectable markers of class. In some historical periods or in some cultures, the markers are quite obvious and explicit, such as particular dress codes for an occupation or caste (Sennett, 1992). Class does not fit neatly into the visible diversity nor invisible diversity category, particularly when class background and current class do not align. As mentioned in the beginning, Americans will deny class but detect and label it with astounding accuracy.

The idea of class as style can proceed in two ways. In the first, class is understood to be anchored in economics, but realized in the many layers of status built upon that economic base. Weber (1978) expanded beyond Marx's notion of class as a two-tier system anchored in economics and identified 'class, status, and party' as three dimensions of stratification that tend to be related but are distinct in their source and enactment. Thus, economic wealth is often tightly coupled to occupational status and prestige and to political influence. Nonetheless, social scientists are often interested in the cases where status does not crystallize and generates 'status inconsistencies' that might allow radical insight; for example, black men whose gender privilege and race oppression could radicalize them (Lenski, 1954). Bourdieu (1977) contemplates disconnections of economic capital and cultural capital, such as newly rich industrialists who lack the style to be accepted as elites in terms of status, while the 'shabby gentility' retain status despite diminished economic circumstances. He uses the term 'cultural capital' to capture intangible resources (e.g. knowledge of the arts, high style) that are distinct from economic capital but nonetheless pay the dividends of high class standing – another, somewhat subtle mechanism whereby class inequality is reproduced.

The second approach to class as style leaves behind the basis in – or interplay with – material economic situation. Unfortunately, class as style without economic anchors may be the way in which class is most likely to be picked up by diversity programs in organizations. If class origins are seen as 'outside' the organization's control, a view described above, then class enters only as a matter of presentation of self. Class can thereby be reduced to another arena in which to carry out traditional human resource programs of enhancing communication, managing conflict, supporting teamwork, and so forth. But the class-as-style approach need not be detached from the structural locations of class; style offers the visible cues to the class structure that supports organizational operations. Within the class-as-style approach, we discuss three issues: accents, dress and manners; universal versus particular speech and reasoning styles; and appreciation of class differences. These issues raise questions for diversity work about assimilation and the hiding of class background, connecting class to the idea that diversity represents an opportunity to learn from different vantage points about how work can best get done (Thomas & Ely, 1996), and the need to appreciate – rather than erase or overcome – class backgrounds.

Accents, Dress and Manners

Advancing in organizations is often about 'looking the part'. Phrases like 'dress for success' have entered the vernacular of organizational life. A certain kind of polish is expected among leaders. People from privileged backgrounds often enter organizations with this kind of style already in hand. They have a ready cultural vocabulary and a certain cultural flair. Those from less privileged backgrounds may seek, quite consciously, to acquire this style along the way. Or they may be encouraged to adopt this style and reluctantly comply (Hoyt, 1999). Executive coaching sometimes focuses on adding this patina of style to an individual's skills and accomplishments to create for the individual a 'package' that is more likely to win a promotion competition. In ascending a pyramid, there are fewer and fewer openings for many talented contenders, so style often becomes a tie-breaker.

Style acquired consciously may not come across 'quite right', in comparison to the style of those 'of the manor born', as Bourdieu and Passeron (1977) argue in their examination of the acquisition of cultural capital and of 'habitus', or taken-for-granted aspects of one's class. Thus, a woman on an executive career path might save up to buy some jewelry to look the part, but she would have to be careful that the jewelry is not 'gaudy' but reflects good 'taste'. The role of cultural capital is seen most clearly when it is decoupled from economic capital. For example, most museums have 'free nights' to encourage the general public to visit irrespective of ability to pay. The class habitus of those in lower classes might not dispose them to attend the museum even for free, because the museum has been marked as a place that is not theirs. The arts have a special place in the style markers of class. Serving on the board of a cultural institution is a pathway to the elite (Ostrower, 1995). A recent portrait of a businessman in a daily newspaper (Talcott, 2004) quite candidly captures the process of polishing one's cultural references and speech style to be not just a CEO but the compelling CEO at the head of a takeover.

> It was just a few years ago that Kenneth Lewis would show up late to cocktail parties and make a beeline for familiar faces. Around the office, he paused a bit awkwardly in conversations, or frequently lapsed into silence. But these days the chief executive of Bank of America Corp. is all about being social. He's introducing topics like art and wine into his cocktail banter and is even watching videos of his speeches to count how many times he says 'um'.

In the workplace, the assimilation project usually involves leaving the marks of lower-class origin behind (Blake-Beard, Felicio & Scully, 2004; Hoyt, 1999). Cases of people being gently nudged to 'lose their accent' abound. Employees try to see the right movies and read the right books so they can enter informal conversations and display their sophistication. The balancing act is quite fine, because overdoing this exercise and appearing too studied or too 'snooty' can backfire. Reading the class code carefully and getting it right is a difficult game.

Universal Versus Particular Speech and Reasoning Styles

Class is particularly evident in speech styles, beginning with those of young children. A widely cited series of studies of speech patterns was conducted in the 1960s in the UK (Hawkins, 1969). Bernstein (1977) relates them to class repro-duction. These studies showed how class-based socialization produces different ways of locating oneself in a frame of action and describing it to others. He dis-tinguished these as 'universal' versus 'particular' styles of speech. He showed boys from elite and working-class backgrounds a series of pictures, like cartoon frames, and asked each to describe what they saw. The elite boys used universalistic or 'elaborated' stories, such as:

> Three boys are playing football and one boy kicks the ball and it goes through the window the ball breaks the window and the boys are looking at it and a man comes out and shouts at them because they've broken the window so they run away and then that lady looks out of her window and she tell the boys off.

The working-class boys used particular or 'restricted' stories (putatively harder to understand without seeing the pictures and thus anchored in the moment and not in the experience of being a teller with a wider audience), such as:

> They're playing football and he kicks it and it goes through there it breaks the window and they're looking at it and he comes out and shouts at them because they've broken it so they run away and then she looks out and she tells them off.

While both convey essentially the same information, the former 'sounds smarter' and appears to have a more cosmopolitan than local standpoint that draws others in.

Organizational changes such as teamwork, participatory management, labor/management teams and quality circles increasingly involve managers and work-ers talking together across class lines. Participant observation in one such joint team setting revealed how the universalistic and particularistic codes of speech bumped up against each other (Scully & Preuss, 1994). Both managers and workers came to the meetings enthusiastic about cooperating, making work conditions better and improving performance by soliciting everyone's ideas.

The workers often arrived with particular problems from recent experience and used shorthand to describe them. 'Big Blue [nickname for a machine] was sticking up. That guy never did come by', or 'Mike's guys don't have the rolls yet'. Managers barely shield their impatience with the uncontextualized specificity of these issues. They want to get to the 'big picture', not just the issues from the past few hours. They like to generalize the issues into broader categories and use concepts like 'production pacing', 'sourcing streams' and 'reciprocal responsibility'. Workers, in turn, get impatient that managers are talking a lot but not saying anything important or relevant to the daily work; the next day, everything will be the same. Both sides may be talking about (and hoping to fix) the same thing, but their socialized class styles and their standpoints make it difficult to connect. The result is lost opportunities for learning and improving organizational performance.

The communication style of managers is considered to be the preferred and 'smarter sounding' one, and, moreover, managers have the power to advance their mode. However, each clearly has its merits, and going back and forth between the specific and the general can be a good way to learn. Diversity work is often about brokering an understanding across differences. In order to connect working-class and managerial styles – and not just coach all to adopt a managerial style – an appreciation of class differences must be developed.

Toward an Appreciation of Class Differences

Markers of working-class background are generally to be 'gotten rid of' in order to advance in organizations. People from these backgrounds often wrestle with a complex mixture of shame and pride about their origins (Hoyt, 1999). In diversity work regarding gender and race, the appreciation of diversity – and the deep opportunity to learn how to work better by really paying attention to diverse approaches – is a cutting edge approach (Ely & Meyerson, 2000; Thomas & Ely, 1996). While women were once to assimilate and behave more like men, women's ways of working have come to be appreciated (e.g. Helgesen, 1995), and from there, the false divide between women's and men's styles has been deconstructed to see where both men and women can innovate beyond a menu of formerly gendered approaches.

No such discourse of appreciation has surrounded class. There is not yet a celebration of 'the working-class way' on the business bookshelf. Therefore, the reason we elaborated on the speech styles above was to open a gateway to such appreciation. The grounded specificity and particulars of working-class speech could be a breath of fresh air in settings that are overwhelmed by managerial fads and consulting jargon. The above findings about universalistic and particularistic speech got a lot of play, but the full set of findings, shown in Table 17.2, show places where working-class kids have an unselfconscious spontaneity. As organizations engage in exercises like scenario building (Schwartz, 1996), they might want to consider having not just top managers in the room but representatives from the working class, who may bring 'longer, more imaginative' extrapolations.

TABLE 17.2 *Appreciating class differences*

Task	Middle-class kids	Working-class kids
Tell the story of the picture frames	Universalistic	Particularistic
Role-play the story	Initially refuse	Jump right in
Make up story using doll-like figures	Tighter, constrained within strong narrative frame	Freer, longer, more imaginative

In the educational domain, Annas (1993) identifies what is distinctive about the writing style of her working-class students. Pertinent to the point above that elites get to define what constitutes merit, she suggests a different metric of merit that would recognize what working-class students contribute. We quote this passage at length, because our organizational writing and imagination is starved for examples of appreciating class.

> We need to redefine what we mean by an expository essay, since our present definition of a good essay – linear, hierarchical, and pointed – is not necessarily amenable to the way, for example, many women think, as Gilligan and Clichy have pointed out. I would speculate that that form is also not necessarily the best one for men from marginalized groups. Writing issues that come up around class and race as well as gender include an articulateness in speaking that students can learn to transfer and translate into their writing and an interest in and ease with particularity, detail, and vivid sense-based language, which can be encouraged and can serve as models for the middle-class students, who are more often mired in vagueness and abstract language. Students from marginalized groups often are suspicious or have a struck-dumb response to 'high' language and they often quite rightly have a sense that the classroom itself and the reading and writing they're supposed to be doing is alien and uncomfortable ... I'd like to suggest that we look closely and critically at the land of academic discourse for which we serve as customs officials.

Meeting rooms and memos in the corporate world perpetuate this style stratification begun in the educational system. Moreover, Annas (1993) shows that class must necessarily be intertwined with race and gender, which is elaborated from the perspective of class as process. While class as style can be the most depoliticized variant on class, if we connect it to appreciating class differences, rather than erasing them, then it has a potentially powerful impact. Those who have traditionally been 'outsiders' to a system have a unique vantage point. 'Outsiders within' (Collins, 1999: 86) can draw strength from their history of exclusion and initiate provocative dialogues that organizations need in unstable times (Proudford & Thomas, 1999). As Lorde (1984: 112) writes, 'those of us who have been forged in the crucibles of difference ... take our differences and make them strengths'. These ideas, derived from the experiences of African American women, extend to – and already embrace – class. Appreciating race, gender or class differences should not be about anointing a few more winners in the meritocracy, but about rethinking how widely distributed merit may already be – and therefore how rewards must be much more widely redistributed. The features of organizations that will enable or inhibit an appreciation of class are part of the class-as-process approach.

CLASS AS PROCESS

Class distinctions are maintained – and sometimes contested – through the everyday activities of organizational life. The historian Thompson (1968) traces the emergence of class as a historical process, rather than as a structure. The working class participated in their own creation, rather than passively having a structure imposed upon them (Marsden, 1977; Thompson, 1968). The process approach to class merges elements of the structural and the style approach. The structural approach sees class as a root fact of social life and traces processes (control, conflict, reproduction, radical change) that flow from it, while the process approach sees class as itself constituted by and through these very processes. Elements of style may be part of this process – how class is enacted and its meanings reinforced.

While class as structure tended to locate the class of workers paid wages for production, quite clearly it can leave out of view the many kinds of work that are not remunerated in traditional ways. Continually returning to the economic base of class makes sure that the notion of class is not trivialized, but leaves out those who are marginal to the economy as it is officially counted. By treating class as a process, the door is opened for domestic workers, sex workers, farm and migrant workers, and all the kinds of work that happen in a global, postcolonial world. Gibson-Graham, Resnick and Wolff (2000: 2) portray the process approach to class:

> The processes of producing, appropriating, and distributing surplus labor are identified as the 'processes of class.' Around these processes social practices are organized, struggles are galvanized, and identities and experiences transformed. Setting forth this singular (and simple) understanding of class … allows us to highlight, amidst the confusing welter of class meanings, a salient meaning deriving its emotional power from the knowledge and experience of exploitation. It creates a strategic point of confluence between the desire to produce a politically enabling discourse of economy and the intense feelings attached to the experience and witness of the laboring body.

This approach to class is less likely to stand outside members of the historically oppressed classes and wonder when and if they will form class consciousness and more likely to listen to the particular stories and appreciate the small but potent moments of mobilization that animate class identity. The class-as-process approach is a window into issues such as how class is 'inside' the organization, how class operates simultaneously with other identities and how mobilization occurs. The implications for diversity in organizations include how everyday procedures in organizations subtly reinforce class lines, how class is both like and unlike other dimensions of diversity, how the reproduction of class is a strong force but one that can be countered by forms of workplace resistance (Prasad & Prasad, 2000) and how workplace mobilization efforts need to make class explicit.

Class as 'Inside' the Organization – and Supporting the Organization

From a process perspective, class is not an exogenous factor inherited by organizations. Instead, organizations are where class is constructed and enacted *and* where the invisible work of marginalized classes is consumed by elites. For example, elite women advance because of the domestic work done by women outside the organization, but capitalized upon inside the organization (Holvino & Scully, 2001). Organizations hungrily consume the efforts of elite women who are freed from domestic burden. Professionals have the resources to fund these solutions, but working-class employees do not. Managers can escalate the hours worked by professionals because 'invisible' labor is maintaining the domestic sphere, into which work hours make incursions. When managers do not understand class-based issues in the domestic spheres of their employees, they often miscalculate where working-class employees, for example, need more or fewer hours of overtime in order to manage their livelihoods and their time (Lautsch & Scully, 2004).

From a structural perspective, organizations set wage structures and create ladders of mobility, as discussed above. A class as process perspective is distinct in looking at the flows of people across those positions (Wright, 1985). Many organizational governance procedures relate to evaluating, ranking and rewarding employees; most organizations now use merit-based promotion and pay systems (Murphy & Cleveland, 1991). Organizational culture includes the language, stories, myths and gossip whereby employees make sense of, contest or defend promotion decisions and status. A considerable body of research has developed on cognitive biases, supervisor memory, critical incident recall, mutual feedback and other procedural elements that can cloud or improve the effectiveness and/or credibility of performance evaluations. These procedures regulate class stratification in organizations.

Other procedures govern how work gets done and who gets to decide about work procedures. Organizational leaders often chart new directions, such as adoption of new technology, without consulting workers; they then sell workers a package. Organizations that include workers earlier in the strategic decision chain, such as participation in technology selection and not just technology implementation, have better outcomes (Thomas, 1994). Workers who cannot participate in meaningful work may find meaningful resistance.

Organizational processes also enact and cement social identities at work, such as gender relations and gendered notions of work (Acker, 1990; 1999). The three prongs of this process approach were adapted by Holvino (2000) who shows how class in organizations is manifested through: (1) requirements for particular educational degrees for managerial and technical positions (where sometimes experience would serve as a qualification), (2) class symbols such as office location and size, décor, different lunch rooms, reserved parking spaces, and (3) cross-class interactions, which are often strained and fraught with missed connections. Holvino describes a diversity training exercise in which a group of workers and a group of managers were asked to draw a picture of their organization. The workers drew a large boot coming down on workers. The managers drew a ship under sunny skies with the occasional cloud or shark in the waters. Each side was surprised, and a bit hurt, by the other's depiction, but the exercise facilitated more candid cross-class communication than typically happens. Because class is so hard to name and acknowledge, organizational life is full of cross-class misunderstandings and 'micro inequities' (Rowe, 1990).

The normalization of class distinctions happens in organizational settings, enabling class differences to persist. For example, it is often understood that upper-level employees will attend off-site meetings and conferences, but workers will not. Nonetheless, workplace restructuring often demands complex skills from workers. At one manufacturing company that sent a small group of workers from the manufacturing line to a conference on total quality management, the ripples of excitement over this unusual opportunity – and the attendant upper-class perquisites like a day away from the office, a nice lunch and reimbursement for travel expenses – were felt for a long time. In another plant, where all the proponents of work practice restructuring were English speaking and all the practitioners on the line were Spanish speaking, opportunities like the conference were harder to orchestrate, and serve a reminder that class is always intertwined with other social identities.

The Simultaneity of Multiple Social Identities

As an ongoing construction, class is lived by people with multiple social identities. Class is not one bifurcated dimension but a process of social identity enactment that varies for different clusters of identity. Class connects to a mix of historically privileged and historically oppressed identities. On the one hand, class can be a dimension that pulls white people back into a discussion about diversity. On the other hand, a rich treatment of class must move beyond the modal 'worker' as a white heterosexual man in the industrial sector (e.g. Zavella, 1991).

When class finally finds its place in organizational diversity work, three problematic moves may follow. First, when class is connected to diversity work, some worry about the risks that class will be made an individualistic trait rather than a collective position and class demands will thereby be depoliticized and managed away (Marsden, 1997). In contrast to how mainstream HR departments approach social identities, unions have worked hard to make class a collective identity and to help workers see beyond the one organization where they work to achieve solidarity. HR departments often cool out protest.

Second, a debate over whether class is the ultimate or central or most defining element, versus race or gender, may arise. Wilson (1977; 1990) has provocatively argued that class disadvantage is the great dividing line and that policy must focus on programs for the lowest classes across all races, whereas affirmative action has tended to benefit the black middle class. This framing makes the important move of keeping the urgent material basis of class in view, but the potentially damaging move of making class 'more important' than race. Class should be used to provoke a rethinking of how work gets done and who (at the juncture of many social identities) gets the returns, not to spur a new round of 'oppression Olympics' among social identity groups (Gamson, 1995). A potential blindspot of class analyses can be a stance that class trumps all other dimensions of identity as it is the most fundamental, economically situated identity. This stance does not help for building alliances across members of different social identity groups committed to working on diversity and justice. It does not recognize that class is lived simultaneously with other social identities in a way that cannot be mathematically pulled apart. For example, working-class African American women cannot 'net out' class from their other life experiences (Bell & Nkomo, 2001). As hooks (2000: 8) notes, 'Class is still often kept separate from race. And while race is often linked with gender, we still lack an ongoing collective public discourse that puts the three together in ways that illuminate for everyone how our nation is organized and what our class politics really are.'

Third, class prejudices sometimes emerge. Tensions within the working class around gender and race and how white men have had access to the most highly paid blue-collar jobs have been well documented (e.g. Padavic & Reskin, 1990). It does not follow that working-class people should be regarded as racist, sexist and homophobic, but this prejudice is common. Working-class people often respond with indignation at the hypocrisy of middle- and upper middle-class liberals who talk a progressive line about social identity politics but act to exclude. In a rare inquiry into the simultaneity of class and queer identity, Kadi (1997) tells of how welcoming her working-class family was to her same-sex partner and how she resented the assumptions of her liberal elite friends that she and her partner would encounter bigotry. Similarly, Gamson (1992) engages working-class white people in discussions of race and affirmative action and finds – as he expects – a rich treatment of the issues, not simplistic racist statements. The redistributive impact of affirmative action is often supported by elites but lived by members of the working class, so their reflections on values and tradeoffs carry a wisdom that could inform policy and cross-race relations, were it ever solicited.

Class and New Processes of Mobilization

The canonical form of mobilization from the grassroots to contest inequality was once unionism. Even as the fate of unionism is uncertain, new forms of employee voice have emerged, particularly groups formed around social identities, such as women's networks, African American caucuses, or gay, lesbian, bisexual and transgender groups (Scully & Segal, 2002). These groups use their knowledge of the internal language and workings of organizations to find levers for change.

A concern is that they may supplant the efforts of unions and the ways in which unions integrated the concerns of diverse members (Hyde, 1997; Piore, 1995) with less collectively and economically oriented social movements (Laraña, Johnston & Gusfield, 1994). These employee groups might indeed threaten unionism, or alternatively, they might occupy a different niche and fill a need for new forms of employee voice (Freeman & Rogers, 1993).

Employee groups around the dimension of class are strikingly absent from the organizational landscape. In part, it may be because unions have played that role. But more likely, their absence stems from the silence and denial surrounding class or the lack of a language of pride about working-class status or origins. Sometimes class enters sideways. For example, in one large insurance company, a veterans group was formed that linked working-class white and black men (those mostly likely to have served in the military).

These employee groups often seek better treatment and advancement opportunities for their members. Occasionally they tackle more radical agendas to transform organizations (Scully & Segal, 2002). Groups formed around a class identity might have a particularly radical project – for example, one that addresses not how to advance, but why there are advancement ladders and steep pay differentials in the first place (Blake-Beard et al., 2004). Taking class seriously prompts a critique of capitalism that does not necessarily follow from taking other dimensions of diversity seriously, a provocative claim elaborated by Acker (1999). Part of the mainstream project for women and others who differ from the white, male, heterosexual dominant worker is to 'fit in' and appear an unthreatening and loyal employee. But to discuss class – even to name it – is already to look like a renegade and to move down a path toward critique of the fundamental organization of work and the distribution of gains in a capitalist society.

Dissent and social change are the ultimate objects of interest for many researchers who incorporate class into their analyses. This chapter has focused on potential grassroots efforts from the working class, but two other agents in the force field must be considered. First, not all the impetus must come from the working class. Members of the elite can and should be allies in redressing inequality – and very occasionally are (Rothenberg & Scully, 2002). Second, against these change efforts, significant strategic prowess is exerted by organizations to anticipate and counter political contestation from inside and outside, an element of organizational 'strategy' evident from a critical or class-anchored perspective (Levy, 2004). Many of the concepts and issues introduced in this chapter – legitimation of inequality, class consciousness, fragmentation and individualization of the working class, assimilation into middle- and upper-class style, etc. – have been developed and invoked precisely to explain why so little dissent and change happens. At the same time, this chapter also shows that there are opportunities for workers to confront the inequities of class on many levels (workplace, organizational and societal), tackling many sources of class reproduction (economic, ideological and organizational) and employing many tactics (forging alliances across differences, reasserting labor's legitimate contributions and desert, linking local concerns to broader societal issues, etc.).

IN CLOSING: AN EMANCIPATORY VISION

If we take these three approaches to class together, with the many issues that arise under the rubric of class analysis, what do we have? The result may be a way of seeing hidden inequality, looking at the deep origins of inequality, and seeking remedies that arise from and respect people from across class positions. In an anthropology course on class analysis at Stanford University in the 1980s, Donham (1999) asked what the disparate treatments of class had in common. What held together a set of works that could be called class analyses? The answer that emerged was that they shared a commitment to the 'emancipatory project' – lightening the load for oppressed workers, valuing all kinds of work, and sharing the dividends of labor more justly across all members of society.

NOTE

We thank David Levy and Pushi Prasad for very helpful comments, as well as the National Science Foundation grant IIS – 0085725 for support.

REFERENCES

Abercrombie, N., Hill, S., & Turner, B. S. (1980). *The dominant ideology thesis.* London: Allen & Unwin.

Acker, J. (1990). Hierarchies, jobs, bodies: A theory of gendered organizations. *Gender and Society, 4*(2), 139–58.

Acker, J. (1999). *Revisiting class: Lessons from theorizing race and gender in organizations* (Working Paper No. 5). Boston, MA: Center for Gender in Organizations, Simmons School of Management.

Adler, P. S., & Borys, B. (1996). Two types of bureaucracy: Enabling and coercive. *Administrative Science Quarterly, 41*, 61–89.

Annas, P. (1993). Pass the cake: The politics of gender, class, and text in the academic workplace. In M. M. Tokarczyk & E. A. Fay (Eds), *Working-class women in the academy: Laborers in the knowledge factory* (pp. 165–78). Boston, MA: University of Massachusetts Press.

Apted, M. (2004). The up series (7 up/7 plus seven/14 up/21 up/35 up/42 up). DVD: First Run Features.

Barley, S. R., & Bechky, B. (1994). In the back rooms of science: Notes on the work of science technicians. *Work and occupations, 21*, 85–126.

Baron, J. N. (1984). Organizational perspectives on stratification. *Annual Review of Sociology, 10*, 37–69.

Baron, J. N., Davis-Blake, A., & Bielby, W. T. (1986). The structure of opportunity: How promotion ladders vary within and among organizations. *Administrative Science Quarterly, 31*, 248–273.

Bell, E. L. J., & Nkomo, S. M. (2001). *Our separate ways: Black and white women and the struggle for professional identity.* Boston, MA: Harvard Business School Press.

Bernstein, B. (1977). Social class, language and socialization. In J. Karabel & A. H. Halsey (Eds), *Power and ideology in education* (pp. 473–86). Cambridge: Cambridge University Press.

Blake-Beard, S., Felicio, D., & Scully, M. (2004). Climbing the ladder or kicking it over: Bringing class and mentoring into critical contact. Manuscript.

Bok, D. (1993). *The cost of talent: How executives and professionals are paid and how it affects America*. New York: Free Press.

Bourdieu, P. (1977). Cultural reproduction and social reproduction. In J. Karabel & A. H. Halsey (Eds), *Power and ideology in education*. Cambridge: Cambridge University Press.

Bourdieu, P., & Passeron, J. C. (1977). *Reproduction in education, society, and culture*. London: Sage.

Bowles, S., & Gintis, H. (1973). I.Q. in the U.S. class structure. *Social Policy*, January/February, 65–96.

Braverman, H. (1974). *Labor and monopoly capital: The degradation of work in the twentieth century*. New York: Monthly Review Press.

Brint, S., & Karabel, J. (1989). *The diverted dream: Community colleges and the promise of educational opportunity in America, 1900–1985*. New York: Oxford University Press.

Bullock, H. E. (2004). Class diversity in the workplace. In M. S. Stockdale & F. J. Crosby (Eds), *The psychology and management of workplace diversity*. Oxford: Blackwell.

Burawoy, M. (1980). *Manufacturing consent: Changes in the labor process under monopoly capitalism*. Chicago: University of Chicago Press.

Chang, G. (2000). *Disposable domestics: Immigrant women workers in the global economy*. Boston, MA: South End Press.

Collins, P. H. (1999). Reflections on the outsider within. *Journal of Career Development*, *26*(1), 85–8.

Creed, W. E. D., Scully, M. A. & Austin, J. (2002). Clothes make the person: The tailoring of legitimating accounts and the social construction of identity. *Organization Science*, *13*(5), 475–96.

Daniels, N. (1978). Merit and meritocracy. *Philosophy and Public Affairs*, *3*, 206–23.

Davis, K., & Moore, W. (1966). Some principles of stratification. In R. Bendix & S. M. Lipset (Eds), *Class, status, and power*. New York: Free Press.

Della Fave, L. R. (1980). The meek shall not inherit the earth: Self-evaluation and the legitimacy of stratification. *American Sociological Review*, *45*, 955–71.

Donham, D. L. (1999). *History, power, ideology: Central issues in Marxism and anthropology* (2nd edn). Berkeley, CA: University of California Press.

Edwards, R. (1979). *Contested terrain*. New York: Basic Books.

Ehrenreich, B. (2001). *Nickel and dimed: On (not) getting by in America*. New York: Metropolitan Books.

Ehrenreich, B., & Ehrenreich, J. (1971). The professional-managerial class. *Radical America, 11*(2).

Ehrenreich, B., & Hochschild, A. R. (Eds) (2004). *Global woman: Nannies, maids, and sex workers in the global economy*. New York: Owl Books.

Ely, R. J., & Meyerson, D. E. (2000). Theories of gender: A new approach to organizational analysis and change. In B. Staw & R. Sutton (Eds), *Research in Organizational Behavior*, *22*, 105–53.

Freeman, R. B., & Rogers, J. (1993). Who speaks for us? Employee representation in a nonunion labor market. In B. Kaufman, M. M. Kleiner, *Employee representation: Alternatives and future directions*. Madison, WI: Industrial Relations Research Association.

Gamson, W. A. (1992). *Talking politics*. Cambridge: Cambridge University Press.

Gamson, W. A. (1995). Hiroshima, the Holocaust, and the politics of exclusion: 1994 presidential address. *American Sociological Review*, *60*(1), 1–20.

Gibson-Graham, J. K., Resnick, S. A. & Wolff, R. D. (Eds) (2000). Introduction. *Class and its others.* Minneapolis: University of Minnesota Press.

Goldthorpe, J. H. (1969). *The affluent worker in the class structure.* Cambridge: Cambridge University Press.

Gordon, D. M., Edwards, R., & Reich, M. (1982). *Segmented work, divided workers.* London: Cambridge University Press.

Gouldner, A. W. (1954). *Patterns of industrial bureaucracy.* New York: Free Press.

Gouldner, A. W. (1980). *The two Marxisms: Contradictions and anomalies in the development of theory.* New York: Seabury Press.

Halaby, C. (1978). Bureaucratic promotion criteria. *Administrative Science Quarterly, 23,* 466–84.

Hawkins, P. R. (1969). Social class, the nominal group and reference. *Language and Society, 12*(2), 125–35.

Helgesen, S. (1995). *The female advantage.* New York: Currency.

Hoffer Gittell, J. (2003). *The Southwest Airlines way: Using the power of relationships to achieve high performance.* New York: McGraw-Hill.

Holvino, E. (2000). Class and gender in organizations. *CGO Insights No. 7.* Boston, MA: Center for Gender in Organizations, Simmons School of Management.

Holvino, E., & Scully, M. A. (2001). Bodies and shops: Whose sweat and whose equity? Paper presented in the Postcolonialism Stream of the Critical Management Studies Conference, Manchester, UK, July.

hooks, b. (2000). *Where we stand: Class matters.* New York: Routledge.

Hoyt, S. K. (1999). Mentoring with class: Connections between social class and developmental relationships in the academy. In A. J. Murrell, F. J. Crosby & R. J. Ely (Eds), *Mentoring dilemmas: Developmental relationships within multicultural organizations.* Malwah, NJ: Lawrence Erlbaum Associates.

Huber, J., & Form, W. (1973). *Income and ideology.* New York: Free Press.

Hyde, A. (1997). Employee identity caucuses in Silicon Valley: Can they transcend the boundaries of the firm? Paper presented to the Industrial Relations Research Association, Spring Meeting, New York.

Iacocca, L. (1984). *Iacocca: An autobiography.* New York: Bantam.

Jameson, F. (1982). *The political unconscious.* Ithaca, NY: Cornell University Press.

Jencks, C., Bartlett, S., Corcoran, M., Crouse, J., Eaglesfield, D., Jackson, G., McClelland, K., Mueser, P., Olneck, M., Schwartz, J., Ward, S., & Williams, J. (1979). *Who gets ahead? The determinants of economic success in America.* New York: Basic Books.

Jencks, C., Smith, M., Acland, H., Bane, M. J., Cohen, D., Gintis, H., Heyns, B., & Michelson, S. (1972). *Inequality: A reassessment of the effect of family and schooling in America.* New York: Harper.

Kadi, J. (1997). Homophobic workers or elitist queers? In S. Roffo (Ed.), *Queerly classed: Gay men and lesbians write about class.* Boston, MA: South End Press.

Katz, M. (1990). *Undeserving poor.* New York: Pantheon.

Khurana, R. (2002). *Searching for a corporate savior: The irrational quest for charismatic CEOs.* Princeton, NJ: Princeton University Press.

Laraña, E., Johnston, H., & Gusfield, J. (Eds) (1994). *New social movements: From ideology to identity.* Philadelphia: Temple University Press.

Lautsch, B., & Scully, M. (2004). *Restructuring time: Implications of work-hours reductions for the working class* (Working Paper No. 0018). Cambridge, MA: MIT Workplace Center.

Lenski, G. (1954). Status crystallization: A non-vertical dimension of social status. *American Sociological Review, 19*(4), 405–13.

Levy, D. (2004). Strategies of power: A critical reengagement with strategic practice. Manuscript.

Linder, M., & Nygaard, I. (1998). *Void where prohibited: Rest breaks and the right to urinate on company time.* Ithaca, NY: Cornell University Press.

Lorde, A. (1984). The master's tools will never dismantle the master's house. *Sister outsider: Essays and speeches* (pp. 110–13). Freedom, CA: The Crossing Press.

Luce, S. (2004). *Fighting for a living wage*. Ithaca, NY: Cornell ILR Press.

Mann, M. (1970). The social cohesion of liberal democracy. *American Sociological Review, 35*, 423–39.

Mann, M. (1973). *Consciousness and action among the Western working class*. New York: Macmillan.

Marsden, R. (1997). Class discipline: IR/HR and the normalization of the workforce. In P. Prasad, A. J. Mills, M. B. Elmes & A. Prasad (Eds), *Managing the organizational melting pot*. Thousand Oaks, CA: Sage.

Martin, J. (1982). The fairness of earnings differentials: An experimental study of the perceptions of blue collar works. *Journal of Human Resources, 17*, 110–22.

Martin, J., Brickman, P., & Murray, A. (1984). Moral outrage and pragmatism: Explanations for collective action. *Journal of Experimental Social Psychology, 20*, 484–96.

Martin, J., Scully, M., & Levitt, B. (1990). Injustice and the legitimation of revolution: Damning the past, excusing the present, and neglecting the future. *Journal of Personality and Social Psychology, 59*(2), 281–90.

Marx, K. (1967). *Capital: Vol. 3. The process of production as a whole*. New York: International Publishers.

Marx, K. (1970). *A contribution to the critique of political economy*. Moscow: Progress Publishers.

Marx, K. (1976). *Capital: Vol. 1. The process of capitalist production*. New York: International Publishers.

Marx, K., & Engels, F. (1962). Manifesto of the Communist Party. In *Karl Marx and Frederick Engels selected works*. Moscow: Foreign Languages Publishing House.

Marx, K., & Engels, F. (1970). *The German ideology*. London: International Publishers.

McAdam, D. (1988). Micromobilization contexts and recruitment to activism. In B. Klandermans, H. Kriesi & S. Tarrow (Eds), *From structure to action: Comparing social movement research across cultures* (pp. 125–54). Greenwich, CT: JAI Press.

McCarthy, J. D., & Zald, M. N. (1977). Resource mobilization and social movements: A partial theory. *American Journal of Sociology, 82*, 1212–41.

Miner, A. S. (1987). Idiosyncratic jobs in formalized organizations. *Administrative Science Quarterly, 32*(30), 327–51.

Murphy, K. R., & Cleveland, J. N. (1991). *Performance appraisal: An organizational perspective*. Boston: Allyn & Bacon.

Nord, W. R. (1974). The failure of current applied behavioral science: A Marxian perspective. *Journal of Applied Behavioral Science, 10*(4), 557–78.

Offe, C. (1985). *Disorganized capitalism: Contemporary transformations of work and politics*. Cambridge, MA: MIT Press.

Ostrower, F. (1995). *Why the wealthy give: The culture of elite philanthropy*. Princeton, NJ: Princeton University Press.

Padavic, I. (1991). Attractions of male blue-collar jobs for black and white women: Economic need, exposure, and attitudes. *Social Science Quaterly, 72*(1), 33–50.

Padavic, I., & Reskin, B. F. (1990). Men's behavior and women's interest in blue-collar jobs. *Social Problems, 37*(4), 613–28.

Parker, M., & Slaughter, J. (1988). *Unions and the team concept*. Boston, MA: South End Press.

Parrenas, R. S. (2001). *Servants of globalization: Women, migration, and domestic work*. Stanford, CA: Stanford University Press.

Piore, M. J. (1995). *Beyond individualism: How demands of the new identity groups challenge American political and economic life*. Cambridge, MA: Harvard University Press.

Prasad, P., & Prasad, A. (2000). Stretching the iron cage: The constitution and implications of routine workplace resistance. *Organization Science, 11*, 387–403.

Proudford, K. L., & Thomas, K. M. (1999). The organizational outsider within. *Journal of Career Development, 26*(1), 3–5.

Purser, G., Schalet, A., & Sharone, O. (2004). *Berkeley's betrayal: Wages and working conditions at Cal.* Berkely, CA: University Labour Research Project.

Rainwater, L. (1974). *What money buys: Inequality and the social meanings of income.* New York: Basic Books.

Reskin, B. F., & Roos, P. A. (1991). *Job queues, gender queues: Explaining women's inroads into male occupations.* Philadelphia: Temple University Press.

Rosenbaum, J. E. (1979). Tournament mobility: Career patterns in a corporation. *Administrative Science Quarterly, 24,* 220–21.

Rothenberg, S., & Scully, M. A. (2002). Mobilizing the wealthy in the fight against inequality. *Proceedings of the International Association of Business and Society (IABS).*

Rowe, M. (1990). Barriers to equality: The power of subtle discrimination to maintain unequal opportunity. *Employee Responsibilities and Rights Journal, 3*(2), 153–63.

Ryan, W. (1971). *Blaming the victim.* New York: Vintage Books.

Schwartz, P. (1996). *The art of the long view: Planning for the future in an uncertain world.* New York: Currency.

Scully, M. A. (1993). *Meritocratic ideology and the imperfect legitimation of inequality.* Doctoral dissertation, Stanford University.

Scully, M. A., & Preuss, G. (1994). The dual character of trust during workplace transformation. *Proceedings of the Industrial Relations Research Association,* 12–22.

Scully, M. A., & Segal, A. (2002). Passion with an umbrella: Grassroots activists in the workplace. *Research in the Sociology of Organizations, 19,* 125–68.

Sennett, R. (1992). *The fall of public man.* New York: W.W. Norton.

Sewell, W. H. (1985). Ideologies and social revolutions: Reflections on the French case. *Journal of Modern History, 57*(1), 57–85.

Stewman, S., & Konda, S. L. (1983). Careers and organizational labor markets. *American Journal of Sociology, 88*(4), 173–202.

Talcott, S. (2004). *Boston Globe,* 1 April, A1.

Taylor, F. W. (1911). *The principles of scientific management.* New York: Dover.

Thomas, D., & Ely, R. J. (1996). Making differences matter: A new paradigm for managing diversity. *Harvard Business Review, 74*(5), 64–90.

Thomas, R. J. (1994). *What machines can't do: Politics and technology in the industrial enterprise.* Berkeley, CA: University of California Press.

Thompson, E. P. (1968). *The making of the English working class.* London: Penguin.

Weber, M. (1978). *Economy and society: An outline of interpretive sociology* (G. Roth & C. Wittich, Eds). Berkeley, CA: University of California Press.

White, H. (1970). *Chains of opportunity: System models of mobility in organizations.* Cambridge, MA: Harvard University Press.

Wilson, W. J. (1977). *The declining significance of race: Blacks and changing American institutions.* Chicago: University of Chicago Press.

Wilson, W. J. (1990). *The truly disadvantaged: The inner city, the underclass, and public policy.* Chicago: University of Chicago Press.

Wright, E. O. (1985). *Classes.* London: Verso.

Zavella, P. (1991). Mujeres in factories: Race and class perspectives on women, work, and family. In M. di Leonardo (Ed.), *Gender at the crossroads of knowledge* (pp. 312–36). Berkeley, CA: University of California Press.

18

Outcomes of Appearance and Obesity in Organizations

MYRTLE P. BELL AND MARY E. MCLAUGHLIN

Is beauty more than skin deep? In some contexts, it is definitely perceived to be. Experimental research has shown that people rate slim, attractive targets more positively on many dimensions, including ability and motivation, than those deemed overweight or unattractive (Rothblum, Brand, Miller & Oetjen, 1990). These judgments apparently translate into behavior in the workplace. Further, unlike discrimination on some physical features such as race, sex or age, appearance discrimination is not generally illegal. Instead, such discrimination is perceived as legitimate, necessary and is a socially accepted, fairly common practice. Because physical appearance and weight are readily observable (as are race and sex), stereotyping on the basis of these factors also occurs readily (cf. Cleveland, Stockdale & Murphy, 2000). These stereotypes result in favoritism toward those deemed attractive and discrimination against those deemed unattractive and/or who are overweight, even when job requirements and performance are unrelated to physical attractiveness or thinness (Hamermesh & Biddle, 1994).

In this chapter, we review the literature on relationships between physical appearance (including attractiveness and weight) and treatment in organizations. We begin by broadly discussing research on the effects of appearance on organizational outcomes, including selection, placement and earnings. We discuss effects of physical attractiveness, dress, make-up and hairstyle as aspects of appearance. Next, although weight is a subset of appearance, because of the increasing numbers of people who are overweight or obese worldwide, and the strong negative connotations of excess weight in many contexts, we examine separately the effects of weight on job-related outcomes. Importantly, we consider the limited legislative protection against organizational discrimination based on weight and appearance and the intersection of demographic factors related to them. We end the chapter with recommendations for researchers and practitioners interested in the effects of appearance and organizational treatment.

APPEARANCE

Although beauty and physical attractiveness are imprecise terms, people recognize and agree upon their existence fairly easily and consistently (Cleveland et al., 2000; Hamermesh & Biddle, 1994). Indeed, as noted by Hamermesh and Biddle (p. 1175) 'within a culture at a point in time there is tremendous agreement on standards of beauty, and these standards change quite slowly'.[1] They report one study in which nearly 1300 people were categorized using five categories of strikingly handsome/beautiful, good looking/above average, average, below average or plain, or homely. Over three years of ratings by different raters, 35% of the targets were rated identically for each rating, and 93% of them were rated identically for two of the three years. The probability of such constancy occurring randomly was 'infinitesimally tiny' (p. 1177). Other research has shown similarities in perceptions of physical attractiveness across cultures (e.g. Etcoff, 1999; Langlois et al., 2000). For example, Marin (1984) found that black and white subjects rated black female faces similarly in attractiveness. Similarly, Asians, Hispanics and Anglo-Americans all rated pictures of black, white, Asian and Hispanic subjects similarly in attractiveness (Chen, Shaffer & Wu, 1997; Cunningham, Roberts, Barbee, Druen & Wu, 1995; Wheeler & Kim, 1997).

The relatively constant standards of beauty across time, and, to some extent, culture, race and ethnicity, disadvantage women, people of color and those with visible physical disabilities, in various contexts (e.g. Eagly, Ashmore, Makhijani & Longo, 1991; Feingold, 1990). People have higher expectations of attractive others; attractive people are perceived to be smarter, more honest, sociable and popular, to have higher self-esteem and to be more desirable as marriage and dating partners than less attractive people. There is evidence of similar stereotypes associated with attractiveness in non-Western cultures. For example, Shaffer, Crepaz and Sun (2000) reported similarities between Taiwanese and Americans in their judgments of traits associated with attractive people. These stereotypical perceptions may be activated in social and employment contexts and result in various benefits for those deemed attractive and disadvantages for those deemed unattractive. In addition to general employer preferences for attractive people, employees may experience unjust discrimination and prejudice because of explicit or implicit rules for attire, make-up, facial appearance and hairstyle. We discuss these and their relationships with gender, perceived sexual orientation and race in the following sections.

Effects of Appearance on Job-Related Outcomes

In a recent meta-analysis of the effects of physical attractiveness on several job-related outcomes, researchers found a weighted mean effect size of 0.37 for 68 studies published between 1975 and 1998 in various psychology, management and economic journals (Hosada, Stone-Romero & Coats, 2003). Attractiveness was positively associated with job-related outcomes including hiring, performance ratings and promotion. The attractiveness bias did not vary as a function of the amount of job-related information provided and was equally strong for male and female targets. Importantly, Hosada et al. noted that the degree of attractiveness bias had decreased in later studies.

In numerous and methodologically varied studies, researchers have found that attractiveness often positively influences entry-level employment decisions as well as long-term salary growth (e.g. Cash, Gillen & Burns, 1977; Dipboye, Arvey & Terpstra, 1977; Frieze, Olson & Russell, 1991; Heilman & Saruwatari, 1979; Riggio & Throckmorton, 1988; Snyder, Berscheid & Matwychuk, 1988). Using a United States and Canadian sample of full-time workers, Hamermesh and Biddle (1994) found both a salary premium for physical attractiveness and a salary penalty for 'plainness'. For both men and women, the plainness penalty of 5 to 10% was larger than the beauty premium. Frieze et al. (1991) investigated starting salaries and subsequent earnings for MBA graduates over 10 years. For men, ratings of beauty were correlated with both starting and subsequent salaries For women, beauty was not correlated with starting salaries; however, the earnings of more attractive women grew faster than earnings of less attractive women.

Although both attractive men and women fare better than their less attractive counterparts, physical attractiveness influences job-related outcomes differently for men and women. For women, the effect of physical attractiveness on job outcomes depends on applicant qualifications, job level and job type. Attractive women are advantaged in lower-level jobs and in jobs held predominantly by women but not at higher levels, in professional jobs or those perceived as men's jobs (Ancker-Johnson, 1975; Cleveland et al., 2000; Heilman & Stopeck, 1985; Jackson, 1983a; 1983b; Marlowe, Schneider & Nelson, 1996). Spencer and Taylor (1988) found that women's physical attractiveness detracted from perceptions of their managerial performance. In their study of attractiveness and corporate success, Heilman and Stopeck (1985) found that the successes of attractive women managers were attributed to external factors, rather than ability, but successes of attractive men managers were attributed to internal factors, such as competence. They suggested that the physical attractiveness of managerial women might activate negative stereotypes of femininity that are associated with lower intelligence or competence. Watkins and Johnston (2000) found that 180 undergraduate student participants rated attractive women 'applicants' higher than unattractive women when applicant qualifications were mediocre. Attractive applicants were not advantaged when qualifications were high. They noted that 'an attractive photograph attached to a mediocre resume made an applicant appear of as high quality as an applicant with a high quality resume' (p. 79). Finally, in Marlow et al.'s (1996) study, experienced (rather than new) managers exhibited slightly lower attractiveness and gender biases, but women applicants were 'routinely' disadvantaged, regardless of job qualifications.

Another physical attribute that may be related to job outcomes is height. In a review of the relationship between height and occupational success among men in academe, police work and sales, Hensley and Cooper (1987) reported a positive effect of height on obtaining a job, although height had little effect on job performance. In a study of working managers, Frieze, Olson and Good (1990) found that height had a positive effect on starting salaries for men, but not for women.

Appearance, Femininity and Sexuality

One mundane, yet consequential aspect of facial appearance, the use of make-up, interacts with issues of gender and sexuality. Dellinger and Williams (1997) conducted in-depth interviews with 20 women about the relationship between make-up and appearance at work. Women associated wearing make-up with being perceived as healthy, energetic, well rested and heterosexual. Some women in their sample reported wearing make-up to comply with heterosexual norms of feminine appearance. Lesbian women who wore make-up reported that they wore it so that they would not stand out, or be 'different' from the other women, in yet another way. One lesbian woman who did not wear make-up reported being denied a significant job opportunity, despite clearly being the top candidate for the position, because she was not 'feminine-looking enough'.

Different types of feminine appearance may be viewed as appropriate for different jobs. For example, waiting tables in a nightclub may demand a highly sexualized image, whereas working as a teacher in an elementary school may necessitate a 'mother image', with relatively less make-up. Extremes of both of those feminine images may be deemed inappropriate for professional and/or office employees, although some degree of attractive, feminine appearance may still be expected. When job decisions are made on them, these expectations, such as those of the lesbian woman discussed above, and in the Ann Hopkins case, discussed in the next section, may constitute illegal discrimination.

Prohibitions Against Appearance Discrimination

Requirements for professional appearance in jobs may be legitimate and job related or illegitimate and discriminatory. Because research has indicated that appearance requirements negatively affect women and, at times, racial and ethnic minorities, such requirements must be carefully scrutinized for illegal discrimination. In the US, Title VII of the Civil Rights Act of 1964 prohibits discrimination on the basis of sex, race, ethnicity and religion in employment matters. The Americans with Disabilities Act of 1990 (ADA) prohibits employment-related disability discrimination.

The widely cited case of Ann Hopkins is an example of how the use of femininity of appearance in job-related decision-making may constitute illegal sex discrimination.

Hopkins was a candidate for partner at Price-Waterhouse accounting firm. Her performance leading up to her candidacy was comparable to, or exceeded, that of her fellow (male) candidates for partner. Though she applied in two successive years, Hopkins was denied the partnership both times. A well-meaning partner who considered himself her friend told Hopkins that to increase her chances for promotion she should dress more femininely, wear make-up, style her hair and carry a briefcase instead of a purse. Following her second rejection for partner, Hopkins sued Price-Waterhouse. After lengthy litigation, the US Supreme Court ruled that Hopkins' treatment was illegal sex discrimination.

Numerous other employers have been sued about appearance requirements regarding hairstyle, facial hair and dress codes when those requirements resulted in race, ethnic, sex or religious discrimination. Recently, an employee who was repeatedly harassed about her hair color sued Enterprise Rent-A-Car, long noted for its strict dress codes (including 26 rules for men and 30 for women). The plaintiff, who had been fired, asserted that Enterprise managers told her that the color of her hair was not of her 'own ethnic origin', and was thus prohibited by Enterprise (Hwang, 2003). After the EEOC filed a lawsuit on behalf of a Muslim employee, Federal Express modified its long-standing policy of prohibiting beards. The company now allows employees with 'sincerely held' religious beliefs that require beards or certain hairstyles to request an exception to the company's dress code (Creighton, 2002). Similarly, Alamo Rent-A-Car and Jean Louis David Salons have been sued and have agreed to modify their policies regarding dress codes that conflict with employees' religious beliefs (Creighton, 2002).

A few US cities have implemented regulations against appearance discrimination, without requirements for concurrent discrimination on the basis of sex, race, ethnic or religious or other already prohibited areas. The city of Washington, DC prohibits discrimination on 'personal appearance', described as 'the outward appearance of any person, irrespective of sex, with regard to bodily condition or characteristics, manner or style of dress, and manner or style of personal grooming, including, but not limited to, hair style and beards' (Solovay, 2000: 244). Madison, Wisconsin also forbids discrimination on the basis of physical appearance, including hairstyle, beards, manner of dress, height, weight or facial features. Requirements for cleanliness, uniforms or certain prescribed attire are permissible when necessary for reasonable business purposes and when applied consistently.

Despite the limited specific legislation prohibiting appearance discrimination and the successful use of other legislation that we have reported, most applicants and employees who experience appearance discrimination do not sue. As with other forms of discrimination, non-litigation related costs to both victims and employers may be unrecognized. As noted by Hosada et al. (2003), presentation of job-related information does not reduce the effects of attractiveness on job-related decisions, which may reduce organizational functioning. We now turn our focus to another aspect of appearance that has perhaps an even stronger influence on stereotyping and job-related decisions – obesity.

OBESITY

Definition and Prevalence[2]

Formal definitions of overweight and obesity are vague and fluid, reflecting variance in socially constructed perceptions and numerous attempts at greater precision by formal agencies. Overweight and obesity may be described by weight in pounds compared to height, or by percentages of body fat compared to lean muscle mass. On a continuum, overweight, obesity and morbid obesity are the least to most extreme, with the most to fewest numbers of people in each category. Some agencies (e.g. the US Centers for Disease Control – CDC; World Health Organizationon – WHO) formally define or describe only the category of obese, while others define overweight, obesity and morbidly obese. Although we provide the formal terminology and definitions of overweight, obese and morbidly obese, we also use the term 'fat', which is the preferred term among activists (e.g. National Association to Advance Fat Acceptance).

Obesity is defined by the CDC as having an excessively high amount of body fat in relation to lean body mass. It is also described as occurring when a person is at least 20% above the weight recommended for their height and gender (Roehling, 1999). *Morbid obesity* occurs when a person weighs 100 pounds (45 kg) more than, or double their recommended weight for actual height. In 1997, the WHO agreed on an international standard for measuring overweight and obesity based on the body mass index (BMI). The BMI is defined as weight (in kg divided by the square of one's height (in m) kg/m^2). Ranges for normal, overweight and obese BMI are 17 to 24.9, 25 to 29.9 and 30 or more, respectively.

Weight is increasing among people around the world, reflecting changes in transportation, work (reduced physical requirements), leisure activities (more sedentary activities), and types and quantities food consuption (more high-fat food, fewer fruits and vegetables) and quantities of food consumption. Of the more than 6 billion people worldwide, there are over 1 billion overweight adults (300 million of them are obese). More than half the adults in many countries are obese (WHO, 1997). In the United States, the percentage of obese Americans grew from 15% in 1980 to 27% in 1999, where an estimated 64% of American adults are overweight or obese (CDC, 2004). In most countries of Western Europe, 20–25% of adults are obese. Although many nations, such as China, Japan and parts of Africa, have obesity rates of less than 5%, certain cities in those countries have much higher rates of obesity (e.g. 20% in some cities in China). The WHO estimates that the highest rates of obesity in the world are among Melanesians, Micronesians and Polynesians, where up to 65% of men and 70% of women are obese.

Obesity and overweight vary by race/ethnicity, gender and age, compounding the effects of multiple aspects of diversity and increasing the possibility for marginalization of some groups in work settings. In the United States, 28.6% of African Americans, 21% of Hispanics and 18% of whites are obese. High rates of obesity also occur among Native Americans and Pacific Islanders (WHO, 1997).

Obesity affects 40% of all women in Eastern European and Mediterranean countries and in the United States about 40% of black, Hispanic and Native American women are obese. Older women are more likely to carry excess weight than are younger women: about 70% of women between 45 and 54 years of age are overweight or obese; only 30% fall into the 'normal' weight category (Racette, Deusiner & Deusiner 2003).

Although men have higher incidences of overweight (e.g. somewhat fat), women are more likely to be obese (e.g. very fat). As a result of the greater percentages of obese women, people of color and older people, obesity discrimination, which is legal for the most part, may have an adverse impact on these groups, creating additional risks for employers. Researchers have also considered the discriminatory effects of using insurance weight tables for determining 'normal' weights. These tables were created using weights of middle-class whites whose weights are lower than poor people of color, which is inherently problematic (see Kristen, 2002).

Effects of Weight on Costs to Employers

Being overweight is associated with higher risks for certain health problems, including hypertension, high cholesterol, heart disease, diabetes, musculoskeletal disorders, respiratory problems and certain cancers (Maranto & Stenoien, 2000; Martin, Leary & Rejeshi, 2000; WHO, 1997). Estimates suggest that obese employees cost US employers 15% more in prescription drug costs 55% more in short-term disability costs, and 20% more in long-term disability costs than non-obese employees (Wolf & Colditz, 1998). Wolf and Colditz estimate that over 39 million work days are lost in the United States each year due to obesity. For countries that have national health insurance, funded by taxes (e.g. Australia, Canada, New Zealand, etc.), the costs of obesity are in the societal domain. For employer-funded health care, however, fears of increased medical or benefits costs or absence are often cited as reasons for preferring employees who are not overweight. Such concerns appear legitimate on the surface, but may simply camouflage disdain for or prejudice against those who are obese, particularly when fears of increased costs or absence due to smoking, excessive alcohol consumption or other invisible factors are not similarly expressed. Further, it appears that fat people who exercise and eat properly (but remain fat) may be healthier than slim people who do not exercise or eat properly. In addition, according to the WHO (1997), the complications of excess weight are particularly common in those with high abdominal circumference. Women are more likely to have larger hip, rather than abdominal, circumference, yet they experience more employment discrimination related to obesity than men, again questioning the validity of claims of fears of increased health risks associated with employing obese workers.

The inconsistent concerns about health issues expressed by employers, coupled with other negative acts toward the obese, attest to the general disdain toward those who are fat. Their work experiences (e.g. overt discrimination, open ridicule, public humiliation, being called a 'fat slob' or pressured to lose weight) attest to the social acceptability of expressing of anti-fat attitudes (Solovay, 2000). Rather than being fat, people have expressed preferences for being mean, stupid, being run over by a truck, losing limbs and even death (e.g. National Education Association, 1994; Solovay, 2000: p. 57, citing Gaesser, 1996; Staffieri, 1967).

Prejudice and Discrimination against Overweight People

Persons who are overweight often experience negative employment outcomes and may be considered personally responsible for their weight, lazy, lacking in self-control and discipline, and incompetent (e.g. Kristen, 2002; Larkin & Pines, 1979; Puhl & Brownell, 2003), all attributes that are undesirable in employment contexts. These negative perceptions persist despite research suggesting that weight is a result of genetic factors as well as behavior and environment (Angier, 1997; CDC, 2001). The misguided, erroneous perceptions of overweight people as lazy, incompetent and lacking in self-control apparently contribute to their differential treatment in organizations.

If hired, persons who are obese are often assigned to non-visible jobs, receive more disciplinary actions, have their performance evaluated more negatively, and earn less when compared to non-obese employees (Bellizzi & Hasty, 1998; Register & Williams, 1990; Rothblum et al., 1990). In a large-scale study using the National Longitudinal Survey of Youth, Pagan and Davila (1997) found that overweight women earned less than slim women, but overweight men did not earn less than slim men. Their analyses showed that fat women were more segregated into lower paying occupations than were slim women, while fat men were more dispersed into higher paying occupations. In Gortmaker et al.'s (1993) longitudinal study of over 10,000 randomly selected participants, overweight women had completed less schooling, earned nearly $7000 less annually, had 10% higher rates of poverty, and were 20% less likely to be married than women who were not overweight. Again, consequences for fat women were more negative than those for fat men; fat men were 11% less likely to be married than normal weight men, but experienced none of the other negative consequences experienced by fat women. Register and Williams (1990) found that young women (but not men) who were 20% or more over their standard weight for height earned 12% less than non-obese women.

Experimental research also supports the survey data showing disadvantages in education, job and compensation levels associated with heavier weight. Studies show that overweight people are evaluated more harshly than are normal weight people. For example, Jasper and Klassen (1990) found that their sample of college students rated obese salespeople more negatively than non-obese salespeople and the negative effects of obesity were stronger for female than male salespeople. Bellizzi and Hasty (2000) also found more negative consequences for overweight women in sales than for overweight men. In another experiment using sales managers, Bellizzi and Hasty (1998) found discrimination against fat people in job assignments and discipline. And, in a simulated work setting, Larkin and Pines (1979) found that college student participants were biased against hiring overweight job applicants, despite performance on physical and mental selection tests equal to that of normal weight applicants.

Finally, there is evidence of biases against people who associate with, or who are simply in physical proximity of, overweight people (Hebl & Mannix, 2003). Participants in two experiments rated a male job applicant more negatively when he was seen with an overweight female as compared with a normal weight female. Negative effects of proximity to an overweight female were found regardless of perceived depth of relationship to the female and amount of positive information presented about her. It is possible recruiters might not give strong consideration to an obese job candidate, despite strong job qualifications, because of a conscious or unconscious unwillingness to be associated with obese people, or to work in an organization that is associated with obese employees.

Cross-cultural Differences in Reactions to Obesity within the United States

In the United States, blacks have stronger preferences for heavier women than do whites (Collins, 1991; Cunningham et al., 1995; Jackson & McGill, 1996). Older black women who are obese report being more satisfied with their weight than older obese white women (Stevens, Kumanyika & Keil, 1994). Finally, white women judge overweight women more negatively (in terms of attractiveness, intelligence, job success, relationship success, happiness and popularity) than do black women, and the racial differences in judgments are especially pronounced when white and black women judge women of their own race (Hebl & Heatherton, 1998). Although these differences are noteworthy, because black women (and other women of color) are less likely to be in decision-making (e.g. hiring manager) positions, their lower proclivity to stereotype fat people likely has little impact on fat applicants and employees.

Relevant Legislation Prohibiting Weight-based Discrimination

Very little legislation prohibiting weight-based discrimination exists, and this absence of protective legislation may facilitate expression of and acting upon anti-fat attitudes. Compared to discrimination on the basis of sex, race, ethnicity or religion, in the United States, no federal legislation clearly and directly prohibits discrimination on the basis of obesity. One state and a limited number of cities currently prohibit *any* non-job related weight-based discrimination, including Michigan, Washington, DC, Madison, WI, Santa Cruz, CA and San Francisco, CA. The Michigan statute, known as the Elliot–Larson Civil Rights Act, covers discrimination on the basis of height and weight, among other factors. This statute has been credited with producing nearly 200 weight discrimination complaints in its first 10 years (Martin, 1994) and providing some recourse for targets of weight discrimination. Although the states of New York and Texas have considered bills to bar weight discrimination, neither state has passed such a bill (Martin, 1994).

At a federal level, protections for fat people are extremely narrow. In some cases, obese people may be protected from employment-related discrimination under the Rehabilitation Act of 1973 (RHA) or the ADA. The RHA prohibits discrimination against people with disabilities by federal contractors and recipients of federal financial assistance. The ADA prohibits such discrimination by state and local governments and private employers of 15 people or more. A person is deemed to be disabled if he or she currently has, has a record of having, or is perceived as having a physical or mental impairment that substantially limits one or more major life activities. Thus, the RHA and the ADA prohibit discrimination against persons who are disabled or who are perceived to be disabled, including those whose excess weight contributes to their disabilities or perceptions that they have a disability. Importantly, if an employee or applicant is *perceived to be* more likely to have health problems, or to miss work because of obesity, and is treated differently because of this perception, this may constitute illegal discrimination (Solovay, 2000).

Morbid obesity clearly qualifies as a disability under the RHA and ADA, but most overweight people are not morbidly obese. Indeed, someone could be extremely obese but technically not morbidly obese; only about 1% of the US population is morbidly obese. For these people, there are no federal protections against job-related discrimination because overweight and non-morbid obesity *alone* are not covered disabilities. Even though the morbidly obese are technically covered under the ADA, the courts have been reluctant to rule in plaintiffs' favor (see Solovay, 2000, for discussions), accentuating the need for other actions or statutes. Further, the wording of the ADA that prohibits discrimination on the basis of a 'perceived disability' may actually serve to motivate overt appearance discrimination rather than deter it. That is, instead of employers expressing concerns that an applicant may have health problems or higher absence due to their weight, which may be construed as illegal, employers may instead be more willing to express concerns with the applicant's appearance.

As discussed earlier, some acts now *specifically* prohibit discrimination on the basis of *personal appearance*. These prohibitions against weight and appearance discrimination vary from human or civil rights statutes to employment laws, and are enforced by the local or state courts or various city commissions. For fat employees and others whose appearance differs from what is perceived as attractive or desirable, these state and local statutes may provide some recourse. In addition, some state disability laws (e.g. New York, New Jersey) are more strenuous than the ADA and have been used successfully by fat plaintiffs (Martin, 1994).

Key Cases under Federal and Local Statutes in the United States

As obesity is becoming more of a worldwide issue, US court cases and interpretations may be useful to other countries as they develop laws to address similar issues. One of the earliest and most often cited court cases to be decided in the obese plaintiff's favor was *Cook v State of Rhode Island Department of Mental Health, Retardation, and Hospitals* (1993). The plaintiff, Bonnie Cook, was 5'3" (1.6 m) and weighed over 300 pounds (136 kg) when she applied for re-employment at the state of Rhode Island, for whom Cook had been successfully employed twice before. Despite her previous satisfactory performance, Cook was denied re-employment based on her weight and the employer's perceptions that she could not perform well and would be more likely to be absent because of her weight. Cook sued under the RHA, and the courts ruled that she was morbidly obese due to physiological conditions, as well as being perceived as having a disability due to obesity, and thus was protected from weight-related employment discrimination.

An early case under San Francisco's prohibition against discrimination on the basis of body size (*regardless of* perceived or real disability) provides a striking example of the need for such legislation to protect those who are fat, but clearly qualified to perform the job. Jennifer Portnick, a physically fit woman who was 5'8" (1.72 m) and weighed 240 pounds (109 kg), applied to audition to be a certified Jazzercise instructor. Despite her size, Portnick had been participating in and teaching high-impact aerobics for 15 years, and had demonstrated such ability at Jazzercise that her teacher, a Jazzercise employee, encouraged her to become certified. Portnick clearly was 'fat and fit', contradicting beliefs that it is impossible to be so. Even though she was qualified and strongly recommended, Jazzercise management would not allow Portnick the opportunity to try out for certification as a Jazzercise instructor. Portnick was told that 'Jazzercise sells fitness' and to lose weight because she needed to *appear* leaner (Fernandez, 2002). The case was settled in May of 2002 when Jazzercise Inc. agreed to evaluate instructors on their competence rather than on their appearance.

Other notable fat discrimination cases include Toni Cassista's experience with Community Foods, a health food store in Santa Cruz, CA (which led to the anti-appearance discrimination act in that city; *Cassita v Community Foods, Inc.*); *Ross v Beaumont Hospital* (1988), involving an obese physician who also had performance problems unrelated to her weight; and, *Fairchild v Coca-Cola*, involving egregious discrimination from management and coworkers (Irvine, 1997). Several researchers have compiled thorough analyses of court decisions regarding fat discrimination and indicated the unwillingness of some courts to rule in favor of plaintiffs despite evidence that plaintiffs were perceived as disabled or egregious behavior toward plaintiffs by employers (e.g. Kristen, 2002; Martin, 1994), leading to arguments that weight should be considered a protected class under the ADA (e.g. Johnson & Wilson, 1995; Kristen, 2002; Ziolkowski, 1994).

Should Overweight be a Protected Class?

In arguments for classifying excess weight as a disability, proponents suggest that even if obesity were completely under volitional control, so too are other conditions that cause other disabling health problems (such as smoking, which causes most lung cancer). Because discrimination against employees and applicants who have disabilities due to these and other voluntary behaviors is prohibited, so also should discrimination against fat people (see for discussions Kristen, 2002; Solovay, 2000). These arguments are even more convincing given researchers' failure to document consistent performance differences between overweight people and thin people.

Ziolkowski (1994) recommended that the 'EEOC reconsider its position concerning weight discrimination and amend its regulations to address overweight conditions reaching the level of obesity, defined broadly as twenty to thirty per cent above ideal weight' (p. 684). He and other researchers have argued that because excess weight is (1) associated with higher risks for certain medical conditions, that it is (2) hard to lose and keep off, and that (3) weight discrimination is prevalent, overweight people may indeed have a case for being included as a protected class (Johnson & Wilson, 1995; Kristin, 2002; Ziolkowski, 1994). In other words, because obesity is a permanent, possibly life-threatening condition and people 'suffering' with this condition experience discrimination because of it, as do people with other disabilities, obesity should be a protected class. Although these arguments were specifically applicable to US law, similar arguments could be made for other countries having anti-discrimination legislation or other protection for groups that often experience job-related discrimination.

CONCEPTUAL ISSUES RELEVANT TO APPEARANCE AND OBESITY DISCRIMINATION

A review of the literature on prejudice and discrimination reveals striking similarities between race, sex and age discrimination and discrimination on the basis of weight and appearance. Researchers have suggested that experiences of overweight and unattractive people may be based upon stigma or symbolic fatism, which we consider in the following sections.

Stigma

Research indicates that persons whose appearance or attributes differ from expectations for typical or 'normal' others in a context may be stigmatized and experience negative employment outcomes (Goffman, 1963; Phelan, 2001; Puhl & Brownell, 2003; Stone, Stone & Dipboye, 1992). A key consideration in determining the applicability of stigmatization to the negative experiences of those who are overweight or unattractive is the perception of 'normal'. According to Stone et al. (1992: 389), '*normal* means conforming to expectations about what is usual, typical, or standard. What is considered normal differs from one person, context, and time period to the next' (emphasis in original). Thus, the question of 'what is normal?' is a legitimate one.

Weight and Cultural Differences

In the United States, within the last 50 years, thinness has become preferred, with female models and beauty queens growing increasingly thinner and increasingly further from the proportions and weight of most women. This preference for thinness persists, even though Americans are growing larger and larger. If the process of stigmatization were based solely on deviance from the 'usual, typical, or standard' and this standard became larger, those who are thin, rather than heavy, should be stigmatized. This does not appear to be happening, which calls into question the applicability of the deviation from the standard as a major cause of stigmatization. What instead appears to occur is that stigmatization occurs when the target (job applicant, for example) *deviates from the ideal or preferred* target rather than from the normal target. Thus, even though the US population is increasingly more overweight, perceivers still prefer to hire those who are not overweight. The *ideal*, against which people are judged, is simply not fat in the United States.

In addition to cross-cultural differences within the United States in reactions to obesity, in some other countries, being overweight is viewed as desirable, often representing wealth and affluence. In those cases, overweight is perceived as preferred to being thin. It appears that in economically developed countries, people of higher socio-economic status tend to be thinner, but in less developed countries, people of higher socio-economic status tend to be fatter (Schneider, 2004). Poor people in less developed countries are less able to afford enough high-calorie food to become fat (Schneider, 2004). Thus, people from underdeveloped countries tend to evaluate overweight people more positively and thinner people less positively than do people in more Westernized countries (Cogan, Bhalla, Sefa-Dedeh & Rothblum, 1996; Furnham & Alibhai, 1983; Furnham & Baguma, 1994). We expect that stigmatization in such countries would reflect preferences for an ideal that was heavier, rather than thinner.

Appearance

As with weight, stigmatization on the basis of appearance seems to be more related to the preferences for an 'ideal', rather than preferences for appearance that is 'normal'. In the United States preferences for white, male, attractive workers in high-status jobs suggest this as the 'ideal'. As discussed earlier, ratings of attractiveness exhibit some constancy across cultures, and the preference for male workers in higher-status jobs is well documented around the world. In other jobs, the 'ideal' worker may be women, people of color, as job appropriate and deviance from expectations for this ideal likely results in stigmatization and discrimination.

Symbolic Fatism

In addition to stigma, researchers have suggested that biases against the overweight may stem from 'symbolic fatism', or symbolic, rather than instrumental, anti-fat attitudes (e.g. Crandall, 1994). Symbolic fatism shares some of the same characteristics of symbolic racism (see Kinder & Sears, 1981), such as the belief that group members do not possess self-discipline and self-reliance, and the association of prejudice with intolerance and authoritarianism. In other words, symbolic fatism is associated with attribution of blame to overweight people for their condition, and a lack of tolerance and a dislike of social deviance from ideal norms. One criticism of symbolic fatism as an explanation for the experiences of overweight people, however, is that whereas symbolic racism likely emerged from overt, 'old-fashioned' racism when racist attitudes became viewed as socially unacceptable, in the United States anti-fat attitudes are still 'overt, expressible, and widely held' (Crandall, 1994). Overt discriminatory acts of race and sex discrimination are likely to be met with organizational and interpersonal sanctions, while fat discrimination is often overt, expressible and widely held. Rather than being symbolic, fatism may instead simply be old-fashioned fatism.

Summary of Appearance and Weight-Related Discrimination

We have reviewed the literature on appearance, including attractiveness and weight in organizations, documenting the existence of employment discrimination on these factors and considering the need for broad anti-discrimination legislation. In general, unattractive and fat people are less likely to be employed, more likely to be assigned to non-visible jobs and earn less than attractive and thin people, even though for most jobs, weight and beauty have little or no effects on performance. In contrast to other dimensions of diversity, appearance discrimination and weight discrimination have the ability to affect nearly everyone at some point. The large number of people who are or may be affected by these issues signals the importance of organizational efforts to curb these discriminatory behaviors that are not job related.

Of special consideration are the intersections between weight and other factors, such as age, race, ethnicity and gender. As people age, attractiveness declines and weight increases; everyone has the potential to become physically unattractive or gain weight. Further, obesity and appearance issues intersect with gender and ethnicity; women of color tend to be heavier than white women, making issues of adverse impact of special concern for organizations. Similarly, poor women tend to be heavier than more affluent women, making class issues yet another factor to be considered.

Recommendations for Practice

Given that professional appearance is justifiable in many situations, organizations should focus on legitimate requirements rather than capricious ones that may negatively affect women, people of color, members of certain religious groups or obese people. Any requirements for 'professional appearance' should be scrutinized for the possibility of adverse impact upon certain groups. In addition, the commonly recommended practice of education and training to reduce stereotypes and misperceptions may be marginally effective for appearance and weight discrimination. Even so, as part of diversity training, employees should learn that many fat people are not fat due to overeating, lack of exercise or laziness, but instead may be fat due to metabolic, genetic and/or medical factors. Regardless of the cause of excess weight, training should emphasize that weight is not correlated with job performance; therefore job-related decisions should generally not be made on the basis of weight.

Controlled, employer-sanctioned, interactions (e.g. based on contact theory) are also often suggested for the reduction of prejudice. As have effects of other surface-level diversity (e.g. race, sex), the effects of physical attractiveness on liking and interpersonal interactions may decline after people have had time to interact with each other. It is possible, however, that negative perceptions of obese coworkers may be very resistant to change, even when legitimate performance information available, particularly given the anecdotal evidence of Bonnie Cook's experience at the state of Rhode Island. If so, employers may need to institute more concerted methods to reduce appearance and weight discrimination. Such measures might include independent reviews of interviews, performance evaluations, and promotional recommendations such as are used in attempts to remedy or prevent race or sex discrimination. Employers should also provide mechanisms to ensure that qualifications are reviewed thoroughly and documented prior to interviews, where stereotyping and discrimination may occur.

Employers should strongly emphasize decision-making on job-related factors, which would help reduce appearance and weight discrimination, as well as other forms of discrimination (e.g. race, sex, age, disability, etc.). Increased reliance on objective sources of job-related criteria rather than subjective, and potentially biased, information should help reduce the potential for discrimination on the basis of appearance and weight. Although these recommendations seem elementary, they are needed, as non-job-related discrimination on various factors persists.

Finally, we suggest that organizations add 'weight' and 'personal appearance' to their anti-discrimination and harassment policies. Making a zero-tolerance policy inclusive of weight and appearance would send a strong signal to both managers and other employees that the organization values workers who are diverse in these regards. This would also send a signal to overweight and less attractive applicants (who may be underutilized in other organizations) that the organization would be a good place to consider working. Cox and Blake's (1991) suggestion that valuing diversity may make organizations more attractive as employers to otherwise devalued workers is also applicable to weight and appearance diversity.

Suggestions for Researchers

Researchers interested in this topic have much to consider. Because obesity crosses race, gender, ethnic and other boundaries, research is needed on the influences of multiple group membership for persons who are obese. Weight gain increases with age, therefore researchers must consider the relative effects of membership in multiple groups with varying degrees of perceived negativity. Is age-associated weight gain more negative for white males (dominant group members) or women of color (non-dominant group members)? As research has fairly consistently found that men are less negatively affected by excess weight than women (e.g. Gortmaker et al., 1993; Pagan & Davila, 1997), we expect this to continue, even as men age. What employment experiences are likely for an older, obese, black lesbian? We expect that because black women tend to be heavier than white women, their extra weight would not be held against them as much as it would white women, reducing (though not overcoming) white women's employment advantages somewhat.

What can be learned about obesity and appearance discrimination from what is already known about other aspects of diversity (e.g. race, ethnicity, gender)? For example, future researchers should investigate which factors, if any, may cause effects of surface-level diversity in physical attractiveness or weight to lessen. What existing theories about stigma and 'isms' can be used to help inform researchers about treatment of unattractive or obese people at work? Recent empirical investigations of the applicability of the theory of reasoned action and the applicability of stigma theory to understanding the treatment of obese workers may provide useful information and stimulate further theory-based research (e.g. Stringer, Bell, McMahan & Davis, 2004; Wilkins, 2004).

Are stereotypes and liking based on appearance and overweight more resistant to counter-information than stereotypes based on race and sex? It appears that stigma associated with these surface factors may be more long lasting (e.g. Albrecht, Walker & Levy, 1982; Jacoby, 1994; Rodin & Price, 1995). Finally, stigma theory suggests that deviance from the norm results in stigmatization and disparate treatment. As the population grows fatter, and thus the true norm changes, will stigmatization and discrimination against fat people decrease? Mass media have been attributed with promoting a thin body standard for women (Silverstein, Perdue, Peterson & Kelly, 1986). What effects do representations in the media have on perceptions of the 'norm' as weight increases? Are more fat people being represented well in responsible and varied positions in commercials, television and movies? If so, does this reduce weight-based stigma?

Research on treatment of people with disabilities indicates that persons with disabilities that are perceived as self-caused are treated more negatively in organizations than persons with genetically caused disabilities (e.g. Bordieri, Drehmer & Taricone, 1990; Florey & Harrison, 2000). To what extent does the perception that obesity is self-caused and controllable contribute directly to stigmatization and discrimination against persons who are obese? If presented with information that obesity is determined to some extent by genetic factors (e.g. is not under people's volitional control), is prejudice and discrimination against obese people reduced? Do similarities exist between prejudice and discrimination against gays, lesbians and persons who are fat due to perceptions of choice?

The broad societal issues associated with weight and appearance discrimination and increasing weight of the world's population make further, rigorous study of these issues paramount. As with other issues of unfairness in organizations, researchers have the opportunity to inform practice, and affect laws and judicial decisions, thereby affecting lives of numerous applicants and employees.

NOTES

1 The notation that 'within a culture' at a point in time, standards are stable is an important point. What is considered beautiful varies by culture somewhat, yet reactions to deviance from the standard of beauty are similar across cultures.

2 We use the terms 'overweight', 'obese', 'morbidly obese' or 'fat' in this chapter as appropriate when reporting research or in describing research protections; however, consistent with perceptions and other researchers, we use those terms generally and without regard to specific criteria in other parts of the chapter.

REFERENCES

Albrecht, G. L., Walker, V. G., & Levy, J. A. (1982). Social distance from the stigmatized. *Social Science & Medicine, 16,* 1319–27.

Ancker-Johnson, B. (1975). Physicist. *Educational Horizons, 53,* 116–21.

Angier, N. (1997). Researchers link obesity in humans to flaw in genes. *New York Times,* 1 December, A1, A8.

Bellizzi, J. A., & Hasty, R. W. (1998). Territory assignment decisions and supervising unethical selling behavior: The effects of obesity and gender as moderated by job-related factors. *Journal of Personal Selling and Sales Management, 18,* 35–49.

Bellizzi, J. A., & Hasty, R. W. (2000). Does successful work experience mitigate weight and gender-based employment discrimination in face-to-face industrial selling? *Journal of Business and Industrial Marketing, 15*(6), 384–98.

Bordieri, J. E., Drehmer, D. E., & Taricone, P. F. (1990). Personnel selection bias for job applicants with cancer. *Journal of Applied Social Psychology, 20,* 244–53.

Cash, T. F., Gillen, P., & Burns, S. D. (1977). Sexism and 'beautyism' in personnel consultant decision-making. *Journal of Applied Psychology, 62,* 301–10.

Cassista v *Community Foods, Inc.,* 856, P. 2d 1143, 1144 (Cal. 1993).

Centers for Disease Control (CDC, 2001). Basics about overweight and obesity. United States Department of Health and Human Services: Centers for Disease Control and Prevention.

Centers for Disease Control (CDC, 2004). Overweight and obesity: Defining overweight and obesity: http://www.cdc.gov/nccdphp/dnpa/obesity/defining.htm (Accessed 5 April 2004).

Chen, N. Y., Shaffer, D. R., & Wu, C. (1997). On physical attractiveness stereotyping in Taiwan: A revised sociocultural perspective. *Journal of Social Psychology, 137,* 117–24.

Cleveland, J. N., Stockdale, M., & Murphy, K. R. (2000). Physical attractiveness, interpersonal relationships, and romance at work. In J. N. Cleveland, M. Stockdale & K. R. Murphy (Eds), *Women and men in organizations: Sex and gender issues at work* (pp. 67–76). Mahwah, NJ: Lawrence Erlbaum.

Cogan, J. C., Bhalla, S. K., Sefa-Dedeh, A., & Rothblum, E. D. (1996). A comparison study of United States and African students on perceptions of obesity and thinness. *Journal of Cross-Cultural Psychology, 27,* 98–113.

Collins, M. E. (1991). Body figure perceptions and preferences among preadolescent children. *International Journal of Eating Disorders, 10,* 199–208.

Cook v *State of Rhode Island Department of Mental Health, Retardation, and Hospitals,* 2 A.D. Cases 1476 (1st Cir. 1993).

Cox, T. H., & Blake, S. (1991). Managing cultural diversity: Implications for organizational competitiveness. *Academy of Management Executive, 5*(3), 45–57.

Crandall, C. S. (1994). Prejudice against fat people: Ideology and self-interest. *Journal of Personality and Social Psychology, 66,* 882–94.

Creighton, M. (2002). A look at religion in the workplace: www.laborlawyers.com/ FSL5CS/labor%20letter/LL%20Jan%20002.pdf (Accessed 27 June 2003).

Cunningham, M. R., Roberts, A. R., Barbee, A. P., Druen, P. B., & Wu, C.-H. (1995). 'Their ideas of beauty are, on the whole, the same as ours': Consistency and variability in the cross-cultural perception of female attractiveness. *Journal of Personality and Social Psychology*, *68*, 261–79.

Dellinger, K., & Williams, C. L. (1997). Makeup at work: Negotiating appearance rules in the workplace. *Gender and Society*, *11*, 151–77.

Dipboye, R. L, Arvey, R. D., & Terpstra, D. E. (1977). Sex and physical attractiveness of raters and applicants as determinants of resume evaluations. *Journal of Applied Psychology*, *63*, 288–94.

Eagly, A. H., Ashmore, R. D., Makhijani, M. G., & Longo, L. C. (1991). What is beautiful is good, but … A meta-analytic review of research on the physical attractiveness stereotype. *Psychological Bulletin*, *110*, 109–28.

Etcoff, N. (1999). *Survival of the prettiest: The science of beauty.* New York: Doubleday.

Feingold, A. (1990). Gender differences in effects of physical attractiveness on romantic attraction: A comparison across five research paradigms. *Journal of Personality and Social Psychology*, *59*, 981–93.

Fernandez, E. (2002). Exercising her right to work: Fitness instructor wins weight–bias fight. *San Francisco Chronicle*, 7 May.

Florey, A. T., & Harrison, D. A. (2000). Responses to informal accommodation requests from employees with disabilities: Multistudy evidence on willingness to comply. *Academy of Management Journal*, *43*, 224–33.

Frieze, I. H., Olson, J. E., & Good, D. C. (1990). Perceived and actual discrimination in the salaries of male and female managers. *Journal of Applied Social Psychology*, *20*, 46–67.

Frieze, I. H., Olson, J. E., & Russell, J. (1991). Attractiveness and income for men and women in management. *Journal of Applied Social Psychology*, *21*, 1039–57.

Furnham, A., & Alibhai, N. (1983). Cross-cultural differences in the perception of female body shapes. *Psychological Medicine*, *13*, 829–37.

Furnham, A., & Baguma, P. (1994). Cross-cultural differences in the evaluation of male and female body shapes. *International Journal of Eating Disorders*, *15*, 81–9.

Hebl, M. R., & Heatherton, T. F. (1998). The stigma of obesity in women: The difference is black. *Personality and Social Psychology Bulletin*, *24*, 417–26.

Goffman, E. (1963). *Stigma: Notes on the management of spoiled identity.* Englewood Cliffs, NJ: Prentice Hall.

Gortmaker, S. L., Must, A., Perrin, J., Sobol, A. M., & Dietz, W. H. (1993). Social and economic consequences of overweight in adolescence and young adults. *New England Journal of Medicine*, *329*, 1008–1112.

Hamermesh, D. S., & Biddle, J. E. (1994). Beauty and the labor market. *American Economic Review*, *84*, 1174–94.

Hebl, M. R., & Heatherton, T. F. (1998). The stigma of obesity in women: The difference is black. *Personality and Social Psychology Bulletin*, *24*, 417–26.

Hebl, M. R., & Mannix, L. M. (2003). The weight of obesity in evaluative others: A mere proximity effect. *Personality and Social Psychology Bulletin*, *29*, 28–38.

Heilman, M. E., & Saruwatari, L. R. (1979). When beauty is beastly: The effects of appearance and sex on evaluations of job applicants for managerial and nonmanagerial jobs. *Organizational Behavior and Human Performance*, *23*, 360–72.

Heilman, M. E., & Stopeck, M. H. (1985). Attractiveness and corporate success: Different causal attributions for males and females. *Journal of Applied Psychology*, *70*, 379–88.

Hensley, W. E., & Cooper, R. (1987). Height and occupational success: A review and critique. *Psychological Reports*, *60*, 843–9.

Hosoda, M., Stone-Romero, E. F., & Coats, G. (2003). The effects of physical attractiveness on job-related outcomes: A meta-analysis of experimental studies. *Personnel Psychology*, *56*, 431–62.

Hwang, S. L. (2003). Enterprise choreographs the look of its workers: http://www. naplesnews.com/03/01/business/d818591a.htm. (Accessed 27 June 2003).

Irvine, M. (1997). 270-pound man sues Coke, claims bias over his weight. *Oakland Tribune*, 16 July.

Jackson, L A. (1983a). The influence of sex, physical attractiveness, sex role, and occupational sex-linkage on perceptions of occupational suitability. *Journal of Applied Social Psychology*, *13*, 31–44.

Jackson, L. A. (1983b). Gender, physical attractiveness, and sex role in occupational treatment discrimination: The influence of trait and role assumptions. *Journal of Applied Social Psychology*, *13*, 443–58.

Jackson, L. A., & McGill, O. D. (1996). Body type preferences and body characteristics associated with attractive and unattractive bodies by African Americans and Anglo Americans. *Sex Roles*, *35*, 295–307.

Jacoby, A. (1994). Felt versus enacted stigma: A concept revisited: Evidence from a study of people with epilepsy in remission. *Social Science & Medicine*, *38*, 269–74.

Jasper, C. R., & Klassen, M. L. (1990). Perceptions of salespersons' appearance and evaluation of job performance. *Perceptual and Motor Skills*, *71*, 563–66.

Johnson, T., & Wilson, M. C. (1995). An analysis of weight-based discrimination: Obesity as a disability. *Labor Law Journal*, April, 238–44.

Kinder, D., & Sears, D. O. (1981). Prejudice and politics: Symbolic racism versus racial threats to the good life. *Journal of Personality and Social Psychology*, *40*, 414–31.

Kristen, K. (2002). Addressing the problem of weight discrimination in employment. *California Law Review*, *9*, 57–109.

Langlois, J. H., Kalakanis, L., Rubenstein, A. J., Larson, A., Hallam, M., & Smoot, M. (2000). Maxims or myths of beauty? Are meta-analytic and theoretical review. *Psychological Bulletin*, *126*, 390–423.

Larkin, J. C., & Pines, H. A. (1979). No fat persons need apply. *Sociology of Work and Occupations*, *6*, 312–27.

Maranto, C. L., & Stenoien, A. F. (2000). Weight discrimination: A multidisciplinary analysis. *Employee Responsibilities and Rights Journal*, *12*, 9–24.

Marlowe, C. M., Schneider, S. L., & Nelson, C. E. (1996). Gender and attractiveness biases in hiring decisions: Are more experienced managers less biased? *Journal of Applied Psychology*, *81*, 11–21.

Marin, G. (1984). Stereotyping Hispanics: The differential impact of research method, label, and degree of contact. *International Journal of Intercultural Relation*, *8*, 17–27.

Martin, C. J. (1994). Protecting overweight workers against discrimination: Is disability or appearance the real issue? *Employee Relations Law Journal*, *20*(1), 133–42.

Martin, K., Leary, M., & Rejeshi, W. (2000). Self-presentational concerns in older adults: Implications for Health and Well-Being. *Basic and Applied Social Psychology*, *22*(3), 169–80.

National Education Association (1994). Report on physical size, 10–11. Washington, DC.

Pagan, J. A., & Davila, A. (1997). Obesity, occupational attainment, and earnings. *Social Science Quarterly*, *78*, 756–70.

Phelan, J. C. (2001). Conceptualizing stigma. *Annual Review of Sociology*, *27*, 363–85.

Puhl, R., & Brownell, K. D. (2003). Ways of coping with obesity stigma: Review and conceptual analysis. *Eating Behaviors*, *4*, 53–78.

Racette, S. B., Deusiner, S. S., & Deusiner, R. H. (2003). Obesity: Overview of prevalence, etiology, and treatment. *Physical Therapy*, *83*, 276–88.

Register, C. A., & Williams, D. R. (1990). Wage effects of obesity among young workers. *Social Science Quarterly*, *71*(1), 130–41.

Riggio, R. E., & Throckmorton, B. (1988). The relative effects of verbal and nonverbal behavior, appearance, and social skills on evaluations made in hiring interviews. *Journal of Applied Social Psychology*, *18*, 331–48.

Rodin, M., & Price, J. (1995). Overcoming stigma – Credit for self-improvement or discredit for needing to improve. *Personality and Social Psychology Bulletin*, *21*, 172–81.

Roehling, M. V. (1999). Weight-based discrimination in employment: Psychological and legal aspects. *Personnel Psychology, 52,* 969–1016.

Ross, M. D. v *William Beaumont Hospital* (1988). US 844 F.2d 789.

Rothblum, E. D., Brand, R. A., Miller, C. T., & Oetjen, H. A. (1990). The relationship between obesity, employment discrimination, and employment-related victimization. *Journal of Vocational Behavior, 37,* 251–66.

Schneider, D. J. (2004). *The psychology of stereotyping.* New York: Guilford Press.

Shaffer, D. R., Crepaz, N., & Sun, C.-R. (2000). Physical attractiveness stereotyping in cross-cultural perspective: Similarities and differences between Americans and Taiwanese. *Journal of Cross-Cultural Psychology, 31,* 557–82.

Silverstein, B., Perdue, L., Peterson, B., & Kelly, E. (1986). The role of the mass media in promoting a thin standard of bodily attractiveness for women. *Sex Roles, 14,* 519–32.

Snyder, M. E., Berscheid, E., & Matwychuk, A. (1988). Orientations toward personnel selection: Differential reliance on appearance and personality. *Journal of Personality and Social Psychology, 54,* 972–9.

Solovay, S. (2000). *Tipping the scales of justice: Fighting weight-based discrimination.* Amherst, NY: Prometheus Books.

Spencer, B. A., & Taylor, G. S. (1988). Effects of facial attractiveness and gender on causal attributions of managerial performance. *Sex Roles, 19,* 272–85.

Staffieri, J. R. (1967). A study of social stereotype of body image in children. *Journal of Personality and Social Psychology, 7,* 101–4.

Stevens, J., Kumanyika, S. K., & Keil, J. E. (1994). Attitudes toward body and dieting: Differences between elderly black and white women. *American Journal of Public Health, 84,* 1322–5.

Stone, E. F., Stone, D. L., & Dipboye, R. L. (1992). Stigmas in organizations: Race, handicaps, and physical unattractiveness. In K. Kelley (Ed.), *Issues, theory, and research in industrial/ organizational psychology* (pp. 385–457). New York: Elsevier Science.

Stringer, D. Y., Bell, M. P., McMahan, G. C., & Davis, J. (2004). Onset controllability and its effect on acceptance outcomes for individuals with disabilities. Paper presented at the Academy of Management Meeting, August, New Orleans.

Watkins, L. M., & Johnston, L. (2000). Screening job applicants: The impact of physical attractiveness and application quality. *International Journal of Selection & Assessment, 8*(2), 76–85.

Wheeler, L., & Kim, Y. (1997). What is beautiful is culturally good: The physical attractiveness stereotype has different content in collectivist cultures. *Personality and Social Psychology Bulletin, 23,* 795–800.

Wilkins, V. N. (2004). Workplace weight discrimination: An empirical investigation using the theory of reasoned action. Paper presented at the Academy of Management Meeting, August, New Orleans.

Wolf, A. M., & Colditz, G. A. (1998). Current estimates of the economic cost of obesity in the United States. *Obesity Research, 6,* 97–106.

World Health Organization (1997). Obesity epidemic puts millions at risk for related diseases. Press release 46, 12 June: http://www.who.int/archives/inf-pr-1997/en/pr97–46.html (Accessed 29 April 2004).

Ziolkowski, S. M. (1994). The status of weight-based employment discrimination under the Americans with Disabilities Act after Cook v. Rhode Island Department of Mental Health, Retardation, and Hospitals. *Boston Law Review, 74,* 667–86.

19

Beyond Inclusion and Equity

Contributions from Transnational Anti-Racist Feminism

KIRAN MIRCHANDANI AND ALANA BUTLER

Earlier chapters in this collection have provided analyses of workplace diversity initiatives, programs and policies. In the present chapter we argue that there are two overarching perspectives within which the various initiatives and programs aimed at fostering workplace diversity can be classified – perspectives which highlight inclusion and perspectives which focus on equity. An example of a case study of a Canadian organization which has received numerous awards and accolades for its diversity initiatives is used to illustrate these perspectives. While inclusive approaches to diversity dominate the field of organizational analysis, there has been some attempt to shift the focus of diversity towards an 'equity' perspective, and many contemporary diversity initiatives now merge dimensions from the two approaches. Drawing from anti-racist and transnational feminist theory, however, we argue that neither the inclusive nor the equity approaches to diversity consider the ways in which race, gender and class operate as social relations which are inextricable from one another. Instead, much of the focus in organizational diversity initiatives have involved the targeting of specific 'groups' such as women, minorities, Aboriginal people or people with disability. We argue that feminist anti-racist, transnational theories provide an approach to diversity which allows us to consider the simultaneous impact of various forms of oppression within organizations. Fundamental to this perspective is the recognition not only that individuals are embedded within local racialized, class-based and gendered hierarchies, but that these processes are constructed by globalization and nationalisms.

CASE STUDY: A CANADIAN LEADER
IN DIVERSITY INITIATIVES

Harmony (a pseudonym)[1] is a large Canadian organization which received a
federal government award for its vision and initiatives around employment equity
for the first time in 1995 and once again in 2000. Harmony has also been recognized as one of Canada's 10 best employers for women as well as for visible
minorities. In 2003, Harmony was named one of Canada's top 100 employers in
an annual ranking and was also named one of Canada's best 50 corporate citizens.
Under the direction of the president and CEO of Harmony, four task forces were
set up in the early 1990s to study the situation of each of the 'minority' groups
(women, Aboriginal peoples, people with disability, and visible minorities). The
results of these initiatives were policies which served to provide a 'level playing
field' for employees and eliminate discriminatory practices, while at the same
time conceptualizing 'diversity' as a 'business issue' closely linked to productivity. Each task force was responsible for studying the work experiences of their
focus group. This involved identifying barriers and making recommendations that
would foster the advancement of their designated group within the organization.

For example, one of the task forces set up as part of Harmony's diversity initiative focused on women. The Task Force on the Advancement of Women held
nearly 200 meetings with a total of 3500 employees, and conducted a survey
of 15,352 employees. According to the 1991 task force report, although three-
quarters of the organization's employees were women, 91% held non-managerial
jobs while only 9% held managerial jobs. The president of Harmony noted that
'equity is not a "women's issue." It is a management challenge … every Banker,
woman and man, will benefit from the result.'

Through employee surveys, the task force attempted to understand why women
were under-represented in managerial positions within Harmony. They discov-
ered that outdated assumptions and false impressions about female employees
were frequently in place (such as the lack of commitment of women to the job,
the assumption that women are less educated, the notion that rapid change is
occurring and that equality between the sexes is merely a matter of time). In addition, the task force reported that Harmony had not provided women with the kind
of encouragement, access to career development opportunities, and information
that was needed for advancement. The report also noted that both female and
male employees perceived that they would be seen as less committed to their jobs
when they responded to outside commitments (such as family demands).

Based on these findings, several initiatives relating specifically to women's
careers were suggested, including the appointment of a Vice President of Workplace
Equality (now Vice President of Equity and Employment Engagement), presidential endorsement for programs, training programs and information sessions for all
employees, training for managers, job-enrichment training sessions, designation of
employment counsellors, and the introduction of flexible work options.

A recently published Harmony task force report showed that as of 2003, 32.6% of Harmony's executives were women, rising from 9% in 1991. Harmony provides training in managerial leadership so that women and other employees could gain access to professional development that would prepare them for higher-level executive positions. Harmony also made policy changes that allow employees to achieve a greater work/life balance such as 'People Care' days, extended leaves and elder care. A separate task force was struck to study the issues facing Aboriginal peoples, which identified several recruitment barriers unique to this group. For example, the report noted the need for a fundamental shift in the relationship between profit-centred organizations and the Aboriginal communities in Canada. Only through the establishment of partnerships with Aboriginal communities can recruitment goals be met. Accordingly, the report recommended the development of networks of Aboriginal associations across the country, and recruitment materials specifically focused to attract Aboriginal people. For Aboriginal employees, the report stressed the need to develop training programs for management, develop mentorship programs, revise harassment policies to include harassment based on race, heritage and culture, and set up training programs on advancement for Aboriginal employees.

The 2003 task force at Harmony reported that Aboriginal employees made up 1.3% of Harmony's total workforce, up from 0.5% in 1991. A separate unit was created in 1992 to focus on the economic self-sufficiency of Aboriginal people across Canada. Harmony is currently developing a set of initiatives that links Aboriginal communities, businesses and individuals with increased access to employment, financial services and job training opportunities. Groups were also set up to study issues facing people with disabilities and visible minorities within the organization. Harmony's approach, through these task forces, was to uncover myths and misunderstandings in place about each of the 'minority' groups identified. Analysis was provided on how these myths and misunderstandings are embedded in the 'culture' of the organization; for example, people with disabilities are often treated with a 'charity mentality' and it is frequently assumed that these individuals will hurt productivity, frequently be absent from work, not be able to communicate and miss what is going on at work. Visible minority employees are not seen to be 'part of the team'. This is despite the fact that at every level, visible minorities had significantly more formal education than the overall Harmony workforce as well as above-average performance reviews. The reports stress the need to challenge these myths while at the same time changing organizational practices (such as hiring criteria or performance evaluation methods) which may unfairly exclude particular individuals.

For visible minorities, a recent task force report showed that 8.4% of executives were visible minorities in 2003, up from 5.6% in 1995. The number of visible minority employees also rose from 12.5% in 1995 to 20% in 2003. Since 1993, business plans include goals for hiring, retaining and promoting women, visible minorities, Aboriginal people and people with disabilities. The CEO's Council on the Equitable Workplace sets qualitative and quantitative workplace

TABLE 19.1   *Comparing inclusive and equity approaches to diversity*

	Inclusive approach	Equity approach
Drivers	Driven by internal organizational requirements such as need for larger recruitable pool or more motivated workforce. Proactive measures (Ross & Schneider, 1992)	Driven by legislative requirements such as employment equity or human rights legislation. Reactive measures (Ross & Schneider, 1992)
Focus	Focused on *individuals*. Assumption that every individual is unique (Ross & Schneider, 1992). Differences between individuals, if properly managed, are an asset to the organization (Kandola & Fullerton, 1994)	Focused on harmonizing differences between groups through the differential treatment of certain groups (Ross & Schneider, 1992)
Assumptions	Assumes that pluralism provides the opportunity for organizational success (Kandola & Fullerton, 1994)	Assumes that difference is a problem and assimilation should be encouraged (Kandola & Fullerton, 1994)

equity goals annually, and measures progress towards the achievement of those goals on a quarterly basis.

The different task forces were set up to study the situation of each of the designated groups. In this sense, 'diversity' was defined within the task force reports as referring to members of these predefined groups, and diversity initiatives undertaken in the past decade clearly had the greatest positive effect on 'women' (leaving unclear whether Aboriginal women or women of colour shared gains in the representation within management ranks). At the same time many of the action items put into place were seen to be for all employees. Programs are designed therefore for all employees and diversity is seen primarily as a 'business issue'. As discussed below, initiatives at Harmony represented a merger of two central approaches to workplace diversity in contemporary organizations.

INCLUSIVE AND EQUITY APPROACHES TO WORKPLACE DIVERSITY

As mentioned earlier, there are two dominant approaches to defining diversity; as noted in Table 19.1, these approaches are driven by different assumptions and factors. The discussion of Harmony in the section above illustrates the ways in which these approaches are often combined in diversity programs. Within the 'inclusive' approach, it is assumed that organizations which support differences within their workforce allow all employees to contribute fully to business success; diversity is defined in broad terms to include all employees (Harvey & Blakely, 1996: 1). In contrast, the 'equity' approach assumes that specific groups have been historically disadvantaged within organizations, requiring 'corrective' measures directed specifically towards the members of these groups.

Within contemporary organizational policies on diversity, there is a clear trend in the literature at large towards the endorsement of the 'inclusivity' approach to diversity (Allen & Montgomery, 2001; Duxbury, 1996; Gandz, 2001; Gardenswartz & Rowe, 1993; Harvey & Blakely, 1996; Jackson & Associates, 1992; Kandola & Fullerton, 1994; Leach, 1995; Ross & Schneider, 1992). It is noted that the fact that no individual is excluded from diversity initiatives, given the broad definition of diversity adopted, results in little 'backlash' towards these initiatives. In addition, diversity is linked in a direct way to organizational goals since encouraging diversity supports the business objectives (Ross & Schneider, 1992: 62). Diversity is seen to be a 'business asset' because it allows the organization to attract the best employees and ensure the higher productivity of all organizational members (Duxbury, 1996; Gardenswartz & Rowe, 1993: 397; Litvin, 2002). These factors contribute directly to the company's 'bottom line'. Diversity initiatives may include programs to combat prejudice and discrimination that against certain groups face, but these initiatives are for all individuals in the organization (including white men), since 'diversity' is defined not only in terms as the predefined 'minority' groups, but in terms of all types of difference (Harvey & Blakely, 1996: 3).

The inclusive approach taken by most organizations defines diversity in the broadest sense so that it includes all aspects of social difference. Litvin (2002) notes that the conceptualization of diversity for business reasons comes with the implicit assumption that specific groups are not targeted. Instead, the intent is to move 'beyond race and gender' to include all members of the workforce.

Combs (2002) asserts that the challenge for organizational leaders is to create a work environment that encourages an appreciation for diverse individual characteristics and dimensions. This relatively vague conceptualization indicates how broad a scope diversity can encompass. This inclusive approach is used to convey the idea that all organizational members have some common ground. Dominant group members can participate in this notion of inclusiveness without feeling threatened by the idea (Sanci, 2000).

Within organizations, diversity has come to be regarded as a means of improving corporate performance (Gordon, 1992). By creating a workplace that is more diverse, businesses will be able to attract and retain skilled employees from a North American population that is also becoming increasingly diverse. Owens (1997) argues that diversity in organizations should be discussed in ways that focus on how it can improve productivity and, in turn, the bottom line. Diversity has been acknowledged as a business reality in light of recent and future demographic changes. In tracing the history of the focus on the 'business case for diversity', Litvin (2002) argues that the narrative of managing diversity as a business asset arose in response to the backlash against affirmative action and employment equity. Diversity is represented as a business opportunity that can potentially increase productivity and foster organizational cohesiveness (Carnevale & Stone, 1994; Elmes & Connelley, 1997; Gandz, 2001; Henderson, 1994; Taylor, 1995).

Much of the literature has shown that internal harmony within organizations has been recognized as an important business factor. Managing employee relations in diverse organizations is something that businesses cannot afford to ignore. Barbian (2003) notes that 'the fact that corporate globalism is here to stay turns diversity into a management issue that can make or break your business, and internal harmony within the company with regard to race, gender, disability, age, or economic status, is just as vital as external accord with clients and customers' (p. 44). Diversity has been conceptualized as a competitive advantage in the global economy. Many corporations are multinational and need to promote and maintain foreign supplier relationships.

Studies showing that heterogeneous teams can improve business performance are commonly cited in corporate training materials pertaining to diversity (Mayo, 1999). Diversity is an asset since it provides the benefit of different perspectives that are assumed to improve team performance. Konrad (2003) argues that demographically diverse groups can outperform homogeneous groups on problem-solving and creative tasks because diverse groups contain a greater variety of experiences, cognitive styles and perspectives. Mayo (1999) notes that as work-places become more diverse and team oriented, it will not be enough to simply co-exist with people from different backgrounds, but to cooperate effectively to achieve team and organizational goals. In this inclusive approach to workplace diversity, inequality with respect to job classification and promotion is conceptu-alized in a manner that recognizes it simply as a matter of resource underutiliza-tion. Organizational performance can be enhanced when all human resources are allowed to reach their potential by eliminating barriers.

The conceptualization of diversity as a business asset has also been articulated by corporate sector diversity advocates who argue that organizations need to effectively manage 'diverse' employee resources in order to derive the potential benefits of improved customer, supplier and global relations (Gandz, 2001; Taylor, 1995). Jackson and Alvarez (1992) explain that delivering service prod-ucts will require cultural similarity between the customer and the service provider. A diverse workforce will help marketers to gain the advantage with both local and international customers. Cox and Blake (1991) theorize that organiza-tional diversity can provide a marketing advantage to companies since they argue that minority group members will have a preference for doing business with orga-nizations where they see members of their group represented as employees. Following from this, companies that actively recruit women and minorities can gain access to additional markets. This is another example of how diverse human resources can come to be conceptualized as 'business assets'. Prasad and Mills (1997) argue that the literature of diversity management has served as a 'show-case' for highlighting its legitimacy as a business function; celebrations of the utility of diversity initiatives focus solely on 'its most striking accomplishments and attractive features' (pp. 8–9). Such displays in fact obscure any notions of social justice and instead represent diversity management as a necessary business strategy. Economic showcasing, for example, reiterates the value of diversity as a business asset and lends credibility through the elaboration of exemplars and guidelines (Prasad & Mills, 1997).

The dominance of inclusive approaches to diversity in Canada relates to the prevalence of discourses of multicultualism which encourage cultural diversity as an integral part of the Canadian identity; this approach allows for government grants for cultural activities, ethnic language retention and funds to support the writing of ethnic histories. From 1971 onward, multiculturalism was created and promoted by the federal government as an official state policy. Multiculturalism in Canada is promoted within the framework of bilingualism. Canada is concep-tualized as being composed of various diverse groups, each with its own culture and history; 'diversity' is therefore defined to include all individuals (Multiculturalism Act, 1988).

Critics of the multiculturalism note that it assumes that racial prejudice and dis-crimination is low enough to allow for mutual tolerance of groups, and that there is no one 'dominant' group which is more powerful than the others (Alladin, 1993: 132). Alladin argues that multiculturalism often leads to economic ghettoiza-tion: 'those outside the "founding" linguistic and cultural tradition are encouraged to retain their culture of origin, yet they are often denied the full benefits of being Canadian' (p. 132). Bannerji (1991) asserts that multiculturalism is itself a vehi-cle for racialization since it establishes Anglo-Canadian culture as the ethnic core culture which 'tolerates' the others. Underneath its liberal interpretation is the idea that there is a core group that constitutes the 'real' Canadians who are pre-sumably benevolent enough to tolerate the others. Mohanty (1990) contends that the definition of multiculturalism implies that an apolitical, ahistorical cultural pluralism needs to be critiqued.

In line with this, theorists argue that inclusive approaches to diversity are ineffective without a consideration of the implicit norms in place in the main-stream culture. Mills and Simmons (1995: 180) note that just as multicultural-ism does not challenge the fundamental structure of Canadian society, the inclusive approach to diversity within organizations does not automatically chal-lenge the organizational structures. Litvin (2002) argues that the business case for diversity in fact serves to maintain the status quo instead of fostering signif-icant organizational change. The business case results in cognitive 'iron cages' that limit the possibilities for alternative conceptualizations of how diversity could be actualized within an organization. The pursuit of the business case comes with a particular narrative that is reinforced and held up as the logical pattern of thought and, as a result, there is no substantial challenge to organiza-tional culture.

Roman (1993) argues that multicultural discourse celebrates diversity without adequately analyzing power differentials among socially defined groups. The celebratory nature of multiculturalism may conceal the reality that there are differing social consequences that some 'groups' may face. Li (1990) claims that the differences that multiculturalism encourages are precisely those differences that may result in inequality in the Canadian labour market. As Prasad and Mills (1997) argue, the showcasing of diversity in the literature has inhibited further examination of the more problematic aspects of multiculturalism in the workplace.

In contrast to inclusive approaches to diversity, 'equity' approaches assume that groups hold differential levels of power within the structure of organizations. It is assumed that there is a predefined category of organizational power (through rank, for example) and this should be more equitably distributed. Konrad (2003) argues that failing to raise questions about power relations between identity groups in organizations feeds the contemporary tendency to deny the existence of structural barriers to opportunity.

While inclusive approaches to diversity assume that the power of all organizational members can be enhanced simultaneously, equity approaches focus on the need for the redistribution of organizational benefits and privileges in organizational structures. Within the 'equity' approach, diversity is seen to be an end in itself; it allows for the 'levelling [of] the playing field' (Thomas, 1990: 110) for all employees. Accordingly, diversity initiatives serve to allow for specific stereotypes to be surfaced and questions to be posed about the environment within which such stereotypes were able to flourish.

In these ways, the equity approach allows for a clear focus on the ideological and political potential of workplace diversity to effect social change. At the same time, the 'minority' groups identified (women, people with disability, Aboriginal peoples, etc.) are often assumed to be homogeneous and the relationship between these assumed 'groups' remains vague. As noted earlier, the equity approach is driven by legislative requirements. Legislative discourse has contributed to this tendency to regard certain groups as homogeneous and fixed. A consequence of this legislative orientation is the idea that there are defined 'groups' that need to be targeted for employment equity purposes. For example, the Federal Employment Equity Act of 1986 was enacted to help correct the employment disadvantages of the four designated groups of women, Aboriginal peoples, visible minorities and persons with disabilities. Large employers such as the federal public service, crown corporations and agencies, or federally regulated private businesses with 100 or more employees are required by the Act to determine whether their workforces fairly represent the four disadvantaged groups. These organizations must submit an annual audit and also identify and remove barriers to equity in their workplaces. Within the equity approach, there is the need to readily identify these group members in order to redress their historic inequitable treatment. This leads to assumptions that identifiable groups are fixed in nature and possess certain traits.

Identities are conceptualized as fixed, static and mutually exclusive 'traits' which individuals possess. As a result, effective diversity initiatives involve simply the collection of various groups 'from different regions and ethnicities – all of whom are projected as presumably forming a coherent yet easily demarcated entity' (Shohat, 2002: 68). In focusing on identities as traits, equity approaches to diversity fail to illuminate the ways in which individuals' social locations are embedded within multiple and interconnected norms around gender, race, class, ability and sexuality. Anthias (2002) argues that we need to recognize both the fluidity and hybridity of cultural identities within social structures and social sites. Anthias rejects the notion of fixed social identities and argues for an approach that recognizes that individuals may comprise many social identities that cannot be separated from each other. Friedman (1995) similarly suggests that the binary categories of race should be eliminated in order to move towards a discourse that recognizes the common ground that all women share. Hall (1991) recognizes that identity is formed through political and historical influences. This less fixed view of identity acknowledges that rather than claim a collective identity, individuals within groups can be shaped by their own histories.

Within anti-racist discourse, there is a shift away from the essentialist conceptualization of social identity. Integrative anti-racism considers racism part of the intersection of all types of oppression such as class, gender or sexual orientation (Dei, 1996). Anthias (2002) urges us to recognize differences within individuals in terms of how their identity is constructed situationally and contextually. Instead of constructing group identity in terms of singular identities, Anthias argues that we need to simultaneously interrogate race, gender, class and other forms of categorizations.

In addition, both inclusive and equity approaches to diversity do not highlight the fundamentally globalized nature of the difference and diversity, and the ways in which diversity initiatives are often framed within nationalist discourses. Theoretical debates within transnational feminist anti-racism, as discussed below, reveal the relationships between various forms of oppression and the globalized nature of social and economic structures.

TRANSNATIONAL FEMINIST ANTI-RACISM

There have been a number of attempts in the feminist literature to theorize the relationships between race, gender and class. Examples include attempts to characterize the relationship between various forms of stratification as 'multiple jeopardies'; as interlocking/intersecting hierarchies; and as 'relational'. The focus on 'double' or 'multiple' jeopardy is an attempt to theorize the additive nature of the relationship between race, class and gender. Acker (1999: 53), in line with this approach, discusses the ways in which certain lines of stratification reinforce others. King (1988: 49) argues, for example, that the salience of any one factor in explaining black women's circumstances may vary depending on the particular context; in some cases, race may play a significant role in determining status while in other cases class or gender may do so. Others argue that rather than identifying the separate impact of these hierarchies on individuals' lives, there is a need to develop understandings of how they intersect and overlap. Collins (1990) argues that various forms of stratification web together to form a 'matrix of domination'. Feminist theorists writing on the interlocking nature of race, class and gender also focus on the 'relational' nature of various forms of stratification. What this means, as summarized by Anderson (1996), is that 'gender, race and class are social relations and exist only in relation to each other' (p. 736). Liu (1991) for example, conceptualizes race as a 'gendered social category', arguing that 'race oppression is predicated upon sex oppression' (p. 265; also Anthias, 1998). Anthias (2002) argues that the reproduction of ethnic groups is always situated within a context of differences and similarities in relation to class and gender. The concept of ethnicity is inherently connected to other social relations such as gender and class. Lloyd (2002) notes that ideas about hybridity and plurality of identity have undermined the concept of a unitary social identity. This shift away from focusing on aspects of social identity in isolation from one another has been the result of new scholarship in the area of identity. These approaches to the intersections of race, gender and class suggest a need to move away from demographic (trait-based) understandings of these concepts, and towards their conceptualization as 'processes'. Glenn (1985) argues that such 'processes' take place through representation (symbols, images), microinteraction (norms) and social structure (allocation of power along race/gender/class lines) (p. 9). The focus on processes suggests that rather than a fixed, determinable relationship, the connections between race, gender and class are located in specific geographical and historical contexts. As Shohat (2002) notes:

> any dialogue about the fictive unity called 'Middle Eastern women' or 'Latin American gays/lesbians' – especially one that is taking place within a transnational framework – has to begin from the premise that genders, sexualities, races, classes, nations and even continents exist not as hermetically sealed entities but rather as part of a permeable interwoven relationality. (p. 68)

In addition, while many diversity programs emphasize internationalism (i.e. the difference seen to be arising from different fixed regional or cultural backgrounds), a focus on transnationalism would represent a significant shift. As Kaplan and Grewal (2002) note, the 'term "transnational" signals attention to uneven or dissimilar circuits of culture and capital. Through such critical recognition, the links among patriarchies, colonialisms, racisms and feminisms become more apparent and available for critique or appropriation' (p. 73). Rather than assuming that identities and perspectives arise in a known and fixed manner out of particular cultural or national backgrounds, transnational anti-racist feminism suggests the need for the development of diversity programs which focus on the ways in which difference is constructed and reified within organizations.

RETHINKING DIVERSITY

A feminist anti-racist transnational perspective allows for an analysis of a number of issues which are often masked within discussions of workplace diversity. An analysis of these issues is needed in order to enhance our understanding of the complex processes involved with challenging social inequality. A transnational feminist anti-racist perspective draws the necessary links between the historical influence of patriarchy and oppressions in all contemporary multicultural societies. This approach is dynamic and represents a reconceptualization of the relations of gender, class and race within the ever-present context of globalization. A transnational feminist anti-racist perspective would help us to understand how social identity can be conceptualized in a way that acknowledges the hybridity and intersectionality of race, class, gender, sexuality and disability.

With reference to the Harmony case study, a transnational feminist anti-racist framework would suggest a fundamental shift in the organization's approach to diversity. Instead of the poorly defined concept of 'diversity', initiatives would focus on the types of difference which translate into systemic inequity within the organization. Rather than separate 'task forces' based on predefined groups of people, focus would be on the ways in which stereotypical assumptions about particular individuals are normalized. Categories such as 'aboriginal person', 'immigrant', 'veiled woman', etc., are created on a daily basis through interactions (and particular individuals are automatically assumed to have certain traits), often on the basis of preconceived notions about innate abilities or foreign nations. Any serious attempt to ensure better opportunities for career progression for all groups would involve situating initiatives within previous 'affirmative action' policies which have historically benefited a small group of white women while giving rise to a backlash around assumptions of lowered standards often directed towards all employees defined as outside of the mainstream demographic. Taking such an approach, much of the emphasis of diversity training would be on educating organizational members on world history and geography, including nationalistic rhetorics which involve naming particular cultures as regressive or backward, local colonialisms which affect many Aboriginal people's lives, and class structures which determine access to caregiving assistance.

In addition to these issues, there are several other considerations which such an analytic encourages. First, a transnational feminist anti-racist perspective calls for an interrogation of the relationship between the proliferation in diversity training initiatives and programs, and nationalist discourses within the United States and Canada. Given that the future of North American enterprises is often said to lie in their ability to capture what has been termed 'emerging markets', the knowledge of diverse cultures and norms can be used to integrate local employees as well as colonize workers and consumers abroad.

Second, the notion of 'designated groups' does not allow for analyses of the ways in which identities and knowledge are situated and relational. Beginning with the perspective that difference emerges out of *interactions* allows for analyses of how notions of majority and minority or mainstream and marginal are enacted and reproduced in organizations.

Third, transnational feminist anti-racist perspectives suggest the need to unpack the assumption underlying many workplace diversity programs that dialogue is likely to lead automatically to understanding. Rather than defining stereotypes which exist in organizations as arising out of myths which simply need to be dispelled through education, more useful approaches to diversity would begin with a study of histories of colonialism and slavery through which much of the fixity around our contemporary notions of colour, difference and diversity has been formed. As Shohat (2002) has argued, 'to map histories of [for example] women and gays/lesbians, we must place them in dialogical relation within, between, and among cultures, ethnicities and nations' (p. 69). The use of terms such as 'difference' and 'equity' to describe systemic inequalities masks the prevalence of racism and sexism which pervade organizational settings and interactions.

Finally, the focus on social location within transnational feminist anti-racism suggests the need for issues around class to be central in workplace diversity programs and initiatives. For example, diversity training initiatives are often only available in organizations to core, permanent employees. Diversity training initiatives also tend to be directed towards front-line and lower-level employees, rather than higher-level or senior executive management. Higher-level executives with a degree of relative organizational power are often able to 'exempt' themselves from having to attend compulsory diversity training. In many organizations, diversity training initiatives are not provided to employees across all departmental functions, but may remain restricted to employees participating in front-line customer service interactions. These employees tend to be on the lower end of the pay scale, further emphasizing the importance of class. This may further serve to marginalize diversity training initiatives within organizations. Finally, given the increasing use of contingent, short-term, temporary or part-time workers within organizations, many of whom are people of colour or recent immigrants, any analysis of organizational diversity needs to be conducted within the framework of the highly differentiated and unequal positions occupied by core and peripheral workers in contemporary organizations.

NOTE

1 This case study is based on an analysis of public documents published by Harmony.

REFERENCES

Acker, J. (1999). Rewriting class, race and gender: Problems in feminist thinking. In M. M. Ferree, J. Lorber & B. B. Hess (Eds), *Revisioning gender*. Thousand Oaks, CA: Sage.

Alladin, I. (Ed.) (1993). *Multiculturalism in the 1990s: Policies, practices, implications*. Edmonton: ELSA Press.

Allen, R., & Montgomery, K. (2001). Applying an organizational development approach to creating diversity. *Organizational Dynamics, 30*(2), 149–61.

Anderson, C. D. (1996). Understanding the inequality problematic: From scholarly rhetoric to theoretical reconstruction. *Gender & Society 10*(6), 729–46.

Anthias, F. (1998). Rethinking social divisions: Some notes towards a theoretical framework. *Sociological Review, 63*, 505–33.

Anthias, F. (2002). Diasporic hybridity and transcending racisms. In F. Anthias & C. Lloyd (Eds), *Rethinking anti-racisms: From theory to practice* (pp. 22–43). London: Routledge.

Bannerji, H. (1991). Racism, sexism, knowledge and the academy: Re: Turning the gaze. *Resources for Feminist Research/Documentation sur La Recherche Feministe, 20*(3/4), 5–11.

Barbian, J. (2003). Moving toward diversity: After many years as a niche initiative, diversity training is gathering strength as an essential business practice. *Training, 40*(2), 44–8.

Carnevale, A., & Stone, S. (1994). Diversity beyond the golden rule. *Training & Development, 48*(10), 18–22.

Collins, P. H. (1990). *Black feminist thought*. New York: Routledge.

Combs, G. W. (2002). Meeting the leadership challenge of a diverse and pluralistic workplace: Implications of self-efficacy for diversity training. *Journal of Leadership Studies, 8*(4), 1–17.

Cox, T. & Blake, S. (1991). Managing cultural diversity: Implications for organizational competitiveness. *The Executive, 5*(3), 45–57.

Dei, G. S. (1996). Critical perspectives in antiracism: An introduction. *Canadian Review of Sociology and Anthropology, 33*(3), 247–68.

Duxbury, L. (1996). Men and women working as partners: A reality check of Canadian organizations. Centre for Research on Education on Women and Work, Carleton University.

Elmes, M., & Connelley, D. (1997). Dreams of diversity and the realities of intergroup relations in organizations. In P. Prasad, A. Mills, M. Elmes & P. Prasad (Eds), *Managing the organizational melting pot: Dilemmas of workplace diversity* (pp. 148–67). Thousand Oaks, CA: Sage.

Friedman, S. (1995). Beyond white and other: Relationality and narratives of race in feminist discourse. *Signs, 21*(11), 1–21.

Gandz, J. (2001). A business case for diversity. *Gateway to Diversity, 1*(1), 1–54. London: Richard Ivey School of Business. Also available online at www.equalopportunity.on.ca/eng-g/documents/BusCase.html (Accessed 30 May 2005).

Gardenswartz, L., & Rowe, A. (1993). *Managing diversity – A complete desk reference and planning guide.* New York: Irwin.

Glenn, E. N. (1985). Racial ethnic women's labour: The intersection of race, gender and class oppression. *Review of Radical Political Economics, 17*(3), 86–108.

Gordon, J. (1992). Rethinking diversity. *Training, 29*(1), 23–40.

Hall, S. (1991). Ethnicity: Identity and difference. *Radical America, 23*(4), 9–20.

Harvey, E., & Blakely, J. H. (1996). *Information systems for managing workplace diversity.* North York: CCH Canadian Limited.

Henderson, G. (1994). *Cultural diversity in the workplace: Issues and strategies.* Westport, CT: Praeger.

Jackson, S., & Associates (1992). *Diversity in the workplace: Human resources initiatives.* London: Guilford.

Jackson, S. E., & Alvarez, E. (1992). Working through diversity as a strategic imperative. In S. E. Jackson (Ed.), *Diversity in the Workplace,* (pp. 13–29). New York: Guilford.

Kandola, R., & Fullerton, J. (1994). *Managing the mosaic – Diversity in action.* London: Institute of Personnel and Development.

Kaplan, C., & Grewal, I. (2002). Transnational practices and interdisciplinary feminist scholarship: Refiguring women's and gender studies. In R. Weigman (Ed.), *Women's studies on its own* (pp. 66–81). Durham, NC: Duke University Press.

King, D. (1988). Multiple jeopardy, multiple consciousness: The context of black feminist ideology. *Signs, 14*(1), 43–71.

Konrad, A. (2003). Defining the domain of workplace diversity scholarship. *Group & Organization Management, 28*(1), 4–17.

Li, P. (1990). Race and ethnicity. In P. Li (Ed.), *Race and Ethic Relations in Canada* (pp. 3–20). Toronto: Oxford University Press.

Litvin, D. (2002). The business case for diversity and the 'Iron Cage'. In B. Czarniawska & H. Höpfl (Eds), *Casting the Other: The production and maintenance of inequality in organizations* (pp. 160–89). London: Routledge.

Liu, T. (1991). Teaching the differences among women from a historical perspective: Rethinking race and gender as social categories. *Women's Studies International Forum, 14*(4), 265–76.

Lloyd, C. (2002). Anti-racism, social movements and civil society. In F. Anthias & C. Lloyd (Eds), *Rethinking anti-racisms: From theory to practice* (pp. 60–77). London: Routledge.

Mayo, M. (1999). Capitalizing on a diverse workforce. *Ivey Business Journal, 64*(1), 20–7.

Mills, A. J., & Simmons, T. (1995). *Reading organization theory: A critical approach.* Toronto: Garamond Press.

Mohanty, C. (1990). On race and voice: Challenges for liberal education in the 1990s. *Cultural Critique, 8*(2), 179–208.

Owens, R. (1997). Diversity: A bottomline issue. *Workforce, 76*(3), S3–6.

Prasad, P., & Mills, A. (1997). From showcase to shadow: Understanding the dilemmas of managing workplace diversity. In P. Prasad, A. Mills, M. Elmes & A. Prasad (Eds), *Managing the organizational melting pot: Dilemmas of workplace diversity* (pp. 3–25). Thousand Oaks, CA: Sage.

Roman, L. (1993). White is a color! White defensiveness, postmodernism and anti-racist pedagogy. In C. McCarthy & W. Crichlow (Eds), *Race, Identity and Representation in Education* (pp. 70–84). London: Routledge.

Ross, R., & Schneider, R. (1992). *From equality to diversity: A business case for equal opportunities*. London: Pitman.

Sanci, L. (2000). *Racial harassment in the workplace*. Unpublished MA thesis, Ontario Institute for Studies in Education, University of Toronto.

Shohat, E. (2002). Area studies, gender studies and the cartographies of knowledge. *Social Text, 20*(3), 67–78.

Taylor, C. (1995). Building a business case for diversity. *Canadian Business Review, 22*(1), 12–15.

Thomas, R. R. (1990). From affirmative action to affirming diversity. *Harvard Business Review*, March–April, 107–17.

20

Trade Unions and Equality and Diversity

ANNE-MARIE GREENE AND GILL KIRTON

Union membership has generally been falling across the developed world in recent decades, largely as a consequence of economic restructuring; in particular the decline in the traditionally highly unionised manufacturing sector, a growth in the lower unionised service sector and increasing levels of 'atypical' employment (Howell, 1996). The latter two trends are associated with higher female and minority ethnic levels of employment, rendering the recruitment and retention of these two groups of workers as imperative to the survival of unions. This imperative has driven many unions to develop strategies aimed at redressing historic inequalities in the representation of 'minority' groups in union democratic processes and structures and also to improve their ability to represent diverse interests in their relationship with employers. Thus, unions can no longer simply be conceptualised as unitary class-based organisations; rather the challenge facing them currently is to develop ways of becoming pluralist organisations capable of representing diversity of interests based on cross-cutting social identities. Indeed, activists have begun to make this demand of their unions and women, black and minority ethnic, disabled and lesbian and gay members have all become more vocal over the last couple of decades in pressing for change (Briskin, 2002; Colgan & Ledwith, 2002).

On grounds of space constraints this chapter focuses on gender and 'race'[1] issues as key aspects of social relations inside trade unions and as key elements of the external trade union agenda of developed countries. In addition, this focus is justifiable to the extent that women's struggle for representation has often set precedents for other minority groups within trade unions (Ledwith & Colgan, 2002). At the same time we recognise that other dimensions of workforce diversity, such as disability, sexuality and age, are also (or should be) part of the trade union agenda in seeking to democratise relations inside unions and to represent workers effectively.

The chapter discusses issues of diversity in the context of the trade union movement of Europe, with some illustrative material from other developed countries. The chapter is divided into three parts; in order to frame the discussion the first part considers conceptualisations of equality, the second examines the issue of diversity inside trade unions, and the third considers the trade unions' role in representing diverse interests.

CONCEPTUALISING EQUALITY

Jewson and Mason's (1986) conceptualisation of liberal and radical approaches to equality policy has proved an influential framework for analysing and evaluating the equality strategies of organisations. The liberal approach holds that equality exists 'when all individuals are enabled freely and equally to compete for social rewards' (Jewson & Mason, 1986: 307). The role of the policy-maker is to ensure that the rules of the competition do not discriminate and that they are fairly applied to all participants. Equality policies formulated according to this approach devise fair procedures avoiding direct and indirect discrimination. Examples of liberal measures in the trade union context include provision of child care at conferences and demographic monitoring of membership by gender and ethnicity (Kirton & Greene, 2002). Examples of liberal measures in the employment context include formalised, consistent recruitment and selection procedures, child care facilities and literature in minority languages. At the heart of this approach is the belief that fair procedures will result in fair outcomes.

The radical approach seeks to intervene directly in organisation practices in order to achieve a fair distribution of rewards. The policy-maker is therefore primarily concerned with outcomes, rather than with procedures. The absence of fair outcomes is therefore taken as evidence of discrimination. The role of the policy-maker is to devise interventions and make decisions that will redress inequalities of outcome. In this view, in the trade union context the under-representation in decision making of women and minority ethnic people is evidence of inequalities and radical equality measures include reserved seats on decision-making bodies, separate women's committees and black/minority ethnic committees.

The liberal approach can be criticised for failing to deliver equality (Webb, 1997), while the radical approach is often perceived negatively as reverse discrimination, special treatment or tokenism (Cockburn, 1989). However, advocates of equality usually regard the liberal approach as weaker and less effective, while the radical approach with its more direct intervention is often favoured. In response to these criticisms, Cockburn (1989) suggests an alternative concept of a transformational equality strategy, which involves 'short' and 'long' agendas. The short agenda treats the symptoms of discrimination and disadvantage and involves measures to minimise bias in procedures such as recruitment and selection. It is therefore resonant with the liberal approach. The long agenda is a project of transformation for organisations, which acknowledges the need of disadvantaged groups for access to power, and has echoes of the radical approach (Richards, 2001). Cockburn (1989) argues that a transformational strategy containing short and long agendas avoids the dichotomous approach of Jewson and Mason's (1986) liberal and radical formulation, where equality policies have either one aim or another.

We believe that the liberal/radical formulation is often useful to characterise individual equality measures and to pinpoint and evaluate their intended and actual outcomes. We argue that at times the direct interventions of the radical approach are necessary to effect change, but that liberal measures are not necessarily weaker or any the less important in the longer term. However, we recognise that the liberal/radical dichotomy can be a straitjacket in terms of understanding and evaluating equality policy because of its failure to reflect the multiplicity in the experiences of disadvantage in employment and consequently the range of equality measures marshalled in response (Cockburn, 1989). Therefore, the concept of transformation is undoubtedly useful because it is dynamic and it makes clear that fundamental change within organisations (including trade unions) is necessary in order to achieve equality. Liberal and radical policies contribute to this transformation but are not by themselves sufficient.

EQUALITY AND DIVERSITY INSIDE TRADE UNIONS

Male domination of union decision making is the prevalent norm and generally this means white, male domination. This exists despite substantial female membership in most countries and substantial minority ethnic membership in some countries.

Table 20.1 shows women's representation in 15 European Union countries where data was available. Interestingly, it is not possible to draw up a similar table showing representation by 'race'/ethnicity because the information is simply not available. Indeed the ETUC (2003) reports that many national union confederations are specifically opposed to ethnic monitoring. Some British unions have recently begun monitoring the ethnicity of new members, but presently most are only able to offer estimates of the size of the minority ethnic membership (Kirton & Greene, 2002). The lack of information available on minority ethnic membership is problematic with regard to developing strategies to increase diversity in decision making.

TABLE 20.1 *Women's representation in trade unions in 15 European Union countries*

	Trade union organisation	Trade union membership % women	Women delegates to congress %	Executive committee % women	Reserved seats for women
Austria	OGB	32	34	13	Yes
Belgium	CSC	48	18	27	Yes
Denmark	LO	48	30	19	No
Finland	SAK	46	38	20	No
France	CFDT	43	37	30	No
	FO	40	45	21	No
Germany	DGB	30	34	19	No
Ireland	ICTU	45	31	17	Yes
Italy	CISL	45	31	15	No
	UIL	18	20	15	Yes
	CGIL	50	40	38	No
Luxembourg	LCGB	32	15	20	No
	CGT-OGB	32	15	16	No
Netherlands	FNV	29	25	21	No
Norway	LO	45	37	27	No
Portugal	UGT	47	22	22	Yes
Spain	UGT	30	19	24	No
	CC.OO	34	23	24	No
	ELA-STV	33	40	25	No
Sweden	LO	46	36	33	No
	SACO	48	39	55	No
	TCO	63	40	70	No
UK	TUC	40	35	32	Yes

Source: European Trades Union Congress (ETUC), 2002

Diversity in Decision Making

Over the last decade at least, there has been a lot of rhetorical commitment to equality (primarily gender) by unions in many countries as evidenced by national policy statements, but there has also been action (such as described below) to increase participation of diverse groups in decision-making bodies. However, much of the effort has been directed at national-level bodies – the 'showcase' of unions – and as important as this is, it has had mixed, often limited, impact on workplace and branch structures where much of the 'everyday' union business is conducted.

At present, lower rates of female participation in union decision making, when compared with male participation and with the number of women in membership, is a global problem (see Table 20.1). Research in, for example, Australia (Elton, 1997), Canada (Briskin, 2002), Central and Eastern Europe (Petrovic, 2001), Western Europe (ETUC, 2002), the UK (Kirton & Greene, 2002) and the United States (Delaney & Lundy, 1996) bears this out. Even in Sweden, often held up as one of the world's most egalitarian societies (with regard to gender), trade union women are generally concentrated in subordinate positions in the union hierarchy (Curtin & Higgins, 1998). In addition, in many countries the form of male power inside trade unions is specifically white, male. Research in Canada (Briskin, 2002), the UK (Kirton & Greene, 2002), and the United States (Cobble & Bielski

Michal, 2002; Delaney & Lundy, 1996) shows that members of minority ethnic groups are also under-represented in decision-making structures. For instance, most British unions have very few, if any, black paid officials and very few black activists on executive committees (Labour Research, 2001).

The absence of women and other diverse 'minority' groups in union decision making is said to create a 'democracy deficit' (Cockburn, 1995), which prevents unions from fulfilling their aim of achieving social justice. Indeed, Young (1990: 92) argues that participatory democracy has both instrumental and intrinsic value, because it requires that a diversity of interests is voiced and because it provides an important means for the development of capacities for thinking about one's own needs in relation to the needs of others. Thus 'democracy is both an element and condition of social justice' (Young, 1990: 91). It can be argued therefore that female and minority ethnic participation and involvement within trade unions needs to increase in order that these groups can develop policies and agendas to address their specific concerns (Cockburn, 1995).

Explaining the Relative Absence of Diversity in Decision Making

This discussion brings us to consider explanations for the relative absence of diversity in union structures. The literature has established that women and other 'minority' groups encounter a range of structural and cultural barriers to their participation in unions. For women, there are three main barriers: the structure of women's employment, the gendered division of domestic labour, and trade union structure and culture.

The first barrier concerns gender segregation, which creates gender-specific bargaining concerns and priorities (Bradley, 1994; Kirton & Healy, 1999). Unions have failed to recognise this and have generally taken a gender-neutral approach. This either intentionally or unintentionally privileges male bargaining concerns, rendering unions unattractive to women. Further, women's over-representation in 'atypical' employment (e.g. part-time, casual or temporary) makes women difficult for unions to organise and also creates obstacles to women's participation. This explanation is rightly critical of union policy and practice although more recently many unions in developed countries have sought to become more 'woman-friendly' and to address women's specific bargaining concerns. Further, it is possible to argue that unions have deliberately concentrated their efforts (until fairly recently) on organising men underpinned by the patriarchal ideology of the primacy of the male breadwinner. This also relates to the traditional union view that women are intrinsically difficult to organise because they have low attachment to paid employment and are therefore not interested in trade unionism. For example, one key group of women workers that unions have historically neglected is part-timers, whose membership rates in the UK (where women have a strong propensity for part-time work) are lower. Yet recent research (Walters, 2002) has highlighted that female part-timers are just as favourable to trade unionism as other workers, yet they are often not asked to join the union.

The second barrier concerns patriarchal relations in the household, which construct an unequal gendered division of domestic labour, with the result that most women are 'time poor', having at least two 'jobs' – their paid work and their unpaid work looking after the home and family. This means that union participation (a third job?) comes at a high price for women. This explanation is supported by research, which has found female union activists (particularly at senior levels) to be 'atypical', meaning older, child free and often partner free (Cockburn, 1995; Kirton & Healy, 1999). Unions cannot be held responsible for gender relations in the home, although they can (and do) develop policies and practices to help women to balance their various roles (e.g. providing child care at union events).

Finally, trade union structure and culture is the barrier that has gained more purchase recently, especially among feminist commentators. It is this explanation that is most critical of unions, rather than blaming wider societal structures or even women themselves. At its most simplistic level this explanation draws attention to the way that union practices, having been constructed by men, are built around men's needs and masculine ways of operating. For example, the timing and location of meetings are often inconvenient or less appealing to women; for example, evening meetings in 'smoky pubs'. Requirements for job mobility and to be continually 'on call' are also seen as proportionately more difficult for women to meet (Bradley, 1994; Kirton, 1999). At another level it is argued that union culture is infused with patriarchal ideology, which manifests itself in all kinds of subtle ways, to the extent that women often describe a feeling of symbolic, rather than actual, exclusion from trade union domains: for example, the absence of female role models; the behaviour of some male trade unionists towards women; and sexual harassment (Cobble & Bielski Michal, 2002; Cockburn, 1995; Franzway, 2002; Healy & Kirton, 2000).

There is less literature specifically about black and minority ethnic under-representation, although research on women in unions has now become more sensitive to cross-cutting identities, including race and ethnicity (Munro, 2001). This body of research suggests that the above three barriers explaining women's under-participation also have some bearing on the relative absence of minority ethnic members from decision making in the context of developed countries. First, unions have a 'white' image, and have failed to deal aggressively enough with racism both inside and outside the union movement, rendering them less effective in representing and protecting black workers. Also, labour markets tend to be segmented by 'race' and ethnicity and the privileging of male areas of employment has often also meant white, male. Second, black women have complained of their marginalisation within both mainstream structures and 'race' and black member structures (McBride, 2001), underscoring the patriarchal nature of male power in both arenas. Third, racism inside trade unions can be both deliberate and unintentional, but acts to symbolically exclude black workers.

When seeking to explain the absence of ethnic diversity internationally, there are multiple problems. There is certainly a common (historical) problem of racism inside unions and in the labour market (Briskin, 2002; Delaney & Lundy, 1996). However, the labour movement of each country varies in how it understands race and ethnicity and responds to racism, depending on ideological and political orientations, as well as on the ethnic structure of the labour market (Wrench, 2003). For example, in Sweden in the 1960s blue-collar unions pushed for the recruitment of Swedish women, rather than immigrants, to fill labour market shortages, arguing that immigration allowed employers to adopt exploitative practices which undermined the pay and conditions of Swedish workers (Mahon, 2002). Similar exclusionary policies were supported by the TUC in the UK until the 1970s (Phizacklea & Miles, 1987) and it is only recently that the AFL-CIO in the United States reversed its anti-immigration policy and instituted a campaign for an amnesty for 6 million undocumented workers. It has since seen a rise in its membership of immigrants from Latin American and Caribbean countries. Thus, the union movements of different countries are differentially implicated in the historical construction of racism and racial disadvantage. More recently, though, the union confederations in many countries are seeking to tackle racism inside unions and in the labour market (see ICFTU website for examples at www.icftu.org).

The explanations for women and minority ethnic workers' lesser participation in union affairs are interrelated and complex and to some extent are contingent on the national context. However, trade unions in many countries have adopted a range of strategies for addressing inequalities inside unions.

Strategies for Increasing Diversity

These strategies fall into the following categories: (1) equality conferences; (2) equality committees; (3) reserved seats on executive bodies; (4) trade union education aimed at particular groups and issues; (5) guarantees of proportional representation; (6) new approaches to conducting trade union business; (7) equality officers. The first four types of strategy can be characterised as radical equality measures as they are forms of separate organising, which is given detailed consideration below. The fifth strategy could be regarded as liberal or radical depending on how the policy of proportional representation is formulated. The final two types of strategy can be characterised as liberal equality measures, since the aim is more one of dismantling barriers (6) and providing information/support (7).

As indicated earlier, research has tended to focus on women. Trebilcock's (1991) comprehensive international review of strategies for increasing women's participation finds radical equality measures adopted in relation to women in a large number of countries around the world. For example, Trebilcock (1991: 419–20) found that regular women's union conferences take place in many countries including Germany, Ireland, New Zealand, Norway, Switzerland and the UK and reserved seats for women are found in some countries including Australia, Canada, Norway and the UK (see also Table 20.1). However, countries with a tradition of declarative gender equality, such as the former communist states of Central and Eastern Europe, appear less comfortable with the radical concept of special measures to achieve higher women's participation (see Petrovic, 2001). Indeed, Petrivic's (2001: 31) survey in the region on behalf of ICFTU finds considerable opposition and hostility towards special measures for women, captured by the following quote from one respondent: 'There are no women's issues, only trade union issues. I guess those in Europe have nothing better to do than to make up things that do not exist.'

Many countries have also developed liberal and radical strategies to increase race and ethnic diversity in union decision making, but adoption is more variable. There can be no doubt that the progress that has been made in many countries on women's representation in decision making has arisen as a consequence of special measures, especially the more radical women's separate organising (Briskin, 2002; Parker, 2002). Based on women's experience it is possible to argue that race equality inside unions will only be accomplished by adoption of similar measures.

Separate organising and special structures

We argue that a radical strategy based on separate organising of 'minority' groups offers the greatest potential for union transformation and democratisation. It can be defined as 'a strategy of empowerment' (Briskin, 1993: 91): a means to an end (inclusion in and influence on democratic processes and structures), rather than a goal in itself. In some contexts (such as the British and Canadian), what began as women's separate organising has also influenced approaches to organising based around race, sexuality and disability (Briskin, 2002). Separate organising has been central to new conceptions and forms of union democracy (Briskin, 2002; Kirton & Greene, 2002; McBride, 2001; Parker, 2002) and in this sense can be regarded as transformational.

The radical strategy of separate organising is, however, not without its critics. Measures such as reserved seats and special training courses are often charged with being tokenistic or patronising gestures, which rather than leading to democratic transformation simply marginalise the issues and the people involved (Kirton & Greene, 2002). In addition, separate organising is often viewed as embodying essentialist notions of women or 'race' and ethnicity, which deny the differences among women and minority ethnic groups. A further criticism is that recognition of diversity dilutes unity and solidarity, and with it union strength and power. Separate organising is viewed as a distraction from 'real' union business and therefore is politically unacceptable and resource draining. These criticisms are advanced both by the white, male majority, as well as by women and minority ethnic trade unionists.

Alternatively, to rebut these criticisms, it can be argued that inequalities are historically embedded in the structural and cultural fabric of trade unions and to redress these requires radical measures. Further, unity within diversity is possible (Briskin, 2002) and that trade unions are better able to promote social justice for all if diverse social groups are included in democratic decision making (Young, 2000). In other words, social group difference can be drawn upon as a resource if inclusive mechanisms are developed through which the voices of diverse social groups can be heard. This more positive view of separate organising seems to have informed the approach in some countries.

Research has demonstrated the benefits of women's separate organising: for example, women-only courses give women the skills and confidence to partici- pate (Greene & Kirton, 2002); women's committees create a space in which women can define their own agenda (Healy & Kirton, 2000; Parker, 2002); some women who initially get elected to reserved seats later get elected to mainstream seats (Braithwaite & Byrne, 1994). However, in the UK, despite the passage of more than two decades of separate organising, and some progress, the gap between the proportion of women who are members and those who are *senior* officials still remains fairly wide in most unions. This experience suggests that separate organising has limitations as a vehicle for transformation and that change is likely to be incremental rather than revolutionary. In contrast, other countries are less enthusiastic about women's separate organising. Reserved seats for women, for example, have been adopted in only a minority of European countries (see Table 20.1). Furthermore, Sweden has moved away from separate organis- ing. It established separate women's structures in 1947, but following a recom- mendation by its Women's Council the blue-collar union organisation LO abolished these in 1967. This resulted in a decline in women's involvement, reversed only in the 1990s when LO women developed informal separate organ- ising strategies (Mahon, 2002). After developing in the 1970s, separate organising has also recently declined in Italy as rivalries among women and between women's groups and the mainstream progressively emerged and different politi- cal orientations grew in importance (Beccalli & Meardi, 2002). The Italian expe- rience underscores the way in which gender does not stand alone as a unitary organising category, but intersects with other identities, including class and political affiliations.

There is less agreement that separate organising is the way to tackle race inequalities inside unions (Kirton & Greene, 2002). The British public services union UNISON has been at the vanguard of developments in black separate organising in the UK (Virdee & Grint, 1994), where it has proved a successful vehicle for giving voice to black member concerns and advancing a 'black' trade union agenda. However, as recently as 1996 the British TUC's 'Black Workers' Conference' recognised the ongoing controversy surrounding black members' separate organising over its acceptability and effectiveness as a tool for tackling black under-representation. Minority ethnic or separate black organising also features in trade unions in other developed countries, such as Canada (Leah, 1993) and the United States (Cobble & Bielski Michal, 2002). For example, the Canadian Labour Congress set up a department responsible for increasing access to leadership posts of people of Asian and African origin. It also held its first conference for Aboriginal workers and workers of colour in 1998 (www.icftu.org/). In Sweden, in 1997 a 'network for immigrant union activists' was established to articulate immigrant concerns in public debate and to support and encourage immigrants to become more active in their unions (Mahon, 2002). The union federations in Australia and New Zealand have created reserved seats for 'indigenous peoples' and encouraged affiliated unions to do so (www.icftu.org/).

Despite some positive examples of what separate organising can achieve, it is important to recognise that it is not a panacea for redressing the absence of diversity inside trade unions and the outcome might not be as radical or transformational as intended. Just as likely is that separate organising could be used as a strategy by the white, male-dominated oligarchy to maintain the status quo. Separate organising might actually legitimate confining 'women's issues' and 'black issues' to powerless domains and ensure that these issues continue to be perceived as of only marginal importance to the mainstream business of unions (Healy & Kirton, 2000). Further, greater diversity in decision making will not change union cultural practices if the masculine character remains intact (Creese, 1995). To accomplish greater equality and diversity, separate organising must meet certain preconditions, which Briskin (2002: 37) summarises as maintaining a (delicate) strategic balance between autonomy from the traditional structures and practices of the union movement and mainstreaming into those structures. The former creates opportunities for trade union culture and practices to be redefined, while the latter is necessary to prevent further marginalisation or ghettoisation of under-represented groups.

In summary, it is clear that women and minority ethnic workers constitute an important source of trade union members. However, they are poorly represented in decision-making structures in all developed countries because of a range of structural and cultural barriers impeding their participation. The unions have a chequered history with regard to tackling internal inequalities, although liberal and radical measures to redress women's and minority ethnic workers' under-representation have become more commonplace. In many countries unions have now recognised that they cannot effectively represent 'minority' groups while a situation of internal inequality remains.

REPRESENTING DIVERSE INTERESTS

Against this background, we now turn to the external role of trade unions, which varies between countries, depending on a number of factors discussed later. However, while the specific interventions may differ, we concentrate on two main areas of union activity, which are common across countries. First, campaigning activities, where, for example, unions lobby government (aiming to improve equality legislation) and get involved with other political and social movement campaigns. Second, collective bargaining, where unions seek to improve terms and conditions of employment.

Campaigning Activities

Trade unions have traditionally engaged in activities extending beyond the workplace; for example, unions have played a key role in campaigns for a national minimum wage (NMW), which seven countries in Europe still do not have. In the UK for example, the TUC was involved in direct discussions with the Confederation of British Industry over the levels set for the NMW first introduced in 1999, and has continued to campaign for improvement of the rate and extension of coverage. Similar union campaigns over low pay have occurred elsewhere, for example in Canada (Briskin, 2002), Sweden (Mahon, 2002) and the United States (Cobble & Bielski Michal, 2002). In the United States, AFL-CIO lobbying of Congress saw the first increase for five years to the federal MW in 1996, while campaigns around 'living wages' have been successful in raising wages of the lowest paid in the regions (Cobble & Bielski Michal, 2002: 238). Low-pay campaigns disproportionately aid women and minority ethnic employees because they are over-represented among the low paid. For example, in Eire, the introduction of the NMW in April 2000 saw a 2% reduction in the gender pay gap (EIRO, 2001).

Trade unions also have a role in lobbying governments for enhanced legislative provision on equality issues. In the UK for example, trade unions were engaged in discussions over the 1999 Employment Relations Act (which included a number of equality-related provisions), while the TUC has campaigned successfully for improvements to this legislation at EU level, for example gaining enhanced coverage of parental leave rights. In Italy, unions have campaigned actively on issues such as sexual harassment, enhanced maternity benefit, and, in 2000, a union-promoted law on parental leave was passed (Beccalli & Meardi, 2002: 120). As one of the European Social Partners, trade unions through the ETUC have influenced a number of EU directives, which have equality dimensions, including those concerned with working time and fixed-term workers. Trade unions have also campaigned over race equality issues. For example, the Florence Social Dialogue Summit in October 1995 saw for the first time the European Social Partners adopting a Joint Declaration on the 'Prevention of racial discrimination and xenophobia and promotion of equal treatment at the workplace', indicating recognition of racism and the need to take joint action in order to fight against it.

In addition, some trade unions work in coalition or alliance with community and social movement groups (civil rights, environmental, NGOs, charities, etc.). Such coalitions are seen as key to moving beyond sectoral and workplace-based interests towards wider social change and a framework of social rights, affecting many disadvantaged groups in the labour market (Ledwith &

Colgan, 2002: 20). In Canada (Hunt, 2002) and Australia (Franzway, 2002), the connection of women's trade union activity with wider social movement causes was clearly important for the progress of lesbian and gay rights. There are also many examples of assistance and support provided by trade unions for migrant workers. For instance, a number of Italian unions have set up special services to help workers apply for residence permits and social housing, which aid the integration of minority ethnic workers into the labour market (EIRO, 2003).

Short or Long Agenda, Liberal or Radical Approach?

While the foregoing examples present a positive picture of trade union campaigning activity, it is also important, however, to recognise the limitations. Much trade union campaigning can be seen as tinkering – having an indirect effect on equality dimensions, rather than impacting on direct equality aims. While low-pay campaigns can raise the wages of some women and minority ethnic employees, they do not directly confront the causes of the gender and 'race' pay gaps, particularly labour market segregation. More radical policy interventions that attempt, for example, to change the classification of particular jobs (offering increased challenge to existing gendered and racialised job and skill demarcations) are found very rarely within trade union campaigning. Thus the specific gender or 'race' equality dimension of the intervention is downplayed, such that pay is presented as more of a 'family wage' and class (blue-collar) issue than one of gender and race equality. Looking across the countries discussed in Colgan and Ledwith's international collection of papers (2002),[2] it is interesting to note the extent of strategies aiming to avoid the backlash associated with what can be seen as 'special treatment'. In the chapters on Canada (Briskin, 2002) and the United States (Cobble & Bielski Michal, 2002), the need for policies on *gender* rather than *women* is emphasised. This is significant in so far as it may be argued that a focus on gender can dilute (whether intentionally or unintentionally) policy measures because as gender equals men *and* women, it could lead unions to privilege low pay generally over the gender pay gap, thus removing the focus from those most disadvantaged. Further, in Sweden, Mahon (2002) notes how equality initiatives that disproportionately benefit women are initiated on the basis of class rather than gender. Similar broad egalitarian rather than explicitly feminist strategies are also noted within the Italian trade union movement (Beccalli & Meardi, 2002). This has led some commentators to argue that union campaigning in the United States and elsewhere has been 'more effective … in advancing needs of women, when those needs are seen as compatible and even complementary with those of men' (Cobble & Bielski Michal, 2002: 245). The problem is that while such strategies have the advantage of avoiding accusations of special treatment, the realities of discrimination remain unacknowledged. Therefore the policies have less potential to be of a 'long agenda' type and be more transformative.

Equality Bargaining

Globally, the proportion of the workforce covered by collective bargaining is variable: for example, as high as 98% in Austria and as low as 15% in the United States (EIRO, 2003). In addition, the scope of the equality agenda within collective bargaining also varies and is determined by a number of contextual factors. These include the history and traditions of collective bargaining in the country, industry or organisation; state and management objectives in industrial relations and how these relate to economic policy and business strategy; and the balance of bargaining power between employers and unions. Furthermore, the relationship between law and collective bargaining varies widely. For example, in countries such as France, Germany and Greece the law plays an important role in regulating conditions of employment. Meanwhile in other member states – most notably the Nordic countries – collective bargaining plays an equally important role. Additionally the legal support for collective bargaining varies from country to country (e.g. collective agreements are not legally binding in the UK whereas they are in the United States).

Collective agreements may also be at national, industrial sector, company or workplace level depending on the collective bargaining arrangements in the particular national context. For example, in eight EU countries (Austria, Germany, Greece, Italy, the Netherlands, Portugal, Spain and Sweden) the sectoral level is currently the dominant wage bargaining level, while in France, Luxembourg and the UK the company is the key pay bargaining level. In Japan and the United States, the predominant bargaining level for pay and all other issues is the workplace level (EIRO, 2003). The level of bargaining has been found to have implications for the content and scope of collective agreements. Kravaritou (1997) finds that across the EU, gender pay differentials are narrower in countries where centralised systems of collective bargaining exist (national or sectoral level), and are wider in those countries with decentralised systems of collective bargaining (organisational or workplace level). One explanation is that nationally agreed levels of pay provide greater consistency of treatment, while local pay agreements and individual contracts allow more space for employer discrimination, particularly given the existence of gender segregation (Anker, 1997).

Developing Colling and Dickens' (1989: 390) definition of equality bargaining beyond a gender focus, we define equality bargaining as 'the collective negotiation of provisions that are of particular interest or benefit to disadvantaged groups and/or are likely to facilitate equality at work'. Within each country equality bargaining objectives may also vary from one union to another, depending upon the composition and characteristics of union membership and the type of employers with whom they bargain and employers' own objectives and strategies. Therefore, there is a huge variety of equality issues covered by collective bargaining, for example pay and benefits equality, job segregation, job access/security, work/life balance, harassment and anti-sex and race discrimination policies. A few examples of agreements and bargaining issues are now discussed to provide a flavour of the types of equality issues unions focus on.

Bargaining on gender issues

The OECD estimates that the gender pay gap is 16% worldwide based on average full-time hourly wages (ICFTU, 2003). In Europe, as in other parts of the world (Colgan & Ledwith, 2002), aspects of equal pay form part of national bargaining agendas (EIRO, 2002a), varying in scope and content according to national bargaining arrangements. Some examples are worthy of specific mention, such as the Finnish national agreement which introduced a positive action (and arguably more radical) intervention in 2000–1 in the form of 'equality allowances' at industry sector level, in proportion to the number of women in the sector, in order to improve women's wages (EIRO, 2002a). Given the extent of gender segregation, progress on equal pay also requires that attention be paid to job evaluation and job classification. This is reflected in the case of Belgium, where, in 2002, inter-sectoral agreements committed the social partners to maintaining efforts to achieve greater equality between men and women. This includes reviewing job classifications in order to ensure they are not discriminatory (EIRO, 2002b). Linked to earlier discussions about the unions' wider political role, in the UK, the TUC has been spearheading a campaign to promote equal pay audits in public sector organisations, including provision of activist training (http://www.tuc.org.uk/learning/tuc-4146–f0.cfm).

Trade unions have also been active on the issue of work life balance. Indeed this is a high-profile campaign of the TUC, which has a dedicated website (http://www.tuc.org.uk/changingtimes) and issues a fortnightly update by email. Following this initiative individual unions have developed campaigns and resources to promote the issue (Kirton, 2003). However on a European level, there are few collective agreements on the issue (EIRO, 2002a: 50).

Bargaining on race issues

In Europe, 11 union confederations (out of 24, covering 17 countries) specifically include migrant and minority ethnic workers' issues in their guidelines on collective bargaining (ETUC, 2003). General statements on equality and on equal access to training, promotion and other workplace benefits are the most frequent elements in such guidelines; however, some federations reported progress on more specific issues such as agreed changes in working time to accommodate religious practices. The problem is that where bargaining is decentralised we do not really know how much difference national (or in this case a transnational declarative) union policy makes. Once again this highlights the possible effects of different bargaining levels.

The conditions of work of migrant and immigrant workers are often central to equality bargaining relating to ethnicity and race, because huge numbers of migrant workers are employed all over the world, often within low-paid, low-status jobs. For example, Mahon (2002) reports how Swedish unions were instrumental in gaining early bilateral agreements enshrining equal pay for migrant workers. Mahon (2002) also provides an example of local agreements where employers have met the total costs of language courses for migrant workers in order to aid integration into the labour market. Wrench (2002: 86) details how the largest Danish union HK (representing commercial and clerical employees) has adopted an ambitious ethnic equality programme, which includes ensuring that local and national collective agreements specifically promote ethnic equality.

Short or Long Agenda, Liberal or Radical Approach?

Equality bargaining on gender and race has achieved some positive outcomes, but its effectiveness can be questioned. While agreements are made, putting them into practice and achieving equality of outcome is often a more difficult task. Their operation is affected by a number of factors including different bargaining levels, the power of unions in relation to other industrial relations actors, and the prevalence of patriarchal and white male cultures within unions and workplaces. Therefore, the content of collective agreements often reflects a liberal approach to equality. Commentators have reflected on the ways in which bargaining agreements may often act to support existing (particularly gender) stereotypes. Kravaritou's comparative European study (1997) indicates the ways in which collective agreements remain male oriented and perpetuate a masculine norm. For example, agreements focus on women coping with their dual role, rather than making more substantial challenges to the status quo, such as radical reorganisation of work and the redistribution of caring and domestic roles. There are a number of explanatory contextual factors for the limited radical action taken by trade unions, which are now discussed.

The context of trade union activity

Trade unions self-evidently exist within a broader social context, being particularly influenced by the political and industrial relations environments. Thus, there are many factors shaping the perceived priorities for trade union campaigning, which may not include equality issues. Also the outcomes of trade union equality bargaining are influenced by membership levels and collective bargaining coverage. Obviously, where membership density and collective bargaining coverage are higher, union action can have more of an impact.

Therefore, an evaluation of trade union activity has to be situated within the context of wider political and public discourse and national culture and traditions. For example, there may be different interpretations of what equality is, which may have implications for the content of collective agreements and the nature of campaigns. As an example, liberal equality campaigns and collective agreements based on equal (same) treatment may actually work against more transformational bargaining agendas aiming to improve the conditions of disadvantaged groups. Union action on the issue of migrant workers is a useful example here. Wrench (2003) points out that in Germany, unions campaigned during the 1970s and 1980s to ensure migrant workers were covered by the same regulations as German workers (e.g. equal pay and equal rights to representation). However, more radical positive action measures could not then be countenanced, including some anti-discrimination measures, because this would be perceived as 'special treatment' seemingly contradicting the espoused policy of equal treatment. Also, within a traditional analysis of the trade union role as protector of members' jobs, it may seem logical that unions might oppose or resist immigration and the employment of migrant workers (Wrench, 2003: 16) in order to avoid the risk of depressing the pay of nationals. There is some evidence of this in Norway and Belgium amongst others, where unions have opposed 'open border' policies, and in Austria, Hungary, Finland, the UK and Germany where worries about 'cheap labour imports' are noticeable in the bargaining discourses of unions (EIRO, 2003: 18). While migrant workers still have not gained a central place on collective bargaining agendas, in some countries agreements may even serve to reinforce disadvantage. In Austria, a number of sectoral agreements actually *allow* discrimination against migrant workers in favour of Austrian citizens in recruitment and dismissal (EIRO, 2003: 19).

The differing legal context also needs to be considered as part of the context of trade union activity. For example, the legal status of migrant and immigrant workers differs from country to country and accords them differing citizenship status (see Kirton & Greene, 2005: 251–84). This has an impact on public policy, illustrated for example by the ways in which some countries routinely undertake demographic monitoring of ethnicity, such as the UK and Eire, while others are vehemently opposed to monitoring, such as Denmark, France and Austria (ETUC, 2003). Indeed in France, recording racial or ethnic origin would run counter to both social and legal norms, based on an assimilationalist concept of citizenship (Wrench, 2002). In addition, Wrench (2002) argues that in some national contexts, unions may be unsympathetic to cultural diversity. While in the UK a public discourse of multiculturalism exists, this is not the case in a country like Denmark where there is often vehement political opposition to multiculturalism. Therefore, this offers possible explanations for why Danish unions have tended to bargain on an equal (same) treatment basis with less emphasis on anti-discrimination (Wrench, 2003).

The changing orientation towards work/life balance policies is another example of the influence of wider public discourse on union activity. Criticism concerns the gender-neutral discourse underpinning many work/life balance policies (Kirton, 2003), which often do not explicitly recognise that women are predominantly primary carers of the family. Indeed, Swan (2002) traces the change in government and trade union rhetoric in the UK over the last decade from 'family-friendly', to 'work-home', to 'work-life',[3] arguably at each stage rendering the gendered aspects of the 'balance' debate less visible. Similarly, at the European level, work/life balance includes 'social life, personal development and civic participation' (EIRO, 2002a: 49). Work/life balance policies therefore do not necessarily aim to challenge the distribution of care and domestic responsibilities, nor structural gender inequalities such as segregation and the pay gap, which produce the material inequalities that push women towards privileging family roles and men towards privileging paid work (Kirton, 2003). Indeed at a European level, there are very few collective agreements concerning pregnancy, child or elder care, with much more policy action over more generic holiday and career break entitlement and working hours (EIRO, 2002a). One reason for the gender-neutral orientation of work/life balance is to avoid the risk of it being perceived as a 'women's issue' (special treatment). For example, in a recent British TUC newsletter (TUC, 2003), the focus of union action on work/life balance is most often male. While on the one hand this might be considered more transformative in the sense of attempting to restructure the balance of work and caring and domestic duties, on the other hand it could also be charged with neglecting to recognise that it is still predominantly women who juggle dual roles at work and in the home. Therefore, even in the new bargaining arena of work/life balance, the male interest is often prioritised (intentionally or unintentionally).

The white male cultures of trade unions also hinder equality action. As discussed in the earlier part of this chapter, the most common 'remedy' for the problems of male- and white-dominated union structures is to increase the number of women and minority ethnic representatives and officials. It is argued that this will enable 'minority' issues to be taken up in bargaining to ensure that organisational policies and practices do not privilege the interests of white men (Colling & Dickens, 1989). We have already noted the slow progress that is being made in the union movement worldwide to increase the diversity of representation; however, once in position, there are now a number of studies which indicate the difficulties that 'minorities' face in getting new issues onto the bargaining agenda. Case study research indicates the ways in which women's voices are marginalised, the trivialisation of what are seen as 'women's issues' by other (male) union officials, and the difficulties women face in being seen as 'real' and credible union activists (Danieli & Greene, 2003; Kirton & Healy, 1999). Therefore, the patriarchal cultures of trade union structures and processes act to thwart more transformative equality bargaining.

CONCLUSION

This chapter set out to examine gender and race diversity and equality within trade unions, and the trade unions' external role in representing diverse interests in the workplace and the wider polity. We have argued that the liberal/radical formulation (Jewson & Mason, 1986) is useful for characterising and evaluating individual equality measures. However, in terms of an overall equality and diversity strategy it is clear from the discussion that the long agenda of the trade union project internally and externally is one of transformation of labour markets and organisations (Cockburn, 1989). Such transformation is essential in order to reduce inequalities and allow disadvantaged groups the access to power necessary to shape the internal and external equality agenda.

The internal picture of trade unions across Europe and in many other countries around the world is one of women's and minority ethnic members' under-representation in decision making caused by a range of structural and cultural barriers. However, the importance of women and minority ethnic workers as sources of members, combined with pressure for change from the groups themselves, has prompted unions to develop a raft of liberal and radical equality policy measures aimed at increasing internal diversity and equality. These measures aim to redress the gender and race democracy deficit, as well as make the unions more effective at representing workforce diversity. The efforts of the past 10 years or so have led to an increase in women's presence in union decision making, but in most countries there is still some way to go before they are represented in proportion to the size of female membership. There is even further to go when it comes to minority ethnic members.

It appears from the experience of many countries that the most effective tool for reversing under-representation is the radical measure of separate organising, which has the most potential to be transformational. It remains controversial, particularly in relation to race and ethnicity, and its perceived appropriateness or utility varies over time and space. Separate forms of organising are unlikely to disappear in the near future, because there is evidence that women and minority ethnic members have become more influential in unions as a consequence of separate organising, rather than as a consequence of more liberal measures. Change is crucial, if trade unions are to have any significant impact at workplace and societal level in advancing the equality agenda. However, separate organising is certainly not a panacea; change has been slow and incremental and the problem of under-representation in decision making has not been solved. Therefore, it is likely that separate organising as well as other more liberal equality measures will remain important at least until such time as diverse groups are fully integrated in union decision making.

While it is unlikely that we will see the concerns of 'minority' groups become central to the external trade union agenda unless greater internal representation of diverse groups occurs, it is true to say that unions in many countries are paying increased attention to diversity and equality issues. Outside of their internal structures, trade union equality agendas are often less radical and transformational. Nevertheless, there is evidence that equality is now an important area of trade union activity both in the wider societal, political and legislative spheres through campaigning activities, and at the workplace through collective bargaining. This chapter has outlined examples of this activity, and, clearly, some of this action has achieved positive gains for those who face disadvantage in the labour market. In spite of this it is important to retain a critical perspective when evaluating trade union activity. Inequality is a persistent problem within the labour market and society more broadly and in the face of a changing context of inequality unions need to continue to develop strategies to combat employment discrimination and disadvantage.

A critical perspective on equality measures is essential in order that unions can learn from failures and build on successes. We have argued that campaigning and bargaining agendas more typically fall into the liberal or 'short' agenda approach. While trade unions can be criticised for this, it is important to recognise that they are by necessity (particularly in periods of low membership and decreasing influence) pragmatic, defensive organisations. The wider social, political, legislative and employment context within which unions operate is often hostile, meaning that more progressive, radical agendas often exist at the level of national policy and rhetoric, but in practice the bargaining agenda is often defensive. Therefore it is difficult to evaluate how widespread are actual agreements containing specific equality measures, especially when bargaining occurs at company or workplace levels. Despite limitations, it is also clear that unions can play an important role in spearheading, developing and monitoring equality agreements and policies, many of which have led to real gains for disadvantaged employees at both national and organisational levels.

NOTES

1 We acknowledge that the categorisation of peoples into 'racial' and ethnic groupings is a subject of debate (Barot, Bradley & Fenton, 1999). We employ the term 'race equality' because it is widely used in the British union context and we also use 'black' to describe minority ethnic workers of colour, because this is the term favoured by (black) British trade unionists.

2 Canada, Sweden, Malaysia, India, Italy, Germany, the UK, South Africa, the United States, Australia.

3 A wider trend also experienced in for example the United States, Australia, New Zealand.

REFERENCES

Anker, R. (1997). Theories of occupational segregation be sex: An overview. *International Labour Review, 136*(7), 315–40.

Barot, R., Bradley, H., & Fenton, S. (1999). Rethinking ethnicity and gender. In R. Barot, H. Bradley & S. Fenton (Eds), *Ethnicity, gender and social change* (pp. 1–25). Basingstoke: Macmillan.

Beccalli, B., & Meardi, G. (2002). Italian labour's changing and singular ambiguities. In F. Colgan & S. Ledwith (Eds), *Gender, diversity and trade unions: International perspectives* (pp. 113–31). London: Routledge.

Bradley, H. (1994). Divided we fall: Unions and their members. *Employee Relations, 16*(2), 41–52.

Braithewaite, M., & Byrne, C. (1994). *Women in decision-making in trade unions.* Brussels: European Trades Union Congress.

Briskin, L. (1993). Union women and separate organizing. In L. Briskin & P. McDermott (Eds), *Women challenging unions* (pp. 89–108). Toronto: University of Toronto Press.

Briskin, L. (2002). The equity project in Canadian unions: Confronting the challenge of restructuring and globalisation. In F. Colgan & S. Ledwith (Eds), *Gender, diversity and trade unions: International perspectives* (pp. 28–47). London: Routledge.

Cobble, D. S., & Bielski Michal, M. (2002). Working women and the US labour movement. In F. Colgan & S. Ledwith (Eds), *Gender, diversity and trade unions: International perspectives* (pp. 232–56). London: Routledge.

Cockburn, C. (1989). Equal opportunities: The long and short agenda. *Industrial Relations Journal, 20,* 213–25.

Cockburn, C. (1995). *Strategies for gender democracy.* Luxembourg: European Commission.

Colgan, F., & Ledwith, S. (Eds) (2002). *Gender, diversity and trade unions: International perspectives.* London: Routledge.

Colling, T., & Dickens, L. (1989). Equality bargaining – Why not? *Equal Opportunities Commission Research Papers*, London, HMSO.

Creese, G. (1995). Gender equity or masculine privilege – Union strategies and economic restructuring in a white-collar union. *Canadian Journal of Sociology, 20*(2), 143–66.

Curtin, J., & Higgins, W. (1998). Feminism and unionism in Sweden. *Politics and Society, 16*(1), 69–93.

Danieli, A., & Greene, A. M. (2003). Fragmented identities and patriarchal common sense: The case of male and female trade union negotiators. Paper presented at the 21st Standing Conference on Organisational Symbolism (SCOS), Cambridge, 9–12 July.

Delaney, J., & Lundy, C. (1996). Unions, collective bargaining and the diversity paradox. In E. Kossek & S. Lobel (Eds), *Managing diversity: Human resource strategies for transforming the workplace* (pp. 245–72). Cambridge, MA: Blackwell.

EIRO (2001). Low wage workers and the working poor: EU and Norway: http://www.eiro.eurofound.ie/2002/08/study/TN0208101S.html (Accessed 31 May 2005).

EIRO (2002a). Gender, pay equity: A comparative study January 2002: http://www.eiro.eurofound.ie/2002/01/study/TN0201101S.html (Accessed 31 May 2005).

EIRO (2002b). Comparative overview of industrial relations in Europe in 2002: http://www.eiro.eurofound.ie/2003/03/feature/TN0303101F.html (Accessed 31 May 2005).

EIRO (2003). *EIRO Observer Bulletin*, May issue: http://www.eiro.eurofound.ie/pdf/eo03-3.pdf (Accessed 31 May 2005).

Elton, J. (1997). Making democratic unions: From policy to practice. In B. Pocock (Ed.), *Strife, Sex and Politics* (pp. 109–27). London: Routledge.

ETUC (2002). *Women in trade unions: Making the difference.* Brussels, ETUC.

ETUC (2003). *Migrant and ethnic minority workers: Challenging trade unions.* Brussels: Labour Research Department and ETUC: http://www.etuc.org.

Franzway, S. (2002). Sexual politics in the Australian labour movements. In F. Colgan & S. Ledwith (Eds), *Gender, diversity and trade unions: International perspectives* (pp. 275–91). London: Routledge.

Greene, A. M., & Kirton, G. (2002). Advancing gender equality: The role of women-only trade union education. *Gender, Work & Organisation, 9*(1), 39–59.

Healy, G., & Kirton, G. (2000). Women, power and trade union government in the UK. *British Journal of Industrial Relations, 38*(3), 343–60.

Howell, C. (1996). Women as the paradigmatic trade unionists? *Economic and Industrial Democracy, 17,* 511–43.

Hunt, G. (2002). Organised labour, sexual diversity and union activism in Canada. In F. Colgan & S. Ledwith (Eds), *Gender, diversity and trade unions: International perspectives* (pp. 257–75). London: Routledge.

ICFTU (2003). Equality through pay equity. *Trade Union World Briefing March 2003*: http://www.icftu.org/www/pdf/PayequityE.pdf (Accessed 31 May 2005).

Jewson, N., & Mason, D. (1986). The theory and practice of equal opportunities policies: Liberal and radical approaches. *Sociological Review, 34*(2), 307–34.

Kirton, G. (1999). Sustaining and developing women's trade union activism: A gendered project? *Gender, Work & Organization, 6*(4), 213–23.

Kirton, G. (2003). Progress on work-life balance? European Industrial Relations Observatory: http://www.eiro.eurofound.ie/2003/02/Feature/UK0302103F.html (Accessed 31 May 2005).

Kirton, G., & Greene, A. M. (2002). Positive action in trade unions: The case of women and black members. *Industrial Relations Journal, 33*(2), 157–72.

Kirton, G., & Greene, A. M. (2005). *The dynamics of managing diversity: A critical approach* (2nd edn). Oxford: Butterworth–Heinemann.

Kirton, G., & Healy, G. (1999). Transforming union women: The role of women trade union officials in union renewal. *Industrial Relations Journal, 30*(1), 31–45.

Kravaritou, Y. (1997). Equal opportunities and collective bargaining in the EU. EIRO: http://www.eiro.eurofound.ie/1997/04/study/TN9704201S.html (Accessed 31 May 2005).

Labour Research (2001). Where are all the black officials? (14–15 August). London: Labour Research Department.

Leah, R. (1993). Black women speak out: Racism and unions. In L. Briskin & P. McDermott (Eds), *Women challenging unions* (pp. 112–25). Toronto: University of Toronto Press.

Ledwith, S., & Colgan, F. (2002). Tackling gender, diversity and trade union democracy: A worldwide project? In F. Colgan & S. Ledwith (Eds), *Gender, diversity and trade unions: International perspectives* (pp. 1–27). London: Routledge.

Mahon, R. (2002). Sweden's LO. Learning to embrace the differences within? In F. Colgan & S. Ledwith (Eds), *Gender, diversity and trade unions: International perspectives* (pp. 48–72). London: Routledge.

McBride, A. (2001). *Gender democracy in trade unions*. Aldershot: Ashgate.

Munro, A. (2001). A feminist trade union agenda? The continued significance of class, gender and race. *Gender, Work & Organisation, 8*(4), 454–71.

Parker, J. (2002). Women's groups in British unions. *British Journal of Industrial Relations, 40*(1), 23–48.

Petrovic, J. (2001). The male face of trade union in central and Eastern Europe. The secret of invisible women. Brussels: ICFTU.

Phizacklea, A., & Miles, R. (1987). The British trade union movement and racism. In G. Lee & R. Loveridge (Eds), *The manufacture of disadvantage* (pp. 21–30). Milton Keynes: Open University Press.

Richards, W. (2001). Evaluating equal opportunities initiatives: The case for a 'transformative' agenda. In M. Noon & E. Ogbonna (Eds), *Equality, diversity and disadvantage in employment* (pp. 15–31). Basingstoke: Palgrave.

Swan, E. (2002). Work-life balance: Recovery from overdosing on work. Paper presented at an ESRC seminar on Problematizing Diversity, University of Manchester, March.

Trebilcock, A. (1991). Strategies for strengthening women's participation in trade union leadership. *International Labour Review, 130*(4), 407–26.

TUC (2003). *Changing Times News*, No. 24, 18 July: http://www.tuc.org.uk/work_life.

Virdee, S., & Grint, K. (1994). Black self-organisation in trade unions. *Sociological Review, 42*(2), 202–26.

Walters, S. (2002). Female part-time workers' attitudes to trade unions in Britain. *British Journal of Industrial Relations, 40*(1), 49–68.

Webb, J. (1997). The politics of equal opportunity. *Gender, Work & Organization, 4*(3), 159–67.

Wrench, J. (2002). *Diversity management, discrimination and ethnic minorities in Europe: Clarifications, critiques and research agendas* (Themes No. 19), MangfåldensPraktik, Centre for Ethnic and Urban Studies, Norrköping.

Wrench, J. (2003). *Breakthroughs and Blind Spots: Trade union responses to immigrants and ethnic minorities in Denmark and the UK*. Esbjerg: University of Southern Denmark.

Young, I. M. (1990). *Justice and the politics of difference*. Princeton, NJ: Princeton University Press.

Young, I. M. (2000). *Inclusion and democracy*. Oxford: Oxford University Press.

21

Critical Diversity Management Practice in Australia[1]

Romanced or Co-opted?

AMANDA SINCLAIR

Working on diversity in organizations and classrooms appears to be a welcome opportunity to do research and intervene to promote fairness, equality and toler-ance. In this chapter, I explore Australian experience of working with diversity to show how the diversity management discourse – with its universalizing language, expectations and justifications – can forestall and silence debate about race and gender issues and, in many cases, entrench the institutional status quo.

The chapter begins with an overview of the practice of diversity management in Australian organizations, revealing the increasing popularity of the term 'diver-sity' and its ostensible rising acceptance as a principle of good management. Despite the original intention of diversity management being to work towards creating greater equality of treatment and opportunity (Linnehan & Konrad, 1999), I show how the development of a diversity discourse in management prac-tice has subordinated those ideals. Taking three elements of the discourse: the business case for diversity; managing diversity doctrine and dimensions of diver-sity, I argue that, frequently, diversity has been manufactured into a malleable set of extensions to managerial prerogative.

The diversity discourse encourages us all to interpret and espouse organizational diversity as simple compelling logic. Of course, it is never this. Hidden behind its marketed neutrality as just good Human Resource practice are contested issues of moral philosophy and political ideology. I argue that the only way to teach and practice with diversity is by keeping at the forefront alternative critical perspectives on those features of diversity that the discourse renders benign, generalisable or uncontestable. The path for practitioners is to engage critically and reflexively with diversity: to illuminate the distribution of power, to reveal the subtle ways in which gender and racial oppression continue and to interleave into the evolving business ideology around diversity, disruptive reminders about the real values at stake.

Over the last decade and a half, diversity and diversity management have become widely encountered items in managerial language. This should surely be a cause for optimism among those working to make workplaces free from discrimination. Yet in this chapter, I argue that the discourse that has evolved and accompanies the management of diversity has in fact reinforced a world view – a set of assumptions and expectations about differences in organizations – that takes us further from understanding and working with the real substance of diversity – namely, social and structural relations.

I begin with a brief review of the history of diversity management's progress into partial legitimacy, including how the term diversity continues to be interpreted as code for something else – affirmative action, EEO, multiculturalism. Focusing on the Australian context and drawing on the experiences of practitioners, the state of diversity management practice is assessed. In Australian workplaces there continue to be many cases of diversity initiatives unravelled, of organizational and cultural change forestalled by economic pressures or undercut by new leadership, of diversity marooned in the tidal flats at the edge of organizational life.

Underpinning the often parlous and compromised state of diversity management practice are limitations entrenched by the management of diversity discourse. These limitations are elucidated using three recognizable features of the discourse: the 'business case for diversity'(Litvin, 2002) which converts diversity into an economic good; the 'managing diversity' ideology which rests on flawed assumptions; and the diversity category itself, which unifies and renders equivalent 'dimensions' of diversity, de-politicizing and disenfranchising what are separate and often conflicting interests.

Elaborating these discursive features, I seek to show how the discourse 'works' – succeeds in appropriating diversity to certain sorts of agendas but concealing other experiences (Foldy, 2002). I also draw on examples to show how diversity fails – fails to encompass the lived diversity experiences of people, and fails to engage decision-makers and power-holders in any really substantive process of change. The diversity discourse too often plays right into the wrong hands, reifying experiences of 'otherness' among those without power (Prasad & Prasad, 2002) and reducing opportunities for systemic change.

As an antidote to the limitations of the discourse, I argue the need for the articulation of critical perspectives on diversity. In Table 21.1 below[2] and drawing on my own and colleagues' experiences teaching and working with diversity, I outline the shape of working as a practitioner on diversity in a reflexive way – a *modus operandi* that is conscious of power and one's own capacity to either be co-opted or resist managerial and organizational urges to render diversity a tool to enhance control of 'the other' (Czarniawska & Höpfl, 2002). While the diversity management discourse has tainted diversity's capacity to be the banner under which systemic change happens, discourse and practice continue to be available for critique by theorists, and thoughtful practitioners.

DIVERSITY'S POPULARITY IN THE AUSTRALIAN PRACTICE CONTEXT

In the decade starting in the early 1990s, the term 'diversity' has seen a surge of popularity in Australian managerial and public policy contexts, alongside the demise of Equal Employment Opportunity (EEO) and Affirmative Action (De Cieri & Olekalns, 2001; D'Netto, Smith & Da Gama Pinto, 2000; Sinclair, 2000a). I begin with an overview of legislative, political and managerial influences which have contributed to the decay of discourses of equality (Summers, 2003) and their partial replacement by a diversity discourse in Australian public and business domains.

Australian academics have been discussing the management of diversity since the mid 1990s (e.g. Bertone, Esposto & Turner, 1998; Burton & Ryall, 1994; Cope & Kalantzis, 1997; Dagher & D'Netto, 1997; De Cieri & Olekalns, 2001; Kramar, 1999; Patrickson & O'Brien, 2001 conferences in 2000 and 2001 culminating in reports and a special issue of the *Asia Pacific Journal of Human Resources*, 2003). However, there is little systemic information about diversity management in Australian companies. More detailed case studies of diversity management within particular industries and organizations remain relatively rare (some exceptions include Dagher, D'Netto & Sohal, 1998; Gillespie, 1999; Krautil, 1995; Smith, 1998; Wilson & Sinclair, 1997).

Equipped with neither comprehensive audits of Australian diversity management nor with extensive case data, the interpretations offered in this chapter are largely based on personal experience: working with and listening to diversity networks; working as a consultant on diversity myself; and on discussions and interviews with consultants and academics working on diversity in the major business centres of Melbourne and Sydney. I have sought to locate and critically evaluate diversity management's progress within a broader Australian political and ideological context but also to capture the practice rather than the theory – the interpretations, doubts and hopes of those who advise and manage diversity initiatives in organizations. Nevertheless, the views expressed are my own unless surrounded by quote marks – in which case they come from an interview conducted with a diversity practitioner.

Australia was regarded as an innovator in EEO and women's policy when, in 1986, the Commonwealth government introduced Affirmative Action legislation. While it did not impose quotas, the legislation did require private sector organizations with over 100 employees to annually report to government on the current status of women and minorities, and on their plans and progress on improving equality of opportunity in the workplace. Legislation outlawing discrimination on the basis of race and sex had been introduced in 1975 and 1984 respectively. By the late 1980s and early 1990s, EEO was a well-supported principle particularly in the Commonwealth and most state public sectors with agencies, educational institutions and many private sector organizations with an EEO officer, responsible for collecting data and training employees in anti-discrimination legislation. Much of the focus continued to be on women, except in a few large workplaces such as car manufacturing with very multicultural workforces and a history of workplace tension between ethnic groups.

By the late 1990s a conservative Commonwealth government was seeking to wind back the amount of regulation on business, reviewing the Affirmative Action legislation and putting more energy into supporting diversity. Resources were withdrawn from various women's advisory units (such as the Office of Women's Affairs) and women's issues relegated to the over-burdened Sex Discrimination Commissioner and Human Rights and Equal Opportunity Commission (HREOC) (Summers, 2003). The Affirmative Action Agency was replaced in 1999 by the Equal Opportunity for Women in the Workplace Agency (EOWA) which, relenting to business pressure, positioned itself as supporting business to realize the benefits in making better use of female employees through 'strategic human resource management' (Sinclair, 2000a).

Meanwhile diversity was burgeoning within the Department of Immigration and Multicultural Affairs (DIMA), later expanded to include Aboriginal Affairs. The Commonwealth public sector has been particularly active in sponsoring a focus on what has been termed 'productive diversity'. In Australia, the term was introduced into public policy at a 1992 conference organized by the Office of Multicultural Affairs, by the then Prime Minister, Paul Keating. Subsequent conservative governments have embraced productive diversity which

> recognises the economic value of Australia's culturally diverse society ... and is generally defined in terms of ... capitalising on the linguistic and cultural skills, knowledge of overseas business markets and experience in business practices often available in people born and educated overseas; and removing impediments to the effective management of a culturally diverse workforce (e.g. cross-cultural awareness, vocational English training, etc.). (Department of Immigration and Multicultural Affairs, 2000)

In the area of productive diversity, the Commonwealth government has sought to re-brand increasingly contested policy domains of multiculturalism and racism (towards Indigenous Australians, migrant groups and, most recently, refugees) under the heading of selling the (economic) benefits of diversity (Bertone & Leahy, 2003). Culminating in business conferences held in the late 1990s and sponsored by DIMA, the focus was on establishing and proselytizing the 'business case for diversity'. The Commonwealth government had established a high-powered multicultural advisory group consisting of representatives from various ethnic and other communities from all states of Australia. To some degree the progress that was made in selling the benefits of diversity and harmony (e.g. through Harmony Day) has been undermined by recent government policy, including the extended mandatory detention of asylum-seekers. Several high-profile and former supporters of the Commonwealth government's diversity policies have publicly criticized asylum-seeker treatment as inconsistent with international human rights standards and have resigned from advisory roles.

Australian business has been slow to recognize that individual or systemic discrimination in the workplace exists, let alone that it is an important business issue (Crawley and Sinclair, 2003; Sinclair, 1998; Sinclair & Wilson, 2002). Indeed, it could be argued that the shift away from an EEO and anti-discrimination focus towards diversity in the late 1990s was partially the result of business pressure to reduce bureaucratic surveillance. The reduction of reporting requirements that accompanied the overhaul of the Affirmative Action Act in 1999 is one example of the success of lobbying to reduce the 'burden' of legislative compliance on business.

Surveys of CEOs and HR practitioners (De Cieri & Olekalns, 2001; D'Netto et al., 2000; Nicholas, 2000) reveal a growing awareness of diversity but sparse commitment to overarching strategies or programmes. The most commonly reported diversity activity is diversity training, followed by targeted employment strategies for under-represented groups (more likely in the public sector) (D'Netto et al., 2000). Confrontingly, the researchers of one study of 227 medium and large firms found that most of their respondents, 80% of whom were CEOs, said they had no diversity policies, did not keep records about the diversity of their workforce, were doing little to foster diversity capabilities in their organizations, rated diversity as of little significance in their plans for growth and, most devastatingly, were relatively satisfied with the virtual absence of corporate activity in diversity management (Nicholas, 2000).

Despite this sobering lack of CEO commitment to diversity, HR practitioners have more informally initiated considerable diversity activity. Several corporate networks formed around diversity from the early 1990s. The InterCompany Network (ICN) assembled representatives from Esso, Hewlett Packard, The Body Shop, Ericsson and Siemens Australia among others. Its successor, the Corporate Diversity ThinkTank, comprises a cluster of HR specialists from large corporations such as IBM, the National and Commonwealth Banks, whose jobs include responsibility for diversity. However, much of this diversity work goes on at the edge of roles that are already 'overburdened' (Sinclair & Wilson, 2002), part of an ascendant wider business ideology that further marginalizes diversity within the already marginalized HR as 'non-core' business issues.

Academics have voiced varying concerns about the productive diversity public policy discourse alongside the also troublesome rhetoric of multiculturalism (see Appo & Härtel, 2003; Hage, 1998). Like the phase 'practical reconciliation' in indigenous affairs, critics argue productive diversity takes the focus away from systemic bases of discrimination putting the onus on individuals to fix the burden of their difference or disadvantage through 'practical', 'productive' solutions. The implication is that economic incentives will magically remove long-standing racist or discriminatory attitudes. A further question for practitioners with an interest in EEO and gender is where women's rights sit within a policy squarely focused on cultural diversity.

Despite these concerns, state and federal public sector organizations have been among the most energetic in diversity management. State police and other emergency service organizations, law and justice departments, local government authorities have programmes targeted at women, indigenous employees and those with a disability. There are diversity networks linking government and semi-governmental authorities in most states. Such initiatives have been driven by a variety of factors: progressive state governments, increasing numbers of women at graduate and senior levels of the bureaucracy and a general view that public sector organizations should reflect the demographics of the communities they serve. For example, the Victorian Police Commissioner has made this a key argument for targeting the recruitment of mature age, minority background and female police (Office of Public Employment, 2004). Managing diversity programmes have also been introduced as vehicles through which to dismantle traditionally homogeneous cultures and associated problems of corruption and bullying in the military, fire and police services.

In the private sector, the other major influence on the rise of diversity's popularity has been the influence of international, largely American and a few UK-based companies whose head office is driving diversity. Examples of Australian operations with diversity programmes and diversity managers have included Hewlett Packard (now with Compaq), Mobil, Shell, BP, IBM, Ford, Cadbury Schweppes and large broking and consulting organizations such as Deloittes, some of whom have experienced discrimination litigation. Although many of these programmes are badged as 'diversity', the focus of most local activities is women. For example, in the Asian region, both Shell and Hewlett Packard have adopted targets for increasing the proportion of women at senior levels and managers are measured and rewarded for their performance. According to one diversity practitioner: 'There are a lot more people using the word "diversity", especially consultants and in organizations. In the public sector there is significant use of the word, especially "equity and diversity", to describe large scale programs, most of which are virtually EEO with another name.'

Many of the large companies with Australian headquarters, including banks, legal and professional services firms, have diversity programmes. While many have a focus on women, some also have initiatives aimed at expanding opportunities for indigenous employees and those from non-English-speaking backgrounds. In another case, an organizational diversity initiative grew out of an incident where an employee was caught making racial slurs about a Jewish client. It is also common to have work/life balance programmes, with provisions for part-time work, job-share, child care and elder care, all shelved under the diversity banner. According to an observer, there is 'an increased use of the word and increased focus on diversity programs but these are often driven by someone in HR with little power'.

To summarize, momentum for a discourse shift from EEO to diversity has come from government policy, from global firms with a head-office-driven diversity agenda and from an increasingly pervasive corporate ideology which condemns government intervention and seeks to maximize managerial autonomy. At the same time and among managers there remains widespread suspicion that 'diversity is just EEO by another name'.

Practitioners offer varied assessments of what diversity might offer, according to their own disciplinary backgrounds and experiences. One interviewee volunteered that 'diversity is a safe place to park gender for a while' while they work on other aspects of difference such as establishing a disability programme. This strategy then allows the organization to be steered back to gender in the broader sense – not just women. At the same time, practitioners are coming to diversity equipped with a variety of conceptual and theoretical frameworks. Consultants with an interest in cross-cultural and indigenous issues sit alongside feminists with a history in EEO and eager managers, firmly committed to the 'can do' managerial camp and impatient with theoretical reservations or reforming agendas.

In my research for this chapter, several features characterize most diversity work done by consultants and organization managers on diversity in Australia. The purpose of this summary is not to denigrate individual efforts but highlight the systemic nature of the difficulties. While there are isolated exceptions where organizations engage consultants to embark on relatively open-ended 'reflective journeys' around diversity issues for sustained periods of years rather than months, more typically practitioners are:

1 Engaged to work on diversity in programmes that are misunderstood or devalued by senior managers. Leaders are usually supportive at the early stages where the focus is on data gathering or preliminary diversity training for the middle or bottom of the organization. However, only a few leadership groups remain engaged if the focus narrows to requiring change in dominant norms and practices (Sinclair, 2000b). Turnover among CEOs has also meant that at any one time there is rarely more than a handful of leaders strongly committed to diversity.

2 Doing corporate work on diversity that contains tensions around the dimensions of diversity that are being targeted without clear articulation of those tensions or how they might pull in opposite dimensions. For example, diversity programmes are initiated because it feels unsafe or impossible to explicitly target gender issues.

3 Conducting 'awareness raising' activities but with significant resistance to taking diversity training much further (see also Foldy, 2002; Prasad & Prasad, 2002). Few diversity training initiatives are empowered to label and work on the existing culture as 'the problem'.

4 Hired to do diversity work by an overworked HR manager who needs support and is sometimes regarded suspiciously by senior managers. Although there have been cases in the past of diversity programmes initiated and supported by local CEOs (Bob Joss at Westpac, Bruce Thompson at Hewlett Packard), they remain rare in Australia.

5 Engaged in diversity work prompted by the need to comply with international head office policy or legislation, or following a publicized and expensive case of discrimination (again most typically in the United States where lawsuits and payouts are large).

Overall, work associated with diversity continues to be a marginal activity for most businesses. The diversity practitioner is often condemned to a perilous existence on the edge of managerial legitimacy and this, of course, puts great pressure on those individuals to do the diversity work managers say they want, rather than assisting the organization to identify and face deeper structural problems. It is this cluster of pressures which have prompted me to explore with colleagues ways of undertaking diversity work that are more critical and reflexive. The remainder of this chapter turns to deconstructing the managing diversity discourse and offering alternative theoretical insights. I also offer some suggestions for the practitioner preparing to undertake diversity work in organizations.

DIVERSITY DISCOURSE

Our ideas and values around differences in organizations have increasingly been shaped by a diversity discourse (Litvin, 2002). Diversity discourse refers to the ways the word diversity and other words typically used to frame and define diversity produce in themselves a particular set of meanings, understandings and expectations – in effect 'regimes of truth' (Hollway, 1989: 39). Discourse theorists argue that the factual content of ideas or concepts is created and given meaning and legitimacy as 'the truth' or 'reality' by the rhetorical and linguistic strategies used to support them. Analyses of discourse shows how theories come to be 'infused with unexamined commitments to particular moral and social orders' (Arrington & Francis, 1989: 4). One effect of the managing diversity discourse has been to legitimate and institutionalize a particular form of organizational response (managing) to what the discourse has constructed as 'the problem' (other people's differences) (Litvin, 2002: 161).

Within the discourse, diversity is almost always prefaced with another word, such as 'valuing', 'managing' or 'the business case for'. One conference was subtitled 'Delivering the Diversity Dividend'. These discursive techniques are not accidental or incidental. They immediately establish diversity as needing to be bounded or managed, in turn inviting and achieving legitimacy for the managing diversity regime implicit in the phrase. Diversity itself is only given a conditional legitimacy via these discursive prefaces; that is, diversity is legitimate only in so far as it is 'managed', given a 'business case for' or 'delivering a dividend'. Without these markers, diversity stands on its own, an ambiguous and perhaps ominous idea. We see how discursive devices mirror and assist in allocating power and structure, establishing meaning and expectations. Diversity on its own is open-ended and threatening, immediately requiring prefacing and control within a familiar managerial context.

Diversity programmes in organizations put together words including inclusion and tolerance, and diversity is often prefaced by 'cultural'. These patterns of word couplings also have political effects. They mark out certain sorts of difference for exotic status, as deserving special signification and as requiring special management, which do not apply to differences which enjoy the privilege of invisibility. For example, Asian or Indian racial features become emblematic of cultural difference whereas whiteness or Caucasian features remain unmarked in this way.

In Table 21.1 and in the following section, I tease out three recognizable elements from the managing diversity discourse. Drawing on both organizational

TABLE 21.1 Comparison between diversity discourse and alternative critical perspectives

Diversity discourse	Critical alternatives
The primacy of 'the business case':	
Diversity a business issue – about making money	Diversity is about power and politics
Managing diversity is justified on economic grounds, as means to increased productivity	Managing diversity is often driven by a desire to reduce friction, conflict and the costs of resistance
Managing diversity sits in and accepts market economic paradigm	Fight for diversity can only be understood within framework of political philosophy which recognizes values, rights
Market arguments are leverage for establishing 'airtight case' which will drive organizational change	Market arguments de-legitimize moral/justice/rights debates Demanding market justification establishes higher hurdle for diversity
Managing diversity mirage of consensus:	
Managing diversity assumes diversity is there to be managed by managers who are above it	Managing diversity enables managers to preserve own (unexamined) homogeneity
Aim is harmonious inclusion and belonging, respect	Inclusion and harmony are mirages sustained by exercises of power and control Inadmissibility of real and regular experiences of domination, repression
Tolerance an overarching value	Tolerance problematized as a luxury that the tolerators have, i.e. to withhold or be tolerant
Good diversity climate evidenced by harmony	Diversity evidenced by conflict and subversion (resistance not decimated)
Collusion with fantasy that change occurs through managerial directive (e.g. hiring, promotion, training)	Diversity will be resisted because it threatens power-holders and invites competition for resources, status and power Suits power-holders to minimize diversity
Managing Diversity individualizes – looks to 'fix' lack of diversity with insertion of individuals – 'body count' approach	Causes of lack of diversity in history, culture, society – structural factors
Responsibility for change with diversity change agents/diversity managers	People with diversity will always be marginalized, their optimism and naivety exploited
Diversity equivalences and subsumes differences:	
Diversity creates a singular, unitary category	Not one diversity but many conflicting overlapping subjectivities of difference
Managing diversity works towards 'integrative' approach subsuming diversity as single solution to immigration, globalization, multiculturalism, etc. (universalism)	Diversity is culturally situated and culturally meaningful or meaningless
Multiple 'dimensions' of diversity managed via a single approach	Diversity models compare non-equivalent experiences. It is inappropriate to treat as somehow equivalent experiences of a Chinese immigrant and indigenous woman
Managing diversity framework implies all differences are acceptable	All differences are not equally valid or benign

and classroom cases, I elucidate how the discourse works – constructing 'others' as the problem, requiring managerial solutions and demanding economic justification before acting. I argue that the language of diversity conceals and masks real experiences of racism, discrimination and oppression, often taking audiences further from grappling with the real values at stake. By identifying some alternative perspectives to elements of the diversity discourse, I begin to show how a critical diversity management practice can be articulated.

The Business Case for Diversity

In Australia, whole conferences have been devoted to establishing 'the business case for diversity'. Making the business case is what business says it wants and needs before it can act. In most diversity change efforts, the first step is assembling data on how much poor diversity management is costing the organization and how much it will gain (in market share, reputation and ease of recruiting) by managing diversity better. A recent newsletter from a consulting firm asserted that diversity is about money. One employee is quoted as saying diversity is not about being black or white, it is about 'green'(the colour of the United States dollar bill). The authors of the report go on to argue that diversity has taken on a respectable hue among many United States corporations. It continues on with the bold new revelation that being diverse will make you money, but eventually concludes that the evidence for this remains intuitive and anecdotal.

What is the problem with giving such primacy to 'the business case'? First, it immediately capitulates to economic justification as the only reason for being concerned about diversity. By chronically prefacing diversity with the business case, diversity becomes conditional on a calculation. Any moral or justice arguments for diversity management get jettisoned, labelled as tired old affirmative action or EEO. Indeed practitioners are often fearful about mentioning social justice or phrases with 'moral' in them. Allowing the business case to set the terms of diversity management defines what is discussable and non-discussable rendering invalid the language and principles of rights and equality. Diversity is, they say, all about 'strategic HR management' not about people and how they are treated.

Accepting the corporate terms of the debate as economic, diversity then has to economically justify itself. It has to solve turnover, it has to avert legal actions and complaints, it has to make it easier to recruit the best (least troublesome) employees. The business case turns on elaborate defences of diversity as a source of innovation, organizational flexibility and market responsiveness. Yet many accepted aspects of organizational operation, for example remuneration packages, never have to be put through this process of scrutiny. As Litvin (2002) has argued, accepting the imperative to argue the business case simply reinvigorates and legitimizes the status quo, acceding to a higher level of scrutiny and economic calculability than other spheres of activity. The end result is to reduce possibilities of substantive change. Managers have played this game many times before and there is no absolute standard of data that suffices to persuade. The diversity business case is a set-up and the bases are stacked.

Buying into the business case also betrays a misunderstanding that values and beliefs are changed by rational economic argument – not even the economists believe this. It perpetuates the fantasy in the diversity community that if only we can get enough hard data about diversity's benefits, diversity management will be a shoe-in. The business case diverts diversity practitioners in never-ending efforts to please senior managers, while those managers get on with the real business of holding onto power.

Another example, this time concerning indigenous Australians, shows how the business case irretrievably hooks diversity to economics. A well-respected white leader who consults to business and indigenous groups on improving indigenous employment opportunities was arguing at a conference that the way to get 'a foot in the boardroom door' was to cite the growth of indigenous markets. Statistics show a burgeoning population growth rate in indigenous communities and specifically in rural and regional areas in stark contrast to what is happening in white fertility rates. Yet despite this resurgence in birth rates, Aboriginal Australians remain a bare 2% of the population with employment rates around half of the white population. Given the small size and economic disadvantage of the indigenous population in Australia, basing the argument for change around labour and consumer market power seems a particularly cruel and ill-fated strategy. Indigenous people in Australia are rightly cynical about political efforts to re-cast an important moral obligation into a business calculation dependent on market power.

Further, there is little evidence that 'getting in the door' with the diversity business case is necessarily followed by an opening of the door to more substantive change. In many cases I have witnessed, a powerful argument is made for improving the record of retention of senior women, typically by a CEO or executive who has 'done it' in their organization. Typically this kind of presentation injects an immediate but short-lived belief that such changes are straightforward and simply require women to adapt better to the organizational culture. Couching such changes in simplistic commercial or marketing terms fosters false expectations. It encourages power-holders to externalize 'the problem' onto the diverse groups who just need to 'fit in' better.

The Managing Diversity Mirage of Consensus and Harmony

Managing diversity is firmly embedded in a structural–functionalist paradigm (Burrell & Morgan, 1979) where consensus is the norm and conflict the exception, where rational managers move towards sensible, profit-enhancing objectives. The way managing diversity is discussed enhances and reinforces the expectation that diversity is another managerial problem to be solved by the usual tools of objective setting and top-down organizational change. In an Australian example, Mobil put a great deal of effort and resources into a Managing Diversity programme.

The case was framed as being about 'Diversity and Inclusion' and the company followed the best textbook advice with the development and implementation of its programme, sponsored by an Asian-born and supportive CEO. But inclusion may be in conflict with diversity. If inclusion is interpreted to mean harmony and pleasant feelings of belonging, what happens to conflict, which may be a true marker of working with diversity? The outcome was a culture in which inclusion triumphed but there was little diversity.

The real experience of diversity sits in another world. This is a world where small- and large-scale domination is a fact of daily life, where subjugation and repression are constant experiences. The form that this subjugation takes varies from the more overt abuse of racism, sexism and vilification through to more subtle but sinister forms of domination. Among my MBA students – female and male, from various racial backgrounds – I hear and read accounts of routine victimization and vilification, where being spat on, abused and excluded are daily experiences for certain students. Women from Asian backgrounds are assumed to fit a passive and silent stereotype with no particular experience to contribute. In one case a young woman had extensive experience as a senior broker in international firms. When a class was asked to physically form itself into syndicates, the group made stereotyped assumptions and did not bother to find out about this woman's background or experience. She was isolated and then rejected when she tried to approach an all-male group.

The effects of sustained domination of women and their marginalization also accrue in ways that are less visible. One senior woman in a professional services firm joked to me that most of the professional women were on IVF (*in vitro* fertilization or assisted conception) programmes. Women in the firm had felt such pressure to work long hours and not take breaks to stay on career track that they had left it too late to conceive without assistance. These women were now condemned to having their sexual and reproductive lives ruled by scientifically induced cycles which had become necessary because of organizationally dictated career paths. In this example, not only are women's hours of work, habits of interaction and norms annexed by the male model and controlled by the organization, but so are their bodies and reproductive cycles as well.

In these situations, many individuals deemed 'different' avoid facing what is going on and shield themselves from seeing the hostility around them. Bosses are protected from hearing and seeing sexist or racist behaviour. Anybody who names what is going on is excluded. Senior professional women know that accurately labelling their exclusion will be career suicide, so most do not, but leave quietly to 'pursue other interests'. Complaints are avoided and cultural norms continue, unabated and further entrenched.

Examples also come from my teaching experiences, where the pressures of group dynamics ensure class participants collude to convert discussion of gender relations into non-threatening exchanges about men feeling 'role confusion'. In other classes with a strong domestic student–international student divide, I had challenged the group publicly with 'what is going on?' Met by silence, I would be inundated after class with particularly Asian students keen to explain why they felt 'nothing was going on' and in so doing elucidating precisely what was going on but was too painful to see or say. What is going on goes like this: 'White is right. White is top. White knows best.' Private emails and one-on-one conversations follow. The class diversity discourse did not allow students to identify or express their 'private' experiences of racism.

Students and organizations want diversity without the conflict. They want the solution without having to fully experience the problem. They want the organization or group 'fixed' but without having to look at their own power and privilege. The diversity discourse plays into this by reifying that diversity is about 'other' (Prasad & Mills, 1997).

Diversity Subsuming, Neutralizing and Equivalencing Differences

Discourse analysis highlights that the way words like diversity are used is not accidental, or benign. With the use of the word diversity, an overarching category is created under which all other possibilities are subsumed and become like each other or equivalent. Everything – race, gender, class, religion, sexuality – becomes just diversity. Diversity is also singular – it is almost never used in the plural as diversities. The reason is that it is simpler to keep diversity as a singular 'variable' to be controlled and it supports the assumption that all diversity is in effect the same and can be managed by a single approach which itself remains above scrutiny.

Calás and Smircich (1993) were among the first to warn that interleaving women and gender into 'globalization' discourse had profound and 'dangerous' implications. In their research with MBA students, Tomlinson and Egan (2002) also found that combining globalization and cross-cultural management discourses made possible avoidance of 'more confrontational and disputational categories of difference, such as race, gender and class' (p. 95).

Yet the idea of diversity as a catch-all solution to a range of structural challenges for organizations is enormously seductive. Bennett and Bennett (2001) describe their project as working towards an 'integrative approach to global and domestic diversity'. To aim for an integrative approach may seem like a helpful strategy, but at another level it universalizes, overriding the very substance of diversity, that is difference, with the assertion of false unity. There are important points of conflict between and within diversities. As many writers argue, the experiences of women are not all the same, and black women are not comfortable that white feminists speak for them (Moreton-Robinson, 2000).

As the following quote shows, the universalizing 'integrative' impulse (Prasad, 1997) is a key characteristic of unconsciously colonizing managerial discourse:

> The pursuit of workplace diversity is a strategic response to the globalization of business activities and the growing multiculturalism of workforces and marketplaces … Diversity in the future will be driven by the imperatives of competitiveness, demography, immigration and globalization, and these will supersede the social activism and legislative interventions of the past. (Gandz, 2001)

The message behind this rhetoric is barely concealed: 'look at the things diversity is going to solve and then thankfully we can wave goodbye to social activism and legislation'.

In defining diversity, theorists commonly have come up with maps of concentric circles with all sorts of differences arranged at inner and outer layers – from whether or not one has done military service (the outer, less visible and permanent markers of difference), to one's sexual orientation and, at the inner layer, one's race and gender (the most visible and least amenable to change markers of difference) (Loden & Rosener, 1991). Putting all such differences in one map and on one page is seductive for audiences. It equivalences all differences or bases of 'otherness' and it also encapsulates them, fostering the unspoken assumption that all difference can be bundled together and managed with one managing diversity programme. As I have argued elsewhere (Sinclair, 2000a), there is no evidence that a programme aimed at enhancing cultural diversity will necessarily foster a better climate for women; openness to age diversity does not guarantee openness to many racial groups.

An assumption often made within the managing diversity framework is the value of all differences (Linnehan & Konrad, 1999). In organizations and classrooms this creates confusion about how to treat, for example, the 'different' view that homosexuality is evil. When one of my students voiced the view that his religion denounced homosexuality, a gay student took the teachers to task for not publicly denouncing what was interpreted as homophobia. Values of equality and freedom of expression that are assumed underpinnings of managing diversity are not uncontroversial, especially when in conflict with religious beliefs.

Certainly some 'dimensions' of diversity are more faceable and palatable than others. There have been Australian examples of diversity programmes introduced in organizations which very quickly uncover significant discrimination against women. Such initiatives start out their life as collusion with a diversity audit, or some cross-cultural work. Sometimes gender is outlawed as part of the diversity work by female HR or commissioning managers who are themselves in camouflage and subscribing to what one practitioner described as 'the organizational myth of gender neutrality'. In these circumstances, problems to do with gender become more heavily masked by the language of diversity. The more eagerly diversity is massaged to avoid offending corporate audiences, the more neutralized and inert diversity becomes. The discourse and expectations it creates take managers further from confronting and working with what is going on.

From the practitioner's perspective, a major risk in diversity work is becoming complicit in a 'diversity change programme' that is just marketing, that continues to consolidate power in elite management's hands but makes those hands look more benevolent and enlightened. At the same time and based on my experience and that of colleagues, I argue that developing alternative critical insights on diversity and the discourse that accompanies it has enabled working in diversity in a way that feels closer to the original intents of reducing oppression and discrimination and fostering genuinely more open and humane workplaces.

TOWARDS A CRITICAL DIVERSITY MANAGEMENT PRACTICE

In Table 21.1 theoretical elements of the diversity discourse and critical alternatives are identified. Part of developing a critical practice in diversity management may be working with groups to help them both tease out the strands of the discourse and identify alternative ways of viewing diversity practices. In this section, and drawing on discussions with practitioners, I discuss more specifically some themes of practice, and some suggested ways of working critically with diversity.

Grounding diversity work in a theoretical framework and locating the various structural and systemic factors that mitigate individual agency and explain institutional and individual resistance to diversity (Agocs, 1997)

The discourse of diversity management portrays diversity as a benign solution to an unproblematized and often undiscussed set of organizational conditions. The job of the diversity practitioner is not to accept this diagnosis but to draw on wider theorization – from sociology, political science, feminist and gender studies, for example – to help the thoughtful organization come to a better understanding of what is going on and why it is hard to change.

For one diversity consultant:

> I use my theory to say in ways that they can hear that they are not gender-neutral. I use the theory to highlight the systemic issues. I disrupt their discourse that this is normal. I disrupt their certainty. They are like chooks in the chicken house. I try to get them all off their perches of certainty and flapping and prevent them going back to roost in the same place.

Rejection of 'the business case' requirement as the reason for diversity and interposition of moral, rights-based or social justice arguments for reducing oppression and discrimination

Most practitioners find the need to resist organizational demands for a business case and have their own sometimes explicit, other times implicit, understanding of why diversity work is important. Part of this is having a broader understanding of who the diversity work is for – beyond who is paying for the work. Some practitioners simply start with the clear need to validate the subjective experiences of individuals and particularly those marginalized. This allows the practitioner to also have ways of judging the success of an intervention that is not tied to organizational metrics of reduced recruitment costs or increased sales. From the practitioner's perspective an intervention can be judged worthwhile when the 'individual emails and evidence that comes back is of people feeling validated and empowered – you know that you reside in the hearts and minds of those individuals'. Others have well-theorized justifications about their work that may come from disciplinary training, for example in social work, sociology or gender studies.

Awareness of power and how to locate one's work to ensure it does not get buried or sabotaged

A well-understood principle of diversity management change efforts is ensuring the CEO and executive team are as supportive and involved as possible in the project. For the practitioner working critically, it is even more important to pursue one-on-one time with key decision-makers to understand their motivation for the project and identify opportunities to strengthen their understanding and commitment.

It is also valuable to use one's own power which is often significant at the early stages of a project. This can take the form of not accepting the initial client's diagnosis or definition of the brief but being confident to draw on one's own experience of other organizations to prompt the client to re-frame 'the problem' and the scope of one's work towards solutions. As discussed above, it is vital to conduct a careful specification about who is the client and to whom the final report should go. Thinking about these issues in advance ensures that a report with difficult findings is harder to 'bury'. An important part of the diversity practitioner's work is upholding the interests of those without power to have their experiences validated and not negated through protestations of the need for confidentiality: people who are already marginalized should not be further disenfranchised by diversity work. As one experienced consultant advised: 'Make sure the report is on the books and they can't say certain things haven't happened. Send the report out as widely as you can and set up the contract so it can't be kept confidential.'

Strategies for working with and containing harmful knowledge

People who work in diversity often uncover or are told about harmful, even brutal, and illegal behaviour. Senior managers may know about such behaviour but it has been normalized. The practitioner then becomes the container for this knowledge and has to make difficult judgements about confidentiality and what sorts of information require notification of other authorities. Supports are necessary when the practitioner is working in very hostile environments, for example having networks of other colleagues who work in similar contexts and making sure visits to the work site are buffered by time in a more sympathetic environment.

Ways of understanding self and insight into the contradictory desires to belong and to subvert and challenge

For most diversity practitioners, effective work springs from active processes of reflection about one's own identity and intents. It entails grappling with personal experiences of being different or 'on the outer' while recognizing human needs to be accepted and find belonging in our chosen work. The best experiences diversity consultants describe are being deep into organizations, trusted by senior managers and confidants of leaders. The paradox is that practitioners are unlikely to be embraced and accepted into the fold for their diversity work, positioned as they are on the edge of organizations, bearers of difficult insights and radical change agendas. Summarizing this dilemma one said: 'I want to be able to do this work which challenges the status quo and I want to be accepted by the status quo.' Diversity and diversity practitioners are pinioned by the spike of their own desires – to both critique and be accepted, 'wanting to be myself, and be validated'.

Critical diversity work inevitably highlights questions of power and identity, thus practitioners need to understand how these issues play out for themselves, to be reflexive about their own needs for belonging, status and approval, and the multiple and shifting influences shaping their sense of identity and efficacy.

CONCLUSION

The dilemmas for people who advise organizations in the area of diversity management have never been greater. The ostensible acceptance of diversity as a good belies the entrenched structural obstacles to implementing greater openness to difference in workplaces. Complex, global influences, such as increasing concentrations and disparities of wealth and international subcontracting of high-risk activities to unregulated workplaces, create new divisions and ways that prejudice and discrimination are manifested. They are nurtured, not mitigated, by current economic orthodoxy which focuses attention on the individual and dismisses structurally created inequities. A dose of diversity management will not overcome these obstacles and a recognition of structural factors should be the starting point for all diversity work.

The widely articulated planks in the diversity discourse may have made it harder, not easier, for the diversity practitioner. The discourse colludes with, indeed reinforces, a world view which leaves the basic purposes and task of managers outside debate. The discourse casts diversity as an economic good that is only justified where a 'business case can be made' and it legitimizes false ideas that all diversities can be bundled into one category for treatment by managers whose own racial or gender markers are invisible.

The job of the diversity practitioner is, then, to stand outside the discourse, not to become an unthinking exponent of it. It is to ask questions which take organizations beyond knee-jerk capitulation to the business case, to articulate the conflicting interests and power inequities that characterize organizational life, not to suppress them in an illusion of harmony. Drawing on insights from critical theory provides antidotes to many of the most simplistic tenets of the diversity discourse. Critical theory prompts us to ask who we are working for and why – whose experiences are being privileged and whose are routinely silenced, whether our work illuminates and changes oppression or simply gives management new tools and additional legitimacy to intensify control of people's lives.

Working towards long-term client engagements allows diversity to become the way in to deeper personal work with executives, with opportunities to work in more challenging ways. Under these circumstances, diversity can be a vehicle through which to do rewarding and organization-changing work: 'where you are engaged to go on a reflective journey with companies who see that they have failed, who are not so tight and frightened about the findings, and are prepared to have them discussed'.

NOTES

1 The core ideas of this chapter were first presented at the ANZAM/IFSAM Conference, Gold Coast, 12 July 2002. I would like to acknowledge my co-panellists at that conference, Judith Pringle and Allison Konrad, and the audience whose provocative questions helped me develop the ideas expressed here. I also would like to acknowledge colleagues and friends working on diversity management in Australian organizations, particularly Duncan Smith and Dr Sue Lewis for their openness in sharing the challenges and perils as they see them. Their voices contributed to these accounts of the state of diversity management practice in Australia although the conclusions expressed here are my own.

2 An earlier version of this table appeared in a paper by A. Sinclair entitled 'Doing Critical Research for the Government' presented at the 2nd International Conference on Critical Management Studies, Constructing Knowledge Stream, in Manchester, July 2001.

REFERENCES

Agocs, C. (1997). Institutionalized resistance to organizational change. *Journal of Business Ethics*, *16*, 917–31.

Appo, D., & Härtel, C. (2003). Questioning management programs that deal with Aboriginal development programs in Australia. *Asia Pacific Journal of Human Resources*, *41*(1), 36–50.

Arrington, C., & Francis, J. (1989). Letting the chat out of the bag: Deconstruction, privilege and accounting research. *Accounting, Organizations and Society*, *14*(1/2), 1–28.

Asia Pacific Journal of Human Resources (2003). Special issue, *41*(1), April.

Bennett, J., & Bennett, M. (2001). Developing intercultural sensitivity: An integrative approach to global and domestic diversity. Paper presented to the Diversity Symposium, Diversity Collegium, Bentley College, Waltham, MA.

Bertone, S., Esposto, A., & Turner, R. (1998). *Diversity and dollars: Productive diversity in Australian business and industry* (Information Paper No. 58). Committee for Economic Development of Australia.

Bertone, S., & Leahy, M. (2003). Multiculturalism as conservative ideology: Impacts on workforce diversity. *Asia Pacific Journal of Human Resources*, *41*(1), 101–15.

Burrell, G., & Morgan, G. (1979). *Sociological paradigms and organisational analysis*. London: Sage.

Burton, C., & Ryall, C. (1994). Managing for diversity: Report commissioned by the Industry Taskforce on Leadership and Management Skills. Canberra: Australian Commonwealth Publishing Service.

Calás, M., & Smircich, L. (1993). Dangerous liaisons: The 'feminine-in-management' meets 'globalisation'. *Business Horizons*, March–April, 71–81.

Cope, B., & Kalantzis, M. (1997). *Productive diversity: A new Australian model for work and management*. Sydney: Pluto Press.

Crawley, A., & Sinclair, A. (2003). Indigenous human resource practices in Australian mining companies: Towards an ethical model. *Journal of Business Ethics*, *45*, 361–73.

Czarniawska, B., & Höpfl, H. (2002). *Casting the Other: The production and maintenance of inequalities in organizations*. London: Routledge.

Dagher, J., & D'Netto, B. (1997). *Managing workforce diversity in Australia* (Working Paper 5/97). Department of Management, Monash University.

Dagher, J., D'Netto, B., & Sohal, A. (1998). Managing workforce diversity in the Australian manufacturing industry. *Journal of Human Factors and Ergonomics in Manufacturing*, *8*(2), 1–15.

De Cieri, H., & Olekalns, M. (2001). Australia. In M. Patrickson & P. O'Brien (Eds), *Managing diversity: An Asian and Pacific focus* (pp. 21–8). Milton, Queensland: Wiley.

Department of Immigration and Multicultural Affairs (2000). Introduction to the 21st Century Business: Delivering the Diversity Dividend Conference, November.

D'Netto, B., Smith, D., & Da Gama Pinto, C. (2000). Diversity management: Benefits, challenges and strategies. Report to the Department of Immigration and Multicultural Affairs under the Productive Diversity Partnership Programme, 16 October.

Foldy, E. (2002). 'Managing' diversity: Identity and power in organizations. In I. Aaltio & A. Mills (Eds), *Gender, identity and the culture of organizations* (pp. 92–112). London: Routledge.

Gandz, J. (2001). *A business case for diversity*. Richard Ivey School of Business, University of Western Ontario.

Gillespie, J. (1999). Profiting from diversity: The Westpac experience. In G. O'Neill & R. Kramar (Eds), *Australian human resources management: Current trends in management practice, Volume 2* (pp. 207–16). Warriewood: Australia: Business and Professional Publishing.

Hage, G. (1998). *White nation: Fantasies of white supremacy in a multicultural society*. Sydney: Pluto Press.

Hollway, W. (1989). *Subjectivity and method in psychology: Gender, meaning and science*. London: Sage.

Kramar, R. (1999). Managing diversity. In G. O'Neill & R. Kramar (Eds), *Australian human resources management: Current trends in management practice, Volume 2* (pp. 193–206). Warriewood, Australia: Business and Professional Publishing.

Krautil, F. (1995). Managing diversity in Esso Australia. In E. Davis & C. Harris (Eds), *Making the Link Number 6*. Affirmative Action Agency and Labour Studies Foundation, Macquarie University.

Linnehan, F., & Konrad, A. (1999). Diluting diversity: Implications for intergroup inequality in organizations. *Journal of Management Inquiry*, *8*(4), 399–414.

Litvin, D. (2002). The business case for diversity and the 'iron cage'. In B. Czarniawska & H. Höpfl (Eds), *Casting the Other: The production and maintenance of inequalities in work organizations* (pp. 160–84). London: Routledge.

Loden, M., & Rosener, J. (1991). *Workforce America! Managing employee diversity as a vital resource*. Homewood, IL: Business One Irwin.

Moreton-Robinson, A. (2000). *Talkin' up to the white woman*. St Lucia: University of Queensland Press.

Nicholas, S. (2000). Corporate awareness of diversity in the workplace: The mind of the CEO. Report to the Department of Immigration and Multicultural Affairs under the Productive Diversity Partnership Programme.

Office of Public Employment (2004). *Focus: Cultural diversity in the Victorian public sector*. Melbourne: Office of Public Employment.

Patrickson, M., & O'Brien, P. (Eds) (2001). *Managing diversity: An Asian and Pacific focus*. Queensland: Milton, Wiley.

Prasad, A, (1997). The colonizing consciousness and representations of the other: A post-colonial critique of the discourse of oil. In P. Prasad, A. Mills, M. Elmes & A. Prasad

(Eds), *Managing the organizational melting pot: Dilemmas of workplace diversity* (pp. 285–311). Thousand Oaks, CA: Sage.

Prasad, A., & Prasad, P. (2002). Otherness at large: Identity and difference in the new globalized landscape. In I. Aaltio & A. Mills (Eds), *Gender, Identity and the Culture of Organizations* (pp. 57–71). London: Routledge.

Prasad, P., & Mills, A. (1997). From showcase to shadow: Understanding the dilemma of managing workplace diversity. In P. Prasad, A. Mills, M. Elmes & A. Prasad (Eds), *Managing the organizational melting pot: Dilemmas of workplace diversity* (pp. 3–27). Thousand Oaks, CA: Sage.

Sinclair, A. (1998). *Doing leadership differently: Gender, power and sexuality in a changing business culture.* Carlton: Melbourne University Press.

Sinclair, A. (2000a). Women within diversity: Risks and possibilities. *Women in Management Review, 15*(5/6), 237–45.

Sinclair, A. (2000b). Teaching managers about masculinities: Are you kidding? *Management Learning, 31*(1), 83–101.

Sinclair, A. (2001). Doing Critical Research for the Government. Paper presented at the 2nd International Conference on Critical Management Studies, Constructing Knowledge Stream, Manchester.

Sinclair, A., & Wilson, V. (2002). *New faces of leadership.* Carlton: Melbourne University Press.

Smith, D. (1998). The business case for diversity. *Monash Mt Eliza Business Review, 1*(3), 72–81.

Summers, A. (2003). *The end of equality: Work, babies and women's choices in 21st century Australia.* Sydney: Random House.

Tomlinson, F., & Egan, S. (2002). Organizational sense-making in a culturally-diverse setting. *Management Learning, 33*(1), 79–97.

Wilson, V., & Sinclair, A. (1997). Diversity management at Hewlett Packard Australia. Melbourne Business School Case Study Services, Carlton, Australia.

Conclusion

Reflections and Future Directions

JUDITH K. PRINGLE, ALISON M. KONRAD AND PUSHKALA PRASAD

The Handbook of Workplace Diversity is intended to redefine workplace diversity as a field of study that is dedicated to (1) the inclusion of a multiple voices, (2) reducing intergroup inequality in organizations, and, thus, the societies they operate in, and (3) initiating a dialogue between diverse theoretical traditions on this topic. In this volume we have aimed at crossing disciplinary, philosophical and national borders. We were especially concerned to move the discussion of workplace diversity out of the US dominance as much as possible. In this objective, we have only been partly successful; nevertheless an important start has been made to truly make the discussion more diverse (*sic*!). More than half the contributions come from outside the United States – Canada, the UK, Australia, New Zealand, the Netherlands, South Africa, Sweden – and cover a range of ethnicities. Below, we describe the contributions and perspectives included in each section of this handbook.

PART I THEORETICAL PERSPECTIVES ON WORKPLACE DIVERSITY

Workplace diversity research is informed by a wide variety of theoretical perspectives. Psychological perspectives have contributed theories of social cognition, social identity and intergroup relations. Human resource management perspectives have emphasized the value of diversity as a strategic management issue, arguing that fully developing the potential of a diverse group of employees brings about a business advantage through fostering team creativity, innovation and problem solving. Human resource managers have implemented formal diversity management programs in large numbers of organizations, and research has examined the impact of these programs.

Many theoretical perspectives are far more critical. Feminists are more skeptical of the workplace diversity movement and highlight the ways in which the literature obscures the impact of patriarchy and dilution of the commitment to reducing intergroup inequality. Postcolonial theorists bring an alternative critical perspective to the study of workplace diversity by arguing that the colonial experience can provide a useful framework for revealing hidden patterns of neo-imperialism in relationships between dominant and marginal groups. Critical theory and cultural studies highlight ways in which embedded and taken-for-granted hegemonies reinforce asymmetric relationships between different identity groups. Post-structuralists examine diversity issues as part of wider discursive organizational arrangements that are responsible for constituting specific identities and reproducing legacies of domination. We hope that including a fuller range of theoretical perspectives in this single volume will help to raise awareness of the breadth of conceptual work that has been accomplished among workplace diversity scholars.

PART II METHODS FOR STUDYING WORKPLACE DIVERSITY

In this part, authors have presented some key methodologies used in the study of workplace diversity and discuss some of their implications for empirical work. This material provides valuable frameworks, tools and strategies for future researchers. Specifically, the two chapters on quantitative measures provide a set of formulas for assessing the extent of diversity within a collectivity as well as a summary and critique of the best quantitative measurement instruments available for studying workplace diversity issues and processes, including information on reliability and validity. The chapter on conducting qualitative research from a feminist perspective describes the advantages of qualitative methods in general, the issues commonly raised when conducting qualitative research on workplace diversity, and strategies for dealing with these issues from a feminist standpoint. We hope that these chapters provide useful guidance for future research. We also hope that by including a discussion of both quantitative and qualitative methods in a single volume, this handbook will enhance appreciation for the full range of methods among scholars working in both the quantitative and qualitative traditions.

PART III DIMENSIONS OF WORKPLACE DIVERSITY

Workplace diversity has multiple dimensions, including (though not limited to) gender, race/ethnicity, age, disability status, sexual orientation, religion and nationality. Bringing reviews of multiple dimensions into a single text illuminates the parallels among various types of intergroup dynamics as well as the distinctions between them. The theoretical approaches used in each area of research are similar in many ways, and highlighted similarities and differences may bring to light potentially valuable avenues for future research. For example, conceptions developed by scholars of ethnicity might be adaptable for use in research on gender. Additionally, research is beginning to focus on the intersections between different dimensions of diversity, highlighting issues such as gendered racism, racist sexism and gendered ageism. By bringing work on the various dimensions of diversity together into a single volume, we hope that this handbook will stimulate such cross-fertilization as well as the development of more research examining the intersections between multiple dimensions of diversity.

EXISTING LACUNA

Limited Understanding of the Socio-political Context

At present, there is a gap in the diversity research literature linking workplaces with the historical or socio-political context of the countries. This absence can be attributed to assumptions of similarity among organizations around the world generated in part by the globalization discourse, an unconscious attitude of ethnocentrism, or simply an unawareness of the significance of local contexts. Lounsbury and Ventresca (2003), amongst others, argue for new structuralism in organization theory that includes efforts of lobby and societal groups, and shifts in local politics over time. We extend this plea to advocate that research into workplace diversity attends to the politics of location, including history, culture and societal concerns, to develop a more critical discourse on the dynamic and reciprocal impacts of diverse social identity on and in workplaces. There have been various attempts but little sustained success to create the meso-level analysis (House, Rousseau & Thomas-Hunt, 1995) that workplace diversity requires. Alvesson and Wilmott (1996: 64) conceptualize 'human beings as historical embodied, traditional and embedded creatures' not as individuated organizational agents. Scholars and managers alike must recognize the embeddedness of instrumental reason in the normative (and historically constituted) frameworks of society (Alvesson & Wilmott, 1996: 78). Our studies of diverse workplaces then need to become critically reflexive works that clearly acknowledge our own positions.

Privileging of Management Views over Employees' Experiences

Another glaring omission in the research literature is insufficient concern about the employees' own views and experiences relating to diversity. One reason for this omission is the hesitancy of managers to allow researchers access to study employees' experiences for fear that studies will document the existence of hostile environments for which management can be held legally liable. Hence, an unintended consequence of public policies offering employees protection for discrimination and harassment has been the closing of organizational doors to scholars wishing to improve our understanding of intergroup relations in organizations in order to hone more effective practices and policies. Moving past this stalemate will require developing a language of diversity scholarship that simultaneously voices the experiences of historically disenfranchised identity groups and approaches managements in a non-threatening manner.

One attempt to create such a language has been the development of the 'business case for diversity'. Business case discussions focus on the interests of managers, viewed primarily as agents of capital, to maximize firm profitability. Whether employees are motivated by calls to maximize shareholder wealth is doubtful, however. Litvin (Chapter 3, this volume) argues for a new case for diversity focused on providing 'an opportunity for everyone in an organization to learn from each other in order to enrich their lives, achieve their goals, and develop the skills necessary for human survival'. We encourage further development of Litvin's logic to create a case for diversity that provides a fairer balance among the interests of all organizational stakeholders.

Limitations of the Business Case for Diversity

Much of the corporate support for workplace diversity has been generated by consultants and some academics who have espoused a 'business case for diversity' (Litvin, 2002). The business case for diversity argues that human rights and equity issues can be advanced by linking diversity with enhanced trade, consumption and economic performance. While this stream of thinking has certainly showcased diversity (Prasad & Mills, 1997) and brought it considerable organizational support, its claims remain somewhat questionable at best. In fact, the business case for diversity has been sharply critiqued by a number of scholars (Kirby & Harter, 2002; Litvin, 2002; MacLaren, 1994) as being narrowly focused on the bottom-line effects of diversity, and objectifying diverse social groups at work.

The notion that diversity is to be embraced mainly because of positive trade and commercial gains is also somewhat problematic. The European Union (which is sometimes hailed as a classic case of a state benefiting from dissolving national boundaries and thriving on diversity) is a case in point. While new laws limit discrimination among Europeans themselves, most European countries have tightened their immigration policies toward non-Europeans, while European organizations (in France, Belgium, Sweden, Denmark and the Netherlands) continue in their notorious practice of discrimination toward immigrants from North Africa, Asia and Latin America.

Our point here is quite simple. Economic and commercial arguments favoring diversity at work (while they have some merit) should not be the *only* reasons for supporting diversity. Rather, diversity is a necessary element of the contemporary social contract that organizations have with the societies in which they function. Given the increasing boundaryless nature of organizational contexts, firms in today's world cannot (ethically or pragmatically) ignore the need to include and respect different social identity groups. It is our hope that the chapters in this handbook can start a serious conversation that is helpful to managers, executives, employees, prospective employees and consultants who are interested in making this happen.

Atheoretical Nature of the Writing

Research and writing on workplace diversity have been justly criticized for being atheoretical, often with a blatant focus on everyday organizational practices and outcomes. A major reason for this state has been that the theoretical roots from which researchers are writing and acting have not been made explicit. We have encouraged that exposure through our discussion of the genres within workplace diversity research and urge this reflexive disclosure to be part of all research and scholarship, at least within this area of organizational studies. We present in the following table the result of a much contested discussion: the placement of the chapters in this volume within the dimension identified in the Introduction: power awareness, identity fluidity, level of analysis, positivist or non-positivist paradigms.

TABLE I *Handbook chapters in non-positivist genres*

Nature of identity	Power awareness	
	Low	High
Fixed		Class – Scully & Blake-Beard
		Gender Perspectives – Billing & Sundin
		Feminist qualitative research – Thurlow, Mills & Mills
Fluid		Postcolonial – Prasad
		Critical and post-structuralist – Jones & Stablein
		Practice – Sinclair
		A new case for diversity – Litvin
		Masculinities – Hearn & Collinson
		Globalization – Mir, Mir & Wong

Among authors in the non-positivist genre, those who treat identities as relatively stable and not particularly open to negotiation due to powerful social and historical forces are placed in the 'fixed' category. These discussions include the chapters on gender perspectives, feminist qualitative methods and class. We also place Sinclair's discussion of critical perspectives on diversity practice in this cell due to her focus on discursive practices which limit the ability of the critical diversity practitioner to create emancipatory organizational change.

Non-positivist authors who focus attention on the ways identities can be achieved or lost through social interaction are placed in the 'fluid' category. The chapters on post-structuralism, masculinities and postcolonial perspectives are included in this cell. We also place Litvin's plea for a new case for diversity here due to her desire to change organizations by developing a new discourse for our field. All of our non-positivist authors are located in the high power awareness column because they have devoted substantial space to discussions of social and historical forces resulting in unequal access to resources across identity groups. It is important to note, however, that concepts of power themselves can be quite varied among the non-positivist genres. Thus, while conventional critical theory and certain branches of feminism see power in stark and concrete terms, others (e.g. post-structuralism and postcolonialism) see power more as a relationship than a property. In other words, in these latter genres, power itself is seen as more elusive in nature and residing (albeit in unexpected ways) even among those groups that have traditionally been regarded as being 'powerless'.

Irrespective of key differences among them, one common characteristic among most of the non-positivistic genres is their commitment to understanding the *processes* whereby the dynamics of diversity are enacted. As such, they tend to favor approaches that are historically attuned and are concerned with richly textured analyses.

We categorize the positivist chapters in the handbook as in the following table. Conceptual discussions in which psychological perspectives predominate are placed in the 'micro' category. Within this category, discussions making power relations a central focus of concern are categorized as high in power awareness. These chapters include (1) the discussion of race, which focuses on prejudice and discrimination against people of color, (2) the discussion of sexual orientation, which focuses on homophobia and heterosexism as processes which privilege heterosexuals, (3) the discussion of disability, which focuses on ablism and negative views of workers with disabilities, and (4) the discussion of appearance and obesity, which focuses on the privileges accruing to more attractive individuals who fit society's weight norms.

TABLE 2   *Handbook chapters positivist genres*

Level of analysis	Power awareness	
	Low	High
Micro – individual	Psychological perspectives – Kulik & Bainbridge	Race & ethnicity – Proudford & Nkomo
	Age – Perry & Parlamis	Sexual orientation – Creed
		Disability – Stone-Romero, Stone & Lukaszewski
		Appearance and Obesity – Bell & McLaughlin
Meso – interpersonal/group	Human resource management – Kossek, Lobel & Brown	Sex and gender – Benschop
		Intersection of gender and race – Mirchandani & Butler
Macro-structural		Trade unions – Greene & Kirton

Chapters included at the meso level examine organizational practices and how they affect individuals. We classify the chapter on HRM practices as low in power awareness because research in this area has utilized a strategic HRM perspective which emphasizes the importance of maximizing organizational performance, although Kossek et al. are obviously cognizant of power differentials between identity groups in organizations. We classify Benschop's discussion of sex and gender as a meso-level perspective high in power awareness due to her focus on organizational practices intended to improve the outcomes of a historically disadvantaged group, specifically women. Mirchandani and Butler's discussion of intersections between gender and ethnicity focuses at the level of the organization, while simultaneously paying attention to both micro and some macro features.

At the macro level, Greene and Kirton's discussion of trade unions examines societal institutions and their impacts on diverse identity groups in organizations. We categorize their work as high in power awareness due to their emphasis on the power differential between employees, managers and owners.

Positivist work has favored psychological models. We have categorized Kulik and Bainbridge's chapter outlining psychological models as low in power awareness because these models (with the exception of status characteristics theory) do not consider power differentials between groups to be the key causal mechanisms resulting in intergroup prejudice and discrimination. Within the workplace diversity literature, however, psychological models have been applied primarily to understanding the experiences of identity groups that historically have been denied equal access to organizational opportunities and resources. Psychologists are documenting that the psychological processes of powerful and powerless individuals are qualitatively different (Dépret & Fiske, 1999; Ruggiero & Major, 1998; Stevens & Fiske, 2000). This work has important implications for the experiences of dominant and non-dominant groups in organizations, and more work is needed to document non-dominants' views of dominants.

Positivist research examining the organizational level of analysis is less common and draws primarily upon conceptual frameworks from the field of management. The least well-explored terrain is the macro-structural level and the societal institutions shaping organizations and the experiences of their members. Greene and Kirton's examination of the influence of trade unions provides some needed insights, but many societal institutions remain relatively unexamined in the workplace diversity literature, and more research is needed to enhance our understanding of the social and historical context influencing diverse workplaces.

FUTURE DIRECTIONS FOR DIVERSITY RESEARCH

Many of the chapters in this volume have emphasized the *interplay* among multiple identities, oppressions and inequalities in organizational contexts (e.g. Mirchandani and Butler, Prasad et al. Scully and Blake-Beard, etc.). We would further venture that diversity research in the future cannot afford to ignore these interplays given the rapidly increasing demographic changes and geographical movements of people. Taking such interplays seriously, however, would also require an expansion of our methodological horizons, since they call for less reliance on single dependent-variable studies or single-site ethnographies. Rather, we might have to increasingly engage in research that is process oriented and better able to capture the multiplicity of identities and oppressions that constitute diversity at the workplace. We are eager therefore to encourage the rupturing of methodological boundaries in creative and rigorous ways.

Combining methodological forces – if done in a theoretically grounded fashion – can serve us in insightful ways. Statistical research can tell us much about concrete patterns in organizations, with respect to the career stagnation and wage disparities experienced by socially marginalized groups. Interviews, however, can give us glimpses into the identity formation of diverse groups, while observation can indicate some of the ways in which divisions between dominant and other groups become institutionalized in organizations. Additionally, some methods are simply underused in this area. Some of these include archival research and historical analysis, both of which analyze public and private documents that contain multiple voices and traces of identity struggles in the workplace.

The future of research on workplace diversity will always be driven by demographic, political and economic forces. Nevertheless within these shifting currents researchers can position themselves to investigate what may be at times eddies in the mainstreams. Increasing mobility of labor globally is likely to increase and provide research sites to open up understanding. For example, the EU presents an excellent site of inquiry because an essential element of EU citizenship is the free movement of workers within the EU (www.eurofound.eu.int). Globally migratory trends may ebb and flow but are always occurring. The management and organizational literature on diversity would also gain much by looking at some recent trends in anthropology, sociology and history which focus on the rise of transnational work patterns across the world. Transnationalism is concerned with the increasing mobility of workers/employees/professionals who lead endlessly migratory lives, moving wherever desirable employment opportunities are to be found (Ong, 1999). Transnationalism challenges established notions of diversity and multiculturalism by focusing on the transitory nature of global work patterns and by calling into question many of our taken-for-granted notions about organizational and national boundaries and cultural space.

There is a need for an increase in critical approaches to be melded into the pragmatics of the daily management of diversity. Intensive case study of micropolitics that are then linked to the specifics of the wider historical and socio-political environment would vastly increase our understanding of the dynamics of workplace diversity.

Finally, an important goal for us has been to build a foundation for a congenial dialogue across epistemological perspectives within the workplace diversity field. We have tried to demonstrate in this volume that we can work together and honor the contributions of scholars working from all paradigmatic traditions. We invite scholars who share our aims to work together in order to build a strong collective stream of research which assists organizations to become more thoughtful, more humane and less exploitative toward the diverse set of stakeholders whom they affect.

REFERENCES

Alvesson, M., & Wilmott, H. (1996). *Making sense of management: A critical introduction.* London: Sage.

Dépret, E., & Fiske, S. T. (1999). Perceiving the powerful: Intriguing individuals versus threatening groups. *Journal of Experimental Social Psychology, 35,* 461–80.

European Foundation for the Improvement of Curig and working conditions: Industrial relation developments in Europe 2002: www.eurofound.eu.int/publications/files/EF0338EN.pdf (Accessed 24 January 2005).

House, R., Rousseau, D., & Thomas-Hunt, M. (1995). The meso paradigm: A framework for the integration of micro and macro organizational behavior. In B. Staw & L. L. Cummings (Eds), *Research in organizational behavior (17,* pp. 71–87, 104–9). Greenwich, CT: JAI Press.

Kirby, E., & Harter, L. M. (2002). Speaking the language of the bottom-line: The metaphor of 'managing diversity'. *Journal of Business Communication, 40,* 28–49.

Litvin, D. R. (2002). The business case for diversity and the 'iron cage'. In B. Czarniawska and H. Hopfl (Eds), *Casting the Other: The production and maintenance of inequality in organizations* (pp. 160–84). London: Routledge.

Lounsbury, M., & Ventresca, M. (2003). The new structuralism in organization theory. *Organization, 10*(3), 457–80.

MacLaren, P. (1994). White terror and oppositional agency: Towards a critical multiculturalism. In D. T. Goldberg (Ed.), *Multiculturalism: A critical reader* (pp. 45–74). Oxford: Basil Blackwell.

Ong, A. (1999). *Flexible citizenship: The cultural logics of transnationality.* Durham, NC: Duke University Press.

Prasad, P., & Mills, A. (1997). From showcase to shadow: Understanding the dilemmas of managing workplace diversity. In P. Prasad, A. Mills, M. Elmes & A. Prasad (Eds), *Managing the organizational melting pot: Dilemmas of workplace diversity* (pp. 3–27). Thousand Oaks, CA: Sage.

Ruggiero, K. M., & Major, B. N. (1998). Group status and attributions to discrimination: Are low- or high-status group members more likely to blame their failures on discrimination? *Personality and Social Psychology Bulletin, 24,* 821–37.

Stevens, L. E., & Fiske, S. T. (2000). Motivated impressions of a powerholder: Accuracy under task dependency and misperception under evaluation dependency. *Personality and Social Psychology Bulletin, 26,* 907–22.

Index